T0311864

From War to Genocide

Critical Human Rights

Series Editors
Steve J. Stern ❦ Scott Straus

Books in the series Critical Human Rights emphasize research that opens new ways to think about and understand human rights. The series values in particular empirically grounded and intellectually open research that eschews simplified accounts of human rights events and processes.

The Rwandan genocide shocked the world and galvanized human rights research. Based on inside material from the International Criminal Tribunal for Rwanda, as well as the author's field investigations, this book offers compelling new evidence on a crucial issue. How did genocide actually emerge and become state policy? By examining the political and military context before and during the genocide, the specific actors and their motivations, and the sequence of events, the author challenges the standard accounts of causation, planning, and responsibility. At the same time, this book is unsparing in its criticism of the callousness of the actors who are most culpable of genocide. *From War to Genocide* is one of the most important books to appear in any language on the development of genocide at the highest echelons of power.

From War
to Genocide

Criminal Politics in Rwanda,
1990–1994

André Guichaoua

Translated by
Don E. Webster

Foreword by
Scott Straus

The University of Wisconsin Press

Translation of this volume has been made possible through support from the Open Society Initiative for Eastern Africa (OSIEA).

The University of Wisconsin Press
1930 Monroe Street, 3rd Floor
Madison, Wisconsin 53711-2059
uwpress.wisc.edu

3 Henrietta Street, Covent Garden
London WC2E 8LU, United Kingdom
eurospanbookstore.com

Originally published as *Rwanda, de la guerre au génocide: Les politiques criminelles au Rwanda (1990–1994)*, by André Guichaoua, © 2010 by Éditions La Découverte, Paris

Translation by Don E. Webster, copyright © 2015 by the Board of Regents of the University of Wisconsin System

Printed in the United States of America

This book may be available in a digital edition.

Library of Congress Cataloging-in-Publication Data

Guichaoua, André, author.
[Rwanda, de la guerre au génocide. English]
From war to genocide : criminal politics in Rwanda, 1990–1994 / André Guichaoua; translated by Don E. Webster.
    pages   cm. — (Critical human rights)
        Originally published as Rwanda, de la guerre au génocide: les politiques criminelles au Rwanda
            (1990–1994), by André Guichaoua, ©2010 by Éditions La Découverte, Paris.
        Includes bibliographical references and index.
        ISBN 978-0-299-29820-3 (cloth : alk. paper)
  1. Rwanda—History—Civil War, 1994—Causes. 2. Rwanda—History—Civil War, 1990–1993.
    3. Rwanda—Politics and government—1962–1994. 4. Genocide—Rwanda—History—20th
    century. I. Webster, Don E. (Lawyer), translator. II. Title. III. Series: Critical human rights.
DT450.435.G8513   2015
967.57104'2—dc23
2015010239

ISBN 978-0-299-29824-1 (pbk.: alk. paper)

with a typeset of peace
Figure Foundation
bound the burden end

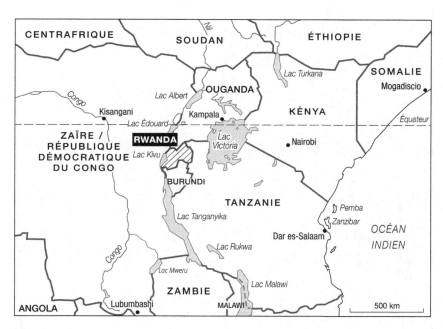

Map 1. Map of the region

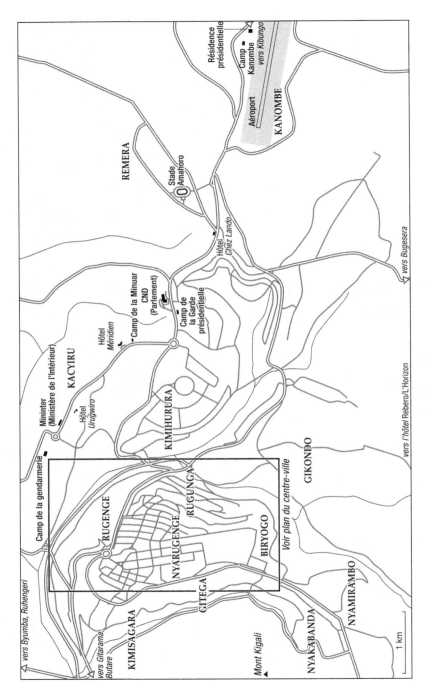

Map 2. Map of Kigali-ville, including the residential neighborhoods, April 1994

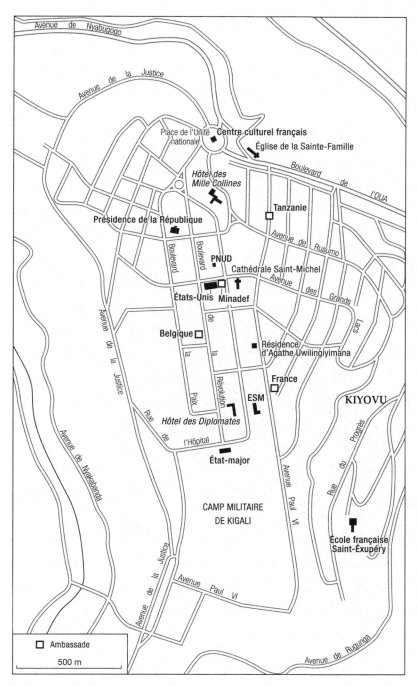

Map 3. Downtown Kigali (plateau), April 1994

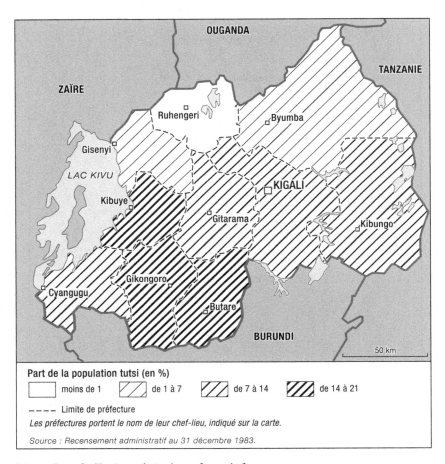

Map 4. Rwanda, Tutsi population by prefecture before 1994

Contents

Foreword

Scott Straus

André Guichaoua's book is one of the most important works to have appeared on the Rwandan genocide since that terrible event occurred in 1994. Until now, the extraordinary material contained in *Rwanda, de la guerre au génocide*, as well as Professor Guichaoua's insightful analysis, remained accessible only to readers of French and Kinyarwanda. With the release of this English version, ably translated by Don Webster, the University of Wisconsin Press has done a great service to all who wish to understand one of the twentieth century's greatest atrocities.

Some twenty years ago, the scale and brutality of violence in Rwanda shocked the world. Haunted by their experiences a year earlier in Somalia, the United States, Britain, and other countries, as well as key actors at the United Nations, refused to become entangled in another African conflict. They chose instead to withdraw their international forces and to allow the killers to inflict their terrible violence on hundreds of thousands of civilians. That failure to stop genocide in Rwanda remains a stain on the record of the international community.

Back then, very few outsiders—citizens, journalists, human rights activists, and scholars—understood the drivers and dynamics of the mass violence. Many of the images that emerged from Rwanda and that circulated in media outlets defied comprehension. Images of macheted corpses on the side of the road, swollen bodies floating in rivers, and churches as the sites of mass graves seemed to confirm the worst stereotypes of Africa. Many public commentators reverted to old clichés about Africa to make sense of the violence. They attributed it to an "ancient tribal hatred" between Hutu and Tutsi. Atavistic animosity drove the killings, it was said; that idea remains popular today.

For a decade thereafter, scholars with knowledge of Rwanda and human rights activists labored to show how problematic such a lens was. Historians demonstrated how colonialism had shaped the categories of Hutu and Tutsi, and they showed how Rwandan political leaders in turn had manipulated the colonial constructions to serve particular political purposes. "Tribal hatred" was a very poor and inaccurate lens to understand the specific political history of ethnicity and the kinds of influence that European actors had on the development of those identities.

At the same time, human rights activists began to document the ways in which the violence was systematically organized, the ways in which state authorities fomented killing as a policy, and the ways in which the modern tools of state administration, media, and civil defense contributed to the violence. Rather than a spontaneous outburst of ancient hatred, the Rwandan case was described as a preplanned, meticulously implemented genocide—one that the international community failed to stop.

That new consensus in turn reigned. It became the foundation for a set of accusations that prosecutors at the United Nations–backed International Criminal Tribunal for Rwanda (ICTR) levied against the genocide's presumed architects. They set out to prove the guilt of the top-level authorities who were most responsible for planning and executing the genocide.

The Rwandan case in turn emerged as a parallel to other highly planned, meticulously organized genocides, such as the Holocaust. That too was the image that the new government in Rwanda cultivated, a government currently led by the Rwandan Patriotic Front, which is the organization that led the rebellion and that had unseated the genocidal government in 1994. In their public communication on Rwanda and in their official memorialization, the Rwandan genocide became the story of a racist regime that would rather exterminate the Tutsi minority than share power with it. Indeed, a certain orthodoxy about the history of the genocide has developed inside Rwanda, and to question that orthodoxy is to risk accusations of genocidal "denial."

To be sure, some studies of the genocide, in particular at the local level, have complicated that picture. Those studies showed how fluid and dynamic the genocide was in particular locations, a set of findings that called into question the model of a meticulously organized and implemented genocide. But overall the narrative of a preplanned genocide held sway both at the international level and in Rwanda.

Missing from the discussion was a careful analysis of the national actors who were responsible for planning and implementing the genocide. Much of the existing analysis turned on connecting high-level elites to the development of particular institutions—such as the media, the civil defense force, and militias—that during the genocide became pivotal in how the violence was executed. Other analysis turned on the key national-level actors who appeared to be the ones calling the shots in the first few days of the genocide. But a detailed picture of how a genocide plan developed, who developed it, when it was developed, and how it was implemented at the national level remained opaque. We did not know exactly how genocide became state policy.

Enter André Guichaoua. A sociologist by training, Guichaoua had conducted research in Rwanda on issues of rural development in the 1980s and early 1990s. He thus had gained perspective on the country and its authorities prior to the onset of civil war in 1990 and the genocide in 1994. That experience afforded him an insight into the nature of the state and key political actors that had escaped many scholars who studied Rwanda only after the genocide took place.

Guichaoua in turn became one of the leading expert witnesses for the prosecution at the ICTR. In that role, Guichaoua gained access to a collection of testimonies, investigations, and reports that had previously been unavailable to other scholars. Combined with that access, Guichaoua was able to draw on the rich source of his own informants, in particular Hutu elites who were not implicated in the genocide but who had insider perspectives on what had happened.

As a function of his access to the prosecution's evidence and his connections, Guichaoua began to piece together the period before the genocide and the critical days and weeks after the triggering event on 6 April 1994, when President Juvénal Habyarimana was assassinated. Guichaoua's focus was primarily the key national-level actors—in the Rwandan military, in the party of the president, and in the government. The result is *From War to Genocide*, a detailed, sophisticated account of how the policy of genocide took shape and came to be.

There is an enormous amount to learn in these pages. Before I read Guichaoua's analysis, I had been studying the genocide for more than fifteen years. But through this book, I came to understand the events in a way that I never had before. This is simply essential reading for anyone who wishes to understand what happened at the center—at the seat of power—both before and during the genocide. What this book does that no other has before it is to show the process by which genocide became state policy. And in so doing, Guichaoua calls into question the standard account of how that process happened.

Guichaoua excels in describing the political biographies and the political rivalries that existed among the political elite in Rwanda. *From War to Genocide* similarly shines in describing the evolution of political strategies on the eve of the genocide. In particular, while much has been written on Hutu Power—a coalition of Hutu-led political movements that sided with the president's party—Guichaoua shows the evolution of the political strategies that were the foundation for that movement. He shows the gradual radicalization among key political and military actors, and he shows how the political field in Rwanda narrowed into a bipolarized environment, which in turn contributed to an ethnicized vision of how to retain power. These developments were gradual and probably not initially planned, but they in turn became critical in how political and military elites responded in April 1994 in the key days and weeks that set the genocide in motion.

Indeed, one of the most significant contributions of this book is to examine the fateful days that followed the assassination of President Habyarimana, an event that is clearly of tremendous significance in the way that Guichaoua narrates the events. Through his research, Guichaoua shows how key Rwandan actors in the presidential family, or who were loyal to it, sought revenge in the hours after the assassination. In Guichaoua's account, they do not appear to have anticipated the assassination, and after it, in a vengeful mindset, they set out to decapitate the political opposition.

Guichaoua further details the ways in which these actors sought to gain the upper hand, to maneuver around the moderates and democrats, including even some within their own camp, who favored negotiation, and to put in place a government prone to a hard-line, anti-RPF coalition. By their logic, political advantage lay with the Hutu majority, and they would play that card against the Tutsi rebels, who represented the minority. Here was a political logic that lent itself to genocide but was not imagined initially as genocide.

Guichaoua's evidence also shows how a policy of genocide still did not emerge as the official stance of this newly installed Interim Government until somewhere around 12 April, by which time it had abandoned the capital in Kigali to the encroaching Rwandan Patriotic Front. He shows how the evolution of that policy depended on a number of developments. It depended on the dynamics of the war with the Rwandan Patriotic Front, which was unrelenting in its advance and apparently wanted to impose a military solution. It depended on the chaos and the intrigues that the assassination of President Habyarimana caused at the heart of the government. It depended on the abdication of the international community and specifically the diplomats and United Nations personnel who could have intervened to protect civilians but did not. And it depended on a political logic of framing the struggle as one between an overwhelming ethnic majority and a militant minority, a logic that dated back to the origins of Hutu rule in the early 1960s.

In contrast to a model of preplanning and methodical implementation, Guichaoua's account demonstrates the gradual emergence of a policy of genocide, and he emphasizes the ways in which the result was neither inevitable nor devoid of the political and military context in which the key decisions were taken. In his hands, the genocide was part of a strategic interaction between those who sought to retain power in the aftermath of Habyarimana's assassination and those who sought to gain it through military means, that is, the Rwandan Patriotic Front (RPF). The genocide cannot therefore be separated from the political context of democratization and the military context of civil war. In describing that process, Guichaoua shows how contingent that process was, even if it was inscribed in a political logic that dates back to the revolution period.

This book is a major contribution to an understanding of the genocide in Rwanda, challenging accepted narratives about how the genocide came about. In particular, the story that Guichaoua tells differs in significant ways from the narrative that the RPF government in Rwanda has canonized. To read this analysis is to have a very different view of how a policy of genocide emerged.

From War to Genocide also constitutes a broader contribution about how a genocide policy develops. Guichaoua's account offers a portrait of a genocide that will aid scholars who wish to understand genocide, mass atrocity, and political violence from a comparative perspective.

A clear misreading of *From War to Genocide* is to claim that because Guichaoua shows a context-dependent evolution toward a policy of destroying the Tutsi population he denies genocide. That is far from what he does. Rather, he shows that a genocide policy may develop, but that policy may develop over time without clear preplanning and forethought. The result is therefore a nuanced account of genocide rather than a plotted, teleological, or static version of the events.

Much has been written about the Rwandan genocide and its aftermath since 1994. That is as it should be. The genocide itself was one of the great human rights crimes of the twentieth century. Moreover, the violence was not one-sided. The RPF rebels committed atrocities as they advanced against the genocidal forces and afterward as they established their political control over the country. Those actors in turn committed atrocities in neighboring Democratic Republic of Congo. All told, the violence that this region experienced in the 1990s and into the 2000s is among the most harrowing and disturbing. Scholars, journalists, filmmakers, and activists should be drawing the world's attention to the region and its history.

From War to Genocide stands out in that crowded field. It fills gaps in the empirical record and provides nuance to the trajectory of action in Rwanda's fateful hours of violence. It does not answer every question and will not satisfy every reader. No book does. But this book takes us a very long way toward understanding Rwanda's horror.

Preface to the English Edition

The present volume is the culmination of almost twenty years of research on the circumstances and tragic unfolding of the Rwanda bloodbath. It draws from a broad range of materials. In addition to offering a sustained inquest into the part played by critical events and personalities, it gives pride of place to the wealth of testimonies given before domestic and international judicial bodies by Rwandan actors and expert witnesses, including my own.

This English-language edition is an abridged version of the original French text. In the event of any differences in translations or interpretations the French version shall prevail. Readers may consult the website that was mounted to complement the French publication (http://rwandadelaguerreau genocide.univ-paris1.fr/). It incorporates many of the items that have been left out here, such as the "boxed-in" explanatory commentaries and transcriptions of testimonies and related papers. The boxes provide additional factual background for the events recounted herein, including relevant biographical information about many of the persons mentioned in the text. The website also includes over five thousand pages of various source materials ("annexes"), assembled with a view to making documentation of one of the most dramatic episodes of the last century readily accessible to a wide audience.

What makes *From War to Genocide* unlike any other dealing with the 1994 genocide goes beyond the broad range of materials consulted. If the book has any merit, it lies in what it tells us about the inner dynamics and contested unfolding of the killing process.

By September 1994, Rwanda was a country that had lost much of its population. A million were dead; two million were living in exile. Among those who stayed in their devastated homeland were survivors of the massacres and Hutu who had resisted the flight into exile, all trying to locate their missing and their dead, struggling simply to get on with their lives. By year's end, various international commissions of inquiry began to take form, all seeking to make sense of what had happened, followed by countless academic colloquia. The participants went to great lengths to come up with explanations for the tragedy. Why genocide? Could it be construed as the outcome of ethnic hatred? Of overpopulation in conditions of resource scarcity? Of blind obedience to authority? Of murderous connections between state authorities and genocidal ideologues? Of the influence or intervention of foreign powers? Whether simplistic or sophisticated, these hasty speculations focused on why these massacres happened but not on how they occurred.

The summoning of expert witnesses before the International Criminal Tribunal for Rwanda (ICTR) in Arusha, Tanzania, often led to additional field investigations, a reflection of its exacting standards of inquiry. The aim was no longer to ask why genocide had occurred but how it had been perpetrated and to parse the evidence a bit more critically. A host of questions arose. How and when was it decided that the genocide should take place? Who made the critical decision? Who set in motion the killing machine? Who kept it going over the course of three agonizing months? Who were the killers? How did they kill? Who were the victims? In what circumstances? In response to whose orders or threats? What were the motives? And with what means, and whose support?

The ICTR Office of the Prosecutor chartered a procedural path that led to months of protracted investigations on the hillsides and in the prisons. Dozens of missions were carried out to countries where perpetrators, victims, and witnesses alike had found refuge. These expert witnesses amassed an abundance of recorded statements and source materials of various sorts, including memoranda and diaries, all of which had to be carefully reviewed and compared, sometimes translated, and then analyzed. The results of this research have been the focus of contradictory debate before the Trial Chambers of the ICTR and have contributed to many of the latter's judgments.

The history of the war and the genocide was thus reconstructed bit by bit, blow by blow, to reflect its complexity. My primary objective here is to trace how the "genocidal government" was initially set up and eventually managed to take over and instrumentalize the massive apparatus of state authority. In so doing, I have tried to lay bare the ambitions, calculations, and actions of those who undertook the massacres while bringing out episodes of individual resistance to the killings, which more often than not reveal valiant efforts to save Tutsi lives.

No effort at uncovering the truth and aiding the quest for justice can succeed unless we try to contextualize the war and its tragic epilogue. This is basic to an understanding of the "politics of genocide" and the first step toward identifying and holding the principal perpetrators to account. What emerges from this tale of woe is that the much-touted notion of a *projet génocidaire* is of little help in explaining the rise of the new regime. Nor can it be taken as the defining trait of President Juvénal Habyarimana's Second Republic; his government, as we shall demonstrate, can hardly be identified with the extremist Hutu forces that committed genocide. On 6 April 1994—the date conventionally agreed upon to mark the onset of the crisis—the government that held power was in no way prepared or willing to engage in mass murder. Neither the prime minister nor the military high command could be counted among the *génocidaires*. It took another full week for a group of extremist Hutu elements to neutralize the army's loyalist officers and to install the Interim Government, which made genocide of the Tutsi a matter of "public policy." And then it would take yet another week to "cleanse" the local and provincial civil service and drag the prefectures of the central and southern regions into the killing spree.

The end was neither inevitable nor planned. While the downing of the presidential plane on 6 April touched off a sequence of events that set the conditions for mass murder, it was not the primary cause of the genocide. Over the course of days and weeks, the deadly logic of confrontation could be pushed to such extremes only because the main protagonists refused to consider any possible alternative. Indeed, the costs in human life and material destruction seemed wholly acceptable to them, given the ultimate objectives they had set for themselves. Therein perhaps lies the greatest lesson of the Rwandan tragedy.

Most of those responsible for the genocide have been arrested, tried, and convicted. Others will certainly follow, because there is no statute of limitations to hold them beyond the reach of prosecutions for genocide, crimes against humanity, and war crimes. Sadly, the conflict that erupted in Rwanda in 1994 eventually engulfed the entire region of central Africa in the First Great African War of 1998–2003, causing over a million civilian casualties. The conflict continues to this day, with deadly armed confrontations repeatedly breaking out in the eastern Congo. Thus, the struggle against impunity remains more than ever an absolute imperative for those who value and who would seek to restore a lasting peace and hope for the peoples of the region.

ANDRÉ GUICHAOUA

Paris, January 2015

Preface to the Original Edition

More than fifteen years have passed, yet the genocide perpetrated against the Tutsi in Rwanda stands as the defining image conjured up by the mere mention of this small central African country. Admittedly, the pain and horror of this tragic episode in 1994 will forever mark the lives and character of Rwanda's people, just as surely as it has sullied the conscience of an international community that refused to intervene to stop the massacres.

Today, however, it is difficult to ignore the paradox inscribed in the rapid pace of reconstruction, on the one hand, with the rise of an authoritarian social order, on the other. The former is fueled by the immense scale of investments that drastically churn up the landscape, especially in urban centers. In counterpoint, a starkly authoritarian social order emergent in the increasingly divisive political context in Rwanda is on the rise, apparently as a result of the intensity of economic and political transformations wrought by the new Tutsi elites who have since acceded to power. This situation is all the more surprising because these elites insist on imposing their own conception of "truth, justice, and reconciliation" and deploy an impressive arsenal of sanctions and incentives to build "national unity."

Explanations abound for the persistence of such intense contestations, and I will try to address them in the chapters that follow. I should emphasize from the start, however, that from 1994 onward there have been intense polemics, even when it comes to factual matters. Here also, despite the multiplicity of investigations and commissions charged with exploring the causes and the blame to be apportioned for the genocide, significant aspects of this war, which started in October 1990, have still not been clarified. Much remains to be explored to reveal or unravel the chain of events that engendered this catastrophe. Consequently, faced with the puzzling refusal of international actors to pursue this effort at truth seeking to its logical conclusion, and given the regime's firm commitment to expunging from the historical record all episodes and eyewitness accounts likely to cast doubt on its own self-serving discourse of "liberation," civil war has now resumed in the realm of propaganda. The Kigali regime draws its legitimacy from its military victory over the former genocidal forces and plays upon the guilty conscience of all those who allowed the genocide to run its course. Supporters of the former Hutu-dominated regime, on the other hand, never cease to denounce the victors' hegemony inside the country and insistently draw attention to their efforts to suppress the truth so as to camouflage, if not to justify, their own crimes.

To make sense of this rather exceptional situation, it is important to note that the current malaise mirrors political choices from years past from which stemmed grievously mistaken assumptions. In this context, no task is more important than to expose and lay bare those fragments of "truth"—whether confirmed or contested—that emerge from the record over a period of time, now available in sufficient volume and with requisite particularity to facilitate a coherent analytic framework.

Before getting started, I will review a few key historical moments from the final years of the Second Republic that paved the way to the crisis. On 1 July 1987 the celebration of the twenty-fifth anniversary of Rwanda's independence took place with over one hundred foreign delegations in attendance. The broad cross section, representing all manner of political persuasion, praised Rwanda's achievements in economic and social development. More significantly, and without the least hesitation, they endorsed the regime of President Juvénal Habyarimana for its accomplishments in matters of "governance," the novel concept then promoted by international aid organizations in search of good pupils to showcase as outstanding achievers in development. Undeniably, of the three autocratic guarantors of regional stability, along with Jean-Baptiste Bagaza in Burundi and Mobutu Sese Seko in Zaire, Habyarimana was the darling of the international community—or, rather, the least objectionable.

The founding of the First Republic under President Grégoire Kayibanda brought to an end the struggle for independence and formalized the collapse of the Tutsi monarchy, hitherto used as a prop by Belgian colonizers. The Second Republic followed in 1973, when Col. Juvénal Habyarimana, a northerner, engineered the coup d'état that lifted him to power. Adopting a developmentalist ideology, the Habyarimana regime enjoyed the active support of the West, most notably the Belgians and the French. Additionally, assistance poured in from international donor agencies and nongovernmental organizations (NGOs) of various ilk, especially the Catholic Church, which, since independence, has remained highly influential in shaping policies.

More fundamentally, however, the regime's most salient characteristics—an authoritarian populism rooted in mass mobilization, "forced-draft" participation, and demagogic closeness to the peasant masses—have exerted a powerful attraction for sympathizers of "Third Worldism" and the technocratic elites. Rwanda was then commonly referred to as the "country of a thousand aid agencies."

The celebration of 1 July 1987 marked the end of the glorious years of the Second Republic, entirely centered around the ruling party, the National Revolutionary Movement for Development (MRND), and its founding president, Juvénal Habyarimana. The years that followed were difficult, marked not only by great economic constraints but also by a strengthening of "civil society" organizations and the rise of democratic demands. Then on 1 October 1990 came the turning point: an estimated five thousand "refugee warriors" fought their way into the country under the banner of the Rwandan Patriotic Front (RPF), a political-military movement created by Tutsi exiles who had put down roots in Uganda in the wake of the setbacks suffered in the years immediately preceding and following independence. A long and bitter civil war followed, which ended tragically after three months of brutal confrontations and at the cost of hundreds of thousands of deaths in the months following the crash of President Habyarimana's plane on 6 April 1994.

This study picks up where my most recent analyses of regional conflicts left off.[1] It expands on the theme of the politics of genocide begun in my earlier work on the role of local authorities.[2] Here the unfolding of the Rwandan conflict is analyzed at the level of the central political authorities: government and party officials and the various high-level decision makers. The focus is on the functioning of the state; the complex conduits of power introduced by multiparty politics; and the political and military conduct of the civil war, including grass-roots mobilizations, shifts in political allegiances, negotiations, institutional adaptations, targeted assassinations, bombings, exactions, and killings. Of course, a major portion of the analysis is devoted to the role of the MRND, which, after the relatively brief interlude of multiparty politics introduced by the new constitution, adopted on 10 June 1991, recovered de facto quasi-exclusive power on 9 April 1994 with the installation of an Interim Government purportedly speaking on behalf of the "Hutu people," the incarnation of a victimized nation. The narrative follows the trajectories of several notable political figures from the MRND party who played highly influential roles during the Second Republic.

My aim, in essence, is principally to establish the facts and then to infer the underlying strategies. The narrative draws from numerous accounts by civilian and military actors. It gives careful consideration to their "agendas," in both senses of the term; that is, their annotated diaries and also their personal strategies. This applies to a number of key figures over the course of the war. It also helps clarify a number of episodes and reactions that had long remained obscure or little known. In particular, it throws into relief the attitudes, policy goals, and perceptions held by those most directly implicated in the issues at stake in the conflict. Not the least of the merits of this multidimensional approach is to offer the reader fresh perspectives on the roots of the tragedy.

First, I examine the internal political sphere, which hinges around the rival formations spawned by the advent of multipartyism in 1991 and the ensuing political divisions within certain state organs. This is where a wide-angle look at the political arena may help us understand its convulsions, for until then, the single party and its leaders dictated all aspects of the public life, and a large portion of the private life, of Rwandan citizens. This preeminence persisted under multipartyism. During the years of political liberalization and of civil war (1991–94), the question at the heart of all the debates concerned the hold that leaders and members of the MRND exercised over the political and economic gears and thus also the means of suspending or loosening that hold. The *mouvance présidentielle* nonetheless remained at the center of national political life and stood as the principal point of reference for the opposition to define its position.[3] Outside the political sphere, public opinion tended to fluctuate in accordance with the ebb and flow of the democratic tide. The country moved apace with struggles whose rhythm and modalities were beholden to the civil war and the evolutions in its two major protagonists, presidential power and the armed Tutsi rebellion, both as ferociously opposed to unleashing political forces beyond their firm control as they were to any genuine sharing of power.

In brief, my aim is to underscore the complex dialectic involved in the struggles for power going on at the domestic level and the deadly stand-off between the two political-military adversaries, one identified with northern extremist officers of the Forces armées rwandaises (FAR, Armed Forces of Rwanda), the other represented by the Tutsi-dominated Rwandan Patriotic Army / Rwandan Patriotic Front (RPA/RPF). Whether the latter could be expected to attain its central objective—the (re)conquest of power—did not depend solely on the support of Tutsi refugees from Uganda and other neighboring states; a critical tactical issue, from the standpoint of the Habyarimana government, had to do with the uncertainties created by the rise of a vigorous domestic opposition to the mouvance présidentielle.

The second perspective concerns the obligation to clearly articulate the various levels of analysis in the political landscape and its structures and actors.

Simply put, understanding the linkages and the course of events demands a keen appreciation of the strategies of identifiable but nonetheless poorly known decision makers in civilian or significant military command. In their minds, and each in their own way, personal ambition and the "overriding national imperative" always overlapped in one way or another. And the conflation was even more intense for those principal figures who emerged during the Second Republic in key positions. This is where the rules for creating legitimacy and preserving the social order were defined and elaborated. They ended up believing in a fate that would propel them to the commanding heights of the state; in short, they saw themselves as the embodiment of a truly "national destiny."

From this perspective, it is important first to understand the rules of the game prevailing in the clientelist system operating at the twilight of the Second Republic along with its peculiar modalities, including the selection of candidates to high office. It is equally important to appreciate how, at a later stage, those candidates' competing strategies for ascendancy within the hierarchies of power, for co-opting and appropriating political, financial, economic, military, and diplomatic resources, affected these same rules of the game and juggled the risks and the stakes.

President Habyarimana was at the very heart of this delicate system, which he had patiently constructed around his person, but he himself was at its mercy when the "creatures" he sired and commanded became major players in his retinue, sufficiently independent to embody competing poles of authority. In peacetime, taming ambitions was relatively easy. It depended largely on the distributions of bounty and official posts, the sources for replenishment and accessibility, both dependent on the strength of their links with the central core of the clientelist system. Juvénal Habyarimana could shatter or loosen those links at any moment.

In the context of the instability created by multipartyism and then by civil war, the strength and the intensity of these poles evolved in relation to the fluctuating circumstances, and, beset and somewhat shaken by the challenges, mastery of the system became much more problematic. In particular, the range of political resources available to the various protagonists in the conflict broadened significantly. Among them could be counted "legitimate" means, to the extent this distinction still made sense, as well as exceptional or usually prohibited practices and "criminal" activities.

The creation of youth wings by the parties and their evolution provides ample illustration of this development: initially, militant consciousness-raising via various socioeducative activities or sporting events; then support for activities geared toward partisan mobilization, organization in militias, and military training; and finally, loans of armed groups to "private" entities and propagation of groups whose activities involved pure banditry.

However, when the protagonists sensed that outright criminality had become necessary in order to achieve their objectives, they did not view their crimes as "violations" but rather as acts of war. At that time, for them, those crimes—propaganda and incitement to racial hatred, threats to property and persons, pillage, targeted killings, explosions, mass killings leading to extermination of an ethnic group characterized as the enemy—could be deemed a functional necessity wholly derived from vital, strategic decision making. The intensive mobilization of such resources and means of action was then limited to the actors who mastered them and who could cast off all moral prohibitions and rules imposed by a state of law. This explains how the authorities or the general staff had recourse to the entire panoply of weapons and were able to envisage and order the annihilation of any individual or group identified as obstacles to their political plans.

We should also recall that recourse to brutal and radical methods was routine in this region of the African continent, plagued as it was by serial political crises and civil wars in decades past. Mired in the afterbirth of failed transitions to independence, almost all accompanied by extreme forms of violence and hefty tolls in human and material loss (e.g., in Uganda, Central Africa, Congo-Zaire, Burundi, and Rwanda), these crises—with constantly shifting stakes—fed on each other and, over time, inscribed themselves in the memory of the elites and at every level of the population like current or inevitable episodes.

In the aftermath of the downing of President Habyarimana's plane, the aggressor raised the stakes to their highest levels, thus unleashing the energies of Hutu extremists. Since the second half of 1993, the latter had adopted a staunch anti-RPF, anti-Tutsi stance. Within hours of the plane crash they emerged as the most forceful, and they responded by decapitating the moderate political opposition to capture power for themselves. After a deliberate, complicit neutering of external actors (including, preeminently, UNAMIR [United Nations Assistance Mission for Rwanda] and foreign troops), the absence or failure of a negotiated end to the conflict, rapidly confirmed, conferred an absolute and definitive character to the war: from all corners it was described as "final."[4] For the belligerents, no longer was there any sense of limitation in the means and the scope of action undertaken in pursuit of victory.

Consequently, this approach, anchored in the strategies and objectives undertaken by the protagonists, seeks to explore the nature and magnitude of the parties' mobilization of political resources during the war, which then gives rise to a rather unique approach to the question of "planning" the crimes or the "conspiracy" that led to them. Supported by a meticulous factual reconstruction of events, it demonstrates why the evolution and the immediate environment of the unfolding war, the reprise of hostilities during the night of 6–7 April, and the unleashing of genocide cannot be uncoupled. Above all, it also points to when and by whom genocide was brokered and guided (*see box 1*).

Postscript: As the reader will be able to see, the review and cross-checking of source materials were accomplished systematically. However, despite the efforts made to provide trustworthy documentation, to corroborate the information and the accounts relied upon, and to reread, revise, and correct the final text, it is inevitable that errors, imprecisions, or misstatements may have slipped through. Let me take this opportunity to beg your indulgence and to apologize in advance if this is the case.

André Guichaoua

Paris, February 2010

Acknowledgments

My sincere thanks go to Don Webster for his excellent translation from the original French to this English version and to René Lemarchand for his judicious editing. I am also very grateful to Jean Majeres for his careful review of the manuscript and to Noël Twagiramungu, who coordinated the translation of the Kinyarwanda edition and whose critical oversight of successive drafts of the text in its three languages enhanced the end results.

The financial contribution of the Open Society Initiative for East Africa (Foundation Open Society Institute), which made this publication possible, is gratefully acknowledged.

Don Webster and I also greatly benefited from the academic and technical support and advice we received from the editorial team at the University of Wisconsin Press. The excellent collaboration we enjoyed with them ensured the final quality of this publication.

Abbreviations

AFDL	Alliance des forces démocratiques pour la libération du Congo (Alliance of Democratic Forces for the Liberation of the Congo)
ARD	Alliance pour le renforcement de la démocratie (Alliance for the Strengthening of Democracy)
ARDHO	Association rwandaise pour la défense des droits de l'homme (Rwandan Association for the Defense of Human Rights)
BACAR	Banque continentale africaine au Rwanda (African Continental Bank in Rwanda)
BBTG	Broad-Based Transitional Government (GTBE, Gouvernement de transition à base élargie)
BCR	Banque commerciale du Rwanda (Commercial Bank of Rwanda)
BNR	Banque nationale du Rwanda (National Bank of Rwanda)
CDR	Coalition pour la défense de la république (Coalition for the Defense of the Republic)
CEPGL	Communauté économique des pays des Grands Lacs (Economic Community of the Great Lakes Countries [Burundi, Rwanda, Zaire / Democratic Republic of the Congo])
CETA	Conférence des églises de toute l'Afrique (Nairobi) (AACC, All Africa Council of Churches)
Cimerwa	Cimenterie du Rwanda (Cyangugu) (Rwanda Cement Factory)
Civipol	United Nations Civilian Police (Police civile des Nations unies)
CND	Conseil national de développement (National Development Council, the Rwandan parliament)

CNDD-FDD	Conseil national pour la défense de la démocratie / Forces pour la défense de la démocratie (Burundi) (National Council for the Defense of Democracy / Forces for the Defense of Democracy)
CRR	Commission des recours des réfugiés (France); CNDA, Cour nationale du droit d'asile, since 2008 (Commission for Refugees, National Asylum Court since 2008)
DAMI	Détachement d'assistance militaire et d'instruction (France) (Group for Military Assistance and Training)
DGB	Développement global de Butare (Butare Global Development)
DRC	Democratic Republic of the Congo (RDC, République démocratique du Congo)
EO	École des officiers (Officers Training School)
ERN	Evidence Registration Number
ESM	École supérieure militaire (Kigali) (Senior Military Training School), formerly the EO
ESO	École des sous-officiers (Butare) (Noncommissioned Officers Training School)
FAR	Forces armées rwandaises (Rwandan Armed Forces)
FDC	Forces démocratiques du changement (Democratic Forces for Change)
FDD	Forces pour la défense de la démocratie (Burundi) (Forces for the Defense of Democracy)
FDLR	Forces démocratiques de libération du Rwanda (Democratic Forces for the Liberation of Rwanda)
FPR	Front patriotique rwandais (RPF, Rwandan Patriotic Front)
Frodebu	Front pour la démocratie au Burundi (Front for Democracy in Burundi)
G1	Unit of the army or gendarmerie general staff responsible for personnel
G2	Unit of the army or gendarmerie general staff responsible for intelligence
G3	Unit of the army or gendarmerie general staff responsible for operations
G4	Unit of the army or gendarmerie general staff responsible for logistics
G5	Unit of the army or gendarmerie general staff responsible for ideological or political training
GI	Gouvernement intérimaire (Interim Government)

GOMN	Groupe d'observateurs militaires neutres de l'OUA (Group of Neutral Military Observers of the OAU)
GP	Garde présidentielle (Presidential Guard)
HCR	Haut-commissariat des Nations unies pour les réfugiés (UNHCR, United Nations High Commission for Refugees)
HRW	Human Rights Watch
ICTR	United Nations International Criminal Tribunal for Rwanda (TPIR, Tribunal pénal international des Nations unies pour le Rwanda)
ICTY	International Criminal Tribunal for the former Yugoslavia
IDP	internally displaced person
IG	ingénieur de guerre (military engineer) (graduate of the War College in Hamburg, Federal Republic of Germany)
ISAR	Institut des sciences agronomiques du Rwanda (Butare) (Rwandan Institute for Agronomic Studies)
MAGERWA	Magasins généraux du Rwanda (Rwanda General Stores)
MDR	Mouvement démocratique républicain (Democratic Republican Movement)
MDR-Parmehutu	Mouvement démocratique républicain / Parti du mouvement de l'émancipation hutu (Democratic Republican Movement / Party of the Movement for the Emancipation of the Hutu)
MFBP	Mouvement des femmes et du bas-peuple (Women and Lower People Movement)
Minadef	Ministère de la Défense (Ministry of Defense)
Mineto	Ministère du Tourisme et de l'Environnement (Ministry of Tourism and the Environment)
Minicomart	Ministère du Commerce, de l'Industrie et de l'Artisanat (Ministry of Commerce, Industry, and Handicrafts)
Minifaprofe	Ministère de la Famille et de la Promotion féminine (Ministry of Family and Gender)
Minifop	Ministère de la Fonction publique (Ministry of Civil Service)
Minijeuma	Ministère de la Jeunesse et du Mouvement associatif (Ministry of Youth and Associative Movement)
Minijust	Ministère de la Justice (Ministry of Justice)
Minimart	Ministère de l'Industrie et de l'Artisanat (Ministry of Industry and Handicrafts)
Mininfor	Ministère de l'Information (Ministry of Information)
Mininter	Ministère de l'Intérieur (Ministry of the Interior)

Miniplan	Ministère du Plan (Ministry of Planning)
Miniprisec	Ministère de l'Enseignement primaire et secondaire (Ministry of Primary and Secondary Education)
Minisanté	Ministère de la Santé (Ministry of Health)
Minitracom	Ministère des Transports et des Communications (Ministry of Transportation and Communication)
Minitrape	Ministère des Travaux publics et de l'Énergie (Ministry of Public Works and Energy)
Minitraso	Ministère du Travail et des Affaires sociales (Ministry of Labor and Social Affairs)
MONUSCO	Mission de l'Organisation des Nations unies pour la stabilisation en République démocratique du Congo (United Nations Organization Stabilization Mission in the DR Congo)
MRND	Mouvement révolutionnaire national pour le développement (Revolutionary National Movement for Development)
MRNDD	Mouvement républicain national pour la démocratie et le développement (National Republican Movement for Democracy and Development)
MSF	Médecins sans frontières (Doctors without Borders)
NGO	nongovernmental organization
NRA	National Resistance Army (Uganda)
NSGJ	National Service of Gacaca Jurisdictions
OAU	Organization of African Unity (OUA, Organisation de l'unité africaine; African Union or Union Africaine since 1999)
OCIR-Café	Office des cultures industrielles du Rwanda–Café (Rwandan Office for Industrial Cultivation–Coffee)
OCIR-Thé	Office des cultures industrielles du Rwanda–Thé (Rwandan Office for Industrial Cultivation–Tea)
ODJ	*ordre du jour* (agenda)
OFPRA	Office français de protection des réfugiés et des apatrides (French Office for the Protection of Refugees and Stateless Persons)
OHCHR	Office of the United Nations High Commissioner for Human Rights
ONAPO	Office national de la population (Office for National Statistics)
ONATRACOM	Office national des transports en commun (National Public Transport Authority)

ONU	Organisation des Nations unies (United Nations)
OPS	operational sector (*secteur opérationnel*)
Orinfor	Office rwandais de l'information (Rwandan Office of Information)
ORTPN	Office rwandais du tourisme et des parcs nationaux (Rwandan Office for Tourism and National Parks)
OTP	*originaire du terroir présidentiel* (native to or originating from President Habyarimana's home turf)
Pader	Parti démocrate rwandais (Rwandan Democratic Party)
Palipehutu	Parti de la libération du peuple hutu (Burundi) (Party for the Liberation of the Hutu People)
Parerwa	Parti républicain rwandais (Republican Party of Rwanda)
Parmehutu	Parti du mouvement de l'émancipation hutu (Party of the Movement for the Emancipation of the Hutu)
PAS	Programs of Structural Adjustment
PD	Parti démocrate (Democratic Party)
PDC	Parti démocrate chrétien (Christian Democratic Party)
PDI	Parti démocratique islamique (Islamic Democratic Party)
Peco	Parti des écologistes (Green Party)
PL	Parti libéral (Liberal Party)
PM	Police militaire (Military Police)
PPJR–Rama	Rwanda Parti progressiste de la jeunesse rwandaise (Progressive Party of the Rwandan Youth)
PRD	Parti pour le renouveau démocratique (Party for Democratic Renewal)
PSD	Parti social-démocrate (Social Democratic Party)
PSR	Parti socialiste rwandais (Rwandan Socialist Party)
PVK	Préfecture de la ville de Kigali (Prefecture of Central Kigali)
Rader	Rassemblement démocratique rwandais (Rwandan Democratic Rally)
RANU	Rwandese Alliance for National Unity
RCD	Rassemblement congolais pour la démocratie (Congolese Rally for Democracy)
"Recce"	Battalion Reconnaissance Squad (Escadron de "Reconnaissance")
RNC	Rwanda National Congress
RPA	Rwandan Patriotic Army, armed wing of the RPF (APR, Armée patriotique rwandaise)
RPF	Rwandan Patriotic Front (FPR, Front patriotique rwandais)

RRWF	Rwandese Refugee Welfare Foundation
RTD	Rassemblement travailliste pour la démocratie (Labour Rally for Democracy)
RTLM	Radio-Télévision libre des mille collines (Radio-Television of the Thousand Hills)
SCR	Service central de renseignement (Central Intelligence Bureau)
SORWAL	Société rwandaise d'allumettes (Butare) (Rwanda Match Company)
TNA	Transitional National Assembly (ANT, Assemblée nationale de transition)
UDPR	Union démocratique du peuple rwandais (Democratic Union of the Rwandan People)
UNAMIR	United Nations Assistance Mission in Rwanda (MINUAR, Mission des Nations unies pour l'assistance au Rwanda)
UNAR	Union nationale rwandaise (parti pro-monarchiste) (Rwandan National Union [monarchist party])
UNCHR	United Nations Commission on Human Rights
UNHCR	United Nations High Commissioner for Refugees
UNISODEC	Union sociale des démocrates chrétiens (Social Union of Christian Democrats)
URAMA	Urunana rw'abanyarwandakazi mu majyambere; Union des femmes militantes pour le développement (Union of Rwandese Women for Development); in Kinyarwanda, Mouvement national des femmes rwandaises pour le progrès
ZDF	Zimbabwe Defence Forces

Chronology

1923. The League of Nations confers Belgium with a mandate to administer Ruanda-Urundi, formerly a colony of Germany.

1925. Ruanda-Urundi is formally annexed to the Belgian Congo and placed under the authority of a vice governor general.

1943. *17 October*. The young king (*mwami*), Rudahigwa Mutara III, and his chiefs are baptized. Soon thereafter, with support from the Belgian administration, Mutara III replaces all of his Hutu chiefs with Tutsi chiefs.

1957. *24 March*. Publication of the "Manifesto of the Bahutu," denouncing the privileges of the Tutsi monarchy and Hutu exclusion from the economic, political, and social spheres.

1959. *3 September*. Tutsi monarchists create the National Rwandan Union (UNAR), which calls for independence.

18 October. Creation of the Party of the Movement for the Emancipation of the Hutu (Parmehutu).

1 November. Start of the "social revolution." There are violent clashes between supporters of Parmehutu and UNAR, which was supported by the monarchy. With support from the colonial authorities, Parmehutu installs new administrative officials (mostly Hutu) in the communes.

1960. *30 June*. Communal elections confer power on Parmehutu, with more than 70 percent of the vote, whereas UNAR, with only 2 percent, virtually disappears from the political scene.

1961. *28 January*. In Gitarama, newly elected burgomasters and communal counselors elect a legislative assembly and proclaim the republic. Dominique Mbonyumutwa is elected provisional president of the republic.

25 September. After organizing a referendum to formally establish the republic, legislative elections confer Parmehutu with the majority.

26 October. Grégoire Kayibanda (Parmehutu) is elected president of the First Republic. Massacres and exile of Tutsi continue.

1962. *1 July.* Rwanda proclaims its independence.

1963. *July–December.* Military units of Tutsi refugees based in Burundi launch repeated attacks against the new republican authorities. Anti-Tutsi pogroms take place inside Rwanda. Thousands of Rwandans seek refuge in neighboring countries.

1965. After his reelection as president, Grégoire Kayibanda transforms Parmehutu into a de facto single party. Juvénal Habyarimana enters the government with portfolios for the Ministry of Defense and the National Guard.

1966–67. Following several attacks from Tutsi refugees based in Burundi, which in turn lead to anti-Tutsi massacres inside Rwanda, the two countries sign an accord to neutralize the activities of armed groups of Tutsi refugees on Burundian territory.

1973. *5 July.* Maj. Juvénal Habyarimana launches a "moral" coup d'état. The constitution is suspended, and the Second Republic is inaugurated.

1975. *5 July.* The Committee for Peace and National Unity, made up of officers who had swept Juvénal Habyarimana to power, is disbanded, and the MRND, the single party, is founded.

18 July. The government signs a "military assistance agreement" with France for reorganization and training of the Rwandan gendarmerie.

1978. *24 December.* First presidential election of Juvénal Habyarimana.

1979. Rwandan refugees in Uganda create the Rwandese Refugee Welfare Foundation (RRWF), which adopted a political structure the following year, becoming the Rwandese Alliance for National Unity (RANU). Many of its members joined shortly after Yoweri Museveni's guerrilla war in Uganda.

1980. *April.* An attempted coup d'état by Théoneste Lizinde and Alexis Kanyarengwe, former "Friends of 5 July."

1982. *October.* Forced repatriation to Rwanda of forty to fifty thousand Banyarwanda (persons of Rwandan origin) resident in Uganda and flight of many others to Tanzania and Zaire.

1983. *19 December.* Reelection of President Juvénal Habyarimana.

1986. *26 July.* The Central Committee of the MRND takes a stance on the refugee question after most of the Rwandans who had been expelled in 1982 return to Uganda. The party acknowledges the principle of the right of return and plans to issue passports and laissez-passer entrance documents permitting regular visits to Rwanda.

1988. *5 February*. President Habyarimana speaks in Semuto (Uganda) and creates with President Museveni a Joint Rwanda-Ugandan Ministerial Committee on the problem of Rwandan refugees. During that same period, the RPF takes root in Uganda.

17–20 August. The Association of Banyarwanda in the Diaspora and the Committee for Refugees in the United States sponsor a conference and meetings of various movements representing Rwandan refugees in Washington, D.C.

19 December. Habyarimana is reelected president for a third term.

1989. *9 February*. A presidential decree authorizes the creation of a Special Commission on the Problems of Rwandan Refugees, and meetings of the Rwanda-Ugandan Ministerial Committee get under way.

1990. *May*. Publication of the report of the Special Commission on the Problems of Rwandan Refugees.

27–30 July. Meeting of the Special Commission on the Problems of Rwandan Refugees in Kigali, with participation from representatives of the United Nations High Commission for Refugees (HCR) and the Organization of African Unity (OAU). They work out the details of a "plan to definitively resolve the question of Rwandan refugees living in Uganda."

September. Visit of Pope John Paul II. Creation of the National Commission of Synthesis (Commission nationale de synthèse), with a mandate to draw up a draft national political charter.

1 October. The Rwandan Patriotic Front–Inkotanyi (the "valiant warriors," a nickname adopted by the RPF soldiers) attacks.

17–19 October. The presidents of Uganda, Rwanda, and Tanzania meet in Dar es Salaam, and the Mwanza accords take place.

Late October. The RPF withdraws to Uganda. With a faltering intervention by Zaire and the withdrawal of Belgian troops, French military assistance becomes decisive for ensuring the triumph of Rwandan government forces (FAR). Beginning with the military operation "Noroît," France actively supports Rwanda from October 1990 through December 1993.

1991. *7 and 25 January*. Eight Tutsi detainees are sentenced to death by the State Security Court.

23 January. The RPF attacks Ruhengeri town and liberates prisoners from the central prison (including Maj. Théoneste Lizinde).

January–February. Massacres of Bagogwe Tutsi in the northern Volcano region.

4 February. Under pressure from conservatives within the party, a new MRND government is set up.

5 February. Publication of the "Hutu Ten Commandments" in the magazine *Kangura.*

19 February. The heads of state of Burundi, Rwanda, Uganda, and Tanzania, the prime minister of Zaire, the secretary-general of the OAU, and the director of external relations of HCR convene in a summit in Dar es Salaam. They issue a statement on the "lasting solution to the problem of Rwandan refugees."

29 March. Under OAU supervision, Rwandan government officials and the RPF sign a cease-fire agreement in Zaire. Most of the 3,500 civilians arrested in the police sweep of October 1990 are released.

10 June. Adoption of the new constitution introducing multipartyism.

August. Meeting in Nairobi of representatives from Rwandan Christian churches with representatives of the refugees (in fact, the RPF) to promote dialogue and reconciliation. Representatives of the governments of Tanzania, Kenya, Zaire, and Burundi and the churches of Uganda also participate. Draft of the future "contact committee."

8–9 September. Regional Summit on the Rwandan Crisis held in Gbadolite, attended by the presidents of Burundi, Nigeria, Rwanda, and Zaire, the secretary-general of the OAU, the first vice president of Tanzania, and the Ugandan minister of foreign affairs.

13 October. Appointment of a prime minister, Sylvestre Nsanzimana (former minister of justice), and repeated attempts to form a new government.

13–15 December. Adoption of laws "announcing a general amnesty and a solution to the refugee problem" and "announcing an amnesty for certain infractions."

31 December. Formation of a new MRND government (plus one representative from the PDC) under the leadership of Prime Minister Sylvestre Nsanzimana.

1992. *3 February.* The first beneficiaries of the law on amnesty are released from detention.

10 March. Wave of anti-Tutsi repression and state of siege in Bugesera.

16 April. Formation of a multiparty government under the leadership of Dismas Nsengiyaremye (MDR) comprising the MRND, MDR, PL, PSD, and PDC, in which the MRND and the opposition parties are equally weighted.

18 April. Party congress of the "renovated" MRND.

22 April. President Habyarimana resigns from the army so that he can be eligible to put forth his candidacy in the next presidential election.

24 May. Initial contacts between the Rwandan government and the RPF in Kampala.

5 June. Cease-fire agreement between the RPF and the three opposition parties in the coalition government, despite MRND opposition.

12, 26 July and 11 August. Under OAU guidance, successive negotiation sessions between the Rwandan government and the RPF (in Arusha, Addis Ababa, and then again in Arusha).

1 August. Cease-fire.

11 August. Deployment of the Group of Neutral Military Observers of the OAU (GOMN).

18 August. Signature of the first protocol of agreement, the "Rule of Law" (the Arusha Peace Accords).

26 August. Signature of an addendum to the 1975 agreement on military assistance, with France extending its scope to the entire army.

30 October. Signature of the second protocol of agreement, "Power Sharing."

1993. *9 January.* As amended, the protocol "Power Sharing" of 30 October creates a post of vice prime minister, set aside for the RPF, and introduces a code of "political ethics," which political parties not participating in the Arusha negotiations are invited to sign. In turn, they would each gain a seat in the National Assembly.

8 February. Renewal of hostilities by the RPF with a massive attack in the north of the country. Over a million "internally displaced" persons encamp on the outskirts of Kigali.

15 March. Reprise of negotiations in Arusha.

2 June. In Burundi, first presidential elections with universal suffrage, installing Melchior Ndadaye (Hutu).

9 June. Signature of the third protocol of agreement, titled "Refugees and Displaced Persons," in Arusha.

3–4 July. Extraordinary MRND party congress and election of Matthieu Ngirumpatse as party chairman.

18 July. Agathe Uwilingiyimana (MDR) forms a new government.

3 August. Finalization in Arusha of the fourth (and the fifth) protocols of agreement (concerning the armed forces and miscellaneous issues).

4 August. Signing of the Arusha Peace Accords between the RPF and the government of Rwanda.

5 October. The United Nations Security Council adopts Resolution 872, authorizing the deployment of UNAMIR (United Nations Assistance Mission in Rwanda).

21 October. Melchior Ndadaye, the president of Burundi, is assassinated during an attempted putsch by Tutsi soldiers. HCR estimates that by late November there are 659,000 refugees, of which 375,000 are in Rwanda.

1 November. The deployment of UNAMIR troops begins.

15 December. Withdrawal of the French military contingent "Noroît."

28 December. RPF troops and representatives arrive in Kigali and are cantoned at the parliament building.

1994. *1 January.* Rwanda takes a seat on the United Nations Security Council as one of the eight nonpermanent members.

5 January. President Habyarimana is sworn in as president, but the setting up of the transitional government and the new Transitional National Assembly pursuant to the Arusha Peace Accords is delayed and rescheduled.

March. Lists of party representatives who will participate in government and the Transitional National Assembly are drawn up, along with repeated delays in setting up the transitional institutions.

6 April. Installation of the transitional institutions is scheduled for "8 or 9 April." UNAMIR's mandate is renewed for three months, and a summit of regional heads of state is held in Dar es Salaam, with presidents Arap Moi (Kenya), Habyarimana (Rwanda), Ntaryamira (Burundi), Mwinyi (Tanzania), and Museveni (Uganda) participating. Afterward, the aircraft transporting the presidents of Rwanda and Burundi for their return trip is shot down upon its approach to Kigali, around 8:20 p.m. that evening.

7 April. As RPF troops stationed near the border with Uganda advance toward Kigali, exchanges of live rounds start around 4:00 a.m. At 5:15 a.m, violent clashes are reported near the president's office; around the same time, Presidential Guard commandos seek out opposition figures in their homes and begin systematic assassinations. Among the first victims are Agathe Uwilingiyimana, the prime minister (MDR); Charles Shamukiga, an MDR member and consul to Luxembourg; Frédéric Nzamurambaho, minister of agriculture (PSD); Faustin Rucogoza, minister of information (MDR); and Landoald Ndasingwa, minister of labor (PL). UNAMIR is immobilized by the Presidential Guard, which controls the city. Ten Belgian "blue helmets" who arrived to protect Agathe Uwilingiyimana are disarmed and taken to Camp Kigali, where they are killed. Interahamwe militias, the youth wing of the ruling MRND party, surround and block off certain key neighborhoods, kill opposition figures and "infiltrators," and pillage and steal.

8 April. As clashes with the RPF spread throughout the capital, negotiations are under way within the army. In the evening, the Interim Government headed by Jean Kambanda (MDR) is formed. Soldiers and Interahamwe militiamen commence systematic massacres, primarily targeting Tutsi.

9 April. French paracommandos take control of the airport, where violent combat continues (Operation Amaryllis). A new president of the republic is named, Théodore Sindikubwabo, former MRND speaker of the parliament, and the new Interim Government is installed. Paul Kagame issues a statement challenging the legitimacy of this government. The RPF launches attacks against Byumba and Ruhengeri towns. Massacres spread throughout the country. Evacuations of foreign nationals begin.

10 April. The Interim Government is sworn into office. The first Belgian airplanes arrive.

11 April. The Interim Government flees Kigali for Murambi (Gitarama prefecture).

13 April. Intense gun battles resume in Kigali. The activities of the Presidential Guard and militiamen now spread to the country's interior, and prefectures where the situation was calm are now swept up in the torrent. The national radio calls for immediate negotiations with the RPF and a unilateral cease-fire to take effect the next day.

14 April. The RPF tacitly agrees to a cease-fire to facilitate the evacuation of the last remaining foreign expatriates. Hostilities progressively take hold in Kigali over the course of the afternoon. The withdrawal of 450 Belgian soldiers is announced. The RPF delivers an ultimatum for the departure of all foreign troops by midnight.

15 April. Meeting in Kigali between a delegation from the RPF and a "coalition of officers representing the Rwandan government."

16 April. Another meeting is set for the RPF and the "government."

17 April. The RPF insists that the Presidential Guard be disbanded and that the "puppet government" be dissolved as preconditions for any negotiation.

19 April. Violent clashes in Kigali. The city of Butare is now also "aflame." Gitarama prefecture alone remains relatively calm.

19–20 April. The Belgian "blue helmets" depart Kigali.

22 April. United Nations resolution modifying UNAMIR's mandate and reducing UN ground forces to the bare minimum (120 civilians and 150 soldiers under the command of Gen. Roméo Dallaire). The mandate is now exclusively political.

23 April. Violent combat in the north of the country (Byumba and Ruhengeri prefectures).

24 April. Delays in the Arusha negotiations because of the absence of the government delegation. The RPF announces a unilateral cease-fire for midnight the next day.

27 April. In the morning, violent combat resumes in Kigali. The RPF announces that it has taken control of Rwamagana, in the south.

30 April. The RPF takes control of the border crossing at Rusumo, at the border with Tanzania. In New York, the Security Council condemns the massacres (four countries, including the United States, object to the use of the term "genocide" in the resolution), and Secretary-General Boutros Boutros-Ghali makes a vain request for armed intervention or a weapons embargo.

1 May. The RPF seals the border with Tanzania, forcing the FAR to move westward.

2 May. An apparent cease-fire in Kigali. The RPF advances toward Kibungo.

3 May. In Kigali, intense exchange of fire with heavy arms between the RPF and the Presidential Guard.

4 May. The "Battle of Kigali" is fully under way.

5 May. Continued fighting in Kigali; increasingly stronger attacks against the last centers of refuge for civilian Tutsi.

6 May. Signing of a cease-fire with the RPF in Gbadolite. Violent clashes in Kigali. Ruhengeri is surrounded.

11 May. Meeting in Byumba between José Ayala Lasso, United Nations high commissioner for human rights, and Gen. Paul Kagame, commander of the RPA.

16 May. The RPF cuts off the road from Kigali to Gitarama, where the high command of the FAR had just relocated.

17 May. The Security Council approves Resolution 918, authorizing an international interventionist force for humanitarian assistance (5,500 troops).

22 May. The RPF seizes control of the international airport in Kigali and the military base at Kanombe.

23 May. The presidential palace in Kigali is captured. Eight African countries offer to participate in UNAMIR II.

24 May. In Geneva, the third extraordinary session on the situation in Rwanda of the United Nations Commission on Human Rights begins. The following day, a motion is adopted without vote to appoint a special rapporteur to investigate the possibility of genocide.

2–3 June. The RPF captures Kabgayi. Three Catholic bishops are kidnapped and killed. The following Sunday the White Fathers condemn RPF massacres (listing sixty-four priests killed).

6 June. Opening of the Thirtieth Summit of the OAU in Tunisia, where debates on Rwanda draw much of the attention; the FAR attempts its final, major counterattack near Kabgayi.

8 June. The RPF acknowledges the deaths of the three bishops.

10 June. Partial withdrawal of the government to Gisenyi.

12 June. The OAU condemns "crimes against humanity" committed in Rwanda.

13 June. Gitarama falls to the RPF. At the OAU Summit in Tunisia, Secretary-General Salim Ahmed Salim characterizes the killings as "crimes against humanity." Boutros Boutros-Ghali questions the role of the international community (only three thousand soldiers, without equipment, are available for deployment).

14 June. Tunisian president Zine el-Abidine Ben Ali announces the signing of a cease-fire agreement negotiated by President Mobutu at the close of the OAU Summit.

15 June. Start of the cease-fire. Alain Juppé proposes an intervention by France in partnership with several other European and African countries.

16 June. The cease-fire in Kigali is violated. Alain Juppé announces plans for an "armed humanitarian intervention."

17 June. At the United Nations, Boutros Boutros-Ghali expresses support for the French initiative.

19 June. The French ambassador explains the objectives of the French intervention to members of the RPF in Kigali.

20 June. Debate at the UN Security Council on the French motion for intervention in Rwanda. China and Russia oppose, unless the parties to the conflict consent, and the OAU refuses to support the French initiative.

21 June. Jacques Bihozagara leads an RPF demonstration in front of the French Embassy in Brussels. The first detachment of French troops arrive at the Rwandan border with Zaire.

22 June. Alain Juppé receives Jacques Bihozagara in Paris. The United Nations Security Council authorizes the French intervention in Rwanda until 21 August, awaiting the mobilization of troops for UNAMIR II.

23 June. Beginning of Operation Turquoise: 2,500 soldiers progressively enter and take up positions in Goma and Bukavu, in Zaire.

26 June. Measured reaction from the RPF concerning the French intervention.

28 June. Special Rapporteur René Degni-Ségui presents his "Report on the Situation of Human Rights in Rwanda" to the United Nations Commission on Human Rights.

1 July. A UN commission of inquiry into acts of genocide committed in Rwanda is established.

3 July. The RPF captures Butare.

4 July. The RPF captures central Kigali.

5 July. French troops establish a "secure humanitarian zone" in the south-west of the country.

6 July. On behalf of the RPF, Faustin Twagiramungu initiates contacts to establish a government of national unity.

7 July. Kigali international airport reopens.

11 July. Massive movement of refugees toward the border with Zaire.

14 July. The RPF captures Ruhengeri. Faustin Twagiramungu returns to Kigali.

15 July. Some five hundred thousand refugees cross the border into Zaire.

16 July. Thirteen ministers and the president of the self-proclaimed Interim Government take refuge in the French humanitarian zone.

17 July. The RPF captures Gisenyi. Six hundred thousand refugees overwhelm Goma. The United Nations humanitarian airlift is suspended when the RPF fires on the airport in Goma. Some ten thousand FAR soldiers, interspersed with the refugees, cross the border into Zaire. Initially, most are disarmed by Zairean soldiers; later, entire columns cross the border with weapons, vehicles, rocket launchers, and semi-automatic weapons. Accompanied by the army chief of staff, the members of the Interim Government take refuge in Zaire. The RPF appoints Pasteur Bizimungu president of the Republic of Rwanda for a period of five years, and Faustin Twagiramungu is confirmed as prime minister, as anticipated by the Arusha Peace Accords, which had designated him prime minister of the transitional government.

18 July. The RPF proclaims a de facto cease-fire.

19 July. Faustin Twagiramungu's government is sworn into office.

22 July. The new Rwandan government calls for the return of refugees and a return to work by all civil servants. Upon arrival in Kigali and all across the country, newly returned Tutsi refugees seek to occupy abandoned homes and farmlands. The United Nations and related humanitarian agencies make appeals for contributions to ensure the survival of the Rwandan civilian population through December.

24 July. Prime Minister Joseph Kengo Wa Dondo of Zaire visits Goma. The border with Rwanda is reopened.

25 July. UNAMIR Force Commander Gen. Roméo Dallaire travels to Gisenyi to meet with the RPF and Zairean authorities to organize the repatriation of refugees.

28 July. Creation of an international commission of inquiry tasked with identifying persons responsible for acts of genocide committed in Rwanda.

29 July. Press conference of President Pasteur Bizimungu in Kigali. US Assistant Secretary of State for African Affairs George Moose visits

Kigali. Withdrawal of the first contingent of three hundred French soldiers of Operation Turquoise.

30 July. Start of Operation Support Hope. Two hundred American soldiers are deployed to the Kigali international airport.

1 August. Appointment of a three-person commission to investigate genocide and atrocities committed in Rwanda (Atsu-Koffi Amega, former president of the Supreme Court of Togo; Habi Dieng, minister of justice of Guinea; Salifou Fomba, professor of international law in Bamako). Sixty British soldiers join Operation Support Hope in Kigali.

2 August. An agreement is reached between the new Rwandan authorities and French armed forces to transform the "secure humanitarian zone" into a demilitarized zone under the authority of UNAMIR II starting 22 August. The French army estimates that twenty-eight thousand ex-FAR soldiers have retreated across the border to Goma. The United Nations high commissioner for human rights outlines a plan to dispatch human rights observers to the region.

10 August. President Pasteur Bizimungu, Prime Minister Faustin Twagiramungu, and several members of the new Rwandan government travel to Gisenyi, to the border with Zaire, to reassure the refugees.

11 August. Adoption of a resolution by the United Nations Commission on Human Rights calling for an international tribunal, among other measures. Belgian diplomats return to Kigali.

15 August. Canadian general Guy Toussignant takes over the command of UNAMIR, with a force of 1,624 soldiers (of the 5,500 authorized by the Security Council).

19 August. Over fifteen thousand Rwandan refugees cross into South Kivu in a single day.

20 August. Closing of the border with Zaire to prevent the mass exodus of internally displaced persons from the Turquoise zone.

21 August. Withdrawal of the last detachment of French soldiers to Zaire upon the expiration of the United Nations mandate and their replacement by UNAMIR II troops.

22 August. Reopening of the border with Zaire in the face of the massive influx of refugees leaving the Turquoise zone.

23 August. A United Nations official announces that over one million persons have been killed since 7 April.

26 August. Members of the United Nations commission of inquiry into genocide and the atrocities committed in Rwanda arrive in Kigali.

30 August. Rwanda retakes its seat as a nonpermanent member of the United Nations Security Council. HCR requests that French soldiers remain in Goma.

2 September. The authorities in Zaire distance themselves from the former Rwandan government and announce that all Rwandan refugees on Zairean soil should leave the territory by 30 September.

7 September. United Nations Special Envoy Shaharyar Khan, in Kigali, anticipates the renewal of hostilities by the former government army from Zaire. A new wave of refugees crosses the border into Tanzania at a rate of twelve thousand per week.

10 September. William Clarance, in charge of coordinating the activities of United Nations human rights observers with UNAMIR, arrives in Kigali.

15 September. Strong differences of opinion rack the government in Kigali on the question of the recomposition of the Transitional National Assembly (as designated under the Arusha Peace Accords).

16–17 September. An international conference on Rwanda in The Hague is organized by the Conseil de l'Europe and the OAU and attended by President P. Bizimungu. UNAMIR estimates that the number of internally displaced persons within the country exceeds two million.

19 September. HCR estimates that approximately 2.1 million Rwandan refugees reside in neighboring countries: 270,000 in Burundi; 500,000 in Tanzania; and 1.33 million in Zaire (850,000 in Goma, 450,000 in Bukavu, 30,000 in Uvira).

23 September. HCR publicly condemns massacres against the civilian Hutu population committed by RPF troops since its conquest of power; the United Nations secretary-general requests further investigations.

27 September. In light of HCR's position—discouraging refugees from returning—and the total failure of the repatriation efforts organized by UNAMIR from Butare, the UN secretary-general requests that no further public appeals be made. HCR releases information at its disposal acknowledging thirty thousand persons killed in Rwanda since the RPF officially took power in Kigali.

28 September. During an informal meeting on Rwanda held in Paris, representatives of the US government—the United States is the only Western power to have maintained its embassy in Kigali—confirm HCR's information about the killings. An official US government report of 1 October takes up the matter. US representatives oppose the release of funds set aside by the World Bank.

29 September. HCR and the United Nations ask the Zairean authorities to reestablish order in the Rwandan refugee camps, where international aid workers face constant threats from "bandits."

30 September. Departure of the last 250 French soldiers of Operation

Turquoise and withdrawal of the last contingent of US aid workers based in Uganda.

22 October. Under the auspices of the HCR representative for Central Africa, the two prime ministers of Rwanda and Zaire meet to discuss the refugee situation and, on 24 October, sign a tripartite agreement for the voluntary repatriation of refugees.

28 October. The Rwandan representative on the UN Security Council objects that, in addition to the crime of genocide, an international criminal tribunal for Rwanda would also prosecute war crimes committed between 1 January and 31 December 1994 and instead proposes a national tribunal "with international assistance."

8 November. The United Nations Security Council adopts Resolution 955, creating the International Criminal Tribunal for Rwanda. Upon a motion from the United States and New Zealand, thirteen states vote in favor of creating the tribunal, with China abstaining and Rwanda opposing. The reasons for Rwanda's opposition are (1) the inclusion of war crimes, in addition to genocide, in the tribunal's jurisdiction; (2) the tribunal's temporal jurisdiction (extending to 31 December 1994, the date initially anticipated, whereas the Rwandan government sought to limit the tribunal's temporal jurisdiction to July 1994, when it took power in Kigali); and (3) the refusal to apply the death penalty, which is permissible under Rwandan domestic law. The international tribunal for Rwanda would be an extension of the one already created to prosecute crimes committed in the former Yugoslavia. South African judge Richard Goldstone would be the chief prosecutor, and the two tribunals would also share a common Appeals Chamber, composed of five judges. Hotly contesting the decision of the Security Council, the Rwandan ambassador in New York announces plans for an "international tribunal" organized by Rwandan authorities.

8–9 November. A French-African summit is held in Biarritz, but Rwanda is not invited, "to avoid the entire summit turning into a referendum on Rwanda." A protest summit condemns "French complicity in the Rwandan genocide."

14 November. MSF (Médecins sans frontières, Doctors without Borders) suspends operations in Rwandan refugee camps in Bukavu.

24 November. F. Twagiramungu announces that the Rwandan government has finally agreed to cooperate with the international tribunal created by the United Nations.

25 November. The Transitional National Assembly, composed of delegates from the political parties, is set up (seventy members). The eleven seats formerly assigned to the MRND and the mouvance présidentielle are divided between the army (five), the gendarmerie (one), and the other parties.

30 November. The United Nations Security Council condemns the activities of militiamen and soldiers in the refugee camps in Zaire and extends UNAMIR's mandate for another six months. As described in an HCR press release, the number of refugees in Bukavu has increased by several thousands in response to efforts by RPA soldiers to dismantle camps for internally displaced persons in the former secure humanitarian zone (Kibuye and Cyangugu prefectures).

1995. *9 January.* The summit of Central African leaders requests that Rwanda begin negotiations with its foreign-based opposition.

22–23 April. Forced evacuation of camps for internally displaced persons in the former Turquoise zone (the army massacres several thousand persons in Kibeho).

22 May. The European Union suspends assistance to Rwanda in the aftermath of the massacre at Kibeho.

13 July. Boutros Boutros-Ghali visits Kigali and requests initiation of a dialogue with the refugees.

18 July. Boutros Boutros-Ghali travels to Gbadolite, in Zaire, where there is discussion of military training in Rwandan refugee camps organized by ex-FAR soldiers and Interahamwe militiamen.

16–30 August. Zaire begins forced repatriation of refugees from Rwanda and Burundi.

1 October. President Arap Moi announces that he will not permit arrests of persons accused of genocide residing in Kenya until those responsible for shooting down President Habyarimana's airplane are identified.

28–29 November. Regional conference in Cairo, presided over by Jimmy Carter, Julius Nyerere, and Desmond Tutu, with the presidents of Burundi, Rwanda, Uganda, Tanzania, and Zaire in attendance.

6 December. Rwanda expels 38 NGOs, suspends the activities of another 18, and allows 102 others to continue their work.

12 December. The United Nations Security Council adopts Resolution 1029, prolonging UNAMIR's mandate until 8 March 1996.

1996. *2 March.* Arrests in Cameroon of eleven Rwandans suspected of committing genocide (including Théoneste Bagosora and Ferdinand Nahimana).

19 April. Departure of the last remaining UNAMIR "blue helmets."

20–21 June. Second round-table conference on Rwanda in Geneva. The American delegation claims that they are prepared to support a "cleanup" of the refugee camps in Zaire, along with intense screenings of returning refugees and removal from border areas of those who remain.[1] Kenya orders the closing of the Rwandan Embassy in Nairobi following Kigali's refusal to lift immunity for a staff member suspected of involvement in an assassination attempt against former Rwandan interior minister Seth Sendashonga, an RPF member, who was a refugee in Kenya.

16 July. Beginning of forced repatriation of several thousand Rwandan refugees in Burundi. Those initiatives are curtailed on 23 July under pressure from HCR.

1–5 August. Return of roughly three thousand refugees (Tutsi) from Burundi following a military coup d'état by Maj. Pierre Buyoya.

20 August. One after the other, the Burundian army forcibly dismantles the camps of Rwandan refugees, who are then repatriated to Rwanda. During the last two weeks of August, more than forty thousand Rwandan refugees return from Burundi. By the end of 1996, almost all of the ninety thousand Rwandan refugees who had fled to Burundi are repatriated.

September–early October. In South Kivu (Zaire), groups of Tutsi Banyamulenge ("people of Mulenge"; old migrants native to Rwanda who fled to eastern Congo—throughout the zones of Fizi, Uvira, and Mwenga) launch military operations in Uvira. Rwandan and Burundian refugee camps are attacked.

October. Col. Théoneste Lizinde, a former intelligence officer in the Habyarimana regime who defected to the RPF in 1992, where he performed similar functions, is assassinated in Nairobi.

16–18 October. Combat intensifies between the Zairean army and Banyamulenge rebels of the newly formed Alliance of Democratic Forces for the Liberation of the Congo (AFDL, Alliance des forces démocratiques

---

1. "U.S. Rwanda/Burundi Special Coordinator Richard Bogosian broached the concept of selected camp closures during the June Rwanda Operational Support Group Meeting in Geneva. Our allies are awaiting a formal proposal from us on this issue" (Confidential, Rwanda Refugee Camps in Zaire, 2 August 1996, Clinton Presidential Library, declassified ISCAP Appeal, 18 March 2014). This proposal was deemed an approval of the Rwandan military intervention that began the following October. Cf. also M. Richard McCall, Chief of Staff of U.S. Agency for International Development, *Statement of the United States*, Round Table on Rwanda, 20–21 June 1996; Rwandan Delegation to the Geneva Round Table, *Response of the Rwandese Delegation on the U.S. Strategy Proposal on the Rwanda Refugee Dilemma*, 20–21 June 1996.

pour la libération du Congo), which is supported by Rwandan and Ugandan troops.

22 October. The government of Zaire accuses Burundi and Rwanda of attacking Zaire in South Kivu.

25 October. The spokesperson for the rebel forces fighting the Zairean army in Kivu announces in Kigali that their objective is to overthrow President Mobutu.

25–26 October. AFDL and its Rwandan allies launch offensives against the refugee camps north of Goma. The Rwandan and Burundian refugee camps are dismantled.

29 October–3 November. AFDL captures Bukavu and Goma. The Rwandan army enters Goma.

8 November. The three special rapporteurs of the High Commission for Human Rights in the subregion issue a press release condemning the fate reserved for returning refugees, in particular, the killings committed upon their return.

15 November. The United Nations Security Council authorizes deployment of a multinational force in East Kivu for humanitarian purposes. The Rwandan army takes over the Rwandan refugee camp at Mugunga, the largest in North Kivu.

17 November. Start of the forced return to Rwanda of hundreds of thousands of Hutu refugees. Hundreds of thousands flee in the other direction, farther toward the interior of Zaire.

November–December. Various agencies of the UN, the ICRC (International Committee of the Red Cross), and other NGOs try to save and help the refugees fleeing ahead of advancing AFDL troops, backed by the Rwandan army. The discovery of mass graves in early December by representatives of several NGOs provokes condemnation of AFDL. United Nations Security Council Draft Resolution 1080, authorizing international intervention in eastern Zaire, is blocked by the United States.

1997. January–February. Campaign of murders against foreigners who were religious or humanitarian aid workers: three Spanish aid workers with Médecins du Monde on 18 January 1997 in Ruhengeri; Guy Pinard, a Canadian cleric, on 2 February 1997 in Ruhengeri; five observers with the United Nations Human Rights Commission on 4 February 1997. "On 18 January, armed men, some of them in military uniform, attacked three buildings in the town of Ruhengeri that were occupied by foreign staff of Save the Children, Medecins sans Frontieres, and Doctors of the World. Driven away from two of the buildings, assailants gained entry to the third, where they murdered three Spanish medical workers and seriously injured an American, who later was obliged to have his injured leg amputated. The government soldiers in the immediate vicinity failed to intervene but later arrested the guard of the premises who had witnessed the whole attack; an RPA soldier shot him the next day, supposedly because he was trying to escape custody. In another case, insurgents killed a Belgian nun when they attacked the school she directed in Satinsyi commune, Gisenyi prefecture, on April 28 and were reportedly also responsible for murdering a Chinese engineer in Kivumu commune, Kibuye prefecture on June 24. A teacher, reportedly once an RPA soldier, shot and killed a Canadian priest during a mass in Kinigi commune, Ruhengeri prefecture on February 2. The attacks on foreign nationals, including attacks on human rights monitors described below, caused many NGOs to withdraw their staff from insecure areas in the west and northwest. This reduced the number of outside witnesses and diminished the amount of information available about incidents of violence" (Human Rights Watch, World Report 1998, RWANDA, Human Rights Developments, p. 1).

Confronted with the passivity of the authorities—which frequently resulted in both witnesses and evidence disappearing—and with lapses and failures in the domestic legal proceedings, many suspected that Rwandese army or other state officials were implicated in the killings (see chap. 7, note 5, and *annex 51*).

2 March. AFDL troops and their Rwandan allies overrun the Rwandan refugee camp at Tingi-Tingi, where over 150,000 persons are sheltered.

13 March. Even as AFDL captures one village after the other, Rwanda opposes an international peace conference for the Great Lakes region.

15 March. AFDL troops take control of the city of Kisangani.

26 April. AFDL troops capture Lubumbashi. Several human rights organizations condemn the killings and disappearances of several tens of thousands of Rwandan Hutu refugees.

30 April. Start of an HCR airlift to repatriate Rwandan refugees from Kisangani. These forced repatriations of Hutu refugees, delivered directly into the hands of Rwandan authorities without protection or follow-up, provoke strong debate within HCR, which is curtailed by Sergio de Mello, assistant high commissioner for refugees.

9 May. After waiting in vain in Kigali for one week for authorization to cross over to South Kivu, a team of UN experts mandated to investigate the killings imputed to AFDL forces and the Rwandan army returns to Geneva.

8 June. Newly installed president of the Democratic Republic of the Congo (DRC), the former Zaire, Laurent-Désiré Kabila, authorizes the UN to conduct investigations into the disappearances of Rwandan Hutu refugees on Congolese territory.

20 June. The first members of the UN commission of inquiry into allegations of massacres in eastern DRC arrive in Kinshasa. Special Rapporteur Roberto Garreton is rejected by the DRC government.

7 July. DRC authorities obstruct investigations by the UN commission of inquiry. UN Secretary-General Kofi Annan renews support for the ongoing investigations. During his visit to Namibia, Laurent-Désiré Kabila accuses the Western countries of leading a campaign of lies against AFDL.

11 July. The UN raises the matter of "crimes against humanity" and condemns repeated obstructions from DRC authorities that impede the work of the commission of inquiry. The UN Secretary-General decides to change the composition of the team of experts.

20 July. Meeting in Kinshasa of representatives of thirteen African nations (Angola, Central African Republic, Congo, Eritrea, Ethiopia, Gabon, Mozambique, Namibia, Rwanda, Uganda, South Africa, Zambia, and Zimbabwe). They issue a press release condemning the campaign of "defamation" against the DRC in regard to the allegations of massacres of Rwandan refugees.

Mid-July. Extended military operations against Hutu militiamen in the prefectures of northwestern Rwanda.

18 July. Arrests in Kenya and transfers to the ICTR in Arusha of seven Rwandans accused of genocide.

1 August. Following Rwanda and the DRC, Burundi rejects the UN special rapporteur for human rights, Paulo-Sergio Pinheiro.

25 September. The minister of defense announces the return of all Rwandan soldiers from Congo-Kinshasa, except those "remaining pursuant to an accord with Laurent-Désiré Kabila."

27 September. The DRC government prevents the UN commission of inquiry, still stuck in Kinshasa, from traveling to Mbandaka, which it had been requesting to visit since 13 May.

1 October. In light of the obstruction of its mission in the Congo, the UN secretary-general recalls the commission of inquiry to New York.

19 November and 4 December. Hutu rebels launch an offensive in the prefectures of northwestern Rwanda.

1998. *29 March.* Violent clashes between Hutu rebels and the RPA in the prefectures of northwestern Rwanda.

10 April. Given the obstructions in the field, the UN suspends the commission of inquiry into alleged massacres of Hutu refugees by AFDL and its allies.

8 May. The day after UN Secretary-General Kofi Annan's visit, Rwanda suspends the UN human rights commission in Rwanda. Conjointly, the Security Council publicly releases a report on the massacres of Rwandan Hutu refugees in the former Zaire. The report accuses AFDL and the Rwandan army of crimes against humanity.

16 May. Seth Sendashonga, RPF member and former minister of the interior in the government first assembled by the RPF in July 1994, is assassinated in Nairobi. He had resigned his post and fled to Kenya in August 1995, and he had survived a previous assassination attempt on 26 February 1996.

11 July. Increasingly fearful of a coup d'état, Laurent-Désiré Kabila terminates the duties of the Rwandan general James Kabarebe, chief of staff ad interim of the Congolese Armed Forces.

27 July. Expulsions of Rwandan officers attached to the Congolese army and release of political staff with Rwandan allegiances.

2 August. In Goma, at the border with Rwanda, a major of the Congolese Armed Forces (FAC, Forces armées congolaises) announces that the army is going to remove Kabila from power. As the uprising takes root and becomes widespread, during the night from 2 to 3 August, the Rwandan Armed Forces and Banyamulenge remaining in Kinshasa attempt to seize the presidential palace.

3 August. The attempt to overrun Kinshasa and topple Kabila fails.

4 August. Rwanda starts a blitzkrieg and launches an audacious airborne operation, flying their troops from Goma in eastern Congo to Kitona, some 1,800 km away on the other side of the DRC, on the Atlantic coast. In the advance toward Kinshasa, Rwandan troops capture several towns and occupy the Inga Dam, which supplies Kinshasa with electricity. At the same time Ugandan troops occupy Beni (Nord-Kivu) on 8 August and Bunia (Oriental province) on 13 August.[2]

12 August. Creation in Goma of the Rassemblement Congolais pour la Démocratie (RCD, Rally for Congolese Democracy). The RCD ruled

---

2. For more information, see International Court of Justice, Case concerning armed activities on the territory of the Congo (Democratic Republic of the Congo v. Uganda): judgment of 19 December 2005 = Affaire des activités armées sur le territoire du Congo (République démocratique du Congo c. Ouganda): arrêt du 19 décembre 2005, The Hague, 2005.

North Kivu as a proxy of the Rwandan Government from 1998 to 2003. In mid-August, with the end of Kabila's power seemingly close at hand, this scarcely veiled aggression is incrementally transferred to rebel movements, assembled and armed by the coalition of neighboring States (Rwanda, Uganda, and Burundi—although Burundi will later claim to have withdrawn). Rwandan authorities appreciate this transposition as much as the troops themselves, because it at least partially resolves the complex question of demobilization of soldiers from the perspective of the international financial organizations.

21 August. Intervention of the armies of Angola and Zimbabwe alongside the FAC, premised upon the mutual agreements for defense among the countries of the South African Development Community.

23 August. Kisangani, the country's third largest city (Oriental province), is "freed" by the Ugandan troops. The RCD effectively controls all the cities in North-Katanga.

25 August. With support from these allied troops, Kinshasa regains control over the border southwest of Angola, where Luanda seeks to attack UNITA (União Nacional para a Independência Total de Angola, or National Union for the Total Independence of Angola), Jonas Savimbi's rebel movement, from the rear. The blockade of Kinshasa is broken and almost all the cities of Bas-Congo revert to the Rwandans. However, there is no question of them pushing the offensive eastward, where the rebel coalition continues to progress quickly.

27 August. Namibia announces that it militarily supports the authorities in Kinshasa.

11 September. Considering that President Kabila had turned to neighboring powers for assistance and that the Sudan was its long-time enemy, Uganda defends its military actions on the territory of the RDC as lawful self-defense.

28 September. Chad acknowledges its military support to the FAC.

30 September. Uganda supports the creation of the new MLC rebel group (Mouvement pour la libération du Congo, Movement for the Liberation of the Congo) and its takeover of Equator province. The north of Congo eclipses the control of the authorities in Kinshasa.

12 October. The FAC declares itself finally ready to launch a counteroffensive with support from Sudanese troops, reinforced by Ugandan and Rwandan rebels, but they are powerless to prevent the fall of their headquarters to Kindu. Rebel offensives continue in Kasaï and in Katanga.

6 November. Rwanda acknowledges its military involvement alongside the rebel forces.

13 November. Uganda acknowledges its military involvement alongside the rebel forces. After this joint recognition, they decide to create a unified command to manage and exploit the resources of the occupied territories. While mediations from African countries get underway, the front more or less stabilizes and the partition of the country takes hold, and there are seven countries (Angola, Zimbabwe, Namibia, Tchad, Rwanda, Uganda, and Burundi) that continue to involve themselves in a war of position on Congolese territory. But even if rebel forces and their allied foreign troops administer half the territory, they actually only control the cities. Everywhere else armed groups or militias take root, which fight them and/or negotiate to offer their support to the highest bidder.

1999. *May–June.* The Rwandan military offensive is relaunched in the DRC.

10 July. Heads of state of the six countries involved in the conflict (the DRC, Zimbabwe, Namibia, Angola, Rwanda, and Uganda) sign a cease-fire, but none of the Congolese rebel groups are included.

14–17 August. Violent military clashes in Kisangani between the two occupying armies of Rwanda and Uganda, which were previously allied.

2000. *June.* Renewed clashes with the Ugandan army for control of Kisangani.

29 December. In a radio broadcast communiqué, Army Chief of Staff Kayumba Nyamwasa confirms that the RPA had launched a defensive "counterattack," retaking Pepa, Pweto, and other positions in the region following attacks jointly led by DRC government troops, ex-FAR troops, and the Forces for the Defense of Democracy (FDD, Forces pour la défense de la démocratie) of Burundi and Mayi-Mayi Congolese militias, which were supported by Zimbabwean forces based in Katanga province.

2001. *January.* The Zimbabwe Defence Forces (ZDF) reinforce their troops on the southeastern front of the DRC, particularly in Katanga province, in order to contain the joint offensive of RPA troops and DRC rebel forces.

17 October. Roberto Garreton, UN special rapporteur on the situation of human rights in the DRC, resigns. Although appointed in 1994, his investigations of crimes imputed to the AFDL and the Rwandan army in 1997 and 1998 could never be completed.

28 October. Meeting between the ministers of defense of Uganda and Rwanda in Kabale to devise measures to reduce the tensions between the two countries.

6 November. The heads of state of Rwanda and Uganda meet in London to resolve the tensions between their two armies at the border.

17 December. The minister of local administration and social affairs circulates the results of a recently undertaken census indicating that

1,074,017 persons were killed in the massacres and the genocide committed in Rwanda between 1 October 1990 and 31 December 1994. Of all the victims of the genocide, 66 percent are men. According to the census, almost all the persons killed were Tutsi. The identities of 951,018 of the victims could be established.

2002. *19 April.* The "Sun City Accords" on the Congolese transition demonstrate the isolation of a DRC subjugated by Rwandan authorities.

30 July. Subject to strong international pressure, particularly from the Americans, President Kagame agrees to sign a peace accord between Rwanda and the DRC in Pretoria. This accord calls for an immediate cease-fire and the withdrawal of Rwandan troops from the DRC.

5 October. Rwanda formally achieves the complete withdrawal of its troops from the DRC.

31 October. Angola, Namibia, and Zimbabwe, having provided decisive military support to the government in Kinshasa for its war against the rebel movements backed by Rwanda and Uganda over the preceding four years, manage to complete the withdrawal of their armed forces from the DRC.

1 November. Presidents Kabila and Kagame agree to a ninety-day delay in implementation of their 30 July accord on the withdrawal of Rwandan troops and neutralization of Hutu rebel forces in the DRC.

2003. *16 April.* During a press conference held in Nairobi, the high commissioner for refugees, Ruud Lubbers, states that "the refugees could return to Rwanda without fear" and adds that all repatriation must be voluntary.

26 April. A constitutional referendum in Rwanda signals the end of the "political transition" started by the 1993 Arusha Peace Accords.

25 August. Presidential elections. The incumbent president, Paul Kagame, wins with more than 95 percent of the vote.

29 September. Legislative elections confer the RPF with complete hegemony.

8 December. The HCR delegate states that by the end of 2004 almost all Rwandan refugees on the African continent will have been repatriated, including those in West Africa and southern Africa.

From War to Genocide

The Social and
Political Context

At the risk of treading on familiar ground, this chapter attempts to sketch out a few basic facts about Rwanda's
social and geopolitical map. It lies at the heart of Africa's central highlands and
shares with neighboring states many of the features that have long impressed
foreigners, especially its high population density and the presence of pheno-
types that have contributed to serve as a basis for a variety of naturalist or
culturalist approaches. Psychoracial characteristics attributed to the inhabitants
are often seen as the underlying factors behind other determinants of conflict,
such as demographic explosion, land scarcity, and rising social pressures.
These various lines of reasoning all suffer from the same drawback—to some
degree or another they make the wrong inferences from an arbitrarily reconstructed perception of political realities.

The Sociodemographic Framework

Landlocked in the heart of the African continent and surrounded
by several bigger neighbors, Rwanda is, like Burundi, a small mountainous
country of 26,338 square kilometers, bereft of mineral resources but blessed
with a temperate climate and a fertile soil (see map 1). A hardworking peasantry
has developed a relatively prosperous agricultural economy centered on sub-
sistence crops (bananas, beans, sorghum, etc.) and two export crops (tea and
coffee), which generate the bulk of its foreign export earnings. At the beginning
of 1994 the total population was estimated at 7.9 million inhabitants, that is, a
density of 300 inhabitants per square kilometer, with a growth rate estimated

at 3.1 percent per year, according to the 1991 census. The urban population barely reached 400,000, with three-quarters residing in the capital city, Kigali. Ninety percent of the total workforce was engaged in agriculture. In relation to arable land, the population density then stood at 417 inhabitants per square kilometer, reaching figures twice as high in the most fertile zones of the mountain crest, an exceptionally high number in sub-Saharan Africa. Even if land in cultivation increased significantly from year to year, rising from 500,000 to 800,000 hectares between 1970 and 1994, this did not necessarily mean "new" land but rather an equivalent reduction in pastures or fallow land. Indeed, the entire country was transforming itself into a "crowded world." Given the intense competition for land in the western prefectures, nationwide efforts at redistribution began in the 1970s. The aim was to diffuse those high densities by encouraging internal migrations toward the eastern prefectures, until then considered "underpopulated," particularly the Mayaga (in the center), and then mainly toward the Bugesera (in the southeast).

Other factors also contributed to these contrasting regional developments. When the country formally acceded to independence (1962), the core region in demographic, economic, and political terms was in the south, in Astrida prefecture, later divided into Butare and Gikongoro prefectures. The political and intellectual elites were distributed between Nyanza (seat of the monarchy until 1961), the city of Ngoma/Butare (the intellectual capital), and Kigali (the administrative capital). After the proclamation of the First Republic (1961–73), rising political tensions led to the virtual closing down of the border with Burundi and the neighboring city of Bukavu, in eastern Congo, much to the economic disadvantage of the southern prefectures and to the benefit of Gitarama and Kigali in the central region. The Second Republic (which began in 1973) reinforced this trend by making Kigali the real hub of the country. Among the new power holders from the north were a number of high-ranking civil servants who took up residence there. At the same time, new poles of economic development emerged in the north around Gisenyi and Ruhengeri prefectures, attracting new infrastructures and investments.

The Second Republic actually intensified the opposition between north and south. The presence of separate regional ethnicities—the so-called Kiga in the north and the Nduga in the south—further contributed to deepen the split: Rukiga was the name commonly given to the three northern prefectures of Gisenyi, Ruhengeri, and Byumba, while the Nduga label came to designate all others. This regional differentiation eventually became the basic frame of reference during periods of relative civil peace.

Not that ethnic opposition wholly disappeared. The size of the Tutsi population in the southern prefectures was in itself a strong and distinctive element. Thus, according to the census figures taken during the 1980s, the prefectures of the Rukiga held only 7 percent of the country's Tutsi population.[1] In Ruhengeri prefecture, for example, Tutsi were only 6 percent of the total population.[2] At the other extreme, among the southern prefectures, Butare stood out, with a Tutsi population approaching 25 percent and varying from 10 to 20 percent in the others. Almost a quarter of the total Tutsi population was concentrated in Butare prefecture, approximately 130,000 persons. When updated, these figures tend to suggest that Rwanda's Tutsi population in 1994 exceeded 800,000.

Map 4 illustrates the extent to which regional and ethnic distinctions overlapped, even if perceptions and their actual incidence remain heavily influenced by a history of interlocking spaces that did not necessarily correspond with the prefecture's administrative borders (ancient kingdoms, "natural" regions, pastoral spaces and areas of colonization, zones of influence of grand lineages, markets, etc.). Also, it is worth noting that ethnic differences did not have the same meaning or the same emotional resonance in all regions.

These considerations are important to bear in mind, as they have a direct bearing on the basic policy choices made by the protagonists; as we shall see, they have had a major impact on the conception and implementation of most of the political and military strategies behind the numerous conflicts that have been part and parcel of the history of this region since the 1960s.

Ancient Conflicts and Continuing Violence

Such conflicts did not just happen. There are antecedents and stages in their unfolding. It is important that they be properly contextualized at both the domestic and international levels, taking into account the chronic instability that swept across the Great Lakes region. Not only are the two small landlocked countries of Burundi and Rwanda marked by almost fifty years of recurring political-ethnic crises, but their surrounding larger neighbors also found themselves embroiled in domestic conflicts of their own, as shown by the early postindependence history of Uganda and the current Democratic Republic of the Congo (DRC, formerly Zaire). This overview may assist in appreciating the intensity of the convulsions generated by repeated recourse to extreme forms of violence.

It may be helpful to recall how, over time, different identity markers were affixed to Rwandan populations. If, in precolonial times, the ethnic categories Hutu, Tutsi, and Twa pointed to clan and family ties and situated individuals in the context of a single national community, colonial historiography introduced a pseudoscientific differentiation that transformed ethnic distinctions into a racial opposition. This racialized conception of ethnicity, which still structures the outlook and self-perceptions of many Rwandans, is rooted in the now-discredited notion of the foreign origins of the Tutsi population. From that perspective, the Bantus—a term normally used to designate a linguistic community but now applied indiscriminately to the Hutu peasantry—had supposedly settled in areas largely untouched by the country's first occupants, the pygmoid Twa. Both Hutu and Twa were in time confronted with the arrival of Hamite pastoralists, Tutsi and Hima, who supposedly imposed their dominion over the country's central highlands.

Through much of the colonial period, this pattern of binary social division between conquering Hamite foreigners and subjugated Hutu serfs constituted the organizing framework for identifying rulers and subjects, chiefs and subalterns. All of the commanding heights, whether in administrative or technical realms or in economic activity, were reserved for candidates of Tutsi origins.

It is easy to see why the beneficiaries of this highly skewed recruitment system ended up enthusiastically endorsing its underlying ideology, using history, race, and religion to justify their privileged position. In 1946 Rwanda and its recently converted monarch were consecrated to the Christ-Roi and turned into a shining beacon of Christianity for the African continent.

Cumbersome Political Heritage

Although Burundi and Rwanda shared similar characteristics in terms of size, ethnic map, traditional institutions, limited natural resources, and colonial heritage, in each state the consolidation of authoritarianism gave rise to contrasting patterns of ethnic domination. While Burundi acceded to independence under Tutsi rule, in Rwanda the Belgian-assisted 1959 revolutionary upheaval handed power over to representatives of the Hutu majority. A backward glance at the past helps illuminate the nature of the forces at work in each state.

After World War II, in 1945, the prospect of emancipation from colonial power was clearly on the horizon and was to be legitimized through a democratic transition. In the midfifties electoral consultations were held, providing Hutu *évolués* for the first time with opportunities to voice their resentment of the political oppression and economic exploitation embodied in Tutsi hegemony.[3] The accidental death of the *mwami* (king) Mutara Rudahigwa in 1959 and the subsequent dispute surrounding his succession gave rise to violent accusations against the Belgian *tutelle* (guardianship), seen by many Tutsi elements as responsible for their ruler's death. With the loosening of administrative controls, a flurry of associations appeared on the horizon, some of which mutated into political parties. After weeks of unrest and repression by administrative authorities, the attacks mounted by a group of Tutsi youth against the pro-Hutu leader, Dominique Mbonyumutwa, touched off a series of local uprisings of Hutu peasants accompanied by considerable bloodshed. This became known as the "social revolution" of November 1959. The movement gained further impetus when the colonial authorities installed new administrative cadres (mostly Hutu) in the communes. Despite the objections they raised among Tutsi, the communal elections of June and July 1960, followed by the referendum of September 1961, intended to legitimize a republican form of government. The elections also ushered in a de facto takeover of power by the upcoming Hutu elites and the consecration of a new social order.

During the three decades that followed, numerous elections gave added legitimacy to the new political order because or in spite of the insistence of the authorities that they stood as the representatives of the "majority people" (*rubanda nyamwinshi*), the Hutu. The ideology behind this arbitrary display of authority implied the downgrading of the Tutsi to the rank of second-class citizens.

Indeed, for the ruling Parmehutu (Parti du mouvement de l'émancipation hutu, or Party of the Movement for the Emancipation of the Hutu), it was not enough to simply abolish the Tutsi's political and economic privileges; the country had to be returned to its only legitimate heirs, the Hutu. Exacerbated by the maneuvering of the colonial authorities, this heated situation explains the violence that accompanied both the "social revolution" and the proclamation of independence under republican rule. Fearing for their lives, tens of thousands of Tutsi fled to neighboring countries.

The continuous exodus of Tutsi refugees became the vehicle through which ethnic antagonisms contaminated the political transition in neighboring Burundi, until then deemed exemplary. After July 1963 armed Tutsi groups used Burundi as a base for launching repeated incursions into Rwanda to regain power. Each of these attacks contributed to the sharp deterioration of Rwanda's domestic climate. Anti-Tutsi pogroms resulted in hundreds of victims and led to the exile of several thousand others. In December 1963 a large group of armed refugees from Burundi crossed the border into Rwanda to launch a deadly raid on Kigali, only to be stopped in the nick of time just outside the capital. Amid the panic that seized the Hutu population, even more bloody reprisals were inflicted upon the domestic Tutsi population, indiscriminately branded as infiltrators or potential accomplices. The ensuing repression is said to have cost the lives of ten thousand persons, including the principal leaders of the monarchist parties. It provoked another wave of several tens of thousands of refugees.

In 1966 and 1967, with support from the Tutsi officers who had just taken power in Burundi, the leadership of the refugee movements reengaged in military incursions into Rwanda, followed by anti-Tutsi killings inside Rwanda. Once more, thousands of Rwandan Tutsi fled the country, seeking refuge in neighboring states, until finally authorities of the two countries managed to negotiate an agreement to neutralize the activities of armed refugee movements. On the hillsides in Rwanda, the killing of Tutsi was viewed as a form of preemptive or punitive self-defense against potential enemies. The killers were for the most part drawn from among young MDR-Parmehutu militants, who, with support from the authorities, attacked, pillaged, and burned the homes of their victims. The main objective was to eliminate or to force an entire family to flee before erasing all traces of the former occupants and then redistribute their property.

Beginning in the mid-1960s, relations between "the false twins" went from bad to worse. Just as the influx of Tutsi refugees from Rwanda had raised fears of a Hutu insurrection among Burundian Tutsi, thus threatening the stability of the institutions born of independence, with the consolidation of power in Tutsi hands in Burundi, many viewed with growing concern a possible replay of the Rwandan scenario. The October 1965 abortive coup attempt in Bujumbura led to the execution of a number of leading Hutu. Meanwhile, the country's new strongman, Capt. Michel Micombero, who midwifed the birth of the republic in 1966 before proclaiming himself president, made no bones about his intense security concerns. These were translated into tragic reality when tens of thousands of Hutu were systematically exterminated between June and August 1972 in what can only be described as a genocide.[4] Many of those who managed to escape the killings ended up as refugees in Rwanda, where their presence only strengthened the conviction among the Rwandan population that the Burundian army was waiting to unleash new massacres and possibly restore the monarchy. These fears were widespread throughout Rwanda, thus encouraging the Burundian Hutu to take immediate steps to organize themselves as a resistance movement.

The military coups d'état of 1973 and 1976 in Rwanda and Burundi that led to the inauguration of the Second Republic, along with off-and-on massacres dating back to the period of independence, had cast a pall over the region. Eventually, however, a period of relative calm began to emerge. Without challenging the monopoly of power held by elites selected on an ethnic basis in both countries, the reformist equivocations and the developmentalist phraseology of the new regimes contributed to a relaxation of national and bilateral tensions.

To fully grasp the roots of the drama at the heart of this discussion, it is important to look back at a series of critical events that took place in the 1980s, a pivotal period in the region's history: the restoration of stability in Uganda (1986), the loosening of the central state power in Zaire (1989–90), the fall of Jean-Baptiste Bagaza's authoritarian regime in Burundi (1987), and the strengthening of significant protest movements in Rwanda toward the end of the 1980s significantly altered the regional political climate.

Political overtures initially centered on the taboo subject of the refugees. The issue was prudently, though explicitly, approached in the "Agreement on the Free Circulation of Goods and Persons," which Burundi, Rwanda, and Zaire had signed in 1985 in the framework of the Communauté économique des pays des Grands Lacs (CEPGL, Economic Community of the Great Lakes Countries). It was also the topic of discussion between Rwanda and the new Ugandan authorities in 1986 (see chapter 2). Consequently, some six hundred thousand Ugandan refugees in neighboring countries were able to return to their homeland between 1986 and 1990. Almost all of the Zaireans who were refugees in neighboring countries were able to return to their homeland; and the sixty thousand Burundian refugees who had fled interethnic massacres in two northern communes of the country in August 1988, where the death toll exceeded ten thousand, were repatriated the following year.[5] In fact, all that remained was the problem of "old case" Burundian and former Rwandan refugees.[6]

In this context, the large majority of national political figures and foreign observers familiar with the two countries imagined that it was finally going to be possible to debate the onerous legacies of the past, which, when power changed hands with independence, had created regimes where ethnic segregation still held sway.

Paradoxically, the eruption of ethnic violence in August 1988 in two communes in the northeast of Burundi, Ntega and Marangara, paved the way for a very candid debate on "overcoming ethnic divisions" and "democratization." The surprise brought on by the outbreak of clashes and their extent (over twenty thousand deaths in a two-week period) amply demonstrated that a series of incidents, seemingly fortuitous, could degenerate quite rapidly into larger conflagrations, recalling most of the characteristics and outcomes of past crises. Particularly noteworthy were the strong connections between the two countries: intense propaganda and political mobilization campaigns before and during the incidents by partisans of Burundian pro-Hutu movements who were refugees in Rwanda and the special relationship they enjoyed with Rwandan officials.

At both the regional and international levels, these interethnic clashes generated much concern and swayed President Pierre Buyoya, a Tutsi officer who had just taken power in Burundi, to set the country on a course toward greater political stability. Indeed, this setback was proof of failure on two accounts. The first, clearly the most significant, concerned the foreign donor community and the technocratic elites who anticipated that rapid "modernization" of Burundi, greater regional integration, and accessibility to the larger world would engender new political habits and more harmonious social relations. However, at the close of two decades geared toward development that had experienced a particularly favorable economic environment and benefited from broad financial and political support from international organizations and from a multitude of NGOs, there was a resurgence of what some described as "secular atavism" and "barbaric violence." The second failure, a corollary of the first, demonstrated the utter senselessness of the politics of denying the "ethnic problem."

More fundamentally, the military regimes in place in the two countries had succeeded in reducing political debate to technocratic issues about the pace and modalities of development, which, given the similarity of economic policy in Burundi and Rwanda, everyone knew depended on largely intractable regional and structural constraints. In Rwanda, where power devolved in the hands of elites first from the south and then from the north, it seemed clear that the practice of democracy could not continue to limit itself to competition between rival factions of the "majority of the people" (the Nduga in the south versus the Rukiga in the north). More important was to recognize the right of expression of minorities. In Burundi, after twenty-five years of intense competition among Tutsi officers from various hills in Bururi province accompanied by three coups d'état, the imperative of "ethnic rebalancing" could no longer be postponed. In both countries the calls for democratic liberalization denounced the politics of appropriating revenue drawn from export crops by monoethnic groups of Tutsi or Hutu, depending on the country, and the aggravation of inequalities. More profoundly, they questioned a social and political order governed by social rank and imposed solidarities, denounced as "clanism, regionalism, and ethnicism."

Even so, any questioning of the fundamental basis of these authoritarian systems immediately provoked leaders to reaffirm their initial popular legitimacy and their founding principles. In this regard, whether suppressed or legitimized, depending on the country, ethnic entitlements or discriminations fulfilled a central and necessary function in the political sphere: they stood as constitutive elements for the organization of state systems inherited from the colonial period.

As a decisive political tool used by those in power to enforce unity in their camp, as well as an essential wellspring of solidarity among the oppressed—who dared not risk betraying their group—ethnic manipulation was a standard strategy. It proved a highly convenient tool to gain political, economic, or social advantage or to sway outcomes in even the most inconsequential situations. Indeed, in an environment of rising intergroup tensions, any allusion or incident that could take on an ethnic connotation could instantly provoke the "evil eye" between neighbors, colleagues, parishioners, and other members of the two ethnic groups, whether in the marketplace, in bars, in the workplace, or in church. Little prodding was needed to make it spill over into open clashes, planned assaults, or killings.

An Inevitable Recourse to Violence?

For this reason it is never sufficient to blame propaganda, the approval of authorities, the influence of alcohol or drugs, or the relative youth of the killers to try to explain violence; nor does it help us understand the pointless nature of the massacres and the cruelties inflicted upon the victims. Aside from the sense of horror evoked by repeated acts of violence, it is well to note the extent to which the perpetrators internalized their experience of genocidal killings, as if each new episode of lethal rage renewed links to past events and reinforced behaviors that had, in some manner, acquired the status of a political reflex or, at the very least, had become a predisposition for it. Indeed, references to the past involved coded messages. They were a means to summon conditioned responses, customary roles, and deeply felt reactions. In both countries, each generation and almost every family, whether Hutu or Tutsi, could refer back to dates when horrors became indelibly engraved in memory. It was among them, in fact, that social bonds were constructed—and deconstructed—yielding a singular political culture. Hence a peculiar disposition for violence emerged between groups that coalesced, defining themselves in antagonistic terms.

Recurrence of these episodic, large-scale massacres between Hutu and Tutsi on each side of the Kanyaru (or Akanyaru) River—marking the border between Burundi and Rwanda—set in motion a seemingly inexorable, if not contagious, chain of events between the two countries. These outbursts and an obsessive foreboding, whether real or imagined, born of a sense of inevitability served to fuel anticipatory violence: kill or be killed. And when the apprehension of imminent killings and disasters became political fodder, it evolved into murderous practice. In both countries, and since the period of independence, denouncing the other ethnic group's supposed plans of extermination featured constantly in the ethnicist propaganda for numerous political groups. Countless politicians and ideologues entered the political arena with one goal in mind: to assert their influence by ensuring that their prophesies of doom would not remain mere rhetorical flourishes. The springs and gears for persistent civil war had been well calibrated since 1959. One could find them at work in both individual and collective action when massacres occurred in Burundi in October and November 1993, following the military putsch and the assassination of Melchior Ndadaye, who only three months before had been the first democratically elected president. Then Burundi sank into bloody civil war that persisted for over a decade before allowing ballots to take precedence over bullets in handing power over to the most disciplined faction of the armed Hutu rebellion.

The same scenario came into focus in Rwanda during the crisis that swept across the country between April and July 1994, unleashing the most extreme genocidal furor ever experienced. The violence was later exported throughout the region after the start in 1996 of what has come to be known as the first "Great African War." The Tutsi rebels newly installed in power in Kigali then announced their determination to nip in the bud the genocidal risk posed by surviving elements from the former regime's army and the Hutu refugee camps along the border with Zaire. At the same time, they also aspired to install a friendly regime in Kinshasa that would then permit access to the land and mineral riches of its towering neighbor. Paradoxically, the new authorities in Kigali tolerated the rise to power of Hutu rebels in Bujumbura, thus bringing to an end thirty years of Tutsi hegemony. The core group of these rebel forces was identified with the National Council for the Defense of Democracy / Forces for the Defense of Democracy (CNDD-FDD), which played a decisive role in the Burundian civil war. Much of the credit for putting together the CNDD-FDD—now Burundi's ruling party—goes to Léonard Nyangoma, who, on 14 August 1994, right after the rise to power of the Rwandan Patriotic Front (RPF) in Kigali, announced the creation of the new rebel organization. From the very beginning it received decisive support from officers of the defeated Rwandan Armed Forces (FAR, Forces armées rwandaises), many of whom had found refuge in regroupment camps in eastern Zaire along the border with Rwanda.

In the end, the conflicts that burst forth in the African Great Lakes region between 1990 and 2000 are considered the most bloody on the planet since World War II: the human losses in Rwanda, Burundi, and the DRC are estimated at more than four million, with civilians accounting for most of the victims. This figure does not include the millions of refugees who joined the earlier outflow of internally displaced persons (IDPs).[7]

The political calculations of the protagonists of these tragedies must be examined in light of these antecedents and experiences. Indeed, in the case of

Rwanda, no one can doubt that after four years of civil war, each of the players had enough information to appreciate the potential risks of their strategic choices—without necessarily anticipating their extent—and that implementing them was not left to improvisation. However, as we shall see, throughout the conflict each lull in the fighting opened fresh opportunities to commit atrocities. Along with wanton destruction of property and persons, killings and bombings never stopped, mostly directed against civilian targets. Hopelessness and spiraling hatreds were relentless, as if they were meant to disabuse Rwandans of any prospect for a peaceful solution and to extinguish all hopes of living together in the future. A similar strategy prevailed in April 1994. When the tides of war and massacres gathered momentum, the belligerents refused all opportunities for negotiation, insofar as that was still possible. The imperative was to drive home the idea that there was no future for those who refused to rally to one side or the other. The legacy of former antagonisms, exacerbated by propaganda, fused with and reinforced attitudes born of day-to-day lived experiences. This was especially true of the younger generations, for whom recourse to violence was no longer an imposition but a vital choice.

The "Habyarimana System"

On 5 July 1973 the coup d'état that toppled Grégoire Kayibanda, a Hutu from Gitarama prefecture and the first president of an independent Rwanda, brought Army Chief of Staff Juvénal Habyarimana to power (*see annex 1*). The result was to shift the regional power base to soldiers from the north, then dominating the army. But the new head of state aspired to broader national legitimacy; he wanted to reestablish national unity, which he felt had been shattered by the MDR-Parmehutu. Various decisions meant to overcome ethnic privileges were promulgated. Among them, a system of quotas guaranteeing a certain number of seats and posts to persons duly identified as Tutsi was presented as a concession to minority rights and as an effort to anchor "democracy" in a sharing of power that gave explicit recognition to ethnic and regional disparities. More broadly, the population was encouraged to engage in development activities intended to reduce national divisions. The "moral revolution" of 1973 enlisted the entire country—farmers, civil servants, and leaders—in a broad mobilization. "Community works" (*umuganda*) were intended to raise the status of manual labor among urban dwellers while promoting solidarity on the hillsides.

From a political perspective, within the Committee for National Unity and Peace, the so-called Group of Friends of 5 July 1973 (including Théoneste

Lizinde and Alexis Kanyarengwe), whose members played a key role in Juvénal Habyarimana's rise to power, started to openly contest the growing concentration of power in the hands of the new head of state. Anxious to curtail the influence of this emerging camarilla—most of whom embraced the ideology of MDR-Parmehutu—on 5 July 1975 Juvénal Habyarimana created the MRND (Mouvement révolutionnaire national pour le développement, or Revolutionary National Movement for Development). And he turned it into a political vehicle wholly subject to his command.

The new single party had as its primary objective to reestablish state authority through a system of parallel control: party representatives would combine administrative and political functions, thus ensuring a firm hold over populations left rudderless by shattered political structures. Mandatory enrollment in the MRND would thus incorporate all Rwandans in the fold of the nation irrespective of ethnicity, region, or religious faith. Priding itself on the diffusion of a peasant ideology and a prudent management of local resources, the new regime claimed undeniable achievements: lowering of the national debt, a balanced budget, monetary stability, and relative food self-sufficiency, at least until the last years of the 1980s. These accomplishments explain its excellent reputation among bilateral partners, international donors, and NGOs. The second half of the 1970s and the beginning of the 1980s were particularly auspicious, economically speaking. The possibility of substantial benefits was within reach of nearly all social categories: significant expansion of monetary circulation and of trade in agricultural products, numerous opportunities for supplementary income for rural families, increased employment in trade and handicrafts, increased recruitment in the civil service, and so on. No doubt this generalized loosening of economic constraints concealed the burgeoning social inequalities previously unprecedented in Rwandan society; principally, it benefited the OTP, an initialism that designates those persons originating from the president's home turf (*originaire du terroir présidentiel*), and, more broadly, all the dignitaries of the regime.

In this context, the quota-based democracy introduced in 1973 gradually entered the national consciousness as a legitimate formula, prompting Rwandan authorities to claim that the ethnic problem had been definitively solved. Aside from refugees living abroad and certain categories of urban-based Tutsi citizens, no one really took exception to a system that most believed was there to last.

It was impossible to escape the hold of the single-party MRND: to be born a Rwandan citizen meant automatic membership in the party; and party rules were binding on all, as they embodied the will of the authorities. If the presidential network strictly controlled all spheres of power, these remained relatively relaxed, and none held particularly strong or lasting influence. The army, the ministerial cabinets, the territorial administration (the system of prefects), the party, and the business community could flourish within the framework of a relatively balanced division of power and resources.

But the party did not demand of its members endorsement of any particular set of beliefs, whatever their previous ideologies; the presence of opponents, be they "dissatisfied" or "stubborn," was accepted as a matter of course, so long as the tasks assigned to them were accomplished. Regular payment of dues, participation in community works, occasional financial donations, attendance at political rallies, and at least perfunctory conformity to the thousand and one party rules (from the presentation of storefronts to the cleanliness of school-children) largely sufficed. The defining feature of authority and its various networks was to advertise discipline and efficiency as necessary conditions for a lasting social and moral order.

In the name of "development," the authorities first imposed strict controls over the population and their activities in both rural and urban contexts, including limitations on travel from one prefecture to the next, especially to Kigali; taxation on all economic or financial transactions; and meticulous instructions for farmers. The main reason for this continuous and often arbitrary control by administrative officials and technical managers is linked, paradoxically, to the almost total dependency of the elites on the labor and outputs of the peasantry. In light of the country's landlocked nature and its lack of marketable natural resources, "rational management" of the rural workforce, the only resource that was truly available in abundance, was deemed a national imperative. But its limitations quickly became apparent: they stemmed from the narrow productive base of peasant agriculture and the encroaching poverty of most cultivators.

Consequently, beyond the omnipresence of the state machinery and the extraordinary poverty of the political discourse, the symbiosis of the party-state achieved by politician-technocrats produced a civil service beholden to the state and its priorities. Stability encouraged demands for autonomy based on the technical and professional skills that the state was able to marshal quite effectively.

In effect, the MRND leaders did not depend on popular support for power and influence. No politician ever deemed popular support useful; few ever risked cultivating a local political following in order to generate support from a personally devoted activist base. The few exceptions to this rule — Félicien Gatabazi, Frédéric Nzamurambaho, Alexis Kanyarengwe, and Félicula Nyiramutarambirwa from 1975 to 1985 — were quickly dissuaded or severely sanctioned. All appointments and all activities were regulated by the top echelons, which had established an elaborate system for recognizing the merits of those deserving highly prized or lucrative appointments. All aspirants to a share of the pie had to meet their patrons' expectations. More important still was the aspirants' ability to anticipate the evolving and often contradictory demands that were part of the broader clientelist system.

From burgomaster to prefect, from government minister to project director in large state enterprises, flattering praise for the president and a liberal sprinkling of patriotic slogans were the two fundamental requirements for climbing the steps of the political pyramid. Thus, in cases where candidates for office were held accountable to an electorate, the primacy of the political machine tended to eclipse demands from the population. For example, in 1981 92 percent of the deputies in the National Development Council (CND, Conseil national de développement, the name given to the parliament) came from the public sector, whereas 95 percent of the population (i.e., the rural sectors) ended up with no representation at all. Only two Tutsi members and a single Twa were seated in the parliament. The situation was similar in 1988 following a reshuffling in the CND: of the seventy new deputies, sixty-eight had previously been ministers (fifteen out of sixteen members of government), deputies (forty-four), officers, prefects, subprefects, burgomasters, or civil servants. Only two came from the liberal professions. Tutsi representation remained the same. Again, in December 1988, when he was the lone candidate, President Habyarimana obtained over 99 percent of the vote, including the south of the country, an unlikely base of support for his candidacy.

Membership in the central bodies of the party was a powerful sign of distinction because it clearly indicated presidential recognition of personal merit. It usually meant being on the receiving end of the line in the distribution of the most coveted posts, including access to the more tightly restricted circles of influence and, even if fluid, with boundaries constantly shifting, access to those who were influential and thought to weigh in on the major decisions. It was also at this level that mutual favors and exchanges among senior managers allowed them to cash in, in relative security, on the financial advantages of the clientelist system. Thus, high-level corruption involved the appropriation of large amounts of public funds, which in turn could be reinvested in the creation and nurturing of a new batch of loyal clients.

The term "dictatorship" seems oddly inadequate to describe the nature of the links between the rural populations and the machinery of the state, composed, in fact, of their native sons, freshly recruited for management posts (during the 1980s it was indeed quite rare to find city dwellers beyond the first generation). Centralized authoritarian patronage seems much more appropriate in the sense that, for the average citizen, there was simply no alternative to complete submission to authority nor any recourse in the event of some arbitrary turn of fate. Overwhelming obligation to comply was the name of the game in the web of relations between the peasant populations and the various yokes they had to bear. Too many complicities, too many solidarities, too many social counterweights—the sheer legacy of the "social revolution" or, quite simply, a passivity continuously imposed on the "masses" makes routine dictatorship seemingly inadequate for the social order imposed upon this rural population.

More broadly, the solidity of the Rwandan social model seemed to be anchored in behaviors typically found in churches and their parishioners. In this regard, one can speak of an "authoritarian educative paternalism": in the discourse of educated elites, peasants were characterized as a mass that needed to be taught to work rationally and that required constant "animation," "consciousness-raising," and discipline because it was repeatedly caught in dereliction or misapprehension of the very duties that were imposed upon it for its own good. The saying "father of the nation," designating President Habyarimana, illustrates quite well the nature of the bond between the authority and its subjects.

The discipline imposed by this carefully elaborated administrative and moral order exerted a powerful attraction for the aid agencies and the international donor community.[8] They could implement their development projects practically in direct contact with their "intended beneficiaries" and with attentive support from a decentralized administration, which progressively extended central directives through each commune and hill.

The Ethnic Question and the Various Forms of Social Discrimination

Retrospectively, the sociopolitical crisis that took root toward the end of the 1980s barely seemed to have an ethnic dimension. Where economics are concerned, the disadvantaged populations were both Hutu and Tutsi occupying structurally disadvantaged positions, such as landless farmers, rural youth without formal education, and women. Politically speaking, the concentration of wealth and privileges in the northern prefectures, benefiting their Hutu natives and the Tutsi allies of the "father of the nation," was denounced by inhabitants of all the other regions.

There is an obvious paradox in trying to understand how a genocide of such cataclysmic proportions could occur while for over a decade domestic ethnic tensions were apparently at their lowest level since the colonial period and when numerous Hutu and Tutsi intellectuals had begun to ponder the feasibility of social competition unfettered by ethnicity. Out of the political and social struggles led by the burgeoning social organizations toward the end of the 1980s in the southern prefectures and in Kigali emerged a coalescence of interests among Hutu and Tutsi anxious to press their common claims where regionalist interests had once had the upper hand. Still, power remained undeniably "Hutu" to the extent that its legitimacy was premised on the exercise of power by the ethnic majority, and the official system of quotas continued to legitimize discrimination in regard to access to schools, employment, elective posts, or positions of authority.[9]

However, while the institutionalization of quotas had been introduced as a response to a political and social problem, it evolved step by step into a political problem in its own right. That is to say, it was the institution of quotas that rigidified ethnic distinctions and recalibrated their gears. Unequal access to schooling soon became a burning issue. As beneficiaries or victims of an identity derived from their parents, students had to assume the accompanying institutionalized privileges or handicaps once taken on board by an educational institution. When these young people finished their primary schooling and applied for places in the secondary school, they noticed quite tangibly that the norms of evaluation and selection that had until then been common for all had been replaced by criteria that were foreign to the institution and to the values it was supposed to promote. For the younger generations, primary and secondary school, the seminary, and the university became sites of apprenticeship for coping with the arbitrary nature of ethnic quotas. It was the same thing for the "ethnic" concentration in certain professions or branches of activity. Tutsi families sought to place their children in domains where prohibitions and control were less intense, that is, private-sector activities, generally speaking, certain categories of the clergy, the liberal professions, and jobs with foreign employers and international organizations.

Consequently, in matters of access to the more influential positions, the system of quotas and the regional "indices of disparity" could be seen as an archaic system designed to cater to the most reactionary factions of those in power. In the context of a depressed economy and hardening of social relations, quotas functioned mostly to preserve the status quo for the benefit of a privileged category of citizens whose goal was principally to control access to strategic, high-ranking, or lucrative positions in such key sectors as the army, the National Assembly, the Central Committee of the MRND, and parastatal enterprises. One would note, for example, that if the presidency carefully divided its bounty among ethnic elites whose interests were directly aligned with those at the top—including a few influential Tutsi families active in business

and import-export whose members benefited from highly contested favors—
the Central Intelligence Bureau (SCR, Service central de renseignement),
responsible for the ethnic background checks that preceded all appointments
to civil service posts, did not shrink from issuing virulent anti-Tutsi threats.
This practice had its roots in the threat posed to economic and social privileges by the drastic personnel cutbacks dictated by economic adjustment policies. Finally, the principle of redistributive justice, which at the beginning was
intended to justify this system, went through a major reexamination when the
time came to denounce the shameless concentration of privileges claimed by
civil servants originating from Gisenyi and Ruhengeri prefectures.

An MRND in Crisis, Faced with Regional Rivalries

In this context, the MRND's mandate was unusual. Put in
place to prolong the "social revolution" of 1959 by a "moral revolution" that
would reunify Rwandans from all regions and ethnic groups in a single institutional body, the incessantly repeated objectives of "peace and national
unity" achieved remarkable success. Many were the freshly minted political
leaders who had grown weary of the internal divisions brought out by MDR-
Parmehutu rule. So there was little inclination to resist the new party system
or to challenge President Habyarimana's efforts to reduce ethnic tensions and
rally support of the Tutsi population. However, while he succeeded in neutralizing ethnicist tendencies in his own camp, the president was less adept at
overcoming regional antagonisms and keeping under wraps the killings of
many leaders linked to the First Republic, which cost him the support of the
southern prefectures despite his efforts to deflect accusations of "patricide."[10]
Similarly, Habyarimana failed in his efforts to turn the MRND into a
breeding ground for politicians exclusively dedicated to serving the regime;
nor did he prove more successful in trying to stimulate intramural rivalries
among them. This staged competition between northern and southern nota-
bilities, civilian as well as military, exasperated the officers from the north
who had brought him to power. It culminated with the promulgation of the
constitution of 20 December 1978, which further concentrated power in
Habyarimana's own hands. Although he already combined the responsibilities
of president of the republic and head of the government with the prerogatives
of minister of defense and chief of staff of the FAR, to these titles the constitution added that of president of the MRND, going so far as to specify that the
party chairman would be the only candidate for presidential election. In this

deleterious climate, the simmering rivalry between natives of Ruhengeri and Gisenyi, further compounded by competition between two northern sub-groups, Bashiru and Bugoyi (i.e., those hailing from Bushiru and Bugoyi, respectively, both located within the prefecture of Gisenyi), fueled the attempted coup d'état of April 1980, provoking the removal of the main Group of Friends of 5 July 1973 (Alexis Kanyarengwe and Théoneste Lizinde).

Very few details have seeped into the public domain about this crisis and its consequences. Suffice it to say that the members of the network of civilian and military figures who were closest to Habyarimana were competing with an alternative network, national in scope, that was constructed around the highly influential minister of the interior, Alexis Kanyarengwe, particularly in the army.[11] The significance of these two groups was evident from their intense rivalry to influence the president's decision-making process. When rumors spread that Alexis Kanyarengwe was engaged in maneuvers to upstage the president, the latter felt that the group of "technicians" and soldiers surrounding him were a threat to him as well. Thus, in April 1980 Juvénal Habyarimana ordered the arrest of Théoneste Lizinde, the feared director-general of the Central Intelligence Bureau. The following 28 December, the president dismissed Alexis Kanyarengwe from his government post, causing him to flee to Tanzania for fear that he too would be arrested. In early 1981 Lizinde, tried and condemned to death, was incarcerated in Ruhengeri prison. After that, suspicions continued to swirl around all those who had been close to the ousted figures.[12]

The suppression of the "northern conspirators" carried extensive ripple effects. In fact, aside from the disappearances and the killings of most of the dignitaries of the First Republic, by the end of the 1970s Habyarimana had promoted a group of brilliant politicians from the south, but they were progressively sidelined for having transgressed the cardinal rule of the regime inaugurated by the newly created MRND with its system of minister-technicians. Whenever they became popular and sought to cultivate a personal base like any true "politician," they were ousted. A dramatic illustration is given by the joint disqualification of two figures as radically opposed as Frédéric Nzamurambaho and Félicien Gatabazi. The former, a hardworking minister fully committed to helping his rural constituents, rising in popularity thanks to his candor and his constant presence in their midst, had the misfortune of being nominated by his peers to preside over the CND. The result was immediately to unleash the vengeance of the president's family, who deemed him too independent. The latter, adept at savvy political maneuvering, was sidelined after he dared directly to oppose Aloys Nsekalije, one of the officers closest to the presidential clan; another strike against him was to seek support from Nzamurambaho and most of the southern politicians.[13]

By reasserting his personal power, Habyarimana also reinforced his isolation. By ousting Lizinde and Kanyarengwe, the president broke ranks with the Bugoyi "clan" (which also included such important personalities as Alphonse Libanje, Stanislas Biseruka, and Jean-Berchmans Birara) and with Ruhengeri. With the heart of the power constellation seriously weakened, he turned to the only secure political base. Blood relations and personalities from his own region of origin—the Bushiru, wholly isolated in Gisenyi—replaced all the other forms of solidarity, in particular military friendships, which, up until then, had ensured a privileged alliance between the powerful lineages of politicians and officers from Gisenyi and from Ruhengeri.

It cannot be overstated that, for the northern prefectures in particular, the linkages rooted in their common turf (*terroir*) or subregion created strong cultural and political solidarities—or, inversely, bitter rivalries. The impact of these bonds under both the First and Second Republics proved to be of far greater consequence than the north-south opposition. At each turning point in history they were essential determinants of the alliances linking the major lineages. Moreover, each terroir had its own particular reputation. One could distinguish between "powerful" terroirs—Buhoma, Bukonya (Ruhengeri), and Bugoyi (Gisenyi)—and those in decline—the Bushiru (*see annex 1*).

It is in this context that the authoritarian and almost monarchical drift in presidential power reinforced itself to the benefit of those closely aligned with Habyarimana and the extended clan of his wife's family. His consistent strategy of ethnic and regional balance had thus been undermined by his partisan political base. Ultimately, this contradicted the objective and functional criteria originally invoked to establish legitimacy for his exercise of power.

For the general-president, the stakes were high: he had to squelch any putschist aspirations of the established lineages of politicians and officers from Ruhengeri—and do so in a manner that would not create martyrs—in order to avoid alienating this rival, though necessarily allied, prefecture. Juvénal Habyarimana dared not purge the army or confront other officers or civilian leaders. All were continually under strict surveillance by three key personalities: Col. Laurent Serubuga, the irremovable army deputy chief of staff; Élie Sagatwa, the private secretary and unofficial chief of staff of the president; and the indispensable Protais Zigiranyirazo, brother-in-law of the president and prefect of Ruhengeri prefecture (24 December 1974–13 October 1989).

Concerned with lessening his isolation, Habyarimana made overtures to candidates from Bukonya—Alexis Kanyarengwe's region of origin—by admitting Col. Léonidas Rusatira and Minister of Foreign Affairs and Cooperation François Ngarukiyintwari to the Central Committee of the MRND. And then in March 1981, he brought another person from Bukonya into the government.

In addition—and this was certainly one of his most important decisions—Habyarimana engineered the rise of a new civilian figure who could neutralize, or effectively "blot out," Alexis Kanyarengwe, take control of the prefecture, and ensure its loyalty over the long term. Thus, Joseph Nzirorera emerged from anonymity to become the key figure during the second period of the Habyarimana regime, his sparkling ascendancy sealing a renewed alliance between the two prefectures. The transformation of this young civil servant, ambitious and venal, into a national figure fully beholden to the president was put forth as an example of the regime's success before he came to embody, more than anything else, its excesses and irregularities and its most extreme propensities run amok (*see box 2*).

Toward the end of the 1980s, after a decade of power in the hands of mostly southern-based elites and with power held almost twice as long—twenty years—by northern elites, the regime seemed to run out of steam. It became clear to many Rwandans that "democratic" rule could not continue to limit itself to competition between rival northern and southern segments of the "majority people." Consequently, the sociopolitical crisis was not simply the failure of an exhausted regime. The increasingly open demands for democratic liberalization challenged a social and political order based on rank or group and imposed solidarities, including the notorious triptych "clientelism, regionalism, ethnicism." These demands also raised the question of the right to free speech by all participants in the social order, Hutu as well as Tutsi.

An initial stumbling block had to do with the fact that the MRND's centralizing and authoritarian tradition was the product of a common heritage. All the same, even though the struggle against clientelism was not on the agenda, its hold on society expanded with the loosening of political constraints. Another obstacle was the fact that no leader and no institution enjoyed legitimacy on a national scale. A third stemmed from the priority set on the consolidation of a democratic base, with the ethnic question relegated to the sidelines, a risky move that could easily spin out of control. Sensing their limitations, few leaders and politicians had given up the option of manipulating to their advantage ethnic or regional loyalties, irrespective of the discredit they might incur.

A final obstacle derived from a self-centered attitude widely shared among northern leaders. Faced with the dangers posed by the emergence of new social forces, they were fully prepared to defend tooth and nail their vested interests in the maintenance of the presidential power structure.

2

The Refugee Question
and the RPF's Choice
of Armed Struggle

Before turning to changes in the domestic arena, it may be useful to recall the international context of the military intervention by the Rwandan Patriotic Front (RPF) and its military wing, the Rwandan Patriotic Army (RPA).[1]

On 1 October 1990 several thousand RPF soldiers launched an offensive from Uganda that profoundly shook the foundations of the Habyarimana regime.[2] Technically they belonged to units of the Ugandan army and consisted mainly of Rwandan refugees from the Tutsi diaspora who had settled in this neighboring country since the 1960s. They had fought in the guerrilla war that carried Yoweri Museveni to power and were led by high-ranking Rwandan officers of Tutsi origin who held commanding positions in Uganda's National Resistance Army (NRA).

The 1 October offensive generated great confusion. It took military intervention from France, Belgium, and Zaire to contain the attacks. Not until the end of the month was a measure of calm restored to a country badly shaken by an increasingly tense political situation marked by a growing north-south polarization. Regional polarities would persist in years ahead but were now inscribed in a much more complex political matrix. Besides the ups and downs of the democratic transition, the invasion dramatically raised the stakes associated with the Tutsi rebellion.

A New Player Enters the Scene

On the basis of information received from Kampala, officers of the Rwandan Armed Forces (FAR) high command in Kigali had already raised and debated the possibility of such an attack. What came as a shock, however, were revelations about the political ambitions of the rebellion and the divergent levels of military preparedness between the two belligerents.

Much to the surprise of the Rwandan authorities, who had taken regional détente for granted, the aggressive move by Rwandan refugees based in Uganda occurred at a time when negotiations on the refugee issue had just been concluded, in August 1990, under the auspices of international organizations. These negotiations were meant to facilitate a voluntary return of all Rwandan refugees officially tallied by the United Nations High Commission for Refugees (HCR). No less surprising was the sense of shock caused by the death of charismatic RPF leader Fred Rwigyema two days into the attack and the resultant leadership void. This situation significantly undermined the rebels' military action and thus forced them to reconsider their strategic plans, and this despite the FAR's apparent inability to deal effectively with the rebel aggression; conspicuously absent were the defensive strategies needed for an effective counterattack.

Equally puzzling was the political response from President Habyarimana, who was outside of the country when the attack began. Hurriedly returning home, he made a brief stopover in Brussels on 3 October to seek military assistance from Belgium. The next day, immediately following a presumed attack by infiltrated commandos in the streets of Kigali during the night of 4 October, he ordered a wave of massive, arbitrary arrests of various categories of Tutsi opponents, real or presumed.

After 4 October, with the arrival of the first units from France, Belgium, and Zaire, the likelihood of defeating the RPF was no longer at the center of the debate.[3] Official concerns shifted to the domestic and regional implications of the crisis and the rising tension between the presidents of Uganda and Rwanda.

The insurgent Tutsi of the NRA had certainly benefited from the recent and rather spectacular defections of certain high-profile Hutu officers (*see box 3*), which expanded the Patriotic Front's social base beyond its refugee core, lending credibility to a truly "national" crusade. However, the military dimension, which implied complicity and support at the highest levels in Uganda, was enough to justify the Kigali regime's efforts to mobilize the "Rwandan nation" against foreign invasion and to seek external military assistance. These efforts quickly won the support of the international community, including the Organization of African Unity (OAU, Organisation de l'unité africaine), whose members were hardly disposed to look with sympathy on an armed rebellion, even if its president at the time was none other than Ugandan Yoweri Museveni.

The Repatriation of Tutsi Refugees

In Uganda, the last census taken by the HCR put the number of Tutsi refugees at 82,200. If we add the number of refugees the HCR had already registered by that date (December 1990) in Zaire (12,596), Burundi (67,684), and Tanzania (22,297), along with the tens of thousands in Kenya, West Africa, and elsewhere, we would estimate more than 200,000 persons with formal refugee status. Even if we adopt the most restrictive definition, and the only one likely to be officially recognized (i.e., those refugees who could, if they wanted to, exercise their "right of return"), it vastly underestimates the actual number of refugees.

In the absence of more reliable sources, estimates of the refugee population can be extrapolated in two ways that complement each other: either 550,000, based on the number of Tutsi counted before independence, or 590,000, based on the number of refugees counted in the 1960s. These figures, likely to be closest to the reality, remain far below the 2 million refugees routinely claimed by the Rwandan community abroad, unless we include the Banyarwanda born outside Rwanda (like the Rwandaphones from Buganda) and who never had Rwandan nationality.[4]

Organized in consultation with the HCR, a relatively accurate census of "persons with refugee status" had been compiled in mid-1990, and at the time of the RPF attack, a committee of experts was supposed to conduct interviews to identify those among the refugees wishing to invoke their right of return right away. Slightly more than forty thousand persons came forward. Even so, a "group representing refugees," accompanied by the HCR, was supposed to visit Rwanda from 27 September to 10 October 1990. This mission was to conduct on-site investigations of the conditions of accommodation and security prevailing in Rwanda in advance of the "registering of the dispositions of Rwandan refugees toward the proposed options."[5] The Ugandan contingent unilaterally canceled the visit right before the contingent's departure. Thus, it clearly appears that the 1 October 1990 offensive was intended to short-circuit the negotiations that were under way.

In fact, RPF leaders had little interest in plans to resettle Tutsi refugees of rural origin; those leaders almost unanimously rejected the view that such plans offered the most desirable conclusion to a delicate chapter in Ugandan-Rwandan relations.[6] They saw the work of negotiation undertaken with the support of international organizations as an irritant. Heavy pressure was brought to bear on candidates for repatriation to dissuade them from going along with the HCR repatriation plan. "We left together, we will return together" was a popular slogan among RPF leaders; those who disagreed were quickly isolated.

The invasion was the ultimate trump card for Rwandan rebels. For one thing, they feared losing a large segment of their prospective recruits through the HCR's programs for reinsertion. Nor did rumors of negotiations on the refugee issue between the presidents of Uganda and Rwanda allay the rebels' fears. Again, largely disconnected from political developments inside Rwanda, the rebels were motivated by one single overriding objective: to return to their homeland.

The "Strategy of Negotiated Return" as a Dead End

The RPF's choice of the military option stemmed from a variety of considerations. The first has to do with the shared exasperation felt by the "most long-standing refugees on the planet."[7] After thirty years in exile, they remained without any formal status, they had no particular hope for the future, and their rights were routinely called into question by the host country. Reinforcing their sense of being marginalized, if not abandoned, was their conviction that their fate was not of paramount concern for their fellow citizens. While Rwanda was undergoing a process of democratic liberalization, the refugees remained totally isolated from this transition to democracy and played no part in its awakening.

The prospects for reintegration hardly appeared promising, even if the domestic political context was evolving favorably. Even in the best of circumstances, the refugees' minority status could hardly assure them a significant voice in the context of a majoritarian democracy, let alone defend their interests. The prospect of an RPF fully integrated in the democratic landscape of a country where the majority of its members knew very little about its social, political, and ideological contexts offered few grounds for hope. After having played such a decisive role in Yoweri Museveni's rise to power in Kampala (1986), these former NRA mercenaries had been progressively marginalized or demobilized. In the eyes of those who were not instinctively "democrats," the prospects were not very inspiring. Inevitably, the peaceful path of negotiations and their extension to other countries meant giving the edge to civilians and intellectual elites from the diaspora, who were particularly numerous in Europe and in North America. However, from the standpoint of RPF elites, such solutions would undercut their principal asset, the mastery of weapons, which in effect positioned the "Ugandans" to capture the leadership of the movement.

An additional reason for giving precedence to armed struggle refers to the slim prospects for civilian reinsertion available to this same elite group. Indeed, Rwandan civil servants, faced with the limitations imposed by the newly implemented Programs of Structural Adjustment (PAS), showed an evident lack of sympathy for the requests for integration from refugees who had completed schooling and who often had access to coveted positions in the Ugandan civil service or as local representatives of international organizations. Likewise, it appeared certain that in the ministries and public entities likely to be conceded to figures coming from the ranks of the RPF, the personnel already in place would try to block access and control. The problem presented itself even more starkly with regard to the integration of RPA soldiers into the FAR.

On the other hand, there is no question that those refugees most favorably disposed to a negotiated return were among the Tutsi business elites, domestic as well as foreign based; indeed, at the risk of antagonizing his own clientele, President Habyarimana had made discreet overtures to some of them. Reliable sources confirm that contacts were initiated at the highest levels between the offices of the Rwandan and Ugandan presidents and, relying on intermediaries, even between Juvénal Habyarimana and the RPF leadership.

We should also recall that, around the time of negotiations for the application of the 1985 Economic Community of the Great Lakes Countries (CEPGL) Convention on the Free Circulation of Goods and Persons, the question of the return of "economically independent" refugees, meaning the well-to-do, if not outright wealthy, was never viewed as posing any particular problem. From this perspective, the Hutu and Tutsi Kigali-based business elites shared the same priorities, thereby raising some highly attractive opportunities for economic development for the entire region. It is easy to see why this option held little attraction for the military leaders of the RPF when compared to their own future prospects. They needed little prodding to be reminded that Museveni's rise to power did little to advance their economic interests; given their status as foreigners, they were denied the opportunities for a trade-off between their prowess on the battlefield and their aspirations in the economic sphere, unlike their Baganda and Banyankole comrades. Either by necessity or by virtue, a good number of these officers continued to project an image of austerity as stern-faced revolutionaries in a country where self-enrichment was commonplace.

And finally, the attitude at that time toward the strategy of the "Ugandan" RPF among Rwandan communities in neighboring countries and in the European and North American diaspora was quite ambivalent, garnering only limited support. There was a huge gap between the RPF eight-point political program circulated in October 1990, couched in generalities, and a military agenda that seemed highly improvised:

- consolidating national unity;
- building democratic procedures and institutions;
- building up a dynamic national economy;
- fighting corruption, mismanagement of public goods, and abuse of power;
- granting the unconditional right of refugees to return to their country of origin;
- strengthening social policy in matters of health, education, housing, transportation, and so on;
- providing the right to security and mobilizing the people to protect it;
- increasing regional economic solidarity and cooperation.

These themes, already widely discussed inside Rwanda, hardly demonstrated originality and could not clearly situate the RPF in the tumble of Rwandan politics (other than point 7, which, under the guise of "the right to security," invoked the particularly sensitive question of restoring ethnic balance in the armed forces).

Thus, Tutsi notables, as well as a substantial segment of the Tutsi population in Rwanda, reacted to the news of the attack of 1 October with great misgivings. As it became clear that the initial thrust had failed to break the resistance of the Rwandan army, the blowback effects of the attack provoked considerable alarm. Massive arrests of Tutsi suspects quickly sharpened mutual fears and distrust. There was hardly a voice that deviated, and most Tutsi intellectuals, many of whom felt little affinity with the potential "returnees," joined in the various initiatives in support of "national unity." Further stimulating the denunciation of RPF "foreign-backed invaders," the introduction of multiparty reforms made it possible for Rwandan Tutsi to exercise a political choice among domestic contenders. Some remained in the Revolutionary National Movement for Development (MRND), at least at first, while most joined the new opposition parties. Popular involvement in politics suddenly became more open, as shown by the rising support of many Rwandans for the newly created coalition of the Democratic Forces for Change (FDC, Forces démocratiques du changement).[8] It was essentially on the basis of ethnic solidarity with the "Ugandan" RPF militants, who had been at the forefront of the armed struggle, that support for the RPF—and indirectly for the military option—took root, principally among those of the diaspora. This support then progressively broadened, bit by bit, as the balance of forces at the front lines tipped in favor of the RPF.

The Primacy of the "Ugandan" Stakes

With the deteriorating political situation in Uganda, in the early 1980s several tens of thousands of Banyarwanda fell victim to attacks from militiamen loyal to Milton Obote, the presidential incumbent at that time; the news sent shock waves among the Rwandan diaspora in neighboring states. At this point the problem of Rwandan refugees came into sharp focus on the agenda of humanitarian organizations.[9]

In 1982, hunted down by the partisans of Obote from one side and pushed back toward the Rwandan border from the other, many were the Banyarwanda youth—in particular, the descendants of refugees—who saw recruitment by the "guerrillas" of Yoweri Museveni's NRA as the only way to escape their predicament.[10]

When Museveni took power in January 1986, the Banyarwanda who had joined the ranks of the NRA shared in the bounty obtained by the other Baganda and Banyankole soldiers and acceded to key posts in the military and civilian administrations. The two most notorious among these Banyarwanda, themselves founding members of the NRA, were Fred Rwigyema and Paul Kagame, army chief of staff and head of military security, respectively. But the new Ugandan president, Yoweri Museveni, could not be but highly sensitive to criticisms from those who viewed him as beholden to the Banyarwanda. Even though his prime minister was from the north, many reacted with distaste to what they perceived as an overrepresentation of Banyarwanda in his entourage and within the NRA. His opponents went so far as to claim that he was of Rwandan origins; ironically, in much the same vein, critics of Habyarimana claimed that his family roots were in Uganda.

Paradoxically, the members of this same expatriate elite, buoyed by victory, were most skeptical of the prospects for a sustainable integration once they had fought their way back to Rwanda. Between the prospects for naturalization in Uganda and a decision to take up arms against a poorly trained and poorly equipped Rwandan army, there were few alternatives. The option of confrontation with the Rwandan army was quickly rejected by Museveni, however; his immediate concern was to consolidate control over his own country, not to open up a new front that would weaken the NRA, especially with Banyarwanda officers and recruits playing such decisive roles.

Even so, the privileged positions held by a number of Banyarwanda officers, not to mention their ostentatious behavior, quickly spiked tensions between them and other communities, notably the Baganda and the Banyankole, the president's ethnic group. The most highly placed among the Banyarwanda were obviously those with the most to lose from rising anti-Banyarwanda sentiment. In time this animosity spread to other ethnic groups. The situation was made worse by the continuing efforts of Ugandan power holders to stimulate nationalist impulses, to which must be added the tensions arising from competition for land in regions heavily populated by Banyarwanda. Confronted with the challenges of reintegrating several hundreds of thousands of its own exiled refugees who had returned home, Kampala responded by steadily exerting pressure on Rwandan refugees (and on Kigali), which only heightened their awareness of the tightening vise they were caught in.

It was in this fraught context that in November 1989, Fred Rwigyema and a number of Banyarwanda officers were sidelined in the NRA. Their removal, considered along with the increasing difficulties confronting the Habyarimana regime, put a premium on the option of an armed return to Rwanda: it developed into a well-planned strategy, and its modalities were systematically examined. Whether Museveni and his NRA friends were involved in a "conspiracy" is debatable; suffice it to note that if such was the case, the plotters stood little chance of success without at least a nodding approval from the highest levels of the Ugandan hierarchy. (One need not be supportive to approve, nor is it necessary to oppose in order to disapprove.) Each party was thoroughly familiar with the expectations and constraints of the other; each could resort to all means of pressure or extortion to impose their views. Moreover, there were profound divergences on both sides about the nature of the Rwandan sociopolitical context, from the commanding heights of the presidency to the individual conspirators. Similar divergences emerged in delineating the objectives of the war.

The conduct of the first few days of the conflict reveals that the conspirators' meticulous preparation for the offensive did not exclude a healthy margin for improvisation, almost as if leaders of the rebellion had decided to proceed full throttle not so much to ensure victory but to make a decisive break with the wavering and equivocations that were undermining their cohesion, enervating all of them. And thus to induce cohesiveness among themselves, they forged ahead with a bang.

The beginnings of the war were chaotic, militarily as well as politically. But in the days following the death of Fred Rwigyema, and with Paul Kagame's exclusive control of the movement fully assured, the RPF again turned to the guerrilla tactics that the Banyarwanda leaders had mastered so well. Besides, and here lies the critical factor behind its success, the Tutsi rebellion's wager that President Museveni would support it through thick and thin turned out to be correct. Regardless of the reservations formally voiced by Museveni, military assistance from the NRA never stopped, whether in the form of supplies or through the use of Ugandan territory as a rear base. This became obvious after the cease-fire agreement of 5 June 1992 (which the RPF signed but did not respect), when the RPF blocked the northern and central shipping routes for goods transiting through Uganda on their way to Rwanda. This was still very much a war undertaken and led by Tutsi Banyarwanda and not a Ugandan aggression with refugee proxies. It was indeed the RPF that made the decisions and fashioned its own strategy, thanks to the wide berth that it had in Uganda: strong and enduring links with the regime, multifarious support from the Banyarwanda population, and strong political networks among the Banyankole populations, the president's own ethnic group.

If opportunism was a factor behind the rebels' precipitous decision to attack Rwanda—notably, in order to forestall the repatriation of refugees under the HCR's auspices—their lack of familiarity with the state of affairs in Rwanda was flagrant. But, more to the point, these self-proclaimed, Uganda-based rebel leaders found themselves responsible for the interests of the entire Tutsi refugee diaspora. And yet while aware of this handicap, they proved incapable of overcoming their internal divisions.[11] No concrete solution emerged from the debates about the contents of their political program or the nature of the regime they wanted to install, and this in spite of the strong bonds of solidarity they tended to display when sensitive matters were at stake. At any rate, the goal of restoring Tutsi hegemony served as a unifying bond for a variety of potential supporters—from big traders and businessmen who had been dealing all along with the Habyarimana regime, to all those who did not want to miss out on the opportunity to return home. All ended up rallying behind this military core group in an effort to achieve unity.

Once the outcome of the first few battles became known among Banyarwanda communities in exile, their reaction was enthusiastically to endorse the RPF's choice of arms. This did not, however, lead to massive recruitments, nor did it allay internal tiffs and divisions within the RPF, most pronounced in the weeks preceding Paul Kagame's assertion of his leadership. Dissenting voices were most often heard among those at the very core of the RPF, as demonstrated by the diversity of public statements from its spokespersons.

With no mandate from or political control over the diaspora, the rebel leaders were determined to fight on, just as they once did while serving in the ranks of the NRA. But this time they fought for their own purposes. In the same way that they generally ignored the views and interests of other groupings within the Tutsi diaspora, including those who joined the rebellion from Burundi or eastern Congo and members of the "civilian RPF," the rebel leaders had no intention of consulting with their Tutsi brethren inside Rwanda about refugee issues.[12]

Regionalizing and Planning the War over the Long Term

After its unsuccessful and costly initial offensive, the RPF was understandably crestfallen and isolated, yet it still held a few trump cards: it had officers experienced in guerrilla warfare and a secure rear base in Uganda, a critical source of military support. Moreover, as it set about laying plans for the medium to long term, the RPF was now in a position to make its weight felt not just in Rwanda and Uganda but in the entire subregion. The RPF now had room to maneuver between political and military strategies, depending on how the balance of power evolved in the enemy camp.

The RPF's need to reinforce its regional base was all the more important since, as President Habyarimana himself had admitted, the October 1990 attacks failed because Rwanda had not been attacked from all sides at once. Accordingly, the RPF immediately undertook significant consciousness-raising and recruitment efforts among expatriate communities throughout the region.

Initially, the RPF tracts circulating among refugees in Tanzania and Zaire did little to sway opinion in its favor. The refugees' preferred attitude was to avoid compromising their security in host countries. However, the advent of multiparty politics in Zaire and the pressures from the new political parties to exclude the Rwandaphone community from local and national political debates gave further impetus to the fight for a right of return.

The situation was then quite different in Burundi. In the capital, Tutsi refugees kept a low profile for the most part because of the rapid evolution of the domestic political situation. However, feeling that they had everything to fear from the policies of democratic liberalization and "ethnic balancing" introduced by the government of Adrien Sibomana, who was characterized as a "Hutsi," residents of Rwandan origin became increasingly involved in domestic political debates. Many openly turned for support to the most radical Tutsi fringe in the military and the civil service, their attention fixated on the shifting balance of power in the region. There emerged a reassertion of cross-border solidarities among ethnic groups, both Hutu and Tutsi, in Burundi and

Rwanda. Each state hosted activist elements who sought to champion destabilization in the neighboring country.

The RPF leaders were gravely disappointed when President Pierre Buyoya of Burundi refused to allow them to open a second front from Burundi, which would have given them a decisive military advantage. Denied the opportunity to establish training camps in Burundi, many young refugees fled directly to RPF camps in Uganda and in the north of Rwanda. Around mid-1993, recruitment of "Burundians," the largest and best-organized refugee community, picked up considerable momentum when it dawned upon them that negotiations conducted under international auspices might lead to a new political deal in Rwanda and that the "Ugandan" RPF was positioned to act as their official representative. They assumed that because of their numbers and influence, through their intellectual elites, the traders and businessmen would offset the ascendancy of the military once the war had ended.

On the other hand, links among the various pro-Hutu groups in Burundi and Rwanda considerably reinforced each other. In 1991 Rwandan army units were implicated in the ethnic clashes that swept across Burundi's northern provinces (Muyinga and Cibitoke). Furthermore, the leaders of Palipehutu, an extremist pro-Hutu movement advocating armed struggle, some of whom had taken refuge in Rwanda, benefited from explicit support from Kigali "to retake the country that the Tutsi [had] grabbed [from the Hutu] over four hundred years ago."[13]

Burundi managed to contain the menace posed by armed pro-Hutu groups by relying on firm repression from a mostly Tutsi army. This was facilitated by the isolation of armed groups in the pro-Hutu movement. In fact, because of the ever-present threat of repression and their conviction that power sharing would inevitably lead in the end to democratic elections, many Hutu leaders rejected the military option. Instead, they gave precedence to political mobilization among the Hutu population of the interior, doing all they could to sow doubts about the sincerity of the Tutsi elites. That the Hutu leaders had agreed to concede some political ground did not prevent them from defending their hold over the military, the state, the economy, and, most importantly, the privileges and assets acquired over three decades of undivided power. While the great majority of Burundians aspired to a peaceful democratic transition, Tutsi extremists raised some daunting obstacles. They lost no time training civilian self-defense groups that could rapidly be activated in the service of their continuing hegemony.

After a period of intense diplomatic activity marked by several summits of regional heads of state and under pressure from international aid groups and funding agencies, a fragile cease-fire was proclaimed in Rwanda on 29 March

1991 under the aegis of the OAU after the summit in Dar es Salaam of 19 February, during which a declaration on the "sustainable solutions to the problem of Rwandan refugees" had been adopted.

The policy of liberalization called for by heads of state failed to yield the expected results. Owing to the quickly deteriorating political climate, the incumbent authorities lacked both the confidence and the means necessary to implement reforms. For its part, the RPF took a stance diametrically opposed to that of the Habyarimana regime and to the multiparty government demanded by the opposition.

Civil War and Democratic Liberalization

At the local level, the 1 October 1990 invasion, followed by the mysterious attack attributed to infiltrated commandos on the streets of Kigali during the night of 4–5 October, made an indelible impression. Rapid gunfire reverberated around the military camps in Kanombe, Kimihurura, Kigali, and Kacyiru, provoking great anxiety among the population. This pivotal event, which the ministers themselves characterized as *ikinamico* (theater), still remains open to debate (see map 2).

There are two diametrically opposed versions of the story. The first, which seems the more convincing, challenges the authenticity of the attack and supports the view that it was staged and orchestrated by the two deputy chiefs of staff of the army and the gendarmerie, Col. Laurent Serubuga and Col. Pierre-Célestin Rwagafilita, with the blessing of the president.[14] The other alleges that the persons responsible for the attack were indeed infiltrated commandos of the RPF. This is the official version put forth by the Rwandan authorities, endorsed, notably, by Col. Théoneste Bagosora (Gisenyi). A third, more recent version advanced by French military informants places responsibility on a contagious panic among government soldiers, who started shooting indiscriminately.[15] Whatever the case may be (*see annex 4*), the presumed attack was used to justify heavy-handed reprisals. The fear that befell the entire city provided the army with a convenient pretext for massive, arbitrary arrests of various categories of political opponents, real or assumed: journalists, leaders of civil society associations, lawyers, and others, mostly Tutsi. What they had in common was their deep-seated hostility to the government in power.

The sense of revulsion caused by the huge number of arrests was scarcely diminished by the corralling of thousands of detainees in one of Kigali's largest stadiums. This, as much as the public display of brutality toward the prisoners, unleashed political shock waves.[16] The calls for denunciations and the incitement to ethnic hatred propagated by Radio Rwanda were quickly relayed to prefectural and local authorities. The result was a pervasive climate of fear and suspicion.

The handling of the case files for persons arrested in October 1990 was less than optimal. Efforts at transparency one day were followed by a hardening stance the next, especially after the November 1990 dismissal of the prosecutor general of the Court of State Security, Alphonse-Marie Nkubito, who was deemed excessively lenient. The trials took place in an atmosphere rife with tension. They were held shortly after the RPF raid on Ruhengeri on 22 January 1991 that freed the incarcerated Théoneste Lizinde, one of Juvénal Habyarimana's "friends" when they launched the coup d'état of July 1973 but subsequently, in the early 1980s, accused of seeking to topple him (*see box 3*).

It seemed as though the northern networks of power—some of which had penetrated the intelligence services and some factions in the army and the party—had regained a capacity of expression and action that had been blocked until then. Thus, certain northern extremists, encouraged by the receptive echo found in the press, did not hesitate to name and shame a number of government officials, branding them as "accomplices of the enemy."

Under pressure from Western embassies and with the conclusion of an RPF cease-fire agreement on 29 March, the appointment of Sylvestre Nsanzimana to the Ministry of Justice eventually led to the release of 3,500 prisoners. And on 18 April a presidential decree commuted eight death sentences to life imprisonment. In response to these measures, a number of independent press organs continued their militant mobilization; so did the church and a number of human rights organizations. One of the most vocal, the Rwandan Association for the Defense of Human Rights (ARDHO, Association rwandaise pour la défense des droits de l'homme), created on 30 September 1990, immediately entered a phase of intense involvement in advocacy activities.

Over the course of 1991, several liberal measures were announced, ranging from simplifying the passport application process (henceforth the Ministry of Interior would handle passport applications instead of the offices for state security) to the automatic issuance of a passport to any Rwandan claiming refugee status. There was also a call for all the parties to work together to address the long-standing political demands of the RPF, the establishment of a new legal framework with the December 1991 law on amnesty (of which 5,872 prisoners were able to avail themselves in February 1992), the designation of the first sites for reintegration of refugees, and the proclamation of the setting up of an official administrative unit for organizing the returns. The system of ethnic quotas in the educational and professional sectors would formally be abolished by November 1990, as would the mention of ethnicity on identity cards. All these measures were undeniable signs of a political will to defuse the situation. The framework for reestablishing civil peace having been drawn with the added benefit of vigilant international monitoring, its success depended on the good faith and honesty of the Rwandan authorities.

However, a number of considerations invited skepticism. Besides the "monochromatic" composition of the government put in place by the hard-line elements, the stalemate in negotiations with the refugees, the delay in the planned electoral process, the failure to restore employment for victims of arbitrary arrests, the unavailability of new identity cards (announcements that printers should submit bids for contracts to create the new cards were only published in December 1991, which meant that the old procedures still held sway in the interim), the reinsertion of the mention of ethnicity in the mid-1991 census, and the violent anti-Tutsi campaign launched by some of the media did not inspire a sense of confidence and security among the potential candidates for return.

Much more worrisome, however, were the recurrent cycles of violence against Tutsi in the wake of the RPF offensive and then again after the advent of multiparty reforms. Numerous murders, disappearances, and abuses were reported in Kibilira in Gisenyi prefecture on 11 October 1990 (383 Tutsi killed); in Kinigi (261 Bagogwe, a Tutsi subgroup based in Rwanda's north-west, killed), Mukingo, Nkuli, and Mutura in Ruhengeri prefecture in January and February 1991; in Kanzenze in greater Kigali prefecture in October 1991; in Murambi in Byumba prefecture in November 1991; and again in Kanzenze (over thirty deaths) in March 1992. These killings did not result from wide-spread, spontaneous outbursts betraying some sort of populist, anti-Tutsi exasperation; they were the consequence of mobilization efforts by local authorities, aided in their task by certain government officials. All these events testified to a global deterioration of public order on the hills. Press accounts sometimes explained how these acts of violence benefited from the deliberate decision of local civil servants and judicial authorities to look the other way.[17] The "rich" Tutsi—businessmen, teachers, wage earners, and "wealthy" farmers—seemed to have been especially targeted. Many observers noted that a standard tactic of the Rwandan government in facing off attacks from the Inkotanyi ("valiant warriors," as the RPF soldiers called themselves) was to hold Tutsi elements hostage. Hence the growing anxieties of the Tutsi population at the prospect of military or police activity and the growing ethnic distrust affecting all aspects of daily social interaction.

Intra-FAR Tensions and
the Definition of "the Enemy"

It was in this context, marked by a combination of political overtures and increasing tensions, that members of the high command of the Rwandan Armed Forces, supported by the regime's heavyweights, decided to put their anxiety on public display. On 1 December 1991 they published a communiqué signed by Lt. Col. Anatole Nsengiyumva on behalf of the Office of Military Operations of the Rwandan Armed Forces that denounced the rampant anarchy and the alarming progression of the *inyenzi*.[18] Three days later, on 4 December, Juvénal Habyarimana organized a meeting of operational sector commanders, unit commanders, and military camp commanders, as well as cabinet officers in the Ministry of National Defense and staff officers of the FAR, to review the situation and map out a course of action. The meeting was held behind closed doors in an atmosphere of tension. A number of the officers criticized leaders of the opposition, accused of betraying their country by organizing activities that favored the enemy and by making statements that weakened the army's morale. President Habyarimana decided to establish a working committee to study the problem and to provide conclusions within a month's time. Referred to by several among them as the Bagosora Commission, taking the name of Col. Théoneste Bagosora, who, as the most senior officer at the highest grade, became its presiding officer, the commission was composed of nine other members, including vigorous supporters of the regime and officers known for their independence or their democratic leanings (*see annex 7*). A report was prepared in less than three weeks. Reread and corrected by Maj. Augustin Cyiza, it was adopted by apparent consensus of all members, or at least without anyone distancing himself from it, and then submitted around 20 December to President Habyarimana, who limited its circulation to a select few.

The first part of this text, focusing on the ethnic definition of an external and domestic "enemy," could provoke strident polemics (which eventually happened when parts of it were circulated selectively in September 1992), but the reasons that the president's office limited the report's dissemination had more to do with chapters emphasizing the lack of turnover and advancement in the officer corps and methods of commanding the army. The kicker was the passage recommending democratic liberalization as a solution to civil war. By challenging the lack of social mobility in the officer corps and the army's lack of preparedness in confronting the RPF offensive, the report gravely irritated the president, who at that time also served as the supreme chief of the armed forces. On 31 December he appointed Sylvestre Nsanzimana as his prime minister and, significantly, relinquished control of the Ministry of Defense. Similarly, the fates of the gendarmerie's chief of staff, Pierre-Célestin Rwagafilita (in active service since 1979), of the army chief of staff, Col. Laurent Seruguba (in active service since 1973), and of the chief of staff in the Ministry of Defense, Col. Léonidas Rusatira (in active service since 1970), were virtually sealed.[19]

Doubting the Rwandan government's commitment to democratic reform, the RPF explicitly adopted a strategy of "protracted warfare." It relied on periodic incursions whose impact could only be minimal in the absence of massive logistical support from the Ugandan army, as was the case back in October 1990. On the other hand, the economic constraints resulting from cutting off Rwanda's vital overland access to ports on the Indian Ocean (northern corridors through Uganda and Kenya to Mombasa and central access through Tanzania to Dar es Salaam) and the cost of the war (especially recruitment and munitions) were far more consequential for the economic survival and stability of this small landlocked country. These repeated incursions weighed heavily upon already tense relations among the various political forces poised to challenge the regime and the MRND party-state, given the prospect of a sovereign national conference (*rukokoma* in Kinyarwanda).

3

 A Necessary Political
Transition

The years of "democratic transition," from 1991 to 1993, were a turning point. The rising demands for democracy found expression in different forms, and their diffusion through social, economic, and political vehicles fed the momentum. The stakes were twofold: on the one hand, a recognition of the new rights of the electorate and the arrival of a political and institutional framework that would safeguard them in a lasting manner; and on the other, the deployment of strategies of co-optation and control intended to breathe new life into both former and newly created political structures.

We can discern two significant periods separated by the RPF offensive of February 1993. Until then, the political scene had given pride of place to domestic concerns (e.g., the recognition of multiparty politics; the growing influence of opposition parties); in subsequent months, however, the RPF loomed increasingly large on the political horizon. Its relentless advance went hand in hand with a recalculation of alliances that led to bipolarization, culminating in the decisive confrontation of 1994.

Attacked from within and without, President Habyarimana made a determined effort to remobilize the "Hutu people" from the countryside. At the same time, he did all he could to portray himself as the only leader capable of pushing through a genuine liberalization of the political landscape in the face of a "double extremism": Hutu extremism, which found loyal support within the army and the state apparatus, and Tutsi extremism, particularly among the refugees based in Uganda, where some had allegedly kept alive hopes of restoring the monarchy. Again, ethnicity reasserted its primacy amid economic, social, and political tensions. At the same time, some elements within the ruling circles sensed the need to underplay racial extremism in order to boost the image of moderation the "father of the nation" tried to project; the tacit assumption was that he really had no other choice but to liberalize his regime in return for continuing military and financial assistance from donors.

It is possible that the president hoped to capitalize upon the war in order to neutralize the domestic opposition, ultimately to relegitimize the Second Republic through a negotiated reintegration of at least a part of the Tutsi diaspora. In the end, however, opposition by the FAR, whose initial military prowess, as claimed by the high command, greatly increased its morale and self-confidence, ruled out that option.

In fact, it took little exaggeration to boast of such military success. Disorganization in the army, on open display, unleashed a bitter settling of scores among the top brass, to which must be added marginalization of officers from the south, deaths in suspicious circumstances of brilliant officers from the north, accusations of treachery or putsch attempts, and imprisonment of officers from the north who were privy to the regime's secrets, all of which helps explain the prevailing deleterious atmosphere, as well as the army's poor military performance.

At this stage all the parties clearly perceived what they would have to endure; each camp kept a close watch on the effects of the RPF offensive and tried, as best it could, to identify potential allies. Domestically, the radicalization of the Gisenyi and Ruhengeri factions was accompanied by a strengthening of their hold on the repressive apparatus of the state. The two prefectures soon took on the appearance of "bunkers," where anyone hailing from the other prefectures was deemed as undesirable. The moment that legalization of multipartyism appeared inevitable and automatically emancipated the central and southern prefectures from the hold of the MRND party-state, the Gisenyi and Ruhengeri factions tightened their grip, even though the arithmetic of the quotas governing regional representation was already outrageously skewed in their favor, given their numerical minority. Thus, the elites from the two communes of Karago and Giciye, a bastion of the presidential clan that substantially controlled power, represented some one hundred thousand people, that is, eight times smaller than the "minority" Tutsi population nationwide.

Regional rather than ethnic cleavage emerged as the more decisive for discriminating between the titans of the north against the more liberal figures from the south-central prefectures. Although the focus on ethnicity had the advantage of enhancing the voice of the majority in the quasi-monoethnic bastions of the north, where ethnic and regional ties overlapped, the tendency was to lump together Hutu and Tutsi from other regions as common foes. However, supporters of a truly "national" MRND insisted on the need for an objective alliance with Tutsi elites, a goal that met with Habyarimana's approval, despite the threat that it could give a new lease on life to the MDR-Parmehutu (Democratic Republican Movement / Party of the Movement for the Emancipation of the Hutu, or Mouvement démocratique républicain / Parti du mouvement de l'émancipation hutu), vanguard of the antimonarchist revolution of 1959. The uneasy coupling of these two currents lasted until the MDR-Parmehutu's disappearance on 6 April 1994.

The conviction that the Habyarimana regime was on its last legs was widely shared among RPF militants. But their urge to finish off their enemy on the battlefield was also a reflection of their concern that the democratic opposition inside Rwanda might steal their thunder in a peaceful march to power. Regardless of the prospects for a resumption of hostilities, the leaders of the Second Republic were no less fearful of the threat posed by the new parties. The most challenging was the MDR (Mouvement démocratique républicain, or Republican Democratic Movement), an antinorthern coalition that drew considerable support from its historic legitimacy as one of the instigators of the 1959 revolution. Second in line would be the PSD (Parti social-démocrate, or Social Democratic Party), which articulated demands for political renewal under the two republican regimes. It enjoyed the massive support of Hutu and Tutsi populations in the Butare and Gikongoro prefectures owing in no small measure to the prestige of their two charismatic leaders, Félicien Gatabazi and Frédéric Nzamurambaho. This, in turn, prevented the RPF from making substantial inroads in those prefectures where Tutsi elements were most numerous. It was the same for the PL (Parti libéral, or Liberal Party, which was predominantly Tutsi), heavily represented in Kibungo and Kigali-rural prefectures, with the second highest concentration of Tutsi in the country.

The "blowhards" of both sides dealt new cards to the extremist fringes: on the one hand, Paul Kagame took Fred Rwigyema's place and set a more brutal and determined course for the RPF; on the other, the "power" and "liberal" factions set upon each other in a "war within the war."

Breathing New Life into the MRND

On 5 July 1990 President Habyarimana announced the introduction of multipartyism. On 1 September Édouard Karemera was formally appointed to head the National Synthesis Commission, tasked with collecting ideas from party members in relation to the political reforms proposed by the president. These various propositions were debated and incorporated in the blueprint for the national political charter, which served as the basis for the constitution of 1991. For those efforts, Édouard Karemera earned the name Rukusanya, the "gatherer" (of ideas).

Three months later, on 5 July 1991, following adoption of new statutes for the renovated MRND, the organizational chart stipulated that President Habyarimana had received the mandate of guiding the transition at the helm of the party's presidency, pending the definitive implantation of the refurbished MRNDD (Mouvement républicain national pour la démocratie et le développement, or National Republican Movement for Democracy and Development); Édouard Karemera was charged with establishing new grassroots organs for the party and managing its day-to-day affairs until its first congress. Party leaders at the prefecture and commune levels were instructed to support the Karemera team and to serve as de facto presidents of the renovated MRND in their respective prefectures. Elections for the communal and prefectural committees were held in February 1992 (*see annex 9*). It was only after these elections at the prefectural level that the party managed to have a "political bureau" comprised of their eleven presidents. Habyarimana only called upon this bureau for major decisions until the April 1992 congress, when the national organs were formally installed.[1]

Operationally, the presidency and the state apparatus—above all, the territorial administration—closely monitored this transitional period. The president played a decisive role: he consulted and entertained frequently, he negotiated and rewarded, and he made quite a few promises. His priority was to ensure the loyalty of those party activists, employees, and local figures whom he could count on. The prefects were particularly helpful in this regard, for in spite of their declining authority in relation to the burgomasters, they still had effective means of persuasion. Government ministers relied on all the powers and resources still at their disposal to ensure the loyalties of high-level civil servants, the heads of both parastatal enterprises and development projects.

This attempt to restructure the party was particularly complex and delicate because it aimed at nothing less than the appointment of new leaders and prefectural officials to advertise the colors of the MRND and champion future combats, particularly electoral contests, on behalf of the mouvance présidentielle. This proved an especially tough proposition in a context of diminished patronage rewards. The nomination and appointment of coordinators and provisional members of the prefectural bureaus, to say nothing of the signatures from prominent "founding members" from the various prefectures and socioprofessional bodies solicited to ratify adoption of the statute for the renovated MRND (the party was formally reorganized on 31 July 1991), gave more than a hint of the new dispensation of power. The coming electoral battles required that "popular" figures be placed in the forefront, to the detriment of former activist-civil servants who previously could simply be summoned by the prefects at the drop of a hat.

It is easy to see why only a very experienced politician, skilled at deciphering the meaning of presidential messages, could effectively rise to the challenge of leading the new MRND; this required exceptional personal skills and an aptitude for negotiation. In this regard, Édouard Karemera achieved impressive results as an efficient and greatly appreciated mover and shaker, thus placing him among the important figures emerging from the south. However, schisms within the National Synthesis Commission and opposition from the presidency came together in a manner that denied Karemera the opportunity to parlay his contributions to his personal advantage. The congress of April 1992 empanelled a new National Bureau, composed of President Habyarimana, reconfirmed as president of the MRND; Amandin Rugira (Hutu, Butare), first vice president; Ferdinand Kabagema (Hutu, Kibungo), second vice president; and Matthieu Ngirumpatse (Hutu, Kigali), national secretary (*see annex 9*). Yet none of these party stalwarts, temporarily entrusted to lead the party through its first congress, ultimately figured among its newly installed leadership. Karemera was among those who were passed over, and his absence did not go unnoticed (*see box 4*).

Renovation through the Prism of Multipartyism

The MRND adapted to the demands for democratization under constraint, with the pressure of war weighing most heavily. The party had to confront a multiplicity of political factions and the collapse of its developmentalist rhetoric, revealing its poverty all the more starkly, given the context of scarcity and structural adjustment. It was a question not just of imbibing the new creed of democratic transition but of articulating a set of mobilizing political references beyond "safeguarding the achievements of the social revolution of 1959 and the moral revolution of 5 July 1973."[2] Despite the internal dynamism and the rich debate that began to take root nationally, the new party statutes demonstrated the limits of that exercise. They provided the party with a high-sounding rhetoric that contrasted dramatically with the concerns and aspirations that motivated party activists and officials. But the "exalted" discourse that began to take hold gave no indication that the MRND was populated by dissatisfied activists. The majority of its officials felt that the single-party legacy was a source of national pride and made no bones of the fact that the opposition parties would remain weak. Paradoxically, the mottos of the renovated MRND invoked continuity with its origins (unity, togetherness), both literally and figuratively, and offered no vision of a new beginning that would give substance to expressions of ethnic and regional solidarity. The central preoccupation aimed at blocking the rebirth of the MDR-Parmehutu with a self-enhancing discourse in praise of its own legacy. In addition, there was concern about how best to contain the internal bickerings of the south while trying to resurrect the political axis of the First Republic that linked Gitarama with Ruhengeri.

Thus, continuity won out by default—by refusing to make clear-cut political choices in order to break with the habits of the single party. The paradox is that in a context of extreme ethnic and regional polarization, the revamped MRND claimed to be open to all and tolerant of all ideological currents. Thus, as James Gasana observed, from the prefectural committees up through its national organs, from its permanent staff to its new Interahamwe youth wing, the party ended up with highly diverse bedfellows, some fairly close to its avowed opponents, and even with activists who were receptive to the ideals of the RPF or, at the other extreme, the radical ethnic purists who later marched under the banner of the CDR (Coalition pour la défense de la République, or Coalition for the Defense of the Republic).[3] It was only after the March–April 1992 massacres of Tutsi civilians in the Bugesera region, in the north, that Tutsi left the party in droves to swell the ranks of the opposition, mainly the PL (Parti libéral, or Liberal Party).

In the absence of genuine political objectives, the agreement involved a partial redistribution of powers within the MRND in order to retain the maximum number of persons who would otherwise be tempted to found their own party and/or join the opposition. Habyarimana needed "renovators" from the south. Clearly, it was important to reduce the number of likely presidential competitors.

While the jockeying for power around the mouvance présidentielle went on unabated and the attitude of defiance of various presumptive candidates for the presidency remained unsanctioned, the northerners never ceased to express dissent from the new party opening. All of this testified to the dramatic weakening of authority within the MRND, its leadership incapable of reining in or consolidating its rival clans.

Complex Fragmentations in the Political Landscape

The limited results of the party reorganization applies equally to attempts at restructuring the political sphere in anticipation of multipartyism. The heads of the new opposition parties often came from the ranks of the "frustrated," whether old guard or new generation, from within the MRND. Among them were many who were denied the posts they hoped to obtain or who failed to be anointed as local leaders in anticipation of the upcoming electoral shake-up.

Thus, multipartyism consisted in institutionalizing a double fragmentation in the political landscape, one internal to the MRND, already beset by factions, congealing around those favored in the succession for the presidency, and the other external to the party-state, taking form through partisan mobilizing by those who missed out on the redistributions of rewards along regional or ethnic lines. The attempt to build a large opposition party for the center and south by breathing new life into the former MDR-Parmehutu failed precisely because of the last-minute backpedaling, negotiated away by the president, and because these new opposition leaders, hard pressed to satisfy their strong personal ambitions, feared losing out in a larger, common structure. Many among them preferred to rely on a personal springboard that they could control rather than risk constant challenges from other equally influential figures.[4] We can also point to a third type of fragmentation: the large competing political blocks that understood, as early as 1992, that in order to boost their representation in key institutions, it was preferable to rely on several rump parties that responded perfectly to the mercenary strategies of opportunist politicians. (See Appendix: Box 5, pp. 351–353.)

The New Configuration of Power Sharing

It would be difficult precisely to gauge the popular appeal of the various parties in the absence of anything resembling a polling organization or opinion survey. The former single party still maintained a quasi monopoly of power except where it was forced to make concessions to the opposition. There was some sort of balance of power in the government set up in April 1992, but everywhere else the reach of the MRND was hardly diminished. In the parliament, known as the National Development Council (Conseil national de développement), whose members were elected in December 1989 under the single-party regime, a few deputies joined the opposition parties, but most parliamentarians remained loyal or ambivalent. In the judiciary or the army, whose members were duty bound to remain discreet, only a few figures openly declared their sympathy for the opposition parties; others were content with the new independence, but the MRND machine kept its uncontested preeminence.

The lines of demarcation were more easily drawn at the local or regional level. When the new multiparty government of April 1992 was installed, prefectural seats were divided between the MRND and the other large opposition parties. For the burgomasters, things worked differently. Wherever the MRND's dominance was deemed unacceptable and contested by opposition party activists, the incumbents had no other choice but to give up their posts. And this occurred even before the government decided to reappoint burgomasters by resorting to *grands électeurs*, a sort of electoral college composed by notable figures in the communal administration. This "cleaning up" of the local government institutions affected 38 communes in March 1993 and 8 others in September 1993 without creating an anti-MRND tidal wave. Thus in 1994 the MRND held sway over 100 of the 145 communes in the country, as compared to 24 headed by the MDR, 15 by the PSD, and 1 governed by the PL. Five communes remained without burgomasters because of their particular circumstances (death or resignation of the burgomaster, local contestation, or maintaining a dual power at the head of commune, etc.). We must nonetheless exercise caution in assessing the fluidity in party affiliations for numerous burgomasters (formal inscriptions in opposition parties in 1992–93 and desertions between late 1993 and April 1994) or multiple, overlapping affiliations (e.g., MRND/CDR or MRND / opposition party). In fact, and this plays an important role, personality and the influence on the local population of burgomasters (often on the job for ten or even twenty years) often trump partisan political rivalry.

Presidential Power

It may be helpful at this point to draw attention to several other features of the system of presidential power. The terms used to map out the shape of this power constellation are by now familiar: the president, the presidency, the presidential clan, the family (or the in-laws) of the president, his inner circle, the presidential turf (terroir) and its denizens (OTP), the president's messengers; then, at another level, the presidential party, the closely linked formations, and, more broadly, the mouvance présidentielle. The multiplicity of terms is illustrative of both the personalization of power and its concentration. What these terms fail to convey is the complexity of the communications system gravitating around the presidential hub, including the wide array of messengers and interlocutors in charge of transmitting or obfuscating presidential orders. A few remarks may illustrate this.

To start with the president himself, the problem consists in understanding how he receives information and then how he expresses his opinions, and especially who bears responsibility for making his will and his decisions known.

As for his sources of information, it is enough to identify who approaches him and transmits the message, in full or in parts and how either is presented, and who is in charge of communicating to him technical or political information, whether official or informal.

At the top of the list we can mention his private secretary (and brother-in-law), Élie Sagatwa, working in this capacity since 1973; various successive ministers assigned to the presidency, one after the other, once the post of secretary-general to the presidency of the republic (held by Col. Bonaventure Buregeya [Hutu, Gisenyi]) was abolished in 1980; the chief of staff; the deputy chiefs of staff of the army and the gendarmerie; the head of the powerful SCR (Service central de renseignement, or Central Intelligence Bureau); and, to a lesser extent, the secretary-general of the Ministry of Defense, whose role was more administrative than political or operational. Habyarimana himself occupied the post of minister of defense and the two posts of chief of staff of the army and the gendarmerie, the two components of the FAR, until the advent of the multiparty system—or, more precisely, until the appointment of the first multiparty government headed by Sylvestre Nsanzimana in December 1991. Others among his close associates were able to bypass Sagatwa's scrutiny and communicate directly with the president.

Beyond this group of close collaborators, half–civil servants, half-courtesans, more often than not involved in cutthroat competition for influence, Habyarimana could tap several other circuits of information: the intelligence services, the leaders of his party, such and such a minister, and those whom he met or socialized with in his "private life." In the other direction, sending out presidential instructions and directives remained the principal preserve of Élie Sagatwa in his capacity as the president's private secretary and keeper of his secrets; he could also respond to messages intended for the president that he chose not to transmit, answering in place of the president or on his behalf.

The difficulty thus consisted in knowing to what extent the messages relayed genuinely reflected the president's will and how much credibility to accord to all those who, informed indirectly by others, would claim afterward that their conduct reflected the will of the president. We can make a distinction here between persons who had received a specific authorization or directive and those who had been authorized to speak on behalf of the president. In this second category could be found his close associates and his family and, more generally, those who were said to have the ear of the president. Whether messages involved orders, responses, wishes, predilections, hints, or rumors, the recipients had no choice but to try to make sense of messages that were often subtle and ambivalent. Consequently, it is likely that Sagatwa had considerably less influence than was generally assumed. The president saw to it that he could exercise exclusive control, with members of his entourage cast in the role of "transmission circuits" or "switches." He thus had access to a wide range of communication networks. To make sure that his orders would be properly executed, he decided to keep under his control all major decision-making processes, political and military. In this complicated environment Sagatwa was reputedly less cynical and less imposing than the other members of the presidential family.

As for the question of assessing the significance of presidential declarations and acts, the situation in that regard was hardly transparent and thus neither easily understood nor easy to analyze.

Certainly, the regime was not short on slogans and presidential messages, incessantly broadcast over the national radio and through the official press. Add to these messages the press releases, various public statements that accompanied the daily comings and goings of the president, presidential speeches that he made or had read on his behalf, and statements from the minister attached to the presidency, who served as his spokesperson. To get these messages right required special skills. While insisting on keeping some of his options open, Habyarimana also realized the need to address the concerns and preoccupations of those he was dealing with, directly or indirectly, even if this would eventually give rise to contradictions. It was even more difficult to know the effect of his decisions and messages when they were sent out or contradicted by other figures either in word or in deed. Finally, among the most striking distortions observed in the realm of communications were the contradictions between the language used by the president in international forums and the language used for domestic consumption. The same applies to official statements from the MRND broadcast in French on the airwaves or in the press and their rendering in Kinyarwanda.

In fact, between the president and the mouvance présidentielle there was ample space for autonomous, if not openly contradictory, strategies. The president's main concern was to ensure the coherence of the whole, even allowing some measure of free rein to select others so long as their maneuverings also served his ends. Few doubted that the president was "well informed" and knew how to listen. That he had an intimate knowledge of his convoluted political environment, that he understood better than anyone else the balance of power within the complex and evolving system that he himself had constructed, that he knew how to apportion his time among his supporters and adversaries, and that he was strong willed—these were well known facts among Rwandans. The question was not whether Habyarimana was pro-democracy, or pro-Tutsi, pro-Matthieu or pro-Joseph. It was rather a question of understanding how the specific forces invoking his name were able to consolidate their respective positions and, within the existing multiparty framework, to reposition themselves in anticipation of unforeseen circumstances.

Two conclusions flow from the foregoing. The first is that recourse to a multiplicity of terms to identify those who spoke in the president's name is inevitable. The second is that, until his death, he stood as the central figure in the political system. He saw himself as the only one capable of maintaining the fragile balance among opposing forces. More fundamentally, he always deemed himself to be the one who, in the name of his presidential role, embodied "national unity" in the eyes of the majority of the citizens. Only he was able to decree that the conditions for making peace were at hand and that he alone could impose their implementation.

The structure of the presidential power can be then described as a set of concentric circles.

The First Ring:
The Akazu

Largely defined by bloodlines and the intermarriages linking the president's extended family, the Akazu (literally, "little hut") can best be seen as an incubator for the country's civilian and military elite, coming mostly from Karago and Giciye communes in Gisenyi prefecture. Over the course of the years, beyond their official designations and formally acknowledged roles, members of the Akazu not only became a parallel network of power within the army, the party, and the administration but metastasized as a parasitic outgrowth in the economic and financial system of the country. Indeed, one could find members and close associates of the presidential family at the Banque nationale du Rwanda, the Banque continentale africaine au Rwanda, the Banque commerciale du Rwanda, and the Banque de Kigali. A similar situation occurred at the national headquarters of parastatal enterprises (OCIR-Café and OCIR-Thé), in joint private-state enterprises, in rural development projects (e.g., Gishwati-Butare-Kigali), and in the import-export sector (e.g., La Centrale, La Rwandaise, Kipharma, Agrotec, and Garage NAHV).

The following persons were generally considered the most influential: Protais Zigiranyirazo, Col. Élie Sagatwa, and Séraphin Rwabukumba (the president's three "brothers-in-law"); Col. Laurent Serubuga (former deputy chief of staff of the FAR); Dr. Séraphin Bararengana (the president's brother); Dr. Charles Nzabageragereza (the president's cousin and ex-prefect of Ruhengeri); Alphonse Ntilivamunda (the president's son-in-law); and Joseph Nzirorera. A very special place is usually reserved for Noël Mbonabaryi (a parliamentarian and the president's godfather).[5] Gathering periodically for strategic networking and surviving the introduction of multipartyism, the central core was composed of Sagatwa, Zigiranyirazo, and Nzirorera. Contacts with the most influential soldiers were then relayed by Sagatwa and Nzirorera. When Habyarimana had to contend with the "liberals" who swept Matthieu Ngirumpatse to the heights of the MRND presidency, the game became much more complex, as it became necessary to maintain an equilibrium between the competing tendencies embodied by Ngirumpatse and Nzirorera. Habyarimana thus had to work with an executive crew incorporating these two rivals and a few others chosen for their particular talents, depending on the subject and the objectives. Never was Ngirumpatse considered a full member of the family's inner circle, if only because of the special bond between Habyarimana and Rose, Ngirumpatse's wife, which was an open secret.

Habyarimana was also close to figures remarkably at odds with this central core, such as those working in his cabinet, including Léonidas Rusatira, Enoch Ruhigira, and Siméon Ntezilyayo (former minister to the presidency). But strategic contacts at this level pointed to other approaches, other regions, and other networks, and, above all, they indicated the president's ability to distance himself from the family nucleus (*see box 6*).

In the new climate introduced with multiparty competition, the hold that the presidential family and its inner circle exercised in political and economic spheres was vigorously contested. By 1991 the word *Akazu*, which had become a real media sensation, was used as a term of opprobrium in MDR party meetings each time activists took aim at their privileged political targets. In ancient Rwanda, the term referred to the "court," the circle of close-knit blood relations and associates of the ruling family, but it has a very special connotation, referring to a site at a fair distance from the main house where family members afflicted with contagious diseases were kept, thus investing the term with a symbolic resonance that made for trenchant political rebuke.[6]

The word's psychological impact was connected in some significant ways to the spread of rumors and how these rumors targeted individuals, including or distancing them from the power holders. Thus, among the analyses of the way power was wielded during the final years of the Habyarimana regime, the Akazu came to designate the place where important decisions were taken. The family of Habyarimana's wife, owing to her clan origins, was viewed as particularly prestigious and influential, compared to the rather modest family roots of a president whose rise to power was traceable, more prosaically, to his long military career. Thus, for many, Akazu referred exclusively to the highly restricted circle of the president's in-laws (Agathe Kanziga, Protais Zigiranyirazo, Élie Sagatwa, and Séraphin Rwabukumba). "However, since the aforementioned persons were not competent enough, they recruited those with the required skills from all over the country while keeping firm control over these recruits. We were under a one-party regime, a dictatorship. Political power was controlled through custom-made existing institutions such as the CND [the Rwandan parliament], the Justice Department and the . . . executive."[7]

Among those closest to the hub of power, the president's brother-in-law was incontestably the central figure. As recounted by a minister from the MRND who must remain anonymous, Prefect Protais Zigiranyirazo was "the quintessential embodiment of the *abiru* system" (under the monarchy, the guardians of tradition, key advisors to the king). On those occasions when the intermediaries failed in their attempt to obtain a favor from Habyarimana, Zigiranyirazo would then intercede on their behalf and contact the deputy chief of staff or Sagatwa. Afterward, the telephone calls from Sagatwa would ring out: "The president of the republic has asked that you . . ." Consequently, Mr. "Z" became known as the presidential mafia's "godfather," whose network overlapped and competed with the president's: "It was of public notoriety, and often said that it was 'Z' who appointed and/or dismissed the most senior civil servants, including the ministers," as reported by that same person.

Generally, the denunciations that targeted Zigiranyirazo linked him to Nzirorera, often referred to as the president's "political creature" (*see box 2*). Because of their prestigious family origins and easy access to the president, they shared a mutually beneficial legitimacy for maintaining order in Ruhengeri. In time, the Zigiranyirazo-Nzirorera bond extended beyond their immediate interests and came to reflect deeper affinities (authoritarianism and a love of power, money, and women). Other terms of derision enjoyed wide currency, most of them aimed at the president's in-laws and intended to capture the shady connections and opaque modus operandi of this small coterie of intimates.[8]

In any case, an analysis of the central axis of power cannot be reduced to its most visible components. Nor should we under-or overestimate the political weight of the president's in-laws. Mere acknowledgment of enduring tensions between the two poles of the extended family is hardly enough to conclude that Habyarimana's family was dominated by his wife, Agathe Kanziga. The president never ran out of ways to impose his decisions. It would be naive or uncritical to assume that the "brothers-in-law" were in full control of the various spheres of power. The following example may suffice to illustrate this point.

When 1975 was declared International Women's Year, Agathe Kanziga took it upon herself to organize the "feminist movement" in Rwanda. Her efforts relied on her network of contacts, some dating back to the École sociale de Karubanda and kept alive in Kiyovu, a neighborhood in Kigali.[9] The group of women usually included the wives of ministers and other political figures who would gather for the community public work projects (*umuganda*) on Saturday mornings, as was expected of all citizens, regardless of social rank or status.

Among them, a small nucleus of eminent personalities linked to Kanziga formed what could be called a "government of women," which made and unmade female deputies, pushing women to posts of greater responsibility and visibility and, especially, controlling the official women's organizations, the only ones that were authorized at the time. The "prime minister" among them was Gaudence Nyirasafari Habimana (Hutu, Gisenyi, married in Ruhengeri), a member of the MRND Central Committee, director of the Office national de la population (ONAPO), and a member of the first ring of the Akazu.[10] Second in rank came Immaculée Nyirabizeyimana (Hutu, Byumba), a 1971 graduate of the École sociale who progressively advanced from her initial status of assistant deputy to that of elected deputy and, during the third legislature, rose to the vice presidency of the CND on 8 January 1989. At the same time she was president of the Association Duterimbere, which was entrusted with the mission of promoting female entrepreneurship, especially by facilitating women's access to credit. The third, Louise Mukasine (Hutu, Ruhengeri), who in 1988 became the first president of URAMA (Urunana rw'abanya-rwandakazi mu majyambere, or Union of Rwandese Women for Development, Union des femmes militantes pour le développement; in Kinyarwanda, Mouvement national des femmes rwandaises pour le progrès), the official women's movement of the MRND, was related to Gaudence Nyirasafari Habimana through her husband. In addition, Mukasine's maternal aunt was the wife of Col. Alexis Kanyarengwe.

Although never exposed to the light of day, this discreet *politique du salon* played a significant role, especially during the second half of the Second Republic. However, Kanziga never personally interceded with any prefect or minister for any particular favor. In fact, she involved herself in a broad array of affairs in the public sphere by relying on her husband or, whenever he declined, on her brothers and cousins. Inversely, requests for intervention were made directly to "Mme President," who would then bring the matter up with her husband.

If the presidential family and its close associates truly formed the nucleus of power, its positioning, its operating principles, and its longevity relied heavily on the capacities of the clientelist system, as conceived by the president, to maintain itself, to recruit and garner loyalty from the managers who benefited from it, and to motivate the support of the broader population. Only a limited few among them were in a position to support clients and to dispatch orders.

The Regional Circuit

The geopolitical underpinning of the second ring of influence was the region of Bushiru, encompassing the communes of Karago and Giciye, in Gisenyi prefecture. This area was often described as the *terroir présidentiel*, the president's home turf, a privileged space that served as the breeding ground for recruiting the clan's loyal devotees. Other terms became widely used, such as OTP, for *originaire du terroir présidentiel*.[11] This terrain was itself the object of fluctuating borders. Indeed, beyond the communes of Bushiru, the broadening of presidential networks staked out a zone of presidential influence between Ruhengeri and Gisenyi. That zone served as a recruiting ground for civil servants and officers identified as potential candidates to fill the gaps created by the purges that regularly affected the clientelist pyramid.

The region of Rwankeri, comprising the communes of Mukingo and Nkuli in Ruhengeri prefecture, was part of the broader presidential terroir. It acceded to this status after the arranged marriage of President Habyarimana's eldest daughter to Alphonse Ntilivamunda (director-general of the Ministry of Public Works), the son of Gaspard Munyampeta, a rich businessman of the region.[12] The latter was considered the spiritual father of Joseph Nzirorera, whose education he had financed. When the marriage was being arranged, Nzirorera was Ntilivamunda's godfather, and afterward, the Habyarimana family affectionately called the Nzirorera family their *bamwana*, in other words, their in-laws, a family relationship born of intermarriage.

But as numerous commentators have emphasized, the system of subterranean alliances extended far beyond the family network and terroir présidentiel. It reached into every region and sphere of national activity. For decades the volume of state resources and the contributions from international donor agencies guaranteed the stability of the power configurations. The political difficulties of the regime started with the sharp deterioration of the economic situation and the drop in foreign aid around the mid-1980s, which greatly reduced the flow of resources into the capillaries of the clientelist system and thus seriously threatened its stability.

The Mouvance Présidentielle

Finally, turning to the formal political sphere, the strategy of creating satellite parties in what became the mouvance présidentielle after 1992 deserves special mention. This move allowed the expression of clearly extremist tendencies and gave birth to a curious political gamesmanship within the presidential circle. In fact, the renovated MRND remained a political formation without a true program, more preoccupied with accommodating the regionalist and clannish pressures of its many dignitaries than with working out a political ideology and regenerating its activists and party officials.

Several satellite parties charged with preventing opposing currents from taking root were launched, with due attention paid to the particular characteristics of each prefecture: Parerwa, Pader, and the CDR are cases in point. Parerwa (Parti républicain rwandais, or Republican Party of Rwanda), financed by Laurent Semanza (Hutu, Kigali-rural, MRND), was personally linked to Habyarimana's family and the burgomaster of the wealthiest rural commune in the country.[13] Pader (Parti démocrate rwandais, or Rwandan Democratic Party) was created by Jean-Baptiste Gatete (Hutu, Byumba, MRND), burgomaster of Murambi commune until 1993. In some instances the MRND simply swallowed up certain opposition parties, such as the PDC (Parti démocrate chrétien, or Christian Democratic Party). Finally, the creation of the Interahamwe and the Impuzamugambi youth wings exponentially boosted the expansion and the operational means of the MRND. These youth organizations were a firm and authoritative extension of the MRND's founding principles.

Broadly speaking, two significant political tendencies emerged that also infused the mouvance présidentielle. The first, characterized as conservative, brought together all those who worked hard and with great efficiency to defend the powers and resources that the Second Republic had obtained for them. Here one found for the most part the denizens of the north, whose privileges and whose hold on the country were roundly denounced. The other, consisting of "reformers," endeavored to establish the conditions for a renewal of the regime. They campaigned for a broadening of the social base of the party throughout the country, for "nationalization" and transparency of institutions committed to the rule of law, like the army and the judiciary. They took note of the enduring popular appeal of President Habyarimana and the hold of the MRND apparatus over the state and the economy. They argued that democratic reforms in the country could never take hold unless the MRND itself first democratized. In particular, they thought that because of its deep roots in the countryside, its broad ramifications, and its founding principles, the MRND was better placed than its opponents to promote democratic reforms. Numerous figures who adopted this progressive current continued to maintain personal contacts with the leaders of the new opposition parties.

In addition, the advent of the multiparty system opened up a wide range of resources and advantages for the newly emergent "activists," whose numbers exploded. These recently empowered cohorts raised the operational costs of the existing political scaffolding and increased pressures on the public and private establishments to chip in. The makeovers for venal, discredited, or opportunistic figures, attacked from all sides, then created a new lucrative market.[14] Many openly called for democratization of access to clientelist redistribution, which is to say, "equal access" to the rewards of handouts and corruption. In this regard, multipartyism and the prospect of open elections led to a surge of electoral mobilization, every constituency anxious to participate in the political struggles on an equal footing.

The dearth of significant electoral platforms made it difficult for the various contenders to affirm their ideological differences. In a context of insecurity and dwindling economic resources, the democratic opening paradoxically reintroduced extreme forms of political competition. Old regional antagonisms reappeared but did little to diminish the ethnic polarization brought on by the RPF attack of October 1990. This tendency, as we shall see, crystallized in late 1993, along with the emergence of a radical pro-Hutu, so-called Power wing. With strong, self-proclaimed local bosses at the helm, the parties relied for support on their respective clienteles, focusing on their local or ethnic identity. On the hills, in the absence of programmatic guidelines, membership depended on social, political, and economic factors or simply reflected an attitude of social conformity. Membership in these parties was built upon region, ethnicity, or a personality, generally involving total commitments. Consequently, far from reinforcing horizontal solidarities, "democracy" strengthened social bonds and invited groups to see each other as rivals, if not enemies.

Having sketched out the political landscape, it still remains to define the new rules of the game. Where basic principles are concerned, the basic objective was straightforward: the democratic transition was expected to transform the electoral rituals of the past into a transparent validation of political choices by means of universal suffrage on a level playing field.

Universal Suffrage and the Voice of the "Democrats"

Here we must address the fundamental question of the status of the parties of the so-called democratic opposition. As we have seen, multipartyism was born of the fragmentation of the single party and the emergence of regionalist or ethnic-based formations that were incapable, in the initial phase, of taking root. Nor were they better equipped to successfully face nationwide scrutiny of their policies and programs. Second, the premium placed on opportunistic alliances or confrontations among those figures with presidential ambitions paved the way for a logic of political machines to the detriment of efforts at political canvassing on the ground. There was never any grassroots appeal except to settle the quarrels among leaders clawing their way up to gain access to a job at the top. Lastly, and perhaps most decisively, credible presidential hopefuls who had made the choice, on their own or under constraint, to free themselves from the MRND found themselves in positions of structural weakness in relation to candidates who remained within the fold of the party: they could no longer draw tactical advantage from their previous connections within the army, the territorial administration, the parliament, the judiciary, and the economic sphere (dominated by the state sector or by parastatal enterprises).[15]

Neither the presidency nor the mouvance présidentielle had second thoughts about the use of repression against the "democrats," as happened in October 1990 and after the appointment of the multiparty government in April 1992. And only a fundamental restructuring of state institutions could alter this state of affairs. But the context of war imposed by the RPF was hardly conducive to such a move, since any attempt to upset the applecart was bound to weaken the military, the gendarmerie, and the security services, on which the very war effort depended. For the internal opposition, only two outcomes could be envisaged: elections or a resort to armed struggle, that is, support for decisive military action by the RPF.

While the 1991 constitution gave legitimacy to multipartyism, it did not address the question of elections, but it nonetheless opened the door. Two opposing approaches held sway. For President Habyarimana and the MRND, the principle of organizing general elections was accepted, but even if the 1992 deadline seemed reasonable, there were no pressing constraints; the single party's hold over the state institutions was under no immediate threat, and the delicate negotiations engaged with the opposition on the modalities of the polls would drag on for a while. Oddly, for the domestic opposition, still weakly structured, the solution of a national conference (rukokoma), inaugurating a division of powers and resources among the main leaders of the political parties, initially for the organization of general elections, would be needed in light of the particularly favorable balance of power. In fact, week after week an impressive movement of popular support in favor of the opposition was taking root—tens of thousands of people demonstrated in Kigali on 17 November 1991—giving the impression of being able to sweep everything aside in its wake.

With the nomination of Sylvestre Nsanzimana, a widely respected MRND figure, as prime minister in October 1991, followed by the installation of a multiparty government, including a single non-MRND minister, the presidency clearly indicated its willingness to organize general elections but without submitting to intimidation. Despite the huge protest demonstration of

8 January 1992 against putting in place his government, the prime minister immediately asked Minister of the Interior Faustin Munyaseza to prepare a draft submission of the electoral law, which had been rendered obsolete with the introduction of multipartyism.

The ministry then turned to the donor agencies, including experts and seminars, to finance the development of this draft proposition. An interministerial team composed of representatives from the presidency, the Office of the Prime Minister, and the Ministry of Justice was instructed to develop a document incorporating the key principles of the new electoral law, including a synopsis of its objectives, and to outline a proposal. The draft proposal was circulated for review to all parties.

The draft proposal for the law left none of the political parties indifferent. Almost all of them proceeded to set up their own internal commissions to study it. But organizing a seminar and launching a public debate did not respond to the priorities of the moment in the eyes of the opposition, as many leaders already imagined themselves to be in a position to force Habyarimana to step down in response to the popular outrage.

After several weeks of discussion, the opposition withdrew its demands for a national conference under pressure from the various embassies. Finally, on 3 April 1992 the president agreed to a genuine coalition government (in which his party would no longer hold the majority) with a prime minister from one of the opposition parties, Dismas Nsengiyaremye (first vice president of the MDR). Most importantly, there was agreement to set limits on the constitutional prerogatives of the president and to prepare the groundwork for communal, legislative, and presidential elections. Although the opposition saw these concessions as a victory, nothing was said of the principles behind power sharing. Nor did the opposition provide any hint of the political strategy it would introduce.

With high levels of popular mobilization under way, the opposition parties were confident of winning the elections. Organized by the Ministry of the Interior, the joint seminar took place at the Hôtel des diplomates under the multiparty government of Dismas Nsengiyaremye. With the exception of the MDR and the PL, all the political parties were represented. A few weeks later, a final report and a draft proposal of the new electoral law were forwarded to the Office of the Prime Minister, the presidency, all the members of government, and all political parties.

It fell to the prime minister's office to propose to the president that the draft proposal be added to the agenda—to be established conjointly—of a cabinet meeting. That was never done, because even though the order of the electoral contests, starting at the communal, then the legislative, and finally the presidential level, was unanimously agreed upon by the parties, there were still strong divisions on numerous technical matters (*see annex 12*). Having decided to give priority to an alliance with the RPF, the prime minister and opposition parties found it preferable to bide their time until the transitional institutions had been installed, knowing full well that they would be able to count on decisive military support from the rebellion. As for the presidency and the MRND, they remained uncertain of their electoral prospects.

Nonetheless, the leaders of the democratic opposition feared that an electoral process would effectively be controlled by the MRND. The former party-state continued to benefit from its long history of mobilization among the populace, and the prefectural administration largely remained at its disposal, except in certain prefectures of the south. All the communes in Gisenyi, Ruhengeri, Kibungo, and Byumba were headed by MRND burgomasters. In Kigali-ville, Kigali-rural, and Cyangugu prefectures, the MRND's monopoly was hardly disturbed, with, respectively, one out of three, one out of sixteen, and two out of eleven controlled by the opposition. Only three prefectures were within the opposition's grasp: Gitarama (fourteen MDR, three MRND), Butare (fourteen opposition, six MRND), and Gikongoro (nine opposition, four MRND).

Consequently, new arguments were constantly advanced to put off any decision. Retrospectively, until then, the debate over how to organize universal suffrage in the context of multipartyism was the most significant political turning point the country had known on its path to democracy. Political calculations prevented these elections from being held; and, paradoxically, it was the "democrats" in the opposition who supported those favoring military solutions.

At that time it was not anticipated that the RPF would participate in elections. Given the extent of popular mobilization and support for the opposition, holding multiparty elections at that moment was the principal obstacle to be removed for two reasons: first, because the electoral process refocused attention on internal political challenges and sidestepped, at least temporarily, the refugee question; second, because the domestic Tutsi vote, dispersed among the various opposition parties, and the ascendancy of political parties like the PL, which attracted numerous Tutsi activists, turned them away from the RPF, then viewed as a Ugandan emanation. The latter took full measure of its own political weakness in relation to the MRND and to the growing potential of the opposition, dominated by the MDR. Whatever method would be adopted for the elections, it was clear that a Hutu majority would carry the day: MRND in the north and MDR/PSD in the south. Additionally, universal suffrage would make it possible for Hutu members of the RPF

(Alexis Kanyarengwe, Théoneste Lizinde, and Seth Sendashonga), if they were put forth as candidates, to reinvent themselves thanks to their strong popular legitimacy.[16]

Unable to confront its two adversaries at the same time, the RPF made overtures to the MDR, the better to isolate Habyarimana and the MRND, and thereby facilitate its military campaign against the FAR. Its military leaders were persuaded that they embodied the only credible alternative to ensure the "liberation of the Rwandan people from the grip of the fascist political-military clique" and did not imagine that the MDR and the other opposition parties could frustrate their objectives upon the final victory of their movement.[17]

In this context, the MRND, now deprived of its former monopoly of power, found itself in an unusually uncomfortable position. The party could not oppose the principle of elections, but its president could still set the time-table. And the central preoccupation was to mark time, allow the storm to pass, and then rebound on the slightest errors committed by the party's adversaries. The implementation of the multiparty government of April 1992 was, from this perspective, as much a step back as it was an alternative, appearing less risky than elections, which could have swept everything away, or embarking upon a period of instability by holding a national conference. After the installation of this government, the MRND could again campaign publicly in favor of organizing elections within a short timetable, since it finally became the only party that was demanding it.

For many of the MRND leaders, however, support of the multiparty government was not simply an opportunistic stance. Upon review of the MRND's internal divisions, its leaders took a hard look at their liabilities: after taking notice of the untapped zeal of the party's constituents, the counter-productive effects of repression when faced by significant popular demonstrations (an unheard-of phenomenon in Rwanda), the archaic nature of its diplomacy and public relations and its handling of the media, and the weak profile of its intellectual elite, most of them agreed on the need for a strategy of remobilization and restructuring. Urging speedy elections was the best way to salvage the situation before the trap of an alliance of the opposition with the RPF could be set.

This failed rendezvous at the ballot box caused a decisive break between the population and the political elites. In the eyes of the majority of citizens, anxiously awaiting the advent of electoral democracy, this failure made no sense. In the absence of rules to organize the political succession, the opposition came up with its own rules for power sharing.

Habyarimana was taken aback by the new prime minister's first pronouncements. Dismas Nsengiyaremye did not propose any steps that could have served as a basis for a minimal program of national unity to face off the RPF. Habyarimana, for his part, favored a minimal alliance with the MDR, relying on a few common, clearly articulated demands that would force the RPF to reveal its objectives. At this stage he only wanted the two major contenders to operate in a recomposed political landscape. The aim was to challenge the RPF's ambitions of exclusive power. The MDR, however, envisaged three poles of competition, hoping that the RPF would be satisfied with a formal recognition of the rights of the minority. It was with a sense of contained anger that the president acknowledged his prime minister's refusal to disavow the meetings in Brussels between the opposition parties and the RPF in June 1992 without the MRND being present and despite the decision of the executive committee of the MDR to disassociate itself from that initiative.

The opposition parties spent much time and energy reaching out to their constituents. Ranking high on their list of grievances was the replacement of unpopular and authoritarian burgomasters, unlike the members of the MRND's elite, who were primarily concerned with getting their cut of patronage benefits. In a matter of weeks, the fratricidal rivalries within the opposition parties came out into the open, where they gradually lost the support they needed to implement the transformations that they recommended. And rather than requesting electoral approval of their mandates, they hoped to gain power and to be fully capable of exercising it with support from the RPF. Counting on the dividends of peace, the opposition parties put off organizing elections until after the end of the conflict.

Opposition party figures were, for the most part, quite in favor of immediate negotiations with the RPF, with several among them hoping it might spur things along with a decisive military nudge. With a surprising political naïveté, they gave themselves over to the RPF in order to weaken the Habyarimana regime and to enlarge their own political terrain. In fact, since the beginning of negotiations, it was the RPF that had set up the framework for them and had waylaid the inauguration of the multiparty government.

Launched on 5 June 1992, right in the middle of preliminary negotiations with the opposition parties, the RPF military offensive against Byumba prefecture, modest in scope, nonetheless produced the hoped-for results. Divisions within the government became cruelly obvious. The opposition parties, preferring to pursue negotiations with the RPF, had to battle on two fronts. They had lost the support of a large part of their popular base that was hostile to the RPF, and they no longer held legitimacy within the FAR. From 12 July 1992 to 4 August 1993, difficult negotiations were held to reconfigure the political scene and put the issue of elections on the back burner. All along, the RPF dominated the domestic political stage by playing upon the divisions among parties and moving back and forth between political overtures, military operations, and terrorist attacks.

Incapable of agreeing on common political demands, several opposition leaders did not hesitate to turn to the RPF to strengthen their negotiating positions. By doing so, they conferred an aura of legitimacy on the rebellion. After switching sides, they had few scruples about breaking away from the MRND, which by then had cast considerable discredit upon itself as the incarnation of the worst kind of authoritarian personal power.

4

The Arusha Negotiations and the Reconfiguration of Political Forces

Soon after the RPF invasion in October 1990, a long-drawn-out negotiation process got under way among the parties to the conflict, first informally and then officially. Those negotiations continued in various locations and with multiple representatives, official and unofficial, and ultimately resulted in the Arusha Peace Accords of 4 August 1993. From the beginning of the crisis in October 1990, the Organization of African Unity (OAU, Organisation de l'unité africaine) and heads of state in the Great Lakes region enthroned themselves as the primary orchestrators of negotiations. The OAU annual report leaves few doubts about the host of complicating factors besetting the negotiations:

> 11.16. . . . The OAU felt it lacked the moral authority to condemn the RPF invasion, although at the same time it quite appreciated the outrage that the invasion caused the Habyarimana government.
>
> 11.17. Secondly, the OAU's chair at the time was held by Uganda's president Museveni, whom Habyarimana always saw as the power behind the RPF. As far as Habyarimana was concerned, his country had been invaded by Uganda. . . .
>
> 11.18. . . . A comparable mistrust of Zaire's Mobutu was harbored by the RPF leadership, who fully understood the close and supportive relationship that existed between him and Habyarimana. Mobutu shared Habyarimana's conviction that the RPF was a Museveni creation. . . . But as doyen of Africa's Heads of State, Mobutu chaired the regional organization of Great Lakes states. . . .

II.19. From the perspective of peacemaking, much of the history of the 1990s is the story of well-meant initiatives, endless consultations, incessant meetings, commitments made, and commitments broken. These frenetic activities reflected the real world of the OAU Secretariat, which has no capacity to make decisions independent of its members, to force any parties to do its bidding, or to punish anyone for ignoring its wishes. What the OAU can do is call meetings, hope the invited attend, facilitate agreements, and hope that the participants abide by their word.[1]

Only in July 1992 did the mediator, Tanzanian president Ali Hassan Mwinyi, and the facilitator, President Mobutu Sese Seko, finally succeed in launching a structured negotiation process. It was strongly supported by the OAU General Secretariat, by the concerned regional actors (Tanzania, Uganda, Zaire, and Burundi), by the major Western embassies (Belgium, Germany, France, and the United States), and by international and regional organizations.

Among African actors who gave impetus to this initiative, much credit goes to the representatives of religious organizations. Their role loomed particularly large after the principle of multipartyism was formally endorsed. On 3 January 1992 the Protestant bishops organized a meeting with the representatives of all the political parties. A secret meeting in London followed, bringing together representatives of the Conférence des églises de toute l'Afrique (CETA; known in English as the All Africa Council of Churches [AACC]), a broad array of ecumenical churches of the continent based in Nairobi, and the RPF. Contacts were also established in Kigali between CETA, the MDR, the PL, and the PSD. The CETA met with ministers and the president of the republic and then on 22 January organized a meeting of church representatives in order to work out a mediation strategy. On 27 January a mixed commission of Catholic and Protestant leaders held discussions with representatives of all the parties, which extended until 6 February. A discreet meeting was then held on 25 February in Nairobi between the RPF and the contact committee (churches and various spokespersons).

Also in February, the military high command of the rebellion propelled the RPF toward a two-pronged strategy combining military pressure with internal political measures and terrorist activities designed to destabilize the new government. The deployment of commandos and the recurrence of bombings and land-mine explosions went on virtually unchecked, owing to the powerlessness of the government's intelligence services and the exacerbation of domestic political conflicts. This is why acts of terrorism, including those committed by the RPF (see later in this chapter), were almost always imputed to "death squads" or to a mysterious "third force," both of which were supposedly linked to the mouvance présidentielle. Violence sharply increased with the installation of the multiparty government of 16 April 1992. RPF commandos then launched an extended campaign of bombings, leading to dozens of civilian victims (*see annex 17*).

Peace Talks under Military Threat

In these conditions it is hardly surprising that opposition leaders placed the issue of negotiations at the heart of their agenda. Officially, the talks started in Kampala on 24 May 1992 between the Rwandan government, represented by Boniface Ngulinzira, the MDR minister of foreign affairs, and the RPF; their first order of business was to set a timetable for negotiations. Peace talks between the RPF on one side and the MDR, the PSD, and the PL on the other were then undertaken in Brussels on 29 May, precisely when a mutiny had broken out in Ruhengeri and Gisenyi prefectures, with mutineers fearing that demobilization would automatically follow the signing of a peace agreement. While still in Brussels, on 5 June, while the negotiating parties were busy trying to hammer out a cease-fire agreement, the RPF again took up arms against the FAR, with much of the violence taking place in Byumba prefecture. French soldiers, added to Operation Noroît, helped the FAR to turn back the offensive.[2]

Negotiations were resumed on 6 and 7 June in Paris. The result was an agreement to bring the MRND to the table and to lay the groundwork for the opening of peace talks in Tanzania on 10 July. The issues to be dealt with ranged from national unity and democratization, to the integration of the warring armies, to the installation of a broad-based transitional government, among others. The minister of defense, James Gasana, after reasserting his control over the army, forced the deputy chiefs of staff of the army and the gendarmerie who had shown their incompetence in dealing with the mutinies into early retirement.

The OAU-sponsored negotiations unfolded in three phases, the first in Arusha, the second in Addis Ababa, and the third again in Arusha. The talks produced an effective cease-fire on 1 August, followed by the signing of the first protocol, the "Rule of Law," on 18 August.[3] In response to rising ethnic tensions and a new campaign of bombings against civilian targets, on 26 August 1992 the French ambassador, Georges Martres, and the minister of foreign affairs, Boniface Ngulinzira, signed an addendum to the "special military assistance agreement" with France for organization and training of the Rwandan gendarmerie dating from 18 July 1975. This addendum extended the agreement's applicability to the entire Rwandan government armed forces.

On 30 October the parties signed the second protocol of agreement, "Power Sharing."[4] It would take another eight months before the third protocol could be drafted, during which period the belligerents significantly raised the stakes. Toward the end of January 1993 the MRND organized demonstrations throughout the country, and numerous killings of Tutsi and political opponents took place in Gisenyi, Ruhengeri, Kibuye, and Byumba prefectures. Then on 8 February, a week after a highly publicized meeting between Presidents Habyarimana and Museveni in Entebbe, the RPF, invoking the ethnopolitical incidents of January, broke the cease-fire and launched a massive attack in the sous-prefectures of Kirambo and Kinihira in Ruhengeri and Byumba prefectures. This new RPF military offensive brought its troops within twenty kilometers of Kigali's northern outskirts. This forward thrust could have had major consequences had it not been for the timely reinforcements of French soldiers to beef up the FAR units.[5] Following the arrival of a company of French paratroopers, armed with heavy mortars, from Bangui, the belligerents agreed to a truce on 22 February 1993. By that time, one million internally displaced persons (IDPs) had found refuge in the vicinity of Kigali, creating an ideal recruiting ground for extremist anti-Tutsi groups.

Under heavy pressure from Western embassies and the apostolic nuncio, high-level negotiations resumed on 6 March in Dar es Salaam between a Rwandan government delegation led by Prime Minister Dismas Nsengiyaremye and the president of the RPF, Alexis Kanyarengwe.

The prospect of a possible settlement led to various domestic political realignments. On 30 March Major General and Head of State Habyarimana resigned the presidency of the MRND, thus easing his load of official titles. Additionally, on 15 April the mandate for the government of Dismas Nsengiyaremye was extended for another three months, while the choice of prime minister for the future transitional government, which fell to the MDR, generated strong tensions among its leaders. It was in this context that on 18 May an RPF commando assassinated Emmanuel Gapyisi (*see annex 15.1*), one of the MDR's principal leaders, widely acknowledged as a possible candidate for the prime minister's office; his role in creating the NGO Peace and Democracy, which called upon the internal opposition to combat the Habyarimana regime and the RPF in equal measure, was a key factor behind his popularity.

After the third protocol, "Refugees and Displaced Persons," was signed on 9 June 1993, the United Nations reinforced the OAU's Group of Neutral Military Observers (GOMN) by creating its Observer mission to Uganda-Rwanda on 22 June, which was mandated to monitor their common border.

Political maneuverings went into high gear with, on the one hand, a reshuffling in the leadership of the MRND during the party congress on 3 and 4 July and, on the other, Dismas Nsengiyaremye's removal as prime minister

(MDR), followed by the nomination of a new government under the direction of Agathe Uwilingiyimana (MDR) on 18 July. Assembled in an extraordinary party congress days later on 23 July, the MDR rank and file disavowed these nominations and voted to exclude all the MDR ministers of the new government from the party, as well as Faustin Twagiramungu, the party's own president. Many among those most committed to the negotiation process found themselves sidelined from the political scene and constrained to flee the country, facing threats to their lives. Defense Minister James Gasana (MRND) and the expelled prime minister, Nsengiyaremye, are cases in point (see later in this chapter).

On 3 August the drafting of the fourth protocol ("The Integration of the Armed Forces of the Two Parties") and the fifth ("Miscellaneous Issues and Final Provisions") was finally completed, allowing for the signing of the Arusha Peace Accords between the RPF and the Rwandan government the following morning.[6] This was followed by the formal appointment of Faustin Twagiramungu as prime minister of the Broad-Based Transitional Government (BBTG) on 5 August. The agreement devolved control of political institutions and the military to the opposition parties and the RPF working together.

Although the news was received with a sigh of relief, there was no outpouring of enthusiasm. At no time had the electorate been invited to voice its concerns about the peace accords or to validate them; most citizens remained intensely preoccupied by the seemingly endless political games going on and the unlikely alliances resulting from them, not to mention the sense of shock caused by the murder of Emmanuel Gapyisi, the first in a long series of political assassinations.

The core element of the peace agreement concerned the deployment of United Nations forces to Rwanda, which had been approved by the Security Council on 5 October 1993. The United Nations Assistance Mission in Rwanda (UNAMIR) took over from the observer mission created in June of the same year. Its mandate, lasting six months, consisted in overseeing the cease-fire between the Rwandan government and the RPF that had been concluded on 8 February 1993, monitoring the repatriation of refugees and the resettlement of displaced persons, as well as the demilitarization of Kigali. Initially it was composed of 1,260 soldiers. The Security Council decided to send an additional battalion on 6 January 1994, resulting in a total of 2,500 soldiers coming from twenty-four countries, placed under the command of the Canadian general Roméo Dallaire. Bangladesh sent 937; Ghana sent 841; and Belgium, 428. With the RPF categorically refusing to allow UNAMIR to incorporate French troops during the negotiations, it was finally decided that Belgian troops would form UNAMIR's "central core."

The deployment of UNAMIR troops began on 1 November 1993, and on 15 December 1993 the French military detachment of Operation Noroît withdrew, leaving only twenty-four military advisors. While the political parties went through a sudden surge of activity—the badly split PL holding two rival congresses, the PSD another, and the MDR getting preparations under way for an extraordinary "reconciliation congress"—RPF troops, accompanied by political representatives, arrived in Kigali on 28 December. As agreed upon at Arusha, some six hundred soldiers (some say eight hundred) took up residence in the CND parliament building.

Aside from the dramatic changes initiated in Arusha, 1993 came to a close with the emergence of major political reconfigurations. These were directly influenced by the evolution of the military situation on the ground and the consolidation of a new balance of power.

The RPF's Ideal Positioning

For the RPF the negotiations significantly raised the electoral stakes, from which the RPF had everything to fear. Its long-standing strategy of toppling the Habyarimana regime was now a central plank in the democrats' platform, a situation that developed independently of its efforts—without itself having to put forward any particular policy program or set of political objectives. With its military offensives under way it also stepped up its campaign of destabilization in the domestic political theater and succeeded in targeting extremists within the MRND. For their part, the latter certainly did not hesitate to organize killings of Tutsi civilians.

RPF responsibility for attacks against civilian targets came to light rather late (*see annex 14*). Between July 1991 and September 1992, forty-five explosions of landmines and antipersonnel mines were recorded and documented by the Rwandan national gendarmerie. Although hardly renowned for conducting criminal investigations, the gendarmerie came up with a generally reliable body of evidence in collaboration with the Office of the Public Prosecutor. At that time, the reports from the Rwandan gendarmerie emphasized:

- the alternating pattern of a campaign of bombings inside the country and RPA/RPF offensives on the battlefront;
- the objective of provoking internal tensions within the multiparty government of Dismas Nsengiyaremye and within the mouvance présidentielle itself;[7]
- the large number of bombings in zones with large Tutsi populations,

which presumably were expected to generate support for RPF initiatives, particularly in prefectures where it could not establish a base (like Butare);

- additionally, the large number of bombings against strategic targets (petrol-carrying trucks and the electricity station in Cyangugu).

It is noteworthy that the targeted sites (markets, bus stations, the Kigali Central Post Office, minibuses, taxis, hotels, and bars) revealed an intention to maximize the number of civilian victims. Only two explosions targeted military minibus transports (Gashora commune, Kigali-rural, in February and March 1992).

The first wave of bombings intensified with the installation of the multi-party government in April 1992 and continued through the end of the year, then practically drew to a halt until the beginning of 1993, coinciding with the RPF military offensive in the northern prefectures that February. Then a second campaign took place between March and May 1993. The number of persons arrested while transporting mines across the borders with Tanzania and Zaire in late 1992 pointed to the RPF's involvement, which led to a change in strategy.

At the same time as the attacks, acts of banditry and especially targeted killings persisted, and those responsible were much more difficult to detect (*see annex 15*). Note, however, that the strategy of infiltrating the opposition parties (especially the youth wing of the PSD) and then the official presence of the RPF in Kigali opened up new possibilities for instrumentalizing violence to the RPF's advantage.

For many Rwandans, particularly the gendarmerie, suspicion of RPF involvement was a normal response to the news of significant killings. Among the incidents attributed to RPA commandos were a series of attacks in November 1993. The RPF reacted quite abruptly to the electoral reshuffling of communal authorities in September 1993 in the north of the country in the demilitarized zone that it had occupied over several preceding months. Even though it had invested heavily in the electoral campaign, the RPF was roundly defeated by partisans of the MRND. More significantly, it was the very legitimacy of electing RPF members that the majority of the population in the occupied communes seemed to be contesting.

This experience on the ground signaled a decisive turning point, revealing a profound disdain of the RPF's conception of "democracy," as well as anger at the RPF's rejection of the electoral process anticipated by the Arusha Peace Accords for the end of the transitional period. This may explain the tragic events that occurred on the night of 17–18 November 1993, when between forty and fifty-five persons were killed in Nyamugari, Cyeru, Kidaho, and Nkumba communes in Kirambo sous-prefecture (Ruhengeri).[8] Many of the persons targeted were the successful candidates from the MRND and CDR, both of which emerged victorious in those elections; even their family members were not spared.

We should also note the role of RPA commandos from 26 to 29 November 1993 in the interethnic outbursts in the Bugesera, which resulted in five deaths and led to displacement of some three hundred persons, who took refuge in the Catholic parish church at Ruhuha. The commandos came from Renga, on the other side of the border with Burundi in Busoni, Kirundo province, where the RPF had installed one of its principal recruitment centers, which was used as a transit point for its Rwandan recruits.

Again, during the night of 30 November–1 December 1993, seventeen civilians were killed in Kabatwa, in Mutura commune, Gisenyi prefecture. The commando unit, composed of some twenty or so persons belonging to the RPA's "Charly" unit, based in Butaro, was headed by Maj. Gashaija Bagirigomwa and Capt. Moses Rubimbura (*see annex 15*). For this massacre, UNAMIR, having already concluded that the RPF was responsible for the one in Kirambo sous-prefecture, deferred investigation, because, as explained by General Dallaire, the UNAMIR force commander: "If we investigated and found conclusive proof that the RPF had committed the murders, we'd be in tricky territory in which one of the ex-belligerents appeared to be deliberately destabilizing the country; if we investigated and were not able to point the finger at the RPF, the media and especially the RTLM [Radio-Télévision libre des mille collines, or Radio-Television of the Thousand Hills] would view us as either being in league with the RPF or totally incompetent."[9]

On 4 February 2004 Maj. Brent Beardsley, former deputy to General Dallaire, gave the following testimony before the United Nations International Criminal Tribunal for Rwanda (ICTR): "In November 1993, we realized that a third force was working alongside the Rwandan government. . . . It was determined to discredit UNAMIR, to sink the Arusha Peace Accords. It was prepared to kill for that. . . . A series of events led us to this conclusion. The coup d'état in Burundi, the destabilization in the South of the country, the anti-Belgian propaganda on RTLM[,] and the two massacres in November forced us to conclude that there was a group that was determined to block implementation of the Arusha Accords."[10] Beardsley's conclusions about a "third force" determined to block the peace process are very much on target. But his observation relies on a deliberate conflation of those responsible for these events, possibly because of the "damned if you do, damned if you don't" reasons advanced by Dallaire. As we shall see, many of the same kinds of unproven assumptions lie at the root of other uncritical arguments about the share of responsibilities for the bloodshed.

Even so, this is not to deny the existence of attacks and violence orchestrated by militias of parties close to the mouvance présidentielle or the exactions committed by groups of soldiers drawn from the FAR. In many of the MRND communes, just as with those within the sway of the opposition parties, there was fairly open propagation of forms of partisan terror, with victims targeted for their opposition to the governing currents or for refusing to submit to the various rackets and the extortions. Among these activities, and often rooted in sheer banditry, were frequent grenade attacks. Such weapons were freely available to all and sundry for ridiculously derisory prices in local markets. Documentation from the Ministry of Defense mentions the large number of grenade explosions that were imputed to soldiers anxious to settle scores, most of those soldiers enjoying impunity.

In reality, there was a "third" and a "fourth" force, one aligned with the "hardliners" of the mouvance présidentielle, the other aligned with the RPF, each situated at opposite ends of the political continuum. The only thing they had in common was their opposition to the Arusha Peace Accords.

In this regard the RPF and its adversaries from the mouvance présidentielle had recourse to terrorist activities that were in keeping with other forms of military and political action. But, as we see in annex 14, the crimes against civilians committed between 1991 and 1993 with landmines and antipersonnel mines were the signature handiwork of the RPF. Toward the beginning of 1994, UNAMIR detected "infiltrators" by the hundreds and then by the thousands across the country, especially in Kigali, without bothering to confiscate their weapons (*see annex 17*).

Practically positioned as an arbitrator, the RPF was able to profit from the clashes between rivals; looking for opportunistic alliances to suit the particular conjuncture was part of its modus operandi. Predictably, the result was to exacerbate social tensions. For the RPF stalwarts, it was to their advantage to discredit their adversaries and then wait to be recognized as the only legitimate alternative to the Habyarimana regime before undertaking the final offensive.

The Split in the Domestic Front

In April 1992 Juvénal Habyarimana, after steadfastly resisting for as long as possible, finally accepted an "opposition prime minister" and refocused his attention on controlling the mouvance présidentielle and the MRND, where competing ambitions now surfaced openly. The restructuring in the administration, the breakdown in the intelligence services, and the schisms in the armed forces began to seriously undermine his position and impose limits on his ability to maneuver. To conserve his standing, he had to first regain the upper hand with the MRND, but numerous party officials more or less openly favored his resignation of the party presidency. He also had to seek support from the party's youth wing, which was an indispensable resource for expanding party membership. On 22 April 1992 Juvénal Habyarimana stepped down as head of the armed forces and announced his retirement from the FAR so that he could retain the presidency of the MRND and remain eligible for the presidency of the republic. At the same time, he took control of the Interahamwe and put in place a new group of leaders. This takeover of the MRND "youth wing" was highly contested by its initial promoter, Désiré Murenzi, a member of the central committee of the party who then decided to break away from it.

The newly emerging situation was particularly complex for the mouvance présidentielle, which faced significant pressures from the opposition parties. The latter had attempted to broaden their influence in the communes through *ukubohoza*, that is, the organization of protest actions, such as destabilization by unseating titular incumbents (*see box 7*).

But the mouvance présidentielle was itself split between those who advocated a strategy of liberalization, which could include replacing the entrenched northern-based party officials, and those officials who actively and jealously defended their turf and began to fill the ranks of the viscerally anti-Tutsi CDR. To the domestic and the external fronts could be added the Arusha battlefield, where an alliance between the opposition parties and the RPF gravely frustrated the MRND bosses. With each step forward in the negotiations, the mouvance présidentielle felt doubly dispossessed. Ironically, numerous figures characterized the process as "negotiations between the RPF and the RPF," to the exclusion of the MRND.

On the one hand, the MRND contingent feared that the opposition alone would be credited with the success of the negotiation process. This clearly emerges from the rancor expressed when the cease-fire agreement between the government and the RPF was signed on 12 July 1992, an agreement that the population, weary of war, had welcomed. On the other hand, the MRND also sensed that the objective of the negotiations was to officiate its political demise.

In these circumstances, it is no wonder that Habyarimana's authority was constantly under attack, and his supporters, including those in the army, worried about his apparent weakening, if not helplessness. His incapacity to sway the government delegation charged with the negotiations was the most stinging of the criticisms evoked by his lack of authority.

Col. Théoneste Bagosora, chief of staff at the Ministry of Defense, was among the most critical. He explicitly positioned himself as a political asset while at the same time campaigning to be promoted to major general, the rank that Habyarimana alone had been qualified to hold until his recent withdrawal from the army. In this regard, we can begin to appreciate the place of the Ministry of Defense and the FAR in the new context of civil war, recalling that the army served as the arena for airing the most vociferous expressions of national division and where these conflicts carried deadly consequences.

A brief overview may shed light on the depth of the army's reach.

Shake-Ups in the High Military Command

From 1973 onward, the central preoccupation for Major General Habyarimana consisted in controlling the actions and ambitions of his peers— now his subordinates—who had carried him to power (*see annex 1*) or, more likely, who, once placed before the fait accompli, had ratified his coup. From the start there was an intraregional competition between officers from Gisenyi and Ruhengeri, which explains why, in July 1975, with the creation of the MRND, the president armed himself with a political instrument entirely subject to his will. In so doing, and without neglecting the army, he anchored the Second Republic with a mix of civilian and military moorings, thus affording him the option of relying on them alternatively or jointly or even playing one against the other.

By the end of 1980, after a failed attempt to overthrow the government led to the incarceration of the prime suspect, Maj. Théoneste Lizinde, and the escape of his assumed coconspirator, Col. Alexis Kanyarengwe, all declared or potential rivals were out of sight. Col. Laurent Seruguba, the assistant chief of staff at the headquarters of the Rwandan army and the "number two" in the military hierarchy after Habyarimana, was certainly in a privileged position, though he was not viewed as the president's eventual successor. A rather embattled and self-effacing figure, he was entirely at the president's service. His longevity at the head of the general staff was clearly linked to his docility, in sharp contrast with the vaulting ambitions of the strong personalities in the third promotion (1962–64), that is, the third graduating class, at the École des officiers (EO), among them Théoneste Lizinde, Stanislas Mbonampeka, Théoneste Bagosora, and Pierre-Célestin Rwagafilita.

Finally, two officers from the president's home region distinguished themselves: Col. Stanislas Mayuya and Col. Aloys Nsekalije. The first, highly respected for his integrity, originally from Gisenyi, and a graduate in the fourth promotion at the EO, was commander of the Kanombe military camp and the paracommando battalion, one of the elite units of the Rwandan army. The second, like President Habyarimana, was among the first promotion at the EO. Nsekalije was the scion of an old, well-established family in Bushiru that had offered hospitality and land to Catholic missionaries, the founders of the Rambura Mission, and also to President Habyarimana's family, arriving in the wake of these missionaries at the beginning of the twentieth century. As the last survivor of the Group of Friends of 5 July 1973, an implacable minister before becoming a parliamentarian, he developed a fiery reputation and openly cultivated his own clientelist networks.[11]

Stanislas Mayuya was killed in March 1988 in front of his office by Sergeant Biroli, the head of security at the Kanombe military camp. The latter's death during an interrogation session generated the wildest rumors about the hand behind the killing. Initial suspicions centered on Colonel Serubuga, the deputy chief of staff, but were eventually discounted after three officers were arrested— but never convicted. As for the second, Colonel Nsekalije, he was sidelined in 1990 by being elected to serve in parliament.

What we have is an army that is conspicuously weak and politicized but also shot through with diverse opinions. At this critical stage of the country's transition, few officers hesitated to voice their political choices or preferences in the conduct of the war or to share their views about their superior officers. These same officers were facing the trials of war at a time when the northern "hawks" did everything they could to manipulate to their advantage the same ethnicist references and code words of the 1960s. The army had numerous younger officers, many of whom had received training in military schools abroad; some of them obtained highly sought after command posts, but almost all of them were subject to the same clientelist, ethnic, and regionalist logic that both governed and divided the military.

In February 1991 one of Sylvestre Nsanzimana's first decisions as minister of justice was to free the three officers falsely accused of having orchestrated Colonel Mayuya's murder.[12] They were later reintegrated in the army by a decision of the Governmental Council on 21 October 1992 with around twenty others who, like them, had been unfairly dismissed from the army. For his part, the new minister of defense, James Gasana, a civilian member of the MRND, tried to loosen the reins of this army that had been bound up by so many presidential networks. He was determined to rebuild a truly "national" army and to raise the morale of the men. Supported by the multiparty government of Dismas Nsengiyaremye, which had been put in place in April 1992, he significantly restructured the military command, reorganized the intelligence services, and redistributed resources among the various units. In April 1992, after Habyarimana left the army (*see annex 19*), the issue of how to fill the positions of chief of staff and major general became the central concern of the armed forces. In May Habyarimana had made it known that he wanted to place Théoneste Bagosora at the head of the armed forces, but, faced with opposition from the minister of defense and the prime minister, the president finally installed Laurent Serubuga as an advisor to the defense minister.[13]

James Gasana refused to back down and announced the forced retirements of Colonels Serubuga (Gisenyi), Rwagafilita (Kibungo), Bagosora (Gisenyi), Sagatwa (Gisenyi), Nshizirungu (Kigali-rural), and numerous other officers, unleashing a vigorous opposition from the titans of the north and the hard-line wing of the army, led by Colonel Serubuga. The minister and the government supported the candidacy of Col. Déogratias Nsabimana (Ruhengeri), who had distinguished himself on the battlefront in 1990. As a compromise, Colonels Bagosora, Sagatwa, and Nshizirungu were accorded one-year extensions of their military careers. However, still expressing disapproval of the means by which Bagosora sought to obtain those extensions, Gasana stripped him of all operational authority and took him on board as a civilian in public service, with the post of chief of staff in the Ministry of Defense.[14] As the last surviving officer of the circle of veteran officers from Bushiru, Bagosora thus became the "eyes" of the president in the Ministry of Defense, entrusted with the mission of keeping a watch on his minister, James Gasana, even though he was a fellow member of the MRND.

Thus, the two new chiefs of staff of the army and the gendarmerie, Maj. Gen. Déogratias Nsabimana and Maj. Gen. Augustin Ndindiliyimana (Butare), both graduates of the seventh promotion at the EO, found themselves at the head of the armed forces, whereas practically all of the most noteworthy or visible figures, or those overshadowing the president's closest collaborators, had been eliminated or marginalized.

At the end of this face-off, none of the candidates supported by Habyarimana managed to attain the rank of general, which would have allowed them to escape retirement, but Bagosora occupied a strategic post for purposes of watching and waiting things out. He did not have to wait long to see his attributions expand. In July 1993 Minister Gasana was obliged to flee the country, faced with serious threats from the extremist wing of the mouvance présidentielle. He was replaced by another civilian who was committed to the views of the mouvance but who was hardly familiar with military matters, Augustin Bizimana. The replacement was heralded with drumbeats, and, while no longer in uniform, Bagosora became a privileged insider within the Ministry of Defense for hard-line elements of the regime.

Remobilization of the MRND and Reaffirmation of the President

The political situation was just as delicate as the military situation. The populace had high expectations for the new opposition government of April 1992, particularly given the challenging economic and social context, but now with the installation of multipartyism, citizens realized just how powerless the state had become in the face of the escalating violence. While the opposition made a good show of its staying power, the upsurge of popular enthusiasm that had swept it to power was now missing. Local mobilization in support of the ukubohoza strategy was active and visible, but it involved the most strong-willed activists, anxious to engage physically with their counterparts in the MRND. The majority of the population was far more concerned about the growing paralysis of administrative services and its impact on people's daily lives. Much of this was the consequence of the ceaseless internal squabbles going on at the ministerial level. The competitive efforts made by parties to solidify control of their respective portfolios generated considerable inefficiency and widespread disenchantment. This mood in effect worked to the advantage of the MRND, which embodied the old order and continued to press for elections. As 1992 drew to a close, amid growing insecurity and the spread of partisan clashes, it was clear that the strategy of the anti-MRND coalition could not hold much longer.

This period corresponds to a political turning point, to the extent that the lines for future political clashes were clearly drawn. The MRND could sense the nature of the themes likely to boost its popularity: order, democracy, development. Unity, one of the pillars of the MRND platform, disappeared from speeches under pressure from the northerners and the Akazu. While members of the Democratic Forces for Change (FDC, Forces démocratiques du changement), internally in upheaval, devoted most of their energies to score total victory over the presidential camp at the negotiating table (they were doubtful of obtaining similar results from the ballot box), the MRND and the president again appealed to the "majority people." The subtle distinction between "political majority" and "ethnic majority" that the RPF and the FDC pointed to in justifying their joint repudiation of elections, questioning the political maturity of the peasant masses, only gave greater weight to the "democratic" arguments advanced by all of the pro-MRND currents, united on this point.

As soon as the cease-fire agreement of July 1992 was signed, the MRND took pleasure in reminding the opposition that, though its principal objection to elections was now resolved, it nonetheless preferred submitting to negotiations among the parties rather than to the sovereignty of the people. This is exactly what the president himself denounced in his impromptu speech at an MRND rally in Ruhengeri on 15 November 1992 before tens of thousands of people:

> When I entered, I noticed one thing: I finally understood why those people are afraid of elections [*applause, whistling, and drumming*]. They claim

that they won, but they do not want elections [*applause, whistling, and drumming*]. Just listen to that! I have now understood why they do not want elections. . . .

Farmers/stockbreeders constitute the roots of our party. Get closer to them and talk with them so as to find out their ideas and their problems. . . .

Farmers/stockbreeders constitute the base of our party. It is they who are our militants.[15]

Habyarimana, hardly enthusiastic about directly managing a party that was shattered and unruly, preferred using his office and his personal charisma to regain his popularity with the "masses," ever responsive to his populist rhetoric. At the same time, he devoted himself entirely to strengthening the Interahamwe youth wing, a breeding ground for party activists unswervingly loyal to the MRND cause. He turned to public enterprises or private entrepreneurs for sources of funding, who then placed the Interahamwe at the disposal of politicians the president wanted to back up. This strategy of partisan insertion seemed like a deliberate riposte to ukubohoza and the excesses of the MDR youth wing, especially in the prefectures of the center and the south. One year after the dissolution of the party-state, the scorned symbol of an exhausted authoritarian system, the MRND managed a truly exceptional turnaround: democratization, or "democracy," in the form promoted by either the reformers or the party's conservative wing, became the party's credo or, better yet, its only source of salvation.

The principal division within the MRND concerned its military strategy. The progressives did not foresee a lasting military solution and thought it necessary to negotiate quickly to get to elections, which would then confirm the "real" balance of power. Conservatives and extremists, having everything to lose, wanted to believe that it was still possible to deliver heavy blows to the RPA and reverse the direction of the tide at the negotiating table.

Everything seems to suggest that President Habyarimana was perfectly aware of the reinvigoration in his MRND. It was no longer necessary for him to negotiate the conditions of his departure from power. As he so clearly indicated in his speech in Ruhengeri on 15 November 1992, he had no intention of bowing to the joint demands of the opposition parties and the RPF.

The hallmark of this speech that distinguished it from most of the press releases and official statements issued by the Office of the Presidency was its utter clarity and force of conviction. The president explicitly clarified the extent to which he counted on mobilizing the MRND—and most of all, its most loyal activists, the Interahamwe—for future political struggles, which would include the next presidential election:

I thank the MRND party officials here in Ruhengeri and MRND supporters in this region. Be courageous! The essential thing is to win the elections, and we are going to win them because you are doing well here and there in the prefectures. . . .

When the right time comes, I will send you a message. I will ask the Interahamwe to accompany me. I was told that during my campaign my soldiers will accompany me so as to campaign for me. Is there a problem if they do this? However, I know that it is mostly the Interahamwe who will do my campaign, because I am with them. I wish you long life.[16]

Speeches like this coming from authorities within the MRND toward the latter part of 1992 provoked quite a bit of polemics and were frequently held up to illustrate the presumed refusal of negotiations on the part of the president and his party, the MRND. But this is to make unduly short shrift of the profound communication gap between political leaders confident in their mass appeal and the negotiators in Arusha. The latter, speaking on behalf of the opposition and the rebel army, were busy putting together consensual arrangements intended to unseat an incumbent president supremely confident that he would come out of the electoral process stronger and legitimized anew. That is what James Gasana sought to clarify when he denounced the "opportunist interpretations," the "presumed presidential hostility to the peace accords," and the notorious presidential reference to "scraps of paper":

When he said that signatures on a piece of paper could not suffice to lead to peace, he was simply observing that the government's lead negotiator [MDR minister Boniface Ngulinzira] did not take into account the sovereignty of the people and their longings for democracy. For him, the Arusha Accords should not take the place of popular acclaim but should rather outline modalities for a popular referendum on the situation. For the MRND, democracy governed not only the rules of access to power but also the rules for surrendering power. It was simply out of the question to relinquish power under threat of force or because of the acrobatics under way in negotiations in Arusha.[17]

Here lies the insurmountable conflict between two legitimacies: the democratic legitimacy of the majority and the right of return of a minority. Recall also that the president was quite explicit about the means he contemplated to reach his objective. For all the advances gained by the RPF and the opposition at the negotiating table, Habyarimana made no bones about the fact that, come election day, he would receive massive support from farmers and herders, coupled with that of his Interahamwe and his soldiers.

This opened a major breach, which Prime Minister Nsengiyaremye addressed in his sharply worded letter of protest to the president of 17 November (*see annex 20.3*). Aside from questioning the president's criticism of the Arusha process, Nsengiyaremye went into a detailed narrative describing the troubled political context, in which uncontrollable members of the armed forces, the territorial administration, and the MRND's militias sowed terror and tried to destabilize the multiparty government. He firmly denounced the participation of the armed forces in the president's "electoral campaign" despite legal prohibitions, as well as the impunity bestowed upon those responsible for the killings of Tutsi civilians in Kibilira, Bugesera, and Kibuye. Nsengiyaremye also condemned the attempted mutiny led by a Major Ntabakuze from Kanombe military camp during the night of 21–22 October 1992, which no one in the mouvance présidentielle dared to denounce—not even James Gasana, the minister of defense, who was the mutineers' principal target (*see annex 21*). Finally, Nsengiyaremye wound up his diatribe with a matter of the deepest concern, one that also found the greatest echo among the population, that is, the growing role of the Interahamwe militias and the impunity they continued to enjoy.

This controversy rose to unexpected proportions. During the second half of November 1992, the prime minister organized a meeting of ministers responsible for public order and security; the aim was to adopt measures to suppress the acts of violence committed by party youth wings. By the end of the year, the gendarmerie had already arrested some eighty Interahamwe. This was seen by the president as a thinly veiled attempt by the minister of defense to destabilize the MRND's youth wing. The tension between the two men grew worse when the minister instructed the gendarmerie to intensify efforts to restrict the illegal circulation of firearms, especially after a raid in Kicukiro on 22 December 1992, when the gendarmerie seized a handgun from the son-in-law of the president's godfather, a local leader of the Interahamwe.

The aura of impunity enjoyed by Habyarimana's closest associates, many of them involved in criminal wrongdoing and including, among the worst offenders, Interahamwe militiamen, acted as a powerful stimulus to violent activities among the youth groups.

The Second Protocol, "Power Sharing"

The amended text of the Arusha protocol on power sharing, signed on 9 January 1993, confirmed the most pessimistic predictions of the MRND leaders. The former single party would only be accorded the presidency of the republic and five out of twenty-two ministerial portfolios in the BBTG. Similarly, the Transitional National Assembly (TNA, Assemblée nationale de transition) only obtained eleven seats, as did each of the large opposition parties (RPF, PL, PSD, and MDR). The amendment also made provision for the post of vice prime minister, accorded to the RPF, and a code of "political ethics," which the political parties absent from the Arusha negotiations were expected to sign. In return, they would each be given one seat in the National Assembly. The RPF and the domestic opposition accorded themselves full power, with their combined two-thirds majority in parliament offering them the possibility of modifying the rules of the game. What the MRND and the CDR called the "coup d'état RPF-Ngulinzira" (the name of the MDR minister of foreign affairs, who had represented the government at the Arusha negotiations) clearly established the pecking order.

At the head of the line were the front-runners of the day: the MDR and its domestic allies, who had an assured advantage over the mouvance présidentielle with the support of the RPF. Once the MRND and its supporters could be pushed aside, the electoral calculations guaranteed MDR and its allies, at least in theory, a perennial hold on power when faced with an RPF deprived of a popular demographic base with which to influence matters politically.

We find the MRND in second place, limping along after losing at the negotiating table. But its minority status had been anticipated. Convinced of their popularity and their foothold on the hillsides, most of the MRND leaders were confidently waiting out the transitional period; they figured they would surely rebound with the elections, which had already been scheduled. They knew that it would be impossible for opposition political parties to benefit from what they had won in negotiations, and the MRND leaders could hardly imagine that the opposition parties would make any inroads at all in the mono-ethnic MRND bastions in the northern prefectures. In Kigali and Kibungo, as well as in Kibuye and Cyangugu, the MRND was firmly anchored, thanks to the influence of powerful figures in the political, economic, and military spheres. Only Gitarama and Butare prefectures eclipsed them. However, the scope of the defeat suffered in Arusha forced the MRND to take stock of the sacrifices to come. Some of these powerful dignitaries would be evicted from their posts as a result of demobilization or at the insistence of newly appointed ministers. Too few and too weak to imagine effective ways of recouping their anticipated losses, the MRND leaders were determined to block the progress of negotiations and were therefore highly receptive to possible putschist initiatives.

In addition, aside from the newly created posts of deputy prime minister and secretary for reintegration of refugees, the five ministerial posts accorded to the RPF were all reapportioned from the original contingent held by the

MRND, which thus lost four of its seats to the RPF, including the highly strategic ministry of the interior (*see annex 22*).

Predictably, the new power-sharing deal provoked an angry response from the MRND and its sympathizers. On 19 January 1993 the MRND and the CDR organized demonstrations throughout the country to protest the accords. The arrival of an international commission of inquiry into violations of human rights in Rwanda contributed to stoking the violence.[18] Members of the commission departed on 21 January, at the very moment that the secretary-general of the MRND openly declared that his party purely and simply rejected the accords, making things even worse. Over the course of six days, murderous attacks led by extremist militiamen, with the local population joining in, devastated the northwest of Rwanda. The MRND organized violent demonstrations throughout the country from 20 to 22 January 1993 and proclaimed its intention of bringing all activities to a standstill. The opposition parties refused to be intimidated and organized counterdemonstrations. The result of the weeklong violence and rioting was over four hundred deaths and internal displacement of over twenty thousand persons.[19]

The RPF occupied the third camp. From then on it received the open support of the Tutsi of the interior, who were confidently expecting a slice of power to fall into their hands. Apace with the rising anti-Tutsi violence that the CDR and the Hutu militias resorted to, many Tutsi youth joined the ranks of the RPF, secure in their belief that it was in a better position to ensure their protection than the Hutu parties or even the Tutsi-dominated parties of the interior.

On the strength of its growing international visibility and of its reputation as a major political force backed by military muscle, the RPF used the pretext of the anti-Tutsi violence to launch a broad military offensive on Byumba and Ruhengeri on 8 February. Intervention by the French army was decisive in turning back the RPF's advance. The assault on Kigali failed, and the RPA withdrew toward the end of March, but its military superiority was by now well established. From that point there was a growing fear among the populations of the northern prefectures that they might be sucked ever deeper into the war, with its cortege of victims and hundreds of thousands of displaced persons.

More broadly, the possibility of the Tutsi rebellion actually taking power was entirely plausible in the eyes of the extremist elements within the CDR and the MRND. The RPF offensive cemented the rediscovered unity of the mouvance présidentielle behind Habyarimana, which came together as a bulwark against the RPF. But it also disturbed a good number of the sympathizers, activists, and officials in the coalition of the FDC. The impact was particularly strong across the northern prefectures, where the MDR and the PSD had great difficulty taking root. Depending on the viewpoint, the RPF offensive could be characterized as a success or as an earthquake. Its results were particularly serious in terms of civilian casualties, which amounted to several thousands killed (although this total figure is seriously debated) and exceeded one million displaced persons, most of them resettled in makeshift refugee camps on the outskirts of Kigali. All of the observers agreed that the offensive marked a decisive turning point in the perception of the RPF as "liberator" (*see annex 23*).[20] It is little wonder, then, that a number of opposition leaders at the level of the prefectures began to reach out to the MRND. Examples include Donat Murego (national secretary of the MDR and president of the prefectural steering committee in Ruhengeri), Stanislas Mbonampeka (second vice president of the PL and president of the prefectural authorities in Ruhengeri), and Hyacinthe Nsengiyumva Rafiki (executive prefectural secretary of the PSD in Gisenyi and member of Félicien Gatabazi's ministerial cabinet).[21]

Rising Tensions and Recomposition in the Political Landscape

The Ouster of Dismas Nsengiyaremye

Within a month, the "Power Sharing" protocol and the 8 February 1993 attack had prodded the various protagonists to clarify their ambitions and resources. This meant a careful reexamination of their strategies, including confrontation. The first victim was the MDR, with Dismas Nsengiyaremye as vice president of the party and the country's prime minister. He had hoped to reap the political dividends of the peace accords and expected to stay on as head of the BBTG. The seemingly unstoppable ascendancy of "MDR Gitarama," Nsengiyaremye's prefecture of origin, was viewed with considerable anxiety by the other presidential hopefuls: Faustin Twagiramungu (president of the party and a son-in-law of the late president, Grégoire Kayibanda), Emmanuel Gapyisi (president of the Political Commission of the MDR and also a son-in-law of Kayibanda), Félicien Gatabazi (head of the PSD), and Justin Mugenzi (head of the PL). In addition, the provision of the "Power Sharing" protocol anticipating that the candidate for the post of prime minister would be "presented by the political formation designated to that effect [and] presented to the two parties to the negotiation for approval" and that his identity should be known before the signing of the peace accords provided Habyarimana with a powerful tool for sowing division among and within the opposition parties.[22] There were many candidates who, eager to neutralize the rising power of Nsengiyaremye, the president's principal adversary, were open to making amends with Habyarimana, first among them Faustin Twagiramungu, who, while amenable to a privileged alliance with the RPF, had a weak hold on his own party.

In the end, the complex maneuverings led to a drastic reconfiguring of the system of alliances, and yet there was no telling at the outset how the jockeying for power would finally play out.

The first stage, in January 1993, began with the recall of Boniface Ngulinzira, minister of foreign affairs, from his post as head of the governmental delegation to Arusha—he became the MRND's bête noire during the negotiations—and his replacement by James Gasana, minister of defense, a move dictated by the fact that "the next phase of the Arusha negotiations principally concerned the integration of the RPF soldiers into the Rwandan Armed Forces."[23] With this decision, Habyarimana significantly weakened Nsengiyaremye and deprived the MDR of the opportunity to reap the political rewards of the peace accords. He also recovered his hold on the Ministry of Defense through the appointment of the all-powerful chief of staff, Théoneste Bagosora, a move that Nsengiyaremye and Gasana strongly opposed. What they did not expect was that Habyarimana would enjoy the combined support of the presidents of the MDR, the PL, the PSD, and even the RPF. Nsengiyaremye and Gasana had no choice but to acquiesce (see annex 24). In the MDR, Faustin Twagiramungu needed Habyarimana's support to block the candidacy of Nsengiyaremye for prime minister of the BBTG, and, broadly speaking, the incipient convergence between Habyarimana, Twagiramungu, and Mugenzi (PL) sparked a process that would lead to a shift in alliances. As for the leaders of the PSD, Nzamurambaho and Gatabazi, their immediate priority was to block the return to power of "Gitarama."

With the reprise of negotiations in February, the RPF challenged the legitimacy of the minister of defense as the new head of the governmental delegation. When the RPF launched its offensive on Ruhengeri, it figured that the political divisions would spread to the army and that its decisive military gains would conclusively seal its alliance with the FDC (MDR, PSD, PL, and PDC). The bipolarization around the RPF, some in favor of and others vehemently against its strategy of conquest by force, became the key issue for the domestic opposition parties. Concomitantly, the sidelining of the MDR, the pillar of the opposition, became the central objective of the two main protagonists, both anxious to simplify the play for power around the two major alliances.

For quite a long time the president remained persuaded that the Steering Committee of the MDR would support extending Nsengiyaremye's mandate and candidacy as the head of the BBTG.[24] According to one of Habyarimana's close associates, it was only toward the beginning of July that the president settled upon unseating Nsengiyaremye in a fit of anger following a visit from the Tanzanian ambassador, who inquired when the president would sign the accords, which would seal the decision on the prime minister. When the president stated that he accepted Nsengiyaremye's candidacy in principle and requested the finalized texts for his signature, the ambassador conceded that they were not yet ready. The president assumed that Nsengiyaremye's lobbying of foreign embassies in support of his candidacy was also aimed at discrediting and weakening the president. Thus, he was receptive to nominating any other candidate, including Félicien Gatabazi, the president of PSD, even if doing so required modifications to the "Power Sharing" protocol.

On 12 July the Executive Bureau of the MRND sent a letter to the president of the republic, copied to the leaders of all the parties that participated in government, to inform them that the MDR "could not impose a candidate [Nsengiyaremye] on its partners who was not up to the task of leading the transition to fair and transparent elections, in the spirit of peace and national reconciliation" (*see annex 24*). On 15 July 1993, at the end of its mandate, the Political Bureau of the MDR requested that the Nsengiyaremye government be maintained in place until the peace accords were signed and reaffirmed his candidacy for the post of prime minister in the BBTG. But the very next day Nsengiyaremye and the chief negotiator, Boniface Ngulinzira, were replaced. Habyarimana had understood that the RPF no longer supported Nsengiyaremye, who was determined to conclude the negotiations before his mandate ended on 23 July. According to a close associate of the president, if Nsengiyaremye had personally approached him for support, Habyarimana would have given it, because it would have reinforced the RPF's misgivings about Nsengiyaremye. By presenting himself as "independent," Nsengiyaremye lost all of his allies.

Faustin Twagiramungu, supported by the RPF, advanced the candidacy of Agathe Uwilingiyimana, president of the MDR in Butare, for the post of prime minister, thus clearing a path for his later nomination as prime minister designate under the Arusha Peace Accords to head the BBTG. The MDR then split between two competing leaderships. Its official leadership and its base were receptive to anti-RPF alliances, leaving Twagiramungu at the helm of a minority.

The MRND Party Congress of 3–4 July 1993

To make sense of this reversal of alliances, it is necessary to return to the stakes and issues raised at the MRND party congress, which had just been held on 3–4 July, and the consequences that flowed from it.

The congress was a theater of confrontation between the "liberals" and the "conservatives," but if the ideological cleavage clearly drew the contours of opposing camps, the strategic positionings reflected other considerations that were just as significant. Thus, in Gisenyi prefecture, the MRND remained above all the vehicle of the OTP (natives of the terroir présidentiel) who sought to safeguard their turf. But the strategy of the central core of the Akazu and the local leaders of the MRND was much more complex. From the perspective of power sharing, it was important to shatter the isolation of the MRND and to diversify the political options in order to attract allied parties and prevent rival formations from taking hold. This was Joseph Nzirorera's mission. He presented himself as a rampart, the spokesperson for the hardliners of the regime, whose powers easily exceeded the limits of the MRND. The unofficial successor to Habyarimana, Nzirorera was the one who, subject to the president's orders, implemented the broadening of the mouvance présidentielle with the creation of the Coalition pour la défense de la république (CDR, Coalition for the Defense of the Republic), regrouping the most extremist elements of the MRND and its satellite parties. He was also the one who coordinated the financing operations and made contributions and loans available to supporters during the rallies. This position turned him into the man who most likely had the broadest and the most accurate vision of the ramifications of presidential power.

The "division of labor" between the MRND and the CDR primarily concerned the ethnic question. The CDR openly expressed what the MRND did not wish to announce publicly, given its founding principles, in order to safeguard, at least for a while, its liberal image and its Tutsi constituency. Its virulent ethnicist rhetoric garnered quite a number of MDR activists who would have never rejoined the MRND. In addition, paradoxically, the CDR's activism was well appreciated by both the conservative and the progressive wings of the MRND. The CDR reinforced the former, whipping up passions and internal pressures. As for the progressive wing, it looked to the CDR to siphon off the party's most extremist elements in order to broaden its capacity for influence.

However, even though the majority of the activists in the two parties only saw advantages in this complementarity, many of the CDR officials sought to free themselves of the former single party's dominion and denounced the concessions and compromises that the MRND seemed to be making toward the RPF and its "accomplices." Thus, the CDR accused both the president and the prime minister of treachery after a 9 March 1993 press release from the president's office expressed support for the negotiations under way in Dar es Salaam. The tone sharpened between the two parties, and the CDR withdrew from the Alliance pour le renforcement de la démocratie (ARD, Alliance for the Strengthening of Democracy) on 27 March. The national secretary of the MRND publicly reproached the CDR for its racist ideology and denounced its involvement in the massacres in Gisenyi in December 1992 and January 1993. But this was merely a passing crisis, given the tight links between the two movements. The CDR was much more than just a party of defectors. By the end of 1993 its influence went far beyond Gisenyi prefecture and the conservative wing of the MRND.

The MRND's internal affairs were no less complex in the other prefectures of the north. War and multipartyism strongly affected the MRND's fortunes in Ruhengeri and, by implication, its privileged alliance with Gisenyi. Indeed, the party found itself confronted by the former dissident Alexis Kanyarengwe, who, against all odds, became the Hutu president of the RPF. There was even much speculation about the existence of an RPF "Power" wing, which would have allied itself with the MDR in order to resurrect the Ruhengeri/Gitarama axis, which served as the backbone of the MDR-Parmehutu during the First Republic. Further complicating the situation was the no-holds-barred competition between two new aspiring MRND leaders.

War thrust two major MRND figures to the forefront: Joseph Nzirorera and Casimir Bizimungu. The former was at the heart of the presidential team, and in speaking of the terroir présidentiel, the president's home turf, Mukingo, Nzirorera's native commune in Ruhengeri, was always included. The man who came to personify the excesses of the Habyarimana regime was once the head of the Ministry of Commerce, Industry, and Handicrafts, where he played a key role in organizing the financing of the president's political base. Strategic foresight demanded anticipation of the inevitable uncoupling of the party's resources from state coffers, which had been so muddled until then. The management and board of directors of the large public and parastatal enterprises, as well as the private stockholders, were brought into line.[25] With Sylvestre Nsanzimana's nomination as prime minister, Nzirorera was forced to relinquish his ministerial post. The same dynamic was at hand within the MRND, where the party's renovators unanimously denounced its monolithic nature (*see box 2*).

On Nzirorera's own turf, another minister, Casimir Bizimungu, challenged Nzirorera's preeminence; consequently, when the time came for elections to the Ruhengeri prefectural committee in February 1992, Nzirorera was only elected to the second tier. Nor did he experience much success during the party congress of 18 April 1992, failing to gain a seat on the Steering Committee or the Political Bureau. That congress heralded the return of Matthieu Ngirumpatse (*see box 8*), while Casimir Bizimungu entered in the Political Bureau.

This second figure, Bizimungu, hailed from Nyamugari commune. He had been singled out in April 1987 by his "godfather," Dr. Séraphin Bararengana, dean of the Faculty of Medicine and the president's brother, for promotion to minister of health and later minister of foreign affairs. His hard-line position against the "Ugandan invasion," contrasting sharply with the president's moderate stance, was particularly well received by residents of the northern prefectures, directly threatened by the RPF military ambitions, and earned him the respect of government and army circles. Many officers from Ruhengeri felt that Gisenyi's dominion was at its end and that Ruhengeri's ascendancy was looming on the horizon. Casimir Bizimungu's brilliant personal trajectory, enhanced by his stature as minister of foreign affairs and his ease in dealing with diplomats, made him appear "fresh" and untainted when compared to Joseph Nzirorera. Because his links with the MDR prefectural administration were of special concern for the president, the latter did not hesitate to thwart Bizimungu's ambitions for the Ministry of Defense, instead proposing James Gasana, a civilian from Byumba. This prefecture was at the heart of a struggle for influence between the communes of Gisenyi and Ruhengeri, a state of affairs adroitly exploited by the MRND to bolster its independence and strike alliances beyond the north, particularly with the prefectures most adversely affected by the war: Kigali and Kibungo. Linked to the progressive currents within the MRND, Gasana was the ideal candidate to strengthen this axis.

To everyone's surprise, Gasana rapidly succeeded in imposing himself within army circles and managed to neutralize the extremist elements close to the presidential clan. His professional, transparent management of the ministry earned him the respect of opposition leaders. Having studied abroad in the United States, like Casimir Bizimungu, Gasana enjoyed considerable respect from several foreign embassies. All of these elements combined to make him suspect in the president's eyes and by members of the OTP, who viewed him as a significant threat. Laborious maneuvers emanating from the Office of the Presidency pushed him to withdraw his candidacy for the MRND vice presidency during the national party congress of 18 April 1992. Those efforts were repeated when the party reconvened for its congress of 3–4 July 1993.

The main objective of this MRND party congress was a global divvying up of posts among the regime's major figures in light of the new dispensation created by the "Power Sharing" protocol. Since Habyarimana would continue to serve as president of the republic, Gisenyi was rewarded, and, despite protestations from his entourage, he announced his resignation of the party presidency on 30 March. The question remained of designating a new leadership team and providing for the five ministerial posts that were earmarked for the

MRND. Many considered that the presidency of the party would be a springboard for candidacy for the presidency of the republic at the same time, which would then risk falling to someone who was not a native of Gisenyi. This is how Ngirumpatse viewed matters: faced with Habyarimana's tergiversations, Ngirumpatse finally played his trump card by sending the president a letter in late February or early March to remind him of his intention to resign from the presidency of the MRND, a letter that Ngirumpatse shared with several of his close associates (*see annex 26*).

Ngirumpatse's rather cavalier, and unprecedented, manner of revealing his ambitions before the president came as a shock and left lasting traces, even if it could be explained by the tensions of the moment, when rivalries at all levels were exacerbated in proportion to the dwindling number of available posts. Having tried in vain to block the convening of a party congress by sabotaging the required fund-raising initiatives, the conservative blowhards now realized that the shift in control of the MRND to the benefit of the reformists was inevitable. Indeed, Ngirumpatse had no difficulty whatsoever in gathering those voices together and getting himself elected. The principal concern of the Akazu at that time was to obtain a balance in power so that it could maintain its hold on the party and impose its own candidate, Joseph Nzirorera, on the national secretariat.

All of the machinations turned on the question of how the five posts attributed to the MRND in the BBTG would be filled. The geopolitical balancing can be summarized as follows: Gisenyi had the presidency of the republic; Byumba had the defense minister; Ruhengeri only had a single post of minor significance (minister of higher education) and thus insisted on gaining control of the national secretariat. The competition shifted to a face-off between Casimir Bizimungu, president of the MRND prefectural committee in Ruhengeri, and Joseph Nzirorera, who finally won out. In fact, the congressional delegates were stumped by the election of Ngirumpatse, who unabashedly put himself forward as the candidate to succeed Habyarimana as party president, because he was widely known as the candidate Habyarimana would support if the party fell from his grasp. James Gasana, then minister of defense, analyzed the outcome of the congress as follows:

> Victory for those who favored a shift at the head of the party was shared between the progressives, who had the presidency, and the conservatives, who had the national secretariat. . . . However, this congress would be the final vestige of democratic renewal within the MRND. In fact, election to the post of national secretary of someone so closely linked to the Akazu allowed its allies to completely overrun the party. From that point on, the

national secretariat operated without taking account of contributions from other organs of the party. Nzirorera thus became, de facto, Habyarimana's direct heir as head of the party, and not Ngirumpatse, Habyarimana's de jure successor.[26]

Just to provide a sense of the climate at the conclusion of the congress, we can add that the confluence of maneuvers to obtain Gasana's departure from the Ministry of Defense, which, with the active support of the army had become an independent authority in relation to Habyarimana, reached an unbearable level of intensity, further reinforced by direct, personal threats. And on top of those death threats from the OTP, Gasana also became a major target for the RPF, deeply concerned by his ability to unify the FAR: attacking him was a means to thwart the renewed combativity among the troops. He then sent his family off to Switzerland and informed the prime minister and the president of his wish to join them for a vacation. On 17 July Gasana verbally accepted his reappointment in the new government of Agathe Uwilingiyimana and on 20 July left Rwanda for France, where he managed to obtain a long-term visa for Switzerland.[27] He informed the government of his resignation on 23 July (*see annex 27*).

As it happened, the command of the FAR again fell under the control of the OTP. Extremist elements immediately took matters in hand. James Gasana's departure left unprotected the more moderate, progressive elements within the army, the government, and the party. Within the FAR, partisanship and militancy could flourish again, unhindered by the new agronomist-minister in charge of the Ministry of Defense, Augustin Bizimana, a native of Byumba.[28]

The soldiers-militias symbiosis had now become deeply entrenched (training, provision of weapons, mobilization). The minister of the interior, Faustin Munyaseza, was no longer able to effectively oppose the excesses of this armed wing, now protected as much by the presidency as by the MRND and the Ministry of Defense.

Joseph Nzirorera was fully in control of the MRND, and the other party organs no longer met. In these conditions, Habyarimana resurfaced as the veritable head of the party. All Ngirumpatse, the titular president, could hope to do was maintain his prerogatives of office and try to deflect attention from his previous affront and ingratitude toward the "Father of the Nation."

The Extraordinary Congress of the MDR of 23–24 July 1993

Dismas Nsengiyaremye's replacement as prime minister by Agathe Uwilingiyimana—despite opposition from the majority of the MDR and surprisingly thanks to support from many MRND figures (in particular, an agreement between the new MRND president, Matthieu Ngirumpatse, and Faustin Twagiramungu)—can be considered the major turning point during the period of cohabitation under the multiparty government of April 1992.

The MDR's split into two wings organized around Nsengiyaremye (first vice president), on the one hand, and Twagiramungu (president), on the other, can be traced to a clause in the Arusha Peace Accords that anticipated the designation of a prime minister before their final signature. Nsengiyaremye, in office since April 1992, hoped to succeed himself. Twagiramungu's courtship of the MRND and the RPF, dating back to the beginning of 1993, proved of great help in pulling off this "coup d'état." Among the MDR stalwarts, supporters for a reversal of alliances in favor of the MRND had gained substantial ground since the last RPF offensive in February. This did not go unnoticed by Twagiramungu, who proceeded to make the most of his title as president of the party to advance his own candidacy for prime minister designate of the BBTG with support from those same four parties (MRND, PSD, PL, and PDC).

Sidelined through institutional maneuvering, the MDR vice president, Nsengiyaremye, then convened an extraordinary congress of the MDR on 23–24 July to build support in his party for a rebound on the political scene and unseat Twagiramungu and Uwilingiyimana, who had just been promoted to prime minister. As an ultraminority faction in the party, Twagiramungu and Ngirumpatse, presidents of MDR and MRND, respectively, worked hand in hand to block the congress and persuade Tharcisse Renzaho, the prefect of Kigali, to forbid its convening. While the congressional delegates braved the ban, and Twagiramungu's supporters were overwhelmed, Ngirumpatse unleashed his Interahamwe militiamen to block access to the Kigali Iwacu Centre (Training Center and Cooperative Research) and sabotage the congress. It was finally the gendarmerie, on orders from Col. Théoneste Bagosora (then filling in for the minister of defense, who had absconded), that was mandated to contain the clashes and maintain security. In the end, the MDR congress voted the exclusions from the party of Faustin Twagiramungu; the new MDR ministers, Agathe Uwilingiyimana, Faustin Rucogoza (Hutu, Byumba), Anastase Gasana (Hutu, Kigali-rural), and Jean-Marie Vianney Mbonimpa (Hutu, Kibuye); and their directeurs de cabinet and advisors. The congress then designated Jean Kambanda, a rival of Agathe Uwilingiyimana in MDR Butare, as its candidate for the prime ministership of the BBTG.[29]

The prime minister, Agathe Uwilingiyimana (in office since July 1993), took note of this turn of events and, after a long discussion with representatives of the MDR from Butare, accepted in writing to resign from government (*see annex 28*). Upon returning to her home, she was met by a large delegation composed of Faustin Twagiramungu, Justin Mugenzi, Ferdinand Kabagema, Matthieu Ngirumpatse, Frédéric Nzamurambaho, and Col. Théoneste Bagosora, who were there waiting for her, insisting that she renounce her resignation. With firm support from Uwilingiyimana's husband, Ignace Barahira, this delegation of party chiefs convinced her to draft a press release for radio broadcast indicating that she had only resigned because of threats from congressional delegates.[30] Dismas Nsengiyaremye was thus definitively unseated. That is how Agathe Uwilingiyimana, who really was never President Habyarimana's preferred candidate, found herself as prime minister, thanks to the concerted maneuvers of Ngirumpatse and Twagiramungu, along with the personal involvement of Bagosora.

Retrospectively, this imbroglio brings to light the singular importance of this long day. Besides putting into perspective the events that followed, these maneuverings demonstrate Uwilingiyimana's sense of ambivalence; despite the strength of her convictions, her half-hearted stance on certain issues often led to vacillation in response to opposing pressures. In this case, her final decision appears not so much as a rational choice but as a reflection of her inability to anticipate her fate if she were to fall out of grace with Twagiramungu. In sum, unity within the party was definitively compromised because of or despite the fact that Nsengiyaremye was out of the play.

Several days later, on 31 July, as his case came under formal investigation, Nsengiyaremye left the country and joined Gasana in exile in France. Sources indicate that a judicial inquiry into embezzlement of funds earmarked for internally displaced persons was under way, instigated by Ngirumpatse and Twagiramungu (see annex 29).

Among other versions of this decisive episode, which marks the MDR's implosion courtesy of the MRND, the one that best sums it up is the following: "Ngirumpatse: to get rid of Dismas, promote Faustin, and then get rid of them both."[31]

Ngirumpatse's tenacity in keeping Nsengiyaremye away from the Rwandan political scene reflected his fear of seeing his MDR/MRND coalition fall apart. In his eyes the stakes were huge. Given the fragility of his hold on the "northist" MRND, an alliance with the center and the south necessarily relied on the MDR. Only a broader MDR/MRND coalition would be capable of beating the RPF in military terms (the two protocols on armed forces and on miscellaneous issues required this alliance between the northern and southern officers, whether MRND or MDR sympathizers), as well as politically (since the MDR/MRND coalition would be in the majority throughout the country, with the possible exception of Butare).

Initially, Ngirumpatse clearly believed that by wholeheartedly supporting Twagiramungu he would manage to bring him back within the fold of the mouvance présidentielle, as he did with Justin Mugenzi, the president of the PL. Eventually, when it became apparent that Twagiramungu would double-cross him, Ngirumpatse approached Froduald Karamira and Donat Murego and convinced them that he could help them regain the leverage over the MDR that had been usurped by Twagiramungu, who one way or another would end up being excluded from the transitional government. But regardless of which partner ultimately prevailed, the main objective was to ensure that Nsengiyaremye not succeed in imposing his point of view, which was opposed to an MDR/MRND alliance. Hence the imperative to make sure he remained outside of the country and especially to weigh him down with the accusation of having ordered the killing of Emmanuel Gapyisi, which would also allow the MRND to win over Gapyisi's supporters.

The gradual weakening of those political formations that had been struggling to impose a multiparty electoral system since 1991 was the result of converging efforts by the MRND and the mouvance présidentielle on one side and the RPF on the other: both aimed at recapturing the political-military landscape. In August 1993, after the signing of the Arusha Peace Accords, the logic of bipolarization that inspired the protocols on armed forces and on miscellaneous issues could apply equally to the entire political arena.[32] Two powerful determinants had a significant bearing on the play of political alliances: one had to do with the choice of strategies designed to win over the two opposing military blocks (i.e., the armed wings of partisan factions); the other concerned the influence of foreign powers—regional or Western—on the negotiating process.

The shifts in the political landscape greatly complicated attempts to turn the clock back to the more coherent alignments of 1991 and 1992. The parties' youth militias and politicians called the shots and voiced their priorities in the name of their presumed social base. All democratic controls on the leadership of the parties having disappeared by mid-1993, games of intrigue got the better of political positioning. The two belligerents were able to "go about their business," both literally and figuratively, while dealing with politicians they disdainfully referred to as "the democrats," alternating between menace and seduction while all along engaged in churning up regional, ethnic, and political enmities. Whether they were associated with the radical Hutu "Power" movement or with Hutu "moderates" who identified their destinies with that of the RPF, rank-and-file elements were never more than beggars in their respective camps.

Unspoken Terms in the
Arusha Peace Accords
and Obstructions in the
Political Transition

The Arusha Peace Accords anticipated a transitional period of twenty-two months once the accords were signed on 4 August 1993. The peace agreement was meant to be exacting, expeditious, and binding (*see annex 30*). Certain provisions were already in effect through particular agreements initiated under the terms of the 31 July 1992 cease-fire, like those concerning the release of all prisoners of war and all persons arrested for security reasons.

The transitional institutions (i.e., the presidency, the national assembly, and the government, with Faustin Twagiramungu at its head) were to be installed within thirty-seven days of the signing of the accords, that is, no later than 11 September 1993, as was the case for the High Council of the army high command.[1] Thereafter, all local authorities (burgomasters, sous-prefects, prefects) were to be replaced or reconfirmed within the three months set aside for setting up the transitional government. And then work on three crucial issues would follow: repatriation of refugees, consolidation of the two armies, and national elections by universal suffrage.

The refugees were to return in stages, with arrival of the first group scheduled during the first nine months following the installation of the new government.[2] During those nine months a survey of the candidates and the proposed resettlement sites was to be conducted; financing from donors had to be secured; and agreements with host countries had to be finalized. A timetable of nine months was also set up for demobilization of those elements from both armies (FAR and RPA) not included among the nineteen thousand soldiers and gendarmes of the new, consolidated force. Finally, the electoral timetable would get under way with the renewals in the mandates of communal authorities six months before the end of the transition, to be immediately followed by general elections, which would be organized at the end of a transitional period of twenty-two months, that is, around mid-May 1996.[3]

Clearly, putting the Arusha Peace Accords into effect presupposed a fair amount of honesty on the part of the protagonists. In large part, the range of possible outcomes hinged on a fairly new expression: "hidden agenda." The most salient feature of such agendas is that they tend to confuse fantasy with reality, even if they conferred certain advantages. Since each had to anticipate the other's strategy, every option, even the most diabolical or outlandish, had to be considered and, for this very reason, to some degree became plausible. On the flip side, this mindset justified recourse to defensive strategies and hence to anticipation, which could be just as exaggerated. In this way, each party pushed the limits of what was duplicitous or acceptable and thus repeatedly ignored or transgressed the few prohibitions that still managed to hold violence at bay. Without falling prey to flights of fancy, we should turn our attention to some of the reasons why few, if any, seriously envisaged the Arusha Peace Accords ever actually taking form.

The Implementation Process

The implementation aroused fears on behalf of all the actors. A first element demonstrated it immediately. Indeed, just before the accords were signed a clean sweep was made of the team of advisors and civil servants surrounding Dismas Nsengiyaremye. That they once had the support of numerous MRND figures makes that clean sweep all the more surprising. The consequences, at any rate, were profound.

Although they had been directly involved in finalizing the agreement and negotiating its terms, these advisors and civil servants suddenly found themselves cut out of the picture. The maneuver immediately compromised the tripolar political logic of the accords, and it ruled out the notion that a relatively autonomous political force might emerge to counterbalance the two military powers. If the complexity of maneuvers leading to Prime Minister Nsengiyaremye's withdrawal from the political arena allowed a glimpse of the intensity and subtlety of the intrigues in store, it still remained to be seen how dearly the "winners" would pay to get the RPF to go along with them. In this regard, the agreement to install an RPF battalion on the CND (parliament) compound in the heart of the capital is traceable to the outrageous calculations made by party leaders. The challenge was figuring out where to house the RPF representatives once the peace accords were signed. Pointing to the problems of security in the capital, the RPF representatives demanded that government cabinet meetings be held in Byumba, a city not far from the border with Uganda and the tea factory in Mulindi, where the RPF had set up its head-quarters. The domestic parties shot down the proposal for the very same reasons. Their negotiators felt that the guarantees of security from the United Nations forces would suffice and categorically refused to allow RPF units to be based in the capital. The solution finally negotiated by Boniface Ngulinzira, the MDR minister in charge of the Arusha negotiations, proposed that the RPF forces remain in Mulindi for as long as it took UNAMIR to fully secure Kigali, and pending that, cabinet meetings would be held in the demilitarized zone, in Kinihira (Byumba prefecture), whenever the RPF was expected to participate.

After Nsengiyaremye's government was dismissed, this proposal, which the RPF had already clearly accepted, was renegotiated by Anastase Gasana, the new MDR minister of foreign affairs (aligned with Twagiramungu). With the MRND's consent, Gasana agreed to the installation of an RPF battalion in Kigali on condition that the name of Faustin Twagiramungu be expressly in-scribed as prime minister designate in the peace agreement.[4] Before this re-negotiation, the MDR was only expected to inform the other parties of the name of its intended prime minister without having to formally inscribe it in the text of the accords.

A second element in the political maneuverings underlying the implemen-tation process was the breadth of the negotiated arrangements. The balance of power inscribed in the Arusha Peace Accords had little in common with politi-cal realities on the ground.[5] The accords conferred a certain equivalency upon the two military blocks, however false or forced: one was officially undefeated but remained incapable of prevailing militarily without serious outside support, which, now that French troops had departed, was no longer an option; the other, with undeniable military superiority, had an inexhaustible source of foreign assistance. However, politically speaking, there was great fluidity in its bases of support; the only certainty was that the RPF, which was constructed on a wholly ethnic basis, could not rely on the kind of broadly based popular support that would ensure its victory at the ballot box in the short or medium term. This twofold impasse shaped the future for all parties involved.

When the Arusha Peace Accords were signed on 4 August 1993, the protocol on the armed forces, which set terms for the recomposition of the new national army, specified that the RPF would provide 40 percent of the troops and occupy 50 percent of the officer corps. Factoring in its guidelines for regional balance, the pro-MRND contingent of the former government army, which had been overrepresented at the level of both troops and officers, was practically cut in half. With its 40 percent, to which would be added the few pro-RPF elements from among the FAR, the RPF became the dominant component in the newly consolidated national armed forces. Taking into account those generally sympathetic to the Forces démocratiques du changement (FDC, Democratic Forces for Change), the new armed forces included one-third pro-MRND and CDR elements and two-thirds pro-RPF and FDC elements. The majority of the "older" officers from the north were pegged for demobilization, also reflecting the new balance of power within the FAR, as clearly illustrated by the choice of officers called upon to constitute the military high command during the transitional period (*see annex 32*).

According to the reports sent to the Ministry of Defense about the selection criteria, the uneven distribution of the officers' regional origin was enough to suggest the nature of the dislocation to come, whether eagerly awaited or feared: the Rukiga (Gisenyi, Ruhengeri, and Byumba) claimed four of the eleven representatives, with only one from Gisenyi (all the others were from the Nduga), meaning all of the country's other prefectures, excepting the northern block. Moreover, if neutrality was still a value held in common by the majority of those appointed, most of the officers from the south made no attempts to conceal their sympathies for the opposition parties. This was as much a message for the minister of defense as it was for the leaders of the opposition. Even if they were not beholden to the mouvance présidentielle, none of these officers was really likely to make trouble for the president and Colonel Bagosora or to oppose them.

Just as the embassies and various observers had predicted, one could sense an immediate radicalization among officers and extremist elements from the north, who viewed this protocol as a provocation. In addition, large segments of the population were convinced that government negotiators were literally writing off expenses incurred over the four years of civil war imposed on the FAR and the entire country by the rebellion: tens of thousands of casualties and war-wounded, in addition to over one million internally displaced civilians herded into refugee camps, along with incalculable traumas and economic losses. By the OAU's account, looking back, there was no longer division within the government negotiating team but instead stark ineptitude: "It is hard to think of any agreement more perfectly calculated to enrage virtually everyone in Rwanda with whom the RPF would need to work. It was one thing to say that an 85-per-cent Hutu population did not mean that Hutu rule equalled democracy. It was another to say that the Tutsi, with less than 15 per cent of the population, should be entitled to almost half the army. Even moderate Hutu, caught in an impossible tug of war between the two sides, found that objectionable."[6]

This raises an issue that was still pending when hostilities resumed on 7 April 1994: the RPF chose not to reveal the names of the officers to be appointed to command positions in the future national army. In the eyes of many observers, this was a sign of deep-seated reservations about implementing the accords. This apparent lack of interest contrasted starkly with the extreme agitation displayed within the FAR, whose titular minister was already hard at work on the configuration of the new command. Beefing up the militias took place within that same context: they would be called upon to compensate for the drastic weakening in MRND/CDR links to the new army as a reserve force that would decisively contribute to preparing for elections.

In fact, after Félicien Gatabazi, the executive secretary of the PSD and the minister of public works, was assassinated in February (see below), the stage was set for a military confrontation between forces anxious to settle things once and for all. On one side there was a coalition of radical pro-Hutu forces from the army who were loyal to northern extremist officers who were already retired or soon to be; and on the other was the RPA. For the RPF, the strategy of military conquest was inevitable and the likely outcome just as certain, since the Arusha Peace Accords required a rapid and complete withdrawal of French troops. But time was of the essence. All that remained was to generate a scenario that would warrant this offensive.

The Coming Together of MRND and the Pro-Hutu Wings of the Opposition Parties

For the presidency, the discrepancy between the balance of power inscribed in the accords and the actual political weight of the mouvance présidentielle, which did not even have a blocking minority in the transitional institutions, gave rise to fears of an "institutional coup d'état" during the transitional period. It was incumbent upon the presidency to broaden its political space and to play for time. To that end, it could rely on an MRND both weakened and reinvigorated by the restrictions of the accords. The rebalancing effected by the party congress of July 1993 sheltered the MRND from the internal divisions suffered by the other parties, and the reaffirmation of the president's leadership somewhat deflected the competition between the two heirs apparent, Matthieu Ngirumpatse and Joseph Nzirorera.

As far as the prospects with the electorate were concerned, there was nothing illusory in the MRND's apparent resilience. In the wake of long months of investigation and review by the opposition to "cleanse" the territorial administration, elections were held on 23 March 1993 to replace thirty-eight burgomasters deemed "corrupt, incompetent, or guilty of exactions."[7] The results were not what had been hoped for. The electoral college chosen for the exercise was selected using criteria that were hardly transparent and subjected to intense pressures.[8] The outcome of the poll confirmed the enduring hold of partisan, regional loyalties. Yet the two principal parties (MRND and MDR) managed to expand their bases of support in the strongholds of their competitors (*see annex 33*). These results significantly demoralized party activists from the democratic opposition. Going forward, they dispensed with all illusions of electoral victory over an MRND methodically hitting its mark. Nonetheless, there were still clear lessons for the MRND, given the electoral weight of the two large republican parties. It had no choice but to open itself to leading figures from the opposition, many of whom sensed the time had come to lay the groundwork for favorable outcomes for themselves. At the same time, the MRND showed few scruples in allowing the more radical Hutu elements to migrate to satellite parties.

The rise of a unifying pro-Hutu movement, dubbed "Power," in reaction to fears of mounting RPF ascendancy accelerated dramatically in October 1993 with the attempted, Tutsi-led military putsch in Bujumbura, along with the assassination of President Melchior Ndadaye and leading dignitaries of the new Burundian regime. The rise to national office of the latter was born of the first elections by universal suffrage since independence. Many Hutu in Rwanda experienced this assassination as an affront to their ideals, directed at a man they saw as their own standard-bearer. In point of fact, Ndadaye was a former refugee from Burundi who had sought asylum in Rwanda in 1972; it was in Rwanda that he received his secondary and university educations. His election to the presidency in Burundi was practically viewed as the triumph of a "Rwandan." The impact of the coup in Burundi and its resonance in Rwanda were decisive. The abrupt collapse of a democratic transition at first seen as one of the most promising in the continent set the stage for rising levels of anti-Tutsi mistrust while accelerating the momentum for populist self-defense measures. The lesson of Burundi was clear: quite aside from the role played by civil society in blocking restoration of the Tutsi military autocracy or, for that matter, the international community's unanimous disapproval, it was first and foremost the massive uprising of the "Hutu people" that forced the putschists to abdicate.

The fallout from this failed coup d'état was catastrophic for Burundi: state authority was significantly weakened after the massacre by the army of the principal leaders of the Front pour la démocratie au Burundi (Frodebu, Front for Democracy in Burundi), while ethnic polarization swiftly swept across the countryside. In those provinces where large numbers of Tutsi civilians had sought protection in regroupment camps for IDPs, the social landscape became virtually monoethnic. In some parts of the country, Hutu residents harshly avenged the death of their kinsmen. This scenario was to have major repercussions in the rise of the Power movement in Rwanda, which openly prepared itself for similar confrontations.

Fearing similar treatment at the hands of the RPF, many Hutu leaders in Rwanda threw themselves into the looming political struggle, now increasingly defined in terms of pro-or anti-RPF. Animosity flared up again a few weeks later when several Tutsi leaders of the Burundian putsch found refuge in Kampala with the blessings of Ugandan authorities. In Kigali there was fearful talk of the "Micombero strategy" and the "Simbananiye plan," referring to one of the most dramatic episodes in the history of independent Burundi.[9] Michel Micombero, a Burundian putschist officer, put an end to the monarchy in November 1966 and then proceeded to eliminate a number of top Hutu leaders in the army and in the administration between October and December 1965 and again in September 1969, a somber prelude to an even more appalling butchery, when from May to September 1972 an estimated two hundred thousand Hutu were killed in the course of what some have referred to as "selective genocide."

Hutu youth wings from the rival parties increasingly began working together to enhance coordination in their struggle against the RPF and its allies. During the last quarter of 1993, parties linked to the mouvance présidentielle and the Power movement began to organize their armed militias for joint operations. Toward the beginning of 1994, in the northern prefectures (Ruhengeri and Gisenyi), they underwent military training by Rwandan army officers and were given weapons.

There is no question that the RPF's strategic position was significantly strengthened by the shake-up in Burundi, but the evolution of political forces in Rwanda grew particularly inhospitable. Kigali was now feeling the pressure of one million Hutu IDPs at its doorstep, while tens of thousands of Burundian Hutu refugees had settled in the border regions in the south. Along with the growing polarization of politics in Burundi, the appalling conditions of the internally displaced and the refugees, the difficulties of bringing them humanitarian assistance in a country tottering on the brink of economic or political disaster, and the swirling accounts of massacres and exactions visited on civilians only served to fuel compelling arguments in favor of "Hutu unity." Not even the war with the RPF had come anywhere near that state of affairs. All this played into the hands of parties aligned with the mouvance présidentielle. A defensive ethnic chauvinism crystallized around the Hutu Power movement and paved the way for a broad alliance among the parties opposed to a military takeover of power by the RPF.

On 16 January 1994 the MRND held a huge rally in Kigali's Nyamirambo Stadium. Supporters of MDR-Power and the "Mugenzi" wing of the PL were also in attendance. It was at this point that a coalition of pro-Hutu parties laid claim to holding the majority in the transitional institutions (*see annex 34*). This massive demonstration marked the beginning of unprecedented political collaboration among the leaders of these groups, and the alliance between the MRND and the MDR-Power movement came very close to taking form.

First initiated in October 1993, a number of encounters between the leaders of these two parties ensued, which ultimately convinced President Habyarimana of the burgeoning solidarity among opposition party leaders under the rubric of Power. He then made it known that he wished to engage with a new leadership team for MDR along the lines of MDR-Power where neither Faustin Twagiramungu nor Dismas Nsengiyaremye would have any place. Jean Kambanda, Froduald Karamira, and Donat Murego then set about organizing another party congress. Exiled in France, Nsengiyaremye returned to Rwanda in December 1993 and tried to curb the party's ethnicist digressions. He also mended affairs with Twagiramungu, and then both tried to convene a congress of reunification. In the end, several prefectures failed to nominate delegates, and the congress never took place. The split deepened.

Consequently, the burgeoning collaboration between the MRND and the splinter groups hostile to the RPF from the MDR, PL, PDC, and PSD continued to solidify. Many meetings were held that cemented links among the various representatives of these parties. These meetings were intended to bring about the replacement of Agathe Uwilingiyimana in late February 1994.

Attempts by the MRND and the RPF to sideline the more independent figures from the MDR and PSD—with a view to later share between them what remained of those parties' membership—thus explicitly sought to isolate the only leaders who still had enough credibility to impose the peace process on the two major political-military parties, even though neither really wanted it.

For weeks in December and early 1994, attention was focused on the internal rivalries within the MDR and PL, each camp claiming exclusive authority to name the deputies and ministers who would represent the party in the transitional institutions. In the MDR there was Faustin Twagiramungu, the excluded president, invoking his status as the prime minister designate (truly in anticipation of his authority) on one side, and opposing him was the official leadership, finding its voice through Dismas Nsengiyaremye, the first vice president, supported by Second Vice President Froduald Karamira and Executive Secretary Donat Murego. In this game, neither the pursuit of consensus by Agathe Uwilingiyimana, the prime minister in office, nor her shifting positions made any difference, if only because she was seldom up to imposing her will.

In the PL, the situation was truly deadlocked between the majority, grouped around First Vice President Landoald "Lando" Ndasingwa (the force behind the national party congress of 13–14 November), and those who tried to claw their way to the top in the wake of the second national congress of 11–12 December, seeking support from the newly elected delegates from the recent prefectural congresses. The latter had been assembled in great haste to garner support for party president Justin Mugenzi (whose electoral mandate had lapsed). The two presidents—Faustin Twagiramungu (MDR) and Justin Mugenzi (PL)—with official prerogatives to designate their party's representatives, found themselves de facto in the minority before their party's decision-making organs, but they were fully confident of their ability to overcome legal challenges.

Consequently, as the weeks went on, one faction of Rwanda's erstwhile democratic activists was moved to support the "Hutu" dictatorship of the MRND, while the other faction opted for the "Tutsi" dictatorship of the RPF.

The Stillborn Transitional Institutions

In this context, and for similar reasons, the strategy of bipolarization adopted by extremist elements from both camps relied upon every conceivable means to delay installation of the transitional institutions. In the interval, each sought to alter the provisions of the Arusha Peace Accords in ways that would increase their influence or to gain the upper hand. The MRND was particularly fearful of the following lineup: two-thirds of all posts in the hands of the RPF and the FDC, with the remaining third left to the presidential majority, but with no real guarantee of even securing this blocking minority. "The entire content of the accords can be reduced to a single provision: where there was no consensus, decisions would be made by the vote of two-thirds of the National Assembly and the government, or by two-thirds majority vote in the cabinet. Every political maneuver, the partisan attitude of certain countries, the killings committed during that period, the splits in the political parties, all of that is a result of that single provision."[10]

What followed was a series of failed installation ceremonies—because one side or the other boycotted the proceedings, or as a result of unanticipated public protests by CDR extremists and the Interahamwe, or because of the absence of a quorum, and so on. Serially and alternatively, the parties relied on every delaying tactic.

On 5 January 1994 President Habyarimana's swearing-in ceremony took place but ended with postponements of the installation of the Broad-Based Transitional Government (BBTG) and the Transitional National Assembly (TNA). And yet, just the day before, Juvénal Habyarimana had received Agathe Uwilingiyimana, and together they had agreed on the final lists of deputies provided by the presidents of the parties (Faustin Twagiramungu [MDR], Justin Mugenzi [PL], and Frédéric Nzamurambaho [PSD]).[11] But late that same evening, Uwilingiyimana informed the president's cabinet that, after further discussions, she could no longer accept the PL "Mugenzi" list, which had been challenged by the "Ndasingwa" wing of the same party (Landoald Ndasingwa, a Tutsi, was reportedly pro-RPF), and that she would have to rely on the latest list sent to her by the president of the Constitutional Court. That list resolved the conflict in Ndasingwa's favor by refusing to include the Power deputies put forward by the PL and MDR party organs. This was a change that Habyarimana could not accept.

After the president took the oath of office, which neither Uwilingiyimana nor the RPF deputies attended, he announced that the ceremonies would continue later that afternoon with the installation of the TNA and the BBTG. The Presidential Guard was then dispatched to prevent members of the "Ndasingwa" wing of PL from participating. That afternoon, the president took note that, in the absence of a quorum, the installation of the remaining institutions would be rescheduled. He thus became the lone incumbent in the new transition. Except for Faustin Twagiramungu, who remained just outside the building, neither the pro-Twagiramungu MDR nor the pro-Ndasingwa PL deputies were present at the ceremony. That afternoon, neither Twagiramungu nor Kavaruganda (the president of the Constitutional Court) nor the RPF turned up. After that date, Uwilingiyimana would take the momentous decision that, "having not commenced the transition," the government could no longer legitimately meet (*see annex 37*). This stance was later invoked on several occasions in various "counter–coup d'états" organized by the MRND and especially, as we shall see, during the night of 6 April 1994 (see chapter 7).

An outburst of partisan polemics quickly followed, imputing responsibility for the aborted installation ceremony to Habyarimana or to the opposition. Dispensing with the president of the PL and the leadership majority in the MDR, a common front emerged that brought together the four domestic opposition parties and the RPF: together they threatened to institutional-ize the transition solely on the basis of approval from the president of the

Constitutional Court. Seen as a provocation, this move immediately drew accusations of a pending coup d'état from the parties aligned with the mouvance présidentielle.

By 8 January 1994, faced with the same set of demands from the opposition, Habyarimana stubbornly refused to heed them. Despite diplomatic pressures and a final, intensive consultation that morning, the oath-taking ceremonies for the government and the National Assembly, which the prime minister had scheduled for the afternoon without consulting her government, had to be put off once again when the president failed to appear.

Jacques-Roger Booh-Booh, the UN secretary-general's special representative and head of UNAMIR, sought to bolster Uwilingiyimana's fruitless efforts by contacting all the parties himself. But the impasse, now limited to the internal quarrels besetting the PL, went on until 14 January, when the swearing-in ceremony was again postponed, and then again on 20 January.

On 7, 10, and 13 February three meetings were held at UNAMIR headquarters to discuss the composition of the PL delegation, which then set 14 February for the installation ceremony, leaving the PL with enough time to devise a workable solution. It was then envisaged to set up a government in which a number of seats—those not yet constrained by internal party agreements—would remain vacant pending final resolution by various tribunals. Uwilingiyimana and Twagiramungu blocked this approach because they held a paper-thin minority in their own party (MDR). On 14 February President Habyarimana proposed a code of conduct to be applied to the political parties and the RPF during the transitional phase, anticipating that a general amnesty and complete administrative impartiality would guarantee democratic elections without risks of procedural maneuvering or trickery that could encourage the RPF to seize power. However, the RPF viewed the proposed code as "unrealistic."[12]

On 17 February the Security Council once again threatened to terminate UNAMIR's mandate if the transitional institutions were not installed. In the end, major concessions from one or the other resulted in general agreement on 20 February, in large part echoing the broad strokes of the solution previously worked out between Habyarimana and Uwilingiyimana, particularly in terms of the number of deputies apportioned to each of the two large political blocks: eleven and twelve, respectively, as opposed to eleven and eleven.[13] Numerous other strategic questions were also resolved: the presidency and vice presidency of the National Assembly; the selection of PL ministers; acknowledgment of Twagiramungu's leadership by the MDR Steering Committee; allowing a deputy from the CDR to be seated once it agreed to the code of ethics.

By this date, one could reasonably expect that the global compromise finalized among the domestic political parties would allow the TNA and the BBTG to be installed.

Indeed, with the consolidation of the Power wings of the opposition parties, the privileged alliance bonding the opposition with the RPF no longer held the majority (given the MDR Steering Committee's shift in favor of Murego, Karamira, and Nsengiyaremye; Félicien Gatabazi's "national" repositioning in the PSD; the split in the PL's executive leadership; etc.).[14] And a recalibrated balance of power in the TNA and the BBTG now held sway, reversing the extremely disadvantaged position for the president and his partisans when the Arusha Peace Accords were first signed in August 1993.

Despite all that, Habyarimana lacked confidence in a number of these leaders, recalling the choices that a few of them had made in favor of the RPF in June 1992. While MDR, PSD, and PL faction leaders were principally concerned with the posts they could obtain, the president viewed appointments to government positions as a matter of secondary importance. Such matters, in his view, should be dealt with at the end of the transition period, based on results from the ballot box. It was of greater urgency to carefully outline a political agreement and build consensus among the parties inspired by an "alliance for democracy."

To fully appreciate Habyarimana's stance in confronting the multiple challenges of a minority-blocking coalition in the National Assembly, the lack of confidence in the opposition leaders, and the need for a code of conduct, it bears noting that, above all, he feared becoming the target of a "constitutional coup d'état," when any convenient pretext could fuel an opposition coalition.[15] Behind such fears were motives that could hardly be made explicit or be debated publicly.

His sense of anguish at being indicted was the product of irrational anxiety, most likely brought on by the return of Col. Alexis Kanyarengwe, a longtime rival who had been expelled from Rwanda in 1980 but was now president of the RPF. There were also rumors of possible indictment for the killings of dignitaries from the First Republic, further heightening Habyarimana's fears. To protect him against removal from office, he needed to safeguard his maneuverability for the duration of the transitional period. For that he had to see to it that due attention be paid at least to one of the following three priorities:

- Joseph Kavaruganda, president of the Constitutional Court, would stay in office. After having been one of Habyarimana's most loyal supporters, Kavaruganda had just switched over to the MDR. Be that as it may, aside from validating the appointments to the TNA, the Constitutional Court also had authority to adjudicate any indictment brought against the president.

- The second priority concerned the post of minister of justice, considered highly strategic because the incumbent was responsible for any judicial inquiry linked to possible indictment of the president. However, this post was likely to fall to Aloys Niyoyita, a Tutsi and a member of the PL. He was aligned with the "Ndasingwa" wing and reportedly pro-RPF.
- The third was the qualified majority required for passing laws in the TNA, which was set at a two-thirds vote.

The major gamble during this waiting period revolved around the attitude of the president of the Constitutional Court, who on several occasions had sided with the opposition in negotiations over validating parliamentary appointments. Had Habyarimana trusted him, the transitional institutions would have been put in place within the agreed timetable, that is, at the beginning of 1994. But playing upon the president's personal insecurity was part of the opposition's strategy. All the same, a two-thirds majority vote was still required for any dismissal or appointment of senior state officials.

The assassination of Félicien Gatabazi (PSD) on 21 February was clearly intended to undermine the advances achieved by the domestic political opposition. The wildest rumors and the worst suspicions flared up and degenerated in violent clashes among the parties. This assassination confirmed the president's worst obsessions.

On 22 February what was intended as a last attempt to install the transitional institutions ended in disappointment when the RPF and PSD, as well as the two prime ministers (both the incumbent and the one designated to follow), along with the president of the Constitutional Court, all boycotted the ceremony. In the end, the opposition parties and the RPF accused Habyarimana of planning Gatabazi's assassination.

On 25 and 27 February the president invited all the parties (the two prime ministers and the heads of the parties—majority and minority leaders for the MDR and PL) to meet to discuss the pending issue regarding the representation of the PL, but the RPF refused, and its political leaders withdrew to Mulindi. One of Habyarimana's key concerns was to prevent the Tutsi PL candidate from acceding to the Ministry of Justice post. Ultimately, the PL did not prevail and found itself isolated. Consequently, the final communiqué circulated by the presidency on 27 February stated: "Those persons or groups not satisfied by the above-mentioned compromises will draw the appropriate lessons and conclusions and act accordingly."

On 1 March Jacques-Roger Booh-Booh traveled to Mulindi to appeal to the RPF to return to Kigali, without success. But on 9 March the RPF finally agreed that the TNA should be installed, even without specific provisions for the PL posts.

On 18 March, after intense negotiation, Faustin Twagiramungu sent the president a list of members of government acceptable to all the concerned parties and the next day followed up with the "final list" of members of parliament (MPs) proposed for the TNA. The latter set three conditions for acceptance: again, he refused to allow the minister of justice post to go to a Tutsi PL minister and insisted upon seating a CDR deputy and another from the Parti démocratique islamique (PDI, Islamic Democratic Party) in the TNA.

While the RPF and the CDR continued to independently negotiate a seat in parliament for the CDR under the auspices of UNAMIR, those demands were rejected outright, and the ceremonies planned for 25 March were rescheduled for the following day (with no greater success) when the RPF delegation failed to show up and Agathe Uwilingiyimana presented a list of deputies that failed to include the CDR representative (see annex 38).

On 28 March, when the RPF representatives, the prime minister designate, Joseph Kavaruganda, and numerous other deputies failed to show up, thus bringing the proceedings to an impasse, President Habyarimana declined even to travel to the parliament building. A meeting of diplomatic representatives from observer nations to the Arusha negotiations (the apostolic nuncio and ambassadors from Germany, Belgium, Burundi, the United States, France, Uganda, Tanzania, and Zaire), with Jacques-Roger Booh-Booh presiding, firmly and unanimously expressed exasperation with the obstructions, which in this instance seemed wholly caused by the RPF (see annex 38). The latter, completely isolated but for the personal support of Gen. Roméo Dallaire, reacted aggressively, instead blaming the leaders of the other parties, and threatened to withdraw its participation in the peace process.

Finally, after a firm warning from the United Nations, which again threatened withdrawal of UNAMIR troops if there was no progress, and with foreign embassies raising the specter of suspending aid, a final deadline was set for "before 9 April." This was the date set by the president, and he duly communicated it to his chief of staff immediately before setting off for Dar es Salaam on the morning of 6 April 1994.

All the lost time was not wasted for everyone: with each passing week, the main protagonists prepared themselves and remained on alert, expanding their reach, with efforts to occupy as much ground as possible, and taking precautionary measures in anticipation of every possible scenario. For the mouvance présidentielle, the strategy was clear: the priority was, as much as possible, to reverse the unfavorable balance of power in transitional institutions imposed by the peace accords. This was the opposite of what happened in 1991–92, when the opposition stoked institutional paralysis to undermine the last single-party government and mobilized on several fronts to expand its political influence and impose a government that it could control. The MRND, the CDR, and their allies, including the Power wings of the opposition parties at that point, used any excuse to delay installation of the TNA and the BBTG. They were intent on subverting the arithmetic of the peace accords, which marginalized them, and sought to advance the personal political ambitions of their chiefs. Thanks to the emergence of the Power wings and to the threat of a two-thirds majority coalition of opposition parties and the RPF, the MRND no longer controlled the transitional phase, and its ability to force decision making in the National Assembly was much diminished.

The "last list" of deputies finally accepted left the impression that the combined forces of the RPF and the FDC (MDR, PSD, PL, PDC, and PSR) delegates might not even garner a simple majority. Consequently, they were quite far from the two-thirds majority required to exercise control of the transitional institutions.

Where political maneuvering and blocking strategies were concerned, the margins were quite narrow, and neither of the two camps demonstrated a clear commitment to implementing the accords: as the former commander of the École supérieure militaire (ESM, Senior Military Training School [Kigali]), Léonidas Rusatira, testified before the Belgian Senate, "One was intent on keeping all power, while the other sought to take all power."[16] With undeniable success, the RPF devoted every energy to tightening its hold on the domestic political scene while scrambling for time; the FDC put the time to good use to improve its military capacities and communications strategy.

"Rumors were circulating in Kigali that the RPF arrived with three thousand men, including the six hundred officially housed at the CND. In the north, there were fifteen thousand RPF soldiers waiting for the signal for a coup d'état from Kigali. That explains their patience and their passivity in installing a government."[17] This remark, by a Belgian intelligence officer, encapsulates the RPF's modus operandi during those decisive months. Its "passivity," at least judging by appearances, was forced upon it by a polarized domestic political scene with deeply entrenched partisan rivalries, stoked by political bosses and factions that they created to further their ambitions and prepare for upcoming elections. At the time of the signature of the Arusha Peace Accords, all of the "national" players had already embarked upon the transition and could only think of the elections that lay ahead, elections that held no promise for the RPF. As the weeks passed, a scenario took shape that was reminiscent of 1992, when the multiparty government was first installed: a recentering of political life around domestic priorities, which in effect marginalized the RPF. For partisans of the mouvance présidentielle, the RPF "enemy" aroused concern only because of its military might and for its potential to split the domestic political opposition; for the opposition parties, the natural allies of the RPF, its utility declined as time went on, reducing its role to merely supporting and protecting figures or factions now in the minority.

It was clear that the RPF leaders would draw few benefits in the domestic arena from their recent military triumphs (beginning with the February 1993 offensive, followed by the withdrawal of French troops in December), their diplomatic successes through the Arusha Peace Accords, or their geostrategic advances in Burundi. Given the broad pro-Hutu consensus that developed in the wake of President Ndadaye's assassination in Burundi in October 1993, the political links that the RPF had enjoyed by proxy via the opposition parties were now exclusively limited to its pro-RPF factions (of the opposition parties). More broadly, the difficulty of engaging in public debate with no real independent political base of its own came to light during those brief periods when it withdrew from negotiations and recalled its representatives to Mulindi in late February and March 1994. Back in Kigali, the intense negotiations among the parties were hardly affected, and it was mainly foreign negotiators who ventured to Mulindi to try to get the RPF back on board in the peace process.

Only toward the end of March did diplomats fully grasp the fact that the RPF was exploiting divisions among its negotiating partners, the better to mask and conceal its own strategy of obstruction. Quite revealing in that regard are the negotiations that the RPF had initiated on its own with the CDR, its most obstinate adversary—until it rediscovered its satanic identity at the very moment when the other parties agreed that it should join in the accords.

Playing to unaware or undiscerning observers and portraying its adversaries as being solely responsible for blocking the transitional institutions, the RPF threatened a reprise of the war each time it met with frustration.

The RPF's Strategy: Destabilizing the Domestic Arena

As we have already seen, the strategies of obstructing and delaying the transitional institutions were calculated efforts by the various actors to enter the "transition" from positions of relative strength or, at worst, in the least unfavorable positions possible. As initially conceived, the Arusha Peace Accords would accommodate the interests of three political forces.

Subsequent developments imposed a bipolar framework, however, with the two dominant forces engaged in complex and oddly complementary maneuvers to either weaken the domestic opposition parties or rally them to their sides. This emerged as the only means for each camp to broaden or enlarge its base, to position itself for ascendancy at the end of the process.

This ruse started with the installation of the Dismas Nsengiyaremye government in April 1992, when splits and rivalries emerged within the broad alliance, which included some rather strong characters and barely structured political parties, anxious to break with the political culture inherited from the single-party era. But they too resorted to bare-knuckled tactics: extortion, threats, and physical assaults on party activists and even against common folk became commonplace and went on hand in hand with targeted or random killings of major political figures. The three months of negotiations preceding the resumption of hostilities in April 1994 were marked by a huge upswing in political violence and a proliferation of violent clashes among party militia.

The clarification sought in the political landscape relied on two different approaches, depending on whether it was sought by the mouvance présidentielle or by the RPF. The former focused its efforts on winning back members and party activists who had gone over to the opposition. This aggressive offensive was driven by a lingering fear of an RPF military takeover. Recruitment surged, and it was not even necessary to resort to spectacular ploys or coercive maneuvers. On the other hand, the RPF, hobbled on the political scene, resorted to a defensive approach, first by directing its propaganda at Tutsi inside Rwanda and in neighboring countries, encouraging them to join the RPF and its military RPA wing, and then by switching once again to political destabilization as the key objective, in effect leaving no other option to its allies or former allies but to choose sides.

On 21 February 1994 the assassination in Kigali of Félicien Gatabazi, executive secretary of the PSD and minister of public works, followed by the retaliatory lynching of Martin Bucyana, president of the CDR, the next day played a decisive role in the political radicalization that swept across the Butare prefecture and through the capital.

Gatabazi was among that group of remarkably strong individuals, all brilliant technicians originally from the south, whom Habyarimana had brought into his cabinet with ministerial appointments in the 1970s to counterbalance his rivals from the north. After the attempted coup d'état by Théoneste Lizinde and Alexis Kanyarengwe in 1980, the president relied heavily on this latter group, even as he sought to neutralize its more popular figures and progressively replace them with more docile southern politicians. The ministerial reshuffling of 8 January 1984 that led to the ousting of Félicien Gatabazi and

Frédéric Nzamurambaho, two of the most highly regarded southern figures, paved the way for the second most significant political crisis of the Second Republic. With the arrival of multipartyism in 1991, the instruments used by the former ruling party to exercise control over Butare suddenly collapsed, signaling an almost visceral rejection of domination by this small coterie of northern military and political figures. The opposition parties immediately claimed the majority, particularly the PSD, founded by the two most popular southern figures, who, quite symbolically, regained their former ministerial portfolios with the rise of Dismas Nsengiyaremye's multiparty government in April 1992.

According to Civipol, the United Nations Police Force, which was part of UNAMIR, Gatabazi's assassination had been orchestrated by Habyarimana's close associates. The names of Cap. Pascal Simbikangwa (Hutu, Gisenyi), a member of the intelligence service, and Alphonse Ntilivamunda (Hutu, Gisenyi, MRND), the president's son-in-law, were mentioned, and the driver for Col. Élie Sagatwa, another of the president's sons-in-law, was suspected of having transported the commando. Even complicity of members of the victim's family was considered.

Targeted for investigation by the Kigali prosecutor's office, this array of prestigious suspects explains the PSD activists' reaction in Butare: the very next day, Martin Bucyana, president of the CDR, was assassinated to avenge Gatabazi's death. In fact, on 22 February 1994 Martin Bucyana, targeted as the deserving scapegoat, spotted in Gikongoro, was followed by a vehicle identified with the Développement global de Butare (DGB, Butare Global Development) project driven by PSD activists. After crossing through Butare, he was set upon and lynched by PSD activists and the surrounding population. Several members of PSD were also RPF members.[18]

Given the general political context, suspicions immediately centered on "death squads" attached to the presidency. The possibility of an RPF-sponsored assassination assisted by PSD members was also considered. In support of this view are remarks made by Gatabazi himself, who is alleged to have made the following comment at a PSD meeting in Butare barely a week before he was killed. This comment was viewed by several analysts as his death warrant: "PSD, having never stooped to being a handmaiden for the MRND, will never become one for the RPF."[19] After a private audience with President Habyarimana, during which he shared his personal doubts about the RPF's commitment to democracy, his remarks seemed highly critical of those within his own party who failed to make clear distinctions between the PSD and the RPF.

There are two lines of argument that advance the notion of an RPF-sponsored assassination.

The first, a contextual argument, reconstructs what would have been the RPF's long-term strategy. Moving forward with the transitional government made sense so long as reliable allies for the RPF were in place, which did not appear to be the case with Félicien Gatabazi. The latter did not seem to approve of a new order dominated by the RPF, and he could easily become one of its most formidable adversaries, which clearly distinguished him from the three other members of the PSD Steering Committee: Félicien Ngango and Théoneste Gafaranga were "won over"; as for Frédéric Nzamurambaho, married to a Tutsi woman, he was viewed as sufficiently pliant. Eliminating Gatabazi was seen as a convenient way of making room for Gafaranga or Ngango in the transitional government. But the latter was already pegged to be the PSD candidate for the presidency of the TNA. Thus, he would become the second most important state official, and he could be called upon to replace the president in case of a vacancy. On many occasions the two other candidates had advanced the argument that Gatabazi was already overburdened with responsibilities in the key post of executive secretary of the PSD, which was incompatible with the additional responsibilities of a government minister. However, Gatabazi was already seriously thinking ahead and had considered the option of resigning his post as minister of public works. He could then position himself for appointment as deputy, which could lead to the presidency of the TNA post promised to Ngango while still holding on to his office as executive secretary of the party. Additionally, the disappearance of Gatabazi would reorient the party, bringing it more into line with pro-RPF elements, and would significantly weaken it nationally and deprive it of major financial resources.

The second argument, which complements the first, proposes an alternate reading of events immediately leading up to Gatabazi's assassination. That Sunday, the day before he died, Gatabazi was quite candid with his close associates and confided that he was in danger. On Monday, 21 February, when it was already late and he was returning from the interior of the country, he received a phone call from Faustin Twagiramungu, then at the Hôtel Méridien, inviting Gatabazi to join him on the top floor. The latter had spent the entire afternoon in a meeting at UNAMIR headquarters with the secretary-general's special representative, Jacques-Roger Booh-Booh, discussing modalities for installation of the BBTG, which was scheduled for the following morning at 10:00. Aside from Faustin Twagiramungu, also present for the meeting were Frédéric Nzamurambaho (president of the PSD), Landoald Ndasingwa (first vice president of the PL), Agathe Uwilingiyimana (prime minister), and Jean-Népomuscène Nayinzira (Hutu, Gisenyi, president of the PDC). After the meeting, most of them retreated to the restaurant at the Hôtel Méridien, and

Faustin Twagiramungu telephoned several key figures who did not attend the afternoon meeting to ask that they join him to discuss the last few details and to finalize the preparations for the ceremonies scheduled for the next morning. Froduald Karamira and Donat Murego of the MDR could not be found; the MRND's Matthieu Ngirumpatse and the PL's Justin Mugenzi both declined, citing the need to first consult their party leadership, and they referred to the lateness of the hour to excuse themselves. Félicien Gatabazi alone accepted. In the end, no meeting was ever held when he got there, since Twagiramungu spent most of that evening on the telephone. Each returned home, except for Gatabazi, who was ambushed in a fusillade not far from his home around 10:45 that night. He managed to drive his vehicle up to his gate, where he collapsed. Over sixty spent shells were recovered from the scene.

In fact, by the time Gatabazi left the hotel, the commando charged with eliminating him had been informed of his impending arrival and was already in position not far from his residence (*see annex 15*). The assassination was supervised by Cdr. Emmanuel Karenzi Karake (Tutsi, originally from Zaire, RPA/RPF), a liaison officer with UNAMIR and head of the commandos in Kigali, posted to the Hôtel Méridien with four other RPA officers. Three of them actually resided there: Cdr. Salton Bahenda (Tutsi, Zaire, RPA/RPF), Capt. Godfrey Butare (Tutsi, Uganda, RPA/RPF), and Maj. Philbert Rwigamba (Tutsi, Uganda, RPA/RPF).

On 21 February, when the order was given to eliminate Gatabazi, there was no doubt that the killing would be imputed to death squads linked to the presidency. In fact, the night before, Sunday, 20 February, during a raucous meeting in Nyamirambo that Agathe Uwilingiyimana and Faustin Twagiramungu had organized to demonstrate their fortitude in facing down attacks from the MDR Power wing, members of the MRND, CDR, and MDR Power wings used grenades and stones against the vehicles transporting their supporters. Many were injured, and six others were killed at Rwampara, not far from Nyamirambo. Had an UNAMIR escort not been on hand, Uwilingiyimana and Twagiramungu could have met the same fate.

And, as expected, on the morning of 22 February, after news of Gatabazi's death had circulated, PSD president Frédéric Nzamurambaho blamed the presidency for the work of the assassins. The approach adopted for the judicial inquiry and the ensuing initial arrests officially confirmed that view. Rumors immediately swirled around close associates of President Habyarimana.

For its part, the mouvance présidentielle blamed the opposition leaders who had participated in the meeting at the Hôtel Méridien. In that context, CDR president Martin Bucyana's elimination seemed quite natural: his death was indeed widely perceived as an expression of "spontaneous revenge." The

MRND and the CDR, however, put forward compelling evidence: the plot had been hatched by Faustin Twagiramungu, Agathe Uwilingiyimana, and the pro-RPF leaders of the PSD and PL in reprisal for the violent clashes provoked by the MRND and Power party members and militiamen in Nyamirambo on 20 February. At a later stage, when the RPF fell under suspicion, the thesis of an organized plot won out. Ngirumpatse interprets events in this manner: "We understood, finally, that the objective was to trap the leaders of the MDR, MRND, CDR, and PL all together, to kill them all the same night. Just as in the past, when the RPF and its allies had accused President Habyarimana of eliminating his opponents, here was yet another opportune moment to accuse him not only of annihilating the opposition but also of eliminating the most democratic elements of his own party. The method was tried and true and was put to good use each time they needed to get rid of someone irksome."[20] This version serves to illustrate just how bitter the enmity among domestic political party leaders had become and the wide leeway that it gave their common adversary.

No doubt, the RPF had hopes that the internecine infighting provoked by the assassination would have the effect of a poisoned offering—it would deal a telling blow to the leadership of the various parties and provoke a general sense of chaos in the lead-up to the RPF's final offensive. If so, the thesis of a Twagiramungu/RPF conspiracy is difficult to imagine: the RPF was too structured and cloistered to ever allow joint operations of this nature with an opposition that it never really respected or trusted and that it had never truly viewed as partners or associates, unless merely as a ploy to divide them.

The assassinations of Gatabazi and Bucyana provoked violent clashes among party militias, leading to thirty-seven casualties in Kigali. The clashes only stopped when the leadership of the various parties began to take stock of the political dividends that the RPF was reaping from those clashes. In fact, just as in January 1993, after massacres of Tutsi and opposition figures in Gisenyi, Ruhengeri, Kibuye, and Byumba prefectures, by 24 February 1994 the RPF had taken to the Radio Muhabura airwaves with threats of responding to political obstructions from the mouvance présidentielle with further military action. At that point the RPF had already violated the cease-fire agreement with the massive 8 February 1993 offensive on Ruhengeri and Byumba. By late February or early March 1994, the RPF relied on the Ugandan press to prime its partisans for a sure victory. In a press release dated 28 February, RPF president Alexis Kanyarengwe wrote: "The horror must have reached its ultimate height on the evening of 21 February 1994, when killers acting on behalf of President Habyarimana assassinated M. Gatabazi Félicien, Minister of Public Works." In *Uganda Confidential*, 28 February–7 March 1994, one can read:

"The likelihood of Kagame taking Kigali are [*sic*] now multiplied by 100." In the *People* of 4–8 March 1994, in remarks attributed to Paul Kagame, he claimed to have had enough means, equipment, and troops to take Kigali within a single day and that he was ready to do so. This attitude was confirmed by the man himself, directly to Gen. Roméo Dallaire, as reflected in the latter's trial testimony:

> So, in my opinion, the RPF was exceptionally well trained.
> In my analysis even before the war, I said that if they are so well trained and in good shape, they could be waiting for the eventuality of the peace accords to fail. In May—I beg your pardon. Prior to that, Kagame said that if there was no solution, then they had to take a definitive solution.
> BY MR. CONSTANT:
> Q. You meant February, General? I thought I had heard May?
> A. No, I meant February.[21]

On 31 March, in line with its efforts to neutralize the leadership of extremist Hutu groups, the RPA assassinated Alphonse Ingabire, alias "Kayumba," the head of the CDR for Kigali. According to its own internal sources, the RPA had put Kiyago, the head of commandos for Zone E (Entrée), and Sgt. Mugisha, the head for Zone Kosovo (covering the neighborhoods of Kicukiro, Remera, Masaka, and Ndera in Kigali), in charge of the operation. Accompanying them was Lt. Jean-Baptiste Mugwaneza.[22]

Insider information made available to me reveals that this RPF campaign of assassinations was set to begin on 17 February 1994, with PL first vice president Landoald Ndasingwa as its first target. He had already been targeted in three prior unsuccessful attempts, the first on the night of 17 February, and the other two on 18 and 19 February.

The fallout from the assassinations of Félicien Gatabazi and Martin Bucyana seems to have satisfied the RPF's initial objectives, and the remaining plans for the campaign were dropped. Among the other leaders targeted were, notably, Joseph Kavaruganda (the president of the Constitutional Court), Stanislas Mbonampeka of the MDR, Justin Mugenzi of the PL, and the MRND's Pauline Nyiramasuhuko. As one can see, the RPF leadership had a broad range of targets and was actually preparing to decapitate the PL, the last of the major parties that still had formidable leaders, the major arena of struggles for control of the TNA. As for Joseph Kavaruganda, a key figure in terms of the institutional transition, he had become President Habyarimana's sworn enemy.

Recalling that all of the parties engaged in the Arusha process, including the RPF, had convened on 21 February to jointly issue a communiqué fixing the very next day for installation of the BBTG and the TNA, news that only made its way to the UN special representative of the secretary-general around 9:00 that same night, one can readily appreciate how the timing of Félicien Gatabazi's assassination fits into the RPF's overarching strategic objective of derailing the peace accords.

Thus, by the end of February 1994, RPF commandos had partially decapitated the MDR, PSD, and CDR and had sown great confusion in the painstakingly recomposed leadership circles of the domestic opposition parties, gravely exacerbating tensions across the entire political landscape.

The MDR managed to survive, but with its leadership shattered. Finding a replacement for Martin Bucyana at the head of the CDR hardly posed a problem (targeting a southerner was largely symbolic, since the true leaders were from the north). However, it was very difficult to resuscitate the PSD, which, until Gatabazi's assassination, had been so thoroughly dominated by its charismatic leader. The party activists were subjected to intense pressure from the two competing camps, and the burgeoning political split came fully into view with elections for Gatabazi's replacement in the party's secretariat.

Toward the beginning of March 1994, the Political Bureau unanimously selected Augustin Iyamuremye, whose candidacy had been advanced by Frédéric Nzamurambaho of the pro-RPF faction, but the Butare regional committee blocked this move. Its objective was to push through Sylvestre Uwibajije, then ambassador to Burundi. Coming together in a party congress in Butare on 12 March, just as Uwibajije formally launched his candidacy, the party confirmed the vote of the Political Bureau. Thus, the pro-RPF wing shored itself up with support from the party leadership but in so doing relinquished the backing of party activists beyond the southern prefectures.

The MRND Strategy
for Duping the Opposition

For its part, the MRND had not given up on efforts to destabilize the opposition. Beyond their shared objective of encouraging defections from the opposition, all the political leaders were in agreement to harass and criticize Agathe Uwilingiyimana for not fully exercising her duties (*see annex 39*). At the same time, they wanted to force her resignation so that the president could fill the institutional void as he saw fit. Here we had a situation totally unforeseen in the Arusha Peace Accords.

The collapse on the domestic scaffolding was achieved by plotting and duplicity from one side or the other, and, given the tight institutional deadlines fixed by the Arusha Peace Accords, each side was willing to play its trump card. By way of example, consider this:

> On 31 December 1993 a meeting was held at the residence of Prime Minister Agathe Uwilingiyimana with Prime Minister designate Faustin Twagiramungu and ministers from the parties constituting the Democratic Forces for Change (MDR, PSD, PL, and PDC) in attendance. The FDC group was in contact with RPF based in CND and was in favor of the said accords.
>
> The meeting examined various strategies to marginalize the MRND and President Habyarimana. Some participants even advocated an attack to destabilize the armed forces, which I objected to insofar as, at least in theory, by virtue of the law, the armed forces depended on the authority of the head of the government led by a prime minister belonging to the MDR, a member of the FDC. Destabilizing the FAR turned out to be a risky political operation for a government already undermined by the MRND group of ministers who used to block any action that might give credit to Prime Minister Agathe Uwilingiyimana.
>
> At the end of the discussions, an FDC delegation went to the CND to reconcile positions with the RPF in the context of the prescribed time limits for the setting up of transitional institutions [five days later].[23]

These hints of subterfuge and duplicity in the institutional political framework grew even stronger after 5 January, when the president was sworn in but the transition got bogged down in failed attempts to install the TNA, initially brought on by fresh demands from Agathe Uwilingiyimana. Various exchanges of correspondence, some particularly harsh, amplified by pronouncements over the national airwaves, confirmed her refusal to allow routine functioning of a government cabinet that had not been duly sworn in. She regularly held restricted meetings with representatives from the opposition parties and, where necessary, larger meetings including the few ministers concerned by problems of security. Her main interlocutor for matters that needed to be addressed with the MRND was André Ntagerura, its most senior member.

In addition, and its supporters did not seek to conceal it, an "insurrectional" strategy to unseat the prime minister won favor from the more "conservative" elements of the mouvance présidentielle. This was a strategy that the more "liberal" MRND members never sought to explicitly disavow.

Two plainly opposed points of view emerged. The first held that President Habyarimana had largely lost control of the situation, that his moderation or ambivalence had alienated the more extremist wing of his camp, and that the latter plotted openly to push him aside and organize a coup d'état. For supporters of this viewpoint, the split had penetrated to the heart of the Akazu, and even his wife's clan was leaning in that direction. It would appear that many representatives of foreign embassies shared this view, surmising that the president had "lost his grip" and his control over the unfolding events.

The second view instead postulated that the president's deliberate wait-and-see strategy was more in line with his personality, as confirmed by many of his closest associates. By that time, Habyarimana had already regained a large share of his long-standing popularity, which he cultivated with numerous public appearances and declarations, and had taken full control of the MRND by playing upon the rivalry between its president, Matthieu Ngirumpatse, and the national secretary, Joseph Nzirorera. After all, it was to him personally that the party's militant armed wing, the Interahamwe youth, pledged allegiance. Within the army, a broad reassertion of control by officers personally devoted to him was under way in the wake of Defense Minister James Gasana's flight abroad.[24] At the same time, a proliferation of parties and political groups, more or less radical in outlook, all inching toward the mouvance présidentielle, allowed a parsing out of roles on the political scene that then gave the president center stage. The president took turns with one group or the other, offering approval and falling back on his role as the moderator and guarantor of political stability whenever events or the evolving power dynamics required it. Even if there were members of his entourage who did not hesitate to debate or challenge one or the other of his decisions, no one dared to speak in favor of changes that might force Habyarimana from the scene.[25]

In this regard, for the MRND and the mouvance présidentielle, the strategy of institutional obstruction only offered advantages. First of all, it allowed a play for time, which gave each side a chance to recruit and mobilize additional supporters to win over the population. Unfortunately, this also risked provoking the RPF's impatience, which could lead it to take up arms again, as it had done repeatedly since 1991, even at the cost of inviting condemnation from the international community and the broader population.

The possibility of a resumption of hostilities was not particularly alarming. In fact, protected by the Arusha Peace Accords, the MRND and its allies could legitimately position themselves before the population and the international community as entirely justified in defending themselves against the RPF. But, more fundamentally, as it emerges in the account from a former government minister, an opportunity like that would allow the MRND to pressure and lobby firmly in favor of "a renegotiation of the Arusha Accords, which had been overly in favor of the RPF. The government party would undertake such negotiations in a position of strength, as the MRND and its allies felt that with massive support from the population and Interahamwe, the RPF would have difficulties on the battlefield, as it would no longer be able to rely on its fifth column (made up of squads of infiltrators), which would have been neutralized by popular resistance."[26]

This government minister could not have put it better, because it was on exactly these dates, 30 and 31 March 1994, that the minister of defense and the Kigali prefecture office held several preparatory meetings to organize the civil self-defense. Their initiatives linked demobilized soldiers with trained militia-men in efforts to mobilize volunteers at the level of the sectors and cells in the three communes of Kigali-ville prefecture and in the neighboring communes (*see annex 40*).

The push for improving organization coincided with the increasing pace of meetings among the domestic opposition parties, and between them and the RPF, to boost security for their activists and leading figures. The meetings started in early March and were held until the evening of 6 April, but not all the meetings shared the same objectives. The only meeting ever made public was an occasion for the various tendencies aligned with the Alliance pour le renforcement de la démocratie (ARD, Alliance for the Strengthening of De-mocracy) and the CDR together to once again demand an end to the multi-party government of Agathe Uwilingiyimana. The opportunity came on 2 April 1994, when the latter was accused of planning a preemptive coup d'état with several southern-based military officers whom she had gathered at her home the evening before.

The idea for the meeting came from Capt. Bernard Ndayisaba, a security officer for the general staff and for Jean-Berchmans Habinshuti, Agathe Uwilingiyimana's private secretary. The meeting sought to bring together army men and "notables" from Butare prefecture so that they could get to know each other better, discuss the various problems in their prefecture, analyze the restructuring that was planned for the army, and shed some light on how to proceed with regard to the anticipated demobilizations. Above all, there was need to reassure them that they would remain untouched by these measures, which principally concerned officers from the north. The question of reinforc-ing security measures for installation of the BBTG was also broached.

That meeting, conceived as the first in a long series, was intended to facili-tate contacts among various members of the armed forces who were sympa-thetic to the domestic opposition parties. Gendarmerie captain Jean-Baptiste Iradukunda had contacted around twenty or so officers and noncommissioned officers.[27] Agathe Uwilingiyimana was supposed to invite two senior officers from natives of Butare, Col. Alphonse Nteziryaryo and Maj. Gen. Augustin Ndindiliyimana, but in the end neither was invited, as they were seen as too unreliable by some. The same can be said for Col. François Munyengango, who was viewed as too politically aloof. Once all was said and done, seventeen southern-based officers and noncommissioned officers participated in the meeting (*see annex 41*).

After the meeting, later that same night, one of the officers, Édouard Gasarabwe, made a report to his superior officer, Lt. Col. Juvénal Bahufite, operational sector commander for Byumba, who had given him permission to attend the meeting. Bahufite then gave a full account to Army Chief of Staff Déogratias Nsabimana, and the story of the meeting eventually made its way to the RTLM, which then launched an alarming media campaign pillorying the prime minister, already viciously targeted for having denied the CDR a seat in the TNA. The day after the meeting, another participant, Lt. Pascal Baziruwiha, had been summoned before Augustin Ndindiliyimana, who was highly irritated to learn from his G2 staff officer that Agathe Uwilingiyimana, his neighbor and, like him, a native of Nyaruhengeri commune in Butare, had organized such a gathering.[28] He immediately called her to express his disappointment. And then, given the distressingly alarmist climate at the time and fearing the heavy price that could be exacted for nodding approval of the "putsch," the families of Augustin Ndindiliyimana (then on vacation at the family home in Nyaruhengeri) and of Édouard Karemera (who was staying there as well) supposedly sought refuge at the home of Col. Marcel Gatsinzi, commander of the joint military district Butare-Gikongoro. The latter, already having taken in the family of former MRND secretary-general Bonaventure Habimana, could not accommodate them, and the two families turned to the gendarmerie commander, Maj. Cyriaque Habyarabatuma. He too was unable to take in two additional families but nonetheless provided them with an escort, who returned with them to the Ndindiliyimana residence and stayed on to provide security.

A new political rallying cry was born, and the extremist press and the mouvance présidentielle ran amok with it, as did the MRND president.

According to accounts from all those in attendance, neither the tone nor the content of that meeting bore any hint of insurrection (*see annex 41*). By all appearances, any aspiring putschist would have taken care to surround himself with more seasoned followers than this team of inexperienced noncommissioned officers, so clearly lacking in the military or political experience to get involved in such a risky move. As an example of the prime minister's lack of foresight in a matter as lofty as a coup d'état, the only officer who was invited, one who was thoroughly lacking in any real political experience, deemed it prudent to protect himself by first informing his superior officer, who was happy to allow the meeting to go forward, only to deliver news of it the next day to a scandal-mongering RTLM, certain to ignite a media sensation. But as various leaders and MRND ministers, and even Jean Kambanda (the rival of

Agathe Uwilingiyimana who had managed to seize the head of the MDR with the Power wing of the party), have since recounted, it all boiled down to the umpteenth maneuver to destabilize or topple the prime minister, orchestrated by her adversaries in the mouvance présidentielle.

Unlike other MDR figures and opposition leaders, Agathe Uwilingiyimana had few misgivings about organizing a meeting of this nature since, contrary to popular opinion, she was never wholeheartedly committed to Faustin Twagiramungu's pro-RPF stance. Among opposition figures, she was quite explicitly with the "nationalists," much like Emmanuel Gapyisi and Félicien Gatabazi, that is, those who refused to acquiesce to the RPF's grab for power. And when they spoke, she did not refrain from openly expressing her opinions to Habyarimana: "I am not Faustin Twagiramungu," "I am not RPF," "I make my own decisions as prime minister."[29] Even so, in popular opinion, Uwilingiyimana's reputation as a stubborn adversary of the president hinged on the rather straightforward and generally bitter exchanges between them, which were quite removed from the diplomatic language most observers had grown accustomed to. But that certainly did not hinder their working together or sharing similar apprehensions on issues of major concern.

Given the sensitive political context, one cannot avoid observing that hosting a gathering of this nature revealed, at the very least, a certain political clumsiness on the part of the prime minister. Openly receiving soldiers in her home, simply on the basis of regional affinities, makes short shrift of the tacit rule that soldiers should stay outside the realm of politics and refrain from showing partisan allegiance.[30] If proselytism was not on the agenda that evening, then Agathe Uwilingiyimana forced considerable risks upon her guests even if the FAR general staff refused to court ridicule by actually taking measures against the young and inexperienced noncommissioned officers it had branded as dangerous putschists.

Even so, the fallout from the meeting was not negligible. As confirmed by quite a few accounts, many hard-line elements of the regime took the notion of this "southern" threat quite seriously, all the more so given that it occurred at the same time that heads of the opposition parties were meeting with the RPF.

But the cabal did not stop there. In the confusion, Ngirumpatse (MRND president) and Augustin Ndindiliyimana (the gendarmerie chief of staff) were also suspected of collusion with Uwilingiyimana. Their presumed concessions and deals with Tutsi and confirmed "accomplices" were once again subject to scrutiny. Because of Ngirumpatse's consistent support of Robert Kajuga (president of the National Committee of the Interahamwe, previously denounced as an RPF infiltrator by northern elements of the "parallel committee" mounted by Nzirorera) and Kassim Turatsinze (the UNAMIR informer, the "traitor"; see chapter 6), suspicion stemmed, just as it had for Ndindiliyimana, in part from the supposed links between Uwilingiyimana and the MDR officers, in part from her Tutsi military escorts, and in part from her support for joint operations with UNAMIR to search and raid Interahamwe weapons caches.

While both Ngirumpatse and Ndindiliyimana were lambasted as potential beneficiaries of a coup d'état fomented by the opposition with officers from the south—which would have catapulted one to the presidency and placed the other at the helm of the army—Ngirumpatse was accused of being the chief instigator because he alone had the authority to involve the National Committee of the Interahamwe in the plan (*see annex 42*).

Although the deadline for installing the transitional institutions was fast approaching, the opportune disclosure of this putsch attempt offered Joseph Nzirorera an unexpected opportunity to marginalize southerners, pro-RPF, and pro-Arusha elements within the MRND and their supporters in the army. The various accusations were thus reported to President Habyarimana, who summoned Robert Kajuga for an explanation—a truly exceptional invitation for someone maligned as a "delinquent" and a "vagabond" (and a Tutsi to boot)—on the morning of 7 April, upon his return from Dar es Salaam.

This maneuver by Nzirorera would appear to many as a final attempt to influence Habyarimana's decision whether or not to continue with the "transition." Nzirorera knew full well why Habyarimana had relinquished the party presidency to Ngirumpatse: because his vision offered the most realistic prospects for transforming the MRND into a party of truly national scope, which would significantly improve his hopes for a triumphant victory in the national elections, something that was beyond Joseph Nzirorera's capacity as an entrenched northerner. But Nzirorera also knew that the northern-based dignitaries of the regime, their natural political base, would never tolerate a transfer of power that would so radically dispossess them.

This collectively satanic portrayal of Uwilingiyimana, the southern officers (*see annex 41*), Ngirumpatse, and Ndindiliyimana, not to mention the demands made upon the president for punitive action projected by the northern-based officers and echoed by the RTLM, clearly illustrates their determination to force his hand in siding with Nzirorera against Ngirumpatse. The message was straightforward: Habyarimana must abandon his balancing act and, before endorsing the accords, act decisively against the RPF for as long as it shunned negotiation. Now, with Habyarimana having agreed that the soldiers who gathered at Uwilingiyimana's home should be penalized, and with Robert Kajuga summoned for explanations, Nzirorera could rest assured that, at last, he had made some crucial headway.

The notion that these events may have precipitated Habyarimana's assassination cannot be dismissed out of hand. Open conflict at the very top of the party founded by the "father of the nation," that last enduring remnant of stability on the domestic front, beyond its symbolic value, strongly upset the internal and external balance of forces. It considerably intensified the risks of chaos and the dangers conjured by the Arusha Peace Accords.

When Habyarimana traveled to Dar es Salaam to finalize the peace accords, the underlying rivalries between his potential successors had the effect of exacerbating regional tensions and weakening the party leadership at the worst possible moment. The first alternative in these conditions was to accept the denials of the so-called putschists and support Ngirumpatse's strategy, which he had already endorsed by signing the Arusha Peace Accords in the first place. Within the framework of the accords, the concessions that Ngirumpatse supported (especially concerning Faustin Twagiramungu, who had been designated prime minister in the transitional government) definitively suspended the brokering of alliances between domestic parties and political groupings where both the TNA and the BBTG were concerned. In that regard, the voices of the RPF's deputies and the positions taken by its ministers only held sway in marginal decision making. The second alternative was to sideline Ngirumpatse in favor of Nzirorera and, with or without signing on to Arusha, give the "green light" to a firm and lasting cohabitation with the RPF and its supporters in the transitional institutions.

However, while many agreed that the president needed the support of both Ngirumpatse and Nzirorera, all Habyarimana could do at that stage, without running the risk of splintering the MRND, was to ask Ngirumpatse to exercise patience and adopt a low profile to avoid provoking the hardliners in the MRND, who had to be persuaded that signing the peace accords did not mean caving in to the demands of the RPF. At this very crucial moment it seemed that only Habyarimana had the political heft to overcome this conflict and convince the mouvance présidentielle to accept the transition.

As we shall see, this settling of accounts within the MRND between Ngirumpatse and Nzirorera, indirectly implicating members of the National Committee of the Interahamwe and the army high command, weighed heavily on the decisions taken on the morning of 7 April, when MRND leaders met with Théoneste Bagosora (see chapter 7). Once again, the MRND was confronted with polarizing figures. Two putschists, each claiming legitimacy—Ngirumpatse as president of the MRND and Uwilingiyimana as prime minister of the multiparty government responsible for installing the transitional institutions—found themselves involuntarily brought together, each with major responsibilities.

During this extremely tense period, the key issue for the overwhelming majority of Rwandans was no longer a question of pondering who or what would replace Habyarimana. For some, the threat of an RPF takeover justified a politics of national redemption that rallied around the president; for others, the fear of having radical pro-Hutu extremists capture power pushed them into the arms of the RPF.

Strategies of Political Survival for the Self-Proclaimed "Democrats"

During that last week leading up to the implementation of the transitional institutions, the internal opposition made several desperate grabs for protection and survival. As an MDR member has recounted:

I am not aware of any specific meeting to prepare any sort of military contingency plan. However, at the beginning of March 1994, I participated in a meeting of opposition parties to find some sort of compromise position that could lead to implementing the BBTG. During that meeting, it was said that if the government was not rapidly installed, there was genuine concern that the militias might kill off the leaders of the opposition and that, in the midst of the confusion, the president would declare a state of emergency and suspend the Arusha Accords, claiming that the population had rejected them. Dr. Théoneste Gafaranga [Hutu, Gitarama, PSD] suggested that the opposition should create a self-defense force to protect its leaders. He suggested recruiting trustworthy youth and sending them off to Mulindi, where they could get appropriate training by RPF specialists. He claimed that the RPF had already agreed to this approach. However, no decision was ever taken at that meeting.[31]

But, anticipating the radicalization in the political climate that would come with implementing the BBTG, the leaders of the opposition really began to sense an urgency for ensuring their security. In late March, around the 28th, a preparatory meeting was held at the Hôtel Milles Collines with Faustin Twagiramungu of the MDR and various other party leaders, including Aaron Makuba of the PSD, Landoald Ndasingwa of the PL, Frédéric Nzamurambaho and Emmanuel Ndindabahizi of the PSD, and Jean-Népomuscène Nayinzira of the PDC, to explore the means of improving security for party activists and leaders of the opposition.

That is when the idea was floated to organize meetings with opposition leaders and soldiers from their home prefectures who seemed in sympathy with their parties. On 1 April Agathe Uwilingiyimana held the first in a proposed series of meetings when she invited a number of southern officers to her home. One of the main points in the discussion of late March, which apparently was not made known to the prime minister, had to do with setting up a unit for "armed response." She also apparently was not aware that among her guests was a freight forwarder who was responsible for providing weapons to the RPF in Kigali. Arrangements had been made for a delivery of eight hundred rifles from Kenya, and the RPF was supposed to organize training for candidates put forward by the various party youth wings.[32]

Generally speaking, the RPF's intransigence was on full display in order to prod the leaders of the opposition to choose sides. According to an MDR party leader,

> On 2 April 1994 the Tanzanian ambassador organized a meeting with an RPF delegation and members of the MDR to work out a compromise position for implementing the BBTG.[33] I personally participated. The RPF delegation included Seth Sendashonga, Tito Rutaremara, and Abdul Harelimana. I do not recall the presence of Patrick Mazimpaka. All pending matters—composition of the government, getting rid of figures linked to Hutu Power, reconciliation within MDR and the democratic opposition parties, collaboration between the RPF and the democratic opposition—were resolved, except one: the CDR's participation in the transitional institutions. The RPF delegation categorically opposed admitting a CDR deputy to the TNA, which ruined all hopes of getting beyond the crisis.
>
> I told the RPF delegation that their position was blocking the situation and could cause the entire peace process to fall apart, which would lead to more violence. Seth Sendashonga responded that for the RPF not giving in was possible and that the risk of violent outbreaks hardly concerned them. In any case, "you cannot make an omelet without breaking some eggs, and if the MRND is foolish enough to relaunch hostilities, the RPF is ready to respond and will take power in less than a week." I asked him if he had given any thought to the number of victims that might suffer, and he added: "There would not be that many. Maybe five thousand. At the most, twenty thousand." The meeting ended in confusion, with all the non-RPF participants convinced that catastrophe was not to be ruled out and was fast approaching.[34]

Another meeting had been organized with RPF leaders in the late afternoon of 6 April at the Tanzanian Embassy (in the absence of the ambassador, who was participating in the talks in Dar es Salaam) with Patrick Mazimpaka, Seth Sendashonga, Tito Rutaremara, Abdul Harelimana, Aaron Mukuba,

Faustin Twagiramungu, Landoald Ndasingwa, and Boniface Ngulinzira. The objective was to put the finishing touches on the alliance between "opponents" of the mouvance présidentielle and the RPF. Polarization was becoming reality.

As much for the arithmetic as for its political implications, the matter of the CDR participating in the transitional institutions was a huge risk: on the one hand, the opposition's anticipated majority in the TNA, most likely held by only one or two votes, and, on the other, that party's antecedents and extremist positions made it a special case. However, in the eyes of international negotiators and their spokespersons, the American ambassador and the papal nuncio, the absolute priority of the moment was to rapidly install the transitional institutions. Given the gravity of the risks involved, it might have seemed preferable to have the CDR formally included, as opposed to casting it in the role of a victim excluded from the political arena. After the first promising exchanges between the CDR and RPF leaders, organized under the auspices of the United Nations in mid-March, the RPF's categorical refusal to accept any future role for a CDR deputy caused the ambassadors in charge of negotiations to view its intransigence as the main stumbling block behind the failure of the Arusha Peace Accords. The negotiators, including those who usually supported the RPF positions, started to seriously question the RPF's willingness to install the transitional institutions. Albeit for very different reasons, the two United Nations officials in charge of monitoring the implementation of the Arusha Peace Accords, Jacques-Roger Booh-Booh and Roméo Dallaire, shared the same sense of foreboding: the peace process was fast coming to an end (*see annex 39*).

By then, however, President Habyarimana, the MRND, and its allies could reasonably expect that the end of the transition would work to their advantage. As for the RPF, its positioning in the domestic political sphere seemed more uncertain than ever; the future looked dim.

The next phase, marked by the reprise of war, shows that the UN negotiators' observations were well founded. But before embarking upon this tragic shift, it is important to comment briefly on one of the major political forces that was called upon to play a decisive role in this new context, the militia youth wings.

6

Competition for Control
of the Militias

MRND chairman Matthieu Ngirumpatse was a fervent proponent of the thesis that the groups engaged in collective action, including violent action, emerged spontaneously. He would have us believe that the Rwandan political landscape was shaped by the best of intentions. By and large, interactions among Rwandan politicians were driven by friendly intellectual debate, ultimately turning on the relative merits and competencies of candidates vying for office. In a 1998 interview, Ngirumpatse described the Interahamwe as an organization that came into being all on its own: "There was also the MRND youth wing, the Interahamwe, who were not formed by the party, and this is a point that I have to emphasize. In their minds, people should not continue making this conclusion. The Interahamwe, the party's youth wing, was not created by the party. The young people themselves decided to . . . form a party."[1] In Ngirumpatse's book *La tragédie rwandaise,* he also states: "They spontaneously set up their steering committee and submitted their project to President Habyarimana and, subsequently, to the organs of the party."[2]

Such nonsense is surprising when it comes from someone as experienced as Ngirumpatse; even the most cursory review of the Interahamwe history shows how little evidence there is in support of this argument. In fact, their founding fathers met with astounding success and could hardly have avoided attracting attention from political leaders keen to mobilize a militant workforce.

The Interahamwe took form during the last three months of 1991. The initial nucleus was composed of young men in Kigali, Hutu and Tutsi alike, who were members of the Loisirs football team, organized by Désiré Murenzi, at that time director general of Petrorwanda and member of the MRND prefectural committee in Kigali-rural. For him, at that time, the objective was simply to assemble a crew of grassroots party activists to spread the ideals of the MRND, relying on the model of associative movements like the Jehovah's Witnesses. Ranking equally high on its agenda was to gather together youth who had the will and the capacity to counter the attacks on MRND members then occurring in certain neighborhoods of Kigali, like Nyamirambo, under the slogan "Northerners for the North." Along with Désiré Murenzi there was Robert Kajuga (the captain of the football team), Éric Karekezi, and those who eventually became members of the National Committee of the Interahamwe, including Eugène Mbarushimana and Dieudonné Niyitegeka.[3] These members formed what would later become known as the official Executive Committee.

The group generally got together on Wednesday afternoons in a building near the Ministry of Planning belonging to Védaste Rubangura, a wealthy Tutsi businessman in Kigali who made several rooms available to the MRND.[4] The meetings could swell to two hundred persons of diverse backgrounds, political lightweights for the most part, who knew each other fairly well from common sporting or extraprofessional activities. As the meetings progressed, with increasingly numerous participants, the interest and presence of MRND officials became more and more pronounced. Figuring prominently among them were Matthieu Ngirumpatse, Charles Nyandwi, François Karera (sub-prefect for political and administrative affairs in Kigali-rural prefecture), and Enoch Ruhigira (the president's chief of staff).[5] These influential political figures came to get a sense of what was going on and took a keen interest in Murenzi's original initiative. Whenever they attended, they offered words of encouragement to these steadfast party youth, who refused to switch over to the opposition parties.

In December 1991 Murenzi and Ngirumpatse, at that time MRND chairman for the Préfecture de la ville de Kigali (PVK, Prefecture of Central Kigali), informed the activists that President Habyarimana wanted to meet with a delegation of ten persons in order to acquaint himself with their objectives and activities. Led by Murenzi, the delegation included Robert Kajuga, Georges Rutaganda, Phénéas Ruhumuliza, Eugène Mbarushimana, Dieudonné Niyitegeka, Ephrem Nkezabera, Ismaël Kayitare, Jean-Marie-Vianney Mudahinyuka, Alphonse Kanimba, and Joseph Serugendo. Their encounter took place at the Hôtel Urugwiro in Kacyiru. The discussions were quite open and candid. The president expressed his understanding and support. In the wake of this meeting, membership in the youth wing skyrocketed.

The movement selected a name, a uniform, and a badge and created the Provisional Committee, expanding the nucleus of initial founding members: Robert Kajuga (Tutsi, Kibungo) was named chairman; Phénéas Ruhumuliza

(Hutu, Gitarama) and Georges Rutaganda (Hutu, Gitarama) were named vice-chairmen; Eugène Mbarushimana (Hutu, Gisenyi) became secretary-general; and Dieudonné Niyitegeka (Hutu, Butare) was treasurer. The committee was supported by "counselors" heading up the various commissions—more or less fictitious—figuring in the MRND's organizational chart (*see annex 43*). There were plans for expanding the movement geographically beyond the PVK: late January or early February 1992 in Gisenyi prefecture, then late March or early April in Butare, and so forth. Although appointments to the movement's subordinate organs were scheduled for a later date through elections, they never occurred.

Following this initial contact, toward the beginning of 1992, President Habyarimana invited the National Committee of Interahamwe ZA MRND and many other adherents, altogether over two hundred persons, to the Hôtel Rebero/Horizon in Kigali to offer them his best wishes for the New Year. During the course of this gathering, he congratulated the members of the Interahamwe for their dynamism and their commitment but made no mention of the escalation in clashes and violent encounters between the youth wings of the various parties, a development that Murenzi resolutely opposed. He felt that the president's inner circle was co-opting the movement and capturing it for political purposes, which Murenzi also rejected.

Shortly after Murenzi had been summoned and threatened by Élie Sagatwa, in June 1992 a grenade attack occurred in the Petrorwanda parking lot. Heeding this warning, Murenzi told several diplomatic representatives that he feared for his security; after applying for political asylum in Europe, he left on a two-week trip to Belgium. On his return, Kassim Turatsinze (the future UNAMIR informant "Jean-Pierre" [see below]) informed Murenzi that his demise was being planned. In the face of continued threats to his security, a member of the diplomatic corps who had been informed of his situation appealed directly to President Habyarimana and told him in so many words that his entourage was suspected of involvement. The president displayed grave concern but roundly denied all responsibility. The president's indifference was unmistakable. Feeling disavowed and fearing for his life, Murenzi decided to withdraw. He resigned from the MRND at the end of July 1992 and then relinquished his post at Petrorwanda.

In the meantime, strong links developed between Robert Kajuga, the children of President Habyarimana (especially his son Jean-Pierre), and their close associates, including Séraphin Rwabukumba and Protais Zigiranyirazo. From that point on, meetings were held in a conference room at the Ministry of Planning, at that time headed by Augustin Ngirabatware, an MRND member from Gisenyi. Sometime thereafter, his father-in-law, Félicien Kabuga, a businessman and financier of the MRND who was also related to the president's family by marriage, graciously made rooms in one of his buildings available to them.

Sponsorship and Co-optation

Habyarimana's and his close associates' increasingly tighter hold on the Interahamwe was in line with a new presidential strategy. Relieved of direct control of government action by the emergence of a multiparty government and hoping to further distance himself from responsibility for the failures he anticipated, Habyarimana, after surrendering command of FAR on 22 April 1992, repositioned himself in the political matrix: his goal was to outmaneuver those within the MRND who speculated that he might give up the presidency. By pulling the youth wing of the party to his side, he linked the upswing in the MRND's vitality to the thrust of his own riposte. At the same time, from its inception the Interahamwe movement served to spur party activists to counter the activities of the emergent opposition. Deprived of control over the coercive instruments of power, the OTP and the conservative wing of the MRND adopted the same methods as the new opposition parties in dealing with the government and their political adversaries. They organized violent demonstrations and successfully polished their strategy of counter-ukubohoza (*see box 7*). The Interahamwe massively infiltrated the youth wings of rival political parties in order to destabilize them and co-opt their more active members.

Confronted with this presidential initiative, which short-circuited the various echelons of the party, Ngirumpatse had good reason to keep a close watch on the leaders of the movement; there was an agenda. He understood perfectly well that control over the Interahamwe had become a central preoccupation for politicians concerned to have a militant arm to manage the MRND machine and the upcoming electoral campaigns.

Indeed, within the framework of multiparty politics, without an activist background and a personal base in the electorate, the "minor politicians" could not realistically envisage acceding to influential posts or ministerial appointments. Ngirumpatse also knew that the northern party bosses would never permit unhindered development of a structure dominated by activists from the southern prefectures (Kajuga, Ruhumuliza, Rutaganda, Niyitegeka, Mudahinyuka, Mwalimu, etc.). When the Provisional Committee was installed, appointing heads of commissions from the north to advise those mostly southern founding members was a means of tipping the balance in the direction of the "family." This explains the competition among leaders of the MRND to federalize this private resource. And the principal beneficiaries were the new leaders rising within the movement: they could then raise the stakes and exact more attractive perks and remuneration.

Indeed, if Habyarimana supported Ngirumpatse's efforts to impose himself on the PVK and on the newly renewed MRND, he nonetheless sought to limit Ngirumpatse's ambitions while trying to control the movement as it expanded into the prefectures. For his part, Ngirumpatse had no intention of allowing himself to be deprived of a turf he had been among the first to cultivate.

Torn between competing loyalties, the new National Committee was never able to impose its authority. The main reason was a seeming lack of strong leadership at the helm of the MRND and the exacerbated rivalries among the various party notables, preoccupied with strengthening their bases in the prefectures for the most part.

> By adopting the name "National Committee," the Interahamwe steering committee in Kigali had already taken it upon itself to manage the new organization, whereas the MRND felt that the Interahamwe should be part and parcel of and operate under the party in the *prefectures, communes,* and *sectors.*
>
> Thus, the Interahamwe was extended nationwide but as a decentralized organization. Nevertheless, the Interahamwe Committee in Kigali kept the name "National Committee" under the initial plans."[6]

From the first months of 1992, Ngirumpatse had to get involved in stemming the flow of defections of Interahamwe activists, who could be lured away by the extremist, ethnicist rhetoric of the CDR, which had just been created. He then denounced those who wanted to "wear two hats," referring to the CDR and the MRND. To ensure their loyalty, Ngirumpatse arranged for the principal leaders of the movement to be invited to the April 1992 national congress of the MRND as observers. Presided over by President Habyarimana at the CND (the Rwandan parliament), the congress was the occasion for the party, rebaptized the Mouvement républicain national pour la démocratie et le développement (MRNDD, National Republican Movement for Democracy and Development), to incorporate new structures and proceed to the election of new leadership. The invitation was very important for Ngirumpatse because he needed support from the youth wing to shore up his leadership position against competitors in Kigali-ville and especially in order to boost his campaign for the post of national secretary of the MRND.

Édouard Karemera had coveted that post but ultimately lost out by a slim margin. Election to the post of national secretary placed its incumbent at the head of the Political Bureau and, with the endorsement of President Habyarimana, made him the true executive leader of the party.

With their principal party leaders in attendance, the party congress pledged unconditional support to the Interahamwe youth wing and invited the national secretariat and the presidents of prefectural committees to promote the creation of Interahamwe youth wings in their respective zones. As the youth wing of the MRND, however, the movement remained under the authority of the party's founding president, who had no desire whatsoever to see the Interahamwe in thrall to the national secretary, as this would greatly strengthen the latter's influence.

As head of the party's secretariat, Ngirumpatse was uniquely positioned to project his image on a national scale and give it added legitimacy through tours across the country's prefectures, through speeches at meetings and pep rallies, or simply by virtue of his presence at the side of the president. In fact, Ngirumpatse accompanied the president to the MRND rally of November 1992 in Ruhengeri, the occasion for Habyarimana to pay a vibrant homage to Interahamwe youth. But, just like Karemera before him, Ngirumpatse was under tight surveillance by the presidency and the OTP, concerned that the widening of the scope of the party's organization on a national scale might leave them in a marginalized position. Weakened within the party, in which the coalition of the liberal wing and antinorth opponents was in the majority, conservative elements were also on the defensive within the FAR. The efforts made by the reformist minister of defense, James Gasana, to enhance professionalism in the army, following the reshuffling of the high command, started to produce results, depriving the president of his usual networks within the army. The conservative elements within the FAR also saw the Interahamwe as a last resort to maintain control over the party, boost popular mobilization, and avail themselves of an armed, militant force. The Interahamwe thus occupied center field in a playoff for influence among the party barons, each one trying to generate personal loyalty from groups of Interahamwe by relying on their supporters in the National Committee of the youth wing.

In reality, this structure never had any real prerogatives, other than to debate and apply the agenda formulated by the MRND's leadership or, more precisely, by those close to President Habyarimana—in a word, those who had the power to make decisions and hand out rewards: the national secretary and/or the president of the party, the presidents of the party's prefectural committees, and the heads of enterprises or influential businessmen.

Three names regularly surfaced among the recognized authorities: Ngirumpatse, who had followed the movement since its creation and organized its national structure starting in 1992; then Joseph Nzirorera, "the most powerful minister under the Habyarimana regime"; and finally Jean-Pierre Habyarimana, who financed the Interahamwe youth in Kigali and was responsible for their travel arrangements. "He also contributed during the 'animation' sessions by covering the costs for meals and drinks in a café known as Tam-Tam and in a nightclub dubbed Kigali Night."[7] Félicien Kabuga's children are also mentioned among the persons perceived as representing the authorities of the party.

From Activists to Militiamen

As these new sponsorships suggest, the spurt of activity that led to the creation of the Interahamwe youth wing—bringing new blood and new ideas into the MRND—had reached its goal. There were no longer competing political camps, liberal or conservative.

The "youth" were there to shore up the waning energies of "adult" MRND activists. The MRND leaders had a stake in lifting matters of security and civil defense to the top of their list of priorities; these new recruits were mobilized as the shock troops of aggressive activists and were regularly dragged into the waves of violence that accompanied the campaigns of destabilization against the new multiparty government, campaigns that the MRND ministers could not direct openly.

This explains how we find Ngirumpatse at the forefront during the most aggressive demonstrations of the party and its youth wing. He was present when residential areas of Kigali were sacked at the end of the huge, popular rally that the MRND organized in Kimihurura in the park opposite the prime minister's headquarters on 6 June 1992 to protest the start of direct negotiations between leaders of the opposition and the RPF in Brussels.[8] Members of the Interahamwe, armed with machetes, hoes, axes, clubs, bows, arrows, and rocks, headed toward the center of Kigali-ville and up the hill toward Nyamirambo, Nyakabanda, Kimisagara, and other areas, which they then ravaged with impunity. Indeed, it was Ngirumpatse who called upon the party stalwarts and its youth wing to organize huge demonstrations all across the country to denounce, as the MRND phrased it, the iniquity of the Arusha Peace Accords.

Demonstrations often degenerated into violence and acts of civil disobedience, with leaders of the various parties mutually trading accusations and invoking the right of self-defense. This was all the more convenient for the Interahamwe, since state authorities generally displayed great tolerance for the group's members, when those authorities did not themselves provide the group with logistical support. As time went on, maintaining order became more burdensome, and the youth wings began to play an essential role in the surveillance of the neighborhoods, especially in Kigali; their tasks ranged from detecting the presence of unknown persons, noting the departure for military training of youth from the opposition parties in league with the RPF, and keeping track of their returns, hostile attitudes, and so forth.

Recruitment was no longer based on ideology or any particular principles. No dues were required, and the advantages promised varied, depending on the background of the candidate. Unemployed youth, particularly those drawn from the camps for displaced persons, were especially targeted for recruitment, as well as demobilized soldiers. Youth displaced by the war following RPF offensives were particularly receptive, available, and undemanding. All were attracted by the "refreshments" (distributions of beer after rallies), free transportation, travel around the capital, contacts with political leaders and influential MRND figures, and the opportunities those leaders offered to better the youth's own and their family's conditions of life. Aside from which, belonging to party youth wings permitted survival by means of petty criminality, since it protected members de jure or de facto from prosecution.

Already quite numerous by the end of 1992, persons displaced by the war swelled to one million after the RPF offensive of February 1993, with almost all located in haphazard camps on the outskirts of Kigali. In Byumba prefecture, thirteen of the seventeen communes had been totally emptied of their residents; the situation was no different for several communes in Ruhengeri prefecture. In October 1993 the refugee population of communes along the Burundi border rose to two hundred thousand to three hundred thousand in the wake of the massacres triggered by the assassination of Melchior Ndadaye, the newly elected Burundi president. Recruiting volunteers from these camps for military training posed no problem.

It was in this context that in 1993 the MRND finally made good on the promise made earlier (1991) by the president to arm the civilian population along the borders "to silence the arrogance of the Inkotanyi [RPF combatants]," with the party president, Ngirumpatse, voicing approval. According to notes taken by Théoneste Bagosora, it was in February 1993—after the RPF attack on Ruhengeri—that plans were drawn up to organize groups of armed militiamen (see annex 44).

The Interahamwe Youth Wing "Incorporated" into the MRND

The status of the MRND youth wing was a question frequently raised but never formally resolved. The political dimension was not much of a preoccupation and only concerned those national leaders anxious to strengthen their hold over this nebulous creation.

The terms of the debate could be summarized as follows: Habyarimana always opposed integrating the Interahamwe into the party. His main concern was being able to access dispersed groups of mercenary activists who were underwritten or sponsored by figures whom he controlled. That would allow him to maintain the upper hand in the clientelist system, with his family and himself at the top, against Ngirumpatse's modernizing ambitions. Ngirumpatse sought to integrate the Interahamwe into the party, hoping to win elections and have himself elected, but the ascendancy of the Interahamwe was linked to rich financiers preoccupied with conserving the influence that Habyarimana allowed them. Less numerous but equally powerful were those who feared that the formal incorporation of the Interahamwe into the party would strengthen the national secretary to the detriment of Habyarimana. Consequently, between the two MRND party congresses of 1992 and 1993, competition soared between the head of state and the national secretary of the MRND, as each vied to reinforce his influence and popularity. Later, the competition was made even more intense by the no-holds-barred enmity between Ngirumpatse and Joseph Nzirorera. In a way, these rivalries, not to mention Ngirumpatse's vaulting presidential ambition, explain the increasing prominence of the Interahamwe, both the cause and consequence of the waning influence of the party presidency.

Failure to bring the Interahamwe into the party had as one of its indirect consequences the unequal treatment meted out to other youth wings in terms of their legal status. Since the others had sought and obtained legal recognition, they were held responsible for damages whenever there were excesses, which allowed communal police, gendarmes, the army, and state prosecutors to exercise some degree of control over their unlawful acts. Potential financial sanctions of reparations seemed to be dissuasive and could even threaten their very existence. However, lacking an independent legal personality and without formal incorporation in the MRND by party statute or resolution by the party congress, the Interahamwe did not run the same risks. Each member, in his individual capacity, would be held responsible for his acts whenever there were clashes with youth wings of the opposition parties or any other dereliction. At that time, several Interahamwe members had been arrested and were the targets of judicial inquiry initiated by Minister of Defense James Gasana. Thus, the threat was real, even if, as a rule, they were quickly released, thanks to the intervention of the president of the Kigali Criminal Court, Jean-Damascène Hategekimana. But the majority of the cases did not even get that far, given the various interventions and pressures brought to bear. For example, President

Habyarimana personally chastised the minister of defense and mobilized his entourage to block a homicide investigation initiated against Séraphin Twahirwa, patron of the Interahamwe in Gikondo and Juvénal Habyarimana's cousin (*see annex 45*).

It was left to the congress of July 1993 to resolve—or, rather, to refuse to address—this question, much to Habyarimana's satisfaction. The presentation of a proposal drafted by Joseph Serugendo at Ngirumpatse's request was overruled, and the recommendation that the Interahamwe be formally incorporated in the party was thus stillborn. This decision seemed of great importance, as it would formally deprive the Provisional Committee of the Interahamwe—whose members all resided in Kigali-ville—of all authority over prefectural committees throughout the country. The hierarchical relationship between these committees, just like the traffic in information, was controlled by MRND structures. The National Committee of the Interahamwe was thus subject to the de facto authority of the president of the party, just as the decentralized structure of the youth wing made it dependent on the heads of the MRND prefectural committees and corresponding officials at the various levels of the party (communes, sectors, and cells). Local units of the Interahamwe were thus subject to the MRND hierarchy, and coordination with the party's higher echelons was handled by the National Committee or the MRND Political Bureau.

This situation invites us to consider the political profile of each prefecture if we are to grasp the genesis, the strength, and the particular roles of these youth wings. It was largely unacknowledged that the movement initially structured itself in Kigali before being taken over by the political figures who took an interest in it. Although nominally under the authority of the MRND prefectural committee for the PVK, the potential sponsors were sufficiently motivated and numerous that the National Committee was able to negotiate support from multiple donors (a particular political figure, depending on the neighborhood and that person's direct links with prefectural and, in particular, military authorities, given the influential sway of demobilized soldiers in recruitment starting in 1993). Outside Kigali, beyond the titular leaders of MRND prefectural committees, it is important to note the political weight and background of different local leaders, their connections with eminent figures native to the prefecture who were working in the capital, the position of the MRND relative to the other parties, not to mention the attitude and the stature of the prefect in office, particularly in the prefectures headed by figures from the opposition. Thus, in the PVK, when Laurent Semanza succeeded Charles Nyandwi as head of the prefectural committee, the movement very quickly transformed itself into a militia force charged with countering all opposition to the MRND, cloaked by virtual impunity.[9] In Byumba prefecture—where the MRND basked in the popular support of those affected by the war—the Interahamwe could rely on a robust incubator for recruitment among the displaced persons. The Interahamwe youth were just as numerous and as well organized in the two other virtually monoethnic Hutu prefectures of Gisenyi and Ruhengeri. In the latter, they benefited from the competition between Casimir Bizimungu and Joseph Nzirorera for leadership in the party's prefectural committee. However, the situation was a bit more complex in Kibuye prefecture, depending on the specific conditions in each commune (the Tutsi population was relatively greater in the southern communes), and in Cyangugu prefecture, where the youth wings of the opposition parties tried to contest the hegemony of the MRND. Similarly, in Kibungo prefecture the youth wings of the MRND and the opposition parties frequently clashed and vied for control over the communal administrations.

To conclude, we should also highlight the paradox of the virtual absence or, at the very least, the extreme weakness of MRND youth wings in the other prefectures of the south. Thus, in Gikongoro, the party's youth wing could not take root in communes largely controlled by the opposition. Similarly, in Butare, under the administration of prefect Jean-Baptiste Habyalimana (Tutsi, PL), proselytism by the various youth wings and their usually violent excesses were firmly contained and sanctioned. Finally, in Gitarama prefecture, the MRND could scarcely make a public appearance given the hegemony of the MDR youth wing. Three of these prefectures were headed by prefects in the opposition, who were removed and/or killed after the reprise of the war in April 1994.

In practice, the effective control that Ngirumpatse exercised over Interahamwe militias was similar to his broad command of the party, generally speaking. He was powerful in Kigali-ville because of long-standing links with most of the members of the National Committee, but decentralized management of the Interahamwe by influential political figures, forever loyal to the regime that allowed them to so enrich themselves, left effective levers of control in the hands of President Habyarimana, especially in the northern prefectures. Nonetheless, it is noteworthy that many MRND members had little interest in these affairs and distanced themselves from the two rivals who sought to control them. That is to say, while they may have been receptive to the idea of a party youth wing, they condemned the violent methods that the Interahamwe used and abused and the terror they unleashed.

With the July 1993 party congress, the struggle for ascendancy, which pitted Matthieu Ngirumpatse, MRND president and formally "chief of the Interahamwe youth wing," against Joseph Nzirorera, "radical member of the

Akazu and veritable chief of the MRND" (as described in the testimony of an Interahamwe leader), subjected the National Committee of the Interahamwe to sharp, contradictory pressures.

The Control of Financial Resources

Clearly, financing represents the second most important variable in managing the MRND Interahamwe youth wing, since access to and levels of available funding determined capacities for recruitment and for inducing loyalty and commitment from "activists."[10] The entire political machinery of the MRND was mobilized to extract donations, which could then be used as inducements to lure or compensate occasional or experienced activists, especially those of demonstrable commitment, capacity, or potential, that is, access to jobs and diverse financial benefits. Among these can be counted the availability of credit from the Banque continentale africaine au Rwanda (BACAR, African Continental Bank in Rwanda), the Banque commerciale du Rwanda (BCR, Commercial Bank of Rwanda), and the Banque de Kigali, all headed by persons loyal to the mouvance présidentielle. All of the ministers and state institutions and parastatal enterprises controlled by the MRND were, in one manner or another, enlisted to contribute, notably the Department of Bridges and Roadways in the Ministry of Public Works (under the control of Alphonse Ntilivamunda, Habyarimana's son-in-law, who also controlled the unfathomable Roadways Fund), Électrogaz, the Société rwandaise d'allumettes (Butare) (SORWAL, Rwanda Match Company), the Office des cultures industrielles du Rwanda–Thé (OCIR-Thé, Rwandan Office for Industrial Cultivation-Tea), the Cimenterie du Rwanda (Cyangugu) (Cimerwa, Rwanda Cement Factory), and the Magasins généraux du Rwanda (MAGERWA, Rwanda General Stores), among others. Certain establishments, like the Office national des transports en commun (ONATRACOM, National Public Transport Authority), the Dairy of Nyabisindu, Cimerwa, and the Office rwandais du tourisme et des parcs nationaux (ORTPN, Rwandan Office for Tourism and National Parks), openly recruited candidates for Interahamwe military training.[11] In Cyangugu, Yussuf Munyakazi, a wealthy landowner and businessman, housed and supported several dozen militiamen in his warehouses. And it also bears mentioning all the household workers directly employed by many MRND leaders.

There was also unmistakable overlap, if not direct osmosis, between traders and businessmen who financially supported the Interahamwe and those who received preferential treatment in tenders for government contracts with, for example, the prison administration or the military.[12] Several witness accounts describe those practices:

> The second example involves funds obtained from different sources by way of contributions to the Interahamwe ZA MRND; the sources included major figures of the MRND, including, of course, the close collaborators of President Habyarimana (Akazu). The funds were supposed to be deposited in an account at the Banque de Kigali in the names of the Interahamwe and handled by the treasurer of the Interahamwe ZA MRND, Dieudonné Niyitegeka. In reality, that is not the way it happened.
>
> For example, our president, Robert Kajuga, would tell us that he had received a large amount of money from Joseph Nzirorera in the amount of fifty thousand or one hundred thousand Rwandan francs. When there was a problem that needed to be resolved, such as members' travel expenses, Interahamwe threatening to leave the movement and join an opposition party such as the CDR, bribing members of rival parties to join the MRND, or giving financial support to members of neighborhood groups, then Robert Kajuga would bring the matter to the attention of Joseph Nzirorera, who was known to be very generous. He gave generously in order to increase his popularity and support the agenda of the party and the Interahamwe ZA MRND youth movement by establishing the loyalty of our members. . . .
>
> The management and distribution of funds and donations was mainly the responsibility of the new secretary-general, Joseph Nzirorera. He would issue funds to the president, Robert Kajuga, and his two vice presidents, Phénéas Ruhumuliza and Georges Rutaganda, as well as to his personal friends. For example, Bernard Maniragaba used to go directly to him and would, in turn, distribute the monies received in the Gitega neighborhood.
>
> Other Interahamwe ZA MRND groups from Gikondo and Inyange from Remera used to receive funds directly from Michel Bagaragaza of OCIR-Thé. The Kanombe Interahamwe ZA MRND group was sponsored by the head of state, Juvénal Habyarimana; he told us so when he requested to become an honorary member of the Interahamwe ZA MRND during a reception held at the Rebero L'Horizon Hôtel in Kigali.[13]

Several witness accounts complement each other, particularly concerning meetings that were held at the hotel-restaurant Rebero/L'Horizon in Kigali, which was owned by President Habyarimana. One of those meetings was supposedly held in July 1993 for fund-raising purposes to finance preparations for an MRND prefectural meeting in Gisenyi. The way the meeting was organized was particularly interesting in several respects. It was necessary to establish a serviceable explanation for President Habyarimana's refusal to acknowledge his role in organizing a meeting so clearly partisan.

> RP—Why did Habyarimana not want to be associated with the fund-raising? . . .
>
> X—In my opinion, from what I gathered, it was because at the time he was president of the republic, and I think that was when he was no longer the president of the party. . . . So, since . . . under the Arusha Accords, it was not acceptable for the president to be too closely associated with the party. . . . At that time, I believe he had already resigned from the army and the MRND presidency.[14]

With financing clearly linked to identifiable figures, competition among the politicians in managing the affairs of the Interahamwe spread from the national scale to the regional and local levels. The schisms within the party and rivalries among the various figures who were concerned about their electoral chances for the future naturally influenced the collections and redistributions of funds. One could discern rivalries among the titans at the very top of the party leadership, especially after the reshuffling of July 1993, signaling a rift in the command structure. Personal competition between the new party chairman, Matthieu Ngirumpatse, and National Secretary Joseph Nzirorera clearly reflected regionalist cleavages. A parallel committee emerged within the National Committee, in which natives of the northern prefectures of Gisenyi and Ruhengeri aligned with one another to counter Ngirumpatse's hold on the movement.

But this personal involvement by the president and his "family" was necessary in order to pique the interest of the many persons who were invited and to stimulate their commitment and generosity. It also demonstrates the extent to which presidential patronage conferred approval on the activities and services proposed for the Interahamwe and how the president's involvement provided cover for those who took an interest in the youth wing.

The most glaring sign of an emergent parallel committee revealed itself in the realm of financing: funds from the north went to militants from the north! For instance, during a meeting organized by the president, only the two hundred thousand Rwandan francs received in coin were passed on to the treasurer and recorded in the bank account for the movement. Where checks were concerned, with an aggregate value in the range of one million francs, a member of the parallel committee personally took charge, and no formal accounting was ever made to the other leaders (*see annex 47*). Thus, it comes as no surprise that by 1992 the treasurer of the National Committee, Dieudonné

Niyitegeka, had to complain to the national secretary of the MRND about the unjustified allegations of malfeasance made against him over discrepancies between the meager funds deposited in the Banque de Kigali account and the huge sums that the movement's leaders were seen spending. But this native of Butare prefecture was not the only one to complain.

Growing resentment toward Interahamwe and politicians from the south may explain the uneven development of the militias throughout the country. It may also explain the few numbers of those militiamen that actually received military training from late 1993 onward, with the exception of businesses and parastatal enterprises that, although located in the southern prefectures, were controlled by MRND cadres who were originally from the north (e.g., SORWAL in Butare, Cimerwa in Cyangugu, and the Dairy of Nyabisindu).

Military Training and Weapons Distributions

Military training for the Interahamwe youth wing commenced in late 1993 and rapidly became a matter of public notoriety, despite the habitual denials from military authorities and the MRND leaders: "One could hear them returning from political meetings, atop of trucks and buses, singing and screaming at the top of their lungs without the least bit of concern for anyone at all: 'Tuzabatsembatsemba'—'We have come to exterminate.' They knew what they were talking about, especially since the speeches mentioned earlier seem to have invited that. And if they took liberties with this sort of language, it's only because they felt protected and approved."[15]

For residents of Kigali, the training took place in military camps in the Bugesera and Mutara, in the west of the country. The militiamen were transported by buses requisitioned from ONATRACOM or via military trucks or minivans loaned or rented from private sources. Selecting candidates was left to the leaders of the Executive Bureau of the MRND, or, more precisely, the National Secretariat, assisted by officers from Kanombe and the Presidential Guard. Physical aptitude was a key criterion, with former reservists and demobilized soldiers receiving priority by virtue of their previous military experience.

In two of his recorded statements, Ngirumpatse fully confirms that plans for military training were indeed implemented, but he imputes responsibility to officers of the FAR. The latter not only organized the training for these youth "in their personal capacity" but at the same time supposedly used them to boost recruitment for the army. According to Ngirumpatse, militiamen were then sent into battle on the front lines and would not have participated in massacring the civilian population, which was the fault of "people among the population."

However, all of Ngirumpatse's activities in his various leadership positions in the MRND demonstrate otherwise. He was firmly committed to strengthening the offensive capacity of the youth wings, as he plainly set forth in a letter dated 15 February 1993 to President Habyarimana:

> The political bureau has also called for the setting up of defense groups among the displaced persons and in the prefectures under threat. That has not been done. The reasons advanced for not arming civilians are misleading and we are likely to pay very dearly for such a typical career-soldier attitude. That has not prevented the parties and the RPF from accusing us of maintaining the militia! In my opinion, the young must be trained urgently (secretly of course). It is clear that the initial plan to conquer Rwanda, Burundi and eastern Zaïre is under way. The only way to stop this is the participation by all of the people.[16]

Numerous witnesses have confirmed that this recommendation was indeed implemented and that eminent figures in the MRND and commanders who supported this policy (such as Léonard Nkundiye in Gabiro) were personally involved in planning military training. Especially noteworthy were the distributions of weapons taking place upon the trainees' return organized by the MRND national secretary (*see annex 48*).

There were previous episodes of weapons distributions to the civilian population in early 1992, but those were deemed ineffective. Starting with Muvumba commune, in the Mutara, attempts to support self-defense by the peasants were extended to other communes along the front lines, but almost all the weapons fell into the hands of the RPF. When James Gasana took office as minister of defense in April 1992, his main concern was to rectify the dysfunctions and the lack of discipline that seemed to reign at all levels in the army, whose size was rapidly expanding. Thousands of newly recruited youth had joined the ranks—at that time dubbed the *quinze jours* (fifteen day-ers), to underscore the brevity of their training—and apparently had no qualms about selling their guns or their grenades. With the arrival of multiparty politics and Gasana's restraining efforts, weapons distributions to civilians were effectively contained, at least until his resignation cleared the way for the Ministry of Defense to be reclaimed by a more "reliable" MRND appointment and by extremist elements from the army. After that, the recipients were rigorously checked by officials drawn from the president's inner circle: these were trained, well-equipped, "civil-defense" groups and Interahamwe militiamen, to the exclusion of activists from the south.

Despite progress made by late 1993 in improving coordination among the Hutu Power youth wings of the opposition parties, the rapprochement had yet to overcome regional cleavages: "Kwigisha abantu kwirwanaho ngo ni ukwigisha abakiga ngo bazamare abanyenduga!!" (Training the population in civil self-defense amounts to training the people of the north to eliminate people from the south!!).[17] This saying vividly illustrates the tensions that were still raw between natives of the north and those of the south, even extending to the conduct of the war and the civil defense. In fact, the Interahamwe militias never really took root in the southern prefectures until the RPF advance appeared unstoppable and defeat was on the horizon (see chapter 12).

Weapons destined for the Interahamwe included rifles (R4, G3, and Kalashnikov), grenades, pistols, and traditional weapons. Kassim Turatsinze, alias "Jean-Pierre," Ngirumpatse's chauffeur, who was also in charge of weapons distributions, estimated that "more or less six hundred rifles" were already in the hands of Interahamwe in Kigali who had undergone military training.

Numerous documents and witnesses describe in great detail the involvement of the presidency of the party and the National Committee of its youth wing in distributing weapons. Thus, starting in late 1993, Ngirumpatse, along with the leaders of the National Committee, engaged in a game of hide-and-seek with UNAMIR: concealing weapons held by party activists and blocking UNAMIR's weapons recovery initiatives, which focused on raiding the homes of likely suspects, mainly militiamen of the youth wings.

> During a meeting of the National Committee of the Interahamwe ZA MRND, usually held on Wednesdays [exact date unknown], Mr. Matthieu Ngirumpatse made an official announcement that UNAMIR had the right to go into any residence and search it for weapons and would confiscate them. Because of that, he issued a warning and asked Interahamwe ZA MRND who had weapons to be extremely careful and to hide them in such a manner that UNAMIR would not be able to find them. He cautioned that the party would not be able to do anything to help any Interahamwe ZA MRND who got caught.[18]

By early 1994 military training of Interahamwe had picked up momentum in army units that favored their activities with the support of the MRND minister of defense, Augustin Bizimana. The militarized cells were mainly located in Remera, where over 60 percent of Interahamwe were reservists receiving support from Presidential Guards; in Kanombe, where almost all of the militia-men were former soldiers; and in Kicukiro. They were the operational van-guard of the movement and distinguished themselves from the other youth who were assembled or deployed mostly for their "theatrics" and who, it was said, could only be used to patrol the *panya road* ("mouse paths" in Kiswahili).

Consequently, the Interahamwe militias had their role well planned, and this was known and understood by the MRND top dogs, as well as by the National Committee. It was also known at all levels in the prefectures, com-munes, and sectors and wherever political figures made funds available to pay for a retinue of guards or political supporters. All the large parastatal enterprises controlled by the president's men (e.g., Cimerwa, SORWAL, OCIR-Thé, the Institut des sciences agronomiques du Rwanda [Butare] [ISAR, Rwandan Institute for Agronomic Studies], ONATRACOM, the Dairy of Nyabisindu) had organized groups, armed and paid for the specific purpose of maintaining order, if not terror.

By first renouncing his leadership of the youth wing and then withdrawing from the MRND, Désiré Murenzi clearly signaled his disapproval of the presi-dent and his inner circle on a very specific point: using party youth as a security force at the personal disposal of politicians. Three years later, and with the full knowledge of the MRND leaders who purposefully underwrote and shepherded its military profile, their offspring had turned into a monster.

7

The Downing
of the Presidential Plane
on 6 April 1994
and the Military Crisis
Committee

On Wednesday, 6 April 1994, at 8:25 p.m. the airplane transporting Maj. Gen. Juvénal Habyarimana and Burundi president Cyprien Ntaryamira was shot down. The two heads of state who perished in this attack were returning from Dar es Salaam, where they had participated in a summit on regional security dealing with the implementation of the Arusha Peace Accords. It was only because of a mechanical difficulty with his own plane that the Burundi president hastily boarded Rwanda's Falcon 50 plane at the last moment.

As it approached the Grégoire Kayibanda Airport in preparation for landing, the plane was hit by a ground-to-air missile, causing it to explode in midair. The downing of the aircraft claimed twelve victims, whose bodies fell into the gardens of President Habyarimana's residence, located nearby. The other occupants of the airplane were the three French crewmen; Maj. Gen. Déogratias Nsabimana, the chief of staff of the Rwandan army; Ambassador Juvénal Renzaho, advisor to the president; Col. Élie Sagatwa, personal secretary and brother-in-law of the president; Emmanuel Akingeneye, the president's personal physician; Maj. Thaddée Bagaragaza, aide-de-camp; Cyriaque Simbizi, the Burundi minister of communication and spokesman for the government; and his colleague Bernard Ciza, minister of development, planning, and reconstruction.

Hypotheses Concerning the Perpetrators of the Attack

As I mentioned in the preface to the original edition, I happened to be in Kigali the night the plane was shot down and in the days that followed. What I saw and heard during that fateful episode needs to be taken into account.

After my evacuation from Kigali on 12 April 1994, I tried, along with a number of Rwandans, primarily academics and journalists, to collect as much information as possible. As best we could, we tried to track the movements of the principal political and military figures and the key players within the mouvance présidentielle and the RPF on the night of 6 April and into the following day in order to situate them in time and space in relation to the unfolding events.

When we compared the results of our investigations in a seminar organized with several academics and political figures in Belgium during the first week of June 1994, three conclusions emerged:

- The group charged with organizing the attack on the plane was tightly limited in number and operated outside the routine channels of political or institutional authority. Highly placed figures, normally close to the decision makers, had neither received advance notice nor anticipated the incident.
- The disorder, if not panic, that reigned in MRND/CDR/Akazu circles immediately following the attack was in stark contrast with the marching orders dispatched to RPF forces stationed at the CND parliament building.
- The silence emanating from the major embassies and foreign intelligence services betrayed an apparent complicity in dissimulation.[1]

In light of the overall findings of our investigations and in the absence of any irrefutable evidence, our conclusion took note that "at this stage, none of these points of view can confirm matters or suspend doubts."[2] Given the passionate debates surrounding this tragic turn of events, I have always tried to limit my comments on this subject.

The hypothesis of RPF responsibility took on a certain consistency in Kigali on 23 March 1995 during a long discussion with then Minister of Interior Seth Sendashonga, who shared with me some of the suspicions raised by several civilian and military RPF leaders concerning some top-ranking members of the RPA. Just two days later, on 25 March, Minister of Justice Alphonse-Marie Nkubito made similar comments to me. On 6 February 1997 the latter, by then director general of the Bank of Kigali and having once again taken up his activities as a human rights defender, told me that he no longer had any doubts about RPA responsibility for the downing of the plane, based on the accounts he had been able to gather. He had recorded these accounts in detailed notes, which he shared with his contacts at the American Embassy. Again, in February 1997, Michael Hourigan, the head of the National Investigative Team at the ICTR in Kigali, was abruptly told by Prosecutor Louise Arbour to desist from the investigation of the circumstances of the crash—this shortly after a telephone conference organized at the American Embassy, where he cited the name of Paul Kagame as the man who ordered the attack, relying on the detailed accounts of three informants.[3]

It was not until August 2002, however, that this presumption hardened into certainty from my perspective. At that time, as an expert witness for the ICTR Office of the Prosecutor, I came across specific information confirming suspicions of RPF implication in several military operations between 1991 and 1994, including the attack against the plane of 6 April 1994. This concerned documents drafted by high-level Rwandan officers still in active service who, after a three-year inquiry, were able to provide several accounts of how the attack was launched, mentioning names of witnesses and participants who had agreed to divulge what they knew. This information was intended for ICTR prosecutor Carla Del Ponte and Judge Jean-Louis Bruguière, who at that time were collaborating, at least formally, on that file. The documents were thus transmitted to the French investigating magistrate, who, recognizing obvious parallels with and confirmation of elements already in his files, immediately requested that the persons conveying this information cease investigations and any further contact out of concern for their own security and that of the other witnesses. As for the ICTR prosecutor, on 8 October 2002, in The Hague, when I offered to personally deliver these notes directly to her, she refused, indicating that, aside from protestations of innocence sworn to her by Vice President Kagame, he had also presented her with documents of American origin clearly establishing the responsibility of France, and she was satisfied with that.[4]

Since then, and until proven otherwise, the fact that investigations conducted independently happen to uncover the same names and references to the same sequence of events argues for their strong credibility. Further evidence surfaced over the following weeks in the form of the assassination attempts directed at several of those officers suspected to have collaborated in these investigations, not to mention the attempted arrests and kidnappings of others. Little wonder if many sought asylum abroad. Nor is it surprising if innumerable hurdles were raised at every step in the judicial proceedings when it came to gathering additional information, especially when it fell to national and international political authorities or administrative officials to facilitate such initiatives or carry them out.

I would also note that before, during, and after the war of 1994, the RPF never hesitated to rely on all means of blackmail and pressure, up to and including physical elimination, against witnesses who risked divulging its "secrets." This covers the crimes committed as part of its strategy in the conduct of the war and applies even to its own members, who had taken an oath to never betray or deviate from the will of the party. Dozens of persons paid with their lives attempts by the RPF to conceal or suppress incriminating evidence from dossiers relating to political assassinations, explosions, and massacres perpetrated against the civilian population, as well as the attack against the presidential plane.[5] Others are subject to continuous surveillance of their movements and communications and owe their survival to their self-imposed silence on some issues of vital significance to the image the RPF seeks to project.

In this context, and while severe repression (including arrests and convictions, assassinations, exile, and issuance of arrest warrants) had overcome almost all officers of the ex-FAR with whom I had been preparing for the genocide trials at the Arusha Tribunal (see chapter 13), on 2 March 2004 I informed the Rwandan minister of foreign affairs, Charles Muligande, that "henceforth I would investigate and would comment on war crimes and crimes against humanity committed by the RPA, just as I had for the crime of genocide."[6] In so doing, I withdrew from our implicit understanding that resources placed at my disposal would not be used to pursue allegations of RPF wrongdoing. In a quote from a series of articles published by the newspaper *Le Monde*, reference is made to this information on Rwandan officers concerning the downing of the plane:

> Although painting herself as a victim of the regime in Kigali after her dismissal in September 2003 ("It is clear that all that started when we undertook 'special investigations' of crimes committed by the Rwandan Patriotic Front"), Carla Del Ponte, like her predecessor at the ICTR, did not care to establish the responsibility of the RPF. After a meeting with the current Rwandan president in Kigali on 28 June 2002, she was even imprudent enough to confirm the abandonment of investigations undertaken against his movement in writing to General Kagame. . . . Then, later on 8 October [2002], satisfied with her decision, Carla Del Ponte turned down a dossier containing evidence pertaining to the 6 April attack against the plane from the hands of an expert working with her own office.[7]

Questioned by *Le Monde*, the prosecutor denied having refused the documents. She then proposed in a letter the following revised version of her response, emphasizing in capital letters: "If there is something I never refuse, it's evidence. Everything that comes to my desk AND WHICH CAN BE ACCEPTED, I take, because it can assist my investigations or someone else's."[8]

Never having had the slightest intention of involving myself in the specialized technical investigations that remain the province of judicial authorities, after that I simply worked to further elaborate my central argument when, toward the end of 2003, I had an opportunity to establish close links with several sources within the RPA who, to this day, confirm those initial reports.

In light of the high cost of revealing the truth, and because of the obligations I have to witnesses interviewed, the results of my investigations in or about Rwanda have all been handed over to judicial authorities or have since been the object of contradictory debate during my appearances before the Trial Chambers of the ICTR in Arusha. Faced with scenarios, documentation, and witnesses engaging in rival forms of propaganda, the judicial authorities must validate and confront these various contributions to the truth.

Additionally, if the downing of the presidential plane is indeed a decisive moment in the chain of events for the year 1994, it is by no means the alpha and omega of the war and the genocide. The attack against the plane cannot be characterized as the cause of the genocide (*see annex 52*); nor does it explain it (see below). This is, in my view, the misleading exaggeration that emerges from Judge Bruguière's warrants and that have done him so much harm in diverting attention from the factual elements of his investigations.[9] Moreover, although attention to the criminal acts committed by the RPF is indispensable for understanding the logic of this horrendous civil war, they have no bearing whatsoever on the responsibility of the other camp for its own criminal conduct.

Unnecessary, Erroneous, and Fatal Choices

As soon as the death of President Habyarimana became known, events unfolded in rapid succession. To begin with a brief preview of some basic points: on the evening of the attack, an informal meeting at army headquarters brought together numerous officers of the high command, each anxious for information and convinced that they were duty bound to take urgent decisions to maintain security and to reconstitute the general staff. Lurking behind the choice of candidates, major rivalries swirled over the issue of President Habyarimana's succession and how power would be exercised in the interim. While the high command and military sector chiefs showed their willingness to maintain the continuity of the state and to rapidly install the transitional institutions, Col. Théoneste Bagosora, supported by the principal

MRND leaders, tried to dispense with the constitutional framework and impose the Military Crisis Committee. This approach complemented the one favored by the presidential family, determined to make its political adversaries pay for Habyarimana's death and promote a successor it would approve. Thus, as dawn rose on 7 April, the Presidential Guard (*see box 9*) and the units of the army "linked to the presidency," along with Interahamwe militias of the MRND, went on a rampage: they attacked political opponents and Tutsi elements in the residential areas; assassinated the head of government, Agathe Uwilingiyimana, as well as the principal ministers and leaders of the opposition; and killed the Belgian "blue helmets" of UNAMIR, in charge of providing security for the prime minister (of which more later). With the new constitutional framework in a shambles, Col. Théoneste Bagosora and the MRND leaders appointed new Power leaders to head the opposition political parties and, invoking the prior 1991 Constitution, installed an obedient Interim Government, charged with mounting a policy of confrontation with the RPF and massacring the civilian Tutsi population.

With the likelihood of a resumption of hostilities looming on the horizon, and granting that little could be expected from the decapitated mouvance présidentielle without a head of state, an army chief of staff, or staff officers at the G2 (intelligence) and G3 (operations) levels, neither the absence of an identifiable power nexus, the prospect of decisive defeat from a militarily superior RPF, nor even the attitude of the major embassies definitively foreclosed all options. In the aftermath of the plane's explosion, the unifying bonds of Hutu solidarity could be reactivated and the will to face off the Tutsi rebellion reenergized. But to be an effective force, this call for unity would have to come from a cohesive command structure with a clear vision of its means and objectives. Instead, the one fact that seemed to eclipse everything else was the presence of a disorganized, uncoordinated deployment of human resources more bent on strengthening regional factionalism than promoting a coherent alliance.

One of the principal errors made by the mouvance présidentielle was its inability to learn an important lesson from the past, namely, its refusal to admit that major improvements in troop combativity and cohesion in FAR command, as observed in 1992–93, was linked to Minister of Defense James Gasana's reorganization of the general staff and his redistribution of equipment among the units. After his forced departure in July 1993, Gasana's adversaries fought tooth and nail to restore their former prerogatives. Within an hour of the downing of the presidential plane, Laurent Serubuga, at home in Gisenyi, called Théoneste Bagosora at army headquarters proposing to "come and help," along with Pierre-Célestin Rwagafilita. Those making these offers of assistance were none other than the former chiefs of staff who had been forced into retirement by Minister Gasana in 1992–93 with the arrival of the multiparty government and the decisive restructuring of the general staff.

This minority faction in the milieu of extremist officers around the Akazu, the most hardened and determined, with the most to lose if it didn't assert itself, supported by the best armed units in Kigali and the most organized groups of militiamen, unleashed a wave of targeted killings and massacres throughout Kigali.

Therein lies the second error, with fatal consequences. By coupling the obliteration of Hutu opponents and Tutsi civilians with military priorities in national defense, the hard-core extremists—loudly asserting themselves as the only ones capable of safeguarding the achievements of the "social revolution"—provoked a sharp break among the general staff and large sectors of the population. In so doing they also dashed all hopes of support from the international community. More than weaknesses in military preparedness, it was the wait-and-see attitude and the disengagement of a large number of civilian and military actors, bonded by conviction or constraint in this suicidal policy, that contributed to the final defeat of "the Hutu." Consequently, even though the balance of power could still have been turned around, the profoundly mistaken strategy of this minority faction is what led to failure.

This was the "war within the war" that, on a daily basis, allowed the militiamen and the self-defense forces to claim illusory victories against pseudo-enemies, while the FAR, divided against itself, did nothing but retreat in the face of the RPA offensive.

The RPA fully exploited these divisions and very rapidly claimed the upper hand. Its superiority in weaponry and provisions, the homogeneity of its ranks, its cohesion in command, and its clear strategic objectives allowed the RPF to mount an effective offensive and suffer relatively few military losses, even if the domestic Tutsi civilian population had to suffer the tragic consequences.

To avoid simplistic assumptions that tend to lump together all the members of the defeated ethnicity and the entire cast of military and civilian elites, it is important to identify the principal leaders and the forces that exercised or tried to control power and to clarify the distribution of roles and the division of labor that took form between the various actors in this disaster.

The Informal Meeting
of the Army High Command

As soon as word spread of the downing of the presidential plane, officers began to arrive at army headquarters to find out what to do to confront the situation and fill the void.[10] No one doubted the responsibility of the RPA, and the imperative of reestablishing a central authority took center stage, given the obvious and inevitable reprise of war with an enemy that had just brutally demonstrated its strategic objectives. If the putschist ambitions of the RPF had been revealed and condemned long in advance, this did not make the political and military leaders of the mouvance présidentielle, like those closely aligned with the opposition, any less disoriented. As shown by past experience, recourse to armed force to strengthen its position or break an impasse was part and parcel of the RPF's modus operandi. Faced with the RPF's military superiority, the trump card held by the mouvance présidentielle and the domestic forces was the overwhelming demographic majority of Rwandan Hutu. In the eyes of their leaders, this state of affairs made it impossible for minority expatriate Tutsi to administer the country in any lasting manner, especially if the elimination of the domestic Tutsi population deprived it of its presumed political base. Such were the basic parameters to be taken into account by those in charge of reconfiguring the decapitated state (*see box 10*).

On the evening of 6 April, the political alternatives available to the mouvance présidentielle and the domestic opposition were quite fluid. No party, faction, or clan had a candidate groomed for the succession. For almost all those attending the meeting of the high military command, the structure of power had not collapsed. From a constitutional point of view, the multiparty government, with a prime minister at its head, assured the continuity of the state. Likewise, the administrative structure, particularly the territorial administration, was fully capable of responding to this situation. Finally, as far as the officers present were concerned, it fell naturally to Augustin Ndindiliyimana, the chief of staff of the gendarmerie and the only officer with the rank of general, to assume provisionally the functions of the army chief of staff, who had been killed.

In this sense, the proposal from the defense minister's chief of staff, Col. Théoneste Bagosora, to assemble the Military Crisis Committee, which would sidestep the legal framework and impose its leadership, appeared to many as a normal reaction—not a move to set off a putsch but the reflection of a concern not to squander this opportunity to return to the political scene (with the approval of the presidential clan).[11] And if, confronted with Colonel Bagosora's ambition, Maj. Gen. Augustin Ndindiliyimana, chief of staff of the gendarmerie, seemed indecisive, his colleagues lost no time in manifesting their opposition to this proposal and in collectively asserting themselves. Thus, somewhat unrealistically, they anticipated a major step forward toward the transitional institutions, which would then definitively rout these retired officers and overcome the timidity of the chief of staff of the gendarmerie. But that did not factor into Bagosora's tenacity or the obstinacy of the presidential family and the less-than-heroic motivations of Augustin Ndindiliyimana. In fact, in order to prevail in the exceptional circumstances of the moment, Ndindiliyimana would need support from the Akazu and would also have to confirm his hold on the army and assert himself politically.

Support from the Akazu was an absolute prerequisite, since the heart of power was indeed rooted in the Akazu, and, for the time being at least, the elimination of Habyarimana made the family circle a focal point for all major political personalities, senior military officers, and diplomats. This point is extremely important and, as we shall see, explains Augustin Ndindiliyimana's reaction in the face of Théoneste Bagosora's maneuvers.

Augustin Ndindiliyimana's position was particularly delicate. Only several days earlier he had been obliged to disassociate himself from Agathe Uwilingiyimana following a media campaign launched by the RTLM and the MRND that denounced the seditious nature of a meeting at her home with officers from the south—even though Ndindiliyimana was not even invited. The majority of the officers who had assembled at the prime minister's home could be viewed as closely aligned with the opposition political parties. Accepting the presidency of the Military Crisis Committee, as was proposed to him, could easily be seen as a major step in the direction of an impending southern-inspired putsch denounced on 1 April. It is well to remember in this connection that Ndindiliyimana was already chief of staff of the gendarmerie, and during the night of 6–7 April, Marcel Gatsinzi's (Hutu, Kigali-rural) nomination to head the army general staff had catapulted command of the FAR into the hands of the southerners.

Moreover, as fate would have it, Ndindiliyimana and Col. Luc Marchal, the deputy commander of UNAMIR, had previously agreed on 6 April to implement joint patrols of Rwandan gendarmes and UNAMIR Civipol (civilian police) to secure Kigali and search out arms caches. This maneuver targeted stocks of weapons made available to Interahamwe youth and the MRND with the assistance of the prefect of Kigali and certain extremist military officers. These searches, almost always fruitless, since they were known in advance, were viewed as provocations by the "hardened" elements of the regime. If one adds to this that the prime minister, Agathe Uwilingiyimana, who hailed from the same commune in Butare prefecture as Ndindiliyimana did, would become de facto head of the executive branch in the absence of the president, one can well appreciate the difficulties that awaited him.

On the evening of the crash, as the popular emotions caused by the assassination of the president reached an unprecedented pitch of intensity, the question of legitimacy lay, above all, with the "family." Beyond offering condolences, it was important to appreciate the reactions and intentions of the first lady and her brothers and half-brothers as quickly as possible.

The Presidential Family's Reaction

Members of the presidential family had no doubt that the RPF was responsible for shooting down the plane. That certitude explains the depth of feelings expressed and the behaviors those feelings engendered, as shown by the following testimony from the daughter of the president's personal physician, who was also killed in the crash:

> When we were crying in front of our father's body, Mme Habyarimana told us not to cry, because if the "enemies" saw us, they would be happy. She added that one should carry a gun like her son Jean-Luc, who walked about with an R4 gun.
>
> While we were praying, Mme Agathe Kanziga, Habyarimana's widow, prayed aloud, imploring to assist the Interahamwe to get rid of the enemy and that Rwandan soldiers should have arms. I must point out that meanwhile two nuns who are the sisters of the president and the archbishop were in the State House. We heard Sister Godelieve telling the cook that all Tutsi had to be killed.
>
> We heard Jeanne Habyarimana, his mother, and also Séraphin [Rwabukumba] explaining over the telephone that it was Belgians who shot down the plane and that they were fighting on the side of the RPF (the Belgians . . .).
>
> This was often said on the telephone.
>
> We heard telephone conversations with Mobutu, Mitterrand, and the French ambassador. There were lots of messages of condolence.
>
> Sometimes, Mrs. Habyarimana asked us to go out because of certain telephone conversations.
>
> I, Claire—I still remember a conversation of Mme Habyarimana that her opinion should first be sought before taking a decision. That was about the appointment of Gatsinzi as chief of staff.
>
> During the day of 7 April 1994, we noticed that the entire family that was present, including the nuns, rejoiced whenever the death of an opponent was announced. It was the presidential guards who announced such when they returned from carrying out murder.[12]

According to those close to her, after Agathe Kanziga had set the tone for responding to the crisis, it fell to Protais Zigiranyirazo, her older brother, to organize the defense of the immediate interests of the presidential family and to designate the steps to be taken. On that first night, he assumed the role usually played by Élie Sagatwa, the president's private secretary and Agathe Kanziga's half-brother, who also perished in the crash: on that occasion his immediate priority was to make known the orders and expectations of "the family" by telephone. The urgency for the presidential clan was to affirm loud and clear that it was still alive and well despite the loss of two such prominent members, that its interests had to be protected, and that questions of succession could not deviate from the late president's wishes. In concrete terms, it was first of all necessary to send a strong message to the outside world, that is, short of punishing those who, by all appearances, were directly responsible for shooting down the plane, to take revenge on those enemies of Habyarimana who, in one way or another, had contributed to his demise. Still more precisely, it was necessary to sideline all those who were likely to benefit from his disappearance. Second, it was necessary to take precautions to avert other attacks and risks and attend to the security and belongings of the clan members. Recall also that if, in the mind of the slain president, a major stumbling block in the political transition was the threat of prosecution for killing the leaders of the First Republic, Protais Zigiranyirazo had good reason to share the same concern, given the posts he held at that time. Appointed prefect of Ruhengeri on 24 December 1974, just a few months after the trial that had condemned those former dignitaries to long years of detention in the confines of that prefecture's sinister prison, it fell to him to watch over their suffering on a daily basis. Finally, and this risk includes the preceding one, the family could not abide that the political legacy of the Second Republic be tainted or watch, without reacting, as the very persons who, openly or indirectly, contributed to its loss acceded to power.

Insuring the survival of the system built by and around Habyarimana was an urgent and daunting challenge. It could not simply be parceled out while the family itself just watched, its arms folded. Instructions concerning the nature of the response were explicit and could only come from loyal members of the family, then reduced to surviving members from the wife's side: Agathe Kanziga; Protais Zigiranyirazo, her brother; Séraphin Rwabukumba, her half-brother; and the children of the presidential couple. For the record, Agathe Kanziga, her son Jean-Luc, and Zigiranyirazo have all stated that no coordination of this nature was possible during the night of 6–7 April, even after the Presidential Guard and the paracommando battalion had cordoned off the zone of the crash and access to the presidential residence in Kanombe. By their accounts, Agathe Kanziga had no contact with the persons mentioned above that night and would have been all alone with those already at the family home (*see annex 54*).

But if Agathe Kanziga had no need of her brothers to make such decisions, it is highly unlikely that members of the family would have remained on the sidelines if they were all at risk of suffering the same fate as the president and the other collateral victims. Nor can one imagine that in such circumstances these members would not have reached out to their half-sister, sister, or nephews. Protais Zigiranyirazo does not deny this:

> Around 8:35 PM my brother Rwabukumba telephoned me to tell me that the president's plane was just shot down. In my confusion I telephoned Kanombe, to the president's residence. Jean-Luc, the youngest son, didn't yet have confirmation that his father was in the plane that had just crashed in the compound. His mother was in the chapel praying. I telephoned to the French ambassador, who told me that he just found out but that it still was not clear if the president was aboard the plane. I called again to Kanombe. Jean-Luc told me that the warrant officer who always travels with his father was just found, and I drew my own conclusions. We spent the night in a nightmare and in fear, because gunfire could be heard all through the night. I couldn't take the risk of traveling to Kanombe alone, so I waited until the next day.[13]

It would be surprising if, over the course of this extraordinary night, Protais Zigiranyirazo had not taken it upon himself to discuss practical matters by telephone with the members of his family. According to two colonels who were present at army headquarters that night, things proceeded as follows:

> The former [Théoneste Bagosora] transmitted his directives by telephone during the meeting that night and dispatched those he could reach by radio (Presidential Guard commanders, military police, the paracommando battalion); the latter [Joseph Nzirorera] relied on Ephrem Setako—not in the official hierarchy—and mobilized the Presidential Guard.
>
> This is how Bagosora operates: he went to gather his information at the home of the first lady [Agathe Kanziga] and finds out who is dead and what is being planned while the other members of the Military Crisis Committee are still waiting for information from the Presidential Guard. Bagosora received the first phone call, which the switchboard operator transferred to him in the conference room, with conversation in muffled tones. Then when the second call came in, he asked that it be transferred to him in another office. He received at least three phone calls and had set himself up in an office in the HQ; after the last call, he came back into the conference room and asked Cyprien Kayumba to go and pick up [the phone]. When Kayumba returned, he then stated that he too was in favor of the military soldiers taking control of matters.[14]

That night it was Théoneste Bagosora who asserted himself as the privileged spokesperson of the presidential clan while parlaying himself into the Military Crisis Committee to take the full measure of the situation.

The Terms of Revenge

Concerning the terms of revenge and, in direct consequence, the options for the succession, there was no need for lengthy face-to-face debate. By then, the list of persons most hated by the family had been etched in everyone's mind for quite some time: there were those who were first in line, given the roles assigned to them by the 1991 Constitution; those who had played along with the RPF during negotiations; those who had fought against the president most vigorously; and those who, Tutsi or Hutu, had chosen to collaborate with the RPF. This would include Agathe Uwilingiyimana, the "putschist" prime minister; Joseph Kavaruganda (Hutu, Kigali), president of the Constitutional Court; Boniface Ngulinzira (Hutu, Ruhengeri), one of the negotiators of the Arusha Peace Accords; Frederic Nzamurambaho and Faustin Rucogoza (Hutu, Byumba), ministers of the opposition parties; Landoald Ndasingwa (Tutsi, Kigali); Félicien Ngango (Hutu, Kibungo); Vénantie Kabageni (Hutu, Gisenyi); and the president and vice president designates who had been proposed for the NTA.

According to someone close to the family and in line with other accounts, a meeting was held at the residence in Kanombe: "At that time, for people like Zigiranyirazo Protais, Kanziga Agathe, and the members of the MRND Central Committee and other dignitaries of the regime, it was completely normal to identify 'the enemy.' It was necessary to avenge the deaths of Juvénal and Élie Sagatwa."[15] Kanombe was encircled by the Presidential Guard, and no other unit or individual could risk going there without its approval. Among the officers who came to the presidential residence, there was Félicien Muberuka, commander of the operational sector assigned to Camp Mayuya in Kanombe, but especially noteworthy was the arrival of Maj. Aloys Ntabakuze, commander of the paracommando battalion, right after the plane crash (he returned there several times thereafter). He was later followed by Maj. Protais Mpiranya, commander of the Presidential Guard.[16] The trips to the presidential residence by two of the most loyal officers illustrate their willingness to affirm their complete solidarity with the presidential family and to take their orders directly from the source. They personally received the blessings of Agathe Kanziga. According to witnesses, Séraphin Rwabukumba and Protais Zigiranyirazo did not show up in Kanombe that night but "early" or "very early" the next morning. As for many others, the Presidential Guard provided escort for their movements to the presidential residence and in town.[17] Some went to the morgue in Kanombe to see the body of Agathe Uwilingiyimana, and Séraphin Rwabukumba went to Camp Kigali "to see the bodies of the ten Belgian parachutists after they had been killed" (see below).[18] This family-wide conference lasted all through the night, simply judging by their many phone calls back and forth. Agathe Kanziga was determined to participate in all decision making; she made clear her thirst for revenge to all those within earshot.

The ascendancy and the authority of the president's widow were undeniable that night.[19] And, as other witnesses have recounted, the intimates of the family who came to pay their respects in Kanombe were not unmoved: "Ntabakuze [the commander of the paracommando battalion] was among those who went to see the body of Juvénal. He was one of the most crazed."[20]

Thus, it seems clear that in a matter of hours after the crash, the family, the unit commanders, and the leading candidates for the succession, Joseph Nzirorera and Théoneste Bagosora, had already resolved the question of eliminating the opposition leaders.[21] As for the choice of targets, there was no need for debate; all were ready for a job many had wanted to be done long ago. The only concern was to ensure that events would unfold in a manner agreeable to whoever finally seized the reins of power. However, a second condition had to be met to carry the day: in addition to making sure each candidate would get the Akazu's support, it was necessary to confirm his control over the army. In fact, giving this elite unit, condemned to extinction by the Arusha Peace Accords, the ability to pursue these criminal missions meant taking them out of the normal channels of authority. More importantly, beyond the political figures, the Presidential Guard was now in a position to terrorize all of the officers and the units that would dare to oppose these planned assassinations. Not knowing how far the Presidential Guard would go, the opposition figures were not the only ones needing to take precautionary measures on the night of 6 April.

The Conditions of the Succession

It was in such extraordinary circumstances that the family and its armed wing confronted the next most critical issue, the matter of the succession:

The debate within the presidential family was to know who would be in a position to state "Long live the king" in relation to those who were dead or absent. With Nsabimana and Sagatwa on one side and Kabiligi and Ntiwiragabo on the other, the only general staff officer ["G"] who was around was the head of personnel, and he was in Gitarama. So it was left to Zigiranyirazo and Bagosora to fill the void and organize the strategic contacts that night and the next morning. For the Akazu, following the assassination of Stanislas Mayuya in 1988, the options were simple: the "second" after Juvénal Habyarimana would be Bagosora if they opted for a soldier or Nzirorera if the Arusha Accords were to be implemented with a civilian.[22]

This celebrated formula, "The king is dead, long live the king," by which the royal line survived the king, rings true in this context. For the presidential family, what became important after the abrupt demise of Habyarimana was continuity, the perpetuation of power. There could be no void; the succession had to be immediate. It was absolutely essential to validate the notion of descent, of legitimate fealty to the line, before any other process would intervene.

If, between Bagosora the soldier and Nzirorera the civilian, the exceptional context of insecurity conferred a decisive advantage to the former, it would still be necessary for him to fulfill the third condition in order to carry the day: to secure the support of the politicians. This required, first and foremost, the neutralization of the "illegitimate" claimant, the one who had recently dispossessed the "father of the nation" of "his" party and who, just before he left for Arusha, had been denounced as a traitor to Habyarimana: none other than Matthieu Ngirumpatse. The latter was in a position to legitimately lay claim to "regency" and govern in tandem with Agathe Uwilingiyimana. He would thus provide breathing space for the transitional institutions to be implemented in line with the Arusha Peace Accords. For anyone to suggest the names of Ngirumpatse and Uwilingiyimana, the two suspected putschists from the week preceding the death of the president (but with the strongest claim on institutional legitimacy), as plausible candidates for the succession would have been received as a provocation even beyond the milieu of extremist northerners within the MRND and the mouvance présidentielle. Since Ngirumpatse was at the top of the list of "enemies," and given the emotionally charged climate of that night, there was no difficulty in obtaining his withdrawal. He simply refused to stand as a candidate to fill the vacancy.

The "family" summoned the various players, and Théoneste Bagosora found himself in the role of impromptu chief, charged, most notably, with mobilizing the loyal troops and the logistics of security. It was a matter not only of eliminating adversaries but also of entrusting the dignitaries of the regime, that is, the major personalities and the MRND ministers, along with their families, to the Presidential Guard.

Joseph Nzirorera, who had previously informed the commander of UNAMIR that he did not feel safe in his residence, which was located in the vicinity of the parliament building, was apparently one of the first to benefit from this protection.[23] The Presidential Guard managed to round up the MRND ministers, who were then securely installed within the enclosures of its camp near the parliament. Maj. Augustin Cyiza, who was president of the War Council in 1994 and probably one of the best informed, described the situation in these terms: "Escorted by the Presidential Guard, the ministers arrived, fearing a coup d'état, but as soon as they were brought up to speed they acted like excited bees hovering about the hive, swearing to seek revenge on the RPF."[24]

Neither Ngirumpatse nor Karemera was among those "evacuated" to the Presidential Guard camp. The latter eventually made his way to the former's home, but in fact they have never revealed where they found shelter on that first night. For the now-pared-down core of the Akazu, allowing Bagosora to set himself up as the head of the Military Crisis Committee at first seemed like the most effective solution, but Bagosora was unsuccessful in fulfilling the second condition (*see box 11*).

A replacement for General Nsabimana, the army chief of staff who lost his life in the crash, would be resolved by the general staff. Normally, the command would go to the highest-ranking officer, in this case, Maj. Gen. Augustin Ndindiliyimana. However, in the absence of a new head of the army, the chief of staff of the gendarmerie would not automatically be promoted. The option of co-opting him as president of the Military Crisis Committee met with immediate opposition from Bagosora. By initially refusing to serve as a substitute for the deceased chief of staff—and, more fundamentally, by refusing to undermine Colonel Bagosora's designs—Ndindiliyimana helped Bagosora to impose himself temporarily. But it was one thing to preside over a meeting and quite another to install a military committee with emergency powers that would substitute itself for the civilian authorities, an option rejected by the majority of officers present. Nor did Bagosora obtain the support of Gen. Roméo Dallaire or the special representative of the secretary-general of the United Nations, Jacques-Roger Booh-Booh, who, over the course of the night, proved unyielding when Bagosora sought his backing (*see box 12*). Apparently, Bagosora did not obtain the support of the major embassies either.

As Booh-Booh and Dallaire understood the situation, as was also the case with most of the ambassadors in residence, two matters were evident: on the one hand, the Arusha Peace Accords had to be put into effect, because as of 5 January 1994 the presidency had formally entered the transition phase; on the other hand, the prime minister occupied a pivotal role in that process. This analysis was duly presented to Bagosora. As soon as he realized that he was presented with no other choice but to give up the notion of the Military Crisis Committee being answerable to him, his response was to stonewall: Why settle for the constitutional option when the physical elimination of those who personified that option was already being contemplated?

As for naming an interim army chief of staff, Bagosora was also unsuccessful in pleading for his preferred candidate, Col. Augustin Bizimungu, who by that time had served only five months as a colonel. By proposing to select an army chief of staff from among the commanders of operational sectors, Bagosora hoped to control the whole army. Already in regular contact with the unit commanders, he had no reason to doubt their support and presumed that their autonomy would ensure their availability for his special projects, especially the assassinations of certain notables. Indeed, a unit could be selected, assembled, and disciplined, remain fully obedient to its commander, and yet disobey the chief of staff. And the operational sectors were composed of battalions that were heterogeneous at the level of their command, as well as that of the troops. But what Bagosora had not anticipated was that the highest-ranking commander of operational sectors with the greatest seniority was, in fact, Col. Marcel Gatsinzi in Butare, even though his military sector—which had just been created—was not effectively operational.[25] Balthazar Ndengeyinka's account, corroborated by the majority of the participants whom I interviewed, amply reveals Bagosora's isolation:

> Colonel Bagosora proposed that we take the most senior commander of the operational sectors. Immediately, I thought that he was pushing Col. Augustin Bizimungu, who, appointed colonel in December 1993 after all the seniors had been replaced, had become the most senior. But Bagosora forgot that, following the problems in Burundi after the assassination of President Ndadaye, Butare sector, commanded by Col. Marcel Gatsinzi, was deemed an operational sector even if there hadn't yet been any operations, which meant that Colonel Gatsinzi fulfilled those conditions. Colonel Bagosora then balked. I responded, suggesting that it was not fair that operational sector commanders should be the only candidates and that normally the job should go to the most long-standing officer, in which case it should be Colonel Rusatira [see annex 64].[26] Colonel Bagosora coldly replied that, if that was the case, he would prefer Gatsinzi to Rusatira. Consequently, Col. BEM [brevet d'état major] Gatsinzi was named acting army chief of staff [see annex 65].

After the designation of the chief of staff, Colonel Bagosora proposed that the civilian authorities be replaced by a military committee, which would have been a military coup d'état. Everyone who took the floor opposed that and had arguments to support their position. That went on for quite some time. . . .

General Dallaire and Colonel Marchal joined us, and we explained the problems we were facing. General Dallaire finally told us that if we deviated from the logic of the Arusha Accords, there would be nothing for him to do but to leave the country.

Someone had the ingenious idea of consulting Mr. Booh-Booh, the special representative of the UN secretary-general. Colonel Bagosora and Lieutenant Colonel Rwabalinda were designated to do that. When they returned, they informed us that Mr. Booh-Booh also advised us to stay within the logic of the Arusha Accords. . . .

Before that delegation to Mr. Booh-Booh's house had left, we had already agreed to follow whatever recommendations flowed from the meeting with him, and we decided to call a meeting of operational sector commanders and independent units in Kigali for the following morning at ESM in order to update them on the situation.[27]

The sector and unit commanders were informed about the meeting held during the night, and escorts were arranged for 8:00 a.m., even though the meeting started at 10:00 a.m. It took place in the presence of Col. Théoneste Bagosora; Gen. Augustin Ndindiliyimana; Col. Léonidas Rusatira; the commander of the ESM, Col. Tharcisse Renzaho, prefect of Kigali-ville; the commanders of operational sectors, army camps, army units, and the gendarmerie (with the exception of the commander of the Presidential Guard, Maj. Protais Mpiranya); the bureau chiefs of the general staff; the heads of the working groups in the office of the minister of defense; and Gen. Roméo Dallaire, who arrived toward the end of the meeting. The decisions of the night before were confirmed.

It was in this atmosphere of apparent consensus that the group chose members for what formally became known as the Military Crisis Committee and named the chief of staff of the gendarmerie, General Ndindiliyimana, to head it while conferring the task of following up on contacts with the diplomatic community to Colonel Bagosora. The group advised that the multiparty government of Agathe Uwilingiyimana be immediately provided with the means to govern, which would ensure the installation of the transitional institutions. The second paragraph of the communiqué issued by the commanders of the Rwandan Armed Forces, which was drafted at the end of the meeting, is unambiguous on this point: "In this respect, the current Government is requested to discharge its duties; similarly the political authorities concerned are requested to speed up the establishment of the transitional bodies provided for under the Arusha Accords" (*see annex 56*).

According to several of the officers present, Leonard Nkundiye, operational sector commander for Mutara (the only officer from Bushiru who was still in active service, apart from Théoneste Bagosora), took the floor and, contrary to all expectations, called for a return to calm and urged that the operational sector commander for Kigali be requested to retake control of the military situation and to urgently support the Arusha process: "I recall the intervention of Lieutenant Colonel Nkundiye, which confirmed that he fully understood the soundness of this position, and requested that the meeting be adjourned so that the different commanders could go and explain to the soldiers the decisions that had been taken."[28] Bagosora thus suffered his third setback. But, as the members of the committee would later find out, this had been anticipated. According to Colonel Rusatira,

> Colonel Bagosora summarized what had been said the night before and gave the floor to the other participants.
>
> I suggested that the army provide security and support to the government in place so that it could continue its work. Here I'm referring to the government of Agathe Uwilingiyimana. Ntabakuze and Nkundiye supported me. I later realized that Agathe had been killed before our meeting had adjourned. I have a suspicion that these two officers, who were firmly in Bagosora's camp, simply pretended to support me when they maybe already knew at that time that the prime minister had been assassinated. The meeting had been interrupted by gunfire, which we heard not far from the ESM, coming from the direction of Camp Kigali.
>
> Lieutenant Colonel Nubaha, commander of this military camp, approached Bagosora and spoke to him about it. I think this transpired before the arrival of General Dallaire. The meeting adopted my position and nominated members of the Military Crisis Committee, which was supposed to ensure that these decisions would be put into effect.[29]

Suddenly, "toward the end of the meeting, we heard several gunshots." Those shots had killed the "blue helmets" (*see box 13*).[30]

It was only toward the end of the meeting that word of the prime minister's assassination by the Presidential Guard began to circulate in the hall, which explains the absence of its commander, Maj. Protais Mpiranya. It was at that point that participants began to realize the depth of the strategic split between a minority putschist faction and those, now virtually helpless, who favored a political solution in line with the Arusha Peace Accords. The carefully worded and sober discourse of those officers close to the presidential clan, like Leonard

Nkundiye, who appeared to favor the return to the continuity of government as espoused by the majority was then revealed as a mere smokescreen. Lt. Col. Augustin Cyiza offered the following analysis of this situation:

> Since 1992 there wasn't much motivation to fight, with those from the south wanting the two armies [the FAR and RPA] to be fused, and the northerners, who didn't think that the problem was military. On the ground, the soldiers no longer had the motivation to fight, and many would flee before the advancing RPF. After 6 April 1994, some could no longer tell whom they were fighting for after the death of Juvénal Habyarimana. On the one hand, the officers from the north wanted those from the south to suffer the costs of the war; Laurent Serubuga, for instance, was already taking this position when he was the army chief of staff in 1992, that "the south's turn had now come." On the other hand, the killings of southern notables made ethnic "solidarity" impossible. Officers from the south had had enough of being looked down upon by the northerners and wanted to put a stop to it.[31] Although, theoretically, the FAR had superior technical capacity and larger stocks of weapons, the likelihood of coming out on top was very slim. Finally, and most importantly, there was no realistic prospect of alliances or serious negotiation with the RPF, because the core of its leadership was composed of "foreigners" with no links to the interior, without intermediaries, and because its social base was exclusively Tutsi. The Hutu in their ranks were neutralized and under watch. That's how, in my opinion, you have to understand what Colonel Nkundiye was saying when he supported the idea of leaving civilians in the forefront.[32]

When he returned to Gabiro, Colonel Nkundiye's attitude toward officers in his sector was similar to that held by several of his colleagues who never dared to publicly challenge the majority view while nonetheless collaborating with Bagosora to settle scores and wreak the vengeance they had been looking forward to for the longest time. In that, they were responding to orders they had received from the colonel during the meeting at the ESM on the morning of 7 April: according to one of the officers present, Bagosora told Majors Nkundiye, Ntabakuze, and Nzuwonemeye to *muhere ruhande* (eliminate everyone). The only difference between them was that Major Nkundiye could not voice dissenting opinions in his operational sector, owing to the presence of his staff officers. For the other officers, Lt. Col. Aloys Ntabakuze (commander of the paracommando battalion), Maj. François-Xavier Nzuwonemeye (commander of "Recce" Battalion, the Reconnaissance Squad), and Maj. Joël Bararwerekana (Hutu, Ruhengeri, commander of the PM), there was no problem in acting in ways opposite to their public pronouncements. Thus, on

Thursday, 7 April, the military high command ordered the "Recce" Battalion and the PM to deploy in order to halt massacres of the population and to contain the Presidential Guard, and yet the units from those battalions readily joined in the killings organized by the Presidential Guard with the approval of their commander, Maj. Protais Mpiranya. Having lost the chief they were supposed to protect, the Presidential Guard, whose dissolution was anticipated by the Arusha Peace Accords, acting in total disregard of the chain of command, took it upon itself to mete out revenge on all of Habyarimana's presumed adversaries. As for Major Nzuwonemeye, an isolated southern officer, he was in no position to take up a dissenting stance; he felt he had no choice but to go with the flow.

In fact, the Military Crisis Committee's strategy, espoused by Bagosora, was never approved by the participants; while it was being discussed and elaborated on during the night and at the meeting of the high command and unit commanders in the morning, Bagosora never stopped issuing orders. This continued all day on 7 April, which resulted in enough chaos to permit the radical, extremist elements to take over. Thus, he didn't sign the communiqué issued at the end of the meeting until early that afternoon, as the assassinations of members of government and opposition figures went on unabated. The communiqué had yet to be broadcast over Radio Rwanda when the RPF exited the parliament building at around 4:30 p.m. to expand its military reach. The Military Crisis Committee immediately contacted General Dallaire to ask that he "take control of the situation" and intercede with the RPF to get them to return to their barracks. The committee accepted the conditions laid down by the UNAMIR force commander: withdrawal of the Presidential Guard and cessation of killings. Afterward, General Dallaire was supposed to contact the RPF and update the committee the following day to put in place practical steps for a cease-fire.

Colonel Bagosora thus retook the initiative despite the setbacks he suffered during the night. He felt he had a blank check to defy with impunity those who earlier rejected his position: in view of the gap between the majority position of the loyal officers in the Military Crisis Committee and the leanings of the majority of military troops present in Kigali, they felt utterly powerless.

> Everyone knew who had control of the arms stocks in town. They had been arrayed against Bagosora's adversaries, and many of us were in the same situation as those who had already been eliminated. In that situation, how do you complain about someone whom we just removed from the head of our committee, who, to top it off, appeared to us to be in cahoots with the killers? . . .

The members of the Military Crisis Committee did not have the same political complexion as the fighting units then present in Kigali, which was a veritable military force capable of enforcing whatever decision was taken.[33] Discussions turned into a vigorous resistance to Bagosora's proposals, which were deemed too adventuresome by the other members of the committee.

We were all convinced, without the slightest doubt, that the assassination was an RPF initiative. We were careful to take decisions that would provide latitude to better appreciate the RPF's true intentions and devise the solutions that were best suited.[34]

The refusal to ensure the continuity of the state and to apply the Arusha Peace Accords was at odds with decisions whose legitimacy cannot reasonably be contested.

Holding the meeting of the high command at army headquarters was perfectly understandable, because it fell in line with standard practice under the Second Republic, when Maj. Gen. Juvénal Habyarimana combined the titles of president of the republic, minister of defense, and army chief of staff. That the heads of the army, who had gotten used to taking orders and responding directly to the "father of the nation," were coordinating their moves among themselves at a time when the chain of command had been dismantled is not surprising. Moreover, they all knew that the multiparty Constitution of 1992, just like the one of 1991, placed the army under the jurisdiction of the minister of defense, who then reported to the prime minister and the government. Filling in for the minister of defense, Colonel Bagosora, then chief of staff in the Ministry of Defense, had no authority to address a message to the nation on behalf of the Rwandan Armed Forces, bearing the seal of approval of the Ministry of Defense, and thereby ignore the authority of the prime minister, who had been deliberately prevented from delivering the message she had prepared.

Consequently, the legalistic posturing of those MRND leaders in their response to Bagosora about convening the political parties and the modalities for replacing the president of the republic is better seen as a thinly veiled display of cynical opportunism at the service of political convenience. That meeting of the three politicians, Nzirorera, Ngirumpatse, and Karemera, with Bagosora had as its objective the creation of an institutional void that not even the assassination of Agathe Uwilingiyimana could have achieved.

Once again, the sobering commentary—shared by those who, since 1992, simply aspired to peace, only to watch it repeatedly slip away—received confirmation: "The more one is in the minority, the more one turns to war." The continuation of the war was the result of the intransigence of the RPF, battling for the minority Tutsi, and, within Rwanda, of a group even more entrenched as a minority and hell-bent on defending the interests of the Bashiru, those inhabitants of Karago and Giciye communes, which gave birth to the "clan." Few were more cruelly aware of this than the members of the Military Crisis Committee.

In view of the tragic occurrences of that day, which the morning meeting had tried to avoid, the meeting of that afternoon between the Military Crisis Committee and General Dallaire proved extremely tense: the members of the committee were virtually hostages and were incapable of obtaining information or taking action. More to the point, the question of designating a head or an executive able to make decisions had not been settled, and Bagosora was eager to resolve it in his favor, all the more so since UNAMIR suspected his responsibility in the killings of the Belgian "blue helmets," and already Belgium was demanding explanations.

> Since the meeting, the committee had never officially informed itself of what was happening in town. Most of the members had no escorts and couldn't move around to evaluate the situation for themselves, but the rumors that were circulating were alarming. Already, toward the end of the meeting, we had learned that the Belgian "blue helmets" were in difficulty, and the prime minister along with other notables had been assassinated, with suspicions mounting against the hard-core members of the presidential clan, particularly Bagosora. The committee decided to divorce itself from Bagosora, with General Ndindiliyimana acquiescing to presiding over the committee. If memory serves me well, he did not even preside over a single meeting.[35]

This is how Gatsinzi, a key player, the colonel in command of the Butare operational sector, described the atmosphere of the 7 April meeting:

> During the meeting of the evening of the 7th, I sensed antagonism between Bagosora and the rest of the team because Bagosora wanted to chair the crisis committee, even though it was a military committee. We did not agree that he chair the meeting, for he was a retired soldier and also, as directeur de cabinet [chief of staff], he was a politician. We wanted the most senior in rank, that is, Augustin Ndindiliyimana, to chair the meeting. He was at the meeting.
> Bagosora made it clear that as a representative of the ministry that was in charge of both forces, that is, the army and the gendarmerie, he should chair the meeting, but the participants refused outright.
> He then personally attacked some officers, such as Colonel Léonidas Rusatira, saying that when Rusatira himself was directeur de cabinet at the

Ministry of Defense, he was above the chiefs of staff [army staff officers].[36] We pointed out that at that time it was the minister himself who had delegated duties to his chef de cabinet [chief of staff].

In the end, Ndindiliyimana chaired the meeting. Bagosora sulked throughout the meeting and did not really participate.

The decisions taken at the meeting were to see how to restore discipline within the Presidential Guard and facilitate contact between high-ranking government officials, politicians, and the RPF with the help of UNAMIR in order to form a transitional government within the framework of the Arusha Peace Accords.

Usually, it was the chef de cabinet at the Ministry of Defense who maintained the link between the military command and the various political and government bodies, thereby ensuring the implementation of the decisions taken at the meeting. The general staff had no direct contact with those bodies.

Bagosora left the meeting angry.[37]

According to Léonidas Rusatira, the conflict between him and Bagosora concerning the choice of a president for the Military Crisis Committee, a conflict that caused Bagosora's "sulking" and his abrupt, premature departure, occurred at the very beginning of discussions. It was the only real issue at the end of that day and had to be resolved before other points could be addressed.

The first twenty-four hours following the death of the head of state ended with oddly paired balance sheets for the two competing factions within the army, each at odds with the other in trying to manage the crisis.

In everyone's eyes, not only those who reviled him but also his own supporters, Bagosora was the uncontested ringmaster. He had eliminated the principal opposition figures, particularly those whom Hutu extremists characterized as accomplices of the RPF. The army units that supported him controlled the city and organized the terror unfolding in the residential areas. At the Kanombe military camp he was already being addressed as "the president." The concerns of the most extremist elements of Hutu Power were brushed aside, infusing confidence in their ranks that he was actually pursuing their "program."

However, where Bagosora's personal situation was concerned, the situation was much more complicated. The absence of the minister of defense, Augustin Bizimana, and staff officers Gratien Kabiligi and Aloys Ntiwiragabo, who were on a mission abroad, deprived Bagosora of decisive support over the course of the night when he tried to head up the Military Crisis Committee and displace the civilian authorities. That failing forced him to make a show of his force and determination by ordering the killings of the opposition political figures entrusted to ensure the continuity of the state and by delivering up the UNAMIR peacekeepers to the vengeance of unleashed soldiers. The springs of his activism focused on a single objective that he believed he alone could attain: block by any and all means the RPF's designs for the conquest of power. Beyond his provocative diatribes, throughout his long career under Habyarimana's command, and much like his mentor, Bagosora had proved to be a cynical and calculating realist, fully capable of appreciating the stakes and the forces in play. In the reigning circumstances, he was prepared to negotiate a very high price for every concession made to the RPF, to deal just as harshly with the southern opposition, and to impose a recalibrated political transition upon the negotiators and ambassadors seeking to save the peace.

In this context it is easy to understand the serenity displayed by Théoneste Bagosora and Augustin Ndindiliyimana over the course of their long afternoon conversation with Gen. Roméo Dallaire (*see annex 60*). The latter conceded his surprise over the extent of Bagosora's authority ("He was the spokesman; there was no one in the government to turn to who could have represented authority"), his command of the situation ("I've never seen someone so calm, perfectly at ease, given the situation"), and especially the "laudable efforts" he deployed to "take positive action" to bring the assassinations and massacres to a halt. Indeed, given the situation created by the disappearance of the president, Bagosora was in everyone's eyes the sole military authority capable of negotiating with the RPF from a position of strength, and, most notably, he was the only officer capable of ordering the military units and militiamen heading up the massacres to put an end to them.

But the majority of the participants in the meetings of the high command and the Military Crisis Committee that night and the following evening held views totally at odds with Bagosora's own. By refusing to vault him to power or let him head up their committee, the members expressed defiance toward a man they believed capable of doing anything to make sure that power would remain in the hands of the presumptive heirs to the regime, or, to put it another way, to safeguard the interests of the officers from Bushiru and Gisenyi and from the north in general.[38] It is for that reason that Bagosora's peers opposed him and denounced him as an "extremist," not because they imagined that he was busy preparing a genocide. It is important to recall that at that time, and until 12 April, the day that the government left for Murambi (Gitarama), the killings were still limited to the capital in Kigali and to Kigali-rural and a few communes in Gisenyi (the president's commune), Gikongoro, and Kibungo. And it's only toward 18–19 April that the southern prefectures (Gitarama, Butare) "fell in line" after visits from the new interim authorities.

The triple repudiation that the "moderate" officers inflicted on Bagosora progressed in stages. During the informal meeting on the night of 6 April, it was the fortuity of his lack of familiarity with their seniority that allowed the officers to rebuff Bagosora's candidate and nominate one of their own as acting army chief of staff; and then, with support from Roméo Dallaire and Jacques-Roger Booh-Booh, those same officers managed to block Bagosora's personal ambitions without, however, daring to affront him, since there was no candidate to be launched in opposition. All they could do was to put off decision making until a meeting could be called to assemble the camp commanders and operational sector commanders. And even if this meeting strengthened the officers' position by solemnly reaffirming the necessity of quickly implementing the Arusha Peace Accords, their success was ephemeral; only toward the end of the meeting did they realize that Bagosora had short-circuited them by making it impossible to implement the accords. In this context, the third repudiation of Bagosora's ascendancy, inflicted later that evening after some robust debate, at least had the advantage of being quite explicit. The clash clearly identified the protagonists and, after Bagosora's departure, forced his opponents to formulate a program and concrete proposals in line with their vision for the way forward.

But here again, appearances were deceptive. By choosing Augustin Ndindiliyimana as president of the Military Crisis Committee, the opponents selected a spokesperson who, indeed, dared not distance himself from Bagosora. And yet, despite the majority position of the committee members and the legitimacy conferred on them by the meeting of commanders, the prerogatives of the members who were finally installed appeared fragile: they revealed themselves to be powerless in the face of undisciplined units and militiamen who controlled the streets, utterly inept in ensuring protection for their base of support in the political class, and even incapable of being taken seriously as viable counterparts for negotiations with General Dallaire or the diplomatic corps.

Finally, and perhaps most importantly, the committee members didn't take full stock of the implications of Bagosora's sulking when he stormed out of the meeting after having failed to win their approval. The strategic audacity displayed by Bagosora, who now felt isolated, in eliminating the "accomplice" politicians turned out to be a trap. Aside from the French Embassy, which had welcomed the MRND dignitaries and their partisans in Hutu Power, escorted by the Presidential Guard (see chapter 10), the representatives of the United Nations and all of the embassies engaged in the negotiations (Germany, the United States, Belgium, the Vatican) condemned the assassinations of the opposition political figures and supported the position taken by the Military Crisis Committee in reaffirming the demand that "the concerned political authorities [accelerate] implementation of the transitional institutions anticipated by the Arusha Accords." And by the very next morning, when the matter of this implementation was to be discussed, it was to Bagosora that the southern political class and the international community and Belgian judicial authorities turned to account for the assassinations of the day before. So he too was saddled with the imperative of taking new initiatives (on this point, *see annex 61*).

Bagosora's self-imposed obligation was made all the more pressing by the RPF, which made a point of noisily reminding everyone over the course of that afternoon of leaving its cantonment in CND to challenge the Presidential Guard, whose camp was located nearby. To quote from a coded message from UNAMIR: "Point 4: The staff of the RPF ensconced within the enclosures of the CND, protected by UNAMIR, had initially been deterred by UNAMIR, but around 16:30 p.m., local time, which was around 10:30 a.m. in New York, around a third of the group, perhaps 150–200 out of the 600, forced their way out. There was fighting in the streets between these soldiers and elements of the Presidential Guard."[39] This signaled the death knell of the Arusha Peace Accords. The eruption of violence set off a swift reaction by members of the Military Crisis Committee, who contacted General Dallaire in order to immediately commence discussions with the RPF. These discussions were held the next day.

On the evening of 7 April, a window of opportunity was still open. All of the actors, foreigners included, were going to have to position themselves, and this despite the fact that reliable information about these events was scarce and circulated only with great difficulty beyond the tight circles of actual instigators of the events. By all indications, it appeared that the day of 8 April would end up being equally decisive.

The Attack on the Plane, an Enduring Enigma

To conclude, it is important to consider the reasons why this question of responsibility for shooting down the president's plane has so long festered in the shadows. No one has ever claimed responsibility for the attack, but in Kigali's official circles it was inevitably attributed to the RPF. From what I observed on the ground, the perceptions of residents and foreigners, diplomatic personnel and journalists, were more complex. Of course, the RPF was viewed as the only entity capable of organizing such an operation, which, besides, was simply a logical extension of the threats its leaders had been issuing over the previous few weeks, coupled with predictions of a certain, and rapid, military victory. But to openly admit this would surely generate embarrassment or vehement denials. For quite some time, Habyarimana had already lost the propaganda war as far as the *bazungu* (whites) were concerned. It was difficult for them to condemn this rebel movement, generally recognized for its organization and its efficiency. Everyone believed the RPF could quickly take power in Kigali if it wanted to. The refusal either to find out who did what, where, and how or, for many, to admit what they already knew, not to mention the indecision and disengagement of the international community, stems from a tacit recognition of the RPF's superior military power, a fact that no one wanted to imagine, even though many could well anticipate how exceptionally destructive it would be if push came to shove. Without offering the factual elements that we were all waiting for, the "major" embassies girded themselves with a prudent strategy of suspecting a range of likely protagonists or by settling upon a likely scenario, more or less openly, that intentionally exculpated whatever camp they supported. In like manner, and even though very few among them had correspondents on the ground those first few days, the international media generated an array of possible scenarios. But as the days passed, and after the first series of assassinations—those befalling leaders of the opposition and the Belgian "blue helmets" (see below)—with the increasing pace and scale and the systematic nature of the attacks against Tutsi of the interior and their "accomplices," the hypothesis of responsibility of the "Hutu extremists," dissatisfied with the concessions Habyarimana had agreed to in Dar es Salaam, gained credibility and, much later, found its way into the scenario of a planned conspiracy for genocide. The monstrosity of the genocide and the irresponsibility of the protagonists, who flatly refused negotiation, coupled with the cowardice of the international community, all combined to make it hard to give credence to sworn testimonies, however candid they may have been. The euphemisms, the interlacing strategies of denigration and reciprocal demonization between the two camps, the manipulation and fabrication of evidence, the obstruction and squelching of standard judicial procedures, all of these served as ingredients for a well-nursed enigma.

Consequently, despite the exceptional gravity of the incident and its aftermath, none of the requests for an international investigation—whether formulated by the president of the United Nations Security Council, the Interim Government of Rwanda, or the governments of other countries—were ever heeded. The UN had received such a request as early as 8 April—made by France—and on 27 June the Security Council entrusted the secretary-general with this investigation. On 12 April the Belgian government did likewise with a request to the International Civil Aviation Organization, which debated it on 25 April. On 15 June 1994 the OAU summit in Tunis also tabled a resolution to that end. Finally, on 28 June René Degni-Segui, the UN Commission on Human Rights' special rapporteur for Rwanda, requested that a commission of inquiry be empaneled. None of these requests were acted upon, at least not until the end of the war. The most bizarre response was the one received by René Degni-Segui: the reason for the refusal, he was told, was the absence of a budget for such expenditures in the United Nations.[40]

After the victory of the rebellion and the installation of new political authorities, all efforts to follow up on such requests were deemed to have been overtaken by events. Thus, on 16 September 1994, at the international conference on Rwanda in The Hague, Pasteur Bizimungu, who served as the new president of the republic, declared that this matter was "without interest" and as such was not a priority for the authorities. He preferred to leave the matter "in the hands of neutral authorities," who then proceeded to bury it.[41] Except for a letter of 28 March 1996 from the Rwandan Ministry of Transportation and Communication to the regional representative of the International Civil Aviation Organization requesting an expert report on the president's Falcon— which never received a response—no other international entity has ever been approached by the authorities concerned in Rwanda or Burundi.[42] There were repeated requests for the ICTR, created by resolution of the United Nations Security Council on 8 November 1994 "for the sole purpose of prosecuting persons responsible for genocide and other serious violations of International Humanitarian Law," including acts of terrorism, to initiate investigations. However, its spokespersons have consistently maintained that the shooting down of the plane on 6 April is beyond the ICTR's mandate. Let me emphasize, nonetheless, that three successive prosecutors, who undertook investigations on this subject without any real commitment, and in even broader terms concerning the war crimes and/or crimes against humanity committed by the RPF, have preferred to turn a deaf ear to such requests, yielding to pressure from the new Rwandan authorities. More serious still has been their blissful disregard of their obligations: the evidence shows that they did not hesitate to conceal or compromise their findings.[43] The ICTR has consistently opposed all requests for investigations into the downing of the plane (to learn more about the reasons for this attitude, see chapter 13). Since then, as a meek justification for the ICTR's stance on the absence of an "international inquiry," the dossier and evidence concerning what the UN insists upon characterizing as "the crash of the presidential plane" or "the plane accident that cost the lives of the presidents of Rwanda and Burundi" remain tightly controlled.[44]

It was only on 27 March 1998, three weeks after the creation of the Parliamentary Commission of Inquiry "charged with investigations on the military operations led by France, other countries and the UN in Rwanda between 1990 and 1994," that the French judicial system, approached by the families of the French crew for the presidential plane, opened a formal investigation, entrusted to Judge Jean-Louis Bruguière.[45] After substantial debate and hesitation, on 17 November 2006 the investigation reached the stage of formally targeting the RPF and then on 22 November followed with the issuance of nine international arrest warrants against persons close to President Paul Kagame.[46] The upshot was Rwanda's break in diplomatic relations with France on 24 November.

The Rwandan government appointed the National Commission of Inquiry on 17 April 2006, headed by former minister of justice Jean de Dieu Mucyo and "charged with assembling proof of the implication of France in the genocide of 1994." The commission, which was formed before the publication of Judge Bruguière's conclusions, was postponed several times. It gave the impression of directly responding to the French accusations.[47] Its report, completed in April 2008 and finally made public the following 5 August, announced the forthcoming issuance of thirty-three international arrest warrants targeting French political figures and military officers.[48] In tandem with this first commission, on 10 October 2007 another national commission was created to "investigate the circumstances of the attack against the plane of President Juvénal Habyarimana on the evening of 6 April 1994." The work of this second commission, headed by Judge Jean Mutsinzi, would demonstrate French responsibility. The results have since been published in a report bearing his name.[49] In addition, relying on the principle of universal jurisdiction, on 6 February 2008 the Spanish judge Fernando Andreu Merelles issued arrest warrants against forty current high-level officials in the Rwandan Army for acts of genocide, crimes against humanity, war crimes, and terrorism committed in Rwanda and in the Democratic Republic of the Congo (DRC) between 1 October 1990 and 2002. Relying on elements and conclusions foreshadowed by the French inquiry, in his indictment the judge accused the high command of the RPA, focusing specifically on Paul Kagame, with organizing the "attack aimed at extinguishing the life of president Juvénal Habyarimana . . . with the objective of preparing a final assault for taking power, and creating a situation of civil war."[50]

On 23 October 2008, Marc Trédivic and Philippe Coirre, the two French judges who inherited the Bruguière investigation and whose complementary investigations had de facto been blocked by the French prosecutor's office when Paris decided to mend relations with the regime in Kigali, informed the parties of their willingness to release their conclusions.[51] This maneuver opened the path to a public trial in absentia for the full array of suspects. On 28 October Bruno Joubert, President Nicolas Sarkozy's advisor for Africa, and Patrick Ouart, legal advisor to the president of the republic, made a short trip to Kigali and explained the circumstances leading to the arrest of Rose Kabuye, the current chief of protocol of the Rwandan president who was accused of complicity in murder in relation to a terrorist enterprise and participating in a criminal association to prepare acts of terrorism. On 9 November Kabuye deliberately confronted the international arrest warrant against her in Germany, provoking her arrest, and was then transferred to France.[52] After the arraignment and her immediate release under court supervision, her defense was finally able to gain access to the thousands of pages of her French judicial dossier.[53] The Rwandan authorities then decided to suspend publication of the "Mutsinzi Report" (which was supposed to demonstrate French implication in the downing of the plane), initially projected for late November 2008 and subsequently postponed until March 2009.

Thus, fourteen years after the attack, the judicial debate was relaunched without any clear indication of the time frame and the conditions in which the debate was likely to end. It would appear that the willingness of the suspects and Rwandan authorities to "lance the boil" was really intended to block a trial in absentia and gain access to the documentation in the Bruguière investigation before engaging in routine procedural jousting with an oddly sympathetic prosecutor's office, one apparently open to a negotiated termination of the investigation or a recusal of the trial judges upon the first procedural error. In fact, in the opinion of many observers, what makes the debate surrounding the shooting down of the plane such a sensitive subject, bordering on the sacrilegious, is the enormity of the massacres and the genocide that followed. However, judging from the reaction and the commentary from the majority of Rwandan political figures on both sides (civilian and military), very few had imagined that the downing of the plane would unleash such a paroxysm of violence or that the international community would betray such utter powerlessness in containing it when faced with the determination of the protagonists to settle matters between them once and for all. Take, for example, the comments attributed to Seth Sendashonga during a meeting between the RPF and MDR delegations on 2 April: "I asked him if he gave any thought to how many victims there would be, and he added: 'It won't be too many: maybe five thousand, at the very most twenty thousand.'"[54] When considered in the context of a "medium-intensity" war, the perpetrators of the attack on the plane, whatever their identity, in all likelihood would be viewed today as undistinguished warlords with whom the entire international community could cohabit or negotiate.[55]

Undeniably, in Rwanda the various schemes and plans that were hatched may have gotten out of the control of those who set them in motion. Even so, it is still important to understand how, once the plane was shot down, the tragic lockstep of war and genocide appeared to materialize and extend over time.

8

The Civilian Alternative

Théoneste Bagosora's failure to control the Military Crisis Committee, which was apparent by the middle of the night of 7 April 1994, forced him to fall back on an alternative solution: the politicians.[1] This solution had its advantages, though, insofar as it did not sideline Colonel Bagosora and still allowed him to advance the candidate of his choosing, Joseph Nzirorera. But for that advancement to happen, it was necessary to break with the logic of the Arusha Peace Accords, which, paradoxically, would seem to have favored the two bêtes noires of the Akazu and the titans of the north: Agathe Uwilingiyimana and Matthieu Ngirumpatse. The likely duo that was at hand—Ngirumpatse in the presidency and Uwilingiyimana heading the government—presented the worst possible scenario. The reins of power would fall into the hands of two southerners, the former viewed as an adversary of the defunct president and the latter as an outright traitor.

Evading the Logic
of the Arusha Peace Accords

Getting rid of Agathe Uwilingiyimana posed no real problem of principle. In the wake of the president's assassination, the sidelining or elimination of the prime minister was to be expected. No one within the mouvance présidentielle could tolerate the country being handed over to pro-RPF elements, much less to a woman who never shrank from voicing disrespectful, indeed injurious, remarks about the president, especially his in-laws. There was no attempt to conceal the bitter enmity that this aroused among them.

I remember that Jean-Luc had a firearm on him; I saw it when we went to see the body of the prime minister at the morgue in Camp Kanombe. I think she was only draped with a sheet, that she was practically nude, and that she was lying on the ground. I went there with Jean-Luc, Séraphin, and the guards. It was around 1 p.m.; I remember because my sister Alphonsine was angry when I got back. I can no longer tell you what day it was, though.

It was Jean-Luc who wanted to go and see the body to make sure that she was dead, and I went with him. I confirm that Jean-Luc Habyarimana would have tried to fire a bullet in Agathe's corpse, but I persuaded him not to do that out of fear for how the soldiers in the camp would react. I saw that the soldiers had spat on Agathe's body.[2]

But as Matthieu Ngirumpatse underscores, the problem of the "designation of the head of state and the applicable law was the lynchpin for all the questions that were being raised."[3] Persuading the MRND president to resign from his position and implementing a constitutional solution outside the framework of the Arusha Peace Accords would require "understanding" on his part and agreement from the other party bigwigs. It meant reawakening the spirit of sacrifice in the name of national unity not only in Ngirumpatse but also in the other presidential hopefuls, who would similarly be called upon to put aside their personal ambitions.

Indeed, at least five key MRND figures hinted at or made explicit their presidential ambitions. That evening each wondered about what might happen next, or, to put it more concretely, what group of soldiers he could count on to ensure his security and eventually support him through thick and thin. These five MRND members were:

- Édouard Karemera, the "rising star" of 1991. In point of fact, he was no longer a serious contender after 1992, when President Habyarimana pushed him aside in favor of Ngirumpatse. In addition, his principal ally in military circles, Maj. Gen. Augustin Ndindiliyimana, once again demonstrated his indecisiveness and his incapacity to impose his will. But, realistic and determined, Karemera remained prepared, in wait-and-see mode, to accommodate himself to the scenario being prepared by the presidential clan—meaning in effect to position himself as a pro-Hutu radical from the south.
- Augustin Ngirabatware, the intellectual of the presidential clan, undeniably inspired confidence among its members. Minister of planning and son-in-law of the powerful Félicien Kabuga, who himself was also linked to the president's family, Ngirabatware already filled the role of counselor.

Moreover, given the uncertainties of the moment, the family surrounding Agathe Kanziga had dire need of a compass. Aside from which, following his recent familial and political ascendancy, he worked hard to earn the favor of officers originating from the president's home turf. But Ngirabatware had no loyal minions of his own nor any political base within the MRND beyond what his wealthy father-in-law, a native of Byumba, could procure for him.

- Casimir Bizimungu, a brilliant and well-respected politician, promoted and protected by the president's older brother, Séraphin Bararengana, had always been viewed as a competitor by Juvénal Habyarimana, and the Akazu was always a bit mistrustful of him. All of Bizimungu's contacts with the president were blocked by Élie Sagatwa, who was totally devoted to Joseph Nzirorera. Bizimungu cultivated strong links in the military among officers from Ruhengeri who were rivals of those loyal to Joseph Nzirorera and who enjoyed favorable reputations among "progressive" officers from the north and the south. But, after James Gasana fled to Europe, when it appeared that Bizimungu's chances of succeeding him at the head of the Ministry of Defense were fading, he lost most of his supporters in the army, who then openly rallied behind Joseph Nzirorera. Nonetheless, within the framework of an election with universal suffrage, Bizimungu was clearly one of those rare northern candidates capable of attracting supporters beyond the prefectures of the Rukiga region.

- The two last presidential hopefuls, the only ones that truly counted that particular night, Matthieu Ngirumpatse and Joseph Nzirorera, had years ago made their ambitions clear and squarely confronted each other as rivals. But in the political context brought on by the abrupt disappearance of President Habyarimana, the first found himself ipso facto rejected by the Akazu. In the eyes of those who could bestow presidential legitimacy, Ngirumpatse was viewed as weak, ambitious, and ungrateful. The plotting that night between the Habyarimana family and those close to it left no doubt that the presidential clan's primary objective was to prevent matters from falling into the hands of the MRND president, the presumed successor under the terms of the Arusha Peace Accords. The clan's animosity toward him was such that it is entirely conceivable—by Ngirumpatse's own admission—that, had he opted to maintain his candidacy, he would have been the target of the Presidential Guard's "populist fury," just like the other "traitors" in the opposition parties. Ngirumpatse also thought that the RPF would never let him stand in their way. His own supporters in the army were unreliable. Officers from his home prefecture, like Marcel Gatsinzi and Félicien Muberuka, hardly mattered when up against extremist officers from the north. All the same, his traditional supporters within the MRND at that time seemed rather lightweight: control over the activist base had already passed into the hands of the party's national secretary, Joseph Nzirorera, who had the loyalty of the highly mobilized, radical branch of the so-called Akazu of the Interahamwe. Even if the rather favorable reputation Ngirumpatse enjoyed among the party's intellectuals and among southern opponents made him the best "national" MRND presidential candidate for any open electoral contest, that very strength disqualified him during the night of 6 April.

In sum, only one of the five MRND candidates, Joseph Nzirorera, met the three conditions previously mentioned: support from the Akazu, support from the army, and the capacity to impose himself politically. And, by the force of circumstances, he earned the favor of Théoneste Bagosora, the failed candidate!

That is how this crucial moment had played out for the presidential clan—and in northern military and civilian circles—by the time of Bagosora's meeting with the MRND party leaders on 7 April at 8:00 a.m. At the request of the UN special representative, this decisive meeting had been scheduled prior to the gathering of military commanders, who needed to be informed of clear political options.

By virtue of the Arusha Peace Accords, the person aspiring to the presidency of the republic was to be proposed by the MRND.[4] Although they had been approached by Bagosora by 1:00 a.m. on 7 April, the MRND party leaders have all recounted in subsequent statements that they had no inkling of the purpose of that meeting, as they had not conferred with one another beforehand—not even by telephone—and that they left that encounter without having discussed or resolved anything beyond reaffirming their confidence in Bagosora to manage, with the Military Crisis Committee, the transition.[5] As for Ngirumpatse, by his own account, he initially had simply "forgotten" that this meeting had even taken place. He claimed that he had only made a single phone call (to Ferdinand Kabagema, the second vice president of the MRND) between the time that he had been informed of the plane crash on the evening of 6 April and the meeting of political parties that was to take place on the morning of 8 April: "So it was the directeur de cabinet [chief of staff] who told me about the president's death; he said to me, 'It is not known whether he is dead, but the plane has been shot down.' . . . Sometime thereafter, there was a military communiqué . . . urging people to remain calm and to stay at home. Being a civilian, I remained at home."[6]

This blatant lie would certainly shock the conscience of other political leaders, to say nothing of the common folk, who, like them, mostly spent the night on the telephone and who already knew by 5:00 that morning that Presidential Guard commandos and soldiers were up and about and had already taken action in their neighborhoods. In fact, during the course of that night they had had all the time they needed to consult with their respective supporters. They had made it quite clear that they were capable of making the decisions expected of them: Nzirorera and Ngirumpatse, the two rival candidates, "spontaneously" refused to assert themselves as the top dogs (*see annex 64*). The MRND president quickly stated his intention to calm the anxieties that the new political dispensation provoked; then, once that weight was lifted, on behalf of the MRND, both men agreed to give Bagosora free rein to fill the void and manage the transition. Concretely, this meant that they approved of the first phase of the game plan—the targeted assassinations of nonaligned figures—set in motion that night by the presidential clan, which went along with Bagosora. That the two lawyers present at the meeting made no reference whatsoever to Agathe Uwilingiyimana—never mind that she had the constitutional mandate to manage the current crisis—clearly indicates that her fate had been sealed. Heeding Bagosora's instructions, the soldiers not only prevented the prime minister's attempt to go to the national radio station to appeal directly to the population but also blocked any attempt at "legalistic" maneuvering. If one can believe the remarks later confidentially attributed to one of the primary members of that crew, one of the participants said, "We cannot suggest a replacement so long as the prime minister is still around," a statement that served as both a death warrant and a repudiation of Ngirumpatse's mandate: "Matthieu did not resist at all."

Given the fears of a possible, sudden demonstration of bravery from Ngirumpatse and the plans set in motion that night by the "crazed" members of the Akazu (as several officers called them), the implicit death sentence to be meted out to the nonaligned figures could just as well have been directed at him. Article 52 of the MRND statutes hovered and swung above his head like the sword of Damocles. The provision held that any vacancy or incapacity of the president of the party would be filled by its national secretary—in that instance, Joseph Nzirorera. That solution would have had the advantage of avoiding the juridical contortions that were taking form and would have officially, immediately enthroned the "natural" candidate for the presidency of the republic. Even more, it would have authorized a transition perfectly in line with the Arusha Peace Accords in the eyes of the international community. The option of eliminating Ngirumpatse was all the more credible since the various extremists who had taken control of the streets were profiting from this period of impunity to settle their own lingering personal scores (family disagreements, commercial disputes, rivalries over women), exactions easily attributable to excesses, banditry, or even the RPF.[7]

The arrangements that resulted flowed from a motley constitutional, military, and political "brew." The minutes of the meeting of MRND leaders with Bagosora were quite explicit (*see annexes 64 and 66*). At the outset, President Ngirumpatse made it clear that the conditions for the MRND's designation of its candidates for the presidency of the republic simply could not be met (organizing internal elections and then a party congress, gaining the consent of other parties). He mentioned the risks of disorder and the distractions that an undertaking of this nature would provoke in the army. First Vice President Édouard Karemera chimed in by stating that only the FAR was in a position to ensure the continuity of the state. Those same remarks were reiterated even more firmly by Ferdinand Kabagema, the second vice president. The national secretary, Joseph Nzirorera, weighed in with an analysis more bellicose in tone: he envisaged a stage of siege, favored "neutralizing all the forces of evil," and wanted to take steps to first calm the country and the population before attending to the political process. Ngirumpatse's conclusion sealed this surging unanimity by supporting all of Bagosora's initiatives: "This would not be a coup d'état, because it was a government by agreement. Juridically speaking, it is not a legal government. Rushing can be harmful. . . . We must explain to the international community that security takes precedence."[8]

Two points in the discussion were essential. Ngirumpatse began his explanation with an appeal to reason: "We would need two candidates." He then reinforced this affirmation: "What one expects of the MRND is simply not possible in the current situation. We would have to get organized (party congress, etc.) in order to present two candidates."[9] However, according to the Arusha Peace Accords, there was no ambiguity.[10] The presidency of the republic fell to the MRND, which had the obligation to present two candidates in the event of a vacancy. Ngirumpatse, catapulted to the presidency some nine months earlier during a party congress, could have legitimately undertaken to have himself put forward as a candidate by the national leadership of the MRND: it was indeed those same leaders who, since 1992, routinely took the important decisions (consisting of the political bureau, along with the eleven presidents of the prefectural committees). His reluctance thus made no sense, unless it was simply a means to refuse engagement in a collaborative process with the other signatories of the Arusha Peace Accords.

There were immediate consequences for this double withdrawal (of the candidate and from the Arusha Peace Accords). Édouard Karemera declared: "UNAMIR should not brandish and flaunt the accords, they should also help us to find urgent solutions." Similarly, Nzirorera intoned: "There have to be exceptional measures before turning to the Arusha Accords (state of emergency)." Dispensing with all ambiguity, Karemera finally clarified: "*Conclusion*:—It is necessary for the political partners to discuss matters, but not the current government" (*see annex 67*).

Karemera proposed that the vacancy in the presidency be filled by the president of the CND for a period of ninety days by relying on the 1991 Constitution. Bagosora could then take action. The green light was given to eliminate the opposition figures, considered pro-RPF and obstacles to this process, and to then install a homogeneous government composed of the MRND and the Power wings.

Beyond its conformity with the 1991 Constitution, the promotion of the new interim president, Théodore Sindikubwabo, presented various advantages, many of which Habyarimana had already discovered. As an MRND member from the south, he was emblematic of the geographic expansion of the party, and as a man prone to equivocation, he was supple and easily manipulated. In addition, by 1994 he was already advanced in age and rather sickly. He thus allowed the veritable chief of the MRND, its national secretary, Joseph Nzirorera, to exercise power via the structures of the former party-state, regardless of strict compliance with formality. Nzirorera, relying on the vestiges of the 1991 Constitution, was aiming for the presidency of the CND in order to succeed Théodore Sindikubwabo at the opportune moment. For his part, Ngirumpatse, the big loser, had to be content with the possibility of deferred opportunities. He could fairly anticipate that, short of a rapid military demise, beyond the three months accorded to Sindikubwabo thanks to Karemera's juridical imagination, an inevitable return to the Arusha Peace Accords would ensure his ascendancy. Jean Kambanda, the prime minister installed in that position on 8 April by Bagosora and the MRND leaders, clearly analyzed the juridical argument they had invoked to safeguard the situation without "compromising themselves":

> It was explained to me that as a legal expert and lawyer, Édouard Karemera had come up with the ploy. He proposed that the 1991 Constitution should be applied. For this to be done, it was necessary to come up with arguments for not applying the Arusha Peace Accords.
>
> The arguments were found. There was the fact that the accords had been violated . . . [a]nd the fact that the Congress couldn't be convened to designate an MRND candidate and that there was an emergency situation. These three arguments were officially presented as the reason for applying the 1991 Constitution instead of the Arusha Peace Accords. . . .
>
> That is what was officially presented to explain the designation of Sindikubwabo. But on thinking beyond what had been said and observing what was going on, I came to the conclusion that it was a ploy. The real

argument was that the situation was so difficult . . . that no one wanted to burn his fingers. It was necessary to let others burn their fingers for a limited period, and when the situation became relatively calm, then they themselves would take over. I drew this conclusion based on the fact that among the missions assigned to the government by these same people was in particular negotiations with the RPF that would have brought the Arusha Peace Accords back on track, by which the MRND party would then have had to present a candidate for president of the republic.[11]

By the end of the meeting with the MRND party leaders, Bagosora's path was thus sketched out, and two options emerged: either a state of siege and full powers assumed by a military committee with the blessings of the MRND; or, and again with the blessings of the MRND, a return to the 1991 Constitution with the expulsion of the current government and a refusal to implement the BBTG. In either case, the elimination of bothersome political figures could get under way, starting with those who, beyond the president of the MRND, were expected to ensure constitutional continuity: the prime minister, Agathe Uwilingiyimana; the president of the Constitutional Court, Joseph Kavaruganda; and the two potential candidates for speaker (presidency) of the TNA, Landoald Ndasingwa from the PL and Félicien Ngango of the PSD. The presidential clan and Bagosora then organized matters quite methodically.

At the time of the encounter between Théoneste Bagosora and Jacques-Roger Booh-Booh, between 11:30 and midnight during the night of 6–7 April, the two were grievously opposed over the issue of the prime minister. According to Booh-Booh, she was competent to ensure the continuity of power and appeal to the population for calm. After the meeting, Booh-Booh called Agathe Uwilingiyimana to inform her that he would arrange for her to get to Radio Rwanda around 5:30 a.m. on 7 April. By 2:40 a.m. Commander Lotin and the nine Belgian "blue helmets" in his unit had left the airport, heading for Uwilingiyimana's residence to escort her to the radio station, where she would tape an official statement. Because of all the roadblocks they had to cross, they did not get there until 5:20 a.m., only to be welcomed by gunfire. The shots came from a unit of the Presidential Guard that was protecting the presidential residence (behind Saint-Michel Church). Around 5:00 a.m. the unit had moved in the direction of the prime minister's residence nearby to prevent her from getting to Radio Rwanda. Ten minutes later, a FAR armored vehicle took position nearby and fired on her house and on Commander Lotin's "blue helmets." Around 8:20 a.m., her life at risk and without any possibility of getting away, Uwilingiyimana took refuge in the gardens of her neighbor's house. UNAMIR soldiers did not follow her, and, as had happened to the

Rwandan soldiers responsible for her protection, they were forced to surrender by Presidential Guard soldiers and transported by minibus to Camp Kigali. The ten Belgian "blue helmets" were killed while a meeting of the FAR high command and commanders of operational sectors was taking place right nearby at the ESM. With the soldiers closing in, Prime Minister Agathe Uwilingiyimana finally tried to take shelter in a UN compound adjoining her house. Gen. Roméo Dallaire immediately telephoned Iqbal Riza, a former Pakistani diplomat who, since March 1993, had been serving as assistant secretary-general in the UN's Department of Peacekeeping Operations and was following the events in Rwanda, in New York, informing him that it might be necessary to use force to save the prime minister. "Riza confirmed the rules of engagement that UNAMIR was not to fire unless fired upon."[12] Thus, the killers had carte blanche: as long as they did not directly attack the "blue helmets," they could kill whomever they wanted. Around forty minutes after Dallaire's call to Riza, around 11:00 a.m., Rwandan soldiers entered the UN compound, found the prime minister, and killed her, as well as her husband, Ignace Barahira, and her advisor, Ignace Magorane.[13]

At that time, most of the other figures who were being sought had already been killed. Around 6:00 a.m. soldiers arrived at the home of Joseph Kavaruganda, president of the Constitutional Court, and demanded that he accompany them. Initially he refused and called various contingents of UNAMIR to seek assistance. In the hour that followed, however, the soldiers overcame him and took him away to the Presidential Guard camp in Kimihurura, where he was killed. Then around 6:30 a.m. the residence of Félicien Ngango, first vice president of the PSD, was attacked, and he was killed. Around 7:00 a.m. Frédéric Nzamurambaho, the president of the PSD, was killed in his home. Shortly after 7:00 a.m., or a bit later in the morning, according to other witnesses, about twenty Presidential Guard soldiers arrived at the residence of Landoald Ndasingwa, first vice president of the PL, and killed him, along with his Canadian wife, Hélène Pinsky, and their children. Many others met the same fate, like Minister of Information Faustin Rucogoza, who was transported to the Presidential Guard camp around 10:00 a.m. and killed. At that same time, escorts were ferrying MRND ministers to that same camp to ensure their security.

With the assassinations of Uwilingiyimana and Kavaruganda, Bagosora effectively ended the debate that the triumvirate of MRND leaders initially broached about the constitutional legitimacy of the candidates whom they might install.[14] After having also eliminated the leaders of the so-called pro-RPF wings of the internal opposition parties, all that remained was to co-opt figures who were already aligned or submissive to put together an obedient civilian government. Ngirumpatse, Karemera, and Nzirorera, who by their own accounts supposedly never left their homes on 7 April, could then organize the political "transition" in their own manner and continue the debate with the other MRND ministers. Sheltered by the French Embassy, those ministers were able to take stock of the figures who had been killed and piece together the latest information as it trickled in.

A meeting of the ministers present was organized the following morning at 9:00, as requested by the French ambassador, Jean-Michel Marlaud.[15] According to Justin Mugenzi, the ambassador "gave us the last accurate information about the situation, what had happened as the French Embassy had gathered the incoming information. He was the one who confirmed for us the names of ministers who had lost their lives, the one who confirmed the situation as it prevailed in the town, and he urged the ministers, as they were assembled there, to try and do something to get the country out of the chaos into which it was sinking."[16] Of course, none of the ministers dared evoke the legitimacy of Faustin Twagiramungu, the prime minister designate under the Arusha Peace Accords. That matter had been definitively resolved. Working in tandem with members of the presidential clan and the MRND leaders, the putschist officers ultimately made good on their aborted attempt to seize power that night of 6–7 April, albeit in another form. The agenda that the early-morning meeting of the Military Crisis Committee and operational sector and unit commanders had rejected outright on 7 April became reality when, unbeknownst to them, certain unit and company commanders carried out targeted political assassinations or led and intensified the massacres of civilians that had begun the night before. Among those units, at the top of the list, was the Presidential Guard, characterized as "uncontrollable," which gave Bagosora and the Hutu extremists the tool they needed to accomplish what they could never publicly endorse. The Presidential Guard was followed by the Military Police Battalion, the paracommando battalion, the "Recce" Battalion, Maj. Ladislas Munyampotore's "Génie" company (Ruhengeri), and Maj. Aloys Mutabera's "Artillery" Battalion (Gisenyi). This explains why, on the morning of 7 April, all of the units stationed at Kanombe were convinced that former camp commander Théoneste Bagosora had become president.

Kanombe had indeed become the nerve center for the powers orchestrating the massacres and was the preserve of those officers and units that bitterly opposed the military high command and the more legitimate forces. According to Colonel Gatsinzi,

From the 8th, I realized that there was no consensus between the politicians and the military. . . .

In my opinion, regarding the operations at that time, on the one hand, there were the purely military operations (war with the RPF), and on the other, operations executed by the military, including the Presidential Guard, which executed a preestablished plan known by a clandestine network. I had no control over the latter operations. On the other hand, I clearly had power over the military operations at the battlefront.[17]

"Let Civilians Occupy the Forefront"

Given the high command's willingness to install the transitional government as quickly as possible—officially reaffirmed by the Military Crisis Committee on the evening of 8 April—putting in place a civilian government held numerous advantages for the nucleus of soldiers loyal to the Akazu. Having flaunted their de facto authority since the evening of 6 April, all they needed now was to choose civilians sufficiently pliant to implement Akazu policies. Equally important was to pick a government that would shield the Akazu from blame by assuming responsibility for the massacres. Instead of a military team, which inevitably would face accusations of having fomented a coup d'état, this move would immediately confer legitimate authority upon the incumbents, which in turn would ease relationships with those foreign powers monitoring the implementation of the Arusha Peace Accords. From the standpoint of its long-term strategies, an interim civilian government maintaining the same distribution of portfolios among political parties, as originally agreed, was viewed by the Akazu as a blueprint for the future transitional government. Nonetheless, headstrong and still committed to the strategy of the fait accompli that had worked so well for him earlier that same morning, Bagosora had already set up the next day's meetings by evening's end on 7 April. These meetings would advance his plans for seating what he characteristically referred to as "his" government.

Thus, by 6:00 a.m. on 8 April, Augustin Ndindiliyimana had met with the acting army chief of staff to assess the situation on the ground before making his way over to the Military Crisis Committee, which he had agreed to lead. He also met with General Dallaire concerning the preconditions to be brokered with the RPF in the wake of the exit of its troops from the CND and the attack on the Presidential Guard camp, that is, the halting of further attacks against political opponents and presumed "accomplices of the enemy."

On the morning of 8 April, Bagosora took it upon himself to begin assembling an interim government to replace the transitional government, initially with Joseph Nzirorera and then with the other MRND leaders. They convened so that they could choose for themselves which representatives of the parties would succeed those who had just been excluded or assassinated, and they debated constitutional solutions for the current impasse.

Once the constitutional texts were amended and recast by the "turn of events," whatever compromise might come about would depend on the division of labor between Bagosora and the MRND party chiefs. While the trio (Ngirumpatse, Nzirorera, and Karemera) went off to debate matters with Théodore Sindikubwabo, new leaders selected from the Power wings of the decapitated, erstwhile opposition parties were collected from their homes by Bagosora in person or by soldiers under orders from Col. Tharcisse Renzaho, the prefect of Kigali-ville. Jean Kambanda may have had the good fortune of being picked up by his colleague Froduald Karamira, who arrived aboard a military vehicle to explain the situation to him, but several other ministers were simply carted off to the Ministry of Defense under escort without the slightest explanation. For some, it really was not necessary to provide any, as the escorts were clearly expected (for the Power wings of the MDR and PL). But for others, particularly those of the PSD, there was great surprise and incomprehension (*see annex 68*). For the PDC, the situation was a bit more complicated. Indeed, the president of the party, Jean-Népomuscène Nayinzira, had gotten close to the RPF and had been designated as the minister who would represent the PDC in the Broad-Based Transitional Government (BBTG). He was deemed "unreachable" by the morning of 7 April, and Bagosora instead sent soldiers to collect Gaspard Ruhumuliza, the PDC minister then in office, for that morning meeting of party representatives on 8 April. The latter managed to get the soldiers who came for him to find two other leaders, Ambassador Célestin Kabanda (Hutu, Butare) and Jean-Marie Vianney Sibomana (Hutu, Ruhengeri), whom they took along to the meeting of the parties.

Nonetheless, if being among the "chosen" was a source of concern for many of them, even more remarkable is that, once assembled, these "negotiators" seemed fairly at ease and started to debate matters as if the situation was wholly predictable, even though their selective enthronement under the yoke of these extremist officers and MRND leaders, as well as the absence of those killed to make way for them, must have weighed on their minds:

> Efforts were made for a strict compliance with the protocol of understanding of 7 April 1992, amended on 8 April 1994, which made it difficult to set up a strong government, since the parties independently chose their candidates. In reality, those who were consulted to participate in the government were faced with a fait accompli, as some key politicians had already died or could not be found. It follows that the government was

little more than a preselected team with limited power. Real power lay elsewhere. While MRND cadres had a dominant position in the administrative hierarchy, the FAR was in thrall to soldiers close to the presidential circle.

Moreover, during the entire process, it was felt that Ngirumpatse, Karemera, Nzirorera, and Bagosora acted behind the scenes and seemed to influence the course of events but did not want to come to the fore. The general assumption was that the MRND's ploy was to place personalities from the south at the forefront during the crisis, pending a later comeback of influential northern personalities after the establishment of interim institutions.[18]

No one seemed to have been duped by the charade imposed by this "gang of four" — Ngirumpatse, Karemera, Nzirorera, and Bagosora — as so aptly put by one of the party negotiators. They finalized their self-proclamation around 3:00 p.m. and awaited the arrival of the missing few, representatives of the PSD who had only to sign off on the dotted line.

> The meeting was over. When we arrived, the meeting was over. The first thing we were told was, "Oh look, the PSD has arrived." We've already informed the government, who are the persons who will occupy the ministries that you hold. The discussion was over. I don't know who chaired the meeting. We weren't told who chaired it. People were standing, others were seated. That's how it was. . . .
>
> People were seated, people were standing, and Mr. Mugenzi told us, look — when we were asked where our former ministers were, I heard Mr. Mugenzi say, "They are either dead, or they have disappeared." This is the answer we were given, and everybody there insisted because we had all the members of the various committees of the various parties that form the proceeding governments were there. They were all represented except the PSD, so they said, "We have finished our work. We have already supplied the names of our ministers, now it's the turn of the ministries who were assigned to the PSD. Now it's up to you, now, to tell us the ministers who were to replace your former ministers that are either dead or disappeared."[19]

The composition of the government was thus finalized without further debate, and then the participants were all transported to the ESM for formal presentation of this interim government to the members of the Military Crisis Committee who were on hand (since it had not even been formally convened) and to those MRND ministers reappointed in office, all of whom had been assembled there by the soldiers.

This was the only meeting of any significance that was actually "presided over" by the president of the Military Crisis Committee, Augustin Ndindiliyimana. Again, it fell to him to introduce Bagosora, who then formally presented "his" government, after which Ngirumpatse explained its legitimacy and clarified how it would operate.

A. We began with the introductions, but the chairperson of the Military Crisis Committee, Gen. Augustin Ndindiliyimana, took the floor and thanked us for being present. He gave the floor immediately to Colonel Bagosora and said that he was the one who had followed up the file from the very beginning and that he was the one who could explain things to us. So Colonel Bagosora took the floor after Ndindiliyimana. . . .

What I recall is that he explained what had happened since the president's—Habyarimana's—plane was brought down. He referred to a meeting with the diplomats and soldiers, the establishment of the Military Crisis Committee, and later on he explained why we were there, why it was necessary to convene us to that meeting.

Q. Were there other persons who addressed the meeting, to your recollection?

A. Yes, there was the president of the MRND, who took the floor. He was the one who explained to us the mechanism of appointment and the establishment of that government . . . and I have no recollection of who took the floor after Matthieu Ngirumpatse. We just had to wait for the swearing-in ceremony the following day when the government was going to be established.[20]

The Limits of Fait Accompli Politics

As all the accounts seem to suggest, officers of the high command and the Military Crisis Committee were systematically excluded from the process. They had devoted their morning to trying to negotiate with the RPF and spent the entire afternoon debating the means to stop the killings. Thus, they were caught off guard by the machinations of Bagosora and the MRND party leaders, which they met with surprise and hostility. As Col. Gatsinzi recalls,

The following morning [8 April], Ndindiliyimana summoned us to a meeting to tell us that Bagosora had met with the political leaders to form an interim government.

During that meeting, Bagosora arrived with the members of the government, and we realized that he had selected these people himself and had not complied with the decisions taken at the meeting held the night before. . . . We had been presented with a fait accompli.[21]

Other high-ranking officers added the following testimonies: "When Bagosora entered with his candidates, consternation reigned: his squad contained a good number of unknown figures, the prime minister, for instance, with no explanation for the missing leaders; those in the know whispered to us that they were all linked to the Power wings."[22] "Other officers, including Col. Rusatira, surprised by this reversal of the situation and still true to themselves, found the formation of a government that completely ignored the Arusha Accords to be dangerous" (*see annex 30*). They made their views known during a meeting held on 8 April with the politicians: "The response to these officers who felt bound by the Arusha process was that this new government was exactly intended to negotiate with the RPF to implement these accords. Nothing was done, and that explains how the objecting officers were not even invited to the swearing in of the interim government, which, in their eyes, offered no hope for the country. What transpired afterward proved them right."[23]

But the matter was settled; the army men of the presidential "clan" and the MRND leaders had emerged triumphant by brutally eliminating and terrorizing the opposition: "On that day, between 9 and 10 p.m., at ESM, after taking note of the list of ministerial candidates, General Ndindiliyimana, on behalf of his colleagues of FAR high command, announced that the mandate of the Crisis Committee had ended."[24] The only thing that those outmaneuvered officers of the high command could do was to organize a rearguard response, which presupposed support from the other stakeholders in the Arusha Accords, the larger embassies, and the RPF. Not one was willing to provide that. But despite being cornered, expelled, or neutralized, as soon as the balance of power decisively tipped against them, several superior officers nonetheless rejected the fait accompli and publicly called for cease-fire and dialogue with the RPF in a communiqué dated 12 April 1994.[25] Their initiative was then reinforced in a letter that Army Chief of Staff Gen. Marcel Gatsinzi sent to Jacques-Roger Booh-Booh on 17 April 1994, in which he proposed joint patrols, confiscations of illegally held weapons, and monitoring and control of radio broadcasts.[26]

But for the hard core of leaders supporting the MRND, the path had been cleared beyond their expectations. Politically speaking, they found themselves masters of the game with an MRND president, a prime minister from the

Power wing, and all the MRND ministers reinstalled in their posts, that is, in control of half the posts in the government. From the standpoint of the incumbents, the situation seemed ideal: by pointing the finger at the people from Butare, Kibuye, and, more broadly, the southern prefectures, they were able to shift the onus of responsibility for the excesses onto them. In the meantime, the ruling triumvirate—Ngirumpatse, Nzirorera, and Karemera—could bide their time under the protective wing of their all-powerful patron, Bagosora, waiting to see how the situation would evolve, and then tailor their personal strategies.

On the evening of 8 April, exactly forty-eight hours after the shooting down of the presidential plane, the members of the Interim Government collectively regrouped at the Hôtel des Diplomates, escorted by members of the Presidential Guard, before formally taking the oath of office the following morning and taking up their duties. Ngirumpatse and Nzirorera, as well as Bagosora, Gatsinzi, and the general staff of the FAR, installed themselves at the hotel on 9 April. The whole affair had been conducted quickly and efficiently.[27]

Only one major source of anxiety remained. It comes across clearly in Maj. Épiphane Hanyurwimana's minutes from the Military Crisis Committee meeting (*see annex 65*) of 8 April with leaders of the political parties and the proposed members of the Interim Government. The most intriguing element in the document emerges in the few lines entered just below the list of those present. This concerns remarks made by General Ndindiliyimana, chief of staff of the gendarmerie, after the meeting with members of the new government, before they held their first cabinet meeting:

Gendarmerie Chief of Staff
How do we convince them?
if the GOVT is slack: security cannot be re-established ~~Abaturage~~ [the
~~population~~].
They are not up to it[.]
Emphasize security. Even if the ministers must remain at home.
Necessary to ~~lead~~ present them with a fait accompli
We are too polite and indecisive
If not[,] the credibility of the FAR will be totally lost
You do not take power ~~from them~~ [crossed out in the original handwritten text].

In the wake of a full day of negotiations, these remarks reveal the officers' fear that their chosen hard-liners might not deliver the aggressive stance that they were hoping for. The malaise, or the lack of enthusiasm for the massacres, hanging over these newly installed government members quickly drew suspicion and denunciation, as the very credibility of the FAR was at risk. As one of the officers present has written: "My memory is not perfect, but I recall that the idea of putting the interim government in the deep freeze circulated from those very first days."[28] The irony in all this is that it would fall to Augustin Ndindiliyimana, that "moderate" from the south, to express that idea.

Indeed, even if all these civilian ministers, intellectuals for the most part, had perfectly understood the "cover" that they were expected to provide, a good number among them still needed time to grasp the implications of the assassinations and the massacres that the soldiers and militiamen were asking them to justify. Many were unprepared to go along with the murderous strategy they were supposed to implement; they had reason to question where the war would lead and how they would actually fare in the end. If, at that time, the sequence of events remained largely unknown, the members of the Interim Government could hardly ignore the stark reality before their eyes, that is, that the Presidential Guard, the army units, and their Interahamwe militiamen would not stop the killings and that a civilian government headed by southerners had little chance of making itself heard, even if it wanted to.

The soldiers and the heads of the two big parties, the MRND and the MDR, thus followed the cabinet meetings of the Interim Government and coached the ministers in their apprenticeship. To ensure group cohesion and win over the more skittish members, there was need to fully immerse them in their mission and do whatever it took to squelch the doubts that had plagued them in the capital. Thus, on 11 April, a decision was taken to move the Interim Government to the interior of the country. Was this transfer a strategy of confinement for unwilling disciples? One could easily believe so.

The following extract from PSD Minister of Finance Emmanuel Ndinda-bahizi's testimony before the ICTR Trial Chamber provides a revealing account of what the ministers had to go through:

A. The government remained in Kigali up to the 12th of April in the morning, the morning of the 12th of April.
Q. And why did the government have to leave the capital then?
A. The government left the capital on the 12th in the morning; but, to my knowledge, no reason was adduced for that. So that I went to see my children, who were at a friend's at Kiyovu, that was at around 500 meters from the hotel, and when I came back I realized that everybody had gone away. I left. I asked as to what was happening. I was told that they had left. So, there was no official information as to the reasons why the government left Kigali.[29]

Three ministers were even left behind: Agnès Ntamabyaliro, Pauline Nyiramasuhuko, and Justin Mugenzi. The confusion brought on by this move was significant, particularly for the prime minister:

Q. Why do you think it [the move] was a mistake?

A. Because Kigali was our capital. That is where we had our official address. That is where we could contact embassies, foreign embassies. Once we relocated in a village—because Murambi was like a village—we were cut off from everything—and I considered that was the beginning of our defeat.[30]

The surprise provoked by this "unexpected" decision, explained away by deliberately exaggerated security concerns, is easy to understand. Clearly, this was more a reflection of manufactured alarm than any real threat on the capital. Further, since responsibility for the government's security fell to Gen. Augustin Ndindiliyimana, one can then recall his remarks from 8 April about harnessing the government that had just been installed: "How do we convince them? . . . They are not up to it[.] Emphasize security. Even if the ministers must remain at home. . . . [They have to be presented] with a fait accompli."

And exactly as Jean Kambanda himself put it, this move indeed signaled the "beginning of the defeat," the one that he and several others still refused to embrace with those putschists from the presidential clan boldly venturing to bring down the legal order just to keep power, or drag everyone else along in their demise.

9

 Installing the Interim
Authorities

The meeting of the heads of the political parties was both complex and simple to organize. Complex because all the dignitaries of the regime, including the civilian members of the Akazu, had gone into hiding by the evening of 6 April, preoccupied by the unleashing of uncontrolled violence from the Presidential Guard and the Interahamwe militias and well aware that even Théoneste Bagosora could not guarantee— or had no interest in guaranteeing—their safety. He himself had known a period of disgrace in the 1980s and was among the "dissatisfied" of the Habyarimana regime who could be tempted to take advantage of its near collapse to settle scores.

Everyone feared for their lives and their property and sought to take stock of their potential "enemies." One of the most significant examples is Jean Kambanda, a strident adversary of Agathe Uwilingiyimana, the president by default of the MDR in Butare and the candidate proposed by the official leadership of the MDR for the post of prime minister of the BBTG in opposition to Faustin Twagiramungu, the candidate designated by the other parties. By the afternoon of 7 April, Kambanda and his family had sought refuge in the gendarmerie camp in Kacyiru with Maj. Gerschom Ngayaberura and Maj. Pierre-Claver Karangwa, who set them up in a building at the entry of the camp. Oddly, Kambanda felt he was doubly in danger: "I was a candidate for the post of prime minister, and I had political opponents because my party had designated other candidates who were supported by, amongst others, the RPF. So I was afraid that I could be assassinated by the RPF. Furthermore, I was an opponent, a political opponent to the Habyarimana regime. And even the rapprochement that had taken place between the two of us was not known by everybody. So people who supported him could pose a threat to me. So I felt that I was facing several risks."[1]

It was while making a quick trip back to his home to pick up some personal effects on the morning of 8 April that Kambanda learned of his designation as Interim Government prime minister:

> While we were packing our personal belongings to take with us, there was a vehicle, a military jeep, parked quite close to our residence . . . and when the vehicle arrived close to my residence it stopped, and I realized that the person coming out of the vehicle was known to me. It was Froduald Karamira. And when I saw that it was him, I was reassured because I knew that he was a friend. He came, and he told me that I was expected at the ESM, that my party had just designated me as a prime minister in a meeting at the ESM, with other political parties and soldiers. That is what happened.[2]

Putting Together the Interim Government

Formally speaking, the Interim Government complied—as much as the political situation could permit—with the terms of the Arusha Peace Accords and the distribution of seats in the BBTG (*see box 14 and annex 30*): a president from the MRND, a prime minister from the MDR, nine ministerial posts for the MRND (which held "by necessity and provisionally" the RPF's vacant posts), three posts for the MDR, three for the PL, three for the PSD, and one for the PDC. No modifications were made in the distribution of ministerial posts among the various parties. The composition of the Interim Government mirrored the preoccupations of those who conceived it. It had to remedy the divisions within the "Hutu" camp in order to face a "Tutsi enemy" and its "accomplices," which the government would have to confront in the military and especially in the political realms.[3] In response to this double preoccupation, an effort was made, on the one hand, to reshape the facade of national unity behind the assumed ethnic commonalities of the "majority of the people" and, on the other hand, to put an end to the rivalries pitting one geographical area against the other while assuring a fair representation of regional political interests.

The first characteristic of the Interim Government, the most obvious, concerns ethnic homogeneity. The fiction of the sole Tutsi minister, which has been adopted and respected by successive governments of the Second Republic, had been compromised. The second characteristic, unprecedented, had to do with the weight accorded to figures from the south and the center of the country. The interim president and prime minister were both from Butare. After the assassination of the prime minister—who embodied the aspirations of southerners in confronting the Habyarimana system—a very heavy price was exacted by soldiers from the north. Thus, the "settling of accounts" and the symbolic union between the regional interests of the First and Second Republics—respectively identified with south and north—could not be more cruelly obvious: the north had lost its presidential chief, and so had the south after the assassination of the head of the government. The former was replaced by the president of the ex–National Assembly, Théodore Sindikubwabo, who, according to the 1991 Constitution, was supposed to fill any vacancy in power and who was quite flattered to extend his political future. Agathe Uwilingiyimana was replaced by her inveterate rival for the presidency of the MDR in Butare. He could demonstrate a certain legitimacy in this post, since the national leadership of the party had expelled the prime minister, who had accepted her post in July 1993, whereas Jean Kambanda had been presented as the party's official candidate for the post of prime minister designate in the BBTG. Kambanda became prime minister of the Interim Government on 8 April 1994.

The refashioned unity of north and south was symbolized by the following slogan: "War for the Bakiga . . ., politics for the Banyanduga."[4] The reasoning was straightforward. First, officers from the south were not considered trustworthy. Thus, the acting army chief of staff, Marcel Gatsinzi, named despite Bagosora's hostility, was ultimately replaced ten days after his appointment. And the army had to be tightly controlled. Second, politically speaking, the south had to be brought within the fold, and only a homogeneous duo—president and prime minister—would permit this goal to be attained. This being the case, it was important that the onus of responsibility for the killings of opposition members be shared with the southern politicians. Aside from the two posts of president and prime minister, the south was accorded thirteen of the nineteen ministries in government, with the prefectures of Kibuye, Gitarama, and Butare holding eight of them.[5] One could clearly see the rise of Kibuye, which, over the course of the Second Republic, had never had more than a single minister in government. This prefecture, which felt it had been left out of the game during the multiparty era, entered the political arena in full force (displacing Cyangugu). It obtained three and then four important ministries: Finance, Information, Justice, and Interior. Or, to put it in a nutshell, it ended up in control of the nerves of the war: propaganda, impunity, maintaining order, and genocide. Beyond this deliberate strategy, sheer chance also contributed to regional overrepresentation. The parties were requested to

Installing the Interim Authorities

propose their representatives in the Interim Government, and that is how the PL came to put forward Agnès Ntamabyaliro, the MDR Éliezer Niyitegeka, and the PSD Emmanuel Ndindabahizi. The first two were indeed well-known national Power figures, but the only reason why Ndindabahizi was taken on board is because he happened to be present at the home of Hyacinthe Nsengiyumva Rafiki—a northern leader of the PSD who had been named minister of public works and energy—when Bagosora came to take him to the Ministry of Defense.

The third specificity of this government was the lack of congruence between political and regional solidarities. There are several significant examples. Thus, at the highest rank set by protocol, the minister of foreign affairs and cooperation, Clément-Jérôme Bicamumpaka of the MDR, was a native of Ruhengeri. At the lowest level, the minister of youth and sports—an important post in the context of civil war where recourse to militiamen, recruitment, and mobilization of youth played a decisive role—belonged to the MRND but came from Gitarama, the southern bastion of the opposition. One could also mention the minister of labor and social affairs, from the PL in Gisenyi, a prefecture that was virtually an MRND fiefdom. Aside from these symbolic nominations, the effort to reach out to the entire country and to avoid excluding any prefecture was obvious. One could also emphasize the concern to maintain a hefty ministerial representation from well-established MRND turfs (Kigali-rural and Kibungo).

The cross-cutting pulls of regionalism made a northern monopoly on power, or even a decisive concentration, simply unthinkable, just as it ruled out an abrupt shift to the south. The MRND had no intention of surrendering the presidency or of weakening its northern base. The nominations of two natives of Butare to the most eminent posts was mostly an accommodation, initially provoking incomprehension among many northern political and military leaders: "The president of the republic was from the south, the prime minister was also from the south, the advisor who filled in as minister to the presidency [Enoch Ruhigira] was a southerner, as was the advisor for internal security [Gen. Augustin Ndindiliyimana]. It took quite a number of persons to make the voice of the north heard in the Interim Government."[6]

Interim President of the Republic Théodore Sindikubwabo was, from the very beginning, viewed as a "passenger" who could quickly be unseated. He was supposed to bear responsibility for the massacres before a more substantial successor would emerge from the former mouvance présidentielle. The only one who really mattered in the arrangement was Prime Minister Jean Kambanda, who had been associated with the majority Power wing of MDR since 1993.

The fourth characteristic of the cabinet concerns relations among the figures henceforth associated with an unexpected group. The downing of the presidential plane was of critical importance in that respect. A good number of ministers, both the veterans and the newly installed, then felt that the demands of the nation, as expressed by extremist officers from the north, were simply not up for discussion. Nor did the exigency of national unity allow for divisions based on party lines. Everyone had to play the card of military preparedness and popular mobilization. The fate of the nation was at stake. Among the question marks raised by this agenda were the ties established by the government with figures of limited experience and well-known fellow travelers or notorious newcomers.[7] For that very reason, most essential was the link that could be established between the present members, those who were instrumental in their appointments, or those in whose name they spoke.

Many Rwandans had the gravest doubts about the wisdom of these choices and made no bones of the fact that only a strong government would be up to the task. One of them was James Gasana:

> However, the Abatabazi ["liberators or saviors," the term used to refer to members of the Interim Government] were a veritable calamity.[8] Even though they had apparently been chosen according to formal procedures, the choice of candidates was a disaster in light of the horrible situation that had overcome the country. The political-military wing of the Akazu had no need for a government that was strong or efficient; it was a grave error in these circumstances, where it was necessary not only to stop the genocide and restore order but also to neutralize the RPF's catastrophic misadventure. Its very first gestures created diplomatic problems, like accusing Belgium of implication in the assassinations of the two presidents even before gathering evidence. It did not manage to formulate any approach toward pacifying the country or outlining any foreign policy. Its refusal to condemn and halt the Tutsi genocide cut it off from the rest of the world and earned it the imposition of an arms embargo, which led it to deliver the country free of costs to the RPF.[9]

But there is no doubt that this government was indeed the one wanted by the civilian and military components of the Akazu. It was a government that was hurriedly assembled, weak, and ineffective, just like all the important decisions taken right after Habyarimana's demise to ensure that power would not slip away from the presidential clan.

Among those in the government's central core we find Casimir Bizimungu, minister of health, a strident opponent making concessions to the RPF who had gone back and forth between the ministries of foreign affairs and health over the previous decade. There was also Augustin Ngirabatware, minister of planning, whose ascendancy (both political and financial) had been staggering following his marriage to a daughter of Félicien Kabuga. It was a rise in status parallel to his political radicalization: he worked from the shadows in most of the efforts to destabilize the multiparty government; he was a staunch supporter of pro-Hutu activists, especially in the realm of the mass media, where he managed the funds invested by his father-in-law. One could also mention Minister of Family and Women's Affairs Pauline Nyiramasuhuko, an ardent activist close to Agathe Kanziga who was married to the rector of the national university, Maurice Ntahobari, a former president of the CND. With Augustin Bizimana absent from Kigali for the swearing-in ceremony but nonetheless renewed in office as minister of defense (he only returned from Cameroon on 10 April), the military action begun by Bagosora and the commanders of the Presidential Guard and the paracommando battalion was never interrupted. Bizimana's career had been charted by Protais Zigiranyirazo, the president's brother-in-law, and his commitment to the "family" was complete. As soon as he returned to the capital, Bizimana made a tour of Kigali with an obedient cohort of superior officers of the general staff. This first group was virtually in charge of defending the interests of the northern dignitaries and what was left of the defunct regime.

In addition, a number of persons were selected to meet formal quotas and join a movement over which they had little or no control. Among them one could mention the minister of finance, Emmanuel Ndindabahizi, who worked for an accounting firm before entering politics as an advisor to Minister Marc Rugenera of the PSD in July 1993. The same can be said for the minister of agriculture, Dr. Straton Nsabumukunzi, a PSD activist and a doctor at the national university in Butare: he accepted the post mainly to protect himself from possible reprisals from the CDR. These were the PSD activists in Butare who were behind the lynching on 22 February 1994 of CDR national leader Martin Bucyana to avenge the killing of Félicien Gatabazi.

For those who remained outside the Interim Government, along with the dramatic changes in the landscape, the usual paths of political intervention had been up-ended. Competition among the challengers shifted to the privileged sites of power during wartime.

This explains why the Interim Government was so strictly controlled and guided over the course of its hundred-day term. The government met almost nonstop in plenary or in restricted sessions, depending on the day's agenda, affinities, or requirements (see tables 1 and 2 in chapter 11). Subcommittees could include certain "invited guests," depending on their presumed specialized knowledge or "observer" status. This mode of collective, informal operation was imposed upon the Interim Government inasmuch as it was a "coalition of political parties administered by a consensual protocol."[10] It was thus constantly surrounded by various officers and figures, official or disguised advisors, themselves leading a bevy of individuals in search of instructions and with requests for assistance, solicitations for protection, or various authorizations. Even if the decisions guiding the war effort and the day-to-day management of civilian affairs did not come from the Interim Government, the place where it was headquartered (Murambi, in Gitarama prefecture, and then Muramba, in Gisenyi) was a meeting point for a good number of influential individuals and the networks willing and able to support them.[11]

It was in this context that the major figures within the mouvance présidentielle and the allied political parties worked to anchor their personal fiefdoms. Each of the rising new stars—Matthieu Ngirumpatse, Joseph Nzirorera, Augustin Ngirabatware, Casimir Bizimungu, Édouard Karemera, and Donat Murego—nursed high hopes for the future.

Ngirumpatse, along with his family, had taken up residence in Murambi by 12 April, just like all the other members of the Interim Government. He was named chief advisor to the president in matters of foreign affairs during the cabinet meeting of 17 May 1994. It was a compromise solution imposed by the context:

> Matthieu remained president of the MRND of course, but he was poorly situated to take control given the mood: he bore the stain of parricide for having expedited Juvénal Habyarimana's removal. He traveled as often as possible and then took on the post of presidential advisor to protect himself so that he could wait things out from the sidelines and be in the most favorable position to observe what went on. In any case, he had no partisans to lead his campaign. "Sticking" to Sindikubwabo, ensuring his longevity, and catering to his weaknesses could place him in a privileged position. Matthieu Ngirumpatse, as advisor to President Sindikubwabo, was a very wise choice. With Théodore Sindikubwabo, he became the link between those from the south and constituents of the north, like Murego, another hopeful on the sidelines. He took over from the president to neutralize Nzirorera, who was the most serious presidential candidate for the succession.[12]

This is how Ngirumpatse thrust himself into diplomatic affairs, extending or reinforcing the networks that Agathe Kanziga continued to cultivate after leaving Kigali on 9 April and taking up residence in Paris (see chapter 10). At the same time, he remained in active contact with his militant base in the MRND, consisting of activists from the south and among the Interahamwe.

The central preoccupation of the northern nucleus was to give itself time to position Joseph Nzirorera. Making full use of his status as MRND national secretary, he was known to spring into action as the most combative lance in political and military circles and among militiamen. He had regained the essential core of prerogatives previously at his disposal during the single-party era and prepared the groundwork for an ad hoc assembly that would formally enthrone him.

> Nzirorera was the legitimate heir and the symbolic defender of the interests of Karago-Giciye-Mukingo-Nkuli communes, but he had to bide his time on the scene and remain somewhat above the fray, and he could not directly take on the campaign or give himself over to political gamesmanship. He had his reserve cabinet in Gisenyi among the loyalists of the Akazu and left Bagosora, Ngirabatware, Semanza, etc. to manage the affairs of the "family" in Murambi. Bagosora made episodic trips there from Kigali; Ngirabatware resided there more than he actually cared to; Semanza was a full-time resident in Murambi but made frequent trips to Kigali as a sort of roving emissary. . . . His dilemma was the obligation to conserve his leadership of the MRND in the north among militiamen and soldiers who were wildly antisouth and yet maintain a minimum level of credibility in the central and southern prefectures.[13]

The third hopeful was Augustin Ngirabatware: "Occupying an intermediate position, he benefited from a certain legitimacy because of his familial connections to the presidential clan and from support by Félicien Kabuga and Augustin Bizimana. His attachment to the Byumba clan caused him in the early 1980s to express trust in the predictions of the prophetess of Mayaga, who had claimed that the successor would come from this prefecture (in his case, through family links)."[14] However, all too eager to move ahead, Ngirabatware committed a major gaffe that temporarily alienated him from large sectors of the army when he supported fellow Byumba native Augustin Bizimungu's nomination to head the general staff (see chapter 12). Maintained at the helm of the Ministry of Planning, Ngirabatware ended up as spokesperson and observer for the presidential clan within the Interim Government and thus was able to wait matters out while cultivating diplomatic support. In this regard, he was able to take advantage of perks much greater than those of the other ambitious "ambassador," Casimir Bizimungu. The latter was cantoned in the Ministry of Health, which hardly afforded the political maneuverability that would allow him to distinguish himself.

Édouard Karemera, with no specific attribution other than his leadership role within the MRND, very active in his home prefecture, imposed himself as a major actor of the Interim Government and often filled in for the absent minister of the interior. For example, he took the initiative, in accord with Minister of Defense Augustin Bizimana, to have the military press reproduce a tract calling upon the entire population to be "active" in protecting "the Republic and Democracy" against the "grandchildren of the UNAR," which was quite symbolic.[15] The tract was intended to be scattered and distributed by helicopter drops (*see box 15*).

Bearing in mind that by then the lines of battle were drawn around Kigali and the Mutara (*see box 17*), the enemy targets were undeniably the civilian Tutsi populations. Marcel Gatsinzi, the acting army chief of staff, was surprised to discover the tract while he was still exercising authority as chief of staff. He responded by forbidding its dissemination. Édouard Karemera waited until Gatsinzi was dismissed before restarting the operation with the approval of the government.

As clearly shown by this example, the first vice president of the MRND and the MRND minister of defense took initiatives, issued orders, provisioned the means to accomplish those orders, and were obeyed without having to obtain approval from the government, from the army chief of staff, or from any formal body of the MRND, whose president was often traveling. In working order and guided by its most active spokesmen, the recomposed MRND party-state knew how to anticipate the "consensus" of the other parties and the government.[16] This is how Kambanda describes the networks of influence at the top:

> The government had honorary officials: there was the president of the republic, Sindikubwabo Théodore. There was also the theoretical head of government, Jean Kambanda, that is myself, the prime minister. I was called upon for all ceremonial decisions and public functions. The real head of government was Bizimana Augustin, the defense minister. When he returned from his mission to Gabon or Togo, I realized he was the leader. The entire team told me that things were going to be back in order now that he was back. I saw him to be a good organizer, a good orator. I saw that he had a way of making himself obeyed even by those who were most powerful among the military. I noted that his return corresponded to the gradual fading away of Bagosora.[17]

Jean Kambanda's reaction to Augustin Bizimana's presumed ascendancy within the army merits further discussion. The political standing of the minister of defense was quite peculiar. On the one hand, he had support from Protais Zigiranyirazo and the presidential family because he occupied a decisive role in the strategy for positioning Joseph Nzirorera. In addition, as a native of

Byumba, he had the major political advantage of being less associated with a regional base than those who hailed from Gisenyi-Ruhengeri. On the other hand, it was necessary to impose a takeover of the military establishment, especially its high command, which was divided and shattered into rival poles, and impose the authority of the party over the militias. Thus, as soon as he returned to Kigali, Bizimana personally received Interahamwe leader Robert Kajuga in his office at the Ministry of Defense. This action profoundly shocked the officers present, since, throughout Kigali, the Interahamwe seemed to be imposing their authority, even over the soldiers.

Nevertheless, Bizimana never became a key figure or a decision maker on a grand scale. He could allow himself to oppose Bagosora only because he had the support of the MRND leaders, who wanted to turn the page on Bagosora's failure and dissuade him from trying to rebound, as he did on 16 April, when he maneuvered to be recalled to active duty in the army. That did not mean that Bagosora was marginalized but that he was no longer called to play a major role in the new distribution of roles. Bizimana was the incarnation of the collective will of the Akazu hard-core nucleus: "In fact, the members of the Akazu did not view themselves as equal; there were 'those who were actually inside the hut, and those who were only on the compound.' These are the exact terms that Bagosora had used, one day in December 1992, to explain his standing in the Akazu to me. To him, his place in the Akazu was on the compound."[18]

Édouard Karemera, who had not been a minister since the government of May 1987, deemed it necessary to harness himself to the government apparatus toward the end of May 1994 as military defeat loomed on the horizon and the genocidal momentum trailed off in the strategic southern prefectures where most of the "accomplices" resided. He was considered best placed and most committed to grapple with the territorial administration, the civil defense, and the relaunching of the massacres.

Finally, among the other aspirants for influential posts, there was still Donat Murego. Although not formally a member of the Interim Government, he took effective control of the MDR and traded on his utility by underscoring his new "national" implication (Ruhengeri, Kigali, Kibuye, Butare). Thus, he profited from the weakening of the PSD, which had been reduced to puppet politicians, to occupy the entire terrain that used to be held by the opposition.

The drastic reconfiguring of power brought about by Habyarimana's assassination was put into effect in a climate marked by a spirit of revenge and by a necessary realism in confronting a common adversary. That reconfiguration was hurriedly organized, brutally implemented, modified, and intensified as the days progressed. If the sense of urgency was compelling, if a degree of improvisation could not be avoided, the center of strategic decision making never faltered. Although initially taken by surprise, the presidential clan and the northern military and political core demonstrated great determination, and their bosses methodically proceeded to establish their authority over the levers of state. Their solidarity was built upon three short-term political objectives: ensure their political survival and eliminate their opponents, reestablish "national unity" to better confront the RPF, and delay the hour of reckoning among the aspirants vying for the succession.

The synchronization of the killings shows just how the "operatives" were ready to do their dirty work (the Presidential Guard's vengeance and murderous furor were in some measure a natural expression of this unity in the wake of the assassination of their chief) and the degree to which anti-Tutsi activism was deeply ingrained and widely shared among militiamen in Kigali and in the prefectures controlled by hard-line MRND elements (Gisenyi and Ruhengeri). The efficient division of labor among the northern military bosses, MRND party leaders, and Interahamwe militiamen clearly indicates that, at this critical stage, roles had already been handed out and the path to murder well established. The orders for massacres emanating from the various authorities that came together in Kigali on 7 April were easily transmitted to the available or solicited "resource persons" needed to carry them out in the neighborhoods of the city or in several prefectures and communes of the interior.

All that remained to be done was to clearly delineate a policy and identify those needed to implement it.

From Vengeance to Genocide

"Ingoma itica, ntihore ni igicuma" (Power that does not kill, that does not seek vengeance, is, like a gourd, a fragile power).[19] This proverb perfectly sums up the logic that took root after the assassination of the "father of the nation," and it applies to both the strategies for revenge promoted by its supporters and the murderous jockeying for power brought on by the succession crisis.

Civilians and soldiers united, creating the most obstinate faction within the mouvance présidentielle (and the one with the most to lose), forcefully demonstrated that power was neither vacant nor fragile like a gourd. While efforts were under way to restore the prerogatives of the party-state to the MRND, its leaders took advantage of these exceptional circumstances to definitively eliminate the same hated opponents whom northern extremists had so long sought to do away with. Adopting the habits of civil war that first surfaced in 1960, they visited massacres and pogroms upon the Tutsi civilian population on an unprecedented scale.

It was one thing to repay aggression by tolerating or provoking the usual excesses of a besieged citadel for vengeance's sake; it was quite another to meet the RPF's military threat with an internal front targeting all those tagged as its presumed accomplices. It was no longer a question of returning fire but of organizing massacres of the Tutsi population as a "public policy" of the reconfigured Rwandan state. This development was neither fatal nor anticipated; it was simply the price that MRND leaders accepted to pay Col. Théoneste Bagosora in exchange for his withdrawal and to ensure his impunity.

This is the analysis proposed by Maj. Augustin Cyiza, at that time presiding judge of the Conseil de guerre (War Council), who endeavored as best he could to keep track of Bagosora's activities over the course of those two days in April 1994.[20] Cyiza's exposé starts by listing the failures and refusals that Bagosora encountered in his various undertakings: first, he was incapable of meeting the expectations of the presidential family for installing a military government to negotiate with the RPF and to safeguard their interests; second, having seen his strategy rejected by the diplomats Booh-Booh and Dallaire, his isolation was obvious and heavy with consequence during the meeting of unit and sector commanders on the morning of 7 April.

It was Nkundiye's public rebuke and Ntabakuze's refusal to associate themselves with Bagosora's plot that allowed other officers to also oppose it.[21] In reality, Bagosora was rather isolated even with his supporters in Kanombe, a few elements of the paracommando battalion, and the Presidential Guard. But the latter did not support Bagosora; it was simply living up, rather spontaneously, to its very raison d'être: safeguard the regime and neutralize the opposition. As for Ntabakuze's paracommando battalion, it had already suffered a lot during the war, especially in 1990 during the RPF's first offensive, and Ntabakuze was convinced that if the war started up again, it would be lost. Even so, he was still available to make all the "traitors" of the interior pay for the death of the president, and many of the companies under his command approved of the massacres. In fact, what one later referred to as the genocide started on 8 April with the distribution of weapons to civilians by Semanza and Karera at the prefecture office.[22] It was the direct result of the failure of the "Bagosora putsch." Two factors were, indeed, determining:

—Internally, the Bagosora camp risked being marginalized as a result of its role in the massacres of the opposition party leaders. The logic of genocide imposed itself because it was the only way to get everyone involved in the massacres.

—Externally, he wanted to trade Tutsi lives for an RPF cease-fire.

The trap was closing in on him [Bagosora]. On the one hand, the Crisis Committee wanted to halt the indiscipline in the army and the killings of opposition party leaders, that is to say, to send back to the Kimihurura camp a Presidential Guard already engaged in battle with the RPA in Kigali and then urgently commence negotiations with the RPF with assistance from Dallaire and the foreign embassies. On the other hand, it was necessary for him to prevent the "unity of the Hutu" between the northern and southern politicians who were prone to negotiate being achieved at his expense. For the southerners, restoring "national unity" necessarily meant that Bagosora would have to pay for the killings of their brethren. For that very reason he urgently needed to assemble a government of extremist civilians who would continue his policy and support the impulse for revenge among the northern soldiers. The MRND leaders supported him, despite his tactical meanderings, because he offered them access to power, and they knew they would end up on the losing side in a negotiated political solution.

Discredited and somewhat marginalized by the Military Crisis Committee, Bagosora called retired officers back into active service, mobilized the militias, and relaunched the civil defense. On 8 April the first batch of weapons was distributed to the Interahamwe. This concerned a stock of new weapons unknown to the army that had been warehoused in the basement of the prefecture office. The civil defense would be structured with a view to reorganizing the militias and arming them, and would draw upon militiamen, including those outside of the MRND and CDR. . . .[23]

Once set in motion, the genocide simply fed on itself. The operatives had been put in place.[24]

The pact between the parallel military command, controlled by extremist officers, and the coterie of MRND leaders clamoring for ascendancy appeared all the more promising, with its promoters keeping a low profile while acting through intermediaries. Both needed a few days to make the final adjustments among the teams that played the leading roles. Bagosora had to wait until mid-April to definitively neutralize the legitimist officers who rebelled against the Interim Government, recompose the general staff, and encourage the urge to kill. It was this parallel military command that mobilized and provided the necessary reinforcements in troops to launch the killings by militiamen and set up roadblocks. As the killings went on, the officers and the noncommissioned officers from the north monitored the situation to ensure that the tasks were duly carried out. With a heavy hint of Bagosora's central role, Kambanda reported: "As far as the civil defense is concerned, it is difficult to pinpoint the real coordinator of the civil defense at the national level, because there may have been too many levels of power, on the one hand, and the corps itself was made up of components that did not necessarily have any coordination, on the other hand. However, I will try to identify the person I believe was responsible for each of its components."[25]

In many prefectures, on the list of monitors put in place by Bagosora and Bizimana, along with the MRND leaders, figured the same persons who by 7 April had already taken the initiative to track down the "enemy."[26] It was all simply legitimized by the Interim Government. Again, to quote Kambanda:

The civil defense command in the prefectures. It was by a written ministerial decision that the government appointed certain officers in charge of the civil defense on the recommendation of the defense minister, who received his orders from his party, the MRND. This party was represented by three influential personalities who had followed the government to Gitarama and who were members of their party's steering committee. These three were Ngirumpatse, Karemera, and Nzirorera. Mostly officers who had been proposed to be members of the parliament or who were already MPs were appointed [because they were already known by the population they had to mobilize]. For Butare, it was Colonel Nteziryaryo, who may presently be in Burkina Faso. He was not an MP. He was the former director of the communal police in the interior ministry. For Gikongoro, it was Major Simba, who may be in West Africa. He was a former comrade of 5 July 1973. He was the MRND MP for Gikongoro. There were problems in having a good candidate for Cyangugu, and the civil defense was coordinated by a young lieutenant called Imanishimwe Samuel but who was assisted by Prefect Bagambiki and who may be in West Africa and who was the former director of the intelligence service and former prefect of Kigali. For Gitarama, it was Major Ukulikeyesu [phonetic], who may be deceased. He was an MRND MP and was later appointed the prefect of Gitarama around May 94. For Kigali, there was no substantive commander, but it can be deemed that Colonel Renzaho, the prefect of Kigali-ville, was in charge of civil defense, assisted by Commandant Bivamvagara Patrice [Gisenyi] and Commandant Twagirayesu [phonetic], who may have died in Butare and who had specifically been in charge of training. He was an influential member of the MDR.

I do not have specific information concerning Gisenyi, but five soldiers could have been in charge of the civil defense. The most important of them are Laurent Serubuga, former assistant army chief of staff in the Habyarimana regime and former comrade of 5 July 1973; Buregeya Bonaventure [phonetic], former comrade of 5 July 1973, former advisor to President Habyarimana, and former commander of the higher military school [École supérieure militaire]; Nsengiyumva Anatole, a colonel who was the regional commander and the lynchpin in the procurement of munitions and the external transit of the government. . . .

For Kibuye, Karemera, who was the interior minister and the first vice-chairman of the MRND and who may be in West Africa, and Niyitegeka Éliezer, who was also the minister of information, were themselves in charge of their prefecture. There were very many massacres in this prefecture. . . .

For Kibungo, it was Rwagafilita Pierre-Célestin, a colonel and MRND candidate for MP in the broad-based national assembly. He had been minister and assistant chief of staff of the gendarmerie in the Habyarimana regime. My intelligence services informed me of extensive massacres in his prefecture. Witnesses also confirmed it. For Ruhengeri, there were [inaudible] of Tutsis, but I was never able to find out what the civil structure was.[27]

That is what I know about the civil defense command.[28] I should point out that some of these people were not necessarily appointed by the government. It was rather a de facto situation.[29]

The trio of MRND leaders was to ensure the homogeneity of the Interim Government. Clearly, the mandate given to the ministers when they took the oath of office was quite explicit: they were asked to "neutralize whoever sought to provoke troubles in the country."[30] But it was necessary for the more experienced members of the MRND, PL, and MDR to close ranks with their younger and less experienced comrades. The first order of business was to put the entire country on a war footing, that is, to mobilize the territorial administration and tighten the hold on the prefectures of the south. After the government's tour through the less militant southern prefectures of Gitarama, Gikongoro, and Butare on 18 and 19 April, it became increasingly clear that, throughout the country, MRND/CDR party activists were in charge of issuing marching orders in every domain of activity, such as subjugating erstwhile opponents and, where necessary, eliminating stubborn or reluctant civil servants or those who were simply too indecisive. Under MRND guidance a range of tasks was entrusted to the local authorities: accelerate the mobilization of state matériel and human resources, exercise close supervision of the population in supporting the armed forces, and whip up the militia's zeal to "win the war." This policy was openly acknowledged and rigorously applied. Participation was mandatory, and the level of personal engagement became a key criterion for evaluating individuals, activists, or operators. No compromise was ever really tolerated, and no one could be unaware of that. In particular, the allies or the newly co-opted were always at risk of being denounced as traitors by the more radical.

Impossible Negotiations
between the Belligerents

In such extraordinary circumstances, the conduct of negotiations between the new government authorities and the RPF appeared more like an obligatory pantomime to satisfy the expectations of foreign mediators. The restart of the war demonstrated how little regard the belligerents actually had for the signatures they placed on the accords so laboriously concluded in Arusha. Extremist elements of both camps had decided to square off, and the very notion of compromise had no relevance.

Only the international community would have been able to stop the coming tragedy and impose effective solutions. It was clearly possible when thousands of Belgian, French, and American soldiers arrived on the scene or in Bujumbura starting on 9 April. But they had not arrived to stop the massacres, or to save the peace, or to assist UNAMIR, which was under attack after having been manipulated with impunity over the course of several months. In fact, if with its twenty-five hundred poorly equipped soldiers, who were limited by a restrictive mandate, the UN mission in Rwanda was not able to intervene to stop the massacres, then the foreign troops in Kigali (a thousand French and Belgian paracommandos) or based in the region (between fifteen hundred and two thousand soldiers) could do it, with the high command of the FAR, along with the majority of moderate units, ready to support them.

Recall that, during those first few days, the killings in Kigali were the work of some two thousand militiamen and about as many members of the elite military units that were loyal to the presidential clan. If an intervention was not risk-free, there is little question that protection of those spaces where the opposition figures and Tutsi had taken refuge and stopping the large-scale massacres were well within the capability of UNAMIR and the troops that had arrived. But from the very beginning, the massacres were viewed as a spinoff of the war, which was neither within UNAMIR's mandate to halt nor a fortiori the responsibility of the international community, in charge of political solutions for which there was no consensus. Numerous civilian and military observers felt that the refusal to intervene in the massacres was rooted in foreign chanceries. It had nothing to do with military reasons and everything to do with the incapacity of Western powers to agree on a common approach: UNAMIR's hostility to Operation Amaryllis (the emergency evacuation of French nationals), the absence of coordination between Belgian and French troops, the hostility of the belligerents toward outsiders (insofar as Bagosora was opposed to reinforcements of Belgian troops, just as the RPF had set a deadline for foreign interventions in the country). More fundamentally, the United Nations Security Council revealed itself to be incapable of delineating a line of conduct. Nonintervention meant allowing RPF troops to capture power but also leaving hundreds of thousands of men, women, and children at the mercy of their ethnic enemies.

The latest events illustrated the determination of the major actors in the conflict to allow forces on the ground to run amok in the name of a policy that excluded all compromise. For a while at least, mediators and moderates of various stripes were not welcome. One is almost tempted to conclude that the real challenge for the two protagonists, both eager to fight, was to frustrate the ambitions of the command of the Rwandan Armed Forces whose sole raison d'être, until mid-April, lay in the prospect of a political solution to the crisis. Having passed that stage, it looked as though the individual and collective strategies of the warmongers drew their inspiration from an aberrant sense of national destiny. The tragedy simply had to run its course.

Since 1994, both victor and vanquished have pointed an accusing finger at each other and traded blame for refusing to negotiate and for the resumption of hostilities following the assassinations of the Rwandan head of state and several of his close associates. For the foreseeable future, this question will remain a continuing source of controversy. I will simply limit myself here to drawing out the broad strokes.

With the decision to shoot down the presidential plane, the RPF took the initiative in operational terms and thus was in a position to anticipate the range of possible consequences. Two obvious scenarios came into focus. The first involved a low-intensity reaction: temporary neutralization of the adversary's political and military decision-making centers and the availability of mediators to organize the transition with members of the army general staff committed to the Arusha Peace Accords, the pro-RPF wings of the opposition parties, UNAMIR, and the foreign embassies. The second raised the possibility of an immediate, violent response by Kigali-based military units attached to the presidency, compounded by an "enraged populace" mobilized by militias. In assessing the more likely of the two, the RPF had had plenty of time to weigh its strategies and finalize an appropriate response to ensure its capture of power. The RPF also had an excellent handle on the divisions that would determine the balance of forces in the opposing camp for both its civilian and its military components.

The willingness of that coterie of northern soldiers and MRND leaders to squarely face the RPF aggression, and their determination from the very outset to respond with the most extreme measures did not derail initiatives by the majority of general staff officers to stop the killings and to start negotiations, that is, until mid-April. By the early afternoon of 7 April Gen. Roméo Dallaire had established contacts between Seth Sendashonga for the RPF and Théoneste Bagosora and the chief of staff of the gendarmerie, Maj. Gen. Augustin Ndindiliyimana, for the FAR. Dallaire had established this initial contact by around 3:00 p.m.:

> I had planted myself in his office and was out of the office only to take phone calls or, in fact, ultimately, to establish communications between one of the political heads, whose name was Seth, and Bagosora himself. They did talk. There was absolutely no will at all to coordinate or to cooperate or something. It was very cold and icy. They spoke in Kinyarwanda.
>
> And then Habyarimana [*sic*] [Ndindiliyimana] went on to the phone, spoke a little longer, and when he hung up the phone he said, "You know, there's no link." He said, "There's no cooperation with the RPF." And the feedback I got from the other side, from my people on the other side, had exactly the same comment. There's no way these guys want to take control of the situation, and this is degenerating into massacres.[31]

Contact was renewed the next day on behalf of the Military Crisis Committee and the following day by Marcel Gatsinzi, the acting army chief of staff. Up until the last communiqué of the Rwandan Armed Forces of 18 April, not to mention the declaration by the commanders of the government armed forces of 12 April (*see annex 71*), there was really no lack of offers to negotiate or a shortage of receptive gestures from officers of the FAR general staff.[32] Some, in fact, did not hesitate to short-circuit and defy the Interim Government to call for implementation of the BBTG and an application of the Arusha Peace Accords. The situation was described in just these terms by one of the ministers of the Interim Government:

> According to the terms of the protocol, the government should negotiate directly with RPF, but the latter refused. Even on 9 April, we insisted on sending a delegation to negotiate. We mandated the prime minister to do so in collaboration with the minister of foreign affairs. We insisted that the international community should participate.
>
> In response, the RPF clearly stated that it did not wish to negotiate with the Interim Government, which it did not recognize, but rather with FAR representatives.
>
> Colonel Gatsinzi, Colonel Rusatira, and other officers called "moderates" were in favor of a direct and immediate meeting with RPF without the government's approval. They did not advocate any military coup as such but to "ignore the government" so as to prompt the setting up of the Broad-Based Transitional Government. In the end, it was decided

to mandate the FAR to negotiate, but on behalf of the government. In fact, the law prescribed that the armed forces are at the disposal of the government.[33]

The 12 April communiqué indeed represents the position taken by the FAR general staff, since it was signed by its acting chief, Col. Marcel Gatsinzi, and the four staff officers (Col. Joseph Murasampongo [G1]; Col. Aloys Ntiwiragabo [G2]; Lt. Col. Emmanuel Kanyandekwe, filling in for Gratien Kabiligi [G3]; and Lt. Col. Augustin Rwamanywa [G4]). But this was the last significant gesture from this group, since Gatsinzi hardly exercised any power from that point on, and the command of the FAR that those signatories claimed to represent still could not manage to impose its authority over the units directing the massacres. Nor did that group receive any significant support from the political parties and the Interim Government, the latter thoroughly radicalized after giving up on the "pacification" operation—which was supposed to halt the massacres in Kigali—and its flight to Gitarama.

The FAR command felt that it was impossible to respond to the conditions set by the RPF (controlling the Presidential Guard and halting the massacres by militias) without first obtaining a cease-fire. Hostilities had broken out on several fronts by 7 April as RPA troops, supported by the Ugandan Army, advanced toward Kigali. Indeed, the attempts to gain control over the Presidential Guard remained fruitless, and neutralizing the militias was tantamount to a "war within the war," in which the FAR could engage neither politically nor militarily without assistance from at least one of the belligerents.[34]

At the heart of this analysis was a clear distinction between, on the one hand, a war for the conquest or defense of power and, on the other, the outright massacres perpetrated against the Tutsi population. These had, from 11 and 12 April onward, assumed the form of a state policy of genocide. For the FAR command, the extremist, pro-Hutu soldiers and militiamen were waging a "parallel" war against the pro-RPF opposition, both Tutsi and Hutu. The FAR command seemed to think—as suggested by the moniker "government of the Abatabazi [Saviors]" adopted by the Interim Government—that even its most fervent defenders doubted that the war against the RPF could be won. The common objective that unified and motivated the pro-Hutu extremists was that none of their former adversaries should savor the victory of the RPF. If defeat at the hands of the RPF could not be avoided, none of their Tutsi or southern enemies, both of whom betrayed them, should be left to cash in on the spoils of their victory. Many soldiers from the late President Habyarimana's home turf, working in the shadows to sabotage initiatives of the FAR command, even refused to face the RPF in battle now that their supreme chief had been assassinated. Their primary objective was to exterminate the potential political base for the RPF and its allies. These soldiers were not looking to take power; had this been their intention, their support could have been decisive in setting up a military committee with a broad range of powers from that first night of 6–7 April. Without a cease-fire agreement, no one could stop the insurgent units in their campaign of extermination; they were well armed and knew they could count on the exasperation of the MRND's base among the militias. From 11 and 12 April onward, with the arrival on the scene of Interim Government politicians who linked their political futures to a resolution of the war through genocide, the balance of power shifted decisively against the FAR high command.

As indicated in the tract from the political parties calling for an alliance against the monarchy (*see box 15*), the security issues debated during the government meetings of 11 and 12 April were less focused on putting an end to massacres of the "internal enemy" than on halting fratricidal clashes among Hutu of the various parties, including the in-fighting going on among the militia groups. Besides, calls to ensure the security of the population, courage in the pursuit of the war, and resistance to the enemy, including detecting infiltrators, traitors, and *ibyitso*, would seal the sacred union of the forces of Hutu Power against the Tutsi enemy and its accomplices. The first meeting of the cabinet and the heads of political parties held in Murambi on 12 April solemnly marked the end of equivocation by the ministers and the consecration of the "great coalition" of the so-called Hutu parties (see chapter 11).

The alliance MRND/MDR—symbolized by the rapprochement between Matthieu Ngirumpatse and Faustin Twagiramungu in mid-1993—was largely motivated by opportunism, and this also applies to the forced resignation of Dismas Nsengiyaremye as prime minister and his replacement by Faustin Twagiramungu, prime minister designate under the Arusha Peace Accords. The alliance received further impetus with Froduald Karamira and Donat Murego working hand in hand to retake control of the MDR with support from the MRND when Faustin Twagiramungu demonstrated his leanings toward the RPF in September 1993. This evolution easily became apparent in November 1993 after the assassination of the Hutu president, Melchior Ndadaye, in Burundi. Prior to that it was just a simple alliance without much of a programmatic or strategic foundation. After 12 April 1994, the "natural" coalition was effectively cemented. It ordered a halt to systematic massacres of Hutu from the opposition parties, whose perpetrators were threatened with severe punishment after a hoped-for conquest over the RPF, and it directed its energies toward the elimination of Tutsi. Similarly, it was after 12 April 1994 that Donat Murego became the de facto leader of the MDR, with Karamira and Kambanda habitually turning to him for his views as an *inararibonye*, that is, a seasoned, well-experienced politician. This was the true start of the genocide in intention and deed.

We can speculate whether Bagosora and Ndindiliyimana had not deliberately organized the withdrawal of the Interim Government to Murambi (Gitarama prefecture) before the opportunities for negotiation sought by the majority of the military high command were completely exhausted.

Forced to counter the suicidal designs of one faction, combined with the ambitions of the other, the high command dug in and tried to push for negotiations, as confirmed by the 13 April cable that Dallaire sent to Kofi Annan, who was the under secretary-general for peacekeeping at the UN's Department of Peacekeeping Operations from March 1993 to December 1996.[35] In this document, the army high command states, "It is time to stop the war. To that end, the High Command agrees to an unconditional cease-fire from 13 April 1994 at 12:00 midday." But, if the RPF and the FAR indeed agreed to a forty-eight-hour reprieve on 13 April, it was to permit evacuation of foreign residents and not to stop the massacres. All the same, conclusion of a new cease-fire on 14 April hardly changed matters on the ground. The first direct talks between leaders of the RPF and the FAR, held on 15 April 1994 at the Hôtel Méridien and mediated by the special representative of the United Nations, Jacques-Roger Booh-Booh, also had no effect on the situation.

For its part, the RPF could sense that the political weight of those favoring negotiations was no longer sufficient to justify a pause in its offensive. Indeed, even though the order removing him was dated 18 April, General Gatsinzi's 17 April 1994 solemn call to the UN secretary-general's representative (*see annex 77*) reiterating his 15 April proposal was the voice of an already suspended chief of staff, since the announcement of his replacement, Col. Augustin Bizimungu, had already occurred on the 15th. But one could also see how the approach reflected a calculated risk, insofar as the RPF's repeated refusals to negotiate fell in line with the Interim Government's murderous strategy. Each passing day further weakened the position of those members of the general staff who favored a political solution.

When the RPF finally agreed to engage in discussions between 22 April and 14 May 1994, it picked Gatsinzi, who was powerless at that point, as the preferred intermediary; it refused to negotiate with the Interim Government's representative. But there was no longer anything for the two sides to negotiate, and the RPF did not want to hear anything more about a cease-fire.[36]

This is exactly what Dallaire confirmed in his message to Kofi Annan of 24 April, which summarized his conversation with Paul Kagame: "He did not appear receptive to a cease-fire then. His forces were winning the tactical war and were going to continue fighting as long as they were winning."[37] War had now emerged as the ultimate arbiter.

There simply would never be a negotiated settlement. This mindset was clear in Gbadolite on 24 April, since the proposed agreement was signed only by soldiers of the FAR. The RPF opposed having the Interim Government minister and head of the negotiating mission, André Ntagerura, sign it. Tito Rutaremara, who should have signed it for the RPF, never arrived. A similar situation occurred in Arusha on 30 April during negotiations organized under the auspices of the Tanzanian minister of defense and its prime minister. The RPF delegation, composed of Alexis Kanyarengwe, Pasteur Bizimungu, and Tito Rutaremara, refused the Tanzanian offer of an effective cease-fire within forty-eight hours and left without signing anything. Their attitude was perfectly summed up by Booh-Booh: "No party refused to negotiate. But there were always preconditions."[38]

After 30 April each belligerent took diplomatic initiatives that would strengthen its position internally and externally. For the RPF, which, thanks to Uganda, encountered no problems regarding access to weapons, the standard attitude was to refuse all negotiation, and especially all outside intervention, despite the guarantees made by those offering to devote themselves exclusively to assist or save the civilian population (*see annex 77.2*). For the Interim Government, diplomatic action principally consisted in making a strong public showing and to make contacts dominated mostly by pro forma requests for support and/or financing for the war effort. This was the sort of intervention that came directly and almost exclusively from the Interim Government and, behind it, the MRND. In fact, despite conceding the ministerial portfolio for foreign affairs to Clément-Jérôme Bicamumpaka, an MDR member, the MRND/CDR alliance retained exclusive control of diplomatic affairs. The titular minister was constantly monitored and accompanied by special envoys of the government, whether civilian or military, who included the presidents of the MRND and the PL and especially the CDR's Jean-Bosco Barayagwiza, who openly overwhelmed the new, inexperienced minister.

Meanwhile, from her exile in Paris, Habyarimana's widow, Agathe Kanziga, initiated contacts and lobbied several African heads of state. Her actions, albeit done discreetly, undeniably strengthened the Interim Government's diplomatic footing.

10

From Massacres to Genocide

As we have seen, in triggering and then systematically expanding the massacres, the orchestrators relied on army units along with Kigali-based militia forces. Both were directly linked to the principal decision makers always on hand in moments of crisis: military officers beholden to the presidential clan. This is perfectly illustrated by the swift mobilization of Interahamwe militiamen in Kigali on the night of 6–7 April. The army, and especially the Presidential Guard, rapidly established roadblocks to secure the neighborhoods where the presidency, military camps, and essential buildings and services like banks were located and where important figures had homes (e.g., Kanombe, Kimihurura, and Kiyovu; see maps 2 and 3); after that, they concentrated on reducing UNAMIR's mobility and sealing off those areas where persons destined to be expiatory victims of the presidential clan's wrath were living. This is also where the first groups of militiamen moved into position early the next morning (many of those militiamen emerged from the ranks of the Presidential Guard). It was only later, toward the end of the morning of 7 April, that they truly descended on the various neighborhoods to localize the "enemies." And it was only later that afternoon that widespread killings broke out at the roadblocks set up on the major arteries in the capital. "Civilian-manned" barricades, seemingly spontaneous, popped up on secondary routes to block access to and egress from the more humble neighborhoods.

The major thrust to hunt down all "internal enemies" had not yet become routine practice at the roadblocks. In fact, initially, groups of Interahamwe militiamen focused primarily on roving through the various neighborhoods to neutralize the "infiltrators and accomplices" of the RPF, whose homes had already been identified and watched.[1] Regardless of the neighborhood or the street, the task was the same: homes supposedly sheltering "enemies" or where a family member was suspected of having joined the RPF were immediately attacked, and anyone living there was killed—with help from soldiers in some cases. Here we find the first manifestation of the "civil self-defense" strategy organized by prefect Tharcisse Renzaho and the minister of defense (*see annex 44*). Later, when information began to circulate about assassinations of certain high-profile figures, mostly Hutu, all linked to the opposition, the authorities then mobilized security patrols manned by neighborhood residents. Since the beginning of the year, and especially toward the end of February, these informal brigades had conducted regular night patrols to monitor the persons and property in the neighborhood. The definition of the "enemy" broadened to include Tutsi of the interior, Hutu political opponents, and, eventually, anyone who did not approve of the killings. Hutu and Tutsi members of the "mixed" patrols who dared to oppose them were themselves eliminated, not to mention the innumerable victims of the random settlings of accounts between neighbors, all made possible by the disappearance of the most elementary legal and normative constraints.[2]

The logic at work here can usefully be compared to what transpired in Burundi in October 1993 after Melchior Ndadaye was assassinated: in both cases, in the name of a slain Hutu head of state, a "popular rage," assiduously nursed and mobilized by ready pro-Hutu extremists, was unleashed with impunity.

The communiqué from the Ministry of Defense signed by Théoneste Bagosora and broadcast to the nation around 6:30 a.m. is highly significant (*see annex 56*). In "urg[ing] the population to remain indoors pending further instructions," his last sentence required those who feared for their lives to stay put and wait for their executioners at home or at their neighbors' homes, and anyone attempting to flee would find that it was extremely difficult to get past the barricades encircling the neighborhoods.

The assassinations and the setting up of roadblocks started very early on the morning of 7 April, and the militiamen hardly needed guidelines to be operational, as they deemed themselves already on alert and fully deployed for "civil defense." The sorcerers' apprentices who gave birth to these militias, who reared them and enhanced their power, were indeed shocked by their efficiency. As one of the perpetrators later testified: "I spoke to you about our interventions as members of the National Committee of the Interahamwe za MRND on the various roadblocks and other locations in Kigali after the death of President Habyarimana, on 6 April 1994. . . . When we would approach Interahamwe on these roadblocks, aside from congratulating them and encouraging them to continue their good 'work,' members of the National Committee would encourage them by giving them beer, cigarettes, food, and pocket money, depending on the situation and the individual capacities of the committee members."[3] This explains how, despite the curfew imposed by Bagosora, Presidential Guard soldiers, obeying orders, along with Interahamwe militia, were the ones who quickly sprang into action at the start of the killings from the night of 7–8 April. Such was the frenzy to kill that Interahamwe leaders who honored the curfew were viewed as "cowardly" or "deserters" the following day. Soldiers had to accompany and protect the members of the National Committee of the Interahamwe "in their work." RTLM commentators reported on their activities, keeping count of the victims and praising the Interahamwe's macabre exploits.[4] The first victims were the political opponents, various accomplices, and infiltrators, who had already been identified and branded: "It was simply in the order of things that after 6 April 1994, persons who were identified and localized would be eliminated."[5]

In Kigali, the National Committee of the Interahamwe was able to establish itself as a quasi-military force. Such was the power of the militiamen that they could even persuade units of the armed forces that opposed massacring the civilian Tutsi population to change their mind; they could just as easily block military escorts of targeted political or military figures. By all accounts the Interahamwe owed this extraordinary latitude to the open approval and support lavished upon them by the heads of the political parties.

This is how one of their leaders described the Interahamwe's relationship with other militias: "Around February, the Interahamwe received the order to collaborate with Inkuba, the MDR-Power militia, but during the first few days of the genocide, many members of MDR—even some who were identified with MDR-Power—struggled against the Interahamwe and the Impuzamugambi [the youth movement of the CDR]. However, after the message from Froduald Karamira that was broadcast on the radio on 12 April, and following similar directives from other party leaders, the MDR youth wing joined with the Interahamwe. Thus, they put into practice the directive that came down to 'forget past loyalties.'"[6]

With support from the most radical elements of the parties, the militias were fused and consolidated under a unified command that was dominated and piloted by MRND party leaders. This command structure was put together with due attention paid to inputs from local party leaders and financiers, who, while supporting "their" youth groups, could still keep their partisan identity and maneuvering capacity. The state's authority over the assortment of militia groups was thus quite tangible, and the myriad decisions emanating from official representatives of the central power offered ample opportunities to manipulate this partisan rivalry so as to encourage the murderous activities of the militias.

We still need to examine the complexity of the relationship between Interahamwe leaders from the National Committee in Kigali, who issued military directives, and the heads of the parties: whether by necessity or for personal gain, the "authorities" exercised their prerogatives while still according the militias a wide, practically limitless scope for action. The violence, pillaging, and rapes that ensued were the price to be paid for maintaining availability and preparedness among the militiamen, and, inversely, the terror that they spread stifled opposition from moderate elements among the soldiers, politicians, and senior civil servants that the Interim Government still struggled to mobilize. The militia chiefs had no intention of limiting their scope of action, but they could not persist without some degree of cover from the recognized authorities, the only ones who could guarantee lasting impunity (*see annex 87*).

Close supervision by militia leaders in the neighborhoods and at the roadblocks, the potential spoils to be had, and the certainty of impunity were sufficient conditions: participating in the massacres virtually became a self-sustaining occupation until it reached the point where, left without guidance from national political leaders and faced with "functional unemployment" as their exploits downsized the number of "enemies" to eliminate, vying factions of militiamen began to direct their energies against each other in fratricidal clashes.

Consequently, after three days of murderous fury, the massacres declined in intensity because the killers were exhausted and had literally exhausted their targets. Routine domestic obligations and the need for supplies took over, but then there was also the matter of removing decomposing bodies from the houses and roadways, divvying up the booty, and settling how vacant properties would be shared. Even if mobilization remained high, uncertainty began to wear down the killers. Despite the RTLM's calls for killing, the militiamen clearly perceived the existence of divisions among decision makers. The militiamen knew that the army high command did not support the massacres and that a good number of politicians or members of the clergy might be against them. Contradictory orders were issued. Thus, on 10 April, government initiatives were announced to bring the massacres to a halt and to reassert control in neighborhoods throughout Kigali, and the prospect of a political transition, as opposed to a "military putsch," began to take hold. We could also point to the return of the minister of defense, Augustin Bizimana; Prefect Renzaho's sanctions against soldiers guilty of violence in Kigali; the Military Crisis Committee's meeting with the RTLM to stop further incitement to killing (*see annex 65.2*); and Radio Rwanda's broadcast of a communiqué from the

Ministry of Public Works calling its drivers back to work the following morning, 11 April.

From the very first hours of 11 April, the spectacle of thousands of "enemy" corpses piled and stacked for removal by Public Works trucks at the major intersections and on thoroughfares bisecting the more populated residential neighborhoods in Kigali palpably shaped the mood of the remaining citizens. At the same time, international reaction denouncing the massacres became more forceful, and the various embassies' personnel began to prepare their departure. Meanwhile, RPF troops made their way toward the capital from Mulindi, taking control of the communes bordering Kigali-rural and moving to surround the capital from the south—it is little wonder that the newly installed military and political authorities were shocked, if not horrified, by these developments. It was in this context that MRND leaders and the other party chiefs summoned the National Committee of the Interahamwe to ask that they put a stop to the most visible massacres. During this period of relative decline in the killings, it was as if time stood still, because the range of options had yet to be sorted out.

On the one hand, among the party heads and political figures, those who could have still weighed in to restore order kept equivocating between political solutions that they found distasteful and unacceptable and intensifying a war that was probably already doomed. The newly promoted ministers categorically refused to take responsibility for the assassinations and massacres that were inevitably imputed to them, but they could not muster the resolve to express disapproval or influence the course of events. In addition, there were dissenting opinions among the prefects who met in Kigali, a fact underscored by the number of absences. Finally, for its part, members of the high command, several among them marginalized or hunted down, were trying to seal an unconditional cease-fire with the RPF, with support from UNAMIR.

On the other hand, members of the tight nucleus who had sparked the assassinations and the massacres, first among them Bagosora, Ntabakuze, Mpiranya, and Nzirorera, could not allow even the slightest political opening to gain a foothold. Perhaps girded by shared resignation, they all knew that "peace" could only be had at their expense and that all the crimes linked to the reprise of war would be imputed to them. The military and civilian putschists of the night of 6 April thus, for the second time, opted for all or nothing at all and played their trump card, with success.

That very same day, the Interim Government sent out directives, aimed to restart the killings that had trailed off a bit, to the prefects before moving its headquarters to Gitarama. Nzirorera's parting gesture—instructions to distribute weapons to militiamen at the roadblocks—gave the decisive push to a new wave of killings. The balance of forces had now shifted dramatically, giving virtually unfettered control to the Bagosora-Nzirorera faction and their radical supporters.

The Interim Government's Ambivalence and Weakness When Faced with the Massacres

No doubt, the new ministers understood perfectly well who the real organizers of their government were and what motivated them. The ministers may not have known all the twists and turns leading up to their appointment to this newly proclaimed government, but they accepted the roles they were offered. In any case, faced with the need for urgent action in virtually every domain, there was no time for introspection about events and the strategic choices the ministers had to confront, whether or not they agreed with them. As former militants (party members) who had themselves emerged from the MRND, they were all well acquainted with its sacrosanct principle: "Unity of thought; unity of approach; unity of action." Multiparty politics did nothing to uproot the culture of absolute respect for authority that had been inculcated in them.

> The party's militants were trained in such an ethos, and the multiparty system changed nothing as regards their mentality of absolute respect for authority. Thus, an activist had no need for written directives in order to take action once he knew that such orders, instructions, or directives came from authority.
>
> Moreover, the MRND controlled or exercised a very strong influence on the officials of the territorial administration (prefects, burgomasters, counselors, and heads of cell committees), and the multiparty system changed nothing.[7]

Despite its apparent enthusiasm, the government's first days proved to be quite difficult. As soon as its military and civilian sponsors withdrew from the forefront, the co-opted ministers assumed, or wanted to believe, that they actually wielded real "power." They held an informal meeting on the evening of 8 April to organize the next day's oath-taking ceremony, and the government cabinet officially met for the first time at the end of that ceremony, on 9 April. Most of the ministers took the floor, and a broad overview of the political and security situation was presented.

At the end of the meeting, the prime minister assigned tasks and set deadlines that placed diplomatic action and "pacification" at the heart of the government agenda. The priority was to establish the new ministers' authority nationwide: "Monday: prefects; Tuesday: burgomasters; Wednesday: counselors; Thursday: the population."[8] Clearly, active involvement from MRND ministers who were reinstalled in their posts allowed the entire group to quickly get up to speed, despite the inexperience of several among them, most prominently, the new prime minister.

However, it was immediately apparent that things were not going as planned. The day after they took the oath of office, on 10 April, the ministers acknowledged that the situation was out of control. Instigators and proponents of the massacres were clearly identified: "soldiers" and "party youth" (Interahamwe militiamen of the MRND), the RTLM, and Radio Rwanda. Directly accused by the RPF, which denounced "the dictatorial government that only seeks to block implementation of [the transitional institutions] by deliberately flouting the law" and that "organizes the massacres," the cabinet only managed to respond by formulating a final resolution for restoring order, purely formal, since it deferred implementation to those with the "means" to execute it without the least public expression of the government's "will": "The army should arrest those who are killing and pillaging and punish them as required by law."[9]

Here we have one of the major features that shaped the evolution of members of the Interim Government. Constantly under military escort, fearing for their security, their world was limited to the neighborhood of Kiyovu and their living quarters, the Hôtel des Diplomates and the French Embassy (see map 3). Their movements were narrowly confined to those areas, and their access to information was strictly controlled by those who were "protecting" them or, more precisely, monitoring their progress. Concretely, between 9 and 11 April, the last day that the Interim Government was present in Kigali, no collegial framework or procedures were put in place to provide the ministers with information about the events that were occurring in the city and throughout the country. Their sources were limited to a few members of the army high command (via contacts with officers in charge of intelligence operations in the prefectures); to information made available from party leaders; to whatever news the prefects sent to the prime minister and to the minister of the interior, or in this case, to Callixte Kalimanzira, his chief of staff, who was filling in de facto for the missing minister, Faustin Munyaseza; or news that made its way to them from top MRND leaders who remained in regular contact with Radio Rwanda, finally reclaimed; and from the RTLM.

To avoid any doubt about the ministers' level of knowledge, we should emphasize once again that the cabinet meetings held at the Hôtel des

Diplomates included MRND party leaders who were all the more available and accessible, since they were all housed together in the same location.

It was in this context that, on 10 April, the ministers opposed the diffusion over the airwaves of a communiqué condemning attacks against civilians from the Catholic Church drafted by Mgr. Thadée Nsengiyumva, the bishop of Kabgayi, one of the organizers of the former Contact Committee between the churches and the belligerents; above all, he was also the president of the Episcopal Conference of Rwanda.

That decision, which was heavily influenced by Minister of Information Éliezer Niyitegeka, a notorious anti-Tutsi extremist, amply demonstrates the extent of the Interim Government's efforts to ensure "security" and promote "pacification." It was against this backdrop that the ministers learned that the majority of the military high command and unit and operational sector commanders had disavowed the installation of the Interim Government, and, additionally, its leading members sought to negotiate directly with the RPF. Hence, the ministers defended their prerogatives. "The government [was] to remain 'in charge' of negotiations," as mentioned in the personal notes of one of the ministers, emphasizing the primacy of the Interim Government in negotiating with the RPF.

On 11 April the "joint meeting of the government and the prefects" allowed them to take stock of the disorder and the massacres throughout the prefectures, an assessment made all the more compelling because several of the prefects present had already joined in the struggle against the internal "accomplices." In response to this account of the seriousness of the situation, many gave credence to Colonel Renzaho's descriptions of the heroic, spontaneous resistance of the populace in turning back the attacks and infiltrations of the RPF.

Confronted with worsening tensions and the realization of just how serious the military had become, the Interim Government started to fall in line with the most radical elements in regard to the war, but political schisms remained and crystallized in reaction to the firm resistance to the massacres in the southern prefectures that were dominated by the MDR and PSD and where the territorial administrations supported the prefects of Gitarama, Butare, and Gikongoro. The alignment of an MDR prefect, another Tutsi PL prefect, and one from the MRND posed a real problem: the first openly opposed the massacres during the meeting, whereas the second, fearing for his life, refused to travel but arranged for a radio broadcast of a joint communiqué with his colleague from Gikongoro to denounce the massacres. It was necessary to conceal the information, which never appeared in the written account of the meeting, as requested by Augustin Bizimana, the minister of defense.[10] The prime minister concluded the meeting with the comment: "I cannot imagine any moment more dramatic than the one we are living at this moment."[11]

This rather demoralizing atmosphere set the stage for the government's abrupt transfer to Gitarama on 12 April. Already perturbed by concerns for their own security the night before, members of the government lodged at the French Embassy were preparing to flee the country with their hosts just as the last of the Western embassies began to shutter their doors. Others gave into the consuming panic that swirled with the rumors, the gunfire, and the movement of troops in the capital, along with the presumed "infiltrations" of the enemy. In the end, their military and political mentors improvised an evacuation to the country's hinterland in Gitarama, fleeing just as RPF troops began to approach the perimeter of the capital, which only underscored perceptions of the weakness and powerlessness of this government in the eyes of all. This episode of wildly overblown, collective panic—the FAR still controlled the core of the city for several weeks thereafter—allows us to locate and evaluate the axis of decision making (both institutional and individual). Up until that moment, the members of the new governmental entity had certainly taken stock of the situation and, at least by default, the expected mission of the Interim Government, but they had not yet developed a clear vision of the division of labor between the party leadership, the various spokespersons of the army, and the government. This first serious political error certainly demonstrated the fragility of the structure put in place by the promoters of the massacres, but it also turned the spotlight on the Interim Government's hesitations and the decisions it either deferred or refused to take.

Once rid of the Interim Government, Joseph Nzirorera and Théoneste Bagosora put an end to these equivocations. The "pacification" tour was abandoned in circumstances that left no doubt about the policy that they had intended to pursue. To dispel all doubts that might encumber their personal engagement, the militiamen immediately received the weapons and supplies that they had been asking for since the reprise of the war. From that point on, the genocide could, as Augustin Cyiza put it so well, simply "feed on itself" until the Interim Government eventually formally assumed control under the guise of "civil self-defense."

Most of the members of the new Interim Government, initially wholly consumed by concern for their own security, were not up to speed on the details of the "pacification" tour and had only tacitly signed off on it during that first cabinet meeting held in Murambi. The very ambivalence of the term "pacification" allowed each one of them to jump on board and to pretend to ignore what it ultimately, unmistakably came to embody: exterminate the internal enemy.

The "Pacification" Tour
of 10–12 April 1994

We can now reconstruct this important episode with great accuracy thanks to accounts from several key direct participants, leaving little doubt about how it unfurled and the role of the various persons involved, including those who, after their arrests by the ICTR, long stuck to flat denials, such as Matthieu Ngirumpatse.[12]

The "pacification" tour is a subject of special interest because it draws attention to the stages involved in launching widespread massacres against the civilian Tutsi population. While Col. Théoneste Bagosora was the instigator who wanted the new civilian authorities to sanction the political assassinations and the massacres, the hesitancy of several ministers, amplified by international condemnation, pushed the government to try to put a stop to them, or at least to exercise greater control.

In fact, on the morning of 9 April, right after the oath of office, an emergency meeting of the government was held to discuss matters of security and the massacres. Unanimously, it "was decided that those responsible for the troubles and the killings should be identified and handled appropriately," that the killings had to stop, and that the corpses of the victims had to be gathered up and disposed of. The prime minister was charged with contacting the heads of the army units. Justin Mugenzi was given the task of informing the MRND leaders, who then summoned the Interahamwe leaders. Accompanied by a paracommando military escort made available to them by Bagosora, on 10 April they made a tour of the main roadblocks to deliver these messages to the militiamen and, toward the end of the afternoon, returned to make a detailed report to the MRND leaders, who instructed them to continue with their task the following day. Shocked that the same message was not being broadcasted on Radio Rwanda while RTLM persisted with its calls to identify the "enemy" and many soldiers and gendarmes obviously continued to obey other orders, the Interahamwe leaders resumed their mission and were stupefied upon their return, around 2:30 p.m. on 12 April, to learn that the government had fled in the meanwhile and that Joseph Nzirorera alone remained at the Hôtel des Diplomates. In the midst of preparing his own departure and pressed to catch up with the Interim Government in Gitarama, he calmed them by promising a delivery of weapons that very same evening.

Tasked with calling for an end to the killings, the Interahamwe leaders went out again with a stock of weapons and munitions to arm the militiamen!

This paradoxical outcome clearly shows a decisive shift in favor of the strategy of radical confrontation and its corollary, the genocide option, set in motion by the Nzirorera-Bagosora faction. In many respects, 12 April was a crucial day: practically all foreign embassies closed down; the Interim Government fled to Gitarama; its military and political sponsors took matters directly into their own hands; the population began to flee en masse; and, finally and especially, the high command of the Rwandan Armed Forces issued its remarkable communiqué (*see annex 71*). In their desperate appeal to the RPF and UNAMIR, the command called for an end to hostilities and an immediate cease-fire so that "loyalist" troops could put an end to the massacres and neutralize the militiamen and the army units that were organizing them.

This communiqué, the last one signed on behalf of the leadership that the military high command had put in place the night of 6–7 April, voiced defeat. Even if it confirmed Bagosora's and the extremist officers' isolation in relation to the high command, it also highlights the utter inability of those superior officers to impose their authority over the militias and the army units that remained insubordinate (mainly the Presidential Guard and the paracommando and Recce battalions) and their inability to go beyond the wait-and-see attitude of many other officers. All this made it unlikely that the RPF would recognize those officers as credible interlocutors for negotiating a cease-fire. While the RPF issued an ultimatum to foreign forces to evacuate their nationals, and while UNAMIR remained paralyzed, the moment for the facedown approached. Nzirorera and Bagosora needed to have the entire country take on the burden of the crucial choices they had made on the morning of 7 April and impose them on all.

Various accounts from Interahamwe leaders complement each other in faithfully reconstructing the context for the decision to distribute weapons to the militias: it was simply the reflection of mutual acknowledgment among the real decision makers. That complicity would persist until war's end.

The Interim Government was beset by double-speak and weakness; manipulated by its sponsors, it had neither the intention nor the will to resort to means routinely associated with government power to restore order or neutralize the extremists. While the Interahamwe had been active in promoting and organizing the massacres from the very first day, they still managed to echo the message entrusted to them by hiding behind symbols of authority (superior military officers, Bagosora's jeep, invoking the names of the MRND party leaders and the government). But every Rwandan knew perfectly well that, where subjects of importance were concerned, an understanding of the underlying intentions, along with a grasp of the real balance of power, was always required to assess the weight of the orders being passed down from above. For the Interahamwe, the double-speak from MRND party leaders was routine, as it had been applied to military training or weapons caches well before the reprise of the war. Anything that was not explicitly forbidden and firmly sanctioned was permissible, especially when the activity corresponded perfectly with the reason this militia had been assembled and trained since mid-1993. Thus, the apparent contradiction in the request made of them was not surprising. On the other hand, this first test was devastating for the credibility of the Interim Government. Barely having settled in, the new authorities were already seriously discredited, and it is no wonder why. Over the length and breadth of the war, relations remained tense between militiamen and this "government of runaways," whose authority and legitimacy were so clearly compromised.[13]

Furthermore, by providing the Interahamwe leaders from the National Provisional Committee with the weapons they were clamoring for, weapons that came from stocks that had been hidden from legitimate authorities until then, Joseph Nzirorera and Théoneste Bagosora endorsed all the killing and pillaging committed since 6 April, effectively giving the go-ahead for continuing and expanding them, and in so doing placed the new and hesitant government authorities with a fait accompli.

Never daring to impose its authority to halt the massacres when that was still possible, and with militiamen openly boasting of having the blessings of these same authorities, the Interim Government had no choice but to concede its weakness and defend the militiamen's exploits. It assumed responsibility for crimes that, at first instance, stripped "popular resistance" of all legitimacy.

Once again, just like the episode involving publication of the tract inciting the population to defend itself (see box 15), it was MRND party leaders and their counterparts in the army who personally took the most important decisions without the slightest deference to subordinate party organs or to any other institutional or collective framework. This proved a huge undertaking. The failure of the "pacification" tour, launched with neither sufficient conviction nor adequate means to predict success, was irreversible. The demands from the National Committee of the Interahamwe were satisfied: henceforth, the militiamen were free to interpret and to exercise their "mandate" and were guaranteed weapons from those who held the keys and had taken the initiative to open this second front: on the one hand, Bagosora and the units loyal to him, and on the other, the MRND via Nzirorera and Ngirumpatse, whose flight with the members of the Interim Government gave a clear signal.

On this point at least, the facts and what possibly may pass as the most important moment in Bagosora's trial at the ICTR coincide perfectly. These few utterances rise above his habitual alibis and justifications and for once have the tone of a true confession:

> Q. . . . What I want to know is whether you admit or you challenge the fact that at a certain point in time Tutsis were killed just because they were Tutsi?
>
> A. At some point in time they were killed because they were Tutsi. At some point in time there was some kind of madness; that's certain. People were killed because they were Tutsi. I agree with that.
>
> MR. PRESIDENT: When did that start?
>
> THE WITNESS: It was after the government fled, after the government fled. I can say that that phenomenon must have started with the flight of the government, with the flight of the displaced people of Nyacyonga.[14] As far as I'm concerned, that would be the reference point. At that time, no one was in charge of another. You—you had the fleeing mass and others who joined them, so nobody was really in charge. There was total disorder, total chaos. So I would say that it was from that moment on.
>
> MR. PRESIDENT: And if you were to give an approximate date for that moment, can you help us with that?
>
> THE WITNESS: I—I would say that from the 12th the government fled. The people—the displaced people of Nyacyonga who were—collapsed. I could take that date as the beginning of the total collapse.[15]

The genocide option was thus endorsed without restrictions from that point on and was never questioned again until the defeat. Even though relying on two different "songbooks," one thanking militiamen for their contributions and the other encouraging them to be "exemplary," the MRND communiqués of 23 and 27 April (*see annex 92*) altered nothing in this fundamental orientation. At no point did the party leadership, which had openly closed ranks against the more timorous or "softer" politicians, ever bother to use the means at its disposal to halt atrocities committed under cover of the MRND uniform and insignia (*see box 16*).

The Stakes and Responsibilities of the Genocide

It is now possible to explain just what is meant by the genocidal "conspiracy," to situate its phases over time, to describe the preconditions for unleashing it, and to identify its various proponents.

The Genocide Risk:
Underestimated or Simply Accepted
by the RPF?

It was incumbent upon the RPF to gauge the risk of large-scale massacres of civilians. Indeed, the resumption of hostilities did not occur by chance, nor was it dictated by circumstances; it was the expression of a mature, thoughtful, and well-prepared policy, one fully evaluated and then set in motion, with numerous advance warnings. The fact that extremist, pro-Hutu groups in league with elements from the military had, since late 1993, openly engaged in assembling and arming militias for "popular self-defense" against the enemy, both internal and external, was a recurrent theme in the national political life at that time, denounced by the internal opposition and the RPF alike. No one can pretend otherwise; this was common knowledge.

In light of statements from RPF leaders prior to that fateful aircraft explosion, several elements seem to indicate that, along with their foreign supporters, they clearly misjudged the level of readiness of the forces they were preparing to confront. Two explanations emerge that are not mutually exclusive.

According to a number of its members or ex-members, the RPA high command's strategic anticipation counted on the real or presumed weakness of President Habyarimana, who apparently was incapable of gaining the upper hand and asserting authority over the array of political formations and currents emerging from the mouvance présidentielle. After the decapitation of the opposition parties and the CDR, the RPA high command apparently deemed the situation all the more favorable for eliminating Habyarimana, viewed as the main obstacle to the conquest of power. Its members felt that the structure of power, entirely organized by and around Habyarimana, would have been "paralyzed" by his disappearance—to adopt the expression of an RPA officer. With no structured or effective riposte expected from the mouvance présidentielle, the RPF would find itself in full control. With UNAMIR providing cover, it could then negotiate with its habitual interlocutors from the internal opposition. As again demonstrated by the meeting at the Tanzanian Embassy at the very moment the assault against the plane was under way, the latter, such as Aaron Makuba (PSD), Landoald Ndasingwa (PL), Faustin Twagiramungu (MDR), and Boniface Ngulinzira (MDR), were absolutely terrorized, even with the RPF promising to guarantee their security (see chapter 5). Beyond the few rare individuals, like Agathe Uwilingiyimana, who still refused to choose between the two military factions, most of the heads of the opposition who had not gone over to the pro-Hutu side were ready for an accommodation with the RPF simply to survive.

There was no mistaking the RPF leadership's disdain for the Akazu, with its talk of "democrats" and the "democratic transition." The Akazu's in-depth knowledge of the depravities of the domestic political scene, regularly updated by accounts from their allies on the inside, did nothing to improve the image of these Second Republic heavyweights among leaders of the RPF. And this explains the RPF's exceptional capacity not only to shape the bitter rivalries among various leaders of the opposition but also to exploit internal conflicts within the MRND.

The international community was no less skeptical: practically none of its representatives gave much credence to the domestic opposition. The RPF knew it could count on a sympathetic neutrality from the majority of foreign embassies or, at the very least, their likely refusal to get involved if war was to start up again.

Be that as it may, those who expected the mouvance présidentielle to fall apart or be temporarily neutralized committed a very grave error. And this, even in spite of the incredible turn of events that allowed those responsible for the plane's explosion to decapitate not just the state but also the FAR. Aside from the head of state, the attack against the plane eliminated Army Chief of Staff Déogratias Nsabimana and the very influential Col. Élie Sagatwa. Furthermore, the minister of defense, Augustin Bizimana, and the minister of the interior, Faustin Munyazesa, were traveling abroad at the time, as was the chief of military intelligence, Aloys Ntiwiragabo, and the head of military operations, Gratien Kabiligi, both away on mission, one in Cameroon, accompanying his minister, and the other in Egypt.

Defying all expectations, neither paralysis of pro-Hutu activists nor a rallying of pro-RPF politicians, finally freed of the "tyrant," would materialize. There was no institutional collapse or splintering in military command and no defection of the officers from the south.

Indeed, resistance to the RPF offensive met with unanimous support within the FAR—albeit somewhat belatedly. In addition, very few had imagined that the offensive and defensive capacity of the militia forces would be so strong. Purely on the military level, this became clear in two ways. Where undifferentiated massacres of the civilian Tutsi population are concerned, the militias first proceeded with targeted and systematic elimination of previously identified RPF activists along with their friends and relatives. And second, they galvanized and filled in for the combat units assigned to the defense of Kigali. The RPF's firm opposition to all negotiation and foreign intervention—which none of the large embassies in Kigali had foreseen—clearly indicated its first and ultimate objective: a total conquest of power.

From Massacres to Genocide

From this perspective, the RPF's misjudgment seems to reflect its inadequate grasp of the political context; but equally worth mentioning is its over-confidence in its military capabilities, rooted in part in its lack of familiarity with the popular mood and the unforgiving terrain on the hillsides. Since the end of 1993, a gradual strengthening of the pro-Hutu block took hold that went far beyond the contours of the mouvance présidentielle at the inception of multipartyism. For example, Agathe Uwilingiyimana herself had to concede that even with the support she garnered personally in Butare as MDR president at the prefectural level, her political program was misunderstood and questioned by most party members, and it was Jean Kambanda who benefited from the unqualified support of the party. Even so, support for the mouvance présidentielle among designated candidates for the future Transitional National Assembly cannot be explained away as the maneuvers of party politics or narrow self-interest. Politically and ideologically, the activist bases of the opposition parties and, more than likely, the majority of urban and rural dwellers had had enough of war, which they blamed on the RPF. More importantly, the various forces that Habyarimana tried to bring together were sufficiently anchored and diversified to survive him, whatever political or military scenario would emerge. And, given the timetable for elections, anticipated with impatience by all, the MRND had no shortage of candidates eager to succeed him.

For months, almost in lockstep with the reconfigurations on the domestic political scene around the Power wings of the MDR, PL, and PSD, the various factions and parties associated with the mouvance présidentielle became more active than ever in mobilizing their political base. The near certainty of an electoral victory at the end of the transitional period gave way to highly diversified political options. Consequently, potential contenders like Ngirumpatse and Karemera could anticipate appealing to northerners and southerners alike and could foresee potential alliances with their current adversaries (Mugenzi, Karamira, Murego, etc.), who were ready to resort to personal bargains and favors and to trade upon their deep regional roots and the fealty of their constituents.

In this context, even if massacring Tutsi of the interior and making them a hostage population was explicitly presented as a defensive maneuver by Hutu extremists to fend off an RPF military takeover, none of the heads of the parties who were signatories to the Arusha Peace Accords dared imagine that this option would actually be pursued to its bitter end with passive acceptance by the international community. And it must have seemed no less improbable that the RPF would anticipate imposing its hegemony over a country with such an overwhelming majority of Hutu, who were virtually universally hostile to the RPF politically. At that time, the genocide option was mostly a warning alarm rather than a strategic plan, even among those who anticipated the reprise of the war and prepared for the inevitable by mobilizing and training militias.

The question that keeps popping up is whether the root of the RPF's strategic error was ignorance or miscalculation of the scale of the forces arrayed against it, or if, and this is the alternative formulation, it was an increasingly sharper perception of this unfavorable imbalance that led RPF leaders to question the gains it so roundly achieved in the Arusha Peace Accords.

This latter scenario would suggest that RPF leaders not only risked large-scale massacres but to some degree consciously anticipated and counted on them as elements of a political-military strategy to prolong and instrumentalize the killings and anti-Tutsi programs from 1991 to 1993 and thus justify their military offensives for an outright conquest of power. From this perspective, as soon as signs of genocide were acknowledged and the RPF could manage to have this internationally recognized, by mid-May the endgame was certain. The decision taken by the United Nations Security Council on 17 May 1994 to impose an arms embargo on the FAR gave the RPF an assurance of military victory. In so doing, the international community validated a posteriori the RPF objective of toppling power and conferred it with a legitimacy that, until then, was still lacking.

Regardless of which of the two is the most convincing scenario, there can be no question that the official narrative of Rwandan history leaves out an essential element: the rebel movement that emerged from the Tutsi diaspora neither started nor conducted a war to "save the Tutsi"; it seized power in Kigali by force of arms at the cost of the lives of its compatriots.

Whether the RPF underestimated or knowingly accepted this risk, it was still the small cluster of officers and politicians linked to the presidential clan that launched those massacres of political opponents and "enemies" of the interior. These officers and politicians were the ones who ordered, and then presided over, a wholesale extermination of civilian lives. They did not do it to "safeguard the republic" but rather to favor the most reactionary currents in that rabid competition for power unleashed by President Habyarimana's assassination and to make sure that their seizure of the state apparatus would be irreversible. Although isolated and in the minority, they succeeded in reaching their goals "by proxy," without visibly appearing in the new distribution of leadership roles, thanks to the installation, in truly exceptional circumstances, of an ad hoc government, tasked with exterminating the ethnic enemy as its central mission. This distinction is important. Although it fell to a "genocidal government," calling for national unity, to effectively mobilize the broad array of state resources (armed forces, civil service, political parties, mass media, civil society, citizenry), the genocidal project remained the province of a small faction (Bagosora-Nzirorera). Able to seize power only by shedding the blood of the country's legitimate leaders (the multiparty government of Agathe Uwilingiyimana), they curbed and harnessed the state apparatus to their aims over the course of a raging three months.

To generalize about the significance and impact of events and deeds and objectives is risky. For each political position, and depending on what would likely ensue or how it could affect the civil war, there were specific, corresponding individual and collective approaches. For pro-Hutu activists, the massacres, pillaging, and violence reflected a sort of populist jubilation after four years of mounting ethnic tensions. Approval from "state authority" unleashed the accumulated hatreds and gave free rein to killing "enemies" without distinction, not just the Tutsi. Eliminating those who opposed not just the massacres but also impunity and disorder and conflating them with the "enemy" for that very reason created a rare opportunity to transgress social hierarchies as a badge of military valor; this was a major enticement for massive recruitments of killers, who then boosted their ascendancy at an ever-mounting cost in human life.

The range of those who refrained varied, depending on the individual, the positions they held, and the place and the time. For most of the population, acquiescence or approval was a product of opportunism, wait-and-see equivocations, fear, or a sense of overwhelming powerlessness and resignation. And finally, and this particular history still remains poorly documented, various forms of resistance to the massacres materialized, with courageous individuals often relinquishing their lives in the same manner as the victims directly targeted. Openly or discreetly, gestures of solidarity cropped up, and networks emerged to save neighbors or friends and acquaintances and to weaken or oppose the genocidal momentum.

Paul Kagame, leader of the Tutsi rebellion since October 1990 who became head of state in 2000, put forward the thesis of a foundational genocidal project that would ideologically consummate the revolution of 1959.[16] It relied on long-standing, periodically revived "genocidal" practices throughout the subregion, along with the development of a genocidal ideology.[17] However, although broadly shared by the new elites in power, the thesis of an ideological predisposition traceable to the previous regimes does not suffice to explain the sociopolitical and institutional mediations that resulted in actual genocide.[18]

In fact, leaving aside partisan arguments and a posteriori evidence, it is difficult to demonstrate the existence of a genocidal "conspiracy," to delineate stages in its unfolding, and to specifically identify its participants and practical organization. And this for two reasons.

The first reason is that there was no state conspiracy: not in 1990, when thousands of political opponents, both Tutsi and Hutu, were arrested, nor between 1990 and April 1994, over the course of the civil war or even when massive hostilities definitively broke out.[19] The analysis of OAU experts on this point is very well argued:

> 7.4 . . . It cannot be demonstrated that the countless manifestations of anti-Tutsi sentiment in these years were part of a diabolical master plan. It seems to us from the evidence most probable that the idea of genocide emerged only gradually, possibly in late 1993 and accelerating in determination and urgency into 1994. . . .
>
> 7.6 The fact that the Rwandan government reacted vigorously to the invasion in itself proves nothing about genocidal intentions. What government anywhere would have done otherwise? . . .
>
> 14.3 . . . It is even arguable that a coup by the radicals against the coalition government, not genocide, was the original aim in the immediate wake of the crash.[20]

This is exactly how Gen. Roméo Dallaire explains it: "My own observance was that by the end of that day [7 April] I had concluded that what we were facing was not an ethnic killing, but it was literally a decapitation of a philosophy. That is to say, the moderate leaders, be they Tutsi or Hutu, were all being targeted, and, generally speaking, that was the picture that we presented. So it was like getting rid of all the moderate leadership in one fell swoop, and the impression was by then from the information that they had been quite successful."[21]

Before the attack against the presidential plane, the government was headed by a prime minister from the opposition and contained a good number of ministers with known democratic convictions; in the armed forces, the general staff and high command had not been won over by genocidal thinking.[22] Similarly, the territorial administration was "divided" between various political formations, especially in those prefectures and communes with relatively higher numbers of Tutsi. Finally, nowhere were the militias strong enough to topple the governing "order" and impose their own authority in areas where the targeted populations resided. This political situation was all the more remarkable in that, over the previous four years, legitimate authorities were confronted by a civil war launched from outside the country, interspersed with bombings against the civilian population and targeted political assassinations. The RPF was behind the most notorious incidents. Moreover, it was responsible for over a million internally displaced persons fleeing massacres against the Hutu population in those communes that the Tutsi rebellion had attacked and occupied.

The second reason is both simple and grotesque: mass killings were to be expected, and there was no special need for an elaborate plan, so long as the territorial administration was pruned, cranked, and readied to follow well-chosen marching orders. What the international community finally characterized as "genocide," after so many weeks of ceaseless killings, was really a question of scale.[23]

A similar analysis was quite explicitly advanced by the OAU rapporteurs:

7.12 The situation, in other words, was abundantly clear. The only thing that was not clear was exactly how far the plotters were prepared to go. Large numbers of observers had little doubt that massacres were virtually inevitable if not deterred somehow. But would the radicals take the un-thinkable quantum leap to a full-blown genocidal attack against every Tutsi in the country?

7.13 The fact is that the overwhelming majority of observers did not believe that a genocide would be launched. More precisely, they could not bring themselves to harbor such a belief.[24]

General Dallaire offered a similar reading of the circumstances:

Q. In the video you are saying that they could have been planning the elimination of the political opponent of people you referred to as moderate. But it is difficult to envisage, if I understand, or your term, a planning of all that happened.

A. No, what I said was that it was difficult to see, to foresee the scope of the killings, that the killing of 600, 800,000 people could have been planned. So, in my mind, it was going from 50,000, which we saw regularly in Burundi, 100,000, 150,000, yes, you could say that people participated, there were militia involved, and that it continued with self-defense groups who killed a good number of people. That is correct. That was plausible. That was something that could be done. But as to whether the plan that existed made provision for the killing of 1.5 million or 1 million or 800,000 or 500,000 Tutsi, as far as I'm concerned, the only aspect I saw, I couldn't conceive the existence of such a plan.

Q. If I understand well, and here comes my second question, your position has evolved between 1994 and today.

A. No, because today I still believe that this figure of 800,000, it's difficult to believe in a plan to kill 500,000 people or 800,000 people. But, as they say in the definition to describe a massacre and genocide, the difference is not only the number. But as far as I'm concerned, the fact that people were allowed during months to kill 800,000 people, I think as far as the planning and management of the whole event is concerned, I am overwhelmed.[25]

Dating as far back as the beginning of 1991 (even before the Interahamwe existed), certain clusters within the mouvance présidentielle routinely visited massacres and pogroms upon civilian Tutsi. In October 1993, after Tutsi soldiers assassinated Hutu president Melchior Ndadaye in Burundi, thousands of Tutsi casualties at the hands of an "enraged Hutu populace," followed by thousands of Hutu killed in repressive military action, gave Rwandan protagonists an idea of the scale (several tens of thousands) that such massacring could attain, whipped up over several days, when irresponsible rabble-rousers deliberately risk exacerbating deadly passions. The Burundian political leaders who called for massacres of civilian Tutsi to avenge the assassination of the first democratically elected Burundian president were a small minority. Before this pivotal event, they had no particular influence over a population that, at the end of a rather exemplary transitional process and for the first time since independence, had embraced its right to vote with serenity and conviction. If we were to survey the promoters of massacres and genocide, the situation was not remarkably different in Rwanda in April 1994; there were perhaps about thirty persons, whose names and profiles (see chapter 11) correspond somewhat to the list published by Human Rights Watch in 1999 (*see annex 94*).

But the four years of war allowed the génocidaires to develop and to gain experience. At first they realized that their intimate knowledge of the country's political landscape and the weariness and malaise of war, which is to say time, played in their favor; on the other hand, the RPF could only manifest its military superiority by direct action on the ground. Already, on three prior occasions, it only managed to circumvent political deadlocks by resorting to military offensives, which, incidentally, could have led it straight into Kigali had there been no foreign military intervention.[26] After French troops left at the very beginning of 1994, the RPF started up again with threats to get rid of the "tyrant" within "forty-eight hours," with really only UNAMIR in a position to deprive it of a victory on the ground. In addition, thinking back to the killings and pogroms from 1991 and 1992, the radical politicians and officers had already had numerous occasions to hone their "techniques of execution" with impunity, despite the outcries they provoked.

These radical politicians and officers continuously complained that the RPF did not want peace and would seek to completely usurp power at the first

From Massacres to Genocide

opportunity. Habyarimana's assassination confirmed this scenario and propelled them to the vanguard as the most committed defenders of the "achievements of the revolution of 1959." Then they fully demonstrated their determination to take power for themselves and make the RPF pay dearly for its predicted victory. No one was willing to intercede or negotiate during the course of this war, which many viewed as total and final (RPF combatants dubbed it *simusiga*, "leave nothing behind," i.e., scorched earth). The carnage endured for three months.

Orchestrating Genocide

It was only after President Habyarimana's assassination, followed by six days of vicious political maneuvering, that this extremist faction managed to impose a supposedly defensive genocidal strategy, which it later molded into official state policy around an interim government. The massacres and the genocide were thus quite clearly the work of this northern political-military faction from the president's home turf, which, starting around 7 and 8 April, with support from "co-opted" units of the army (the Presidential Guard, the military police, and the paracommando and Recce battalions) and the top leadership of the MRND, progressively took control of the levers of power to impose an "alliance" of all Hutu, from north and south. Driven by either conviction or opportunism, MRND ministers and radical elements from the party's prefectural committees, as well as all the Power leaders who defended its ideals within their own parties, rallied behind this same faction and were swept along. So we can appreciate why, as already observed, over the course of events set in motion by the death of the president, there seems to have been no central decision making or even consistency of approach among uncontested chiefs. This is also why, with genocidal forces "readied" only in the north and in the capital, the prefectures of the center and the south—where the Hutu opposition held sway—could fall into line only after the new governmental authorities reshuffled the administrative leadership at the highest levels. That explains why the organizational structure of genocide (targeted assassinations, control of the state apparatus, effective propaganda, adequate means of extermination, etc.) had to be put in place at the right moment. The organizers reinforced and propelled each other gradually within a framework of deliberate, incremental advances, combining explicit strategic decisions from 10 to 12 April with sometimes baffling improvisations. These were intended to obtain or impose solidarity from other forces for the genocidal enterprise. An analysis of the sequence of events leading to the carnage shows how specific individuals and groups of potential killers were made available to carry out assassinations and mass killings.

Coordination and support, but also divergence and clashes among these individuals and groups, melded in action; as the killings were under way, it became clear that the methods, targets, and objectives of the génocidaires were specific to each group and varied in relation to the neighborhoods, communes, prefectures, and the orders received, or simply because there was no more order, and impunity reigned.

During those first few days, before the assassinations and killings were openly endorsed, allowing authorities of dubious legitimacy to impose some institutional framework, the killings and the murderous competition among those spearheading them called for a hierarchy to mark off territory and zones of control for apportioning the booty of their exploits (pillaging, extortion, women). Competition went far beyond what conventional forces of order could control. The Presidential Guard had conferred exceptional status upon groups of Interahamwe militiamen holding sway over large swaths of Kigali (particularly those composed of ex-soldiers), but even they had difficulty asserting control in those overcrowded, poor neighborhoods where other militia groups were also strongly implanted.

Consequently, the thesis of a scrupulously planned genocide is simply not consistent with the "run for your life" reflexes and strategies of the majority of Hutu civilian and military leaders routinely denounced as its architects. All the more so if the notion of conspiracy relies on the point of departure so often offered up, explicitly or implicitly, as proof par excellence of "planning": the shooting down of the presidential plane, notoriously propagated as the trigger for genocide, by Hutu extremists that no jurisdiction, national or international, has ever prosecuted, since the culprits have never been identified.

Moreover, the consequences and implications of shooting down the plane had not even been "anticipated," judging from the difficulties encountered by potential instigators of genocide in initiating or sustaining contacts during those first crucial hours: the impromptu meeting of members of the army high command, who "arrived at headquarters when they heard the news"; the default designation of an interim army chief of staff, selected by the happenstance of seniority; the high command's disavowal of an attempted putsch by the presumed "mastermind"; the need to hurriedly organize contacts and meetings to settle the issue of succession and to locate and appoint preselected candidates; the difficulty in finding available political leaders, which explains the malaise of certain candidates who were prodded into the Interim Government, this same government whose military strategists sought to "put in the deep freeze" as soon as it was assembled, even before the oath of office was administered; and so on. A number of episodes even reveal crazed behavior or even a falling apart: for example, the shots fired randomly by Presidential Guard soldiers stationed at the presidential residence in Kanombe right after the plane crash; the nocturnal flight to the Presidential Guard camp by the government's extremist wing, followed by its abrupt transfer to more secure lodging (which happened to be the French Embassy) the following afternoon; the MRND president's refusal to take over as head of state because he too, fearing for his life, sought to renounce political responsibility; the panic that struck members of the Interim Government on the morning of 12 April, with one group being evacuated to Burundi by the French army as another group sneaked away to Gitarama under military escort; the disarray of those ministers who, left behind, searching for transportation and petrol, had to look for or catch up with the colleagues who abandoned them. A final illustration bears mention if only because it is so ludicrous. In fact, repeated calls from members of the presidential family, isolated in their Kanombe compound, requesting evacuation by the French Embassy, followed by the president's widow's furtive escape to Bangui and onward to Paris, paints a rather pathetic image of the "first lady," that awesome strategist who would have engineered her husband's demise to block implementation of the Arusha Peace Accords and take power for herself! Fate was neither kinder nor more glorious for other presumed instigators of the massacres—the brothers, half-brothers, and relatives of Agathe Kanziga— since by 11 April, when French Lt. Col. Grégoire de Saint Quentin arrived in Kanombe to evacuate them, they were no longer there, having already reached Gisenyi by their own means out of concerns for security.

If all this planning, as seemingly elaborate as it would have to be, still left some things to chance, then improvisation would have attained truly alarming results.

In fact, in order for the genocidal project to take form, launch itself, and morph into some organized political form(s), its promoters would have had to reach a reasonably coherent consensus among participating groups of génocidaires: among soldiers, between civilians and soldiers, between northerners and southerners, among the prefectures, and between the parties vying with each other.[27] From this perspective, we would have to posit that shooting down the presidential plane made genocide possible because a series of elements were thrust into motion as if by chemical combustion. As if Hutu extremists needed a full week to concretize the genocidal project and to fashion and adopt the structures necessary to sustain it over the course of three months. The debate about the plane's explosion turns on a tendentious question: knowing who was behind it would lead to apportioning responsibility for the events that followed it. However, those who implemented the genocide did so not because the plane was shot down but to ensure their political survival, which had come under attack from all sides even though the rebalancing they were able to manage by brutal, preemptive measures risked ending in failure.

Even if in refusing a negotiated political settlement RPF leaders assumed the risk of genocide, the shooting down of the plane can in no way be deemed the cause of genocide. Given the climate brought about by the power vacuum, the genocide was the culmination of a political strategy implemented by extremist Hutu groups that felt that with the downing of the aircraft and the inevitable reprise of war, the moment had come to settle the conflict with the RPF militarily and to do away with the political forces supporting the RPF inside the country. Participating in the genocidal enterprise clearly established a line of demarcation between unforgiving enemy camps. It would meld the "majority Hutu people" around those who had made this extreme choice, from which there was no turning back. That choice would definitively lead them to defeat because it did not reflect (or no longer reflected) the cleavages and fault lines that characterized Rwandan society at the dawn of the 1990s.

In all that transpired from the evening of 6 April onward, we can parse and observe a criminal strategy taking form, with decisions and events (and especially the assassinations of political figures) compounding with each passing day, culminating in the most radical maneuvers sought by the most extremist elements as "final war" took hold.

On this basis, a clear distinction can be drawn between the assassinations and the genocidal killings that began the night of 6 April and those committed after the Interim Government effectively took over, after 9 April. During those first few days, individual and collective acts of violence in Kigali and in many prefectures were imbued with vengeance for sacrificial victims, with war crimes and crimes against humanity shepherding the extremists' strategies for recomposing the political landscape, where the latter seized upon the vacuum in power to impose themselves as they prepared for the inevitable showdown with the RPF.

This characterization of the targeted assassinations and the generalized killings of political opponents and Tutsi from the early morning hours of 7 April is clearly borne out in accounts from the two most senior officials attached to the UN's peacekeeping mission in Rwanda, Gen. Roméo Dallaire, the force commander, and Jacques-Roger Booh-Booh, the secretary-general's special representative. As we observe in Dallaire's sworn trial testimony:

> Q. General, you said you had information concerning the fact that Presidential Guard members apparently visited neighborhoods with lists. . . . Does it match the killings of dignitaries, or these were other people?

A. Our analysis at that time already was that they were people of authority who seemed to belong, as far as we know, to the opposition or who belonged to the moderate camp.

Q. Would you agree with me that these were not widespread massacres; rather, they were targeted killings? This is what you are saying?

A. Yes, the report indicated that those were targeted killings. Moreover, in my report, I describe the fact that although there were roadblocks and there were people who were killed at those roadblocks, at that time what we could see was literally a decapitation of the leadership of people with moderate leanings, be they Hutu or Tutsi, from both ethnic groups.

Q. So these were not massacres at roadblocks, which we will look at later, based on ethnicity?

A. No, the ethnic term, as used by my headquarters, came some days later.[28]

And from Booh-Booh's witness statement:

Despite assurances from the Military Crisis Committee of endorsing the peace agreement and the restraint of their forces, the FAR, gendarmerie, and Presidential Guard have not returned to their barracks. If not actually conducting the terror campaign, they are they are [*sic*] at a minimum assisting, observing, and not taking any action to maintain law and order. Interahamwe and other mobs are continuing their campaign of ethnic and general violence. . . . Despite assurances to restrain their forces, the Military Crisis Committee either cannot control large portions of their forces or are implicated in the terror campaign.[29]

After three days of political wavering and following the Interim Government's transfer to Gitarama under the supervision of party leaders, its members then explicitly embraced, organized, and accelerated the spread of large-scale massacres, later legally characterized as acts of genocide.

Indeed, earlier assessments were cruelly inadequate to describe the nature of the crimes; it was no longer a question of violence and killings spearheaded by extremist groups or self-proclaimed authorities seeking vengeance or a settling of scores in their reach for power but rather a deliberate, systematic policy in which all citizens were personally summoned to participate in exterminating an ethnic group. From 12 April through mid-July—within the framework of a "public policy" aimed at mobilizing the broad array of state resources under government supervision—each of the various players, wherever located and in whatever capacity, had to renew their commitment to state policy and whatever was required to sustain it. This allows us to better appreciate how political actors responded to the course of events.

Rising political and social tensions, hidden agendas, and the mobilizing and grooming of combatants within the confines of the military establishment made descent into war and massacres and genocide possible. But, eschewing unnecessary fatalism, it is still important to emphasize that the length, scale, and direction of the war were neither inevitable nor predetermined. Over the course of days and weeks, the logic of violent confrontation took root only because the main protagonists refused all other options and because the huge cost in human life and the material devastation were acceptable in their eyes, given the ultimate objectives, which may explain how such gross errors of judgment came about.

It is easy to acknowledge that a floundering and collapse in the international mechanisms made renewed warfare inevitable. That political disengagement or implicit approval from some of the more influential foreign actors may have facilitated massacres and genocide is a convincing argument, but the intensity of the conflict and the will to push the confrontation to its ultimate end reveal a multitude of decisions taken piecemeal, day after day, by those who, in both camps, were responsible for conducting the war.[30] It is only by careful examination of their initiatives over months and weeks that we can take the measure of their responsibilities, and not by second-guessing after the fact.

For these reasons, it is simply incorrect to take what was at root a criminal undertaking, hatched by a handful of plotters, and brush off responsibility across a broad range of institutions, parties, organizations, and groups, all too easily characterized as "genocidal structures" or "criminal organizations." Beyond a limited number of institutional actors advocating a strategy of harsh ethnic exclusivity and those individuals who, in one way or another, waged this "war within a war," it is imperative to reconstruct the individual paths and collective processes that prodded institutions and those responsible for them toward ruin, in thrall to the politics of extermination and recourse to violence.

11

 The Interim Government
at the Center of Power

Paradoxically, once transferred to Murambi, the Interim Government's period of apprenticeship came to an end. From that point on, it was called upon to take charge of the "final war." Reassured by all the party chiefs, who had also arrived in Murambi, the ministers quickly regained their composure. With guidance from the more experienced politicians, the first cabinet meeting of the Interim Government was held on 12 April, shortly after its arrival at the government training center, where the ministers would also be lodged. Quite revealingly, that first meeting was referred to as a "working session" or "cabinet meeting of ministers and political parties."

The first line from the handwritten notes taken down by Minister Pauline Nyiramasuhuko consists of a trail of slogans: "intambara, ubutwari, ubushake, ubushobozi, ubwitonzi" (war, courage, willpower, competence, wisdom).[1]

The tone was set. A good distance from the battlefront, fear dissipated, and the moment for steely resolve had arrived. The themes permeating the minutes from the string of Interim Government cabinet meetings all the way through the final debacle were fairly predictable: the conduct and the financing of the war, the diplomatic action, and the mobilization against the internal enemy. Also, there was the long series of trips abroad to purchase weapons.[2] This first meeting of the government and political parties is emblematic because it showcased the way the government operated over the next three months. The Interim Government operated in symbiosis with "the parties" under the yoke of the MRND and the triumvirate directing it. This scenario is perfectly illustrated by an ironic (or cruel) saying that emerged in Kinyarwanda: "Bakora kigare" or "Bakorera kigorofani," which translates as "They work like a bike" or "They work like a wheelbarrow." It targets those who are guided by others without themselves knowing where they are headed.

The "Real Mandate" of the Interim Government, Fully Embraced

If we can rely on his own words, the prime minister, Jean Kambanda, fully embraced his official mandate. The government was in charge of organizing the massacres, and the Interahamwe militiamen were its armed wing. The monitoring of its policies and follow-up activities was left to the tight core of senior military officers and MRND leaders who had been piloting events since President Habyarimana's demise. These were the same men who provided strong moral support for restarting the massacres on 12 April. Minister of Defense Augustin Bizimana, along with many other influential politicians, relied on radio messages calling for the unity of the Hutu. According to them, partisan interests had to be pushed aside to focus on the struggle against their common enemy: the Tutsi. Nzirorera, the national secretary of the MRND, relied on "direct action," whereas the MRND president, Ngirumpatse, sought the same ends "by omission." Between Nzirorera and the MRND vice president, Karemera, who did their part of the work methodically and with conviction, apparently undistracted by second guessing, and Ngirumpatse, who at times seemed indecisive, solidarity reigned supreme and was clearly focused on strategy, with slight variations only where personal ambitions and political calculations were concerned.

Installing the Interim Government at Murambi, just outside Gitarama town in the center of the country, was not the least bit fortuitous. It could even come across as provocation on the part of the radical core group behind the new authorities and clearly reveals the challenges and risks they were confronting. Massacres had not started in the southern prefectures, and the prefect of Gitarama had not hesitated in opposing them the day before, when he was called before the cabinet. After all, this was a prefecture where the MRND had been de facto banished since 1993, when MDR candidates were elected in virtually every commune, and not a single MRND figure would even dare venture to cross by road if traveling to Kibuye. Finally, the MDR youth wing had no intention of abandoning leadership to the Interahamwe za MRND. Prodding Gitarama into the war was the very first task that fell to Jean Kambanda, the MDR-Power prime minister. If he could not manage the triumph of "Hutu unity" in the prefecture that gave birth to the MDR, where the "social revolution" of 1959 got its start, it would be a fortiori impossible to even think of facing up to Butare, his home prefecture. There are a number of reasons for this: MDR was in the minority and held little sway in the more rural communes; Agathe Uwilingiyimana's killing profoundly shocked the local population, and the prefect, a Tutsi member of the Parti liberal, had deliberately refused to attend the meeting with the Interim Government the day before, telling the prime minister that he did not recognize his authority or the authority of the government he was heading.

The stakes were quite high, since, for the Abatabazi, the ultimate fate of the war would be played out not in Kigali but in the interior of the country, among the "majority people." Establishing legitimacy for the recomposed state meant reanimating its popular base along the lines of the old party-state. That would entail a return to habits and routines that only the MRND, in tandem with the territorial administration, had truly mastered, from the very apex of the state down to the level of the cell, across the country.

This objective was clearly apparent when MRND ministers immediately demanded reinstatement of payments and bonuses that, prior to the reforms of multipartyism, were routinely made to *responsables* (administrative heads of the cells, the smallest administrative unit in the pyramidal structure of the territorial administration) in cells throughout the country (*see annex 96*). Squarely addressed during the second government cabinet meeting of 10 April, the matter, so decisive in reviving the fighting spirit of those political apparatchiks closest to the population, was again at the heart of discussions in the cabinet on 14 April in Gitarama.

Pacification:
—*first* sensitize the cellules to ensure *civil defense* . . .
Decision
—All the parties to pacify bring the people to resistance kurwanya umwanzi [struggle against the enemy]
—Message to the members of the cells
Kuko badufasha kurwana intambara,
ko government yemera ko ali umwenda [because they can help us to fight the war; the government should acknowledge that the unpaid bonuses are a debt].[3]

Despite the absence of the minister of the interior, who, though fortuitously left behind, never returned from his trip to Dar es Salaam with President Habyarimana, regaining control of the territorial administration was well under way, and that was the key means of rallying the masses.

After coming together, having noted the challenges ahead, and realizing there was no other way out, the members of the Interim Government were, oddly enough, among the first to line up for battle duty. Operating under the yoke of the heads of the political parties and virtually outpacing the soldiers, who were still divided, the ministers pushed the matter of the "Rusatira-Gatsinzi initiative and their supposedly 'moderate' associates."[4] The mandate to be given to the FAR to negotiate with the RPF was put at the top of the agenda during the ministers' first cabinet meeting in Gitarama (*see annex 97* [12 April]).

A Remarkable Voluntarism

Before probing any deeper into the Interim Government's performance, a few words about its modus operandi may be useful. The Interim Government worked at a fast pace, convening at least 37 cabinet meetings over the course of the 101 days of its existence (see table 1), an average of one meeting every three days, without counting those discussions and deliberations that continued informally. The consensus among the parties required for government action could never have materialized otherwise.

The periods of greatest activity were concentrated in two specific phases. The first, when the government was first installed and war broke out again, called for daily meetings. The second, just before the final defeat and the flight and retreat to Zaire, involved weekly meetings, first on Thursdays, then on Fridays, and a few additional sessions, as well as what appears to be a three-day marathon toward the end of April.

Discussion here is limited to those dates where meetings are specifically identified, which is to say, anytime the notation "cabinet meeting" or "meeting of the government" appears in the notes and agendas of the various ministers. These diaries were our principal source of information about the functioning of the Interim Government (*see annex 97*). Also included in the survey are references to "expanded meetings" (with prefects, party leaders, deputies, and military authorities in attendance) and "restricted sessions."

Restricted sessions were held in tandem with cabinet meetings and were intended to clarify or resolve particularly sensitive pending matters. They often addressed personal problems linked to individual members of government or concerned a particularly significant individual or perhaps financial issues, and in most instances they addressed urgent military affairs. But, here again, even when restricted sessions were noted in the agendas and diaries, there were still numerous "interministerial" meetings immediately before or after the government cabinet meetings, depending on the matters to be

Table 1. Government cabinet meetings held by the Interim Government over the course of its existence

1994	Monday	Tuesday	Wednesday	Thursday	Friday	Saturday	Sunday	Total Meetings	Days
April			6	7	8	**9**	10		
	11	**12**	**13**	**14**	**15**	**16**	**17**		
	18	19	20	**21**	22	23	24		
	25	26	**27**	**28**	29	30		15	22
May							1		
	2	3	4	**5**	6	7	8		
	9	**10**	11	**12**	13	14	15		
	16	**17**	18	19	**20**	21	22		
	23	24	**25**	26	**27**	28	29		
	30	**31**						8	31
June			1	2	3	4	5		
	6	7	8	9	**10**	11	12		
	13	14	15	16	**17**	18	19		
	20	21	22	23	**24**	25	26		
	27	28	29	30				6	30
July					1	2	3		
	4	**5**	**6**	**7**	**8**	**9**	**10**		
	11	**12**	13	14	15	16	17		
	18							10	18
Total								**39**	**101**

Note: Indicated in gray is the period from the swearing-in of members of the Interim Government in Kigali through the flight to Bukavu of the president, the prime minister, and the last few ministers who had taken shelter within the Turquoise zone in Cyangugu. Indicated in bold are the dates of the cabinet meetings

Table 2. Government cabinet meetings held by the Interim Government in Bukavu and in Goma before setting up the government in exile

1994	Monday	Tuesday	Wednesday	Thursday	Friday	Saturday	Sunday	Total Meetings	Days
July		19	20	21	22	**23**	24		
	25	26	**27**	28	**29**	30		4	13
August	1	2	3	4	5	6	7		
	8	9	10	11	12	**13**	14		
	15	16	17	18	19	20	21		
	22	23	24	25	26	27	**28**		
	29	30	31					2	31
September				1	2	3	4		
	5	6	7	8	9	10	11		
	12	13	14	15	16	**17**	18		
	19	20	21	22	23	**24**	25		
	26	27	28	29	30			14	30
October						1	2		
	3	4	5	**6**	7	8	9		
	10	11	12	13	14	15	16		
	17	18	19	20	21	22	23		
	24	25	26	27	28	29	30		
	31							8	31
November		1							
Total								**28**	**105**

Note: Dates shown are between 19 July 1994, when the Interim Government ministers first reassembled in Zaire, and 1 November 1994, when the government in exile was installed. Indicated in gray are the daily working sessions on the reshuffling of ministerial departments and the setting up of the government in exile, presided over by the president of the republic and the prime minister, with ministers, party representatives, and officers who were present in Bukavu participating (see annex 98). Indicated in bold are the dates of the cabinet meetings.

addressed or resolved, when visitors arrived in Murambi, and especially during periods of intense government activity, when the cabinet met virtually non-stop in day-long sessions. In practice, only the most personally committed, or those directly implicated in matters under consideration, kept up that rhythm; sometimes the plenary sessions did not include more than a handful of persons, to which might be added occasional visitors who simply popped in to gather information without staying through to the end. These points will be addressed farther on in our discussion of the modalities of power in wartime.

Whether any particular minister was present for the entirety or for any portion of a cabinet meeting is hard to tell. In any case, given the requirement of "consensus among the parties," most of the important cabinet meetings were held after preliminary consultations of the various political parties (to work through their individual positions), or they were followed by meetings to ratify the decisions that were taken. Since consensual agreement was required between the Interim Government and the parties on all sensitive or important matters, the formal designation of "minister" was not mandatory for the functioning of the government. Furthermore, decisions running counter to the wishes of figures of considerable weight who kept to the sidelines—such as Matthieu Ngirumpatse, Joseph Nzirorera, Donat Murego, Froduald Karamira, and Stanislas Mbonampeka—would languish without being implemented. No wonder both the president of the republic and the prime minister actively sought their counsel before and after cabinet meetings without necessarily reducing the cabinet to a mere echo chamber, as the vibrancy of the debates there clearly suggests.

Additionally, since these ministries were actually controlled by political parties, which, in turn, "consigned" them to appointee ministers, the handling of internal issues could vary, depending on the personal style of each minister and his standing in his party. Their approach could be quite rigid or more informal, uniform or ad hoc.[5] Thus, although technically subject to the MDR prime minister's authority, in the absence of the incumbent minister—who was simply reappointed, pending his expected return—the Ministry of the Interior carried on, business as usual, under the stewardship of the MRND party hierarchy, or, more precisely, its national secretary and first vice president, who fully embraced the task. At first the chief of staff, Callixte Kalimanzira, handled the day-to-day affairs, so there was never any faltering in operations or void in leadership, and he was already used to taking orders from the Akazu, even when he served under Minister Faustin Munyazesa. Afterward with Édouard Karemera's arrival at the head of the ministry on 25 May, there was a marked strategic shift toward supporting the war effort: it was necessary to mobilize popular support to make up for the reversals and divisions in the military. Also, in the event of military defeat, the means to rally reliable political support had to be in place to revitalize institutions and prepare for future struggles. Even so, ministers perceived to be weak or who were imposed at the insistence of the parties were openly supervised by more dependable figures from their own parties or assisted by others designated ad hoc.

This was the approach in two crucial domains: in foreign affairs and in regard to the military. In both cases, parallel power networks could, depending on the stakes and the matters concerned, short-circuit the ministers and/or their cabinet. Also, the presidency or the prime minister could authorize specially appointed delegations to represent or to negotiate in the place of the titular officeholder. The ruse became extremely delicate when clarifications of sensitive points abroad had to rely on a diverse array of messengers, or when those in charge of cranking up and oiling the genocidal machine dispatched officials abroad on missions simply to neutralize them. Apparently some ministers actually welcomed these foreign junkets, as they never fully embraced the Interim Government's policy, or certain aspects of it, and especially since the potential "alibi" provided by these trips abroad might insulate them politically if ever a day of reckoning required explanations for all the massacres that were ordered.

Generally speaking, absenteeism rapidly became a major distraction for ministers with little reason to expect political rewards or mobility from their duties, or for ministers with more technical profiles for whom the wartime atmosphere at Murambi and then in Muramba (in Gisenyi prefecture) provided little scope or motivation. Schooled in discretion, and without necessarily disavowing the government policy, certain ministers no longer wished to flaunt their presence at large public gatherings, or make public appeals on the radio, or chime in with the calls to action at prefectural or local assemblies. Absenteeism was also a way to avoid being seen in Kigali or on the "pacification tours," with the attendant obligation to openly embrace the policy of massacres. Some of the more experienced ministers, those with no illusions about the ultimate fate awaiting this Interim Government, refrained from the thousand and one maneuvers or plots that the residents of Murambi seemed to favor and instead buried themselves in dry, routine, bureaucratic activities.

Promoting Cohesion among the New Interim Authorities

In the beginning, neophyte ministers had to find their footing and adapt to the technical demands of their duties, and this, coupled with the sense of urgency generated by renewed warfare, justified the long daily cabinet meetings. Apparently, they essentially served as a forum for a mutual exchange of information among members, who, blessed with military escorts, were among the privileged few who could circulate, telephone, and maintain contacts with those "in the know." However, the Interim Government's grip on events remained weak; most decisions were taken elsewhere: by the army high command or a parallel line of authority linked to Bagosora; by top MRND party leaders and the militias; or even by foreign meddlers. Members of the Interim Government proceeded by trial and error: they had to find out what the real decision makers expected of them and how to carve out their own spheres of influence; and through it all they could expect little more than lukewarm respect in diplomatic circles and from UNAMIR and outright rejection by the RPF.

The first nine cabinet meetings held between 9 and 17 April thus suggest a cautious, "on-the-job training" for the group, whereas the block of MRND ministers and their political bosses were immediately effective in their efforts to take control of the centers of power that emerged within the first few hours of the disappearance of the head of state and the army chief of staff. It was not until 11 April that a somewhat structured working agenda emerged, which took form once the Interim Government took up headquarters in Murambi. The government started to impose its authority on the territorial administration by convening the prefects on 11 April, then met with the burgomasters. Matters of security took absolute priority: struggling against RPF infiltrations; ensuring the security of the population; and especially receiving reports and updates from the prefects concerning the massacres (*see annex 97* [11 April]). The government's hold on the levers of power was strengthened on 12 April during a joint meeting with the heads of the political parties. The focus of the discussions was on internal and external mobilization, covering such issues as propaganda and diplomacy, including relations with the UN, OAU, Belgium, and UNAMIR; logistics and financing for the war (i.e., organizing missions abroad to buy weapons); and "managing the war and the resistance," detecting infiltrators, traitors, and Ibyitso, the name given to alleged accomplices of the RPF (*see annex 97* [12 April]). It was really a matter of divvying up the tasks between members and nonmembers of the government.

The government cabinet meeting of 13 April inaugurated a third phase, clearly the most important, since the objective was to install an army high command that would support the new political dispensation and give a hand to the MRND minister of defense, Augustin Bizimana, recently returned from a mission abroad. He and the party heads were anxious to clarify the attributions of Bagosora, who, although knocked out of the running for the presidency, had set about rebooting his networks with demands to recall a number of retired OTP officers into active service (himself most of all) and by organizing the civil defense. Bizimana and Bagosora saw eye to eye on one point at least: the necessity of neutralizing the army high command and general staff, as configured by the Military Crisis Committee on 7 April. On the agenda for the cabinet meeting was replacing Col. Marcel Gatsinzi, the acting army chief of staff, and reaffirming the Interim Government's authority over the high command, which, just the evening before, had again sought to negotiate directly with the RPF; coordinating activities between the Interim Government and military authorities; starting a voluntary fund for the army; and creating a crisis general staff composed of soldiers and government officials in order to bolster their resolve and their links with the population (*see annex 97* [13 April]). This was followed by two cabinet meetings, on 14 and 15 April, devoted to questions of logistics and operations (provisions, finances, etc.), in turn paving the way for numerous parallel meetings concerning shake-ups and transfers in the territorial administration and the army general staff, all of which was debated over the course of the cabinet meeting of 16 April. The discussions continued until the next day. The Interim Government had thus clearly outlined what its policy would be over its three months of existence and set out a program for the implementation of decisions.

The most noteworthy of these decisions concerned the nomination of prefects. It was the subject of a communiqué read over Radio Rwanda by Éliezer Niyitegeka, minister of information and spokesperson for the government. He congratulated the prefects who fulfilled their "duties" zealously and announced the removal of two prefects of the "opposition" (Butare and Kibungo) (*see annex 100*). It had become necessary to assert the Interim Government's authority in those areas where its "messages" were not getting through or were getting through only poorly. Then a three-day round of tours throughout the country was carefully orchestrated for most of the Interim Government ministers and party leaders so that they could impart the new agenda to the territorial administration in Gitarama and Gikongoro (on the morning and afternoon of 18 April) and then in Butare (on 19 and 20 April). The objective was to ensure that these dormant prefectures would finally heed the wake-up call. In Butare prefecture, the government ministers categorically dismissed those who opposed the genocide and intimidated state employees (soldiers and civilians alike) who dared resist them.

This government imperative—establishing networks to back it up throughout the country—was accomplished by dispatching ministers to monitor "pacification" in their home prefectures.[6] It was supervised by the prime minister himself, who followed up with regular trips throughout the country. To strengthen the government's central authority over a decentralized administration, territorial administrators and executive civil servants were constantly rotated and shifted about as the war progressed, and decision making in this regard figured routinely as an agenda item in cabinet (*see annex 97* [10 June]).

But, as clearly seen in decisions taken by the cabinet on 16 and 17 April, the government's increasing control over the state was not limited to the territorial administration. By reserving a place within its structure and in various ad hoc committees for party leaders—who also doubled as leaders of the youth militia—and for the officers in charge of the war, the Interim Government did not dominate all decision making but still placed itself at the heart of the structure of power. In this regard, the meeting of 16 April signaled a major evolution in the relationship between the Interim Government and the military establishment.

The Military under Civilian Control?

Despite the initial difficulties, the division of labor proposed by Col. Léonard Nkundiye on the morning of 7 April to "push the civilians out in front" while leaving it to the soldiers to manage the war finally took root with no major shocks.

Through the installation of an Interim Government, its military and civilian godfathers reconstituted the model of the MRND party-state. And given the context of wartime, necessarily, the army was accorded overwhelming preeminence. The fusion was plain to see: by 9 April, Gen. Augustin Ndindiliyimana was seated in the cabinet and, in the absence of the minister of defense, organized meetings for the prime minister and the heads of different units within the army to try to halt the looting and killing. With his military colleagues, without the least consultation, on 12 April he also ordered the transfer of the Interim Government to Murambi. Then on 13 April, after the meeting with the political parties, it fell to those officers who had contributed to installing the Interim Government to work with him in putting together a "crisis general staff composed of soldiers and government officials" to "strengthen their determination and their links with the population," since "[undisciplined soldiers] were just hanging around the roadblocks to hitch rides."[7]

Upon his return from a mission on 10 April, the MRND minister of defense, Augustin Bizimana, thus encountered a reconfigured high command, now deeply splintered. Rivalry within the high command and the wobbling at its highest levels were on open display. On the battlefield, to the north and the east of the country, the situation got worse each day.

Bizimana's first decisions were consistent with the joint strategy initiated by Bagosora and the MRND party chiefs: he had the army chief of staff sign off on reinstating officers previously forced into retirement by his predecessor and expedited promotions for several key northern officers such as Léonard Nkundiye (*see annex 101*). Coming from someone dubbed the "yes man" of the extremist officers, these measures immediately provoked a climate of bitter animosity among many senior officers. Faced with this deteriorating situation, the government backed down, fearful that a significant number of units and soldiers, especially those from the south, might break ranks or worse.

Even if the prime minister agreed with Bizimana on a replacement for the acting army chief of staff, it could not have escaped him that, regardless of the candidate ultimately selected by the cabinet, the new chief of staff would never emerge by unanimous acclaim, and those who lost out in the competition would retain considerable clout. In addition, surprisingly, Bizimana's personal preferences held little sway with the military establishment. In the context brought on by the disappearance of the head of state and the army chief of staff and the reprise of the war, a civilian minister whose standing did not even rise to his predecessor's—James Gasana—did not have enough legitimacy to impose a chief of staff of his own choosing.

In anticipation of the removal and replacement of Marcel Gatsinzi as chief of staff, at least two candidates had to be considered. Bizimana chose to propose two of his close associates, even though he clearly had a favorite. He proposed Gratien Kabiligi (Cyangugu) and Augustin Bizimungu (Byumba). Kabiligi was commander of the operational sector in Byumba when Bizimana was prefect (July 1992–July 1993) and had just been named staff officer for operations (G3) in the general staff, but he had a reputation as more of a unit commander than a potential chief of staff. Bizimungu was a good soldier and was very popular. He did not know the intricacies of the general staff any better than Kabiligi, but he bore no blemishes in regard to human rights, whereas Kabiligi was openly viewed as heading up military training for the Interahamwe. In addition, and this aside is purely anecdotal, a native of Byumba like Bizimana would satisfy the criteria of the soothsayer who had predicted that a "man from Byumba" would ultimately succeed Juvénal Habyarimana.

The cabinet weighed in in favor of the minister's choice and promoted Bizimungu to major general by decree of 18 April, following his appointment as chief of staff. At the same time, Kabiligi was named brigadier general. Additionally, with a single stroke, Colonels Marcel Gatsinzi and Léonidas Rusatira were also promoted to general, apparently to assuage the implicit demotion for the former and to compensate the latter for the shocking and generous promotions that were its corollary. Reflecting on these nominations, Minister Éliezer Niyitegeka commented: "We, 'the government,' managed to snatch Bizimungu from the midst of all these other colonels; now he had to work for us. . . . Minister Bizimana and the other MRND ministers pushed to advance Augustin Bizimungu's candidacy; Gatsinzi's and Rusatira's were supported by ministers from the other parties."[8]

One glaring omission in the list of those promoted: Théoneste Bagosora, who had been campaigning for promotion to general for quite some time. The government felt that after his failure of 7 April, a promotion would only have further inflamed divisions within the high command. He did not even garner support from the "family." Augustin Ngirabatware, linked by marriage to Félicien Kabuga, one of the most eminent businessmen tied to the Habyarimana regime, solidly backed Bizimungu. He was practically viewed as a "son" of Kabuga, who had arranged for him to be sent to the Officers Training School in Brussels. The support from Byumba (Kabuga and Bizimana) was amplified by sponsorship from Gisenyi (Augustin Ngirabatware and Protais Zigiranyirazo), and the new army chief of staff basked in the congratulatory embrace of senior officers from the president's home turf.

These promotions and the lobbying and bartering that went along with them failed to settle any of the former rivalries; indeed, just the opposite. In fact, when Augustin Ndindiliyimana and Déogratias Nsabimana were promoted to major general in December 1993—aside from the requirement that one officer come from the gendarmerie and the other from the army—a balance was achieved by taking one candidate from the north and another from the south. These factors outweighed the criterion of length of service at the highest grade. Although he was the more senior officer, Léonidas Rusatira never obtained backing from the presidency, which already had its northern candidate in the person of Nsabimana, and also lost out with the southern opposition, which was inevitably drawn to Ndindiliyimana. Nominations for the rank of brigadier general for Colonels Gatsinzi and Rusatira were proposed in cabinet in Murambi by those who, albeit timidly, still favored moderation. They had no support from Minister of Defense Bizimana, who had little regard for the 12 April communiqué of the FAR command, largely piloted by Gatsinzi and Rusatira. Various sources indicate that Bagosora bitterly opposed these two promotions. Paradoxically, however, it would appear that these nominations for Gatsinzi and Rusatira flowed directly from their roles in publishing that very same communiqué of 12 April. No doubt, the intention of the government was to bring them back within the fold, without, however, placing them in strategic positions. The new power brokers had to maintain appearances of cohesion among the most long-standing senior officers, several of whom scorned the authority of the new major general with demands to rectify the "scandalous promotions." Colonel Rusatira had been repeatedly overlooked in the past and in April 1994 had already served eight years as colonel; in this regard, he had far surpassed the four-year requirement to move up to the rank of brigadier general. Two other arguments weighed in favor of Rusatira. First, since he was viewed as an MDR party sympathizer, it was fitting to cater to the newly installed MDR-affiliated ministers in the Interim Government. In addition, there was some incentive to balance the promotion of a northerner from Byumba (Bizimungu) with a northerner from Ruhengeri. As for Gatsinzi, who was a few months short of the required seniority to apply for promotion, it was appropriate to soften the blow of his rapid and abrupt removal from the general staff. In any case, both newly promoted generals only benefited from the administrative perks of higher rank without any real expansion of authority.

As for the other two young colonels who were promoted together in December 1993, Bizimungu and Kabiligi, they were, respectively, products of the thirteenth and twelfth graduating classes of the École supérieure militaire, far behind the two former colonels (Rusatira, who graduated with the sixth class, and Gatsinzi, with the ninth). Neither of the two appeared on the list of officers who were next in line. Kabiligi had risen to the rank of colonel in 1993, at which point he was only in twelfth place on the list of lieutenant colonels eligible for promotion. Both had already been conferred with significant responsibilities. Bizimungu had just been pegged to be commander of one of the four brigades maintained by the Arusha Peace Accords, and Kabiligi was commander of operations in the general staff. In their case, the promotions were coupled with prestigious assignments in the general staff of the gendarmerie for the former and commander in the operational sector for Ruhengeri for the latter, replacing Bizimungu.

For the two "senior" colonels promoted brigadier generals, Gatsinzi and Rusatira, the imposition of a candidate not even listed by promotions commission at the higher rank of major general was indeed a slap in the face. The affront stung all the more because Rusatira was first in his class and presumably at the top of the list (as the most prized graduate in his class), whereas Bizimungu was at the bottom of his class. Aside from which, the nomination of an underrated lieutenant colonel to brigadier general scandalized the other colonels.

Even if the superior officers were familiar with the distinctions between administrative rank and substantive attribution—distortions linked to complex variables of politics and merit—tricky manipulations of this nature degraded personal relationships of mutual respect among colleagues. Thus, it is no exaggeration to suggest that arbitrary decisions taken by civilians (Minister Bizimana and the other MRND ministers) somewhat at odds with the military mindset could explain, at least to some extent, the FAR command's dispirited military performance during the war.

With the culmination of the restructuring in the military high command, the relationship between civilians and military men had significantly evolved over the course of a fortnight. The division of labor changed fundamentally: it fell to the "civilians" to resolve matters for a military institution that was internally divided and seriously challenged at the battlefront.

Judging by appearances, by mid-April a government of political parties reshuffled by the military, one that Bagosora confidently called "his government," represented, domestically and abroad, the very embodiment of "power." Even if he was not the exclusive incarnation, he was certainly at the new government's heart: Murambi was indeed the locus of major decision making. Other sites may have had wide margins of maneuver, but they never truly rivaled Bagosora's government: the new FAR general staff and the Kigali-ville prefecture office, where defense and the massacres were concerned; Gisenyi, with the close circle around the presidential family, who maintained strong powers of persuasion and diplomatic prerogatives through links to the exiled widow of the slain president; the local party machines, dominated by patrons, or financiers, with various interests; and finally, the militias, justifying their criminal exploits as a heroic defense of the nation.[9]

The Interim Government was well aware of the relative autonomy retained by the various entities mandated to implement its program. The new positioning of Bagosora illustrates perfectly the precarious reciprocity those relationships entailed.

The Privileged Autonomy of Théoneste Bagosora

Already in retirement, administratively speaking, but retained as chief of staff in the Ministry of Defense without formal reappointment, rebuffed in his efforts to continue in active military service (and thus denied promotion), and frequently undercut by his own minister of defense, the putschist rejected by the majority of his peers could no longer claim to hold center stage. Nevertheless, he still had not lost his influence among large sectors of the army. For several months now, extremist officers from the north, holding command posts, had maintained privileged relationships with Tharcisse Renzaho, who controlled the capital.[10] In addition, the reach and impact of orders issuing from the government in Murambi to the army headquarters in Kigali could be limited or eclipsed simply by virtue of the daunting logistical constraints routinely confronted by the general staff in its conduct of the war.

Judging by numerous accounts from soldiers and officers, from 7 April onward meetings were regularly held at the Kigali prefecture office, the Hôtel des Diplomates, the Ministry of Defense, the FAR headquarters, the homes of certain key political figures or members of the army (like the militia leader Claver Kamana), or, better yet, the "headquarters" of Angeline Mukandutiye, a member of the MRND prefectural committee and Interahamwe president in Rugenge sector. These meetings demonstrate the existence of a "natural" framework for collaboration among important decision makers, all familiar with each other, and all hell-bent on uncompromising, strident opposition to the RPF and implementation of the Arusha Peace Accords.

Depending on the location and the day, among the various participants could be found Colonels Tharcisse Renzaho, Théoneste Bagosora, and Gratien Kabiligi; Majors Morgan Hategekimana of the Presidential Guard and Protais Bivamvagara, who headed up the civil defense; Lieutenant André Miruho from Camp Huye; François Karera; Captains Innocent Sagahutu and Pascal Simbikangwa; Minister Éliezer Niyitegeka; Stanislas Simbizi and Jean-Bosco Barayagwiza of the CDR; or members of the National Committee of the Interahamwe. Renzaho, who was both a colonel and a prefect, was to some extent the perfect amalgamation: in the context of war, he could invoke military authority in addition to his administrative prerogatives, and as a loyal MRND supporter, he had at his disposal the party's youth wing militiamen. If we add that Renzaho was both experienced and highly competent, it is easy to see how effectively the military cadres recruited for defense of the capital could be mobilized. An observer summed it up quite well: "Responsive to Théoneste Bagosora, Tharcisse Renzaho, and the extremist officers, in Kigali the prefecture office really functioned like a minigovernment headquarters. The funds at its disposal served them as a sort of 'ministry of finance,' and the availability of material and human resources, especially manpower, satisfied logistical and administrative demands."[11]

Bagosora built up a parallel command structure that was operational well before 6 April where communications were concerned and particularly effective that night, but this structure also continued to make decisions that eclipsed the general staff, unbeknownst to it. Logistics and the instruments of power were, for the most part, issued and controlled by Renzaho, who, according to the prime minister, carried on like a veritable minister of the interior who "behaved like everyone's boss":

> No one could live like that in Kigali without the consent of Renzaho, who acted as the coordinator of the Interahamwe in Kigali. He was the only political official to remain in Kigali. He was a soldier and at the same time a politician. There was no administration, no civil servants in Kigali. The war was the affair of the army; civil defense was his affair. He was therefore someone to be congratulated in our circles. He was active. He was also subtle. Renzaho behaved like everyone's boss. He was a colonel. It was not by chance that it was soldiers of his rank and age who had been chosen to be in charge of civil defense, even elsewhere. They were respectable. Having known war in the past, they were experienced and versed in war. They knew their region.[12]

At this point, we could argue that the question of the government's authority over the army need not even arise. Indeed, the policy of "Bagosora's government" was exactly what this government pursued, as set in motion by the minister of defense and his fellow ministers from the MRND and by the prime minister. None of the divergences that emerged between the army chiefs and the Interim Government leaders could stand in the way of this course of action, given the organizational or logistical mesh between the two entities. The same applies to the government's relationship with the militias, even if, unlike the army, the absence of a unified command led to distinct regional variations.

The Question of Controlling the Militias

By 7 April militiamen were relatively autonomous, and the leaders of their National Committee in Kigali were themselves wholly committed to the war effort and thus hardly inclined to oppose the excesses that went along with it—which benefited them in any case. They had no reason to curb the violence any more than the army and the gendarmerie had. All were fully engaged in the killings and never worried about sanctions. The ritual calls for a return to calm found in those initial communiqués from the armed forces and then from the Interim Government almost seemed to justify the outbursts of "populist rage" that made hostages of the Tutsi population. At least for a time, the militias occupied and defended the "homeland" from the "enemy" by striking against its presumed domestic supporters while the RPF, meanwhile, methodically deployed its ground units. The military command made a spectacular show of preaching and lauding the supposed unity of the Hutu, whereas irreversible ruptures were taking hold between northerners and southerners, between the enthusiasts of a war to the finish and those who opposed that suicidal strategy but found themselves powerless to contain the extremist factions that sabotaged any negotiated political resolution.

The presidential nucleus and its loyal devotees, extremist soldiers and MRND party leaders, ultimately managed to throw their weight behind "fighting units" of soldiers, gendarmes, and militiamen spearheading the massacres. This was the same coterie lurking behind the Military Crisis Committee, outmaneuvering it, which then went on to dominate the Interim Government and the army general staff.

Militiamen held the streets in Kigali and progressively extended their reach into the prefectures. For a number of reasons, these militias were the most dedicated forces and the ones most actively engaged in the Interim Government's central mission: massacring the Tutsi and their "accomplices." Their lack of discipline and the excesses and inevitable exactions were simply incidental costs for their services. This observation, already touched upon in chapter 6, directly contradicts the contention that the militias were a force unto themselves beyond control of all authority, civilian or military, and exclusively responsible for their depredations. This impression gained credence because the killings were committed so openly, plain for all to see, most often on public thoroughfares, with corpses piled up and lining the roadways. It was reinforced because groups of individuals or various gangs were highly visible in terms of reputation and practice, and even if there were chiefs or higher-ups ordering them about, individually they could still extort, attack, or kill whomever they pleased without appealing to any higher "authority." In the absence of any nationwide system of coordination or of monitoring and reprovisioning, this indiscipline, and the material gain that the killers could make of it, became the motor driving the momentum in the killings, guaranteeing its results and whipping up competition and mutual emulation among other groups. Nonetheless, depending on the particularities in the various prefectural contexts, it was soldiers in active service (as in Kigali), retired officers (reinstated and called back to duty to head up the civil defense), and various local sponsors (politicians, wealthy businessmen, etc.) who maintained support and covered expenses for supplies, without which the militiamen would be unable to act. And the assignment of tasks (or the order of their priority) was constantly supervised by the prefecture security committees (*conseils de sécurité préfectoraux*) or other groups acting on their behalf.

New Directions in Mobilizing for Civil Defense

By ministerial decision of 12 May, based on recommendations from the MRND minister of defense, the government specifically appointed certain officers to take charge of the civil defense. For the MRND and the northern officers, this was an opportunity to recycle previously retired officers like Maj. Aloys Simba, former "friend of 5 July 1973" and MRND parliamentarian from Gikongoro; Maj. Jean-Damascène Ukulikeyeyezu, an MRND parliamentarian who was later appointed prefect in Gitarama on 4 June 1994; and Col. Pierre-Célestin Rwagafilita, the MRND candidate to represent Kibungo in the National Transitional Assembly and former deputy chief of staff of the gendarmerie.[13] In Kigali there was Col. Athanase Gasake and in Butare Col. Alphonse Nteziryaryo, who was also director of the communal police in the Ministry of the Interior. Pauline Nyiramasuhuko would later recommend that the minister of the interior appoint Nteziryaryo prefect of Butare as the PSD candidate in order to maintain the illusion that the PSD still formally controlled the prefecture. This resulted in his nomination on 17 June 1994. Once again, genocide was indeed the business of the territorial administration, the politician-soldiers (Bagosora, Bizimana, and Rwagafilita), and, at every level, the MRND and its Interahamwe youth wing.

With the installation of the new minister of the interior, Édouard Karemera, and the dispatch of the government's directives to the prefects, policy evolved and took a markedly radical turn.

Édouard Karemera was a man of order, efficient and determined. Kigali prefecture, as described above, must have come to mind for him when it became clear that acts of pure criminality, embroiling militiamen across the length and breadth of the entire country, were becoming less and less acceptable to the Hutu population, which also began to suffer pangs of vulnerability and instability. On 25 May the prime minister and the minister of the interior officially released directives and a covering memorandum of instructions for restructuring the civil self-defense (*see annex 104*), with the apparent objective of funneling the murderous propensities of the militias and rationalizing their use. By placing responsibility for civil defense squarely upon the prefects, several of whom were soldiers, the authorities also sought to revive failing energies for its policy of massacres and to galvanize a last nationwide surge before the final military collapse. The civil self-defense was conceived to embody the alliance among the people, its self-proclaimed government, the armed forces, the parties, and the militias.

According to the directives on "self-organization of the civilian self-defense," it was incumbent upon Interahamwe youth wings in all communes and sectors to provide "resource persons to train members of the civilian self-defense core groups politically and ideologically" because they best exemplified the "objective criteria for selecting youth to be trained" and already incorporated a good number of reservists, as previously advised in the 25 May ministerial memorandum to the prefects. The objective was to place as many of these youth as possible under military supervision.

In relation to the "pacification" campaign that had been under way, the objective remained the same (the term was still a masked call to arms for the massacres), but the point now was to make better use of available resources and to accelerate elimination of "enemies" as the RPA offensive intensified in Kigali and shifted toward Gitarama and the outskirts of Butare. Here, the blank check given to the militias—by now fully anointed—had become obvious. Officers were appointed to head up civil self-defense committees in each prefecture and to organize military training and distribute weapons to militiamen. Thus, the 25 May 1994 covering memorandum from the minister of the interior titled "Implementation of the Prime Minister's Directives on the Self-Organization of the Civil Defense" de facto gave local leaders of the civil self-defense committees power of life and death over any member of the population deemed wanting or hesitant in "defense of the endangered homeland" (see annex 104). As the late historian Alison Des Forges put it well, establishing an official framework for the civil self-defense had the advantage of circumventing in one stroke the political parties, the military hierarchy, and the territorial administration in order to openly confer power and legitimacy on the militias, which is to say the most aggressive and committed foot soldiers of the massacres.[14] No higher law, no hierarchy could be invoked to contain the zeal of these recruits, prone to attack any and all who, in one way or another, sought to diminish the zeal of self-defense blowhards. One of the principal uses of these directives was to exert additional pressure on the "weary," increasing in number in the administration and especially in the army, who began to seriously question the logic of all these killings, a sentiment that would overcome many Rwandans as the Interim Government once again fled farther north.

This reinforced mobilization for civil self-defense also allowed tighter control over the militias in order to limit their predatory excesses. Renewed appeals to personnel in the Ministry of the Interior and the local administrative cadre sought to arouse the populace, whose waning participation in the patrols had virtually surrendered control of the roadblocks to militiamen and gangsters.

Putting in place civil self-defense units organized by platoon and section attracted many new recruits, especially those drawn by the prospect of acquiring firearms. Among them were citizens from every walk of life: small store owners and traders, civil servants, administrators and teachers from the universities, and so on. Beyond the duties of "pacification" that fell to members of the civil self-defense, the volunteers recognized the opportunity to see to their own security and thus better safeguard their own belongings.

The Interahamwe figured among the principal beneficiaries of weapons that were delivered to the Ministry of Defense in June, of which roughly a quarter (around 2,500) were directed to the Ministry of the Interior for use in civil defense.[15] However, those hasty recruitments by communal authorities were hardly effective when the military command turned to the militias for help in turning back the RPA advance on Gitarama during the first half of June. The government camp suffered heavy losses in the face-off that occurred in the northern communes of Butare, which clearly illustrated the weak military capacity of citizens' civil self-defense.

It was also during that last government cabinet meeting that the minister of the interior requested that each minister be "assigned" to his home prefecture to personally supervise implementation of consciousness-raising initiatives and mobilization of popular support. Even if no one dared publicly oppose his assignment, which, no doubt, the more willing members had already anticipated, several among them remained quite ambivalent. Characteristically, this peculiar task (routinely reviewed and updated in cabinet meetings) was never documented in writing in any diary or personal notes of proceedings that have since come to light.

The "Government of Genocide"

Although rather intense, the characterization "government of genocide" pegged to the Interim Government now seems quite justified. The prime minister himself acknowledged as much when, realizing that he had been "appointed to go and organize the massacres," he sought to hide himself behind the official trappings of his mission.[16] And if, as was also the case with his fellow ministers, he played no role whatsoever in assembling this Interim Government, he nonetheless embraced its "real mandate" with genuine determination once he realized the scale of the resistance it was encountering in some of the southern prefectures. Extension of the massacres fell in line with the escalation of the military conflict: going forward, the priority was to solidify the front against the RPF in the capital and to the east of the country, where it was advancing rapidly, and to boost mobilization nationwide.

Nevertheless, the phrase "government of genocide" still begs clarification.

First, it becomes clear that, contrary to the various theses that postulate a failed state after 6 April 1994 or even before then, leading to the onslaught of generalized chaos, there was never any power vacuum in Rwanda—at least, by one outrageous example, given the immediacy of the reaction from those would-be putschists during the night of 6 April. Even if competition among potential successors to the deceased president brought on a brief interlude of wavering, the major actors in the two military blocks and their corresponding civilian factions never lost control of the internal political situation. They were the ones who set the stage and spiked the momentum in military hostilities and civil war and provoked actions (demonstrations, tracts and statements, pogroms, exactions, killings, etc.) to exacerbate tensions and the forces of destabilization conducive to their global strategy for capturing or retaining power. Similarly, in the capital and in the prefectures of the interior, if the lack of resources palpably affected the central services or, even more drastically, the social services after the transfer of the government to Murambi, the administration continued to operate practically everywhere—as evidenced by the massive volume of memoranda circulating through the various echelons of the hierarchy—especially where mobilizing the population for partisan purposes was concerned.

Second, this observation is not the least bit undermined by our previous allusion to the mediocrity or inexperience of persons making up the Interim Government or the parallel systems of authority at play. Recognition of the lack of professionalism of a good number of ministers, if not outright incompetence among a select few, is incontestably apt. We could point to Kibuye prefecture, virtually unrepresented in governing circles since the founding of the republic, now oddly blessed with four of the most important ministries, and speculate that in wartime, candidates most likely to hanker for the most thankless posts are precisely those from previously neglected prefectures where ambitions had been frustrated for decades.[17] These newcomers distinguished themselves by their excessive zeal in the performance of their new duties, whereas the seasoned veterans, accustomed to power, gingerly hesitated if they joined in or simply refused.

But most ministers were hardly called upon to exercise any of the technical skills required by their respective domains of attribution (e.g., higher education, agriculture, family and women's affairs). Instead, they contributed as delegates of their parties and their prefectures of origin, and mostly in regard to the compelling matter of civil defense and pacification. Their efficacy was judged by the depth of their commitment in supporting government policy, that is, concretely, in monitoring and supervising their personnel in the war effort, especially in mobilizing their constituencies to that end. These are the matters that consumed members of the Interim Government in endless debate, going so far as to weigh the merits of dismissals and appointments even at the lowly level of sector counselors.

Even so, the argument that the Interim Government seemed to function by default because ministers engaging in its "à la carte" methods of operation were often absent (at impromptu meetings, interminable discussions, and a profusion of informal sessions) does not give due respect to how the government was galvanized or pulled along by the tight nucleus of more consistently engaged members who appropriated significant influence in their own right or on behalf of parallel lines of authority, like the president's or the prime minister's inner cabinets with their various advisors. For the most part, these misgivings concern the policy that was followed, how engaged the members were, and the government's lagging credibility abroad but do not seem to question its murderous efficiency and its doggedness, even if suicidal, in pursuing its objectives. This observation comes through quite clearly, albeit rather crudely, in statements and accounts from participants.

Discussions among government authorities and party leaders reveal an abysmal level of insensitivity, as when some of the top intellectuals of the country referred to the unfolding mass killings as if they were the engine of a second popular revolution:

> For example, I remember Mr. Donat Murego, who, though a doctor of political sciences, talked about the killings and the war "as a means of completing the 1959 revolution" and a way of preparing his party for future elections.
>
> I was deeply perturbed by the last official cabinet meeting in which I participated in Murambi (Gisenyi) [on 11 June]. . . .
>
> At the same meeting, the minister of defense, Augustin Bizimana, asked the participants whether the government should yield to the request from soldiers to eliminate two Tutsi bishops, Mgr. Jean-Baptiste Gahamanyi of Butare and Mgr. Wenceslas Kalibushi of Nyundo (both were refugees in Gisenyi), in order to avenge the three Hutu bishops killed on 5 June 1994 by the RPF, namely, Thaddée Nsengiyumva of Kabgayi, Joseph Ruzindana of Byumba, and Vincent Nsengiyumva of Kigali.
>
> I was greatly shocked that such a discussion could be held so openly during a meeting of the council of ministers, and I categorically objected to the request from the minister of defense. . . .
>
> Among those in attendance, I remember Mugenzi, Pauline Nyiramasuhuko, Karemera, and Mugiraneza.[18]

On this level of insensitivity there hardly seems to be any real distinction between those ministers of authentic intellectual repute and the ones who were simply pushed ahead. Pauline Nyiramasuhuko herself distinguished "the politicians who had ideas," on the one hand (i.e., the party chiefs who, at this stage of the conflict, preferred to remain on the margins of day-to-day state affairs and who devoted themselves principally to preparing the endgame), from the management team for the war and "pacification," on the other. And even so, among the group as a whole, the ministers who were hotheaded and aggressive (Éliezer Niyitegeka, Callixte Nzabonimana, Pauline Nyiramasuhuko, and Rafiki Nsengiyumva) could be distinguished from the political toilers (e.g., Emmanuel Ndindabahizi, Straton Nsabumukunzi, André Rwamakuba) and the "political stealths," as Jean Kambanda described them, that is, those who would never put themselves out front (e.g., Gaspard Ruhumuliza, Jérôme Bicamumpaka, Jean de Dieu Kamuhanda).

Most of the ministers took their work seriously: the government functioned, convened, kept itself informed, deliberated, made decisions, and issued orders on a full range of issues, including challenging military matters, which the ministers were at pains to master. This legitimacy and the prerogatives that went with it were jealously claimed, even as far along as mid-July, with ministers insisting upon the fiction of power despite defeat and exile.

The only argument of any substance would point to more powerful decision makers who would have had the means to force the hands of the ministers over the course of their mandate. That argument comes in two versions. The first version points to the conditions under which the ministers were appointed on 8 April and the tentative commitments of these "anointed ones" during those first few days of the Interim Government's existence. Certainly, up until the oath taking on 9 April, we could surmise that a few among them reasonably anticipated being killed if they refused. All the same, having realized that they had been selected to make southerners bear responsibility for the initial crimes and massacres, or at least share responsibility, several did indeed voice their hesitations about the massacres. But it was only after their transfer to Gitarama that the ministers reemerged as cheerleaders for the killers and set about implementing the policy, as was expected of them, right where it was needed, that is, in the countryside, not in Kigali.

The second version, advanced, notably, by one of the ministers of this Interim Government, postulates an unofficial power undercutting the good intentions that he lends to this government: "Due to the continued massacres, it seemed to me that there was a weak official power alongside a much more powerful unofficial power composed of members of Akazu like Bagosora, Nzirorera, Casimir Bizimungu, Augustin Ngirabatware, and others who had solid networks within and outside the country, because despite our directives and the measures that the minister of defense claimed to have taken accordingly, the massacres continued."[19] This argument is sound where convergence of official and parallel lines of authority is concerned, but nothing seems to suggest that there was any fundamental divergence between these two. As Alison Des Forges reminds us, the party chiefs generally convened with the members of the government, and ministers expressed themselves on behalf of their party, giving no hint of possible discord.[20] If there were aspects of the political game that eclipsed members of the Interim Government, as there must have been, the policy of "pacification" was not one of them, for it proceeded in complete symbiosis with the parties, utterly unperturbed.

Similar reasoning could apply to the argument that ministers were deliberately misinformed or were denied information about the unfolding of the massacres. However, practically all of the agenda items listed for government cabinet meetings contained the point of order "propaganda": clearly, the ministers were in control of that. The Interim Government routinely accorded a major role to managing how its activities were reported in the media, even if there were mixed results. Consequently, in setting up discreet, limited ministerial working groups, information and propaganda were clearly identified as special concerns. At the same time, numerous missions were dispatched abroad to explain the government's position, missions where the ministers or designated spokespersons often served as envoys to negotiate financial assistance or weapons purchases.

Thus, clearly, it is difficult to contradict the statement that "civilians were thrust to the forefront"; at the very least, they got caught up in the game.

- The territorial administration was under tight government control and, more precisely, controlled by the persons in charge of "pacification" in the prefectures. Competition between individuals and between the parties for control of the prefectures, communes, and sectors necessarily complicated matters and could unleash intense local rivalries, but resolutions were negotiated within the government, between the parties. Additionally, the authority of the Ministry of the Interior and the prefects was reinforced during this period of the conflict by a sort of intramural competition that transferred power to administrative personnel most zealously engaged in the government's war effort, irrespective of official, formal hierarchy.
- Squabbles among the parties were the daily fare of the government, but beyond rivalries over allocations of resources and posts, solidarity prevailed in regard to objectives and means. This concurrence was paradoxically reinforced by the overwhelming influence of the MRND, which claimed privileged links within the army and a quasi monopoly of the territorial civil service, extending over more than two-thirds of the country. And finally, the MRND kept President Théodore Sindikubwabo under the constant surveillance of his advisors. MRND party leaders also controlled Radio Rwanda and had sparked the creation of the RTLM.

- The discreet withdrawal of the presidential family to Gisenyi and the martyrdom of its chief reinforced the legitimacy and the hold of the presidential party. Beyond the advice of the "family," disseminated within the Interim Government and through diplomatic links to certain heads of state by Augustin Ngirabatware, the "Gisenyi group" raised its profile on 25 April with the creation of the National Defense Fund, commissioned to provide assistance to the government (purchases of weapons, vehicles, and military uniforms for the army and the militias). Among its promoters were Félicien Kabuga, Matthieu Ngirumpatse, Édouard Karemera, and Anatole Nsengiyumva. On 20 May Félicien Kabuga formally informed the Interim Government of the creation of this fund and described the manner in which it was to be used (*see annex 105*).
- Finally, and especially after it was unleashed, genocide as the order of the day had to be forced upon the FAR and in prefectures dominated by the opposition, where it faced detractors, "weak" politicians, and "hesitant" cadres. It became necessary to reactivate the engine of death whenever the energies and the convictions about its strategic efficacy began to taper off. Aside from mobilizing the human, logistical, and material resources necessary to accomplish the genocide, the government was constantly obliged to uphold the legitimacy of these "populist outbursts," at least ideologically, both within the country and abroad. To do that, it had to infuse and sustain them with ad hoc rhetoric (pacification, civil self-defense, etc.) to avoid having the killings degenerate completely into barbarism, banditry, and wanton exactions at the roadblocks and on the hillsides.

In large measure, once begun, "the genocide fed on itself, and there was no need for massacres to be 'planned,'" just organized from day to day.[21] Once formed, focused on simple objectives, and then freed from all normative constraints, the militia forces did not need to be "reprogrammed." On the ground, the most important thing was to maintain or regularly replenish their energies with rewards of various sorts (rackets, pillaging, rapes, direct remunerations, or redistributions of bounty).

Assembled in conditions imposed by necessity and urgency, from 9 April to 19 July the government became a group "unto itself" in which various individuals played significant roles yet for various reasons conserved distinct allegiances. Even where it did not control all sites of power (in particular, with groups of soldiers and politicians that directed it from the outside or from a distance), the government laid claim to constitutional legitimacy and never sought to distance itself from the various powers behind the scenes: the Akazu and its representatives in refuge abroad; Théoneste Bagosora and his northern military connections; the quartet of leaders from the MRND; the big bosses in the prefectures (Renzaho in Kigali, Rwagafilita in Kibungo, Nsengiyumva in Gisenyi, etc.). On the contrary, it always seemed to anticipate their desiderata or used its own authority to cloak their improprieties. The responsibility of the politicians who subjected an efficient and well-structured civilian administration to the wartime objectives of a small nucleus of military and paramilitary extremists is well established, since they were the ones who strove to neutralize all organized forms of resistance to the genocidal project (e.g., nongovernmental organizations, churches) and to obliterate any social bonds that could transcend the pull of ethnic origins and loyalty.

In sum, what allowed the state apparatus to accomplish its sinister mission over the course of those three months is that the fates of the various state and parastatal actors were linked in a war that was known to have been lost from the very outset and because political and regional cleavages that weakened their collective politics cut across each partisan grouping. Also, the unifying bonds were derived from the strong links inherited from the single-party system, which converged around the highest echelons of the army, the political class, and the administration. Both the Kayibanda regime and the Habyarimana regime relied on elites of various profiles, and the war reinfused the edifice with a certain vitality. The FAR was on one side, the heads of the two major parties were on the other: Nzirorera, Karemera, and Ngirumpatse for the MRND; Murego and Karamira for the MDR. The two parties trumpeted their refound unity in the fusion of their party youth wings, Interahamwe and Inkuba, and then within the structures of civil self-defense.

The deadly cleavage that caused the system to unravel was so deeply rooted in the ethnoregional Nduga-Rukiga rift that neither the MRND, nor the army, nor the administration was ever in a position to overcome it. In fact, in the mindset of most of the cadres from the south, civilian and military alike, imagining power in the hands of a Nzirorera, who embodied all the excesses of the Second Republic but without the populist charisma of a Habyarimana, was no more enticing than the prospect of falling under the boots of the Tutsi RPF. In addition to the two "fronts," external and internal, on which the pro-Hutu factions were already engaged, they also ripped each other apart in fratricidal battle over the succession, which ultimately doomed them.

12

War and the Fight
for Supremacy

In the same way that the war radically disrupted social and
economic hierarchies, arbitrarily tossing power and
riches from one hand to the other, claims for abandoned or vacant property,
indeed outright seizures, became a motivating factor in the war. Pillaging state
resources and amassing war booty galvanized energies among the various
parties. The allocation of booty (posts, cash, provisions) strengthened loyalties
and groomed ambitions. These elements played a determining role in the
competition among parties and individuals vying for ascendancy.

Allocation of Public Resources

Few other tasks facing the various parties were more urgent
than mobilizing their members politically and ideologically. Ensuring the un-
swerving loyalty of party cadres and local administrative leaders at the cell
level was essential for effective political sensitization and awareness building.
To succeed, the parties had to offer their allies a long-term vision, which
meant, concretely, the lure of guaranteed resources in a period that all found
difficult. The size or scope of the various ministries or public entities that were
attributed to a particular party, depending on its capacity to generate resources,
was thus of the utmost importance. War only reinforced this trend.

The constraints of the war called for major accommodations in the
clientelist system put in place by Habyarimana. In order to build "consensus
among the parties," the government had to lubricate the ambitions of those
eager to enter the race for the presidency of the republic or any other major

position of responsibility through missions, rallies, or meetings; access to funding was equally important to facilitate peace deals with the party chiefs. This was really one of the underlying purposes of the missions abroad, whether diplomatic or commercial, undertaken by the various party dignitaries to conclude agricultural and industrial trade agreements and to purchase weapons. Minutes from government cabinet meetings currently at our disposal and several personal accounts provide numerous examples, with indications of the sums involved and the beneficiaries.

First, there were the senior officials, who had to meet their own needs and contribute to their parties' finances. The MRND was naturally the most privileged recipient, with a special place reserved for Col. Ephrem Setako, warrant officer and right-hand man to Joseph Nzirorera. Setako came from the same region as Nzirorera and was just as committed to filling his patron's coffers as he was to filling those of the MRND and his own.[1] Then comes Nzirorera himself and Casimir Bizimungu, then Protais Zigiranyirazo, who gained control over the export of pyrethrum. For the weapons trade, we find the two party heads well recognized for their business savvy: the MDR's Froduald Karamira and the PL's Justin Mugenzi (*see annex 107*). Hyacinthe Rafiki Nsengiyumva of the PSD was not one to be left out: the government accorded him responsibility for the trade in the coffee harvest in place of Straton Nsabumukunzi, minister of agriculture, who was a member of the same party.[2] The portion of the budget that the minister wanted to deposit with the Banque nationale du Rwanda (BNR) was wholly earmarked to finance "missions for selected persons." Fellow party member Emmanuel Ndindabahizi managed to set aside $84,000 for himself, also skimmed from receipts of coffee sales. By 15 June 1994, all of the hard currency held by the BNR had been disbursed. The funds that were "lost," appropriated by one figure or another, amounted to $151,000. What remained of the coffee harvest shipped out by Rwandex-Gisenyi was sold in Goma by Eugène Mbarushimana, secretary-general of the Interahamwe youth wing, in collaboration with Augustin Ngirabatware and Félicien Kabuga, both related to him by marriage. Some $600,000 never reached state coffers. Minister Callixte Nzabonimana made off with the bounty from the sale of colombo-tantalite. The deal was worth approximately $470,000, not a penny of which ever landed in state coffers. Once in exile, under mounting pressure, Nzabonimana "reimbursed" around $50,000 to Prime Minister Jean Kambanda, who was then in a bad way himself.[3]

Finally, the soldiers were particularly well placed to take advantage of the transactions in arms purchases. In fact, the "Bagosora system" was expanded to include Col. Jean-Bosco Ruhorahoza, Lt. Col. Cyprien Kayumba, and Théoneste Bagosora himself. The handler for the account with the OMI

Corporation for acquisition of weapons and munitions, Col. Cyprien Kayumba, pocketed $1 million.

All of these special missions were highly coveted because the transactions were generally made in hard currency, without official documentation, with suppliers seeking to circumvent the international arms embargo. Profit margins and kickbacks were thus generous and guaranteed.

The missions undertaken by Bagosora, Ruhorahoza, and Nzirorera in May 1994 gave rise to genuine highway robbery, perpetrated against state funds. On 23 May all three journeyed to Kinshasa, delegated to meet with Zairean authorities to work through the serious problems of weapons shortages then confronting Rwanda because of the arms embargo imposed by the UN Security Council. Nzirorera then went on to South Africa, where he remained from 27 May to 9 June, eventually meeting up again with Bagosora, who rejoined him there and on 3 June handed over $1 million in travelers' checks. The transaction faltered because distributors demanded payment in hard currency, and the banks refused to honor the travelers' checks.

Ultimately, the problem was resolved when the Rwandan Embassy in Kinshasa made a direct transfer of the required sums to finalize the transaction. The payment was finally accepted, but only on 14 July, after the government had already collapsed in defeat, with the government of Zaire, the titular payee in the transaction, becoming the sole beneficiary in the end. Thus, the required funds were actually disbursed twice, first in the travelers' checks held by Nzirorera, and then again when payment was channeled through the Rwandan Embassy in Kinshasa. Although never cashed, those travelers' checks never made it back into state coffers.

According to Jean Kambanda, these financial matters were wholly managed by the minister of defense—without government supervision—who was among the primary beneficiaries of the public weal (*see annex 107*).

Seventh case: Bizimana, defense minister. He had to manage enormous amounts for the purchase of military equipment. . . . Correspondence between us in September 1994 clearly shows that pending sums for three orders that were paid for but not delivered have to be accounted for. There is the sum of one million American dollars that was given to a Chinese in Hong Kong. This contract was signed by Kabiligi in Nairobi just before the war. Another million dollars was paid in South Africa for the same kind of delivery by the same Nzirorera before the exile, which delivery was canceled in late 1994 or early 1995.[4]

These elements clearly illustrate the predatory instincts that consumed so much of the energies of these officeholders, essentially bankrolled by a government expected to meet their expenditures, however extravagant. Such practices are no different from the rash decisions to raid the pension funds held by the National University of Rwanda or the requisitioning of hard currency accounts, the withholding of salaries and nonpayment of civil service personnel, and the forced collections of donations and dues imposed on traders and on the populace. If these larcenous practices ended up sabotaging weapons acquisitions for the FAR, precipitating or largely contributing to its military defeat, they also illustrate the cynicism and indifference of those who profited from the misery of the populations in whose name they made such harsh demands. We can also notice that, putting aside the case of Justin Mugenzi, the largest amounts were concentrated in the hands of ministers and officers from the north, whereas the natives of those three prefectures had already monopolized control of the vast majority of parastatal enterprises.[5]

Nduga versus Rukiga

The machinations that led to elevating southern-based politicians to the highest echelons of political institutions ran counter to the republic's unwritten law that neither the south nor the north should ever benefit from a concentration of power. The titans from the north brought a great deal of pressure to bear on the government to circumvent this tacit understanding. The government in general, and certain of its members in particular, constantly faced criticism for their powerlessness in the face of the RPF's progression or were suspected of weakness in confronting its accomplices. The rhetoric of Hutu unity was echoed essentially by MRND/CDR party activists from the north, always ready to point out the faults and failings of their southern allies, for whom they had little respect and only limited confidence. The political concessions made to southern politicians were always considered temporary, expected to last no more than ninety days at the very most.

President Théodore Sindikubwabo, a seasoned politician whose wife was Tutsi, was quite offended by the consequent lack of consideration and slights he had to endure. Because of his age and his failing health, many felt that he was not up to the job. Some urged him to hand in his resignation, which would then clear the path for Nzirorera. The latter dared not openly display his impatience, but not everyone was bound by such discretion.

Thus, a serious crisis had broken out by 22 April 1994, or three days after President Sindikubwabo had launched the massacres in his home prefecture, when he solemnly informed the minister of defense and then the cabinet that he intended to resign. Once before in conversation he had asked Augustin

Bizimana for increased security for his family members in Butare, who were facing constant threats "with no success in getting a response":

> Is it necessary, Sir, to reiterate that should any one of the members of my family, a list of whom is already in your possession, suffer death at the hands of this gang of thugs and miscreants, it would be very difficult for me to continue to exhaust my limited energies in service to such ingrates and traitors? . . .
>
> It would be all the more regrettable, Sir, if the rumors currently in circulation that certain persons intend to profit from this crisis to rid themselves of those Banyanduga they find troublesome, this would not only be regrettable but rather catastrophic, because in so doing the enemy objective would be achieved without difficulty; that is, division, disharmony, and self-destruction of the Hutu people.[6]

The rumors Sindikubwabo alluded to pointed to Nzirorera and Bizimana, both of whom were longing to expedite the matter of succession. His warnings served little or no purpose, despite the show of support from the cabinet: on 26 April his daughter's father-in-law, Claver Mpakaniye, was killed by "activists," and on 27 April a house belonging to Emmanuel Kayiranga, his son-in-law's brother, was destroyed after an all-out looting.[7]

In fact, despite the long history of Théodore Sindikubwabo's links to President Habyarimana and his robust ethnic chauvinism, northern extremists openly viewed him as a potential dissident. He was at pains to protect his son-in-law Augustin Iyamuremye, a former chief of security in the office of the prime minister under both Dismas Nsengiyaremye and Agathe Uwilingiyimana and Félicien Gatabazi's successor on the steering committee of the PSD party, linked to its pro-RPF wing, by sheltering him in his own personal residence in Nyaruhengeri under the watchful eyes of the Presidential Guard. He was also suspected of "weakness" in his own prefecture. The emergence of a serious crisis at the top, when the government, already facing strong international criticism, was embarking upon lobbying efforts and negotiations abroad, was particularly embarrassing.

The president's case was not an isolated event: regionalist competition, if not distrust, and ethnic suspicions lingered. Denunciations and exposure of traitors within the ranks only increased. On 26 April Édouard Karemera deemed it appropriate to "discreetly provide some information for follow-up" to Augustin Ndindiliyimana, commander in chief of the gendarmerie; in actuality, he was requesting that he relieve of their duties the Tutsi members of his escort (*see annex 109*). Later, during a "security meeting" in Kibuye on 3 May, when the prime minister was accompanied by Édouard Karemera—in his capacity as first vice president of the MRND—and representatives for PSD and MDR, the speeches were particularly explicit: "Where were they with us? Each leader should reveal his colors because the bell for a decision has tolled. Whoever is not with us is against us. Nobody should say, 'I am going to seek refuge somewhere; I am going to observe the development of the situation, and then later I will reappear and say that I am the mediator.' We have no need for a mediator. They should make up their minds. Are they for the RPF or are they defending the people's cause?"[8] It fell to the MRND first vice president to engage in open confrontation with the president of the Interim Government during a meeting of the party's Political Bureau in Murambi, convened on 10 May (*see annex 110.1*). The participants expressed concern about the evolving political and military situation; some wanted to discuss the organization of the civil defense but also, most importantly, to broach the matter of accelerating the constitutional transition, which appeared on the agenda under the rubric "miscellaneous." The CND vice president, Immaculée Nyirabizeyimana, set to succeed the interim president in the event of incapacity, and the MRND ministers were also invited. Intense debate followed over two consecutive days, 12 and 13 May, and ended with a statement from the Political Bureau that was read over Radio Rwanda by the two organizers of the seminar, Édouard Karemera and Joseph Nzirorera, successively (*see annex 110.2*).

The most important development was the announcement concerning a constitutional amendment "to fill the institutional void after the anticipated three-month period," but the legal terrain was almost immediately overtaken by an urgency to avoid "further delay in filling vacant posts at the institutional helm: the presidency and CND." Yet these posts had been duly filled by provisional ninety-day appointments.

Indeed, the urgency was elsewhere. Théodore Sindikubwabo was in failing health and physically quite weak. There was considerable speculation about his capacity to live up to his duties over the long term. But even more fundamentally, "the MRND political bureau recommended to the government to put in place a crisis committee for the efficient management of the war," as well as a "multidisciplinary committee to reflect upon the various political, economic, and social problems besetting the country and propose solutions for resolution to the government."[9] Thus, the governmental team was explicitly blamed as wholly ineffective, and the Interim Government's inability to regain the initiative in confronting the RPF militarily, as well as on the diplomatic front, provoked increasing anxiety within the MRND.

The risk of ending up in a position where there was nothing left to negotiate was fast becoming the reality. The time for withdrawal and reflection had lasted long enough. A reshuffling was absolutely necessary to reinforce the increasingly compromised armed forces and to quickly remobilize and rein in a civil defense overwhelmed by "pacification," where the vandals and thugs were gorging themselves. Toward mid-May, in fact, the military situation worsened, to the point where the high command of the FAR, wracked by open animosities and faced with the risk of the RPF's imminent takeover of the capital, was also forced to withdraw to Gitarama.

Even though few had any doubt of the RPF's capacity to win the war, the great powers and the United Nations still had to come together to weigh in on the conditions for ending the war. Diplomatic maneuvers, however, seemed to stumble over insurmountable contradictions. The propaganda war had already proclaimed a victor, the Tutsi rebellion, and had morally disqualified the pro-Hutu camp, fast on its way to defeat. On the one hand, to stop the genocide and the massacres it was still necessary to negotiate with authorities already long declared "untouchable." The horror of the genocide and the scorched-earth campaign imposed by the government camp cut off all hopes of political compromise or reprieve, even from the more sympathetic foreign supporters, still quite numerous in Africa. On the other hand, the collapse of the extremist "Hutu camp" and the flight into exile of broad masses of the population generated unimaginable risks and an enduring source of destabilization for the entire region.[10]

The Irreversible Upsets of 17 May

By mid-May, anticipating imminent decisions from the Security Council based on a third extraordinary session of the United Nations Commission on Human Rights concerning the situation in Rwanda, held in Geneva, the authorities began to mobilize.

With four Interim Government ministers returning home from missions abroad—Gaspard Ruhumuliza, André Ntagerura and Agnès Ntamabyaliro (who returned on 14 May), and Justin Mugenzi (15 May)—the agenda for the cabinet meeting in Murambi of Tuesday, 17 May, just a few hours before the UN Security Council met in New York, was particularly laden, and the deteriorating security situation required urgent, decisive decision making at every level of government activity.

Marked by the presence of the president, already quite weakened by illness, and by a short-tempered and unusually aggressive Jean Kambanda, the cabinet meeting got off the ground with the prime minister's summary of the series of reversals recently suffered by the Interim Government (e.g., the arms embargo, the fall of the airport in Kigali, the breakdown in ground communication with the prefectures in the north and the east, financial straits, diplomatic isolation).

As could be expected, this onslaught of bad news only emboldened partisans for renewed and swift radicalization who were anxious for purges within the ranks. It primarily took form around the principal point of debate, that is, the legislative project for civil self-defense initiated only a few days previously by the MRND Political Bureau. Ngirumpatse and Nzirorera had been invited to participate, just as the (seemingly omnipresent) minister of the interior, Édouard Karemera, since he was the author of the proposed measures. The prime minister's account provoked several legal objections primarily rooted in the impossibility of a government cabinet imposing legislation in the place of a National Assembly. The resolution was to adopt the very same program under the guise of directives from the prime minister, complemented by circulars explaining their application from the minister of the interior.

Final decision making and the proposed dismissals of several subprefects were put off until 20 May. The Ministries of Defense, Family and Gender, Youth, Tourism and Environment, and Primary and Secondary Education were delegated to support the Ministry of the Interior in its mandate for mobilizing the civil self-defense. Notes made during those meetings provide some indications of which ministries were most involved in mobilizing the population: "(3) Civil Defense → Minadef, Mifaprofe, Mijeuma, Mineto, Miniprisec" (Civil Defense → Defense, Family and Gender, Youth, Tourism, Primary and Secondary Education).[11] Swift implementation was the order of the day, and a reshuffling in the civil service was launched to revive the massacres.

There were two other major agenda items: the government cabinet received a note from the vice president of the CND, Immaculée Nyirabizeyimana, concerning institutional requirements and deadlines, and President Sindikubwabo formally updated the cabinet about his plans for restructuring it. Ngirumpatse's new status as head of mission would end his tour of duty as roving ambassador and was of no particular or immediate political consequence. However, by linking his future to that of Sindikubwabo—unlike Nzirorera, who sought to distance himself—Ngirumpatse occupied a privileged vantage point that allowed him to anticipate institutional shake-ups. Positions hardened, as the UN resolution was close at hand, as confirmed by the highly anticipated decision from the UN Security Council on the evening of 17 May. Indeed, the vote on Resolution 918, which imposed an embargo on weapons destined for Rwanda and authorized an international humanitarian interventionist force of 5,500 men, sealed the fate of the war and therefore the destiny of the Interim Government authorities.[12]

Purging the Officer Corps and
Relaunching Civil Self-Defense

But the day was not over, and there were still surprises in store. Weighed down by the shock of such bad news, which left them powerless and incapable of taking decisions on par with the current stakes, the members of government were overcome by exasperation, which only intensified as tensions mounted, aggravated by the daily promiscuity of their isolation within the confines of the Murambi compound. Cabin fever enflamed the political-military microcosm; "traitors" were singled out, and heads were expected to roll.

At the conclusion of a meeting of the management commission for the war on 17 May at 3:15 p.m. that included participation from members of the government, as well as party leaders like Semanza and Ngirumpatse from the MRND, a "list of twelve Ibyitso officers" was presented that same evening to Sindikubwabo.[13] It was handed over by Bagosora and Defense Minister Augustin Bizimana, whose role as coordinator of the civil defense had just been reconfirmed by the government cabinet.[14] Quite disturbed, and convinced that the list's authors were indeed serious, Sindikubwabo immediately summoned Augustin Ndindiliyimana—whose name appeared on the list—to Murambi the following morning to alert him of these threats and to seek his advice.

After a preliminary chat with Jean Kambanda, the president informed Ndindiliyimana of the recommendations from the management commission for the war.[15] The latter discussed his own fate with both the president and the prime minister. As soon as he returned to Kigali on 19 May at around 4:00 or 5:00 a.m., Ndindiliyimana summoned Col. Laurent Rutayisire and Maj. Pierre-Claver Karangwa to his office to make sure that they tightened up security measures, without, however, explicitly informing them of his reasons. He also immediately set about making preparations to evacuate his family and to organize his own departure.[16] Sindikubwabo then drafted a second letter of resignation, which, according to several officers, became the object of lengthy discussions with various members of the cabinet.

A few of the targeted officers were discreetly informed of the decision to push them aside or to eliminate them by some of the very same persons called into the meeting so that they could make the necessary arrangements. Thus, Semanza warned Col. Félicien Muberuka, who hailed from the same commune as him and apparently was also a relative, but then when questioned by others he denied the purpose of that meeting.

The matter of purges to be conducted within the Rwandan Armed Forces was a recurrent theme in government cabinet meetings.[17] Threats had been repeatedly directed against several officers, especially "opponents" from the south. There had already been several attempts to eliminate them, with Augustin Cyiza, Marcel Gatsinzi, and Léonidas Rusatira (from the north) at the top of the list. The threats were not only verbal. According to Rutayisire, he was targeted in a botched attempted assassination at the bridge over the Nyabarongo. But that 17 May list was a clear indication of radicalization within the army high command against officers deemed "close to the RPF."

The list also included these targeted officers:

Maj. Augustin Cyiza (Cyangugu)[18]
Maj. Emmanuel Habyarimana (Byumba)[19]
Maj. Pierre-Claver Karangwa (Gitarama)[20]
Lt. Col. Ephrem Rwabalinda (Cyangugu)[21]
Lt. Col. Innocent Bavugamenshi (Cyangugu)[22]
Col. Félicien Muberuka (Kigali)
Col. Balthazar Ndengeyinka (Kibuye)[23]
Col. Anselme Nshizirungu (Kigali)[24]
Col. Laurent Rutayisire (Gikongoro)[25]
Brig. Gen. Marcel Gatsinzi (Kigali)[26]
Brig. Gen. Léonidas Rusatira (Ruhengeri)[27]
Maj. Gen. Augustin Ndindiliyimana (Butare)

For the most part, the list is a compilation of all the officers who had participated in the Arusha negotiations. All except two came from the southern prefectures. Only one among them could be linked to the OTP. Perhaps Bagosora was seeking to definitively silence those key witnesses to his failed attempt to seize power within the Military Crisis Committee, like Ndindiliyimana, Rusatira, and Gatsinzi, who, nonetheless, had never been involved in the Arusha process. We also find the principal instigators of the FAR communiqué of 12 April, which had so outraged the members of the Interim Government. After the final defeat, most of these same officers appeared on a list of "criminals" established by the Interim Government in exile in Bukavu.

Over the course of that decisive 17 May, another list of officers gave rise to vigorous debate and even greater dissensions and displays of bravado among decision makers in Murambi, but its contents only came to light toward the end of the week. With support from President Sindikubwabo, the minister of defense appealed to staff officers, heads of units, and commanders of operational sectors to recall certain retired officers back to active duty owing to the dire military situation. When the minister finally circulated the list of those officers recalled to arms, apparently on 20 May, it was clear that Bagosora, Bizimana's own chief of staff, was not included, whereas Bagosora had been contesting his retirement at the legally required age since June 1992 and had already sought to circumvent the regulation and have himself reinstated on multiple occasions. On 21 May Bagosora asked Nzirorera and Ngirumpatse to protest this obvious discrimination by Bizimana on behalf of the MRND, stressing the importance of "avoiding any major disagreement" with Bagosora on the eve of his departure, as he and Nzirorera prepared for their joint mission abroad to purchase weapons. Bizimana conceded without bearing too much of the cost: Bagosora was indeed immediately recalled to active service in the army but without the promotion to general that he so longed for (*see annex 113*).

This latest affront to Bagosora simply shows the extent to which his political stature had been diminished. A fairly significant portion of the woes befalling the FAR could be directly imputed to him, owing to his isolation within the army and his inability to effectively mobilize support. But, as Nzirorera himself recognized, it simply was not prudent to invite additional dispute with an officer with control over such a wide terrain, as he had in managing the defense of Kigali, where some of the best-equipped units of the army were stationed, along with the National Committee of the Interahamwe and all of the resources of the Kigali-ville prefecture office (see chapter 11).

The government then gave priority to promoting a broad campaign of public safety, articulated as a populist mobilization for civil self-defense. Re-launched under the yoke of Édouard Karemera, who finally entered the public discourse in his capacity as minister of the interior, its command was conferred to Col. Athanase Gasake. The ministerial directives concerning civil self-defense urged a symbiosis between the common folk mobilized by the MRND and the youth wingers already groomed and trained by former military officers, only recently recalled to active duty under the authority of the prefects. But at the same time, also on the broader agenda was the matter of accelerating an exit strategy to terminate the "interim" phase of government, removing President Sindikubwabo and formally installing Nzirorera at the helm before it was too late.

This period of score settling and political clarification stands as a pivotal turning point in several respects. It slightly precedes the flight of a part of the Interim Government from Murambi to Muramba (Gisenyi prefecture) after Nyanza fell to the RPF on 29 May 1994. Military defeat loomed on the horizon, and final initiatives were haphazardly being taken in order to salvage whatever could still be saved.

The most outlandish of these initiatives sought to muster a final push for control on the political and military fronts and to relaunch the massacres against the civilian Tutsi population. If the likelihood of regaining control was meager, at least where the massacres were concerned, here, at any rate, was something fully within reach of the Abatabazi.

An Obligatory Alliance between Édouard Karemera and Joseph Nzirorera

Formally entering the Interim Government on 25 May in this context, Édouard Karemera sought to align his new status as minister of the interior with his concrete efforts on the ground.

Since the very onset of the war, Karemera had taken it upon himself to boost mobilization, to campaign for, cajole, and advise the Interim Government, and to occupy himself with organizing the civil defense. Interahamwe excesses, especially in the southern prefectures, irked Karemera, and fairly early on he became the advocate for more effective supervision and for subsuming this armed civilian component under military command. The MRND first vice president's arrival on the scene served to enhance credibility for this rundown government, already moribund in the eyes of certain of its members, but it also signaled the beginning of the final, great maneuvers.

Indeed, the conflict was at a turning point: the RPF advance seemed unstoppable, and, de facto, the weapons embargo virtually ensured that the country would soon be handed over to it. Nevertheless, the Interim Government still sought to demonstrate that, without negotiations, its defeat could only come at great cost. At this stage of the conflict, discussion along these lines could only lead to partition of the country between zones already fully under RPF control to the east and the high plateaus of Hutu-dominated territory to the west. The Arusha Peace Accords would thus be given effect formally in terms of "power sharing."

Certainly, in this scenario, competition among those vying for ascendancy swung in favor of Nzirorera, who could foresee being swept to the pinnacle of the Hutu half of a divided Rwanda. But, even so, Karemera would hardly be left out. Indeed, whereas Ngirumpatse weighed himself down with vague, intellectual calculations, lamenting how discredited the government he had represented abroad had become, Karemera deemed it essential to make a show of unflinching determination and to boost his popularity by heading up the civilian resistance to the RPF's looming domination. He took advantage of the war to fashion himself a hero, to prepare himself and ready the terrain for the inevitable restructuring that an end to combat would impose on the MRND. But he was still wise enough to remain realistic: nothing would be gained by affronting Nzirorera and his northern base. Thus, Karemera had to support Nzirorera while yet expanding his own grounds within the party. By taking on highly visible and important responsibilities, Karemera could still hope to mobilize the "anti-Nzirorera" lobby whenever the time was right. Prime Minister Jean Kambanda himself perceptively offered the same analysis on 3 May 1994 in Kibuye, with Karemera standing right beside him.

Karemera's return to center stage echoes the logic of the unexpected promotion, during a 1 June cabinet meeting (*see annex 97*), conferred upon Col. Félicien Muberuka, an ambitious officer from Kigali-rural linked to the colonels supposedly "flaunting the authority of the minister [of defense]." The government's nominating him to head the gendarmerie as Ndindiliyimana's replacement relied on political calculations very similar to those made by Karemera: "If we lose, we will at least have half the country" and "we will restore the real hierarchy within the army." Assimilated to other officers deemed "opponents" (he appeared on the list of the twelve Ibyitso officers), Muberuka's positioning within the FAR nonetheless remained unique: although he was a "southerner," his wife, a native of Ruhengeri, made him acceptable among the ranks.[28]

With the Security Council vote of Resolution 918 (17 May) imposing an embargo on weapons destined for the FAR, there was no time for equivocation. Even if it became impossible to "rob" the RPF of its military victory, if diplomats no longer envisaged a reprise of negotiations with a thoroughly discredited pro-Hutu camp, it was still possible to salvage a small portion of the political content of the Arusha Peace Accords, as meager as that portion was, that is, a bit of territory, a few of the "Hutu" authorities, perhaps a bit of legitimacy justified as a humanitarian "necessity," culminating in some manner of partition of the country. On this basis, the interim authorities hoped to still retain a few cards that could be played on an international negotiating table. By 18 May France's minister of foreign affairs, Alain Juppé, had made a proposal before the National Assembly calling for a summit of heads of state of neighboring countries to Rwanda, and on 20 May in Paris he received Faustin Twagiramungu, the prime minister designate for the BBTG. On 20 May the Belgian ambassador to Rwanda, Johan Swinnen, embarked upon a contact-initiating tour to several African countries. Sindikubwabo even made an appeal for help to French president François Mitterrand on 23 May, which found receptive ears in Paris (*see annex 114*).[29]

For its part, the RPF needed to accelerate its offensive in order to conserve its gains, to ensure there would be no turning back. That very same day it managed to capture the Kigali airport and the military camp at Kanombe. The following day, authorized to raise the matter of some five hundred Ghanaian "blue helmets" on standby in Nairobi, Iqbal Riza, the secretary-general's special envoy, was received at the RPF headquarters in Mulindi. Paul Kagame himself responded with virulent diatribes against the organization and, at the same time, ordered his troops to take over the presidential palace in Kigali. This is the context for appreciating the mutual hardening of positions among the protagonists.

The arrival on the scene of Karemera, known as a man of order and linked to a colonel just recently appointed to head the gendarmerie—who, incidentally, boldly announced his willingness to end the careers of those "arrivistes" at the helm of the army (and, in particular, Maj. Gen. Augustin Bizimungu) at war's end—could be interpreted not only as a deepening resolve in facing the rebellion but also as an overture. This new development was sure to seduce a good number of French officers, well acquainted with Félicien Muberuka from their time together during their training in some of the finest French military schools and through their long collaboration when he was operational sector commander for Kigali, when he clearly distinguished himself from the pro-Hutu extremists heading up the better-equipped units in Kigali. With a view toward a possible humanitarian operation under UN mandate whose objective would be to secure the zones not yet taken over by the RPF, anticipating the rollout of UNAMIR II, the Karemera-Muberuka team could possibly be presented as a pair of worthy interlocutors for eventual negotiations.

While waiting for the framework, the leadership, and the objectives of this international operation to be worked out, it was still important to demonstrate the authorities' determination. Although injured on 21 May 1994, Muberuka was still able to make the rounds in Kibuye prefecture with Karemera after his appointment.

Where the Ministry of Interior is concerned, senior officials working there, wallowing without direction during the long, incomprehensible absence of an incumbent minister, were quickly remobilized around the tasks of civil self-defense, which became the priority, and Karemera immediately stepped up efforts to expedite the presidential succession, to Joseph Nzirorera's benefit.

Institutionalization of Civil Self-Defense

Karemera was particularly effective in addressing matters of civil self-defense, as his own notebook of handwritten entries would indicate (*see annex 117*): by 25 May the prime minister's directives on civil self-defense had been issued, and three days later, 28 May, Karemera summoned all the prefects to Gitarama to report on how his instructions were being implemented, to approve replacements for communal authorities proposed in the reshuffling, and to discuss the status of internally displaced persons (*see annex 118*). On 9 June he pressured the government to obtain stronger support from the FAR for civil self-defense and embarked upon an "intensive campaign over the airwaves and in print media with a view to convincing Rwandans of the need to resist, and even to attack, the common enemy instead of fleeing all the time."[30]

Karemera's commitment to institutionalizing civil self-defense was not simply a response to situational necessity. In circulating the directives of 25 May 1994, he wanted to overcome the ambiguities arising from the very inception of the youth wing, which could now be officially incorporated in the newly formed entity. By making the militias the internal armed wing of the Interim Government, this "number three" man in the MRND hierarchy also managed to put an end to the raging competition for control of the movement between Ngirumpatse and Nzirorera.

This institutionalization of the MRND youth wing clearly indicated Karemera's willingness to seize control of an entity shrouded in ambivalence toward him, since its members had played such a decisive role in his losing his place among the top leadership during the MRND party congress of April 1992. But gaining control also had other benefits, because the institutionalization could also be viewed as a whitewashing operation performed by a former loser now posing as the new "godfather" of the youth movement.

Indeed, this was the objective of institutionalization: improve the performance of these militiamen, and legalize the crimes that had established the reputation and swelled the pride of these "true patriots opposing this war and supporting the national army": "This time they adopted that program of civil self-defense, which at the same time institutionalized, legalized, absolved in some ways those who had undertaken slaughtering, massacring."[31] This was also an opportunity for Karemera to address practical matters as a warlord in his native prefecture of Kibuye. This prefecture had already experienced huge massacres because of the large numbers of Tutsi living there, an easy target for the very aggressive campaign against them led by the prefect, Clément Kayishema. By late May the hills of Bisesero had become a gathering point for the targeted civilian Tutsi population, now trapped: all paths of escape had been sealed, whether to the north toward Gisenyi, or to the west toward Lake Kivu, or to the south to Cyangugu. The straggling survivors were determined to defend themselves to the very end with whatever weapons they could cobble together from their surroundings: arrows, bows, spears, or stones. This heroic resistance, which kept at bay the combined forces of local police and militiamen drawn from the entire prefecture and even neighboring ones, provoked a hysterical response from the government. Crushing it rose to the proportions of a national campaign (*see annex 119*).

The government cabinet meeting of 10 June took note of the alarming situation but made no recommendation. The subject again appeared on the agenda for the 17 June cabinet meeting, with clear intimations of urgency. To justify the expenditures of military and civilian resources that would be brought to bear, the government offered pseudohistorical justifications ("these are all just former feudal warriors") and compelling military objectives (the military threat to Gisenyi).

As every shred of documentation demonstrates, it was indeed the minister of the interior, Karemera, who oversaw what he euphemistically characterized as a "vigorous intervention" with support from the prefect and the gendarmerie camp commander. On 20 June, in the absence of the minister of defense and in the name of the government, he ordered Lt. Col. Anatole Nsengiyumva, operational sector commander for Gisenyi, to send auxiliary support to gendarmerie units from Kibuye to help them rout the survivors. He set a timetable of three days for completion of the "mopping-up operation." He instructed the prefect accordingly and demanded that he provide a follow-up report on the situation (*see annex 119*).

The offensive that raged across the Bisesero hills offers a dramatic illustration of the scale of efforts deployed to exterminate the Tutsi population, ranging from coordination at the highest level to joint intervention by the operational sector army commander assisted by contingents from the gendarmerie, the communal police, and militiamen specifically recruited for the task. Note, however, that for all its efforts, this broad coalition had yet to finish the job by the time troops from the French-led Operation Turquoise arrived on 22 June.

But as also betrayed by remarks from Minister Karemera, war was simply a tool in service to politics. The Bisesero operation was an absolute imperative for the viability of the two interlaced objectives he had committed himself to with Joseph Nzirorera: first, the "rational" relaunching of the massacres and the war in order to expand the margins for negotiation, and second, additional time to complete the constitutional transition that he himself had helped to plan back on 7 and 8 April.[32]

The Anointing of Joseph Nzirorera

By the time he took office as minister of the interior, Karemera had but six weeks to prepare for the expiration of the interim period—a fleeting six weeks to ensure that elections would propel Nzirorera to the head

War and the Fight for Supremacy

of the National Assembly, in position to succeed Sindikubwabo, whose interim presidency was limited to three months. Given the wartime context, this was no easy task, and Karemera had to navigate the obligatory stages at a rapid clip. The decisions taken when the five political parties participating in government met in Gisenyi on 6 and 7 June 1994 and confirmed by the cabinet meeting of 7 June anticipated the implementation of the TNA on the basis of the Arusha Peace Accords; the replacement of the late president of the republic would follow, within the same framework, along with assembling and swearing in a transitional government (*see annex 120*).[33]

By this date, given Karemera's willingness to ensure Nzirorera's rise to power, the political circumstances dictated a radically different interpretation of the legal framework, up to and including its manipulation. The situation was the exact opposite of what had been obtained back on 7 April: in order to satisfy the international community, which no longer looked to the Interim Government, it became necessary to anoint Nzirorera as the new president of a "legitimate" TNA, that is, one in line with the Arusha Peace Accords, while at the same time preserving all the prerogatives that the 1991 Constitution conferred upon the president of the CND: most importantly, succession to the presidency of the republic if ever there was a vacancy.[34]

In this instance, the TNA formula weighed out over the CND to deal with the matter of the CND vice president, who then received a proposal to take over as interim secretary-general of the MRND (promoted to the presidency of the TNA). In line with the legal texts, it was also necessary to replace the former members of the CND with representatives drawn from the current MRND roster. Among the new deputies whom the MRND put forward to participate in the TNA were figures heavily implicated in the massacres, including Laurent Semanza (Kigali-rural), Adalbert Muhutu (Butare), and Pierre-Célestin Rwagafilita (Kibungo). And then, invoking the Arusha Peace Accords, the door of the TNA was opened to the new parties of Hutu Power.

All that remained was to settle how each would be represented and to resolve the matter of the CDR, whose participation in the TNA had been denied in March and April 1994. Thus, among the changes introduced in distributing the seats, compared to the list drawn up just before the war started, were two newcomers: the Union sociale des démocrates chrétiens (UNISODEC, Social Union of Christian Democrats) and the Parti démocrate rwandais (Pader, Rwandan Democratic Party). Subtle negotiations influenced the distribution of the seats, with due respect for the relative strength of the parties and how seats would be apportioned between the former mouvance présidentielle (the MRND, the CDR, and the trail of satellite parties created by the MRND to expand its influence) and the parties of the former opposition.

It ended up with four blocks, composed of forty-four, fourteen, six, and six deputies.[35] The four "major" parties—MRND, MDR, PSD, and PL—held on to their eleven seats each, with the RPF's share being reapportioned among the other parties. The thirteen remaining parties were weighted appropriately: CDR, five; PDC, four; Peco and PDI, three; RTD, Pader, and Parti démocrate, two each; MFBP, PRD, Unisodec, UDPR, Parerwa, and PPJR–Rama Rwanda, one each.

The balance of power between the former mouvance présidentielle and the parties of the former opposition, reduced to their only surviving pro-MRND contingent, thus evolved significantly. In the end, thirty-one seats were attributed to the former (the MRND and the allied parties; see box 4), with forty going to the latter (FDC and independent parties). In relation to the first attempt to implement the TNA back in January 1994, the block of parties derived from the mouvance présidentielle thus grew from seventeen to thirty-one seats, claiming 44 percent of the TNA.[36] And to fully ensure that this assembly would conform to the expectations of its promoters, as Karemera has written, it was the prime minister and the minister of the interior who made the final choice of candidates.

Organizing elections was a long and complex process. It required coordination with the refugee camps in Tanzania and arranging transportation for the selected deputies to Gisenyi. To validate such high-level decisions, the necessary quorum was raised: at least fifty-three deputies had to be in attendance.

Brought together in Gisenyi on 4 July at the former MRND Palace, right next to the Palm Beach Hotel—after the preliminary announcements—the fifty-four deputies were actually present and, according to the minutes, took the oath of office administered by Charles Nkurunziza, the government's secretary-general, who had been appointed president of the Court of Cassation, the court of last resort, and ipso facto of the Constitutional Court (replacing Joseph Kavaruganda, killed on 7 April). Even if the final results seemed preordained, three deputies put forward their candidacies for the presidency: Joseph Nzirorera (MRND), Stanislas Mbonampeka (PL), and François Ndungutse (PSD). But in recognition of the need for a firm demonstration of unity among allies of the former mouvance présidentielle and parties of the former opposition, agreement was finally reached on the lone candidacy of Joseph Nzirorera, who was elected by a vote of forty-three of the fifty-four deputies. The two vice presidents came from the PSD and RTD, respectively, with the deputy secretary provided by the CDR (see annex 120).

At the conclusion of the voting—which conferred complete hegemony to the MRND/CDR block—and contrary to the decisions of the parties and the government, the assembly did not proceed with the "election of a successor to the deceased president," nor, as a result, with installing a new government. On this date, in fact, Nzirorera was obliged to reevaluate his personal strategy in light of how the situation had evolved.

The initial concern centered on the desperate military situation enveloping the FAR since its last, failed counteroffensive of 6 June. The option of a final line of defense along the Zaire-Nile crest and adjacent forests was no longer possible: demoralized troops fled toward the border with Zaire, unwilling to fight on.

Additionally, after lengthy negotiations, the mandate for Operation Turquoise (*see box 18*) had been quite narrowly circumscribed. French humanitarian intervention had finally drawn a sobering response from RPF officials after a series of direct contacts with French authorities: French ambassador Jean-Michel Marlaud, who had returned to Kigali on 19 June to "explain the objectives" of the intervention to members of the RPF and, importantly, on 22 June in Paris on the very eve of the official launching of Operation Turquoise; and the minister of foreign affairs, Alain Juppé, received a vigorously negotiated visit from Jacques Bihozagara, who was the spokesperson for the RPF in Europe at that time. Inversely, the meager political results achieved by Stanislas Mbonampeka on a mission for the Interim Government, when he traveled to Brussels on 22 June, and by the minister of planning, Augustin Ngirabatware, during his exchanges at the French Ministry of Foreign Affairs with Ambassador Marlaud (*see annex 121*) left no doubt as to the slightest possibility of saving any Rwandan regime with links to the former mouvance présidentielle.

The Interim Government authorities were perfectly aware of just how sensitive it was for foreign diplomats even to keep up the appearance of maintaining contact with them. The delicacy of the matter followed them into exile. Indeed, as implied by the approach adopted following its retreat to Zaire on 17 July, the Interim Government sought to boost international credibility for its political-military regime with the presence of new figures, "unsoiled," as Minister Pauline Nyiramasuhuko put it. Aside from ethical considerations, the likelihood of judicial inquiry seemed unavoidable after the UN Security Council voted Resolution 925 on 8 June, taking note of acts of genocide, followed by condemnations of "crimes against humanity" in Rwanda from the OAU on 12 June, and especially after René Degni-Ségui filed a report on the situation of human rights in Rwanda with the UN Human Rights Commission on 28 June.[37] Finally, on 1 July, taking note of the information already assembled, the UN Security Council dispatched "as a matter of urgency, an impartial commission of experts," that is, a commission of inquiry into acts of genocide in Rwanda. This was but the penultimate phase of a procedure intended to embark upon "identifying those responsible for acts of genocide committed in Rwanda."[38]

Nzirorera continued to insist upon the inevitability of holding negotiations. It was important for him to formally establish his legitimacy in representing the refugees and the "resistance." However, he abstained from going so far as to cloak himself with the title of president of the republic, which would have appeared a bit outrageous given the military debacle suffered by his camp, and especially since Faustin Twagiramungu, on behalf of the RPF, had embarked upon formally initiating contacts to unveil a new government of national unity (6 July), not to mention that several high-level FAR officers had officially broken ranks with the interim authorities (see annex 122). This hope of retaining some level of representation in the future political dispensation was unyielding, though without pretense, as shown by the agenda item on that very issue for the government cabinet meeting of 11 July.

On the basis of his investiture in the presidency of this TNA, Nzirorera became the supervisor for the Northern Zone of the refugee population in Zaire by cabinet decision of the government in exile on 27 July, while Théodore Sindikubwabo and Jean Kambanda held similar attributions for the Southern Zone.[39] Members of this phantom TNA supposedly then met on several occasions in the refugee camps around Goma without taking any real action. Each zone remained de facto subject to the authority of local chiefs. The authorities and the population in exile in Goma took to addressing Nzirorera with the honorific "Mr. President," even though doing so was an utterly inconsequential gesture.

To conclude the tale of this obstinate quest for power, recall that relations between the authorities from the north (settled in Goma) and from the south (settled in Bukavu) were particularly tense, giving rise to violent clashes and retribution. The leaders of Bukavu, like President Sindikubwabo and the prime minister, hesitated in journeying to Goma, genuinely fearing for their lives. The circumstances of Sindikubwabo's demise, which transpired during this period, still provoke debate. His health had deteriorated even before his flight into exile, which very likely limited efforts to care for him, perhaps lending credence to reports of his death by natural causes. But no information is available about the place and circumstances of his demise nor of what ever became of his corpse. Yet at the time he was being assisted by a lieutenant, serving as his aide-de-camp, and he still retained a detail of armed military escorts. It is difficult to accept that not one among them has ever surfaced to provide such information. The rumor of an assassination ordered by Nzirorera was often bandied about.

The forced alliances from the month of April wound up in bitter divisions, making managing the defeat just as difficult as fighting the war itself. The RPF was taking control of a country that was devastated and depopulated: aside from the hundreds of thousands of victims of genocide and war, some three million refugees were now settled in camps all along the borders under the authority of those very same Interim Government officials. Rwanda and the subregion were becoming centers with the highest concentration of refugees on the planet, left in the charge of an international community that had no choice but to intervene.

Candidates for the Succession, Rising and Falling

With this backdrop in mind, it may be interesting now to return briefly to the interwoven trajectories of a few of the principal protagonists. We shall limit ourselves here to Matthieu Ngirumpatse, Édouard Karemera, and Joseph Nzirorera, the three top MRND leaders who gathered together in Théoneste Bagosora's office on the morning of 7 April.

By the start of the 1990 war, all three were senior civil servants, rising fairly rapidly through the ranks. They all found themselves strategically poised to anticipate a national destiny. Ngirumpatse, a product of the first generation of postindependence *évolués* (those who received some degree of higher education under the colonial system, which then allowed them to occupy posts in the administration), was at a stage in his career that would allow him to flourish politically and capitalize upon his recognized talents, especially in diplomatic affairs. His only drawback was a personal reputation for indecision and ambivalence. Perceived as an intellectual, with great capacity for analysis and a refined sensitivity in human relations, he could seduce the broader public and charm intellectual circles, especially those from the southern prefectures, known to be somewhat critical and rebellious toward the central power. However, especially in the coarser circles of the northern elites, dominated by soldiers and businessmen, he was perceived as rather delicate and fragile. His temperament, like his conjugal embarrassments, was exploited to disparage his capacity to assert himself and to lead. But one can also appreciate how his position of structural weakness, vis-à-vis the Second Republic northern power brokers, demanded a certain prudence and tactical refinements that were not quite as necessary for his rivals, who had more abundant political resources and legitimacy.

No doubt, multipartyism and the (relative) democratization in political life that took root in the early 1990s opened up favorable opportunities for him, and he expected the electorate to embrace him if only he could get the party machine behind him. But with war looming and the exacerbation of political tensions, his hopes for a political opening began to fade. Given the regionalist shape of the political landscape, promoting a centrist candidate was already highly ambitious after twenty years of polarization in wealth and power benefiting the north. But his claim to be the "dove" fending off the "hawks" (in his view, a more appropriate characterization than "moderate" and "extremist") over time became increasingly untenable given the constraints of wartime, as he found himself hemmed in by the practical politics of the party he was formally leading but which in actuality undermined his position.

The final test of his leadership, on the morning of 7 April, confirmed all the warnings about his capacity to rise to the challenge in situations of major crisis. He fully lived up to his reputation: weak and hesitant, he dared not claim his legitimate right to the succession, went along with getting rid of the "troublesome elements," and thus sacrificed the democratic wing of the MRND. Just as his rivals had anticipated, the timorous intellectual would not risk pushing his personal ambition to the commanding heights of a national destiny. Given the exceptional circumstances prevailing on 6 April, he could have proposed a "liberal" political solution, quite in line with the values he claimed to champion, and hold himself out as a bulwark of peace and democracy to defend the Arusha Peace Accords and reverse the spiral into war. Allies would not have failed him, but he never even bothered to seek them out.

While the tragedy was under way, he embraced his duties as MRND party president to safeguard its seeming prerogatives, however illusory, and, as much as possible, sought to protect and enhance his respectability with diplomatic missions abroad, all the while defending the official positions of the Interim Government. Even this calculation ultimately proved to be of little value. Ngirumpatse never ceased to throw a veil of secrecy around the "interim authorities," masking their increasingly murderous exploits, but in so doing he also sought to reaffirm his ascendancy, pretending he was just as steadfast. Throughout the period of the genocide, despite the volume of materials that have surfaced, there is not a single text or statement in which he parts company with the official line or condemns the activities of the militias. And yet he was their chief. With no political backbone, he ended up losing everything; even afterward, in the refugee camps, the respect that usually attaches to the head of a party only outlasted the final defeat by a few months.

In this regard, at least, Karemera prevailed by dint of his boundless determination. He too had to endure the affronts and humiliations from the presidential clan for having exposed his ambition, but at least his dealings with Habyarimana remained workable, though cold. Karemera understood that he had to adapt himself to the intricate rules of the game and a complex network of power relations extending far beyond the person of the president and his family. When the president sought him out to manage the restructuring of a "renovated" MRND, he played his best cards and accomplished this difficult task with skill and aplomb, capitalizing on his numerous contacts and eliciting a mixture of fear and admiration from his adversaries. Now viewed as a serious, long-term contender, he opted to seek his future in the MRND and, like Ngirumpatse, girded himself for more extensive political reshufflings, determined to reserve a greater stake for natives of the south. Even if he may have suspected that the founding president of the party would somehow prevent him from maximizing his investment, he certainly did not expect Habyarimana to push him aside so abruptly in favor of Ngirumpatse. The reward he received in his new legal career showed, however, that he was perceived as a serious politician, and then the rebound that he orchestrated during the 1993 party congress placed him in the upper reaches of the hierarchy but not quite on the front line.

After the president's sudden demise, Ngirumpatse's shrinking stature left the field open to any solid candidate who could embody the founding values of the republic and the aspirations of the south to fend off the heir apparent, Nzirorera. The strategy of backing away, adopted in unison by all three MRND leaders that night of 6–7 April, served him much more effectively than it did Ngirumpatse. Perhaps reflecting his temperament as much as it did his particular interests, the latter championed the massacres as a necessary, and justified, political imperative. For Ngirumpatse, it mattered little that they would leave him "soiled." Like Nzirorera, he spent with abandon, as long as the object was to expand his dominion in the MRND Executive Bureau. He deemed it necessary to not allow leadership to simply default to the northerners, and his capacity to rally support from officers and political figures from the south was much appreciated.

When Ngirumpatse officially became part of the ministerial cabinet in May, he took control of operational matters at a particularly crucial moment and positioned himself as a hero of "national" resistance to the enemy. Even if it was impossible for him to turn the situation around or to rebound effectively, by the time of the flight into exile, his record was not insubstantial in the eyes of the extremists, and he had garnered respect and allegiance from key figures among the refugees.

Up until the very end, including exile, Édouard Karemera had no doubts about the cause he championed, and he was not inclined to question the soundness or legitimacy of the means chosen to defend it. On the contrary, he attributed shortcomings to inadequate populist mobilization, which, in his view, could have compensated for the army's obvious handicaps. His main regret seems to hark back to the initial series of choices—even though he was among the ringleaders—in cobbling together a government that was weak and simply not up to the task of imposing the kind of discipline and determination that could measure up to those of the hated adversary.

Joseph Nzirorera held a privileged position within this broad tableau, which, over the course of his long career as a prodigious son of the "father of the nation," allowed him to enjoy all the perks of power without reserve. He did not have to maneuver or seduce; he had but to demonstrate that he was worthy of the hopes placed in him and defend the seat already reserved for him from those seeking to grab it. The political crisis brought on by the rising tides of democratic reform and multipartyism forced him to withdraw briefly from the political stage and into defense of the increasingly weakened status quo ante. He adopted the strategy of heir apparent, duty-bound to protect a legacy for its rightful beneficiaries and, above all, for its lone intended legatee. In this regard, the main challenge facing him was not getting the succession under way but rather forestalling and blocking competitors who, given the right moment and through artful maneuvers, could force him to "auction" a share of the bounty.

The way that he, along with the president's in-laws, managed to survive Habyarimana's demise bears the markings of an epic storyline. Within a fortnight, the terrain was swept clean for the anointed successor, and the continuity of the system survived intact. By handing the country over to a straw-man president surrounded by a team of neophytes whose veteran MRND ministers remained entirely devoted to him, Nzirorera took no risks and held on to two major assets that would serve him down the road: those very same "interim" authorities would be blamed for having eliminated the legitimate claimants to power; and he would conserve the power to set the time of his own rise to power. Even though he had been a remarkable tactician, this particular strategy was doomed. The adversary was immune to the pressures of civilian massacres, and the killings ended up precipitating a collapse with no redeeming value. Afterward, this spoiled child of the regime had to thoroughly exhaust himself to save whatever he could of the birthright so coveted by the "enemy." When all hopes for partition were spent, Nzirorera relaunched the scorched-earth campaign. He remained unflinching in the face of its horrendous costs in human life, and when that disastrous crusade tapered off in spite of it all, a pathetic ceremony to have himself anointed president of the National Assembly was still the order of the day, remaining ever faithful to the nickname that lionized him: "Total."

With each step in this tragic story, we find all three politicians animated by the same cynicism, the same profound indifference to the wanton killing of civilians and genocide, which for them was but one political card among others that could be played to advance their personal ambitions. With the tragedy consummated, while in exile they made hostages of the refugee population to afford themselves new opportunities for confrontation, described as major strategic stakes (*see annex 123*), until they were finally pushed aside, having learned nothing through it all: "I remain convinced that the massacres were an accident and an unfortunate experience that should not be repeated."[40]

The fourth principal figure, Col. Théoneste Bagosora, was a bit too quick to believe that he would finally succeed Habyarimana. It was an ambition that he had nursed along since the early 1980s, when the grand lineages of northern soldiers were locked in fratricidal struggle, and a weakened Juvénal Habyarimana turned to his extended family and his home turf for support. Calling upon this legitimacy of proximity and the deference accorded military men in wartime, Bagosora managed to impose himself as the ringmaster for the first few days but could only garner support from the president's inner circle and those his brutality could terrorize into submission. Isolated and fearful of one day having to account for ordering the elimination of the legitimate authorities, he opened a second front, against the internal enemy, for which he conferred responsibility to "his" government. The assassinations and massacres linked to avenging the "father of the nation" and waging the war for the succession were then ensconced in a deliberately aggressive genocidal project. Bagosora's own crimes were diminished and washed away by greater horrors committed by those whom he, along with the MRND leaders, put in power, while the political and military situation evolved and the more serious contenders for the succession, waiting on the sidelines, positioned themselves. In fact, incapable of sorting out who should assume power, the contenders gave themselves a ninety-day constitutional moratorium, which then absolved them of blame for the atrocities they had ordered, or so they believed. A genocide to referee the race for power!

Fifteen years later, all four found themselves together again in the Arusha UN Detention Center, preparing once again for a final sorting out by the judges of the ICTR Trial Chambers. Bagosora was arrested by the ICTR on 6 March 1996 in Cameroun and then transferred on 23 July 1997 to Arusha, where he faced charges of genocide, conspiracy to commit genocide, complicity in genocide, direct and public incitement to genocide, crimes against humanity, and serious violations of the Geneva Conventions. Bagosora was indicted along with the former military commander for Gisenyi sector, Lt. Col. Anatole Nsengiyumva; former commander of the Kigali paracommando battalion, Maj. Aloys Ntabakuze; and the former head of military operations for the army general staff, Brig. Gen. Gratien Kabiligi. After a false start on 2 April 2002, along with several postponements and reassignment to a Trial Chamber presided over by the Norwegian judge Erik Møse, the trial dubbed "Military I" truly got off the ground on 16 June 2003 and continued through 19 December 2008, with the pronouncement of a final judgment acquitting Kabiligi and convicting the three other codefendants to life imprisonment. The judgment was subsequently appealed.[41]

Karemera, Ngirumpatse, and Nzirorera were all arrested on 5 June 1998 in Togo, Benin, and Mali, respectively, and subsequently transferred to the tribunal in Arusha. After numerous procedural delays, a joint trial that also included another political figure was discontinued by the Appeals Chamber in October 2004 after a year of testimony. A retrial started on 19 September 2005. They were accused of conspiracy to commit genocide, direct and public incitement to genocide, genocide, complicity in genocide, rape, extermination, and serious violations of the Geneva Conventions, with the prosecutor arguing that these crimes were "in furtherance of a joint criminal enterprise" or the "natural and foreseeable consequences" thereof. The latter refers to the "expanded form" of a joint criminal enterprise intended to destroy the Tutsi population of Rwanda, which "came into existence before January 1994 and continued until at least July 1994" (the amended indictment against the MRND leaders). According to the indictment, its instruments were the structures of the MRND, its Interahamwe militia, the territorial administration, and its various resources, including the mass media. Temporarily suspended in August 2008 when one of the defendants fell gravely ill, at the time it was the first trial expected to continue beyond 2009, the deadline proposed for completion of the tribunal's mandate.[42]

With these two leading cases fully under way or inching toward finality, some fifteen years after the war ended, the International Criminal Tribunal for Rwanda can be expected to complete the essential tasks identified by successive prosecutors to satisfy a United Nations Security Council "convinced that in the particular circumstances of Rwanda, the prosecution of persons responsible for serious violations of international humanitarian law would enable this aim [to put an end to such crimes] to be achieved and would contribute to the process of national reconciliation and to the restoration and maintenance of peace."[43] We can now attempt a preliminary overview of the facts developed on the trial records, and this present study can at least begin to appreciate what justice has been able to establish, "beyond a reasonable doubt," concerning the unfolding of events and the acts, omissions, and dispositions of those involved.

13

Truth, Justice, and the Politics of Memory

The climate surrounding current debates about the role and achievements of international justice in the postconflict period defines its breadth and limitations. Attempts to reinterpret the facts of the genocide—with a view to dismissing the horror as a mere "accident" or an "unfortunate experience"—are not unheard of, although the genocide of hundreds of thousands of Tutsi civilians is beyond question.[1] To this day, efforts to deny the evidence have given a new life to the debate. Assertions of denialism attract increasingly wider audiences and feed into competing propaganda campaigns that continue to do battle, particularly concerning matters of ethnicity. The macabre accounting exercise designed to take an inventory of how many victims each camp has suffered, as if to keep a scorecard of the crimes committed by each side, shows that the important work of international justice since 1994 has done little to cushion the impact of propaganda and the passions it fuels.

With one party denying genocide and the other demonizing the genocidal regime and the previous two Hutu-dominated republics, confrontation has moved to an ideological terrain dominated by ethnicity. It has seemed as though the plethora of investigations undertaken since 1994 by international organizations, national commissions, nongovernmental organizations, foreign courts, international ad hoc tribunals, not to mention the hundreds of books and films and testimonies have counted for nothing. Nevertheless, the debate goes on irrespective of the reams of findings laboriously compiled over more than fifteen years. Is the evidence just not credible or acceptable, or has it been assumed to be beyond the reach and ken of the so-called experts amid these instrumentalized polemics?

A Project for Truth,
Exemplary but Selective

There are a number of explanations, but here we will limit ourselves to those that can be linked to the international judicial body specially mandated to accomplish this mission. We'll begin with a few broad strokes to recall the international framework in which this judicial body was created.

By the end of 1994, the global shock and distress engendered by the events in Rwanda had provoked close scrutiny from various governments and international agencies, some unprecedented in scope and modalities. Numerous commissions of inquiry were assembled to shed light on the Rwandan tragedy and to formulate recommendations in matters of "assistance, reconstruction, and development" or "peace, justice, and reconciliation." Starting in 1995 and up until 2000, these commissions mobilized hundreds of specialists and accumulated thousands of pages of reports and transcriptions of testimony that today form a huge documentary corpus.

However, guided by the institutional demands of their sponsors, the investigations mainly focused on the lapses and limitations of policies and programs and on the global failure of external intervention. They also avoided dealing with aspects of the crisis that were most controversial. Nor did they consider the strategies of international actors that refused to get involved.[2] Generally speaking, these institutions were more interested in justifying the international community's nonintervention, as well as their own, in the face of the Rwandan tragedy than in exposing the consequences of this war and the forces that propelled it and brought it to a conclusion.

At the same time, an impressive outpouring of works of all sorts (books, films, etc.), for the most part scholarly, others better seen as works of fiction, addressed the entire gamut of the genocidal phenomenon, its causes, its unfolding, its protagonists, and its victims, survivors, and horrors. Analytical and commemorative works rose to the level of this exceptional crime, commensurate with the denials and the international indifference that it provoked, although, more often than not, with little or no familiarity with the country prior to the genocide.

This "acknowledgment" of sorts has profoundly influenced how the Rwandan crisis is viewed. It also lays bare the weaknesses already noted in works produced by international actors because of the numerous questions that remain unanswered concerning the responses and the responsibilities of domestic actors in relation to the reprise and conduct of the war. Overall, large segments of the history of this war have yet to be explicated; extant reports and other materials are of little help in filling the remaining gaps, ranging from the military objectives of the protagonists to the underlying motives behind the attacks against civilians, the political assassinations, and the downing of the presidential plane on 6 April. In the absence of satisfying responses, these questions continue to this day to feed rumors and suspicions, encouraging the denunciations and self-justifying fevers of rival camps.

It fell to the United Nations International Criminal Tribunal for Rwanda to build upon this preliminary work and then proceed with more rigorous investigations to gather evidence, identify sources and resources (especially in matters of expertise), establish contacts with institutional partners, and concretely define the contours and priorities of its prosecutorial agenda. External sources were routinely consulted during the early, institution-building stage for the ICTR, before it became the primary locus for amassing, archiving, and exploiting the materials indispensable for its mission.

The Pitfalls of International Justice

Despite having collected an impressive volume of materials, all in the name of truth and justice, the ICTR has managed neither to satisfy the parties nor to quell Rwandan passions. This egregious failing feeds the various misgivings and criticisms directed against the ICTR. These are in part rooted in structural constraints, like the geographic isolation of Arusha, along with its attendant lack of access to media circuits, but they also derive from a lack of familiarity with documentary resources, their existence, and their accessibility. Then there are weaknesses inherent in the institution itself, principally its meager output, as evidenced by the number of trial judgments rendered. By July 2009 there were indictments against ninety accused, thirteen of whom remained at large. Seventy-three accused were tried or were on trial. (By January 2014, there were ninety-two indictments, nine accused still at large, and seventy-five trials.)

With regard to our central concern—analyzing and appreciating the sequence of events and the actors' responses—the quality of the assessments is uneven, and so are the results, depending on the particular emphasis and variation in the prosecution strategy.

Two observations can be made at this point. The first has to do with the strategic choices confronting the ICTR during the first fifteen years of its existence to establish its credibility and its effectiveness. Its less-than-ideal performance at first provoked bitter denunciations from Kigali and from donors and supporters, and for good reasons: it made few arrests; held few, if any, trials; and hardly rendered any final judgments.[3] However, the investigations and the research undertaken during this phase, accompanied by exceptional productivity, provided hopeful signs. After the ICTR began working closely with NGOs and the academic community, the debates and confrontations launched in this context fostered a better appreciation of the stakes involved and set priorities and procedures, thus facilitating preliminary findings. The preliminary result was a rich and diversified collection of documents. This period also allowed the tribunal to recruit a substantial number of legal interns and judicial aides, as well as staff assistants reasonably familiar with the complexity of the Rwandan situation.

At a later stage, during the early 2000s, with the appointment of Prosecutor Carla Del Ponte, the members of the Security Council imposed strict managerial parameters. Finally equipped with a system for archiving and exploiting the materials that had been collected, the principal members of the Office of the Prosecutor were firmly encouraged to accelerate the pace of the trials and to prioritize efficiency and output. The institution did not adapt well to this acceleration: expanding the numbers of indictments and arrests generated blunders or errors of varying gravity that affected procedure, scheduling, the quality of the evidence, and the coherence of the tribunal's objectives. A significant number of case files were irremediably blocked, weakened, or compromised: rushed investigations, poorly drafted indictments, standardized witness accounts, ineptitude in exploiting already available evidence, and gross errors in documentation were accompanied by constantly rotating appointments of chiefs of prosecutions, senior prosecution counsel, and investigators. The result was a high level of frustration, particularly deeply felt by those who expected the tribunal to first organize several distinctive trials and then direct its resources and discretion toward case files where the demands for truth telling and justice were most urgent.

The second observation concerns the determination of the new Rwandan authorities, almost to the point of obsession, to carefully monitor investigations and to only tolerate initiatives that were consonant with their expectations and political objectives. This was met by a parallel set of concerns from milieus close to the accused, especially the high-profile figures. Consequently, access to witnesses, both for the prosecution and for the defense, was constantly negotiated, monitored, and directed from afar by Rwandan administrative or political authorities from either the former or the current regime. In either case, bearing in mind the risks involved, only those witnesses who were identified, advised, and supported by groups or third parties dared involve themselves in the trials. In the same way that officials from the Habyarimana regime made themselves available to the defense, survivors' organizations or repentant prisoners volunteered to assist the prosecution, functioning like subcontractors providing witnesses duly prepared to testify as expected. However, the ICTR was established to give voice to witnesses and victims, free from the organized terror that would otherwise condemn them to silence.[4]

These two observations cannot be disassociated, because the reverberations from internal Rwandan dynamics on this international jurisdiction were deep and lasting.

The Choice of Targets of Investigations

One of the central questions in this regard is the collaboration between Rwandan authorities and the ICTR. The Kagame regime used its prerogatives as an indispensable party to weigh upon, if not substantially determine, policy decisions from the Office of the Prosecutor. This situation has its source in the conditions and the context in which the tribunal was created.

The ICTR was premised on an ambiguity. The new Rwandan authorities, rising to power in the aftermath of war in July 1994, wanted a victors' tribunal along the lines of Nuremberg that would pronounce expeditious judgments against the "masterminds" of the genocide. They did not want a ponderous institution that would deliberate over the course of ten or fifteen years in accordance with its own conception of justice and reconstruction.

In this regard, they were bitterly disappointed during the mandate of South African prosecutor Richard Goldstone, in office from late 1994 through 30 September 1996: nothing he did came anywhere near the Rwandan authorities' expectations. The tribunal set itself up for the long run, with personnel trying to adjust to a new and difficult environment, conducting investigations yet hardly arresting anyone: of fourteen suspects, none were sentenced. What's more, instead of targeting major figures, the first series of arrests essentially targeted regional or local figures, like Clément Kayishema, former prefect of Kibuye; Alfred Musema, ex–tea factory director; Joseph Kanyabashi, the burgomaster of Ngoma-Butare, the second largest city in the country; and midlevel managers like burgomasters Jean-Paul Akayezu from Gitarama prefecture and Élie Ndayambaje in Butare. Even if observers could appreciate the pedagogic and symbolic value of starting the trial process with an "ordinary" suspect like Jean-Paul Akayezu, a burgomaster, it is clear that there were much higher expectations for international justice. As in the case of the tribunal for the former Yugoslavia in The Hague, the mandate of the ICTR was to aim for the commanding heights, that is, for those responsible for the gravest crimes committed over the course of the war. Only the arrest of Georges Rutaganda, the vice president of the Interahamwe youth wing, met that expectation.

In 1996 Prosecutor Goldstone rectified the approach by arresting several high-level suspects in Cameroun: Ferdinand Nahimana and Jean-Bosco

Barayagwiza, presumably the two persons most responsible for RTLM's programming; Col. Théoneste Bagosora, chief of staff in the Ministry of Defense; and Lt. Col. Anatole Nsengiyumva, former chief of military intelligence and operational sector commander for Gisenyi. But Goldstone did not have time to organize their transfers to the prison in Arusha. It was the Canadian prosecutor, Louise Arbour (in office from 1 October 1996 through 15 September 1999), who took charge and appointed a new deputy prosecutor, Bernard Muna, a Camerounian magistrate, duly mandated to implement a prosecution strategy that prioritized political leaders, ministers of the Interim Government, military officers, and media figures.

Thus began a long period marked by cycles of hyperactivity in arrests, which then led to a piling up of the docket before the Trial Chambers. These waves of arrests elevated the figures that the prosecutor's office was required to submit for year-end annual reports, quieting critics, particularly the Rwandans, who were all too ready to lambaste the top-heavy ICTR for its incapacity to get trials under way, much less conclude them.[5] Only a single trial had begun in July 1997, when Louise Arbour authorized Operation NAKI (Nairobi-Kigali), which led to the arrests of nine suspects in Kenya, including the former prime minister of the Interim Government, Jean Kambanda; the former minister of family and women's affairs, Pauline Nyiramasuhuko, the first woman ever accused of genocide and crimes against humanity by an international court; her son, the militiaman Shalom Ntahobari; Gen. Gratien Kabiligi; former journalist Hassan Ngeze; former Butare prefect Sylvain Nsabimana; and an Italian-Belgian national, Georges Ruggiu, former RTLM commentator. Another similar operation, dubbed KIWEST, was organized in 1998 in West Africa. It targeted the top leaders of the MRND who had taken refuge in Mali, Benin, and Togo.[6] It also led to the arrests of Emmanuel Bagambiki, former prefect of Cyangugu, and Juvénal Kajelijeli, ex-burgomaster of Mukingo in Ruhengeri prefecture. Four former Interim Government ministers were also arrested in 1999, three in Cameroun—Jérôme Bicamumpaka (foreign affairs), Justin Mugenzi (commerce), and Prosper Mugiraneza (civil service)—and one in Kenya—Casimir Bizimungu (health). In all, Arbour managed to make twenty-three arrests, which earned her the approval of Rwandan authorities.[7]

Arbour's global prosecution strategy explicitly responded to the objectives of Rwandan authorities. Prioritizing the notion of criminal conspiracy, that is, conspiracy to commit genocide, in March 1998 she presented a joint indictment inspired by the trials undertaken in Nuremberg. The megatrial that she envisaged targeted twenty-nine accused, with Col. Théoneste Bagosora at the head—characterized as the mastermind of the genocide by the prosecution—

and would prove conspiracy at the national level. The judges rejected her initiative, reasoning that the rights of the accused would be violated, since the prosecutions were at different stages of procedure. Some were already in custody and had appeared before the Trial Chamber, whereas others had not yet been apprehended. The prosecutor nevertheless maintained her approach to joint trials but scaled back the number of accused in each separate case by grouping them either thematically (media, government, military) or geographically (Butare, Cyangugu).

Carla Del Ponte, the Swiss prosecutor who succeeded Arbour and held office from 15 September 1999 through 14 September 2003, initially adopted a similar strategy, but her attempts to accelerate the pace of trials quickly fizzled.[8] She tried to outline an ambitious prosecution strategy, clearly delineating the objectives that the ICTR should attain by 2008, the year set by the United Nations for the end of its mandate. In conformity with Security Council Resolution 1329 of 20 November 2000, "taking note of the position expressed by the International Tribunals that civilian, military and para-military leaders should be tried before them in preference to minor actors," the prosecutor established various lists of targets, prioritized in terms of the gravity of the alleged crimes, and regularly announced numerical objectives for the cases she wished to pursue, going from the 140 projected for 2001 and rising to 250 for 2003. In four years, Carla Del Ponte arrested twenty-nine suspects (out of over two hundred who were being sought), including former government ministers Jean de Dieu Kamuhanda (higher education) and Emmanuel Ndindabahizi (finances); generals Augustin Ndindiliyimana and Augustin Bizimungu, in charge of the general staffs of the gendarmerie and the army, respectively, during the genocide; colonels Tharcisse Renzaho (prefect of Kigali-ville) and Tharcisse Muvunyi (commander of the École des sous-officiers in Butare); Protais Zigiranyirazo, a son-in-law of President Habyarimana; musician Simon Bikindi, considered a propagandist for the regime; and Maj. François-Xavier Nzuwonemeye, who commanded the "Recce" Battalion of the Rwandan Army, stationed in Kigali. However, in terms of completed trial judgments, her achievements were hardly any better than Louise Arbour's: seven at the first instance (six in individual trials and one in a joint trial) for a total of eight accused.

Upon taking office on 15 September 2003, Prosecutor Hassan Bubacar Jallow, a Gambian national, initially clarified that preparing cases for trial would take priority over new indictments. Consequently, with the winding down of investigations in 2009, with a total of twelve arrests over the course of six years and ninety indictments in all (of which twelve were for suspects still at large), he had drastically pruned the lists compiled by Carla Del Ponte, thus limiting the agenda set for the tribunal. The prosecutor nonetheless authorized arrests of several notable figures, like Col. Ephrem Setako, the "right-hand man" of Joseph Nzirorera; the militia chiefs Yussuf Munyakazi and Joseph Serugendo; Interim Government ministers Augustin Ngirabatware (planning) and Callixte Nzabonimana (youth); and Lt. Ildephonse Nizeyimana, one of the principal organizers of the massacres in Butare. All of the others were minor actors. The same could be said for the list of the twelve accused who remain at large, of whom only three can be considered major targets: Augustin Bizimana, minister of defense; Félicien Kabuga, the "financier" of the genocide; and Maj. Protais Mpiranya, commander of the Presidential Guard.

In total, over the course of fifteen years, only sixty persons responsible for the most serious crimes and around thirty suspects of secondary importance have been judged or prosecuted by the international tribunal. This is quite a low number when compared with initial projections of some two to three hundred major perpetrators of the genocide.

Of course, such modest numbers did not satisfy the expectations of the Rwandan authorities. We should recall that toward the end of July 1994, coming out of the war, the RPF had published a provisional list of 220 planners of the genocide and the massacres that included around 100 prefects, sub-prefects, and burgomasters. This first, rather low estimate was then superseded by a listing compiled by the first minister of justice in the transitional government, Alphonse-Marie Nkubito (Hutu, civil society), when he assumed office on 19 July 1994. Nkubito listed over ten thousand foot soldiers, or génocidaires, and two to three thousand national leaders and several dozen cadres in each commune (of the 145 communes). The RPF, for its part, claimed that there were over one hundred thousand criminals, relying on Red Cross International's estimates of the actual number of prisoners being held, while justice of a much more expeditious nature was well under way on the conquered, occupied hillsides of the interior. No sooner had the RPF consolidated its grip over the state institutions and the communes in early 2000 than the number of génocidaires — classed in three categories depending on the gravity of the alleged crime — expanded rapidly, until by 2009 it wound up including almost the entire male Hutu population over fourteen years of age in 1994.

Official listings of the "big génocidaires," in terms of numbers and identity, still affect the country's judicial and political affairs. The first "list of First Category suspects," published in November 1996, contained 1,946 names classified by prefecture and profession. The "national" list, with names of those most actively sought, then numbered 110. According to the Organic Law of 1996, the list of suspects had been compiled by the prosecutor general of the Supreme Court, published in the *Official Gazette*, with plans for periodic republication to reflect updates. The first update was issued on 8 July 1999, and, just as in 1996, the list provoked sharp criticisms for incorporating inaccurate information, listing persons who had died even before the genocide, or listing persons who were not present in the country at the time of the events. Several months later, on 19 January 2000, acknowledging those lapses and errors, the prosecutor general published a revised list of 2,133 names (643 names were withdrawn, and 830 were added). On 11 April 2001 a third list of First Category genocide offenders was issued, this time containing 2,898 names (36 names from the second listing were withdrawn, and 801 names were added).[9]

Since 2003, separate lists of those persons residing abroad who were suspected of having committed genocide in Rwanda in 1994 were circulated to facilitate indictment and extradition. For the most current publication (11 May 2006), ninety-three names were listed, along with another twenty or so for whom confidential arrest warrants had been transmitted to INTERPOL.

Even if many of those names replicate the listings of suspects already under investigation by the ICTR or in other jurisdictions, the underlying objective was broader. As Rwandan prosecutor general Gerald Gahima himself noted in January 1999, appearing on the list of suspects did not automatically mean guilty; nonetheless, the publicity and the very existence of the list stigmatized those whose names were mentioned, with no indication of the origins of the denunciation or the nature of the crime. He also acknowledged that deceased persons, including those who died before the genocide, like President Habyarimana, had been listed so that their property could be seized. Noting the numerous disputes between returning Hutu refugees and Tutsi returnees—the so-called old caseload refugees—linked to the new government, many of whom simply grabbed vacant plots at war's end, the significance of this acknowledgment cannot be overstated. Nonetheless, in light of the numerous preparatory missions undertaken by Rwandan authorities to negotiate repatriation among the diaspora communities—including issues such as the return of abandoned property, the removal of names from lists of suspects, or the threat of adding names of opponents—it was obvious that the listing exercise institutionalized a sort of political extortion directed against members of the Hutu diaspora. It rested upon an expansive definition of crimes linked to the genocide and could concern all manifestations of opposition to the new regime, particularly when "sectarianism," "divisionism," and "genocide ideology" entered the Rwandan penal arsenal. Thus, names of persons who had never been associated with the genocide appeared and disappeared in sync with political "messages" RPF authorities wanted to disseminate via judicial channels. To this end, they did not hesitate to fashion baseless indictments, which were then handed over to the ICTR so that it would pick up the clues and follow through with investigations. A number of examples could be mentioned that reveal the effectiveness of this well-hewn stratagem. One particularly notorious case came to light in August 2007 among those targeting Rwandan expatriates in their host countries, prodded by an international arrest warrant and an extradition request from Rwanda. The accused had already figured as a mastermind of the genocide on that first 1994 list. The charges filed against him and substantiated by numerous depositions and "eyewitness" accounts concerned allegations of acts of genocide committed over the course of April, May, and June 1994, despite the fact that this eminent MRND figure had been evacuated by the Belgian Embassy at the very beginning of the war. It was easy to prove that he had never returned to Rwanda after fleeing in early April.

Finally, upon careful review of the choice of targets, three broad categories emerge: those who, though initially targeted, managed to evade international justice; those who were arrested and prosecuted; and finally, those who, despite their reputedly significant roles in the genocide, have never been disturbed by international justice.

A first group of persons were able to evade international justice even though, at one time or another, well-documented charges had been brought against them. This happened for a variety of reasons: because no individual or group made any effort to have them named and shamed and arrested; because the evidence against them turned out to be lacking; because key witnesses refused to testify; because they managed to "disappear" or achieve anonymity; but especially because they managed to benefit, in one way or another, from family networks—regional or political—that spared no effort to whitewash their antecedents or defend them in the face of denunciations. Yet others, in Rwanda or abroad, managed to negotiate accommodations with the authorities in Kigali, thus managing to acquire the most secure passport for impunity. In this regard there are examples of major figures (politicians, high-ranking army officers, businessmen, and traders) who managed to remain unnoticed, thus ensuring that silence would consign them to obscurity. This was not completely risk-free, as painful reversals were always possible, but the likelihood that justice could catch up with them is increasingly doubtful, and this for two major reasons. On the one hand, the Office of the Prosecutor drastically curbed its ambitions, scaling the three to four hundred potential indictments down to ninety; on the other, the lists and charges generated by Rwandan authorities were not above suspicion, and by 2009 rare were the countries that would seriously envision extraditing suspects to Rwanda. A preliminary observation thus emerges: those who, aware that they were being sought by the ICTR, allowed themselves to be arrested to "get it over with," particularly during the period of Carla Del Ponte's intense judicial activism. Others made a serious miscalculation or were simply unable to do otherwise: the majority of those arrested were, obviously, the most accessible or those who simply had never tried to hide.

The second point concerns the persons who were actually prosecuted. Globally, it cannot be denied that the major protagonists of the genocide have been arrested and judged. We can question the range and disparity in sentencing for those convicted, the reasons for the six acquittals, the reasons why, among persons of similar profile, some were arrested and tried, while others evaded prosecution. But broadly speaking, the indictments targeted a wide array of the major architects of the genocide: highly placed civilian and military leaders, politicians, officers, militiamen, senior civil servants in the territorial administration, senior managers of parastatal enterprises, businessmen, and propagandists. They provide a comprehensive record of how the genocide was conceived and implemented by the Interim Government in the name of the Rwandan state in the days following the downing of the presidential plane on 6 April. They also offer detailed information on how state resources were mobilized, by whom, and where, thus illuminating the evolving dynamics of the carnage and pointing to the diversity of local conditions.

What the Office of the Prosecutor has consistently failed to demonstrate is the alleged existence of a "conspiracy" among the accused—presuming an association or a preexisting plan to commit genocide. This is the central argument at the core of its prosecution strategy, borrowing from the contentions initially put forth by academics and human rights defenders. With the exception of two judgments, confirmed on appeal, the Trial Chambers have uniformly found the prosecution's proof of a conspiracy wanting, regardless of the case.[10] Pleaded in all of the thematic and geographically grouped joint trials, the conspiracy thesis has definitively lost luster as the explanatory keystone, though its pertinence endures. And here lies the principal achievement of the trials underway in Arusha. The conspiracy thesis only appears promising when applied in situations and within temporal parameters that are clearly defined: that is to say, when it helps to explain how on which hill, in what commune, in which prefecture, under what administration, the strategies of various actors coalesced to motivate broad swathes of the population to participate in the massacres. If the theory of the masterminds appears so weak today, it is because the day-to-day genocide was the product of multifarious decisions that cannot be traced back to a single "proponent" or to a timeless project. On the contrary, fieldwork has uncovered an extreme diversity of situations and, beyond a few common features, lays bare the "creativity" of the torturers, regardless of their particular status. The collective results of the paroxysm of violence, fear, and ethnic hatred were shaped by well thought out directives and programs. These activities require mobilization of resources, and coordination by specific individuals, within the framework of a particularized division of labor. This reasoning, which views individuals as conscious protagonists with full awareness of the stakes in this war, applies all the more to "spontaneous" or "private" actions of groups or individuals "pursuing their own interests." It is thanks to the trials and the multitude of investigations undertaken against "lower ranked" suspects in Kibuye, Kigali-rural, Butare, Cyangugu, and Gitarama prefectures that it became possible to carefully craft the indictments and support the allegations against those "larger" figures with the means or the audacity to mask their involvement or to have their dirty "work" done by others.

Third, we should consider those presumed masterminds who were "forgotten" by international justice. Indeed, we would reasonably expect that the Office of the Prosecutor would give priority to indicting members of the Akazu (Agathe Kanziga, the wife of President Habyarimana, and her "clan"), which embodied the heart of Hutu Power. However, aside from Protais Zigiranyirazo, the brother of Agathe Kanziga who was arrested fortuitously in Brussels in June 2001 (see annex 125), the matter of the "unpunished," that is, to quote from Stephen Smith, "those who, by reason of their official role or their influential position on the sidelines, should have had to explain their actions, or their refusal to act, during the genocide—and who have never done so," remains equally pertinent today.[11]

In early 2007 most observers assumed that rejections of Agathe Kanziga's requests for asylum in France, first by the Office français de protection des réfugiés et des apatrides (OFPRA, French Office for the Protection of Refugees and Stateless Persons) and then by the Commission des recours des réfugiés (CRR, Commission for Refugees), would be followed by an ICTR arrest warrant.[12] None ever materialized, generating great surprise, all the more so since the CRR rapporteur had implied that a secret arrest warrant for Agathe Kanziga was among those issued by the ICTR under seal. Clearly, that was as inaccurate then as it is now. Similarly, investigations against Séraphin Rwabukumba, half brother of the former first lady and currently residing in Belgium, were abandoned by both the ICTR and Belgian authorities.

The two situations boil down to the same thing: either the ICTR and the relevant domestic jurisdictions (France and Belgium) lack evidence that can support an indictment, or they have chosen not to prosecute these individuals for reasons that have nothing to do with the law. The first explanation was confirmed on 16 November 2009, when the Appeals Chamber in The Hague acquitted Protais Zigiranyirazo. Lacking solid proof, the prosecution based its case, as it often does, on testimony from false witnesses, supplied in bulk by

Rwandan judicial authorities. The prosecution already had information that the accused was not at the scene of the alleged crimes, but it persisted. An aggressive defense team and vigilance from judges in The Hague allowed the accused to regain his liberty.

The second reason is a political trade-off. For the current Rwandan authorities, it is one thing to demonize the former presidential family and to broker private investigations toward that end and quite another to insist loud and clear on a real trial. Indeed, if that were the case, it would be difficult to avoid authentic contradictory debate on the shooting down of Habyarimana's plane on 6 April, possible international involvement or complicity, and the war crimes and crimes against humanity committed by the RPF in capturing power by force. Having thus succeeded, by blackmail or intimidation, in blocking investigations of its own armed forces, and having obtained from Prosecutor Hassan Bubacar Jallow a definitive privilege of immunity for war crimes and crimes against humanity—a privilege further confirmed by the United Nations Security Council on 4 June 2009—no prosecutor has had the moral standing to bring charges against the widow of President Habyarimana.

The intrigue enveloping these matters feeds suspicion. Fifteen years after the events, that an independent international jurisdiction dedicated to bringing out the truth would allow it to be said that the "true" génocidaires and the big "planners" have not been prosecuted is unacceptable. By tacitly admitting that it is in no position, at the close of its mandate, to demonstrate the pyramid of responsibilities, the ICTR undermines the entire corpus of its work. This approach has serious ramifications, because it nurtures the rumors and conspiracy theories already in wide circulation. Given the toxic climate surrounding anything having to do with the former presidential family and their intimates, it is regrettable that, by its very silence, the ICTR unwittingly sustains the notion of secrets shared among guilty parties and protectors so influential that one dares not even name them.

The apparent powerlessness of international justice to arrest Félicien Kabuga, a man generally described as the "financier of the genocide," denounced since 2001 as "enemy number one"—a distinction he usurped from Agathe Kanziga—is even more troubling, especially since the United States has offered a large bounty to any person contributing to the arrest of a man who, according to the ICTR, resides in Kenya. A businessman reputed to have prepared the genocide and financed RTLM and the Interahamwe, Félicien Kabuga entered into the presidential family through marriage: two of his daughters married the sons of President Habyarimana (*see box 6*). Similarly, only through a combination of incompetence, inertia, and high-level protection did his son-in-law, Augustin Ngirabatware, minister of planning in the Interim

Government, manage to evade international justice—until his arrest in Germany in August 2007 (*see annex 84*).

Despite the on-and-off media attention paid to this famous fugitive, it is still appropriate to raise the question as to why the indictments drawn up against him and his son-in-law seem so threadbare, especially since they concern the two men presumably responsible for financing the genocide.

The Elusiveness of Financial Deals

What occurred in this portion of the investigations against the major figures of the Habyarimana regime sheds light on some of the difficulties encountered by the prosecution. From the very beginnings of the ICTR and again in 2000, significant efforts were devoted to documenting the financial aspects of the war and the genocide.[13] Compelling, "self-evident" (written) proof was expected. Investigators filled containers with barely organized documents concerning budgets and expenses in various government ministries, national accounting, movements of capital, and foreign trade. Finally, investigators and the experts could only obtain fairly meager results, like the demonstration of a war economy or the rise in importations of machetes during the period leading up to the genocide (routinely touted as proof of the "planning" of genocide). These elements in and of themselves do not suffice to establish the guilt of the accused in the eyes of the judges.

In May 2001 the case against Alphonse Higaniro, one of the accused in the first Belgian genocide trial, served as a precedent.[14] It demonstrably showed that sustained investigations made it possible to reveal with considerable precision the nature of large-scale financial exchanges among the holdings of parastatal enterprises—controlled by members of the Akazu or their close associates—and many leaders of political groups linked to the mouvance présidentielle (*see annex 25*).[15] Financial investigations were thus relaunched on a new basis.

Once the operational methods characteristic of the various parastatal entities were laid bare, it was easy to trace back transfers from the enterprises to the holders of bank accounts. From the very outset, reviews of the documentation were overwhelming for a number of these bank account holders who made deposits and transfers without the least effort to hide them. This simply serves to illustrate the pervasive sense of impunity among dignitaries of the regime and the complacency of the banking sector in the early 1990s. We can thus appreciate how the presidential clan and their close associates were able to access financial resources dispensed by the large donor agencies (notably, the World Bank) or the suppliers of petroleum. This review also shed light on how the mouvance présidentielle facilitated transfers to politicians and to new political groupings and allows us to examine the transfers of capital and investments abroad throughout the period of the genocide by dignitaries of the regime via Belgium, France, or Switzerland. Principally, the Banque continentale africaine au Rwanda (BACAR, African Continental Bank in Rwanda) and the Banque de Kigali were involved.

But it was one thing to gain access to banking records when the Rwandan minister of justice personally telephoned bank managers with specific instructions and quite another to transfer this documentation, duly organized, to the ICTR. Soon after a formal request was filed in June 2001, investigations were abruptly interrupted by the directors of financial establishments in Kigali who, after consulting among themselves and with the agreement of their foreign directors, refused to hand over the bank statements of the targeted persons and the copies of the checks accompanying those statements. Once informed of this, Rwandan authorities became divided on the matter, some insisting they "wanted to know" and others somewhat indifferent. Then, despite the letters to the minister of justice and follow-up by the Office of the Prosecutor, it was impossible to restart the proceedings and conclude the transfer of the documents. In fact, these investigations might have hampered "national reconciliation" by raising concerns among the economic groups linked to the import-export trade, since those groups now considered themselves sheltered from further investigations. If the methods are a bit more elaborate today, the guidelines remain largely unchanged (*see annex 126*).

In the business sector, "national reconciliation" was swift and selective. The new authorities set the terms and could exonerate whomever they pleased. Starting with the foreign donor agencies that could conceal the former regime's financial improprieties, as well as those of the new regime, the money laundered through host countries was transferred to the new claimants the moment the old regime collapsed; the same holds true for those who held capital or goods, both foreigners and nationals, and wanted to turn the page, ready to participate in the reconstruction of the country. The argument that the mandate of the tribunal did not anticipate prosecutions for corruption served to foreclose investigation into the mechanisms by which national economic resources had been used to advance a criminal enterprise (transportation, remuneration, use of funds, etc.). With claims to practicality and efficient use of resources, the ICTR thus shortchanged its own investigations, and the prosecution found itself deprived of irreplaceable evidence.

We could cite many other examples to show that, like the fluctuating Rwandan "lists" of suspects, those of the ICTR could also be expanded or trimmed, depending on the denunciations and demands of outside political agendas. Indeed, from solicitation to outright blackmail, a whole range of pressures was used, almost always with success, by Rwandan authorities in dealing with the successive prosecutors to block certain investigations or to impose their own choice of targets for investigation. This self-arrogated right of interference was always deemed legitimate by those authorities, even if it directly contradicted the principle of the independence of the prosecutor and reassured those challenging the impartiality of the ICTR.

One-Sided Justice

In addition to prosecuting those presumed responsible for genocide, the mandate of the tribunal also anticipates prosecutions of persons presumed to be responsible for war crimes committed between 1 January and 31 December 1994, thus bringing within its ambit the types of crimes committed by members of the RPA over the course of the war and during the six months that followed its rise to power. The RPF rejected this principle outright from the very beginning.

Adopted by a resolution of the Security Council, the statute of the ICTR makes it mandatory for states—including Rwanda—to cooperate. However, in light of the rather strained relationship between the RPF and the United Nations following the impotence and failure of its peacekeeping mission in Rwanda, maneuverability for those who supported the tribunal was extremely limited. The RPF's total victory over the génocidaires conferred incontestable military, political, and ideological legitimacy upon the "liberators" both in Rwanda and abroad. In fact, from its triumph in Kigali in July 1994, the RPF controlled all the levers of power. There was no mistaking the intention of the victorious commanders to administer the country in the same manner that they had conducted the war, and where relations with the international community were concerned, they could play upon the guilt of a world that had averted its eyes during the genocide.

As early as 1995, the RPF's determination to thwart any threat to its sovereignty found expression in the brutal "pacification" of the former Turquoise zone, then still under UNAMIR's protection. On 9 June 1995 the RPF obtained a drastic reduction of Operation Turquoise's mandate and staffing from the Security Council, as well as a commitment to leave the country within the next six months. By the end of 1996, the RPA sealed once and for all the fate of over two million Rwandan refugees settled in camps along the border by forced repatriation, physical elimination (240,000 were declared "missing" by the Haut-commissariat des Nations unies pour les réfugiés [HCR]), or forced migration to other African countries. By arbitrarily categorizing all refugees as "génocidaires," the RPF accomplished a tour de force in equating expediency with the appearance of morality, with few signs of dissent from Security

Council members, apparently more anxious to mask their own impotence than to question the new regime's claims to impunity. Thus, in 1997, after the United Nations Commission on Human Rights (UNCHR) took note of the assassination of five members of its own mission to Rwanda (*see box 13*), its response was to terminate the mandate of its special rapporteur. A similar decision was taken shortly thereafter in regard to the Special Commission appointed by the Security Council to investigate the massacres of Hutu refugees in Zaire, which the rapporteur, Roberto Garreton, was poised to characterize as genocide.

This brief reminder is essential for understanding why it was unthinkable for the prosecutor, at a time when the ICTR was just getting off the ground, to initiate investigations on the full range of crimes and massacres committed over the course of 1994. He thus initially postponed implementation of his "second mandate" concerning war crimes and crimes against humanity committed by RPA troops and justified his decision by the priority to be accorded investigations against those responsible for genocide.

This presumably selective justice could hardly be challenged while the ICTR still struggled to define a prosecution strategy, languishing without making arrests or even obtaining the budget or level of staffing equal to the tasks at hand. The mandates of both Prosecutors Richard Goldstone and Louise Arbour were marked by highly critical audit reports concerning the management of the institution, leading to successive dismissals of high-level UN functionaries. Rwandan authorities pounced on the weaknesses of this international institution and systematically denounced them. But Kigali's sustained vigilance in regard to the ICTR's shortcomings, real or imagined, also served to delay the inevitable confrontation over investigations of war crimes and crimes against humanity. Kigali's strategy paid off, for neither of the first two prosecutors dared venture in that direction.

The appointment of Carla Del Ponte, a magistrate with a reputation for immunity to political pressure, signaled a remarkable shift in the judicial climate. As fate would have it, at the very inception of her mandate she was confronted with the Jean-Bosco Barayagwiza debacle, which Kigali invoked to break off relations with the ICTR.[16] The new prosecutor was denied an entry visa for Rwanda. This baptism of fire permitted Rwandan authorities to test her capacities for negotiation and to send her a message. Going back and forth between displays of authority and concessions, from the very start she showed little interest in the dynamics of "African realities," an attitude that persisted for the duration of her mandate.

Carla Del Ponte replaced a number of persons occupying key posts in the ICTR, unleashing bitter polemics about her very personal choices in staffing.

She also embarked on a major reorganization plan aimed at streamlining procedures and revamping the targeting strategy for investigations, establishing objectives and timetables covering the entire duration of her mandate. For Kigali, this initiative was laden with risks. In December 2000, as soon as the ICTR announced that "special" investigations were under way against soldiers of the former Tutsi rebellion suspected of war crimes and crimes against humanity for incidents in 1994, the Rwandan government accused Carla Del Ponte of "politicizing her office."

One year later, the prosecutor informed the Security Council of her intentions.[17] Upon her return in December 2001 and then again in April 2002, she announced that arrest warrants would be forthcoming. The showdown that followed took the form of a "witness crisis" for most of 2002. Under the pretext of a misunderstanding between the tribunal and genocide survivor groups brought on by the brusque manner often adopted by certain defense teams toward prosecution witnesses, the stratagem put in place in early 2002 by the Kigali authorities took the form of a series of denials of travel authorizations and the withholding of passports. For months, several of the trials under way at the ICTR were completely paralyzed by the absence of witnesses from Rwanda, a situation that had a profoundly negative impact on the functioning of most of the trials and made painfully clear the ICTR's total dependence on Kigali.[18] After Gen. Paul Kagame informed the prosecutor on 28 July 2002 of his refusal to tolerate any investigation into the downing of the presidential plane on 6 April 1994—another case provoking grave tensions—as well as the other crimes imputed to the victors' camp, all of these investigations were abandoned in September 2002.[19] But this still failed to dissipate the lingering animosity. In December 2002 a new crisis erupted, provoking strong words from both sides. A government press release declaring that, "as of today, the people of Rwanda have lost confidence in Carla Del Ponte's objectives and her capacity to render justice" generated a firm response from the prosecutor: "For me, a victim is a victim. Any crime that falls within my competence is a crime, without consideration of the identity, ethnicity, or political views of whoever perpetrated it. Justice does not bow to political opportunism. No one is above prosecution for the most abominable crimes."[20] This crisis marked the end of all euphemisms: although the Rwandan authorities categorically refused to link this "crisis" with the "special investigations," Carla Del Ponte publicly acknowledged for the first time, during a meeting with British parliamentarians, that her "special investigations" were the principal reason for this noncooperation.

Although well founded, the explanation was still unsatisfying. Over the course of the same year, the Office of the Prosecutor was beset by a number of grave errors: already behind schedule in getting the most complex cases to trial (especially the joint indictments), in attempts to please its RPF interlocutors, it sought to prosecute several officers of the former Rwandan army with spotty evidence, again illustrating its vulnerability to the constant pressure so effectively applied by certain activists in Kigali.[21] Having succeeded to some degree in arraying the entire panoply of Rwandan sensibilities against it, the Office of the Prosecutor lost all support in Rwanda among the more democratic elements—in the government, in parliament, in the military high command—many of whom had been genuinely committed to the existence and independence of the ICTR. Anti-ICTR radicalization and obstruction of the "special investigations" rose to the surface, untrammeled by any counterweight in internal political debate.

If the Security Council finally succeeded in persuading Rwandan authorities to respect their legal obligations and desist from obstructing the proceedings, the council nonetheless managed to avoid sanctions or even criticism. The Security Council declaration of 18 December 2002 was satisfied to call for a "constructive dialogue . . . with a view toward resolving any problem likely to perturb the work of the Tribunals that could arise in the framework of their cooperation."

In April 2003, for the first time and after a series of meetings organized by the prosecution in Arusha, approximately fifteen sites of RPF massacres were listed, four of which were carefully documented and pegged to support indictments.[22] Nothing happened. With support from the American ambassador for war crimes issues, Pierre-Richard Prosper, the Rwandans felt that they were fully capable of looking into and adjudicating any crime purportedly committed by those among their ranks and opposed all investigation undertaken by the ICTR. The prosecutor found herself de facto forced to postpone sine die her "special investigations" and any investigation of the RPF. As discord lingered, casting doubts on the future of the tribunal, it became apparent that the overwhelming majority of the staff in Arusha were unwilling to put at risk the continuity of the institution and the hundreds of jobs it provided.

Despite the concessions Carla Del Ponte was willing to make to placate her interlocutors, Rwanda's hostility toward the prosecutor remained palpable, and in August 2003 the UN secretary-general, supported by the United States and the United Kingdom, recommended the uncoupling of functions between the prosecutor of the ICTR and the International Criminal Tribunal for the former Yugoslavia (ICTY) "for reasons of efficiency." Having no other choice but to maintain her leadership of the ICTY at the expense of the ICTR, she ultimately lost out because of her lack of resolve. By not denying the rumor that the nomination of a separate prosecutor was motivated principally to put an end to the special investigations, Carla Del Ponte, like the Rwandan authorities, implicitly endorsed the view that the newly appointed prosecutor, Hassan Bubacar Jallow, would not venture in that direction despite the reaffirmation of that portion of his mandate by the Security Council. As early as November 2003, Pierre-Richard Prosper called upon the ICTR and the Rwandan government to reopen discussions on their principal point of contention and to agree as to which of the two, the ICTR or the Rwandan government, should henceforth take charge of these investigations. Despite this mediation by the United States, which should have been reassuring for Kigali, the prosecutor and the Rwandan authorities avoided any such discussion during their initial contact. Then, during a press conference held in Arusha on 23 January 2004, the prosecutor publicly reaffirmed that the international tribunal was competent to address crimes possibly committed in 1994 by the ex-rebellion, and, on 29 June 2004, before the Security Council, he expounded upon what had become, retrospectively, his "nonpolicy" on the matter:

> With regard to the allegations against members of the Rwandan Patriotic Front, my office is now evaluating the evidence that has been gathered so far with a view to determining whether there is sufficient basis for prosecution, against whom and for what offences.
>
> I have also engaged in discussions with the Rwandan government on this matter, specifically in regard to what options are available for dealing with any cases that may arise from any such evaluation.[23]

However, contrary to his statement to the United Nations Security Council during its session of 23 November 2004, when he explained that he was reviewing the materials that had already been collected, on 2 December 2004 Hassan Bubacar Jallow requested independent investigations and announced at the Security Council meeting of 13 June 2005: "Work continues in respect of those allegations." After having received an as-yet-unpublished, confidential, well-documented file, he took the decision to select the cases that definitively would be retained for purposes of preparing indictments.[24] At the conclusion of meetings held in Arusha during the week of 31 October 2005, the Office of the Prosecutor declined to commit itself on 7 November, reinvoking the proposition originally formulated by Pierre-Richard Prosper to defer the matter. Thus, the question of the choice of "options" was handed back to the Rwandan government.[25]

At the same time, Prosecutor Jallow kept an investigative team in reserve, assigned to these files, which offered him a pretext to claim that he was checking allegations before deciding on possible prosecutions. In 2006 as well as in 2007, the Security Council was treated to vaguely similar comments:

investigations were under way, they were taking more time than expected, you will be informed next year, and so on.[26] Meetings with academics were even held the day after his statement of June 2007 to gauge his willingness to go forward.

Without anything happening, the epilogue of this long and delicate controversy was finally resolved in March 2008: the ICTR prosecutor submitted two case files to President Kagame likely to set the stage for trials in Rwanda or, failing that, in Arusha based on investigations undertaken by the ICTR. The first concerned the massacre of fourteen persons at Kabgayi, near Gitarama, on 5 June 1994. The bishop of Kabgayi, Mgr. Thaddée Nsengiyumva, the archbishop of Kigali, Mgr. Vincent Nsengiyumva, and the bishop of Byumba, Mgr. Joseph Ruzindana, were killed there by RPF soldiers along with nine priests, a senior priest of the Josephite Brothers, and a child. The second case file concerned massacres committed at Byumba stadium on 23 April 1994 that cost the lives of between one and two thousand Hutu victims assembled there by soldiers of the RPA. In a killing field defined by the space between the Episcopal church, the stadium, the military camp, the École sociale du Bon conseil, the flour mill, and the schools at Kibali and Buhambe, over five thousand civilians were massacred in Byumba during the month of April 1994. President Kagame's response was to be given by the end of May at the latest in order for the prosecutor and the president of the tribunal to inform the Security Council how the case file would be handled.

The ICTR claimed to be prepared to organize a speedy trial, considered largely symbolic, for the killings of the bishops and would put it forward as a clear demonstration of its commitment to judging all crimes before requesting an extension of its mandate through calendar year 2009. In any case, prosecutions were inevitable, given the echoes in international circles about these calculated executions, especially since they had long been carefully documented. Moreover, since the end of the war, they had been openly acknowledged in Kigali, where they were presented as regrettable, though understandable, acts of simple soldiers. The case of the killings at Byumba stadium was just as notorious but was potentially risky for the RPF, since, occurring in a prefecture particularly affected by the war, the case would likely open up a general debate about mass crimes against civilian Hutu. Additionally, it was difficult to replicate the excuse of "simple solders," as with the case of the murdered bishops, since it was already a matter of common knowledge that commander-in-chief Paul Kagame was present at the scene. As the ICTR only had a single factual witness for the Byumba case file, the case was offered to Rwandan authorities for trial with the proviso that the Rwandan prosecutor's office would itself find additional witnesses. Failing that, it should be abandoned.

On this basis, on 4 June 2008 the ICTR prosecutor informed the UN Security Council that the Rwandan prosecutor's office had informed him of its "decision to rapidly indict and prosecute four Rwandan field officers for murder and complicity in murder" suspected of involvement in the killings in 1994 at Kabgayi of thirteen Rwandan clergymen, including three bishops.[27] In light of this unprecedented cooperation, the prosecutor announced that, once the trial was completed, it would terminate any further action on his part concerning "these crimes" of the RPF: "As the Council knows, Rwanda shares concurrent jurisdiction with the ICTR over such offences. I have therefore decided to hold in abeyance further action on my part on the clear understanding that any such prosecutions in and by Rwanda should be effective, expeditious and open to the public. My office will also monitor those proceedings. The prosecutions in Rwanda will of course be without prejudice to the primacy of the ICTR's jurisdiction over those crimes. I hope that the prosecutions will be conducted by Rwanda in a manner that will effectively contribute to reconciliation in that country."[28]

The joint case file assembled by the prosecutor's office in Arusha and the military tribunal in Kigali established that the tragedy "was an accident," involving "personal decisions of soldiers acting without orders."[29] The indictment made no mention of the child who was murdered. Furthermore, no attempt was made to call upon a prosecution witness to confirm or contradict this version of what actually happened. On this basis, the trial proceeded in a fairly predictable manner: arrested on 11 June, the two superior officers were acquitted and released on 24 October 2008, because, according to the judgment, they had no information that would have allowed them to prevent commission of the crime. As for the two captains who had pleaded guilty, they were sentenced to eight years of prison for having acted "on the impulse of emotion." Reviewed on appeal in January 2009, the decision of the High Military Court of Kigali was rendered public on 25 February after the ICTR prosecutor had validated the conclusions and the procedure. The acquittals of the two generals were confirmed, and the sentences of the two captains were reduced from eight years to five years (*see annex 128*).

Two principal points emerged from this trial. The first is that no prosecution witness had been called, whereas the ICTR prosecutor had been informed that two witnesses were available and were prepared to testify (including a relative of one of the victims whom soldiers had separated from the others as they selected the persons they intended to kill).[30] The second concerns the peculiar interpretation of events that the authorities had adopted in deference to Prosecutor Jallow's wish to "effectively contribute to national reconciliation in the country" by holding this trial in Kigali. However, above all, this trial provided a pretext for a campaign of vilification against the Catholic Church hierarchy; to give a semblance of credibility to the claim that the killings were "a reaction provoked by the inhuman and genocidal behavior" of the bishops, the latter were presented as the local master planners of the genocide: "The bishops had power over the officials, the soldiers, and the Interahamwe: one word from them could have saved everyone. But they themselves were among the executioners."[31] Ironically, Mgr. Thaddée Nsengiyumva, then president of the Episcopal Conference, happened to be one of the most active promoters of the Contact Group of Churches, which courageously took the risk of initiating the first series of discussions with the RPF toward the beginning of the civil war before playing a prominent role in promoting peace and an opening vis-à-vis the RPF when war was raging.

As for the second trial, involving mass crimes in Byumba—scheduled to be handled by the Kigali prosecutor's office—it was purely and simply called off for lack of witnesses in accordance with a previous agreement between the ICTR and the Rwandan authorities. This allegation was indeed surprising considering that, according to the report on RPF war crimes and crimes against humanity established by Carla Del Ponte in 2002, eleven factual witnesses were identified for the massacres committed in Byumba, including six—and not just one—for the killings at the stadium. And no one was told of further efforts to identify additional witnesses. Responsibility for such tasks, it should be noted, had been entrusted to the Rwandan prosecutor's office.

Retrospectively, it would appear that Prosecutor Jallow's "nonpolicy"— marked by a total absence of fresh inquests and an apparent lack of familiarity with investigations previously conducted by Prosecutor Carla Del Ponte— would only have served to buy time before the staging of an exit scenario prearranged with Kigali for the end of the tribunal's mandate. This contention can be substantiated by the total absence of any mention of expenses for this line of investigation in the budget for the Office of the Prosecutor. Not the least bit of expense for this budgetary line appeared for 2008; no funds at all were budgeted in 2009, as if the results of these two test trials were known in advance.

This is how crimes allegedly committed by the RPF in 1994 were investigated for purposes of preparing indictments, with questions still unanswered and no conclusive resolution, as emphatically stated in a press release issued by the NGO Human Rights Watch (HRW) on the eve of the Security Council meeting of 4 June 2006. That meeting would officially conclude and approve this particular leg of the tribunal's completion strategy (see annex 129).

Three principal reasons sum up this recurrent powerlessness. The first hinges on the status claimed by the new authorities as "liberators" of Rwanda and for which decency would forbid "placing the génocidaire and his victim on the same level."[32] And, indeed, the juridical framework set up by the new national authorities to prosecute the crimes committed since the outbreak of war in October 1990 (conventional justice, "traditional" justice, and military justice) accords de facto complete impunity for war crimes and crimes against humanity committed by the RPA, as well as the killings, assaults, and pillaging imputed to civilian Tutsi of the interior or to returnees—characterized as "crimes of revenge."[33] This impunity is then crowned by a decade-long, prescriptive statute of limitations covering almost all crimes and offenses except those linked to the genocide, that is, those directed against Tutsi.

The second reason is no doubt the more illuminating. It stems from the strict discipline and the operational regulations that governed the RPF. In contrast with Rwanda's newly emergent state institutions, where it was always difficult to tell who the real decision makers were and thus to reconstitute a chain of command, the degree of centralization that prevailed among the rebel forces makes it almost impossible to investigate any incident, even the most minor infraction, without tracing back to the highest levels of decision making. Thus, it would have been impossible for even a symbolic show trial to insulate the higher-ups.

Harassed by unrelenting criticism of the ICTR's inefficiencies and of the protection supposedly granted to the génocidaires by the great powers—and therefore likely to reap the fury of the Kigali authorities—all the prosecutors were invariably advised by the Security Council to obtain prior approval from Rwandan authorities for the special investigations files targeting RPF suspects; however, they invariably received dilatory responses, if not firm refusals.[34] And when not explicitly dissuaded or disavowed, no prosecutor ever benefited from the support of the UN secretary-general or the Security Council to effectively implement this portion of his or her mandate.[35]

The third reason, and the most publicized, for which the diplomatic impact far exceeds the potential legal consequences, given the suspects most likely implicated, concerns the downing of the presidential aircraft on 6 April 1994. Whereas the first prosecutor, Richard Goldstone, proclaimed loud and clear, albeit a posteriori, that the plane crash fell within the mandate of the ICTR, Louise Arbour even denied having initiated investigations in this regard when her investigators sent her witness accounts placing blame on the RPF.[36] Carla Del Ponte hesitated quite a bit before acknowledging a link between the downing of the plane and the outbreak of massacres, only to later claim that the tribunal had no evidence and then that President Kagame had convinced her of his "innocence." Eventually, she left it to French authorities to shed light on this matter, even though she refused to provide the designated magistrate

(Jean-Louis Bruguière) with the materials he requested, and then denying that as well. As for Prosecutor Jallow, from the very beginning he held that the downing of the plane did not fall within the mandate of the ICTR, all the while allowing members of his office to claim that the various hypotheses concerning responsibility were all open to debate, especially the purported "Hutu extremist" thesis, and this even after the French had concluded their investigations in October 2006 and Judge Bruguière had issued arrest warrants against RPA officers. The ICTR was supposed to have supported the French in that regard (*see annex 130*).

Transitional Justice: A Means to Stifle the Truth?

These various elements, deliberately suppressed or left hanging, and the strategic choices they betray significantly affected the investigative work of the tribunal, as well as the conduct of the trials. Some held that this was the price to be paid for expediency: a simple story of good guys and bad guys. On one side were liberators struggling to enforce their right of return and to recover their identity and all that had been taken from them; on the other was a genocide planned from the inception of the republic, with fascist and racist elites leading an enraged populace.

In view of the breadth and the systematic nature of the massacres, the basic issue, thus stated, was straightforward, easy to understand by foreigners in charge of assembling this tribunal, and likely to be repeated in all cases with minor variations, depending on the survivors available to testify. As long as it was a matter of judging the planners and the immediate perpetrators of the massacres, the prosecution's approach encountered few problems. Things changed, however, with the elaboration of the theory of conspiracy, when the Office of the Prosecutor sought to fuse cases against military leaders, politicians, media personalities, and ideologues within a consolidated narrative framework. Reluctance or refusal to factor in the complexity of political networks and the primacy of regional antagonisms invalidated many of the prosecution's presumptions, which focused on presumed masterminds who in due course were able to demonstrate, with their lawyers' assistance, weaknesses in the cases filed against them.

Indeed, the odd particularity of this genocide hinges on the fact that anti-Tutsi extremists controlled regions that were practically monoethnically Hutu and where massacres necessarily remained extremely limited; the bulk of the Tutsi population targeted by the genocide resided in prefectures where these extremists were not only in the minority but, in fact, truly marginal. Oddly, the implementation of a genocide conceived by northern elites presumably fell to the same southern elites that had been challenging the northerners' hegemony for the last twenty years! It was only after the trials got under way against the political and military figures, described as the presumed "planners" of the genocide, that it became obvious that this simplistic, Manichaean explanatory scheme seriously undermined the full appreciation of the facts linked to the genocide. More to the point, it sapped the arguments marshaled by the prosecution to counter the defense lawyers as they progressively grasped the ins and outs of the Rwandan situation.

Limiting investigations to only one of the two protagonists can best be described as an attempt to muddy the waters; all it does is to confuse our understanding of the sequence of events and how these were linked. If anything, it encouraged the defense teams to construct legal strategies based on purely political considerations, going so far as to even deny the legitimacy of the definition of the crimes imputed to their clients.

Truth telling as reflected in the victors' justice did more than produce biased accounts. The ensuing political and ideological polemics returned to the fore with the completion strategy that marked the termination of the ICTR mandate. The calm purchased by the prosecutors at the price of renouncing a part of their mandate proved illusory: the end result was to compromise the implementation of transitional measures and the transfer of the tribunal's prerogatives to Rwanda. By the end of 2009, no country had pronounced Rwanda's judicial system to be so untainted as to fit the mold of an *état de droit* (rule of law). The authorities thus felt obliged to precipitously legislate bylaws of exception (exceptional measures or arrangements) to save the appearance of legality.

In fact, and even though Prosecutor Jallow bestowed his global approval on the Rwandan judicial system and anticipated future improvements, he still could not substitute his assessments for those of the ICTR judges. The latter, having no commitments to a prosecution strategy, could be tempted to assert their independence, up to and including impatience and disapproval with the Office of the Prosecutor's inertia toward RPF cases.

There were quite a few hurdles to overcome. First of all, there was the question of transferring pending cases to the national jurisdictions where new suspects had or would be arrested or to Rwanda, which had long requested the extradition of suspects, especially those who were not likely to be arrested or tried before the termination of the ICTR. Over the course of several years, many extradition requests were de facto denied in the Netherlands, the United Kingdom, France, New Zealand, Canada, Switzerland, and Sweden because of the serious doubts concerning the capacity of the Rwandan judicial system to respect the rights of the accused and to try them fairly. Since the abolition of the death penalty, introduced in early 2007, the principal legal obstacle to these extraditions had been lifted, but all of these countries were waiting for the ICTR to take the initiative with an initial transfer before proceeding themselves with pending extradition and repatriation applications.[37] In fact, they would have preferred not to burden their legal systems with these expensive trials and were really hoping to relieve themselves, once and for all, of all these "Rwandan cases." Regardless of their previous attitude toward Rwandan requests for judicial assistance, these countries soon realized that there was no end in sight and that Rwanda was relying on these prosecutions to export its own controversies and to settle accounts with tens of thousands of political opponents and refugees scattered across the globe, whether long-standing or only recently dispersed.

Additionally, Rwanda had always sought to have ICTR convicts serve their sentences in Rwanda. Up until 4 March 2008, Mali, Italy, Benin, Swaziland, France, and Sweden had signed agreements with the ICTR concerning the execution of sentences. All of the accused who were finally convicted were serving their sentences in Mali. That is when the ICTR signed an agreement with the Rwandan government to reaffirm that ICTR convicts should rightly serve their sentences in Rwandan prisons. The agreement did not suffice to dampen the controversy in this regard. Only the president of the tribunal could issue an order for an accused to serve his sentence in Rwanda. To this date, no convict has been transferred there. The same month, without having consulted the Trial Chambers, the prosecutor agreed to transfer ICTR cases against the RPF to Rwandan authorities. This decision also provoked open disagreement between, on the one hand, the Office of the Prosecutor and, on the other, HRW and several expert witnesses.

Finally, there was the question of transferring cases against persons already in ICTR custody who had not yet been tried to which Kigali also laid claim. This provoked sharp debate on 24 April 2008, when the judges heard representatives of the government and the Rwandan bar association, as well as the other parties concerned, to decide if the first accused whom the prosecutor sought to transfer to Rwanda would be able to get a fair trial. This review of the legal requirements and, more broadly, the Rwandan political-juridical context, gave rise to lively exchanges between, on one side, the Office of the Prosecutor, jointly supported by the Rwandan authorities and the bar association, and then, on the other, the organizations that wanted to "enlighten" the court on the matter (see annex 131). In the months that followed, five denials rendered by the chambers in charge of adjudicating the transfer requests demonstrated that the judges were not yet convinced by arguments advanced by the Office of the Prosecutor. The Appeals Chamber in The Hague then weighed in and confirmed those refusals. The Rwandan authorities and the prosecutor returned to the matter toward the end of the year with assurances of rectifications and improvements in the governing juridical texts responsive to the objections that had been raised. Toward the end of 2009, despite intense diplomatic lobbying from Rwandan authorities and the prosecutor and the Security Council's almost complete support for the principle of transferring cases, there was still no solution or proposition worth revisiting before the judges.[38]

Another issue, as symbolic as it is divisive, was linked to the demand made by Rwandan authorities to have Rwanda serve as the final repository for the archives of the ICTR. Compliance with this request entailed risks: it meant access to the entire documentation available in the ICTR data banks, including the most confidential information, which would then reveal the identities of heretofore anonymous sources and witnesses. This would benefit the persons whom the tribunal's mandate had clearly deemed to be parties to the conflict, presumably perpetrators of war crimes and crimes against humanity. This serious risk was already present in the cases being prepared against the victors' camp. The hesitancies and equivocations of the Office of the Prosecutor in prosecuting RPA members suspected of war crimes and crimes against humanity constitute a major obstacle in collecting prosecution evidence. How can one claim to guarantee anonymity and protection to witnesses and informants — especially if they still reside in Rwanda — or promise personal and professional security to tribunal staff members working on case files against civilian or military RPF figures if, sooner or later, these case files end up in the hands of those same persons? Moreover, can one really expect that the guarantees of protection, follow-up, accessibility, and recourse that supposedly inhere in the UN system would be applied on equal terms to the other Rwandan cases that it has handled so far (*see annex 131*)? All staff members and witnesses know that, dating back to the tribunal's early days, nothing that happens there escapes attention from Rwandan intelligence services: the appointments, the case files, the procedures, the movements and travels, the documents in the databases, even the closed sessions or sealed files ordered by the chambers![39] The impression one gets is that defending these principles remains purely symbolic. Examples abound to demonstrate that the question of how often these principles are respected, or not, is no matter for speculation.

Consider one example, quite revealing, of the workings of this truth-killing machine — and sometimes quite literally so. In February 2002, in anticipation of the "big" trials against the military and political leaders accused of genocide, eleven high-ranking ex-FAR officers and the Rwandan minister of defense, all fully capable of up-ending the accused's denials of genocide, accepted to cooperate with the ICTR. All were among those who, well before the genocide, had distanced themselves from extremists of both camps and who, at risk to their own lives, had even tried to halt the outbreak and spread of the killings. However, before their selection as potential witnesses was even confirmed, several from among this group whose identities were supposedly protected by the ICTR were targeted in coordinated attacks. One of them, Col. Pierre-Claver Karangwa, was designated a "suspect under investigation" when he first arrived in Arusha on 25 March 2002; another, Gen. Léonidas Rusatira, was arrested and indicted in Belgium on 15 May upon request from the Office of the Prosecutor (he was subsequently exonerated and freed on 18 August when the prosecutor was forced to acknowledge contradictions in the "evidence" that was proffered). Two others faced other warnings, judicial harassment, and repeated threats of prosecution in their host countries. The last few, still residing in Rwanda, saw their careers destroyed; by way of punishment they were subjected to constant blackmail and extortion. Threatened with arrest, a ranking general and former defense minister, Emmanuel Habyarimana, and a colonel, Balthazar Ndengeyinka, had to flee into exile on 30 March 2003. A lieutenant colonel, Augustin Cyiza, vice president of the Supreme Court, was kidnapped by agents of the DMI (Directorate of Military Intelligence) and the police and transported to the military camp Kami in Kigali; he was never seen again.[40] Another officer, Maj. Cyriaque Habyarabatuma, whose heroic role in opposing the genocide in Butare had been unanimously recognized and who was the first officer from the FAR to be reintegrated in the RPA in August 1994, was incarcerated on 8 February 2004 on the basis of denunciations from the same prisoners whom he had caused to be arrested. Within two years, without any of its members giving testimony in Arusha, the group was reduced to naught. The RPF could not tolerate any of these officers, former soldiers of the defeated army, testifying on genocide-related crimes before the tribunal in Arusha, fearing, most likely, that they would also reveal the large-scale violence committed by the former rebel forces.

These examples confirm an observation only too rarely noted: the presence of a fundamental conflict underlying the apparent solidarity between Rwandan authorities and the ICTR. From 1990 onward, everything that the RPF sought by force of arms it obtained: the conquest of power, international approval, and a commanding military and political role in the region. To that can be added, as a bonus from an international community excoriated for its lapses during the 1994 tragedy, an exceptional volume of financial and technical assistance and a guarantee of impunity covering a broad range of incidents in national and regional military campaigns and now extending to army units occupying the eastern DRC. From this point of view, the ICTR—and this also applies to other international entities that have made clear where they stand on one aspect or the other of the Rwandan crisis—has fulfilled the mission entrusted to it within its particular domain, that is, framing the perceptions of the war around its most dramatic feature: the genocide of the civilian Tutsi population.

The Bagosora Judgment, or the Limitations in Rewriting History

The judges of the ICTR have nonetheless managed to set limits on the rewriting of history by the victors. In this regard, the Bagosora trial judgment, issued on 18 December 2008, can be considered the most important aspect of this international jurisdiction.[41] Within the framework established by the prosecution, it establishes a good number of very detailed points of reference, several of which are worth notice. If this judgment, confirmed on appeal, does not completely dispense with partisan polemics, it still has the distinction of clarifying what the judges of Trial Chamber I of the ICTR, after long years of trial and months of deliberation, found to be the judicial truth emerging from the evidence brought before it by the parties.[42]

Practically evolving into a mantra, with its amorphous amalgamation of facts, events, or declarations repeatedly invoked to justify some presumed juridical requirement in the various indictments of the Arusha tribunal, and uniformly crowned by the diabolical figure of Bagosora (characterized as the mastermind), the theory of the planning of the genocide transformed itself into a formula of almost mythic proportion over the years.[43] It has since become a line of demarcation, with "genocide ideology" just a step away from the antechamber of negationism and revisionism, which have now been erected as crimes in their own right by the authorities in Kigali. Better yet, not believing in the "planning" becomes, in the eyes of the authorities, acceptance of the "collective madness" argument to explain the intensity and the extreme violence of the 1994 massacres. That would be equivalent to siding with those who view the downing of the presidential plane and the fury it unleashed as the only reasons for the catastrophe. In other words, not believing in the "planning" practically reverts to believing that the genocide was spontaneous and thus segues into "racist considerations of those who only see in the extermination of Rwandan Tutsi another episode of tribal warfare, just one more taking place on the African continent." With this same mindset, the Bagosora judgment would become the "logical culmination of the thesis of the negation and the inversion of genocide: it negates the genocide of the Tutsi or attributes it to the Tutsi themselves."[44]

Well thought out and elaborately argued, the judges' decision not to include conspiracy to commit genocide in their conviction of Bagosora takes on particular significance. As it turns out, attempts to prove the genocidal conspiracy in sixteen of the thirty-five trials that were finally completed by mid-2009 had again been found wanting, whereas the conspiracy theory had served as the central pillar of the indictment in this leading case.[45] The *Prosecutor v. Bagosora et al.* trial was supposed to judge the alleged mastermind of the genocide, and the prosecution did not hesitate to make allusions to organizing the attack against the presidential plane in its arguments, which then surfaced implicitly as the first manifestation of genocidal plotting.

Let us review some of the principal points in the judgment of 18 December 2008.

The first point consists of a surprising and symbolic reference to the downing of the plane on 6 April, even if, right off the bat, the judges deliberately detached it from the thrust of their reasoning: even after rigorously reviewing the pertinent evidence, the Trial Chamber took note that the downing of the presidential plane was the object of "alternative explanations" but that none of them, at present, suspended the judges' doubts: "7. . . . Some teams have also advanced a number of alternative explanations for the events which unfolded. One of them is based on the view that it was the RPF that shot down President Juvénal Habyarimana's plane on 6 April 1994, and that this event, together with other factors, triggered spontaneous killings."[46]

The second point concerns the notion of a mastermind of the genocide, for which, factually, the judges questioned the pertinence of the evidence. The judgment clearly established Bagosora's personal responsibility for the assassinations of political figures, the spearheading of massacres, and the commission of genocide, but it just as clearly explained its reasons for rejecting the theory of coordination among protagonists and advance planning of operations. Thus, the Trial Chamber reasoned that the assassinations of political opposition figures did not necessarily form part of a "genocidal conspiracy" and could arise from political conflicts in the power struggle or measures taken in relation to the reprise of the war with the RPF.[47] The judges reserved in their sentencing a major place for assassinations of opponents and "Hutu moderates" who had also been targeted by killers from the beginning of the war.[48]

Over the course of these few days, Théoneste Bagosora was supposed to have conducted himself like the veritable director of operations, completely up to the task and motivated, and eager to accomplish "whatever was necessary" to safeguard the collective interests of the Akazu and the titans of Gisenyi, so abruptly undercut by the sudden attack. At the same time, he was, presumably, the consummate politician, moved by imperious personal ambition, manipulating all the others so that he could succeed the man who had dominated him for the last twenty years and finally assume the ultimate title of major general. In fact, however, as we have just seen, the principal decisions that were taken during the night of 6–7 April and the following morning had been made by, or in concert with, Agathe Kanziga and the extended family "because of the actual authority she wielded in the hours following the attack on the plane of 6 April 1994" (*see annex 54*). That Bagosora immediately sought to impose himself and accede to power is logical, but under such circumstances he simply could not have avoided "adopting" the solutions and the desiderata of the presidential family. Nor was it to him that the commander of the Presidential Guard turned in deciding to set in motion the "revenge" and the massacres committed by his commandos and the militias. The Presidential Guard had always been the "private domain" of the Habyarimana family in terms of recruitment and management. Under the direct authority of the family and technically commanded by Col. Élie Sagatwa, brother-in-law and unofficial chief of staff of the president, the Presidential Guard was only formally linked to the general staff. On the evening of 6 April, only two persons were really capable of ordering it about: Agathe Kanziga and Protais Zigiranyirazo. All the same, the immediate deployment of Interahamwe militiamen in tandem with the Presidential Guard, as noted by observers, did not concern Interahamwe in Kigali in general but rather specific units in Kanombe and Remera that were composed of reservists from the Presidential Guard.[49] The question of controlling the Presidential Guard and halting the massacres could obviously not be resolved by the general staff or the high command without approval from Agathe Kanziga or Protais Zigiranyirazo, and neither of them was willing to grant that permission before their scheduled departures, respectively, on 9 April (to Paris) and 11 April (to Gisenyi). After these dates, having established the conditions for a transition in line with their interests and ambitions, Théoneste Bagosora and Joseph Nzirorera were free to plot their own destinies.

The third point concerns the evidence supporting the notion of conspiracy and the intention to commit genocide. This is perhaps the most original part of the judgment and likely the richest.[50] It addresses the pleadings in the indictment: participation in the 1991 commission on "defining the enemy" (*see annex 7*); mobilization, consisting of military training, distribution and storing of weapons, organizing the militias of the various parties, and drawing up lists, especially in Kigali; and the numerous accounts of forewarnings, like the supposed letter (anonymous) of the "moderate officers" of 3 December 1993 and the revelations of the notorious "Jean-Pierre" of 10, 11, or 12 January 1994 (*see especially annexes 16 and 46*). Probably for the first time in the ICTR, this part of the judgment addresses the range of arguments and reviews the evidence routinely invoked to prove the thesis that genocide was "planned," and it does so in a detailed and systematic manner. Relying on thousands of pages of transcripts of extended hearings—over the course of which many of those who supported the allegations had to acknowledge the fragility of their arguments, the weak credibility of their informers, indeed, the deliberately false sworn testimony and the liberties they had openly taken with the facts—the judges deemed most of these allegations uncertain or insufficiently established. The most important part of the judges' reasoning concerns the militias and the civil defense.[51]

More fundamentally, the judges openly challenged the factual underpinnings and the underlying presumptions of a thesis that established "planning" of the Rwandan genocide from a template derived from the Holocaust. None of the evidence of criminal conspiracy was convincing, and none of the presumed members of the conspiracy were implicated, even though the judges, contrary to the arguments advanced by the Office of the Prosecutor, did not refrain from reading history backward, to well before 1 January 1994, to look for proof of this presumed conspiracy.[52]

> 16. Several elements underpinning the Prosecution case about conspiracy were not supported by sufficiently reliable evidence, for instance, Bagosora's reference to preparing the apocalypse in 1992, the Accused's alleged role in certain clandestine criminal organizations, including the AMASASU [Alliance des militaires agacés par les séculaires actes sournois des unaristes, or Alliance of Servicemen Annoyed by Underhand Secular Acts of Unarists, i.e., partisans of the royalist party in the independence], the Zero Network or death squads.[53] The testimony about a meeting in Butare in February 1994, where Bagosora and Nsengiyumva allegedly drew up a list of Tutsis to be killed, was not considered credible. The Chamber has reached the same conclusion with respect to Kabiligi's alleged speech about genocide in Ruhengeri in February 1994. There are also problematic aspects in connection with the anonymous letter outlining a "Machiavellian plan" and the information provided by Jean-Pierre.[54]

In their reasoning, the judges do not deny that the genocide was foreseeable nor that there weren't warning signs, such as, for example, the hate speech and propaganda that went hand in hand with the organization and the arming of groups described as crimes of individuals, groups, and agents of public authority (distribution of weapons, existence of arms caches, assassinations, etc.).[55] But at the culmination of an extended marshaling of this evidence, along with well-substantiated arguments, the Trial Chamber concluded, like all the other chambers before it, that the count of conspiracy to commit genocide was not established "beyond a reasonable doubt."

Bearing in mind the status and profile of the accused, from this point forward we can presume that the judges' refusal to find the "intention to use these forces to commit a genocide" and a fortiori the lack of proof of any pre-existing agreement now invalidate that judicial construction and the popular phraseology that extends it, even though it was so often repeated by most of the media and by a large number of human rights publications and organizations.[56] This long digression by the judges on the decision-making process henceforth established a clear disassociation between intuition and proof.

The fourth point is embedded in important factual conclusions; the judges solemnly reaffirmed the uncontested, objective reality of genocide: "7. The evidence in this trial has reiterated that genocide, crimes against humanity and war crimes were perpetrated in Rwanda after 6 April 1994. The human suffering and slaughter were immense. These crimes were directed principally against Tutsi civilians as well as Hutus who were seen as sympathetic to the Tutsi-led Rwandan Patriotic Front (RPF) or as opponents of the ruling regime." The judges emphasized: "8. Also other persons than Tutsi and moderate Hutu suffered in 1994. The process of a criminal trial cannot depict the entire picture of what happened in Rwanda, even in a case of this magnitude. The Chamber's task is narrowed by exacting standards of proof and procedure as well as its focus on the four Accused and the specific evidence placed before it in this trial."[57] With the reference to "other suffering," which has not given rise to investigation and sanction, the judges acknowledged the one-sided reading of events that the prosecutors imposed on the Trial Chambers by exclusively limiting their scrutiny to the genocide of Rwandan Tutsi.

Finally, the last point demonstrates the Trial Chamber's firm resolve to distance itself from partisan political manipulations that feed on this notion of "planning." Consequently, the decision to acquit Gratien Kabiligi, the staff officer who had been promoted to brigadier general on 16 April 1994, of all the counts against him demonstrates quite clearly that, in spite of all the evidence offered by the prosecution, the simple fact of having occupied senior functions in the FAR did not, in itself, constitute criminal conduct. The judgment insists upon the fact that those responsible for crimes do not implicate the groups to which they belong:

7. . . . The perpetrators included soldiers, gendarmes, civilian and party officials, Interahamwe and other militias, as well as ordinary citizens.

Nevertheless, as the evidence in this trial and the history of the Tribunal show, not every member of these groups committed crimes.[58]

The Rwandan army was no more a "genocidal" army than the Second Republic of Juvénal Habyarimana was a "Nazi regime" or Rwanda was "a fascist country since 1959," as some of the current rewriting of contemporary history by the victors' camp would have us believe.[59]

In fact, as this study and several others demonstrate, prior to 6 April, none of the institutional components of the Rwandan state was linked to the genocidal project; the same can be said for the military high command of the FAR, the parliament or the territorial administration, and the established political parties, including the MRND.[60] For this very reason, the nucleus of loyalists around the presidential clan had to organize the killings of the key figures of the democratic opposition, Hutu and Tutsi alike, and neutralize anyone or anything supporting the Arusha Peace Accords process in the army, the judicial and territorial administrations, and the media in order to clear the path for the genocidal forces. A clear demonstration of this is the initial phase of resistance and wavering, when extremist politicians and officers were forced to personally take matters into their own hands. They launched a broad series of maneuvers and propaganda to gear up and reinforce the killings that were unfolding, and during the second half of April they went so far as to push the Interim Government to tour the southern prefectures, which is where the majority of the Tutsi population lived. These politicians and officers threatened and sanctioned the civil service and military functionaries and all those who refused to start "the work." And before they were able to accomplish their plans, the ideologues and partisans of the genocide had to methodically shatter the institutional anchors of the social order (with priority given to the administration and the judiciary) and sever the human bonds that enabled groups and individuals to survive four years of searing tensions.

Political Manipulation of the ICTR

It is reasonably safe to assume that the principal reason why the RPF supported the ICTR from its inception was to formalize the definitive routing of the enemy and to secure, by the end of the ICTR's mandate, what was unobtainable by other means: a moral legitimacy that would also authorize the rebel leadership to dispense with this exceptional, ad hoc judicial mechanism (judicial tutelage of the ICTR and oversight by the United Nations Security Council). Full judicial sovereignty would be recovered when the

Rwandan juridical system and norms could be realigned with international standards, even if only formally. The closing of the ICTR would permit Rwandan authorities to insist upon its capacity to judge all suspects in Rwanda. Third countries would be able to extradite Rwandan defendants to Kigali and, in so doing, rid themselves of judicial cases that were weighing them down. For the authorities, the page would definitely be turned, and the RPF would see itself exonerated of its own crimes.

If, in approaching the ICTR's projected end in 2010, the illusionist's wand seems to have done the trick for the judiciary, the same cannot be said for moral legitimacy. Curtailing investigations against the RPF or withholding their conclusions, this UN-approved suppression, achieved through diplomatic and bilateral wrangling, cannot lift suspicions and still may not foreclose accountability sometime down the road.

In two domains at least, many observers think that the denials of truth and justice can, over the long term, transform themselves into significant political errors. Thus, reluctance in pursuing the enigma of the 6 April plane crash remains an enduring reminder of the limitations of international justice where truth seeking is concerned and, even more seriously, in clearing the path to future reconciliation. This pivotal event has long occupied a special place in the literature of conspiracy theorists; it also lies at the heart of the argument advanced by the most determined adversaries of the RPF, who deem it the triggering event for the war and the cause of the genocide. More fundamentally, the privilege of impunity accorded de jure or de facto to members of the victorious ethnicity and the unlimited power of the accusers have provoked such resentment of the international justice system that the "vanquished"—those referred to as *izatsinzwe* in Kinyarwanda—still cry out with demands for fair punishment. The astonishing result of this one-sided justice is that it seems to stoke dissatisfaction on the part of both survivors and the accused. This form of transitional justice carries political implications that cannot be left out of the accounting, any more than can be ignored the collective memories of disenchanted or stigmatized populations: their adamant refusal to sacrifice the struggle against impunity on the altar of "unity" and national stability is not risk free. They insist on a justice system worthy of their trust.

The legitimacy of judicial decisions cannot be decreed or self-proclaimed. It must be recognized and shared by its constituency, in this instance the Rwandan people and international "public opinion."[61]

In an environment marred by fear and trauma, overrun by intense political and ideological polemics, this magnified focus on genocide not only invites exclusive explanatory schemas but leaves out the necessary space in the margins where alternative or suppressed themes can be aired. The heavy-handed ideological and intellectual censure thus gives rise to what we might call a "black market" in thought and morality (as when rank criminals in denial are allowed to cloak themselves with the mantle of "political resistance").

That does not mean that the work produced by the ICTR has been in vain or that its achievements are negligible. No doubt, where truth seeking is concerned, anything not already documented or established will likely never be so, at least not in any systematic manner. But a thorough examination of all the witness accounts and investigations collected in the databases would largely suffice for a reconstruction of the Rwandan conflict in terms much less Manichaean than those that triumphed at the end of the war, which does not foreclose deeper exploration in other directions and in other places.

It is clear that neither the prosecutors nor a good number of the ICTR judges wanted war crimes and crimes against humanity committed by the victors' camp to be investigated and prosecuted at the same time as the genocide committed by the vanquished. By according an exclusive priority to the "crime of crimes" and by constantly fending off the criticism of bias, they wanted to make condemnation of the genocide of Rwandan Tutsi a line of political and moral demarcation that would not be trespassed. According to them, this condemnation transcends ethnic and political loyalties and eclipses all partisan co-optation, even those of genocide survivors in whose name current authorities claim to "govern Rwanda."

The importance of postconflict justice hinges on the fact that it must also contribute to reestablishing the humanity of those it identifies as perpetrators of the crimes. By affording the various actors an opportunity to express themselves about the events that they lived through and at least provide fragments of the truth, it affirms that the acts and motivations that it seeks to document— including the most reprehensible—are not beyond human understanding. It thus restores dignity to the victims; and for those it exonerates, it fully restores their rights.

By refusing to investigate and prosecute the perpetrators of infractions and crimes that it had formally identified among the victors, international justice, just like Rwandan justice, runs the risk of discrediting its mission in the struggle against impunity and to restore peace and reconstruct national unity. And in so doing, a new category of citizens has been created: the unpunished, condemned to live shadowed by constant suspicion for crimes they were accused of committing.

All the same, the privilege of impunity thus conferred upon the unpunished by these two systems of justice differs in nature. Where the *gacaca* jurisdictions and national, conventional justice are concerned, the explanation is commonplace: without any attempt at camouflage, they render a political justice that simply reproduces the totalitarian hold that the RPF progressively has imposed on all spheres of social life since its conquest of power.[62] On the other hand, the privilege of impunity afforded by international justice occurred because of lapses by successive prosecutors: because these investigations were not a priority; because opposition to them was too strong; and now, going forward, because the evidence is not strong enough. Among these reasons, it is clear that the last is the most convenient and the least credible, especially for an institution that surely must have the most detailed and exhaustive documentation on the matter. Indeed, just by virtue of its mandate, one way or another, it inherits all the files assembled by private parties, organizations, and national judicial institutions with which mutual assistance and exchanges of information are routine and continuing. And most importantly, international justice accedes to the entire documentation produced by the agencies that the UN system commands, including the most sensitive, which it systematically places beyond reach to please the new authorities in Kigali, such as records from the HCR and the Security Council.

The "war of memory" will thus continue. The retrieval of memory has yet to run its course in the only institution with a mandate and the authority to judge the perpetrators of all the crimes committed over the course of this conflict. Consequently, it is the prosecutors and the United Nations Security Council that will bear responsibility for this failure, but the role played by Rwandan political authorities should not be concealed.

Without returning to the ambivalent relationship that it has always maintained with the ICTR, denying it all legitimacy in one context while at the same time demanding that it operate according to its dictates, let us recall that Rwanda had never incorporated the ICTR statute in its domestic law and that its recent willingness to appropriate the soon-to-be-vacated properties and holdings of the ICTR reflects a deliberate strategy of political manipulation.

The ICTR completion strategy is thus exposed to ambiguity and ill will from the same Rwandan stakeholders who presided over the creation of this institution. In fact, as it embarked upon creating the ICTR, the preamble of the ICTR statute made reference to strengthening the Rwandan judicial system.[63] But the statute did not clarify the manner in which the two systems were supposed to combine their efforts. The statute could have anticipated judging all the suspects and establishing criteria by which the cases would be shared, which Rwanda could never abide. That is why, de facto, the ICTR only took an interest in suspects who could be found outside Rwanda, and the two systems (on the Rwandan side, with the conventional courts and the organic law of 1996 at first, and then with gacaca afterward) coexisted by completely ignoring each other, without the least consideration for potential collaborations and complementarities and without the least indication of concern on the part of the UN for the manner in which the Rwandan system was functioning or the way suspects were being treated in Rwanda. Some of these suspects never benefited from the "privileges" of Arusha (conditions of detention, trial procedures, and length of sentencing) for the simple reason that they never managed to flee the country.

As for the fate of the accused in Rwanda, it is only very indirectly and by pure necessity that the existence of the ICTR was finally able to have some influence on Rwanda's national system: as soon as it became important to deal with the issue of transfers, Kigali declared itself ready for any sacrifice, including abolishing the death penalty, a very costly sacrifice, but one that had the distinction of applying to all the other prisoners, not just those from Arusha. We cannot say as much for other "exceptional" laws that were already voted or undergoing adaptation in anticipation of the accused who would be transferred or extradited to Rwanda by the ICTR or other countries.

Thus, the example of the cooperation agreement between Rwanda and the ICTR anticipates that, where sentences are to be served in Rwanda, the conditions of detention are to be governed by domestic law: lifetime solitary confinement, for example, which the judges in Arusha had deemed inhumane treatment. And the concept of double jeopardy (no one shall be tried twice for the same offense) anticipated by the text is easily avoided by calling upon "new facts" that require adjudication.

There is a long list of contentious points—which will be specified and analyzed following the conclusion—pending before the ICTR closes its doors. The conference focusing on the ICTR legacy in Geneva in July 2009 took note of several points to be addressed before the mission of this institution is completed.[64]

Conclusion

In concluding this analysis of war and genocide, it may be fitting to offer a final observation, in light of the materials reviewed, and to add a few personal remarks based on my hybrid status as both "expert witness" and researcher.

The observation concerns the astounding futility of the strategic choices that the main protagonists ultimately made over the course of 1994. It was utterly devastating to equivocate in relation to the Arusha Peace Accords or to call them into question, as doing so inevitably derailed the transitional agenda. Then, later on, the cynical choice by one side to pursue the military option and an exclusive conquest of power and, by the other, the insanity of annihilating democratic institutions and forces, and ultimately the civilian Tutsi population, set the stage for calamity. With each new setback in implementing the Arusha Peace Accords, the rise in tensions and the violent backlash made all possible outcomes foreseeable, but they were never inevitable.

As we have seen, the decisions that resulted in reprise of the war in April 1994 and then led the Interim Government to open up a second front internally against "accomplices" of the RPF rebellion reveal strategic choices and rank opportunism but nothing mysterious. Even if a few points still merit further elaboration, the key actors are clearly identified, the sequence of events can be retraced and dated and their paths and means identified, along with the evolving delineation of objectives, of resources to be mobilized, and their various operational modalities.

The assassinations of key figures, as well as those first massacres, flowed from explicit directives dispatched to elite military units and groups of militiamen, maneuvers no less deliberate than the orders that were never implemented to stop the killings. The murder of civilians was part of a strategy to take power that, in a matter of days, allowed a group of officers and politicians and their cronies to take over the state apparatus, install a new government, subjugate the army and the territorial administration, neutralize the justice sector, and overrun the media. Once these objectives were attained, these same persons inscribed the genocidal agenda in public policy and mobilized the entire state apparatus to that end. Neither some purported dissolution of state authority nor any allegedly impulsive popular fury can account for the organized, methodical operations that were on display for several months. At both the regional and national levels, very concrete "policies of genocide," systematically promoted and extended over the course of several weeks, refute the presumably deadly, spontaneous activism of a "population" rising up as some undifferentiated, collective perpetrator of the massacres.

The murderous strategy of turning the civilian Tutsi population into hostages is a legacy of the First and Second Republics. Its efficacy was demonstrated during the early 1960s in countering attempts at restoration from monarchist guerrilla forces.

In Kigali, despite the heavy blows inflicted on the mouvance présidentielle by eliminating its president and army chief of staff, its capacity to rebound and fight back should not be underestimated: its successor's thirst for revenge, along with the natural impulses of the army's best-equipped units and fevered impatience among the Power youth wings, could lead some to contemplate whether opening an internal "front" might not dissuade the RPF and lead it to consider a negotiated settlement in spite of its military superiority.

However, concerning those putschists who, having installed a wholly subservient government, practically monopolized the levers of power, we would have expected a more "realistic" approach, especially in light of the two unavoidable questions: With inevitable military defeat looming on the horizon, was it not possible to negotiate and to salvage or conserve matters, and if so, how? And if nothing could be negotiated or salvaged in the short term, how could options or resources be preserved for the future?

There was none of that. This certainly must be the most surprising revelation to emerge from the accumulated documentation and witness accounts. The decision to pursue the genocide option was a response to the urgent necessity to create bonds of solidarity not just between soldiers and southern politicians but also with the instigators of the assassinations of democratic political figures and the Belgian "blue helmets." But beyond this political maneuver, which successfully mobilized the governmental team, justified the fusion of militia forces, and contributed, for a short while at least, to reunifying the "Hutu majority people," we can only be astonished by the suicidal futility of its consequences.

This is not an isolated observation. As we have seen, there were a series of incidents in the war and the genocide of 1994 that stemmed from precisely these kinds of short-term calculations. The political missteps that set the tone in negotiations for implementing the transitional institutions seem to have foreshadowed the murderous delirium that flourished among all these civilian and military dignitaries, the influential mixed in with the less so, practically under siege within the residential confines of Murambi (*see annex 134*), then in Muramba, and their adjacent homes and bars. And many had already embarked upon this course while transiting through the Presidential Guard camp in Kanombe, the French Embassy, and the Hôtel des Diplomates. And while there, constantly monitoring each other's comings and goings, they passed their time in countless cabinet meetings, round-table discussions, sidebars, and confessionals where alliances were knit together or unraveled, feeding on interminable arguments, flaring into deadly rivalries and the hatching of plots. It is through the prism of these political games and wagers, whether sophisticated or hare-brained, that they learned about the war and the massacres they had directed, with a stunning detachment in the face of their horrific immediacy.

As the tide of military defeats and diplomatic fiascos began to rise, feeding the genocidal frenzy became an end in itself. Despite constant purges in the territorial administration and the military command, as well as back-pedaling among the populace despite the innumerable entreaties, there was no strategic surge. What's more, by the end of May, when the uselessness of the massacres was evident, governmental authorities had delineated an ad hoc institutional framework for legitimizing and relaunching the killing. But time had run out, and the operation only served to expose and banalize the horrors of the massacres. The final defeat was all the more decisive when unanimous moral outrage and condemnation capped the military debacle. The futility of the strategic option thus appeared overwhelming.

Finally, most glaring in the behavior of these leaders was their extraordinary refusal to face reality and acknowledge defeat. And, rather than inspiring in them a more lucid sense of reality, their refusal to admit the successive failures only reinforced mounting ambitions and rivalries among them. All this took place with an absolute disdain for human life and without the slightest hint of moral scruple. It was as if wanton killings were the price to be paid for their own defeat by a population they deemed to be complicit with the enemy or too cowardly to resist it. It was unthinkable to question the soundness of the choices they had made.

But perhaps most repugnant is the stubborn refusal of foreign troops already on the ground or nearby, spectators of the carnage, to put aside their differences in order to squelch the spiraling violence. By action or by omission, having supported the campaign of one or the other belligerent over the previous four years, all the large embassies endorsed or applauded the bellicose choices of their respective champion until, confronted with the ensuing disaster, they did what they could to mask its blatantly criminal dimensions.

Finally, to conclude, let us return briefly to my introductory remarks about the "scientific" nature of this study, which arises in the context of a "judicial inquiry" and a scholarly undertaking.

In 1994, after spending fifteen years researching and doing fieldwork in the Great Lakes region, I felt reasonably well acquainted with the social realities on the ground and the dynamics of political transformations in that part of the continent. Much of this firsthand experience is reflected in my numerous reports on the economic, social, political, and ideological developments of the peasantry, the predominant social sector throughout the region.

However, for all my familiarity with many of the political actors and my regular trips to the field, the breadth and intensity of the violent outbursts of October 1993 in Burundi, and even more so the appalling events of April to July 1994 in Rwanda, is what caused me, in a way, to lose my intellectual bearings. No precursor or framework for analysis could have anticipated these moments of murderous folly, where the social fabric is brutally torn apart and the people—whether peasants, urban dwellers, or political leaders—cease to "be themselves," as they so often explained. It was one thing to understand and to document situations of heightened political and social tension, as had occurred episodically in the region, and quite another to explain and find the words to convey these extreme ruptures.

In the face of such convulsive events, accompanied by all manner of social interaction colored by ethnicity, the temptation to surrender to utter powerlessness is hard to resist. The sudden outpouring of unsuspected hatreds and the incredible banality in violence and cruelty were overwhelming. All were inevitable products of collective mobilization. Abrupt reconfigurations in the political landscape, a constant shifting in the poles of power, the opacity in decision making, and the emergence of alternative constructions of social hierarchy and power in wartime have subverted the order of things.

The absence of working national research institutions in the devastated countries, the distance or unfamiliarity of foreign researchers with realities on the ground, and, more generally, the tendency toward partiality or insularity among academics hardly facilitated an adequate response. All the same, the expert reports prepared by international aid organizations to explain the genesis of the conflicts and to outline prevention mechanisms appeared, more often than not, routine-like and opportunistic. This is when I decided to diversify my involvement. I took up assignments from agencies responsible for emergency assistance and, at the same time, did what I could to respond to requests from the ICTR to prepare reference materials to get the initial trials under way and then testify. All this helped me develop strong ties at the ground level, as well as in the new political sphere in Rwanda.

Looking back, the experience greatly facilitated indispensable new insights. In fact, after testifying as an expert prosecution witness for the tribunal in Arusha and then in several national jurisdictions, I was able to continue my work along similar lines for an academic research program, that is, with an approach and methods that I was able to develop on my own, in complete independence.

The ICTR mandate created opportunities for investigation over the long term, despite an authoritarian political environment that was not particularly favorable to any sort of independent investigation. It also guaranteed a degree of liberty available to very few analysts or researchers in postgenocide Rwanda. The Rwandan authorities extended this privilege to me until 2003. It was based on an explicit agreement that I not use this mandate for genocide investigations to embark upon parallel inquiries for the ICTR's "second mandate," that is, war crimes and crimes against humanity attributable to the RPF. Beyond that date, essential portions of my investigations could still continue outside of Rwanda with the support of the ICTR.

Oddly, the second mandate was more constraint than opportunity. Publishing these reports, originally conceived for use in trial sessions, requires a long and laborious process of revision. Factual reconstructions are not always appropriate in the framework of a judicial mandate. And the revision was not simply a process of adding information, because as I tried to demonstrate in the preceding chapter, the disconnect between "judicial truth," which must go through laborious procedures, and the "researcher's truth" is huge and entails real boundaries. First, there is a demarcation in terms of scientific detachment from the different registers, complementary and opposite, on which the expert witness is called to play to "speak the truth" in the judicial context: objective expert, participant, and "witness of witnesses." Next, there is a demarcation, or perhaps a clear distinction, in relation to the political reading of the Rwandan conflict that the tribunal endorses through its prosecution policy and its judgments.

From my perspective as a researcher, it was not bias or deliberate misunderstanding of key elements and, more broadly, entire currents in the history of the Rwandan conflict that caused concern; it was the refusal to rise to the intellectual challenge of closely examining the unfolding of the war and the inception of genocide. It was also the incapacity to appreciate the hidden and profoundly troubling character of this genocide, to understand the consequences of this massive mobilization, to situate the exact impact of ethnicity, that is, to identify the specificities of this major human tragedy, which was unexpected yet failed to surprise the majority of those involved.

But is it really necessary to direct criticisms of this nature against the institution that, for the past fifteen years, permitted all those who were drawn to study this war and this genocide to dispose of an exceptional database, that compiled thousands of accounts from victims, perpetrators, and eyewitnesses and mobilized the expertise of hundreds of prosecutors, lawyers, and judges? Little of the analysis presented in this book could have been done without the experience and the materials made available by this same tribunal.

It may be more to the point to simply concede that, for those truly committed to revealing the truth, the only remaining issue of any real urgency before the ICTR finally winds down is conserving the integrity of its archives, ensuring free access and use of the compiled materials.[1] On many points, the time has not yet come to make pronouncements of who was truthful and who lied, but future generations will surely demand answers. They will consult the documentation, review the witness accounts, and make their own assessments.

The truth that academics and researchers seek cannot be produced within the time limitations of 2004, or 2008, or 2010, the successive deadlines established at one point or another for the ICTR to complete its work. Of course, the ICTR must eventually close, but the task of establishing or revealing the truth will continue. The truth will be written or rewritten. And if, depending on the moment or the context, politics or ideology intercedes to prevent any particular explanation from being articulated, those who will eventually establish a "true" history are those who will have brought forth the most compelling source materials or who will have unearthed new or unexpected revelations to support their analyses.

Updates for the Period 2010–2015

Since the publication of the original French edition of the book in February 2010, new developments have occurred that have significantly reshaped the debate on the Rwanda genocide. I limit myself to a few specific points that help us get a better understanding of the analyses presented earlier. The first is the enduring split between the Rwandan authorities and the ICTR that has crystallized around certain judicial decisions and statements made by judges and deemed incompatible with the official version of history written by the RPF. The second, related to the completion of the special judicial process, with the simultaneous closing of the ICTR and of the transitional justice mechanism known as gacaca, leaves the field wide open for a reassessment of Rwanda's record of "Truth, Justice, and Reconciliation." The third revolves around the use and misuse of the laws enacted to fight against the recurrence of genocide and the resultant international criticism of such moves.

Some Major Dates

6 November 2009—Appeals Chamber acquits and releases Protais Zigiranyirazo.

8 October 2010—Publication by the Office of the United Nations High Commissioner for Human Rights (OHCHR) of the *UN Investigation and Assessment Report on Serious Violations of Human Rights Perpetrated in Zaïre and the DRC between March 1993 and June 2003* (aka *Mapping RDC*).

14 December 2011—Appeals Chamber delivers judgment in the "Military 1" case. Life sentences given to Bagosora, Ntabakuze, and Nsengiyumva are reduced to thirty-five years for the first two and fifteen years for the third. The acquittal of Kabiligi is confirmed.

12 January 2012—French judges Marc Trédivic and Nathalie Poux, in charge of the pursuits for the attack of 6 April 1994, transmit to the parties the findings of technical reports provided by ballistics and acoustic experts.

29 February 2012—Completion of prosecution by the ICTR.

18 June 2012—Completion of prosecution by gacaca jurisdictions in Rwanda.

4 February 2013—Appeals Chamber acquits and releases Justin Mugenzi and Prosper Mugiraneza, ministers of the Interim Government.

1 January 2014—Murder of Patrick Karegeya in Johannesburg. External Security Organization chief and close advisor to Kagame, he had gone into exile in South Africa in February 2008. He and Kayumba Nyamwasa, former head of Military Security, also a refugee in Republic of South Africa since February 2010, were considered the most dangerous opponents because of the support they still enjoyed in the country. He had already been the target of two assassination attempts in June 2010. Since January 2012 these two officers, neither one involved in the French inquest, repeatedly claimed to have evidence of the organization of the attack of 6 April 1994 by Paul Kagame. South Africa has not responded to the French rogatory commission filed in 2014.

9 July 2014—In Paris, Judges Trédivic and Poux completed their investigation, the results of which have been submitted to the prosecutor. The parties, that is, the plaintiffs (the Habyarimana family and the families of the other victims) and the defense (the officers of the RPA), will now take cognizance of the file and report to investigators and judges. The parties may request new procedures or cancellation of certain acts. They have three months to do so before the prosecutor decides to refer the files to the Criminal Court or requests a dismissal.

29 September 2014—The Appeals Chamber delivers its verdict on the cases of Édouard Karemera and Matthieu Ngirumpatse and confirms life sentences.

20 June 2015—General Emmanuel Karenzi Karake, head of the Rwandan National Intelligence and Security Services (NISS), is detained at the international airport in London when British authorities execute an arrest warrant issued by Spain, where he had been under indictment since 2008 along with thirty-nine other Rwandan government officials accused of large-scale killings, including crimes against humanity and genocide, committed between July 1994 and late 1997.

The Failure of the Recognition
of Conspiracy to Commit Genocide
by the ICTR

The decision of the ICTR Appeals Chamber in the cases of Bagosora and Nsengiyumva on 14 December 2011 confirms the deep break between the Rwandan authorities and the international tribunal, now openly accused of supporting "genocidal ideology" for its alleged indulgence against the génocidaires. Among those acquitted were Protais Zigiranyirazo, brother-in-law of Juvénal Habyarimana; the ministers of the Interim Government André Ntagerura, Justin Mugenzi, and Prosper Mugiraneza; and the officers Augustin Ndindiliyimana and François-Xavier Nzuwonemeye. Denial of justice was another accusation leveled against the tribunal, that is, its refusal to condemn the alleged mastermind of the genocide for his involvement in planning the bloodbath and his alleged participation in the attack against the presidential plane.

On this point it should be noted that no prosecutor has dared to take up the issue of the responsibility for the shooting down of Habyarimana's plane, and this despite all the prosecutors' participation in investigations conducted before they withdrew. And yet this is where they would have had the opportunity to establish whether the conspiracy theory was proved beyond all reasonable doubt; conspiring for the purpose of committing genocide was indeed a charge that Rwandan authorities have systematically asked the judges to formalize and address to the most prominent defendants as having been the brains behind the genocide. Had they possessed as much as a shred of evidence likely to convince a chamber of the guilt of one or of several of their most prominent defendants, they would not have hesitated to use it in support of their own version of the roots of the genocide, and this in turn would probably have called into question the ICTR's entire prosecutorial policy.

The wrangling over these legal and political discords took a new turn on 12 January 2012 following the submission to the parties by Judges Trédivic and Poux of the antiterrorist section from Paris of two acoustics and ballistics reports on the attack of 6 April 1994. According to lawyers of the six accused in Kigali, the conclusions of these reports render null and void the whole procedure and the indictments of the judges' predecessor, Judge Bruguière, and put an end to fifteen years of controversies. According to the experts, the missile that shot down the plane of both Rwandan and Burundian presidents would not have been fired from Masaka Hill, as most witnesses and analysts admitted, but from another sector of the commune of Kanombe in an area controlled by the FAR.

While lawyers suspended judgment, awaiting an impending decision, Rwandan authorities immediately put pressure on the ICTR prosecutor, requesting him to initiate a judicial process questioning the verdict of the ICTR on the Bagosora case based on new evidence imputing the responsibility of the attack to the "Hutu extremists." Such recourse was feasible within a period of one year after the decision of the Appeals Chamber, that is, on 13 December 2012. Nothing, however, came from Paris despite the certainties entertained by Rwandan diplomats, lawyers, and their political supporters. But for the RPF regime, the new construction was considered already validated, and the culprits were designated. Indeed, even in the absence of any element to put names to the accused, the official story was now definitively written on the basis of modeling scenarios of experts, indirectly validating the testimony of ad hoc witnesses.

Two years later, no dismissal had yet been requested by the French judges, and the continuing refusal of the French government to put pressure on the judicial process remains a cause of great tension between Kigali and France. This became dramatically evident during the commemorations in 2014 of the twentieth anniversary of the genocide. While the French president was one of only two foreign heads of state to personally receive an invitation from President Kagame to participate in the commemoration, he did not follow up on it, and the French ambassador was not allowed to participate. During the ceremonies, France was denounced for its alleged responsibility in the preparation, initiation, and commitment of the genocide. Everything suggests that the expected return for the invitation was the exoneration of the six Rwandans accused in the French procedure. In the eyes of the authorities in Kigali, this would probably have been the most important legal decision, though by default, that is, without proper identification of those responsible. This decision would have put an end to many questions about the conduct of the civil war triggered by the RPF in October 1990.

In the light of this political context, following the assassination of Patrick Karegeya and the Kayumba Nyamwasa affair, it is easy to understand Kagame's obsession with his own security. However, the situation appears to have changed since 8 July 2014, with the formal closure by the French judges of the endless procedure concerning the downing of President Habyarimana's plane without having been able to question Kayumba Nyamwasa, the sole person accused who is still the subject of an extradition warrant to France and of a pending commission of investigation seeking to obtain his testimony in South Africa. For over a year it has been impossible to find out who within the French and South African administrations (and of course the Rwandan administration) is responsible for blocking this dual warrant, since the three countries seem to be cooperating in keeping Nyamwasa tight-lipped. He claims to be ready to provide evidence of the RPF's responsibility—and thus possibly also of his own?—on condition that he should not then be the sole person charged to bear responsibility for the assassination based on his statements.

Indeed, a dismissal of the case, for whatever reasons, is what the lawyers of the accused have been anticipating for two years. It would allow Rwanda to end the judicial phase of international preeminence and regain full national sovereignty on the basis of a recalibration of its legal system with international standards. Dismissing the case would also finally confer on the RPF the moral legitimacy that it only enjoys by default. The RPF and its leader could then consider themselves to be definitely absolved of the presumed crimes of which they were accused without consequence by the ICTR, foreign national tribunals, and numerous studies carried out by various United Nations bodies. Then, by extension, all charges relating to war crimes and crimes against humanity or genocide would be dismissed (see the entry for 8 October 2010 on the list above).

But as of January 2015, the French judicial proceeding concerning the seven indicted Rwandans was still pending. The public prosecutor has still not made a decision, and the judges continue with the hearings of witnesses.

The Balance of ICTR and Transitional Justice (Gacaca) Eighteen Years Later

On 29 February 2012 the ICTR established the Mechanism for International Criminal Tribunals (MICT) to perform the residual functions of the International Criminal Tribunals for the former Yugoslavia and Rwanda. On 18 June 2012 Rwanda also closed the procedures for its own "popular justice" system. Thus, the fight against impunity initiated in late 1994 to judge the crimes of genocide, war crimes, and crimes against humanity has come to an end concerning the exceptional legal instruments ICTR and gacaca. Whether to pursue legal action will then be up to the conventional justice system in Rwanda and to Rwandan military justice, as well as to the national courts of those countries sheltering implicated Rwandan nationals.

For its part, in Rwanda, when the proceedings undertaken under the gacaca system of transitional justice were formally concluded, the National Service of Gacaca Jurisdictions (NSGJ) listed 1,951,388 trials that had taken place. If we note the figure of around 1.5 million "perpetrators of genocide" tried, of which some 80 percent were found guilty in a country of 7 million inhabitants, that means almost every Hutu male over the age of fourteen in 1994 has been put on trial.[1] Viewed from the aspect of the battle against impunity, the legal response has thus been on the scale of the tragedy of Rwanda in 1994, and the Security Council's main objective would appear to have been achieved.

In October 2012, taking note of the retreat of the ICTR, the research unit of the Office of the Prosecutor in charge of handling those accused of genocide in Kigali took over in hunting those tried and convicted in absentia by the gacaca courts and other suspects considered in flight. It announced that 146 international arrest warrants had been issued on that date, and then, "sooner or later," the figure of fifty thousand or even seventy-eight thousand would be reached. This would include most of the Hutu exiles from 1994.

Since then, Rwanda has increased the international arrest warrants through INTERPOL and raised complaints in the refugees' host countries. If preliminary investigations and pursuits were generally undertaken by the host countries' judicial institutions, only in very rare cases have extraditions been made to Rwanda: several refusals to comply, as recently happened in Britain, France, and other countries, triggered heavy criticism from the Rwandan authorities. The concerns voiced by host countries generally focus on the weakness of the dossiers submitted, retroactive use of the 2004 law to prosecute the accused, the reliability of offenses, and especially the late discovery of crimes attaching to proceedings by the authorities on suspicion of political motivation or settlement of accounts. More generally, the main concern is the lack of independence of the judiciary and judicial practice (characterization of the facts, guarantees of a fair trial actually granted by the judges, etc.) in a country where freedom of expression and civil liberties are more limited.

For its part, the ICTR was then winding up the completion of its ongoing trials and cases on appeal. Thus, after a new postponement until the second half of 2015, when the final judgment of the Butare case is scheduled to be issued by the Appeals Chamber,[2] "the ICTR will continue its efforts aimed at ending the impunity of the people who are responsible for acts of genocide" and will implement, one last time, the "good practice" that it has promoted in the field of international criminal justice.

But beyond the convictions established until the twentieth anniversary of the ICTR on 8 November 2014, the imminent completion of its work also invites a more global and political questioning of other missions carried out by the ICTR, in particular those "contributing to the national reconciliation process and to the re-establishment and maintenance of peace" in Rwanda and in the region. In fact, such noble objectives are now barely mentioned in ICTR literature, nor do they figure among the priorities set by the Rwandan authorities, which still focus on pursuing the "perpetrators of genocide" and their accomplices.

At the formal level, we should first of all emphasize that the international and national justice systems continually and deliberately ignore each other and indeed even overtly oppose one another, so contradictory are their approaches and procedures. From formulation to implementation of their decisions, no coordination or system of consultation was ever established between them. On an institutional level the UN jurisdiction became a kind of heavy and distant countermodel of justice throughout the entire African Great Lakes region. Among the Rwandan population, such justice, meted out in a foreign country by foreigners, aroused only very modest interest, and its pedagogical influence remains tenuous.

We are reminded, for example, that Kinyarwanda was not a language recognized by the court and that no transcripts of the Rwandan witnesses' hearings were ever translated and distributed in that language. It was only on 8 November 2014 that, on the occasion of its twentieth anniversary, the ICTR announced the launch of a multilingual legacy website. For the first time, an extensive selection of indictments and judgments translated into Kinyarwanda is available online. This belated effort does not bring to an end the scandalous lack of Kinyarwanda transcriptions of witness testimonies. And yet, 80 percent of the witnesses used Kinyarwanda to express themselves during these trials.

With regard to the very low impact of its legal decisions relating to national "reconciliation," this can be explained by the fact that neither of the two legal systems, in agreement at least on this point, has ever prosecuted and convicted the presumed perpetrators of war crimes and crimes against humanity from the winning side, the RPF. Indeed, the existence of statutory limitations should have ruled out the opening of proceedings under the gacaca justice system in 2005. Such limitations were by then enshrined in the ten-year prescription rule, which de facto covers all crimes and offenses qualified as "crimes of vengeance," apart from those associated with genocide. Certainly, articles 47 and 48 of the Organic Law establishing these tribunals stipulated that cases instructed by the Prosecutor General's Office and by the Military Prosecutor's Office must be transferred to the cellular gacaca jurisdictions, but for that to happen, specific conditions had to be met: there would need to be some case files; these local jurisdictions should make clear their desire to transfer the cases higher up; the plaintiffs should have the option and be willing to take the risk of denouncing the culprits before their *nyumbakumi* (the base cell for the populace); and the authorities would have to validate the charges. None of this happened.

No foreign national jurisdiction, apart from France and Spain, where such legal actions are bogged down, agreed to take on the accusations relating to crimes committed by the RPF rebellion and its supporters against its own nationals. One of the major reasons for this situation relates to differences in the nature of the chain of command between the losing side and the RPF, a highly structured political-military movement under the control of a high command that received its orders from an omnipotent leader, Paul Kagame, who was always fully informed of the orders given and executed at whatever level of the hierarchy.

The failures of this selective justice are not themselves attributable to the ICTR. The victors' justice to which the ICTR is subject, or has acceded to, despite its ad hoc status as tribunal with an independent prosecutor at its head, illustrates first and foremost its lack of power in the face of international divisions in regard to such extreme conflicts and their spinoff effects. International justice is not responsible for maintaining political order at national or continental levels. It can only act within the framework of its mandates. It is in no position to carry those mandates out without the effective support of the political authorities that defined them, regardless of whether or not a statute of limitation exists concerning the crimes committed by a particular country and its leaders. It is appropriate in this connection to remind ourselves that since October 2010, the Security Council has been waiting in vain for the counterinvestigations that the Rwandan authorities said they wanted to add to the UN *Mapping* report, drawn up at the behest of the OHCHR on the most serious violations of human rights and of international humanitarian law committed in the DRC between March 1993 and June 2003.[3] More recently, in December 2014 and January 2015, following the discovery of dozens of "floating corpses" on the Akagera River and Lake Rweru, Rwanda made every effort to thwart the investigation of the circumstances of such deaths, despite requests to that effect filed with the African Commission on Human and Peoples' Rights and the Peace and Security Council of the African Union.[4]

The Turning Point of 2014: Commemorations of the Twentieth Anniversary of the Genocide under High Tension

In October 2013, after years of procrastination and complacency, the United Nations Organization Stabilization Mission in the DR Congo (MONUSCO, Mission de l'Organisation des Nations unies pour la stabilisation en République démocratique du Congo), strengthened by South African and Tanzanian troops, decided to move against M23, the rebel forces supported by Rwanda in eastern Congo, thereby threatening to stop the looting of mineral resources exported to Rwanda. This unexpected military setback generated sharp divisions among Rwandan higher-ups, especially within the army, while making clear that the era of international diplomatic indulgence toward Rwanda was coming to an end.

It was in this context that the celebrations of the twentieth anniversary of the genocide were held with hope that they would help to restore order and national unity: an additional boost came from the often repeated slogan of the fight against genocide, the "negative forces," the traitors, and their foreign accomplices. The national justice system was also mobilized.

In response to international criticism of the murder of Patrick Karegeya, the Rwandans reacted immediately by alluding to the existence of a vast conspiracy. On 26 January the Ministry of Defense spokesman announced the start of the "trial against terror" intended to prove to national and international opinion alike the joint implication of the Rwanda National Congress (RNC)—the party in exile, cofounded by Patrick Karegeya—and the FDLR (Forces démocratiques de libération du Rwanda, or Democratic Forces for the Liberation of Rwanda) in the grenade attacks that have taken place from time to time since 2010 in Rwanda. This process was aimed principally at Joel Mutabazi, President Kagame's former bodyguard, who was extradited after he was kidnapped in Uganda, where he was under the protection of the United Nations High Commission for Refugees (UNHCR), and who was accused—along with his presumed accomplices—of terrorism, desertion, and conspiracy against the head of state.

Another symbolic example of the radicalization of the authorities concerns a young singer, Kizito Mihigo: his reputation had been raised to the level of national star by the Rwandan authorities, so much so that he was invited to sing an anthem to the victims of the genocide during the official ceremonies. Wrongly assuming that he would be protected by his fame, he expressed the wish to include the victims on the "losing side" in his homage.[5] Not surprisingly, he "disappeared" just before the ceremonies before reappearing in public on 14 April, charged with "implication in the planning of terrorist attacks against Rwanda, a violent attempt to overthrow the government, of assassination of government officials, and incitement of the population to violence," following a troll by police of Internet comments on social media networks intercepted by the intelligence department.[6] In December 2014 he was sentenced to life in prison for his involvement in a terrorist plot.

A second example concerns the battle at the Security Council over the use of the expression "genocide in Rwanda," which should be replaced by "genocide against the Tutsis." This phrase, which has been strongly criticized, especially by the United States, carries a step further the political instrumentalization long practiced by the Rwandan regime, with the paradoxical result that after having decreed the end of ethnic groups, it was now giving them renewed salience. Thus, the Ndi Umunyurwanda (I am Rwandan) program launched in 2013 offers to every Hutu the opportunity to ask forgiveness for the crimes committed in the name of every Hutu and to every Tutsi the chance to forgive in the name of all the Tutsi. Collective guilt for some, collective impunity for others. This approach brings together the underlying foundations of the gacaca people's justice system, which pursued almost every adult Hutu male to be brought to trial and which is wading through a vast program of extradition requests and prosecutions that target the opponents in the diaspora. In the deteriorating domestic political climate, it also invites the Tutsi elite to form a block around the regime and its president at a moment when the debate on the "third mandate" of the president is on everyone's mind. Originally conceived as a tool for international recognition and to cement real national unity, and more recently becoming an aid to forced reconciliation, the national public policy to "promote, manage, and defend the memory of the genocide" is now morphing into a political instrument designed to strengthen the legitimacy of both the government and the underlying political mythology.

The break with the past introduces a line of demarcation imposed on all Rwandans, and beyond, on all those who have business with or have an interest in Rwanda. Since 2003 the battle against genocide has indeed been based on a legal framework that permits the prosecution of those who refuse to accept this break. In the name of the "divisionism, revisionism, negationism" triptych, the concept of criminalization has been extended to include any conduct of noncompliance with orders and commands from military personnel and the political leaders of the RPF determining the everyday life of the country's citizens. More generally, all forms of criticism of the regime are punished, regardless of whether the criticism is of the official history relating the heroic actions of the liberators, the economic miracle that is the reconstruction of Rwanda, or the enlightened government by the head of state, who incarnates the restored national unity and proclaims himself as the guarantor of regional stability.

However, after the trauma of the civil war and genocide, the painful but necessary ordeal of justice, the burdens of reconstruction, and the difficult process of relearning how to live together, the need for personal and collective security in compliance with the fundamental rights of all citizens recognized by law has become a widely shared imperative. Helping Rwandans transform this agenda into reality ought to be a paramount goal of the international community, bearing in mind that the benefits would extend far and wide through the entire African Great Lakes region.

The Arrest of General Emmanuel Karenzi Karake: An Epilogue or a Rekindling of the Fight against Impunity?

Was it a strategic arrest? Calculated to conclusively bury the case and put an end to the harassment of activists battling against impunity and the annoyance of further investigations, perhaps modeled on the scenario of the November 2008 arrest of Rose Kabuye in Germany? (In that case chief warrant officer Rose Kabuye, head of protocol for the presidency in Kigali, was detained in Germany on a French warrant, but requested a "fast transfer to France," where she was formally charged ten days later and released without bail. Eventually she was authorized to leave French territory with no further proceedings.) Or, rather, is Karake's arrest a demonstration of the uncompromising rigor of European police procedures and the exemplary independence of British justice? Only the hearings planned for the later part of 2015 will make that clear.

But the general Karenzi Karake is no ordinary accused. He, in particular, was charged with numerous crimes committed in Rwanda and the DRC during and after 1994, including two massacres that claimed the lives of Spanish nationals in 1995 and 1997. In 2014, Spanish authorities modified the indictment in conformity with newly introduced legislation on universal jurisdiction. The original counts of genocide, crimes against humanity, and war crimes were removed and a new arrest warrant alleging terrorism for the deaths of nine Spanish nationals was issued. On 25 June 2015 the Westminster court granted bail and released Karake on house arrest pending an extradition hearing, scheduled for 3 October 2015.

The arrest of this particular official, known to frequent Great Britain in the past, generated great surprise and strong reactions in Rwanda. With the exception of the French case linked to the downing of the presidential plane on 6 April 1994, this is, in fact, the first time that a member of the victor's camp has ever had to face criminal charges for the killing of foreign nationals (see chap. 7, note 5). In every other case, notably in Canada and Belgium, similar accusations foundered on procedural grounds or the complainants were discouraged from proceeding.

Despite the fevered opposition it kicked up, or perhaps because of this very opposition, this arrest had the potential to mark a decisive turning point in the judicial response to crimes committed as an extension of the war and genocide of 1994. Even though expressly limited to terrorism, the Spanish indictment invokes the factual narrative underlying the original charges, including allegations against current Rwandan president Paul Kagame, who remains insulated from prosecution as head of state. More broadly, this arrest revives scrutiny of the previously suppressed investigations of "revenge killings" of Hutu, as well as the war crimes and crimes against humanity committed in the DRC already alleged or documented in investigative reports commissioned by the UN Security Council. These reports have since been shelved, or rather classified, along with those detailing the economic crimes linked to the pillaging of the country's mineral resources.

Additionally, this arrest revives debate about the refusals by various ICTR prosecutors to implement their "second mandate" despite the proof that was available, evidence that the implicated Rwandan authorities have consistently demanded be turned over to them, along with the complete archives of the tribunal.

Given the current political context and the stakes in Rwanda, the highly anticipated decision of the judges arouses great interest. Surprisingly, the resolution came on 10 August 2015, well in advance of the scheduled hearings, through a seeming "legal loophole" that allowed the Westminster Magistrates' Court to set the accused free.

Howard Riddle, chief magistrate for England and Wales, ruled there was insufficient evidence to substantiate Spain's allegations under UK law. For extradition to proceed, there must be enough proof to sustain the charges under the laws of both the country seeking extradition and the one where a suspect has been detained.

The British court was persuaded by the arguments of Mrs. Cherie Blair, spouse of the former UK prime minister, who led General Karake's defense team, and carefully decided that it was not competent to examine the crimes alleged against the general. Emmanuel Karenzi Karake was immediately released and returned to Rwanda, where he received a hero's welcome.

Again, given the context and the stakes, this unsatisfying end comes as no surprise. Those who follow these matters will simply take note that, here too, yet another judicial authority resorted to procedural grounds to avoid delving into the substance and content underpinning the arrest warrant. The opportunity for an independent court to probe into the grave crimes and massacres at the root of the indictment was studiously avoided. The crimes alleged will remain unexamined and unpunished.

But just getting this criminal case started is still some measure of vindication for all those in Rwanda who have already paid with their lives, or with stiff terms in jail, for having seen, or for having dared to testify about, these crimes, or quite simply for daring to question or try to find out about them.

Indeed, as the Rwandan authorities themselves have reiterated since General Karenzi Karake's arrest, any accusation made against any member of the victor's camp, regardless of who makes it, is deemed a crime of "defense of genocidal ideology."

Appendix: Box 5

Political Parties and Organizations
Officially Registered in 1991

In June 1991 a new constitution enshrining multiparty competition was adopted. At first, five political parties were registered, and their articles of association were published in the *Journal Officiel*. The MDR (Democratic Republican Movement) was the first to announce its birth in March 1991, followed a few days later by the PSD (Social Democratic Party), the PL (Liberal Party), the PDC (Christian Democratic Party), and the PSR (Rwandan Socialist Party). Almost immediately, these groups established among themselves rules for consultation to impose a redistribution of the roles with the MRNDD (National Republican Movement for Democracy and Development).

Then new contenders appeared, in the order of their registration: the RTD (Labour Rally for Democracy), the PDI (Islamic Democratic Party), Peco (Green Party), PPJR–Rama Rwanda (Progressive Party of the Rwandan Youth), Parerwa (Republican Party of Rwanda), and Pader (Rwandan Democratic Party), mostly raised by the MRNDD.

Twelve parties were thus reported in February 1992, and by April 1994 six others had been officially recognized: the PD (Democratic Party), the CDR (Coalition for the Defense of the Republic), the UDPR (Democratic Union of the Rwandan People), the MFBP (Women and Lower People Movement), the PRD (Party for Democratic Renewal, close to the MRND and MDR-Power trend), and UNISODEC (Social Union of Christian Democrats). The RPF wasn't included because of its armed component. Awaiting the integration of its military agents in the new Rwandan army, the RPF considered itself a "political organization." All these parties could be grouped around three major alliances:

1. ARD (Alliance for the Strengthening of Democracy), created on 12 November 1992 and gathering, in the order of their importance, the MRND, the CDR, Peco, Parerwa, and Pader:

- MRNDD (National Republican Movement for Democracy and Development, formerly MRND from 1975 to 1991), president, Matthieu Ngirumpatse (Hutu, rural Kigali)
- CDR (nicknamed "Akazu MRND"), president, Martin Bucyana (Hutu, Cyangugu), killed in Butare on 23 February 1993 and replaced by Théoneste Nahimana (Hutu, Gisenyi)

Both groups maintained "youth movements," respectively:

- Interahamwe ("those who work together"), 1991, president, Robert Kajuga (Tutsi, Kibungo) (see chapter 6)
- Impuzamugambi ("those who share the same goal"), 1993, president, Stanislas Simbizi (Hutu, Gisenyi)

Many of these can best be described as bogus organizations designed to broaden the political base of what was then called the mouvance présidentielle; examples include:

- Peco, president, Dr. Jean-Baptiste Butera (Hutu, Kibungo)
- Parerwa, president, Augustin Mutamba (Hutu, rural Kigali), and vice president, Augustin Semucyo (Hutu, rural Kigali)
- Pader, national secretary, Jean-Baptiste Ntagungira (Hutu, rural Kigali)

Moreover, although not belonging to the ARD, the following parties could be considered as part of the presidential camp:

- MFBP, chaired by Gaudence Nyirasafari Habimana (Hutu, Gisenyi)
- PDI, presided over by Omar Hamidou (Hutu, Kigali) and coordinated by André Bumaya (Hutu, Cyangugu)
- PRD, president, Alexis Nsabimana (Hutu, Gitarama)
- UNISODEC, president, Célestin Mutabaruka (Hutu, Gikongoro)

2. FDC (Democratic Forces for Change), involving the MDR, PSD, PL, PDC, and PSR:

- MDR, president, Faustin Twagiramungu (excluded on 23 July 1993), senior vice president, Dismas Nsengiyaremye (from mid-1993, the MDR was divided into a pro-RPF faction called Amajyogi, led by Faustin Twagira-mungu, and a faction called Abapawa, led by Froduald Karamira [Hutu, Gitarama] and Donat Murego [Hutu, Ruhengeri])

- Inkuba, "the lightning," the youth movement of the MDR, established on 6 July 1993, led by Bernardin Ndayishimye (Hutu, Gitarama)
- PL, president, Justin Mugenzi (Hutu, Kibungo), first vice president, Landoald Ndasingwa (Tutsi, Kigali), second vice president, Stanislas Mbonampeka (Hutu, Ruhengeri), secretary-general, Agnès Ntamabyaliro (Hutu, Kibuye) (the PL suffered from the same internal tensions as the MDR, leading to a split in December 1993)
- PSD, president, Frédéric Nzamurambaho (Hutu, Gikongoro), first vice president, Félicien Ngango (Hutu, Kibungo), second vice president, Théoneste Gafaranga (Hutu, Gitarama), executive secretary, Félicien Gatabazi (Hutu, Butare)
- PDC, president, Jean-Népomuscène Nayinzira (Hutu, Gisenyi), first vice president, Théobald Gakwaya Rwaka (Hutu, Cyangugu)
- PSR, president, Dr. Antoine Ntezilyimana (Hutu, Gikongoro), first vice president, Médard Rutijanwa (Tutsi, Kigali)

The PL, PSD, and PDC also created their own youth movements: the PL's youth group lacked a specific name; the PSD's was known as Abakombozi; and the PDC's was the Young Christian Democrats.

3. "Independent" parties: Democratic Party, PPJR–Rama Rwanda, RTD, and UDPR:

- PD, president, Ildephonse Nayigizente (Hutu, Byumba)
- PPJR–Rama Rwanda, first executive secretary, André Hakizimana (Hutu, Gitarama)
- RTD, chair, Emmanuel Nizeyimana (Hutu, Byumba)
- UDPR, president, Vincent Rwabukwisi (Hutu, Gitarama)

The first three parties kept close relations with the ARD, while the UDPR was closer to the FDC (the UDPR chairman was assassinated in April 1994).

List of Boxes

List of Annexes

Notes

Preface to the Original Edition

1. André Guichaoua, ed., *Exilés, réfugiés, déplacés en Afrique centrale et orientale* (Paris: Karthala, 2004).

2. André Guichaoua, *Rwanda 1994: Les politiques du génocide à Butare* (Paris: Karthala, 2005).

3. After the introduction of multipartyism, the generic term *mouvance présidentielle* identified the array of persons or groups that continued to define themselves in relation to President Habyarimana, remaining loyal to him and linking their interests and ascendancy to his.

4. UNAMIR was created on 5 October 1994 by UN Security Council Resolution 872 and completed its mission on 8 March 1996. Its mandate was to contribute to ensuring security in the city of Kigali, to supervise the cease-fire agreement, and to supervise the general conditions of security during the final phase in the mandate of the transitional government until elections in mid-May 1996. The military commander of the mission was Gen. Roméo Antonius Dallaire (Canada), on active duty since the initiation of the mission through 20 August 1994; he was formally under the authority of Jacques-Roger Booh-Booh (Cameroon), special representative of the secretary-general of the United Nations and head of the mission from 23 November 1993 to 15 June 1994.

Chapter 1. The Social and Political Context

1. These census figures underestimated the Tutsi population because of the changes in ethnic identity requested by the families. The differences are negligible, depending on the year.

2. The prefecture was literally emptied of its Tutsi residents during the various periods of tension and clashes that characterized the "social revolution" (1959) and the first years of the republic. A good number resettled in uninhabited areas in rural Kigali, particularly in the Bugesera.

3. The term *évolués* characterizes the first generations of secondary school graduates recruited by the colonial administration and to whom it turned for support.

4. The "events of 1972" refer to a particularly bloody episode in the country's turbulent history, resulting in the deaths of an estimated two hundred thousand Hutu at the hands of a Tutsi-dominated army following a localized Hutu-led rural insurrection. The scale and intensity of the massacres came as a shock to outside observers and Burundians alike. There is no room here for a full-scale discussion of the sequence of events and the complexity of the underlying causes. Suffice it to say that Burundian society was profoundly and lastingly convulsed by what can legitimately be described as a genocide.

5. See André Guichaoua, "La région des événements," in *La crise d'août 1988 au Burundi*, ed. Jean-Pierre Chrétien, André Guichaoua, and Gabriel Le Jeune (Paris: CRA/Karthala, 1989), 17.

6. On the history of refugees from this region, see Guichaoua, *Exilés, réfugiés, déplacés*, 122–30.

7. In fact, after independence countless numbers of refugees were registered as coming from Rwanda; with the exception of Algeria after 1954, Rwanda was the first African country to produce a substantial number of refugees, or at least the first officially recorded as such. The outflow rose to substantially higher levels with repeated crises throughout the region (1963, 1965, 1969, 1972, 1973, etc.) until the early 2000s. By then the region claimed one of the largest concentrations of refugees worldwide.

8. An authoritarian framework impressed them as a cardinal virtue and the key to efficiency; the negative side of the ledger, including arbitrary or exclusive authority, was largely brushed aside by the international community. Seemingly unmoved by episodes of mass violence, donors consistently viewed Burundi and Rwanda as "stable" and "well-administered" countries, going so far as to use them as reference points for their interventions to restore peace elsewhere in the region in political contexts that were even more chaotic.

9. Other than Col. Épimaque Ruhashya, the only Tutsi among the officers who were members of the Committee for Peace and National Unity, and the two Tutsi deputies in the National Assembly, all of the prefects and burgomasters during that period were Hutu. Without exception, those who were rumored to be Tutsi had identity cards indicating their ethnicity as Hutu.

10. Condemned to death by a court-martial along with seven other detainees in June 1974, the toppled president, Grégoire Kayibanda, died under mysterious circumstances in his home, where he was held under house arrest. Several dozen of the dignitaries of the First Republic also died in inhuman conditions. This was particularly the case for those who were detained together in the sinister "special section" of the Ruhengeri prison under the authority of Maj. Théoneste Lizinde. These unsolved and incomprehensible murders significantly alienated the populations and leaders from the south.

11. The network of civilian and military figures closest to Habyarimana included Alphonse Libanje (director of OCIR-Thé, the state-owned tea plantation consortium),

Jean-Berchmans Birara (governor of the national bank), Aloys Bizimana (administrator for the Banque de Kigali), all natives of Bugoyi, and Jean-Bosco Rugigana (ex-secretary-general of the Ministry of Finance), originally from Byumba, on the one hand, and a group of highly influential officers close to President Habyarimana, in particular Col. Laurent Serubuga (deputy army chief of staff), Col. Bonaventure Buregeya (secretary-general for the presidency, relieved on 16 April 1980), and Col. Pierre-Célestin Rwagafilita (deputy chief of staff of the gendarmerie), on the other.

12. *See annex 1*: it includes a list of the first sets of graduates from the Officers Training School (École d'officiers) and then of the Military High Command School (École supérieure militaire), which shows the regional origins and the interconnections of the various officers.

13. While the president understood the reasons for the southern politicians' opposition, irrespective of their political ambition, these events triggered some lasting enmities. But the accumulation of these political errors seems to suggest a deep-seated fear of southern politicians, provoking emotionally driven decisions. The marginalization of these figures was accompanied by a series of suspicious deaths among them toward the end of the 1980s and by a policy aimed at humiliating southern leaders.

Chapter 2. The Refugee Question and the RPF's Choice of Armed Struggle

1. Note that the separate designation RPA rarely appears in the literature because, in fact, the two are so thoroughly interlaced that any reference to the RPF usually refers to both the RPF and the RPA.

2. There are divergent estimates of the actual number of combatants: between fifteen hundred and seven thousand, depending on the source. In fact, during the first two weeks of the attack, there were no more than four "battalions" involved, at most fifteen hundred men. The larger figure seems to correspond to the total number of RPA soldiers, composed of approximately four thousand former recruits of the Ugandan army and around three thousand "civilians." They were mostly Rwandan refugees, joined by Kinyarwanda-speaking Ugandans or Ugandans of Rwandan origin and a good number of Ugandan officers and soldiers whose units had deserted.

3. The FAR definitively retook Gabiro and the surrounding region in late October. Troops from Zaire had withdrawn by mid-October, followed by Belgian troops in November, whereas the French intervention, code-named "Noroît," was extended, since Rwandan authorities anticipated another general offensive toward the end of 1990.

4. More broadly, three groups must be distinguished: Rwandaphone elements who had lived outside Rwanda since precolonial times; those who migrated during the colonial period, for the most part economic migrants; and refugees of predominantly Tutsi origins who left Rwanda immediately before or after independence. Just as their motives differed, the social boundaries among them are problematic because of cross-cutting cultural and family ties.

5. Namely, "return to Rwanda; remain in Uganda with hopes of being naturalized; or resettle in a third country." See République rwandaise, Commission spéciale sur les problèmes des émigrés rwandais, "Le Rwanda et le problème de ses réfugiés: Contexte historique, analyse et voies de solution," Kigali, May 1990, chapter 4, point 2.

6. This observation was never challenged in diplomatic circles, particularly among Africans.

7. This phrase was usually used by the activists of the diaspora.

8. The FDC brought together under the same roof the political forces opposed to the MRND-sponsored Alliance for the Strengthening of Democracy (ARD, Alliance pour le renforcement de la démocratie).

9. See, for example, the documentation of the International Colloquium for the Protection of African Refugees in Dakar, 1982.

10. Between October 1982 and early 1983, some forty thousand Banyarwanda fled from Uganda to Rwanda. Six to eight thousand of them were stopped at the border after it was closed by Rwanda. Almost all these returnees were able to reenter Uganda after Yoweri Museveni rose to power toward the end of November 1985. Eighty thousand other Banyarwanda had been regrouped in camps in the south of Uganda, of which approximately thirty thousand were moved to other locations in the interior of the country afterward.

11. Notably, during the Congress of Rwandan Refugees held in Washington in August 1988.

12. The influence of Ugandans' hold revealed itself to be quite decisive after the RPF took power; it goes far in explaining the demographic weight of RPF-affiliated Ugandans in Kigali and their almost unfettered control over the country. It was those Rwandaphones from Uganda who allowed returnees from Uganda to expand their numbers in relation to the Burundian or Zairean Tutsi and the genocide survivors. The expression "civilian RPF" referred to Tutsi intellectuals who joined the movement, notably those from Western countries who had neither military backgrounds nor training.

13. *Kangura*, no. 30 (January 1992): 9.

14. See Jean-Baptiste Nsanzimfura and François-Xavier Nsanzuwera, "Le génocide des rwandais Tutsis: Un plan politico-militaire," ronéo (mimeograph), ICTR, Arusha, December 2003.

15. Bernard Lugan, *Rwanda: Contre-enquête sur le génocide* (Toulouse: Privat, 2007), 42ff.

16. The estimates made by independent organizations exceeded eight thousand persons and did not take into account those held in communal jails.

17. See the article "Abategetsi bamwe ni bo bayoboye imvururu muri Murambi" (Certain authorities organized the incidents in Murambi), published in the Catholic journal *Kinyamateka*, 1 November 1991, and various other articles published in the same issue, followed by lists of disappeared persons from the Bugesera.

18. *Inyenzi* (cockroach) is the term that was used to designate the Tutsi combatants who participated in attacks to reestablish the monarchy in the 1960s. They then appropriated the term by using it as an abbreviation for *Ingangurarugo yiyemeje kuba ingenzi* ("combatant of the Ingangurarugo militia," meaning that they were the most valiant). The Ingangurarugo were one of King Rwabugiri's most feared fighting forces.

19. The first president of the republic, Grégoire Kayibanda, appointed Rusatira to the post of chief of staff in the Ministry of the National Guard and the Police (which later became the Ministry of Defense) while Col. Juvénal Habyarimana was in charge of this department. Kayibanda continued to serve under Habyarimana until the first multiparty government appointed him head of the École supérieure militaire in June 1992. *See annex 7.2* for discussion of the significance of the debates generated by this commission.

Chapter 3. A Necessary Political Transition

1. Although it was only an informal party organ, the "political bureau" still remained a privileged site for President Habyarimana's decision making.

2. Article 5, MRND Party Statute, *Official Journal*, no. 16, 15 August 1991.

3. James Gasana, *Rwanda, du parti-état à l'état-garnison* (Paris: L'Harmattan, 2002), 86.

4. Mention must be made in this regard of the role played by foreign embassies and pressure organizations (especially the International Christian Democrats), which threw their weight behind specific parties or candidates in hopes of cashing in at a later date on their political investments.

5. For many years Noël Mbonabaryi occupied the strategic post of director-general of employment in the Ministry of Civil Service and Employment. His approval was required for all recruitments of senior personnel in private industry. He worked closely with the Service central de renseignement (SCR), which was authorized to review all nominations at the senior level in the public and private sectors, as well as political appointments. From 1973 to 1980 this service, headed by Maj. Théoneste Lizinde, was a major instrument of repression. Noël Mbonabaryi died in early 1994.

6. According to Clément-Jérôme Bicamumpaka (MDR, minister of foreign affairs and cooperation in the Interim Government), during a meeting of the party's Studies and Programs commission in February 1992, linguist and senior MDR party official Boniface Ngulinzira proposed the term as a means of designating persons in the president's entourage who had not been officially nominated or elected. The term was then adopted by the MDR Political Bureau and used in various communiqués before it was finally taken over by the political opposition across the board (see the trial testimony of Clément-Jérôme Bicamumpaka, ICTR, 17 September 2007).

7. Witness ADE (MRND member and member of the Akazu), OTP (Office of the Prosecutor) witness statement (Annex I), 11 October 2004, p. 9 (ERN no. K036-0532-0532).

8. These terms include the "Zero Network," which shot to fame after the publication of Christophe Mfizi's open letter of resignation from the MRND, addressed to Habyarimana (*Le réseau zéro*, Kigali, 15 August 1992). Mfizi was a dignitary of the regime who broke with the MRND. He later preferred the term "Z-ist order," a nebulous configuration constructed around Protais Zigiranyirazo and other members of the president's family of in-laws.

9. Agathe Kanziga, who was among the first class of graduates receiving diplomas in the postindependence period (1962), looked beyond this generation to graduates of the École sociale, which she deemed a veritable incubator of candidates. Alumnae were organized in an association of former students, and she searched for talented candidates among them.

10. Gaudence Nyirasafari Habimana attended primary school with Juvénal Habyarimana at the Rambura Parish of Gisenyi and then afterward was educated in Europe, a rare privilege for a Rwandan woman at that time. Parenthetically, Gaudence Nyirasafari Habimana's husband is Phocas Habimana, who directed RTLM (Radio-Télévision libre des mille collines, or Radio-Television of the Thousand Hills).

11. Gasana, *Rwanda*, 37.

12. Note that in Rwanda each person is individually named, without a customary last name or family name indicating paternity or lineage.

13. See André Guichaoua, "Laurent Semanza, the 'great burgomaster,'" expert report, ICTR, Arusha, April 2001.

14. The negotiated defections of former dignitaries of the Second Republic to the RPF had initiated this process in 1990.

15. Although drawn into the same debates and political confrontations, personnel affiliated with the army, the territorial administration, the parliament, and the judiciary were not authorized to join political parties, which muffled any expression of dissent. For the economic sphere, see Guichaoua, *Rwanda 1994*, 120–23.

16. Seth Sendashonga, Hutu intellectual, joined the RPF and became one of its principal leaders.

17. Fundamental law in force as of 17 July 1994.

Chapter 4. The Arusha Negotiations and the Reconfiguration of Political Forces

1. See chap. 11, "Before the Genocide: The Role of the OAU," in the document "Rwanda: The Preventable Genocide," by the International Panel of Eminent Personalities, 2000, Addis Ababa, http://www.refworld.org/pdfid/4d1da8752.pdf (*see annex 5*).

2. The French operation, code-named Noroît, was launched on 4 October 1990 at President Habyarimana's request in response to the RPF offensive. The detachment was composed of a tactical command of 40 persons and two companies of 137 persons each. They were tasked with protecting the French Embassy, ensuring security for French nationals and preparing their evacuation. In fact, between 5 and 12 October, 313 French nationals left Rwanda. In December 1990 only a single company was

maintained in Kigali. See the report of Gen. Jean-Claude Thomann in Assemblée nationale française, *Enquête sur la tragédie rwandaise (1990–1994)* (Paris, 1998), 2:138.

3. This protocol of agreement contains four chapters: "National Unity," "Democracy," "Political Pluralism," and "Human Rights."

4. This second protocol of agreement was subdivided into five sections: "State Institutions," "The President of the Republic," "The Broad-Based Transitional Government," "The Transitional National Assembly," and "Judicial Institutions." It transferred most of the president's prerogatives to an executive council. The executive would henceforth issue from the cabinet of a future transitional government in which all of the large parties would be represented.

5. From 22 February to 28 March 1993 a special operation dubbed Chimère, composed of approximately twenty officers and specialists of the 1er régiment de parachutistes d'infanterie de marine (1er RPIMa, or First Marine Infantry Parachute Regiment) arrived as reinforcements, regrouping all of the soldiers in the Détachement d'assistance militaire et d'instruction (DAMI, Group for Military Assistance and Training), 69 men in all, and the reinforcements of Noroît (whose numbers rose to 688). The objective was to indirectly mobilize an army of approximately twenty thousand men and to indirectly command it. See Assemblée nationale française, *Enquête*, 1:157.

6. Among the final dispositions were the suppression of all reference to ethnic identity in identity cards and acceptance and incorporation in domestic law of certain international conventions on human rights.

7. In April 1992 Christophe Mfizi, the director of Orinfor, published a particularly strident denunciation of what he referred to as the "zero network," giving credence to the existence of "death squads" commanded by the presidency that were determined to destroy the opposition. For purposes of illustration, we can point to the first explosion imputed to the RPF of 6 May 1992 in Butare at the Hôtel Faucon, where the first meetings of MDR prefectural leaders were held after the multiparty government was installed.

8. Numbers determined by the UNAMIR ad hoc commission of inquiry.

9. Testimony of Gen. Roméo Dallaire, *Prosecutor v. Bagosora et al.*, ICTR case no. 98-41-T, 21 January 2004, p. 60 (*see annex 16*).

10. Testimony of Brent Beardsley, *Bagosora et al.*, 4 February 2004, pp. 28–29 (*see annex 16*).

11. All the other officers in the Group of Friends of 5 July 1973 had been expelled or sidelined since the MRND came into being, sealing the personal power of President Habyarimana amid a tight circle of his most ardent devotees.

12. A respected figure, Sylvestre Nsanzimana, a native of Gikongoro and the former minister of foreign affairs under Grégoire Kayibanda who went on to become the first Rwandan rector of the National University of Rwanda, held the post of assistant secretary general of the OAU when President Habyarimana first approached him to sort out the internal political morass.

13. The promotion to head of the armed forces appealed to Bagosora's strongest yearnings, and by rising to the rank of general he would thus escape the fifty-year-old

age limit and would have become the army's highest-ranking officer. But it was also a means for Habyarimana to place Bagosora under his direct control and gain a proxy to counterbalance the authority of the minister among officers from the north.

14. Bagosora's retirement on 23 September 1993 had been announced on 1 January 1993.

15. Extracts of President Habyarimana's speech at an MRND rally in Ruhengeri on 15 November 1992, in ICTR, Arusha, ERN no. KV00-0392E, exhibit no. P-011(E) (2), *Prosecutor v. Karemera et al.*, ICTR case no. 98-44-T (*see annex 20*).

16. Ibid.

17. Gasana, *Rwanda*, 168.

18. This investigative team traveled to Rwanda from 7 to 21 January 1993. See International Federation of Human Rights / Africa Watch / Interafrican Union for Human and People's Rights / International Center for Human Rights and Democratic Development, "Report of the International Commission of Investigation on Human Rights Violations in Rwanda since 1 October 1990," 8 March 1993.

19. Statement of Dismas Nsengiyaremye (made following the decision of the cabinet meeting on 3 February 1993) in "Rapport de la Commission politico-administrative sur les troubles dans les préfectures de Gisenyi, Ruhengeri et Kibuye."

20. Assemblée nationale française, *Enquête*, 1:109–10 (*see also annex 23.3*).

21. An officer who graduated with the third promotion, Stanislas Mbonampeka was commander of the Kigali military camp, where the military coup d'état originated in July 1973. But the camp commander had neither administrative nor operational authority over the units stationed there, which reported directly to the general staff.

22. Article 51, "Power Sharing."

23. Enoch Ruhigira to the prime minister, 23 January 1993.

24. Juvénal Habyarimana often confided to close associates that he did not understand Dismas Nsengiyaremye's refusal to seize the presidency of the MDR from Faustin Twagiramungu.

25. *See annex 25*; Guichaoua, *Rwanda 1994*, esp. chaps. 4 and 5.

26. *See annex 2*; Gasana, *Rwanda*, 208–9.

27. On 15 July, on his own initiative, the French ambassador paid Gasana a friendly visit in his office at the Ministry of Defense. After learning of his intention to travel to Switzerland, Ambassador Jean-Michel Marlaud offered him a diplomatic visa for France, valid for three months, which was delivered to him the following day, personally signed by the ambassador.

28. Director of a management project for the valleys of the Mutara, Augustin Bizimana underwent training in management in 1987 in Canada, where he met Protais Zigiranyirazo. Upon his return, "Mr. Z" arranged for him to be appointed director of the Office du pyrèthre du Rwanda (OPYRWA, Office of Pyrethrum Rwanda) in Ruhengeri. Promoted to prefect of Byumba in July 1992, he became the man whom the presidency could rely on. After James Gasana's flight into exile, Bizimana's nomination to the head of the Ministry of Defense on 30 July 1993 was presented as a solution for continuity (the same prefecture of origin and the same profile as Gasana).

29. Jean Kambanda was born on 19 October 1955 in Gishamvu commune, Butare prefecture. A founding member of the MDR and a rival of Agathe Uwilingiyimana in Butare prefecture, he took the lead in the Power wing of the party after she was excluded.

30. For this point, I rely on information provided by James Gasana in his study, *Rwanda*, 216.

31. Summary drafted on 8 May 1993 following a long conversation between the author and Matthieu Ngirumpatse.

32. The military portion of the Arusha Peace Accords anticipated that the integration of former RPF and government combatants in a single army (where the total manpower would be limited to thirteen thousand men) and in the gendarmerie (six thousand in all in the future) would share equally in the command structure and achieve a 40:60 ratio in troop composition. The RPF claimed to have fifteen thousand men, and the government forces numbered forty thousand, which meant that thirty-five thousand men had to be demobilized.

Chapter 5. Unspoken Terms in the Arusha Peace Accords and Obstructions in the Political Transition

1. The withdrawal of all foreign troops was to immediately follow the arrival of the Groupe d'observateurs militaires neutres de l'OUA (GOMN, Group of Neutral Military Observers of the OAU), with the exception of military aid workers who were in Rwanda pursuant to bilateral aid agreements.

2. Those refugees not requesting financial support or reimbursement could return whenever they wished.

3. The possibility of a one-time extension, justified by exceptional circumstances delaying implementation of the government program, was anticipated.

4. This was also a serious military error that generated lasting suspicion within the FAR command about the choice made by the politicians.

5. This was exactly General Dallaire's perception when he took up his duties at the time (*see annex 31*). This also seems to have been the opinion of the principal Tanzanian negotiators: "The Tanzanian prime minister, Mr. John Malecela, had confirmed this state of affairs to me in Arusha in August 1993, the day after the accords were signed, when he paid me a visit at my hotel and asked me . . . to defend this agreement. He plainly told me that he was fully aware that the RPF had only signed under great pressure and would likely use the slightest pretext to block implementation" (an important Rwandan political figure, personal conversation with the author, 20 January 2006).

6. International Panel of Eminent Personalities, "Rwanda," § 8.12 and, more generally, §§ 8.10–13; *see also annex 5*.

7. See Ministère de la Fonction publique, Commission nationale d'évaluation des agents de l'État, *Administration territoriale*, part A, 31 July 1992, part B, 12 August 1992, part C, 3 May 1993.

8. By the terms of a ministerial directive dated 11 March 1993, the electoral college (*grands électeurs*) would include representatives from political circles and outstanding local figures in religious circles and civil society organizations.

9. Arthémon Simbananiye, a Burundian Tutsi from Bururi province, home of the officers who seized power from 1965 to 1993, managed the Burundian judicial administration from 1965 to 1972 before acceding to other prominent positions. In the minds and memory of Hutu from Burundi and Rwanda alike, "Micombero strategy" and "Simbananiye plan" are forever linked to a presumed plan to kill the greatest number of Hutu possible in order to finally achieve a numeric parity between Hutu and Tutsi.

10. Matthieu Ngirumpatse, "La Tragédie rwandaise: L'autre face de l'histoire," photocopied document, drafted in exile, most likely in 1996, p. 105 (*see annex 26*).

11. The titular presidents of the MDR and PL each presented lists that differed from the ones submitted by the majority organs of their respective parties (*see annex 37*).

12. Jacques-Roger Booh-Booh to Kofi Annan, 14 February 1994, UNAMIR code cable, MIR 345.

13. The "Twagiramungu" and "Ndasingwa" wings of the MDR and PL each obtained six seats, and their opponents obtained five, to which another CDR deputy could possibly be added.

14. Félicien Gatabazi had just informed Habyarimana and the prime minister that the pro-RPF wings of the PSD and PL had agreed to send members of their respective youth wings to Mulindi for military training and to receive weapons that had recently been delivered. He asked them to intervene and demand that all youth wings of all political parties be disarmed.

15. See article 11 of the "Protocol of Agreement between the Government of the Republic of Rwanda and the Rwandese Patriotic Front on Miscellaneous Issues and Final Provisions": "In the event of violation of the Fundamental Law by the President of the Republic, his indictment shall be decided by the Transitional National Assembly on the basis of a 2/3 majority vote of the members present and by secret ballot. However, prior to voting on the indictment, the Transitional National Assembly shall consult the Joint Political Military Commission (JPMC) referred to in Article IV of the Ceasefire Agreement as amended at Gbadolite 16th September, 1991 and at Arusha 12th July, 1992. It may also consult the Facilitator. In case the indictment is confirmed to be appropriate, the President is answerable to the Constitutional Court which alone is competent to decide on his immediate resignation."

16. Hearing, Special Commission on Rwanda, Belgian Senate, Brussels, 29 April 1997, p. 7.

17. Lt. M. Nees, intelligence officer, UNAMIR, 11 February 1994, KIBAT (Kigali Batallion), S2.

18. See the collection of materials in André Guichaoua, *Butare, la préfecture rebelle*, ICTR expert report in *Prosecutor v. Nyiramasuhuko et al.* (the Butare case) (Annex 12), 3:53–83.

19. See Gasana, *Rwanda*, 246.

20. Ngirumpatse, *La tragédie rwandaise*, 116.

21. Testimony of Roméo Dallaire, *Bagosora et al.*, ICTR, 23 January 2004, p. 25.

22. "They were saying, just like when Ingabire was killed, they were saying that the situation was tense, just wait. . . . We're going to strike, everyone stay alert. Someone said: 'What's going to happen? Ingabire, we going to kill him. Who is going to do it? Kiyago, Kiyago is the one who's going to do it. Good, OK'" (RPA officer, personal conversation with the author, 24 April 2005, transcription, p. 13).

23. Witness CR (former government minister), OTP witness statement, 24 February 2005, p. 10 (ERN no. K035-0145-0166).

24. The political context certainly would not permit recalling retired officers back to active service nor any sort of effort to keep on board officers who were deemed close to the opposition, but the presidential clan still had strong men at its disposal, northerners, in every prefecture of the country, and they made up a trustworthy network.

25. Even if, before installation of the BBTG, the mouvance présidentielle dared not compromise its unity when up against its adversaries, such a scenario was still possible further down the road. The extraordinary fluidity in the political arena generated by multipartyism gave way to all sorts of alliances. Consequently, the few converts to the RPF, dubbed "RPF-Power" (Hutu who were pro-RPF), were much more threatening to the presidential clan than "Tutsi" RPF. In fact, between 1992 and 1994, the various negotiating sessions provided opportunities for encounters between Hutu from the RPF (including Pasteur Bizimungu), MRND figures, and officers from Ruhengeri. A similar alliance was also discussed among the members of MDR-Twagiramungu, then linked to the RPF. But the prospect of war would not permit any contact for the time being. On the one hand, Habyarimana remained strong and consistently enforced group solidarity for those in power; on the other, the Hutu dignitaries recruited had hitched their destiny to that of the RPF.

26. Witness CR, OTP witness statement, 24 February 2005, p. 10.

27. The account of this episode relies on information that I managed to obtain from several persons who were directly involved, particularly in Kigali in February 2001, and from subsequent trips and contacts.

28. In the FAR, the general staff for the army and for the gendarmerie were each comprised of four units, G1, G2, G3, and G4, which refer to the heads of each unit. The RPA distributed responsibilities the same way, replacing the term "unit" with "department" and adding a G5.

29. Author's telephone conversation with an eminent MRND figure, 18 May 2009.

30. Note, however, that in this instance the rule only applied to officers from the south. It would have been highly unusual to even remark that political figures and soldiers from the north would meet to discuss politics.

31. Account of an MDR figure, personal conversation with the author, 21 March 2004.

32. See the author's personal conversations in 2001 and 2002 with persons involved.

33. Dismas Nsengiyaremye (former prime minister), Boniface Ngulinzira (former minister of foreign affairs), and Faustin Twagiramungu (prime minister designate for the BBTG set forth in the Arusha Peace Accords), participating in the meeting on behalf of the MDR.

34. Account of an MDR party leader, personal conversation with the author, 21 March 2004.

Chapter 6. Competition for Control of the Militias

1. OTP interview of Matthieu Ngirumpatse, 15 June 1998, ICTR, Bamako (K7 KT 00-0201, K023-6162-6162).

2. Ngirumpatse, *La tragédie rwandaise*, 69.

3. Éric Karekezi (Tutsi, Kigali) was the brother-in-law of Bonaventure Habimana (Kigali-rural), MRND secretary-general from 1975 to 1991. Eugène Mbarushimana came from a large, well-established family in Bugoyi whose "patriarch" had had approximately thirty offspring from several spouses, all of whom received his name— Eugène Mbarushimana. This Eugène married one of Félicien Kabuga's daughters, Winnie Musabayezu. Dieudonné Niyitegeka was a Hutu of a Tutsi mother (Shyanda commune, Butare, MRND).

4. Édouard Karemera also maintained his private law office in the building.

5. Reportedly, François Karera was the one who proposed the name Interahamwe ZA MRND. President Habyarimana personally negotiated George Rutaganda's and Phénéas Ruhumuliza's recruitment into the Interahamwe, while Matthieu Ngirumpatse was president of the MRND for the PVK. The president deemed it very important to co-opt particularly strong supporters from the "enemy" prefecture of Gitarama.

6. Protected witness (Interahamwe leader), OTP witness statement, 6 February– 8 May 2006, pp. 18–19. Various extracts of UN reports and witness statements are available in *annex 48*.

7. Witness T (Interahamwe leader), OTP witness statement, May 2004.

8. On 5 June 1992 the RPF and the three parties in the FDC from the government coalition signed a cease-fire agreement in Brussels, despite opposition from the MRND. This was immediately followed by renewed fighting between the RPF and the FAR in Byumba prefecture, which the MRND then presented as proof of an alliance between the domestic opposition parties and the RPF.

9. See André Guichaoua, "Laurent Semanza, the 'great burgomaster,'" expert report, ICTR, Arusha, 2001.

10. Only the national Interahamwe is analyzed here; the local varieties and derivations were analyzed in other publications devoted to Butare and Cyangugu prefectures, relying on several key examples (large enterprises, local sponsors of youth wings).

11. ORTPN was the bastion of Protais Zigiranyirazo and Charles Bunani, head manager, who had married the daughter of Noël Mbonabaryi, President Habyarimana's godfather.

12. Concerning these different strategies for co-opting support from militiamen, see chapter 8 in Guichaoua, *Rwanda 1994* (*see also annex 25*), which explores how Interahamwe leaders were financed by SORWAL in Butare, where Ngirumpatse was president of the board of directors and Karemera was general counsel. In a division of labor of exceptional sophistication organized under a variety of statutes and designations, we find on one side the principal dignitaries of the regime (those close to the president, the heads of the MRND, many ministers and bankers) and, on the other, virtually the entire national leadership of the Interahamwe but also—and this aspect is certainly the most interesting—the treasurers of various local political organizations and sympathizers such as the CDR. Here we have proof that this was an organized, unified system of predatory redistribution that benefited the broad array of political groups associated with the ARD.

13. Witness T (Interahamwe leader), protected prosecution witness, OTP witness statement, 21 May 2004, pp. 71–73 (official ICTR translation).

14. Witness G (Interahamwe leader), protected prosecution witness, transcription of OTP interview, 31 March 1997, pp. 1–2.

15. The slogan "Tuzabatsembatsemba" can also be translated as "We will exterminate them" or "We will exterminate you." Extract of testimony of Gen. Léonidas Rusatira, Special Commission on Rwanda, Belgian Senate, Brussels, 29 April 1997.

16. Matthieu Ngirumpatse to President Juvénal Habyarimana, 15 February 1993, K050-3816-3818-F; official ICTR translation, K035-7056-7057-E; see P-027 (*Karemera et al.*) (*see annex 48.1*).

17. Diary of Pauline Nyiramasuhuko, ICTR, entries from 31 January, 19–20 February, 22 February 1994 (*see annex 76*).

18. Witness T (Interahamwe leader), protected witness, OTP witness statement, May 2004.

Chapter 7. The Downing of the Presidential Plane on 6 April 1994 and the Military Crisis Committee

1. Some of these elements and opinions can be found in the collection of essays *Les crises politiques au Burundi et au Rwanda*, edited by André Guichaoua (Paris: Karthala, 1995), particularly in the chapter "L'attentat du 6 avril contre l'avion des présidents Habyarimana and Ntaryamira," 675–93.

2. Ibid., 677.

3. On 27 November 2006 Michaël Hourigan provided an affidavit to the ICTR concerning his investigation (*see annex 49*).

4. This concerns a document produced by an obscure organization identifying itself as the International Strategical and Tactical Organization (ISTO), imputing responsibility for the attack on the plane to the DGSE, the French Office of Foreign Intelligence. Its representatives provided the names of French military officers who were supposed to have shot down the plane to the Rwandan Embassy in Canada.

However, verifications by the judicial police relying on the French civil register and the list of officers who graduated from Saint-Cyr were unfruitful. Interpol was also unsuccessful in tracing the organization ISTO in Canada (*see annex 50*).

5. I will limit myself to several notorious examples: Prefect Pierre-Claver Rwangabo, killed on the road to Butare on 4 March 1995; Minister Seth Sendashonga, killed in Nairobi on 16 May 1998; Bishop André Sibomana, awaiting medical evacuation to Nairobi, but the authorities' refusal to issue a passport delayed his departure, leading to his death on 9 March 1998; Minister Alphonse-Marie Nkubito, found dead in his home on 12 February 1997 (*see annex 51*); his friend, the president of the Conseil d'État, Vincent Nkezabaganwa, killed in Kigali two days later on 14 February 1997; the vice president of the Supreme Court, Augustin Cyiza, kidnapped on 23 April 2003 and never seen again. In addition, the killing of foreign eyewitnesses of massacres committed by the RPF has continued until recently, for example, Joaquim Vallmajo, Spanish priest, on 26 April 1994 in Byumba; Claude Simard, Canadian cleric, in Butare on 17 October 1994; four Spanish Marist brothers in a refugee camp in South Kivu on 31 October 1996; three Spanish aid workers with Médecins du Monde on 18 January 1997 in Ruhengeri; Guy Pinard, Canadian cleric, on 2 February 1997 in Ruhengeri; five observers with the United Nations Human Rights Commission on 4 February 1997; the Croatian priest Curic Vjekoslav in Kigali on 31 January 1998; Isidro Uzcudun, Spanish priest, in Gitarama on 10 June 2000.

6. The encounter took place in Arusha, where a meeting of the East African Community was being held.

7. Stephen Smith, *Le Monde*, 3 April 2004.

8. Carla Del Ponte, correspondence, 11 March 2004.

9. Tribunal de Grande Instance de Paris, Office of Judge Jean-Louis Bruguière, issuance of international arrest warrants, Ordonnance de soit-communiqué, Paris, 20 November 2006.

10. *Annex 53* provides a detailed reconstruction of this informal meeting based on accounts obtained from several of the members who were present.

11. Col. Théoneste Bagosora continued to occupy his post without any particular official assignment following his retirement on 23 September 1993.

12. Hearings, Auditorat militaire, Brussels, PV no. 1013, 22 June 1994, archived in the Evidence Unit of the ICTR Prosecutor (ERN no. K036-4476-4479).

13. Protais Zigiranyirazo, curriculum vitae dated 7 November 2001, archived in the Evidence Unit of the ICTR Office of the Prosecutor (ERN no. K022-2712).

14. Written comments from the interested parties, transcribed on 30 May and 1 June 2009.

15. Protected witness, witness statement, archived in the Evidence Unit of the ICTR Prosecutor (ERN no. K035-4596-4647), pp. 74–78.

16. In support of these accounts, there exists, largely thanks to the ICTR, numerous witness statements and, more and more, sworn trial testimony from the principal participants in these events. As the trials proceed, the accumulation of information allows for a more careful parsing of the various accounts. For example, one will find a

systematic review of the testimony, accounts, and alibis in the *Bagosora et al.* trial judgment (*Prosecutor v. Bagosora et al.*, ICTR case no. 98-41-T, 18 December 2008, chap. 3, "Events from 6 to 9 April 1994," and esp. chap. 3.2, "Meetings").

17. Protais Zigiranyirazo provides 10:00 a.m. as the time of his arrival at the presidential residence on 7 April. He supposedly remained there until the president's widow was evacuated on 9 April, before the entire household was transferred to Gisenyi on 10–11 April. He took up residence in his house in Giciye but traveled back and forth between Gisenyi-ville (where the northerners among the Interim Government and several other close associates were headquartered) and Goma (where he had installed his Tutsi wife). Around mid-July he moved to Goma but later relocated to a township a bit farther from the border.

18. Hearings, Auditorat militaire, Brussels, PV no. 1013, 22 June 1994.

19. Decision of the CRR, 15 February 2007, 564776, Mme Agathe Kanziga, widow of President Habyarimana.

20. Maj. Augustin Cyiza, Officer of the Rwandan Armed Forces, personal conversation with the author, 11 January 2001.

21. The ICTR prosecutor's office was unrelenting in its efforts to prove that Théoneste Bagosora had actually participated in meetings at Kanombe camp organized by Aloys Ntabakuze to establish his role as "the mastermind." On the contrary, however, it is Bagosora's presence at such meetings that would have been surprising, as this would exceed his formal attributions. On that date, Bagosora was still a retired civilian. He no longer had a place in the military hierarchy and could not rely on any supposed prerogative of rank or seniority to give any "line order." Nor did he have any delegation of authority from the minister of defense. In the minister's absence and in the absence of the two other general staff officers, Bagosora could assemble the officers and coordinate meetings, but he could not supplant the existing hierarchy and openly worm his way into the command of military operations. This did not preclude him from ordering assassinations and massacres, and, in any case, he was certainly not the only one to do so, but this explains some of the inconsistencies that accompanied their execution. Additionally, nothing proves that specific orders were issued, as a matter of priority, to assassinate those persons who embodied the constitutional order; all of the major political opposition figures met the same fate, excepting those who managed to hide or flee. Similarly, it remains to be proven that the killings of the Belgian "blue helmets" had been planned, or indeed planned with the particular objective of causing UNAMIR to withdraw. These contradictions and questions remain unresolved, even in the wake of the Ntuyahaga trial (Brussels, May–July 2007) and the Bagosora trial (see, especially, *Prosecutor v. Théoneste Bagosora et al.*, ICTR case no. 98-41-T, Judgement and Sentence, Arusha, 18 December 2006, chapter 3, Events from 6 to 9 April 1994, § 854ff. and § 864ff.).

22. Gendarmerie Col. Aloys Ntiwiragabo (Hutu, Gisenyi) was then G2 in the army general staff. Although he belonged to a group of officers known for their fanaticism in matters of ethnic or regional chauvinism, his colleagues suspected him of a disqualifying Tutsi ancestor in matters of lineage. Of the four bureau chiefs of the

general staff, the only "G" that remained was Col. Joseph Murasampongo (G1). Stanislas Mayuya was a colonel, originally from Gisenyi. At that time he was viewed as Juvénal Habyarimana's likely successor (Cyiza, personal conversation, 11 January 2001).

23. "I recall that during that time Mr. Nzirorera was living in a private house situated in front of the CND, on the road to Kinyinya. . . . The house he occupied was a veritable bunker, and everyone was talking about it at the time. I remember that during a conversation, he told me that on the night of 6 April 1994, that is, after the presidential plane crashed, Presidential Guards took him from his private residence over to another house that he owned in Kiyovu. I don't know if he took his wife and his children with him. What I can confirm is that Mr. Joseph Nzirorea was in Kigali on the night of 6 April 1994, judging by his own admissions" (hearing, protected witness, May–June 2003).

24. Cyiza, personal conversation, 11 January 2001.

25. The commander of the École des sous-officiers in Butare was incorporated in the radio network for operational sector commanders in order to provide him with access to information from the front and in order to prepare him to take command of sector operations in the eventuality of an offensive from Burundi in that part of the country.

26. The order of seniority that all of the protagonists had in mind for promotions in rank was arbitrarily set aside, generating strong rivalries and dissensions that unsettled the high command for the duration of the war, particularly since a colonel who had been promoted just months before, during the last commission, was named chief of staff and major general. If we add regionalist discrimination and other long-standing resentments over career development, we can better understand the faltering legitimacy and the challenges suffered by the newly promoted officers, all of which severely hampered the mobilization and combativeness of the FAR.

27. Col. Balthazar Ndengeyinka, personal conversation with the author, 24 August 2002.

28. Ndengeyinka, personal conversation, 24 August 2002.

29. Gen. Leonidas Rusatira, ICTR witness statement, Brussels, 4 March 1999, pp. 7–8.

30. Ndengeyinka, personal conversation, 24 August 2002.

31. This analysis comes through clearly in trial testimony from Romeo Dallaire: "My feeling was that there was, in any case, a number of units that wanted a ceasefire. When the people—my people—went out, they came out with information that there was a good proportion—I cannot tell you if it is 40 percent or 70 percent—but that there was a good proportion of soldiers in the field who no longer wanted combat, who wanted peace, who no longer wanted to continue fighting against the Patriotic Front" (*Bagosora et al.*, ICTR, 26 January 2004, p. 13).

32. Cyiza, personal conversation, 11 January 2001.

33. That force included the Presidential Guard camps in Kimihurura and Kanombe (armored cars, artillery, mortars, paracommandos, etc.).

34. Ndengeyinka, personal conversation, 20 April 2005.

35. Ndengeyinka, personal conversation, 10 April 2005.

36. An incorrect assertion, in any case.

37. Marcel Gatsinzi, PV no. 0142, Ministry of Justice, Kigali, 16 June 1995 (ERN no. K010-9948-9955), p. 4.

38. If the presidential family expected him to save their honor and patrimony, they knew perfectly well that their prerogatives would be diminished in the process, as this rival of Juvénal Habyarimana had many reasons to feel previously "neglected" in their circles.

39. It is noteworthy that the UNAMIR memorandum maintains the fiction of six hundred RPF soldiers cantoned at the CND, whereas it was generally well known that their number had at least doubled. UNAMIR outgoing code cable, archived in the Evidence Unit of the ICTR Prosecutor (ERN no. L000-1689).

40. "I asked the United Nations to make available a ballistics expert to conduct investigations. Meanwhile, it was disclosed that OAIC [International Civil Aviation Organization] could not handle the inquiry because it was a military plane, not a civilian aircraft. So a commission of inquiry would be required. I then asked the United Nations for one, and the response was that there was no budget for that" (testimony of René Degni-Segui, Belgian Senate, Parliamentary Commission of Inquiry Concerning the Events in Rwanda, Report of the Commission of Inquiry, MM. Mahoux and Verhofstadt [534b], Brussels, 6 December 1997).

41. See, in particular, the reports issued by the UN and the OAU concerning the 1994 events in Rwanda, both of which were authored by independent experts: UN Security Council, "Report of the Independent Commission of Inquiry on the Actions of the United Nations during the 1994 Genocide in Rwanda," 15 December 1999; International Panel of Eminent Personalities, "Rwanda." The UN report does not address the question of the possible perpetrators of the attack against the plane; nor does it anticipate the slightest investigation of the matter. As for the report by the International Panel of Eminent Personalities, after acknowledging frustration in the face of an obstinate silence on the subject, the authors explain as follows: "9.14. Inevitably, wildly conflicting stories and accusations about the possible perpetrators have swirled ever since. As part of a systematic attempt to lay the foundation to justify a planned assault on UNAMIR Belgian troops, radio station RTLM immediately blamed the Belgians, among others, [sic] Since then, virtually every conceivable party has been accused of the deed—the Akazu, other Hutu radicals, the RPF, the UN, UNAMIR, the French. The truth is that to this day, this historic event is shrouded in conflicting rumors and accusations but no hard evidence. Mysteriously enough, a formal investigation of the crash has never been carried out, and this Panel has had no capacity to launch one. We address this important issue in our recommendations." These same authors recommend that yet another party be mandated to investigate: "26. The OAU should ask the International Commission of Jurists to initiate an independent investigation to determine who was responsible for shooting down the plane carrying Rwanda President Juvénal Habyarimana and Burundi President Cyprien Ntaryamira" (chap. 24, sec. C).

42. See Assemblée nationale française, *Enquête*, 2:248.

43. In 2006, in the *Bagosora et al.* trial, the Office of the Prosecutor attempted to admit evidence drawn from certain documents concerning the purchase of ground-to-air missiles by the FAR that, up until that point, had not been deemed relevant to the proceedings, eliciting an unequivocal response from the Chamber: "*No allegation implicating the Accused in the assassination of the President is to be found in the indictment, the Pre-Trial Brief or any other Prosecution communication. Indeed, no actual evidence in support of that allegation was heard during the Prosecution case*" ("Decision on Request for Disclosure and Investigations Concerning the Assassination of President Habyarimana," ICTR, Arusha, 17 October 2006, § 3, p. 4).

44. UN Security Council, "Report of the Independent Commission," 17, 47.

45. Assemblée nationale française, *Enquête.*

46. Tribunal de Grande Instance de Paris, Office of Judge Jean-Louis Bruguière.

47. In fact, Rwandan intelligence services had already begun the work of systematically collecting information about the role and the presumed implication of the French military by the end of 2002. Minister of Defense Marcel Gatsinzi, appointed on 15 November of that same year, was then asked to identify soldiers of the ex-FAR who had had contact of any sort with Operation Turquoise and who would thus be able to testify about this implication. Gen. Marcel Gatsinzi was the commander of military recruitment in Butare-Gikongoro at the time of that military operation. Toward the end of 2002 arrests of members of the former territorial administration serving in the concerned prefectures and communes and the prisoners who had been members of the ex-FAR were systematically invited to testify. This approach was initiated following the legal upsets suffered by Paul Kagame after the publication of a book by Charles Onana, *Les secrets du génocide rwandais* (Paris: Duboiris, November 2001). Reacting on behalf of the then Rwandan vice president, Jacques Bihozagara, the Rwandan ambassador in Paris initiated lawsuits against the author and the publisher for defamation and for nonrespect of the presumption of innocence of Judge Bruguière's investigation. This led to a double failure: the first was in April 2002, when the Paris court rejected the complaint for technical reasons; the second was in December of the same year, when the plaintiff withdrew the complaint just before a hearing that was to examine "evidence" from the journalist concerning Paul Kagame's implication in the shooting down of the plane on 6 April. The withdrawal generated a great deal of publicity and was interpreted as an implicit admission of the facts.

48. Republic of Rwanda, "National Independent Commission Charged with Assembling Proof Demonstrating the Implication of the French State in the Genocide Perpetrated in Rwanda in 1994," report and annexes, Kigali, 15 November 2007.

49. See the "Mutsinzi Report," http://mutsinzireport.com.

50. Administración de Justicia, Juzgado Central de Instrucción no. 4, Audiencia Nacional, sumario 3/2.008, Madrid, p. 7.

51. After President Nicolas Sarkozy acceded to power in May 2007, this dossier presented a major obstacle to the policy of "reconciliation" with Rwanda championed by Minister Bernard Kouchner. This push for normalization sought to permit France to recover the influence in Central and East Africa that it had lost to the British and

the Americans, especially insofar as relations between the DRC and Rwanda were concerned. Following the African Union summit at Sharm el-Sheikh, Egypt, in June 2008, President Kagame took the lead in a crusade of heads of state in opposition to "little white judges," to the universal jurisdiction of European courts, and to the encroachments of the International Criminal Court.

52. "B. Kouchner: No, we never tried to block this investigation. Before we arrived [in power in May 2007], the Rwandans asked us to vacate the arrest warrants that Judge Bruguière had issued against their countrymen. We told them that it wasn't possible. The judiciary is independent. A working group composed of lawyers had indicated that if the Rwandans wanted access to the dossier, at least one of the nine suspects would have to surrender to the French authorities. This is what Kagame's former chief of protocol, Rose Kabuye, ended up doing" (interview with Bernard Kouchner, French minister of foreign affairs, *Le Nouvel Observateur*, 5 February 2009).

53. In view of the charges filed against the accused, it wasn't so much the arraignment judge's decision to release her that surprised a number of observers (she didn't even receive the usual order forbidding contact with other witnesses or other accused) but the fact that it was the prosecutor's office that had itself requested that she be released. This was a delicate about-face on the part of the prosecutor, who had demonstrated remarkable dynamism in October 2006 when he was issuing arrest warrants against the Rwandan officers.

54. Unidentified MDR leader present during the meeting, personal conversation with the author, 21 March 2004.

55. In Burundi, for example, those who commanded, executed, or were accomplices in the assassination of President Melchior Ndadaye have never been prosecuted and had, for some time at least, prudently fled to Uganda.

Chapter 8. The Civilian Alternative

1. "These were the first decisions that the presidential family took that night: install a military government to negotiate with the RPF and to protect their interests; gain the upper hand with the foreign embassies and Dallaire; take control of the army. In respect of all three, Bagosora met with stark refusal" (Augustin Cyiza, personal conversation with the author, 11 January 2001).

2. Hearings, Federal Police, Brussels, annex to PV no. 257777/2003, case no. 1007/02, 7 November 2003, archived in the Evidence Unit of the ICTR Prosecutor (ERN no. K007-4271ff.). Jean-Luc Habyarimana categorically denies having made this statement (trial testimony of Jean-Luc Habyarimana, *Prosecutor v. Bagosora et al.*, case no. ICTR-98-41-T, 6 July 2006).

3. Ngirumpatse, *La tragédie rwandaise*, 170.

4. See articles 47 and 48 of the "Protocol of Agreement between the Government of the Republic of Rwanda and the Rwandese Patriotic Front on Power Sharing within the Framework of a Broad-Based Transitional Government" (signed in Arusha on

9 January 1993, in continuation of the protocol of agreement signed on 30 October 1992) (*see annex 63*).

5. Detailed minutes are available for this meeting and for several others that followed. The very existence of these summaries, which are of significant interest, was forgotten until they were found and corrected in May 2002. There are five in all, and they cover the meetings of the Military Crisis Committee from the morning of 7 April through the evening of 8 April. The collection of texts was transcribed, reread, corrected, and revised under my supervision and then annotated by their two authors, who returned them to me on 13 November 2002. I then made them available to the ICTR when my expert report for the *Prosecutor v. Karemera et al.* trial was submitted in February 2006 (see ERN nos. K036-5916-5950, K036-5961-5979, K036-5987-5992). The original texts are currently in the possession of Épiphane Hanyurwimana (*see annex 64*).

6. Matthieu Ngirumpatse, transcript of OTP interview, ICTR, Bamako, 17 September 1998, cassette no. 4, p. 2 (*see annex 66*).

7. For example, former Army Chief of Staff Laurent Serubuga begrudgingly partnered with Tutsi businessman Bertin Makuza, the majority stakeholder in Rwandaform and several other enterprises. When Makuza was being seriously threatened with death, Serubuga demanded that the former transfer all of his assets to him. Makuza initially balked, but, fearing he would be eliminated eventually, he relented and appealed to one of his associates, Maj. Pascal Ngirumpatse, who then used Serubuga's 4x4 Mercedes SUV to transport him and twenty-four other members of his family from Remera to the Hôtel des Mille Collines.

8. Major Épiphane Hanyurwimana, Minutes of the meeting of members of the crisis committee with MRND leaders on the morning of 7 April, Kigali (*see annex 64*, p. 11).

9. See Ngirumpatse, OTP interview, 17 September 1998 (*annex 66*).

10. As of 4 August 1993, the day that the Arusha Peace Accords were signed, they became the *loi fondamentale* (fundamental law). The 1991 Constitution was still in force for the dispositions not taken into consideration or "covered" by the accords, and the latter would govern in any situation where there were contradictions between the two. Article 48, paragraph 3, of the protocol on power sharing anticipated that within three weeks of any declaration of a vacancy in the presidency, the party would propose two candidates. During the fourth week, an election would be held in a joint session under the supervision of the speaker of the TNA. If the party did not present a candidate, all the parties would be able to propose one within six weeks of the vacancy, and an election would be held the following week, with investiture in office to follow one week after the election.

11. Jean Kambanda, transcript of OTP interview, cassette no. 18, 27 September 1997, ICTR T2-K7-18, pp. 28–29.

12. See UN Security Council, "Report of the Independent Commission," 16.

13. International Panel of Eminent Personalities, "Rwanda," § 15.4, p. 41.

14. "I remember quite well what Karamira, the vice-chairman of the MDR, had told me when he came to fetch me from my home in Kacyiru: 'Ibya Agatha byabaye ngombwa ko tubi . . . tubirangiza ngo tubone uko dushiyiraho guverinoma,' which, freely translated, means 'It was necessary to finish with Agathe Uwilingiyimana in order to be able to form our government.' He told this because he thought that for him and for me, it was good news that I was going to become PM at last" (Jean Kambanda, transcript of OTP interview, 19 May 1998, ICTR [T2-K7-66], p. 28).

15. By the French ambassador's account, the meeting was held on the morning of 8 April, "after the ministers arrived." In fact, as we have seen, the ministers and the MRND and Hutu Power figures settled in at the embassy on 7 April and had all the time they needed to organize "their" political transition (see chap. 10, "Les partis pris de l'Ambassade de France" [The Political Leanings of the French Embassy], in the French edition of this book).

16. Trial testimony of Justin Mugenzi, *Prosecutor v. Bizimungu et al. (Gov II)*, ICTR, 8 November 2005, p. 59.

17. Col. Marcel Gatsinzi, Ministry of Justice, hearing minutes, Kigali, PV no. 0142, 16 June 1995, archived in the Evidence Unit of the ICTR Prosecutor (ERN no. K010-9948-9955), p. 6.

18. Witness CR (former Interim Government minister), OTP witness statement, 24 February 2005, p. 13.

19. Trial testimony of Emmanuel Ndindabahizi, *Prosecutor v. Ndindabahizi*, ICTR, 24 November 2003, pp. 38–39.

20. Trial testimony of Jean Kambanda, *Prosecutor v. Bagosora et al.*, ICTR, 11 July 2006, pp. 28–29.

21. Gatsinzi, hearing minutes, 16 June 1995, pp. 5–6.

22. Col. Balthazar Ndengeyinka, personal conversation with the author, 20 April 2005.

23. Léonidas Rusatira, *Rwanda, le droit à l'espoir* (Paris: L'Harmattan, 2005), 54ff.

24. Witness CR, OTP witness statement, 24 February 2005, p. 13.

25. Communiqué issued by the Command of the Forces armées rwandaises, 12 April 1994 (see *Prosecutor v. Karemera et al.*, exhibit no. DNZ-734). We will simply rely on *annex 71*, which sets forth the reactions of the various parties to this communiqué.

26. Letter of Gen. Marcel Gatsinzi, 17 April 1994, ICTR (ERN no. K019-6126) (*see annex 71*).

27. Théoneste Bagosora occupied room 205, which he retained when "Hôtel des Diplomates simply became the annex of the military camp's mess hall," until Kigali was finally evacuated (Paul Rusesabagina, manager of the hotel, personal conversation with the author, 23 November 2007).

28. Written comments from a colonel in the FAR, personal notes of the author, 21 March 2006.

29. Testimony of Emmanuel Ndindabahizi, *Prosecutor v. Ndindabahizi*, ICTR, 25 November 2004, p. 8.

30. Testimony of Jean Kambanda, *Prosecutor v. Bagosora et al.*, ICTR, 11 July 2006, p. 33.

Chapter 9. Installing the Interim Authorities

1. Testimony of Jean Kambanda, *Bagosora et al.*, ICTR, 11 July 2006, p. 26.

2. Kambanda had just informed Augustin Cyiza that he would meet up with him the following day for the convoy heading to Butare that the latter was organizing, but he declined just before its departure, at 9:00 that morning, when he was appointed prime minister. Quotation from Kambanda testimony, 11 July 2006, p. 26.

3. Indeed, the prospect of outright war by the RPA was still viewed as improbable by a number of Rwandan soldiers. (How could the RPF, the voice of a "foreign minority," hope to govern a "Hutu" country?) According to them, it was all the more unthinkable from the perspective of foreign powers, including the United States and Great Britain, the RPF's principal supporters, which would never allow power to be monopolized by a minority Tutsi-led guerrilla force with millions of Hutu exiles lurking just across the border. Clearly, each one believed that at some point or another in the war, a proposal making reference to the Arusha Peace Accords would prevail in the long run.

4. Théoneste Bagosora's agenda, Banque de Kigali, ICTR, page for 15 February 1993 (ERN no. K023-9532).

5. The prefectures of origin for the nineteen ministers are as follows: Kibuye, four; Gisenyi, three; Butare, two; Gitarama, two; Kibungo, two; Kigali, two; Ruhengeri, two; Byumba, one; Cyangugu, one; Gikongoro, zero—in other words, six for the north (the three prefectures of the "Rukiga": Gisenyi, Ruhengeri, and Byumba) and thirteen for the south ("Nduga").

6. Reinstated in the same post that he held under Juvénal Habyarimana, Enoch Ruhigira declined the appointment and had left the country by 12 April. He was replaced by Daniel Mbangura. It was indeed to Gen. Augustin Ndindiliyimana that Colonel Bagosora conferred the task of monitoring the personal security of members of the Interim Government while arrogating control over matters of "logistics" to himself. Ndindiliyimana had neither the material means nor the key information that would be essential for such responsibility: "The all-powerful Col. Bagosora, who had enthroned this false president [of the Military Crisis Committee], kept a close eye on him, and everything was done by his will. No one could occupy that post without Bagosora's approval" (unidentified, anonymous staff officer, personal conversation with the author, 23 February 2007). The quotation is from Maj. Augustin Cyiza, personal conversation with the author, 11 January 2001.

7. As with former journalist Éliezer Niyitegeka, who became a petrol distributor in Kibuye before 1994.

8. Literally, "sent to the front." This was a reference to "liberators" who, traditionally, sacrificed their lives in order to safeguard the kingdom.

9. Gasana, *Rwanda*, 255.

10. "Regarding the responsibility of the government, no member could by his signature or speech commit the government, because it was a coalition of parties governed by a consensual protocol. A decision is by consensus, without which such a decision only bound the person who made it. Thus, according to the rules and regulations governing the functioning of the government, decisions taken by the council of ministers should be recorded as minutes. The minutes should be formally adopted by the council of ministers and extracts of the decisions put down in a report signed by each minister" (witness CR [former Interim Government minister], OTP witness statement, 24 February 2005, p. 14).

11. In fact, the ministers were not comfortable with arrangements for security at the Muramba parish church. Outside of Jean Kambanda and Pauline Nyiramasuhuko, who were resident there, the ministers only went there on Fridays for cabinet meetings. The other ministers were lodged in Gisenyi, where most were housed at the Hôtel Méridien Izuba: "In Gisenyi the Méridien Hotel at some point in time had become the turning point—the boiling pot for all activities, both government and parliamentary. You know, even at some point I was appointed president of the national assembly, and I had to chair some meetings there. . . . But I used to go to Hôtel Méridien because we held meetings there when I was president of the assembly. I chaired a meeting of members of parliament" (testimony of Joseph Nzirorera, *Prosecutor v. Bagosora et al.*, ICTR, 12 June 2006, p. 22).

12. Senior official of the MRND, personal conversation with the author, 7 January 2006.

13. Ibid.

14. Ibid.

15. The Union nationale rwandaise (National Rwandan Union) was a Tutsi-led promonarchical party that came into being before independence.

16. This clarification—"the recomposed MRND party-state"—is essential for distinguishing "the MRND of 5 April from the party of 10 April. Between those two dates there were those who were missing, or who had been eliminated, and those who went into hiding" (senior official of the MRND, personal conversation, 7 January 2006).

17. Jean Kambanda, transcript of OTP interview, cassette no. 16, 26 September 1997, p. 5.

18. Balthazar Ndengeyinka, telephone conversation with the author, 30 September 2008.

19. Literal translation from Kinyarwanda, where the word *ingoma* has two meanings: "drum" and "power." The drum represents power; a gourd, emptied, easily shatters under pressure.

20. The War Council never became operational, so there were few constraints on Cyiza's time. A staunch human rights activist, he maintained numerous contacts and handled various mediation efforts.

21. The public positions of Nkundiye and Ntabakuze were always highly scrutinized because their spouses were originally from Zaire, giving rise to presumptions or suspicions that they were Banyamulenge Tutsi.

22. Semanza was very close to President Habyarimana and the long-standing, irremovable burgomaster of Bicumbi, the most fertile and the most rural commune in the country. This notorious extremist was president of the MRND prefectural committee for Kigali-rural. Famously, he came to be known as *inkandagirabitabo*, the brute, because of the brutal terror he wielded against those who refused to join the MRND in his commune.

23. On the basis of various consistent accounts, the new weapons (Kalashnikovs and Uzis) distributed to militiamen at the Kigali prefecture starting 8 April came from Kanombe, where Théoneste Bagosora had his strongest supporters. Before being transferred to the Ministry of Defense, he headed the camp known as "Colonel Mayuya." This essentially honorific command consisted for the most part in ensuring coordination of administrative management within the parameters of Kanombe. The camp was home to Aloys Ntabakuze's paracommando battalion, the field artillery battalion, the antiaircraft battery, the military hospital, the military stores and barracks, and several other units.

24. Maj. Augustin Cyiza, personal conversation with the author, 11 January 2001.

25. Kambanda, transcript of OTP interview, 26 September 1997, p. 5.

26. Théoneste Bagosora maneuvered to have reinstated in active service the officers who had been forced into retirement by former Defense Minister James Gasana, most prominently himself.

27. Lt. Col. Bonaventure Ntibitura was in charge of Ruhengeri.

28. Col. Athanase Gasake (Ruhengeri) commanded the civil defense nationally under direct orders from the minister of defense.

29. Jean Kambanda, transcript of OTP interview, 27 September 1997, pp. 2–3.

30. Pauline Nyiramasuhuko's diary, ICTR, at the page for 9 April (*see annex 76*).

31. Testimony of Roméo Dallaire, *Prosecutor v. Bagosora et al.*, ICTR, 19 January 2004, p. 45 (*see also annex 60*). The press release broadcast on 7 April 1994 at 5:20 p.m. called for implementation of the transitional government and thus showed support for the application of the Arusha Peace Accords, but the RPF never responded.

32. On 9 April 1994, in an interview that was broadcast by radio, the acting army chief of staff reminded listeners: "The Rwandan Armed Forces urgently and immediately requests that the partners of the RPF use their goodwill to promote the return of a climate of peace and negotiation and that the RPF not give priority to war, because a resort to weapons cannot bring peace and can prove fatal in the end."

33. Witness CR, OTP witness statement, 24 February 2005, p. 17.

34. The OPS commander for Kigali-ville, Col. Félicien Muberuka, made numerous attempts to control the Presidential Guard, at least insofar as they still made sense, as indicated by his telegrams to headquarters all throughout the day on 7 April requesting a halt of "clashes between soldiers and the population" by all camps and sector units (RT INT/OPS/94/1428 of 7 April 1994 from Camp Colonel Mayuya; RT OPS/94/356

of 7 April 1994 from the commandant of OPS Kigali-ville; RT INT/OPS/94/353 of 7 April 1994 from the commandant of OPS Kigali-ville).

35. MIR 750, admitted in evidence before Trial Chamber I of the ICTR as exhibit no. D.NT108.

36. "Current assessment of the situation in Rwanda," 24 April 1994, Kigali, p. 4, § 10 (*see annex 77*). See also Roméo Dallaire, *Shake Hands with the Devil: The Failure of Humanity in Rwanda* (Toronto: Random House Canada, 2003), 326–27.

37. Testimony of Roméo Dallaire, *Bagosora et al.*, ICTR, 21 January 2004, p. 70 (*see annex 77*).

38. Testimony of Jacques-Roger Booh-Booh, *Prosecutor v. Bagosora et al.*, ICTR, 22 November 2005, p. 81.

Chapter 10. From Massacres to Genocide

1. "The RPF strengthened its position by secretly transferring weapons and several hundred troops to Kigali to reinforce the 600 soldiers authorized under the Arusha Accords. The movement developed politically as well, both in Kigali and throughout Rwanda. Assured of a role in government thanks to the Arusha Accords, its supporters, previously hesitant to profess support, began to admit that they were members of the movement. Political cadres that journeyed to the RPF zone to undergo training returned home anxious to recruit new members. By early April, the RPF had 600 cells throughout the country, with 147 in Kigali alone. Each group was composed of 6 to 12 members, which would suggest a total of 3,600 to 7,200 persons who openly or privately admitted their support for the RPF. The greatest number, some 700 to 1,400, were to be found in the capital" (Human Rights Watch / Fédération internationale des droits de l'homme, interviews with a former UNAMIR officer, Plainsboro, New Jersey, 13 June 1996, Nairobi, 22 March 1996 by telephone, Kigali, 14 February 1997 by telephone).

2. Wherever "mixed" patrols with both Hutu and Tutsi members existed, these patrols were clearly distinguished from the monoethnic Hutu patrols, which were usually just direct extensions of the party youth wings.

3. Trial testimony of Witness T (Interahamwe leader, protected witness), unofficial translation, *Prosecutor v. Karemera et al.*, ICTR, 31 May 2006.

4. Ibid.

5. Surveillance and monitoring were systematic. "The youth wings of the PL and the PSD and the Abakombozi of the PSD, most members of the youth wing had received military training with the RPF and were expected to return at some point. And upon the arrival of the RPF battalion, most of them were so arrogant that they provoked people in taxis, in transportation vehicles, and they were saying, 'Our boys are here, we have our own army, we have our own Interahamwe, so what are you going to do now? What are you going to say now?' Those persons, therefore, identified themselves as the accomplice of the enemy, and did so openly. Now, with the arrival of the RPF battalion, there was a very open display of an attitude on the part of those who supported the enemy. They would go out in the morning to the CND and would

be there—they would move around from early morning to about 6:00 PM. And it is in view of those movements that it was concluded that some of the RPF members infiltrated the city under the pretext that those who had left in the morning were those returning. But these people who were monitored—they were being monitored" (trial testimony of Witness T, *Karemera et al.*, ICTR, 31 May 2006, pp. 3–4) (*see also annex 86*).

6. Trial testimony of Witness G (Interahamwe leader, protected witness), *Karemera et al.*, ICTR, May–June 2003.

7. Witness CR (former Interim Government minister, protected witness), OTP witness statement, ICTR, 24 February 2005, p. 5.

8. Handwritten notes, Pauline Nyiramasuhuko, ICTR, ERN no. K004-5913 (*see annex 88*).

9. Handwritten notes, Pauline Nyiramasuhuko, ICTR, 10 April 1994, ERN no. K004-5914, *Prosecutor v. Nyiramasuhuko et al.*, ICTR-88-42-T, exhibit no. D-347(A).

10. Jean Kambanda, transcript of OTP interview, ICTR, T2-K7-15, 26 September 1997.

11. Handwritten notes, Pauline Nyiramasuhuko, ICTR, 11 April 1994, ERN no. K004-5914.

12. "I explained to you that after the death of the president I had no further contact with the [Interahamwe] committee" (Matthieu Ngirumpatse, ICTR, OTP arrest interview, Bamako, 15–17 June 1998, unofficial translation).

13. "I should add that the members of the National Committee of the Interahamwe ZA MRND felt betrayed and abandoned on 12 April 1994 when the Interim Government fled Kigali for Murambi, and then from Murambi to Gisenyi (June 1994), and from Gisenyi to Bukavu-Zaire (July 1994)" (Interahamwe leader, protected witness, OTP witness statement, 19 May 2004, p. 28).

14. Among the camps of displaced Hutu who fled the RPF offensives and occupied zone starting in 1991, Nyacyonga Camp—some fifteen kilometers north of the capital—was by far the largest, with hundreds of thousands piled together in conditions of extreme poverty. Starting on 9 April, as RPF troops descending from the demilitarized zone approached Kigali, the two camps, Nyacyonga and Mugambazi, emptied out into the capital. On 12 April, in the late morning, when they discovered that the Interim Government was fleeing, the internally displaced headed en masse for the main road to Gitarama and fled behind them. With a generalized panic ratcheting up, this massive exodus was marred by extensive looting (to sustain themselves) and marked by expressions of extreme hatred for the RPF and for all Tutsi. Their passage south played a big role in extending the massacres in Gitarama, Kibuye, and Butare prefectures.

15. Testimony of Théoneste Bagosora, *Prosecutor v. Bagosora et al.*, ICTR, 10 November 2005, p. 23 (*see annex 91* for a lengthy excerpt), which provides an opportunity for the reader to follow Bagosora's reasoning. By his account a deadly sequence of events triggered the convulsion in "large-scale, excessive massacres." Nonetheless, we can still observe that even if his perceptions correspond to actual events, factually speaking, everything brought on by the decisions taken by newly installed authorities,

particularly his own role in "the impending catastrophe," is systematically concealed or denied.

16. "But this plane crash was not the cause of genocide. . . . The genocide in Rwanda started in the 1960s. You have to trace it ideologically; it was developing over a long time, and in 1994 it reached a high point. It was a long process" (interview with Paul Kagame, *Le soir*, 6 January 2006).

17. A presence that, as we emphasized in the introduction, was not unique to Rwanda and was not the exclusive preserve of Hutu.

18. *See annex 5* (International Panel of Eminent Personalities, "Rwanda," 39–48, concerning the purported "planning of genocide").

19. Or instead of a state conspiracy, to put it more crudely, a "Nazi regime," as a number of current leaders have characterized it.

20. International Panel of Eminent Personalities, "Rwanda."

21. Testimony of Roméo Dallaire, *Prosecutor v. Bagosora et al.*, ICTR, 20 January 2004, p. 52.

22. The excess of snubs and rebuffs that Bagosora had to endure during the night of 6–7 April and the headlong rush to drag "his" government into war demonstrates this clearly. If Bagosora and the soldiers supporting him had been "ready" and in a position of strength, they would not have been obliged to negotiate with the FAR high command, and would never have been cornered by Gatsinzi's nomination to the head of the general staff or the nuisance of mounting a civilian government. They would have immediately set up a military committee without the bother of useless consultations. In the same vein, the "civilian" political alternative became necessary only because Bagosora was utterly incapable of seizing control of the army.

23. United Nations Social and Economic Council, "Report on the Situation of Human Rights in Rwanda," submitted by M. R. Degni Ségui, special rapporteur of the Commission on Human Rights, in application of paragraph 20 of Resolution 1994 S-3/1 of the Commission, 25 May 1994, doc. no. E/CN.4/1995/7, New York, 28 June 1994.

24. See International Panel of Eminent Personalities, "Rwanda." This formulation has much in common with the summaries of hearing testimony in the final report from the French Parliamentary Commission: "Having been predicted so many times since 1990, by the beginning of 1994 the notion of impending genocide was deemed plausible, but not probable" (Assemblée nationale française, *Enquête*, 1:281).

25. Testimony of Dallaire, *Bagosora et al.*, ICTR, 23 January 2004, p. 55.

26. Those military offenses included one in Ruhengeri on 23 January 1991, one in Byumba on 5 June 1992, and especially the massive assaults in Byumba and Ruhengeri prefectures on 8 February 1993.

27. For detailed discussion of the genocidal project and its political forms, see Guichaoua, *Rwanda 1994*, chap. 8.

28. Testimony of Dallaire, *Bagosora et al.*, ICTR, 23 January 2004, p. 28.

29. Jacques-Roger Booh-Booh to Kofi Annan (assistant secretary-general for peacekeeping operations), Marrack Goulding (assistant secretary-general for special

political affairs), and Peter Hansen (assistant secretary-general for humanitarian affairs), UNAMIR code cable, MIR 727, ICTR, ERN no. L000-4279-4282, para. 11.

30. In regard to political disengagement or implicit approval, Belgium, first of all, qualifies because of its abrupt withdrawal from UNAMIR, but so do France and the United States, for divergent reasons, and more generally the UN Security Council.

Chapter 11. The Interim Government at the Center of Power

1. Handwritten notes of Pauline Nyiramasuhuko for cabinet meeting of 12 April 1994, ERN no. K004-5916, *Nyiramasuhuko et al.* (Media), ICTR-98-42-T, exhibit no. D-351 (*see annex 88*).

2. An urgent order had been placed with a company located in the United Kingdom by 10 April (Myl/Tec, see ERN no. K005-7496 and K005-7534; *see annex 95*).

3. Handwritten notes of Pauline Nyiramasuhuko for cabinet meeting of 14 April 1994, *Nyiramasuhuko et al.* (Media), ICTR-98-42-T, exhibit no. D-351; see also *Karemera et al.*, ICTR-98-44-T, exhibit no. P-497B.

4. Indeed, a number of senior military officers simply refused to accept the Interim Government as a fait accompli. In their "Communiqué of the FAR High Military Command" of 12 April 1994, they openly called for dialogue with the RPF and a halt to the combat. This initiative continued with the letter that Col. Marcel Gatsinzi, the acting army chief of staff, addressed to Jacques-Roger Booh-Booh on 17 April proposing that communal patrols be set up and that illegally obtained weapons be confiscated, and for monitoring and prohibiting incendiary radio broadcasts (*see annex 71*).

5. The situation of Gaspard Ruhumuliza is quite unique in that respect, since he was almost always the only representative of his party, the PDC, present in Murambi.

6. As reflected in my previous studies, the slogans were followed by action, and in a few days, all of the communes had opted for the massacres (see Guichaoua, *Rwanda 1994*, chaps. 7–8).

7. Handwritten notes by Pauline Nyiramasuhuko for cabinet meeting of 13 April 1994, *Nyiramasuhuko et al.* (Media), ICTR-98-42-T, exhibit no. D-553; see ERN no. K004-5919-5919 (*see annex 97*).

8. Account provided by one of the officers present; personal notes of the author, 5 January 2008.

9. After Agathe Kanziga's departure for France on 9 April, the members of the presidential family who remained behind headed for Gisenyi on 11 April, later to be joined by close associates like Félicien Kabuga. The Hôtel Méridien Izuba became their pied-à-terre and meeting grounds, drawing together political and military decision makers linked to the Akazu.

10. For example, on 7 March 1994, after a meeting between the army general staff and the prefect of Kigali, Tharcisse Renzaho sent a letter to the president and to the Ministry of Defense, copied to other officers, without informing the prime minister. This letter recommended arming the population in preparation for war (*see annex 40*).

11. Maj. Augustin Cyiza, conversation with the Author, 11 January 2001.

12. Jean Kambanda, transcript of OTP interview, ICTR, 26 September 1997, cassette no. 14, p. 17.

13. Jean-Damascène Ukulikeyeyezu replaced Fidèle Uwizeye, who had already fled by late May and was officially dismissed on 4 June 1994.

14. Alison Des Forges, *Leave None to Tell the Story*, Human Rights Watch, FIDH (Fédération internationale des ligues des droits de l'homme).

15. See Jean Kambanda, transcript of OTP interview, cassette no. 18, 27 September 1997, ICTR T2-K7-18.

16. "Because . . . starting out, when I was first named prime minister, I didn't see myself as someone who was put in office to organize the massacres, I saw myself as someone who was appointed to be prime minister of the whole country and to restore peace and security, and these were the objectives that had been outlined for the government, and it's in that framework that I tried to work, recognizing that I was given three objectives: restore security throughout the country, negotiate with the RPF to get the Arusha Accords back on track, and then ensure the livelihood of the population, etc., attend to the refugees. That was my intention" (Jean Kambanda, transcript of OTP interview, cassette no. 68, 20 May 1998, ICTR T2-K7-68).

17. The four most important ministries were Interior (planning and genocide); Finance (nerve center of the war); Information (propaganda); and Justice (impunity).

18. Witness CR (former Interim Government minister), ICTR witness statement, 24 February 2005, pp. 16–17.

19. Ibid., 18.

20. Des Forges, *Leave None*, 262.

21. Quotation from Augustin Cyiza, conversation with the author, 11 January 2001. Recall that the massacres in Kibilira commune or in Bugesera required no particular, central organization. They were accomplished with minimal logistical support, administratively or politically: representatives of the authorities requesting or transporting the committed partisans of the MRND, an army of war casualties. The inability to squelch the tenacious resistance of Tutsi survivors in Kibuye prefecture who had regrouped on the hilltops of Bisesero in May and June 1994 and the need to have soldiers brought in from other prefectures clearly demonstrate this structural unpreparedness, despite the haphazard mobilization of the army, the gendarmerie, the communal police, and the militiamen.

Chapter 12. War and the Fight for Supremacy

1. A justification of accounts undertaken by the Interim Government in exile valued the level of Joseph Nzirorera's unreimbursed advances for official missions abroad at $900,000. See "Rapport sur la situation du patrimoine" (Report on state expenditures), submitted by Innocent Habamenshi, Minister of State Holdings of the Government in Exile, upon the request of President Théodore Sindikubwabo, 10 October 1995 (*see annex 106*).

2. The latter had already received payments for various goods valued around $100,000.

3. See Habamenshi, "Rapport sur la situation."

4. Jean Kambanda, transcript of OTP interview (official ICTR translation), ICTR, 1997, T2-K7-72, p. 29 (*see also annex 107*).

5. The governor of the Banque nationale du Rwanda (BNR), Denis Ntirugirimbazi, a native of Ruhengeri, was often accused of having transferred significant bank holdings to Zaire, to Kenya, and then to Luxembourg, with no indications of the ultimate beneficiaries.

6. Théodore Sindikubwabo, President of the Republic, to Augustin Bizimana, Minister of Defense, 22 April 1994 (*see annex 108*).

7. Emmanuel Kayiranga, a businessman, older brother of the big distributor from Butare, Étienne Gakwaya, alias Mwami, then fled to Burundi with his family. Afterward, he made trips back and forth between Bujumbura and Butare to continue to manage his business affairs and was killed during one of those trips.

8. Transcript of Jean Kambanda's speech, 3 May 1994, ICTR, *Karemera et al.*, DNZ-288-B (ERN no. K036-4167-4168), p. 19 (*see annex 103.2*).

9. MRND Political Bureau, closing remarks, 13 May 1994.

10. A preview of this catastrophic scenario had patently shocked the foreign press a few weeks earlier, on 22 April, when 250,000 Hutu refugees fleeing the RPF advance crossed the border into Tanzania in a matter of just a few hours (see chapter 9).

11. Diary of Pauline Nyiramasuhuko, ICTR, 26 February 1994 (*see annex 76*).

12. On 25 May the United Nations Human Rights Commission, without voting, adopted a resolution authorizing a special rapporteur to file a report on the situation of human rights and to investigate human rights abuses and violations of international humanitarian law. It was extended on 8 June by Security Council Resolution 925, which took note that "acts of genocide have occurred in Rwanda and recalling in this context that genocide constitutes a crime punishable under international law."

13. Diary of Jean Kambanda, Banque de Kigali, ICTR, KA000209 CZ (*see annex 111*).

14. This major episode of conflict within the FAR command was reconstructed on the basis of accounts from practically the entire complement of officers concerned: Augustin Cyiza, Félicien Muberuka, Balthazar Ndengeyinka, Léonidas Rusatira, Marcel Gatsinzi, Pierre-Claver Karangwa, Laurent Rutayisire, Emmanuel Habyarimana, and Anselme Nshizirungu. Ephrem Rwabalinda and Innocent Bavugamenshi were already deceased by the time this inquiry was conducted; Rwabalinda died in July 1994, and Bavugamenshi died in October 1996. It was not possible to obtain an account from Augustin Ndindiliyimana.

15. Diary of Jean Kambanda, Banque de Kigali, ICTR, KA000209 DA (*see annex 111*).

16. Augustin Ndindiliyimana's family arrived in Burundi on 14 June.

17. Thus, Col. Balthazar Ndengeyinka, appointed to head a nonexistent military sector on 13 May 1994, was made commander of the operational sector in Bugesera at

that time and was almost immediately relieved of his duties on 29 May, to be replaced by Lt. Col. Édouard Gasarabwe. On 2 June 1994 Ndengeyinka was suspended from the military (*see annex 112*).

18. Augustin Cyiza was president of the Conseil de guerre (Court Martial) and occupied an unusual position in the military hierarchy given his double-edged role as officer and lawyer. As legal advisor to Minister of Defense James Gasana, he participated in various negotiations with the RPF within the framework of the Groupe des observateurs militaires neutres de l'OUA (GOMN, Group of Neutral Military Observers of the OAU).

19. Emmanuel Habyarimana was an officer assigned to the operational sector in the Mutara. He was never personally informed of this decision. Sometime in late May, in the course of one of his trips from Butare to Kigeme on his way to the ESM, he was held at a roadblock in Gikongoro but managed to get away. He found his way to Kigeme and placed himself under General Rusatira's protection, but he too was ultimately dismissed.

20. Pierre-Claver Karangwa, ex–staff officer G2 in the gendarmerie, was assigned to UNAMIR at the time. He was personally informed of his dismissal by Augustin Ndindiliyimana and was replaced by Maj. Stanislas Kinyoni (Kigali-rural), already retired but recalled to active duty.

21. Advisor to the army chief of staff, Ephrem Rwabalinda traveled to Paris for consultations with French authorities from 9 to 13 May 1994. He was killed in an RPF ambush in Gitarama on 7 July 1994.

22. Innocent Bavugamenshi (Cyangugu) was commander of the gendarmerie unit responsible for security details of selected persons. Assigned to protect Prime Minister Dismas Nsengiyaremye in 1992 and 1993, he was accused of having links to the opposition. After receiving threats during the first days of the massacres, he requested a transfer as commander for the gendarmerie detachment in Cyangugu. Once there, despite serious threats from soldiers, he opposed the murderous activism of his predecessor, Maj. Innocent Munyarugerero (Ruhengeri), and tried, without much success, to stop the massacres in the prefecture with the assistance of Major Cyiza. He died in October 1996.

23. Balthazar Ndengeyinka, former technical advisor to Minister of Defense James Gasana, was commander of the operational sector in Gitarama in April 1994. In early July he received a suspension order from the minister of defense from Gisenyi. He was warned of attempts to eliminate him by Col. Félicien Muberuka, who was himself warned by Laurent Semanza. When questioned, the latter refused to admit the meeting's objective, unlike Matthieu Ngirumpatse, who acknowledged it to certain persons.

24. Anselme Nshizirungu had been the military advisor to Agathe Uwilingiyimana.

25. Ex–chief of external security at army headquarters, Laurent Rutayisire had been placed at the disposition of the gendarmerie by Théoneste Bagosora but remained without a specific assignment. He was informed of his fate by Augustin Ndindiliyimana.

26. Marcel Gatsinzi had been an ephemeral army chief of staff between 8 and 14 April 1994.

27. Director of the ESM since 1992, Léonidas Rusatira displayed open hostility toward Bagosora's "putsch" of 6–8 April 1994 and had to seek shelter at the Chinese Embassy after 12 April. He later settled in Kigeme (Gikongoro), where the ESM had been transferred. He was warned of his inclusion on the list by the army chief of staff, Augustin Bizimungu, but took necessary precautionary measures. Dismissed from the FAR on 10 July 1994, he fled to Bukavu on 13 July with assistance from French soldiers in Operation Turquoise. He returned to Rwanda on 29 July 1994 and placed himself at the disposal of the RPA.

28. Félicien Muberuka had figured on the list of potential candidates to head the army for quite some time. His nomination as chief of staff of the gendarmerie benefited from Matthieu Ngirumpatse's support (also a native of Kigali-rural) and apparently would not have provoked objection from Théoneste Bagosora, even in spite of the hostility Muberuka displayed toward the army chief of staff, Maj. Gen. Augustin Bizimungu. This suggests that it was important to promote someone outside the *originaire du terroir présidentiel*. Generally speaking, his career had been going well despite the animosity of the officers from Busuhiru. For example, he was appointed commander of the commando battalion in Ruhengeri for 1980–81, then sent for training to the École supérieure de guerre interarmées (Military Training College) in Paris, where he obtained a Brevet d'études militaires supérieures (diploma in advanced military studies). From 1989 to 1992 he was G4 officer in the army general staff and then took over from Bagosora as the head of Camp Mayuya in Kanombe and as commander of the operational sector for Kigali-ville.

29. Despite the isolation, the international community could still appreciate that there were advantages. By 25 May the United Nations Office of Legal Affairs was unambiguous in its assessment of the legitimacy of the Interim Government (*see annex 115*), despite the vote on the resolution of 17 May concerning the weapons embargo and the reservations expressed by the members of the Security Council.

30. *See annex 97*; diary of Édouard Karemera, minutes of 9 June 1994 cabinet meeting (KA01-0403B through KA01-0403E), *Karemera et al.*, exhibit no. P-226.

31. Testimony of Witness T (Interahamwe leader), *Karemera et al.*, 6 June 2006, p. 22.

32. "Substantial resources are needed to force the RPF to negotiate": handwritten notebook of Édouard Karemera (KA01-0403-0403X and K036-7379-7379), *Karemera et al.*, exhibit no. P-225, pp. 59, 65.

33. Handwritten notebook, Karemera (KA01-0403-0403X, KA01-0403-A, KA01-0403-D) (*see annex 117*).

34. Several cabinet meetings were devoted to reviewing constitutional amendments that were adopted before the reelection of the bureau of the Assembly (*see annex 97*).

35. Ultimately, the guideline of fourteen was not followed (*see* Appendix: Box 5, pp. 351–353).

36. The materials relied upon to obtain these figures come from a variety of sources (mostly witness accounts), but the most detailed account appears in Pauline Nyiramasuhuko's diary (see Guichaoua, *Rwanda 1994*, 422–25). *See annex 76*.

37. Report on the situation of human rights in Rwanda submitted by M. René Degni-Ségui, Special Rapporteur of the United Nations Human Rights Commission, Economic and Social Council, E/CN.4/1995/7, 28 June 1994.

38. The United Nations began to set up this international commission of inquiry three weeks later, on 28 July 1994.

39. Handwritten notebook, Karemera (KA01-0403-R) (*see annex 117*).

40. Ngirumpatse, *La tragédie rwandaise*, 148.

41. In mid-December 2011 the Appeals Chamber of the ICTR upheld the acquittal of Gratien Kabiligi and, quashing several of the Trial Chamber's factual and legal findings, commuted the three life sentences previously pronounced. Théoneste Bagosora and Aloys Ntabakuze are now sentenced to thirty-five years in prison, and Anatole Nsengiyumva to fifteen years. These officers remain guilty of genocide, crimes against humanity, and war crimes. They are still held criminally responsible for failing to prevent the crimes committed by the military or punish the perpetrators. Similarly, the judges confirm that Bagosora, then chief of staff at the Ministry of Defense, was the highest military authority in Rwanda between 6 and 9 April 1994 (additional note from the author, January 2015).

42. Despite successive delays and adjournments caused by the declining health of Ngirumpatse, president of the MRND, and the sudden death of Nzirorera, secretary-general of the presidential party, the trial of the main leaders of the MRND was finally completed in December 2011, resulting in double convictions and sentences of life imprisonment. Matthieu Ngirumpatse and Édouard Karemera, vice president of the MRND and minister of the interior of the Interim Government from the end of May 1994 until the flight into exile to Zaire (now the Democratic Republic of Congo) in mid-July, were convicted of genocide, crimes against humanity, and war crimes. According to the Trial Chamber's judgment, they failed to prevent, halt, or condemn the atrocities committed in 1994 by the most active supporters of the genocide, the Interahamwe militiamen, the youth movement of their party. These sentences were confirmed on 29 September 2014 by the ICTR Appeals Chamber, which reaffirmed almost all the factual and legal conclusions of the trial judgment. Like the defendants in the trial of the military officers at the highest levels of authority, leaders of the ruling party have not been convicted of conspiracy to commit genocide. During the "putsch" of Colonel Bagosora on April 7 and the installation of the Interim Government, the three main leaders of the MRND had wanted to stay in the background, waiting to see how the political and military situation would evolve (additional note from the author, January 2015).

43. Preamble to United Nations Security Council resolution 955 that created the ICTR, 8 November 1994.

Chapter 13. Truth, Justice, and the Politics of Memory

1. *Karemera et al.*, Appeal Chamber, Decision on Prosecutor's Interlocutory Appeal of Decision on Judicial Notice, 16 June 2006, at para. 35: "There is no reasonable base

for anyone to dispute that, during 1994, there was a campaign of mass killing intended to destroy, in whole or at least in very large part, Rwanda's Tutsi population, which was a protected group. The campaign was, to a terrible degree, successful. . . . The fact of the Rwandan genocide is a part of world history, a fact as certain as any other, a classic instance of a 'fact of common knowledge.'"

2. So it was that major powers like the United States and the United Kingdom and most of the neighboring countries, including Congo-Zaire, Burundi, and Tanzania, were nonetheless directly concerned and implicated in the conflict and in the mediations, especially Uganda. After all, the RPA was originally a vital segment of that country's armed forces, the National Resistance Army (NRA), which played a significant role in the launching of the war and, besides its logistical and other kinds of assistance to the RPF, participated in all of the decisive decisions concerning the conduct of the war.

3. The first trial judgment, issued on 2 September 1998, did not become final until the Appeal Chamber judgment of 16 May 2001.

4. Fear continues to keep at bay a great number of witnesses, whether they are sought by the Office of the Prosecutor or by the defense teams. Neighbors or close associates of victims or of the accused residing in Rwanda, and even those living abroad, fear retaliation against their families or themselves from the other party. As a rule, the tribunal only very rarely succeeded in mobilizing sophisticated, truly independent Rwandan expert witnesses, no more than it was ever able to obtain guilty pleas and confessions in any significant number (nine) to be of genuine interest for the prosecution.

5. Where length of pretrial detention is concerned, the record is deplorable, based on the information available in July 2009 for forty-three detainees whose first trials had been completed. For the fourteen who were tried separately in single-accused trials, the average length of pretrial detention was 1,670 days (four years, seven months). The shortest period was 213 days (seven months), and the longest was 2,891 days (seven years, eleven months). For the twenty-nine defendants who faced joint trials, the average length of pretrial detention rose to 2,903 days (seven years, eleven months). The shortest period was 973 days (two years, seven months), and the longest—for Théoneste Bagosora—was 5,032 days (thirteen years, nine months). As for those accused persons who pleaded guilty, there was still an average pretrial detention of 1,012 days (two years, nine months).

6. Édouard Karemera, former minister of the interior; Joseph Nzirorera, former speaker of the National Assembly and former minister of public works; Matthieu Ngirumpatse, former minister of justice who occupied the posts of vice president, national secretary, and chairman of the MRND.

7. Only four trial judgments (three in single-accused cases and one in a joint trial) involving six accused were rendered over the course of Arbour's mandate, which lasted three years.

8. From the very beginning of her mandate, Carla Del Ponte was confronted with major difficulties in obtaining cooperation from Rwandan authorities and pursued, as did Louise Arbour before her, joint trials.

9. *Official Journal of the Republic*, no. 2,279, Kigali, 11 April 2001.

10. The two judgments are the convictions of Jean Kambanda, ex–prime minister, and Eliezer Niyitegeka, ex–minister of information of the Interim Government.

11. Stephen Smith, "Rwanda: L'injustice internationale," *Le Monde*, 19 May 2001.

12. OFPRA, decision of 4 January 2006; CRR, decision of 15 February 2007 (*see annex 54*).

13. A rather banal conclusion to these investigations held out the possibility of seizing the bank deposits of fugitives (UN Security Council, 2 June 2000).

14. Alphonse Higaniro was the director general of SORWAL, a large parastatal enterprise in Butare.

15. Leaders of the youth wing of the MRND were among the principal beneficiaries of the payments. Key portions of the results were published in Guichaoua, *Rwanda 1994*, chap. 5.

16. Former political advisor to the Rwandan minister of foreign affairs and a member of the steering committee for the RTLM, Jean-Bosco Barayagwiza was one of the three accused in one of the leading cases in the ICTR, the "media trial." The Appeal Chamber dismissed the indictment against him and released him on 3 November 1999, hardly a month after the new prosecutor took office.

17. "One of the new areas that we will embark upon concerns allegations of crimes committed in 1994 by the armed forces of the Rwandan Patriotic Front (RPF)" (United Nations, Security Council, 27 November 2001).

18. This maneuver was clearly decisive because, in the Anglo-Saxon system, which was practically adopted as the judicial model by the ICTR, investigations are conducted by the Office of the Prosecutor, and proof relies, for the most part, on the credibility of witness accounts.

19. In Florence Hartman's *Paix et châtiment* (Paris: Flammarion, 2007), Carla Del Ponte provides her own account and confirms the willingness of members of the Security Council to thwart implementation of the mandate of the independent international criminal tribunals.

20. Carla Del Ponte, interview with Agence Hirondelle, December 2002.

21. In the case of Gen. Léonidas Rusatira, former commander of the École supérieure militaire and recognized for having publicly opposed the genocide in April 1994, an indictment was knitted together from a patchwork of witness accounts, wholly inspired by self-proclaimed "auxiliaries of justice," with the Office of the Prosecutor uncritically accepting their assertions. After a meeting organized by the Belgian minister of justice in Brussels, where the accused was awaiting transfer to Arusha, Carla Del Ponte was forced to acknowledge that she lacked sufficient evidence to indict him. He was released on 18 August 2002.

22. This would include the sites of two massacres in Byumba prefecture—the prefecture stadium and Giti commune—in April 1994. A third concerned the murder of bishops at Gakurazo, Gitarama prefecture, the following June. The last was situated in Butare, specifically the arborium, the following July.

23. United Nations Security Council, S/PV.4999, 29 June 2004, p. 17.

24. The central elements of this file were assembled on the basis of in-depth investigations undertaken by Lt. Abdul Ruzibiza and other RPA officers (*see annex 127.2–3*).

25. "In addition to these areas, the allegations made against the RPF have also been under consideration. . . . I have also been holding discussions with representatives of the Rwandan government concerning the options available for the prosecution of any such cases which may arise as a result of these further inquiries" (Justice Hassan Bubacar Jallow, statement to the UN Security Council, 15 December 2005).

26. "I expect that in 2007, these enquiries should conclude and enable us to decide which way to proceed" (Justice Hassan Bubacar Jallow, statement to the UN Security Council, 15 December 2006); "Since my last report to the Security Council some progress has been made in the investigation of the allegations against members of the RPF. We look forward to concluding this matter early next year" (Justice Hassan Bubacar Jallow, statement to the UN Security Council, 10 December 2007).

27. In fact, the allegations were against two senior officers and two captains, whose cases were severed from the joint indictment.

28. Justice Hassan Bubacar Jallow, statement to the UN Security Council, S/PV.5904, 4 June 2008, p. 11.

29. It is, however, highly improbable that high-level officers of the RPA would have been able to decide upon the killings of figures of such importance without going through the RPA's hierarchy.

30. This point is extremely important, because two of the Office of the Prosecutor's expert witnesses had personally informed the prosecutor that the names of the two eyewitnesses of the killings at Kabgayi would be made available to him as soon as concrete measures were taken to protect their security when they testified, and he never responded. The prosecutor indicated on 11 July 2009 in Geneva that he had not transmitted evidence to the Auditorat militaire de Kigali and that the case file had been wholly investigated by Rwandan authorities: "We have not provided Rwanda with any evidence from the Office of the Prosecutor. The evidence that they used was produced by them, but it is consistent with what we have and with the position that we took" ("Arusha, Model or Counter-model for International Justice," conference held at the Université Paris–I / Institut de hautes études internationales et du développement [IHEID, Graduate Institute of International and Development Studies] / ICTR, transcript by Hassan Bubacar Jallow, session 5). However, the records of the Security Council session of 4 June 2009 took note of the fact that "the Tribunal transferred information on some of its Rwandese Patriotic Front (RPF) investigations to Rwanda's domestic courts in June 2008, and four RPF officers face trial" (Ms. DiCarlo, statement of the United States to the UN Security Council, S/PV.6134, 4 June 2009, p. 27). Thus, there was indeed an exchange of information, and unless the statement was made in error, evidence was transmitted to Rwandan authorities and then exploited without the approval of ICTR judges.

31. Preliminary statement of the defense when witnesses testified on 10 September 2008.

32. Servilien Sebasoni, "À propos d'une justice intimidée," *Libération*, 23 May 2006; press release of RPF spokesperson, Kigali, June 2006.

33. The several case files against RPA soldiers that were transmitted to the ICTR for informational purposes deal exclusively with lower-level soldiers, principally sanctioned for the disorder their misbehavior provoked in their units.

34. The spokesperson for the RPF queried if "the ICTR was not created to be dysfunctional" (Sebasoni, "À propos").

35. Many countries in the Security Council did not accept the principle that investigations could be directed against the authorities in power; as a result, representatives of these countries did not always support prosecutors. Confronted with lists of "génocidaires" residing abroad, all of the countries hosting suspects who had not yet been arrested and prosecuted encountered the same pressures. Three countries (Switzerland, Belgium, and Canada) had already held well-publicized trials for genocide, but up to the present day, no national jurisdiction, with the exception of France and Spain, has agreed to process complaints where crimes were allegedly committed by the rebel forces and their supporters. In one instance, the characterization of crimes has been deemed insufficient; in another, the existing judicial framework has been deemed inadequate. As if that's not enough, there have been appeals to the "understanding" of the complainants because of likely risks for their associates and the witnesses so that they would refrain from lodging complaints.

36. According to Goldstone, "I don't understand that [ambivalence]. It's clearly linked to the genocide." "In any case, that was the trigger for the genocide, and it would have been very, very important from a judicial perspective and from the point of view of the victims to clarify that" (Richard Goldstone, interview in *Berlingske Tidende*, Copenhagen, 12 December 2006).

37. On 28 June 2011 the ICTR finally issued its first decision approving the transfer of a case to Rwanda. After a lengthy appeals process the ICTR handed over Pentecostal minister Jean Uwinkindi to the Rwandan authorities on 20 April 2012. Following a number of procedural delays, Uwinkindi's trial began on 26 February 2014. As of this writing, the most recent follow-up report was published 18 March 2015 by the Mechanism for International Criminal Tribunals indicating obstructions to the trial process because of the absence of defense counsel (see *Prosecutor v. Jean Uwinkindi*, MICT-12-25, 18-03-2015 (20-1/879bis).

38. On 30 March 2009 the assistant secretary-general for legal affairs, Patricia O'Brien, did not hesitate to exercise this pressure during a visit to Kigali, stating that transferring persons accused of genocide to Rwanda was "a decision that depends on the United Nations Security Council and the judges of the ICTR."

39. One is reminded of comments from Prosecutor Louise Arbour to Canadian journalist Carol Off: "The Rwandan government was reading my mail. They knew what I was doing. Consequently, if I send someone to investigate the RPF he could be killed. I didn't do it" (Carol Off, *The Lion, the Fox and the Eagle* [Toronto: Random House Canada, 2000]).

40. See Augustin Cyiza, *Un homme libre au Rwanda* (Paris: Karthala, 2004), 209ff.; *annex 132*.

41. See the complete text in *annex 133*: *Bagosora et al.*, Judgment and Sentence, 18 December 2008.

42. The spokesperson for the RPF expressed himself strongly: "No, the judge in Arusha is insensitive to what slowly cooks up, to what is concocted, even out loud, and can only believe in concrete plans! That's ridiculous. That brings at least two things to light: the first is that Rwandans, even the most literate, don't always write down what they plan to do; and it also demonstrates how mistaken it was to place the ICTR in the hands of judges who only know very little or nothing at all about Rwanda. Judges who are easily fooled and manipulated by a handful of armchair academics" (Sebasoni, "Bagosora").

43. "The memory of the victims of the genocide in Rwanda only covers the short period from 1 October 1990 to 31 December 1994, whereas the history of the genocide against the Tutsi covers numerous decades, because one has to go back to its origins if one wants to discover its causes" (Commission spéciale du Sénat, *Idéologie du génocide au Rwanda et les stratégies d'éradication*, Kigali, 4 February 2009, p. 152).

44. Sebasoni, "Bagosora."

45. By the end of January 2015, the tribunal had indicted ninety-three individuals, including sixty-one who were convicted and sentenced. Among these, the ICTR convicted four defendants for the crime of conspiracy to commit genocide. In addition to the prime minister of the Interim Government, Jean Kambanda, who pleaded guilty, the convictions after trial concerned the information minister, Eliezer Niyitegeka, the finance minister, Emmanuel Ndindabahizi, and the minister of family, Pauline Nyiramasuhuko (the Appeals Chamber's review of the trial judgment is anticipated for mid-2015).

46. *Bagosora et al.*, Judgment and Sentence, 18 December 2008, p. 2.

47. "17. The Chamber certainly accepts that there are indications which may be construed as evidence of a plan to commit genocide, in particular when viewed in the light of the subsequent targeted and speedy killings immediately after the downing of the President's plane. However, the evidence is also consistent with preparations for a military or political power struggle and measures adopted in the context of an on-going war with the RPF that were used for other purposes from 6 April 1994" (ibid., pp. 2–3).

48. As in numerous conflicts, the narrow focus on the most dangerous protagonists and on extremists in general led to a marked lack of interest by ambassadors and various mediators in the more moderate voices in government and civil society organizations. Those voices of moderation would probably have been able to shape the course of events but instead found themselves isolated and weak as a result. In the case of Rwanda, during the first days of April, it is highly probable that with the UN forces already on the ground, deliberate interventions by the large embassies, and additional support from easily mobilized foreign military forces, political figures who had distanced themselves from the ethnic blocks would have had sufficient ascendancy to call for a halt to the massacres, neutralize the militias, and regain the upper hand over the mutinied units with support from the military high command of the FAR.

49. It was only during the course of 7 April and especially 8 April that the "parallel committee" of the Interahamwe mobilized and coordinated the other youth groups in tandem with those elements of the army taking orders from officers loyal to the

presidential clan. As soon as the Interim Government left, it was able to link up with the "downtown" committee of Interahamwe led by Prefect Renzaho and Théoneste Bagosora.

50. *Bagosora et al.*, Judgment and Sentence, 18 December 2008, chap. 3, "Allegations of Planning and Preparation of the Genocide," pp. 45–159.

51. Ibid. See para. 2.6, "Creation, Training and Arming of Civilian Militias."

52. To explain its difficulties in proving "conspiracy," the prosecution routinely invoked the limited temporal jurisdiction (calendar year 1994) that the Security Council had established for the tribunal, which would narrow the reach of its indictments, and claimed that the judges adopted an overly restrictive interpretation of this constraint.

53. The prosecutor's formulation, supported by a single witness, a former RPF leader, is that Bagosora abandoned the Rwandan government delegation to the Arusha negotiations, headed by MDR minister Boniface Ngulinzira, in October 1992 in protest over the disproportionate concessions made to the RPF, and that at that time he claimed he was returning to Kigali "to prepare the Apocalypse." However, at that period, he was not yet a member of the delegation to Arusha. Moreover, when he actually did leave Arusha, on 26 December, it is because he had been recalled by President Habyarimana and over strong objections from the minister, head of the government delegation.

54. *Bagosora et al.*, Summary of Judgment, 18 December 2008, p. 4. On the last point concerning the informant "Jean-Pierre," one may refer to *annex 46*, which presents various elements of the substantive proof advanced by the prosecution. Note, however, that the testimony of General Dallaire before Trial Chamber I in the Bagosora trial (in particular, his testimony on 22 January 2004) undermines this evidence and lays bare the incoherence and the absence of elementary verifications that would have justified the reported assertions.

55. See, for example, the document "Warning of Genocide to UNAMIR," dated 20 November 1995, by Shaharyar M. Khan, who succeeded Roméo Dallaire as the head of UNAMIR (*see annex 134*).

56. See, in particular, on the very last publications from Human Rights Watch on this subject: "The Rwandan Genocide: How It Was Prepared," 7 April 2006.

57. *Bagosora et al.*, Summary of Judgment, 18 December 2008, p. 2.

58. Ibid.

59. The current Rwandan authorities and President Paul Kagame himself take the position that a fascist, racist dictatorship was installed after Rwanda became politically independent, with the handover of power to newly elected national authorities. This thesis was extended by a second claim, which flows logically from the first: the genocidal project was a constituent element in building up a Hutu opposition and in the founding of the republic. Hence, the interethnic clashes and massacres of the 1960s and 1973 would have anticipated the "Final Solution" of 1994. From this perspective, the question of "planning genocide" would have been pointless, since the history of the republic could only be a series of episodes of Tutsi martyrdom.

60. Even if the members and the resources of the MRND may have decisively contributed to accomplishing genocide, characterizing the MRND as a criminal organization, which today permits the authorities in Kigali to imprison or prosecute well-known party officials, party employees, burgomasters, and even ordinary citizens simply on the basis of their membership and status in the party, without further proof of the crimes committed, seems to reveal an abusive generalization that the ICTR Trial Chambers have rightly, consistently avoided (see "The MRND is not on trial. The Chamber will have to assess the individual criminal responsibility of the Accused," in "Decision on Prosecution Prospective Expert Witnesses Alison Desforges, Andre Guichaoua and Binaifer Nowrojee," *Karemera et al.*, 25 October 2007, p. 10).

61. At least by "ethical" organizations, like the international human rights organizations that speak on its behalf.

62. Gacaca jurisdictions ("justice in the grass"; grass = *gacaca* in Kinyarwanda) are a system of informal and popular prosecutions organized by Rwandan authorities as an alternative to its ordinary courts, where suspects are brought before members of their communities who then pronounce the punishment.

63. "Stressing also the need for international cooperation to strengthen the Courts and Judicial System of Rwanda, having regard in particular to the necessity for those Courts to deal with large numbers of suspects," UN Security Council Resolution 955 (1994), S/RES/955 (1994), 8 November 1994.

64. See transcripts of the discussions at the international conference "ICTR: Model or Counter-model for International Criminal Justice? The Perspective of the Stakeholders," Geneva, 9–11 July 2009, http://genevaconference-tpir.univ-paris1.fr/.

Conclusion

1. Concerning the question of Rwanda's request to transfer the archives of the International Criminal Tribunal for Rwanda (ICTR): The Security Council decided to keep the archives in Arusha in Tanzania, just as those from the ICTY are kept in The Hague. If the Rwandan request is legitimate, its motivations are less so, because almost all the scanned archives are accessible at the ICTR Information Centre in Kigali. Rwanda, however, seeks to retain the originals. Handing over materials of this nature to one of the parties to the conflict, given the ICTR's mandate to prosecute the presumed perpetrators of war crimes and crimes against humanity, would contravene the duty to preserve the confidentiality of witness statements in a permanent documentary archive, particularly in light of the Rwandan authorities' consistent opposition to any investigation or prosecution of the crimes partially documented in the "special investigations" abandoned in late 2005, upon the insistence of the US State Department.

Updates for the Period 2010–2015

1. The difference between the number of trials and the number of people brought to trial is principally due to the fact that the same person may have been tried several times as renewed accusations were made.

2. After a lengthy pretrial phase of procedural challenges, the Trial Chamber began adducing evidence in June 2001 and the appeal hearing for the appeal of the final trial judgment started on 14 April 2015. When the appeal judgment is finally pronounced, this trial will have lasted more than fourteen years.

3. Based on extensive research carried out by a team of twenty experts over a period of twelve months, this report concluded that the majority of documented crimes could be qualified as crimes against humanity and as war crimes. In particular, the report raises the question of whether certain crimes committed between 1996 and 1997 by the Rwandan army and its Congolese ally, the rebel group of the Alliance of Democratic Forces for the Liberation of Congo (AFDL), against Rwandan Hutu refugees and Congolese Hutu citizens could be qualified as genocide. The report stated that it was the responsibility of a competent court to make such a decision.

4. After this macabre discovery, Burundi tried to enlist the support of the United States, the Netherlands, and Switzerland to help fund and follow up the preliminary investigations. Rwanda then insisted on the filing of a joint application and the transfer of the file to the African Commission on Human and Peoples' Rights, chaired by a Rwandan. After it was sent to the Political Affairs Committee, the file went dead. Speculations about the identity of the victims cover a wide spectrum. One possibility points to Rwandan refugees from the east of the Congo (presumed to qualify as génocidaires or Interahamwe) intercepted in Burundi before being handed over to the Rwandan authorities. Some suggest that the bodies could have been sent back to Burundi in an accusatory gesture for having protected and supported them in the DRC.

5. In "The Meaning of Death": "They, too, are humans. I pray for them."

6. *New Times*, Kigali, 14 April 2014.

Glossary

Abakombozi: "Liberators." Youth movement of the PSD.

Abatabazi: Literally, "sent to the front." This was a reference to the "saviors" who, traditionally, sacrificed their lives in order to safeguard the kingdom. The term was adopted by members of the Interim Government and used to characterize themselves as the saviors of the nation.

Abiru: Under the monarchy, the guardians of tradition, key advisors to the king.

Akazu: Literally, "the little hut," a term designating the royal entourage in the former kingdom of Rwanda. It refers to the relatives and the close associates of the ruling family. After 1991 it was frequently used to characterize presidential family's inner circle of confidants.

Baganda: Native to Buganda, a former kingdom within Uganda.

Bakiga: People from the north.

bamwana: In-laws, a family relationship born of intermarriage.

Banyamulenge: People of Mulenge; old migrants native from Rwanda to the eastern Congo dating back to previous centuries, distributed throughout the zones of Fizi, Uvira, and Mwenga in South Kivu, DRC; sometimes called "Tutsi Congolese."

Banyanduga: People from the south.

Banyankole: People of Ankole, a former kingdom within the south of Uganda.

Banyarwanda: Literally, "those who come from Rwanda"; old or recent migrants who live in the South and North Kivu, in Western Uganda.

bazungu: Whites (Westerners).

gacaca: Literally, "grass" in Kinyarwanda; by extension it indicates Rwanda's community courts in the communes: the "justice in the grass."

ibyitso: Name given to alleged accomplices of the RPF.

Impuzamugambi: "Those who share the same goal." Youth movement of the CDR.

inararibonye: The "one who has seen." Term referencing the old wise men of the hillsides. Refers to someone who is well informed and well experienced.

Ingangurarugo: Among King Rwabugiri's most renowned and feared militias.

Inkotanyi: The "valiant warriors." Name adopted by RPF fighters in 1990, in reference to the brave troops from the period of the monarchy.

Inkuba: "Lightning." Youth movement of the MDR.

Interahamwe: "Those who work together." Youth movement of the MRND.

inyenzi: Cockroach. Pejorative term from the 1960s for Tutsi combatants engaging in armed attacks against the country to reestablish the monarchy. Later reappropriated and turned on its head by these very same combatants as an abbreviation of *ingangurarugo yiyemeje kuba ingenzi* ("combatant of the Ingangurarugo militia," self-avowed to be the best).

izatsinzwe: "Vanquished." A contraction of the expression *ingabo zatsinzwe* (vanquished army), referring to all the Hutu vanquished and enthralled by the RPF.

Kubohoza: "Liberation." Movement taking root with the onset of multiparty politics when opposition political parties directly confronted the dominant MRND by seizing control of institutions or property belonging to the former MRND party-state (often involving mass action to capture other people's property).

mwami: Monarch or king (by extension, *ibwami* referred to the royal court or lineage).

Nduga (or "extended Nduga"): Name given to the remaining prefectures of the country when the northern prefectures of Gisenyi, Ruhengeri, and Byumba are extracted. The majority of leaders and officials of the First Republic originated in those prefectures.

nyumbakumi: Created under colonization, the *nyumbakumi* was in charge of informing the authorities about the travels and goings on within the ten households or family plots in his area of oversight. More widely, he also had to be on the lookout for the risks of conflict. After independence, this function of mediation and surveillance was strengthened by tasks of a political nature on behalf of the single-party regime. *Nyumbakumi* appointed or endorsed in this framework became conduits for relaying information to and from the cell counselors, and farther up the pyramidal administrative structure of the commune.

Power or "Pawa": Generic name adopted by pro-Hutu partisans, derived from the slogan "Hutu Power."

Rukiga: Name given to the three prefectures of Gisenyi, Ruhengeri, and Byumba. Originally, the term Rukiga applied to the cool, mountainous regions of the country, as distinguished from the Mayaga, the hot lowlands. In actuality, northerners also controlled a swath of Greater Kigali prefecture (Kigali-rural), which was largely colonized by natives of Ruhengeri. The majority of leaders and officials of the Second Republic originated from those prefectures.

rukokoma: Sovereign national conference, in which all the politicians and other main actors of a country (such as the representatives of the political parties, the civil society, the professional groups, and members of the army) meet to decide on its future and define a workable political framework.

simusiga: "Leave nothing behind," that is, scorched earth. This expression describes the all-out war that took place immediately following the shutting down of foreign embassies and the withdrawal of UNAMIR.

terroir présidentiel: The president's home turf. This term indicates the terrain or space that served as an incubator, or recruiting ground, for the faithful supporters of the clan. It corresponds to the region of Bushiru, which, broadly defined, covers the communes of Karago and Giciye in Gisenyi prefecture. Presidential networks extended beyond Bushiru, however, and managed to incorporate wide stretches from the prefectures of Ruhengeri and Gisenyi.

ukubohoza: Forcibly "liberating" the people from the MRND.

umuganda: Community or public work projects held on Saturday mornings. All citizens, regardless of rank or social status, were expected to participate.

Index of Names

Critical Human Rights

Printed in the United States
by Thomson-Shore

Printed in the United States
By Bookmasters